John Milton

PARADISE LOST

A Poem in Twelve Books

A NEW EDITION

Edited by MERRITT Y. HUGHES

Hackett Publishing Company, Inc
Indianapolis/Cambridge

Copyright © 1997 by Prentice Hall, Inc.
Reprinted 2003 by Hackett Publishing Company, Inc.

10 09 08 07 06   2 3 4 5 6 7 8

For further information, please address:

Hackett Publishing Company, Inc.
P. O. Box 44937
Indianapolis, IN 46244-0937

www.hackettpublishing.com

Cover design by Lorraine Blake
Printed at Edwards Brothers, Inc.

Library of Congress Cataloging-in-Publication Data

Milton, John, 1608–1674
    Paradise lost : a poem in twelve books / John Milton. — A new ed. / edited
by Merritt Y. Hughes.
        p.   cm.
    Includes bibliographical references
    ISBN 0-87220-673-4 (cloth) — ISBN 0-87220-672-6
    1. Bible. O. T. Genesis—History of Biblical events—Poetry. 2. Adam
(Biblical figure)—Poetry. 3. Eve (Biblical figure)—Poetry. 4. Fall of man—
Poetry. I. Hughes, Merritt Yerkes, 1893– II. Title.

PR3560 2003
821'.4—dc21   2002191310

ISBN-13: 978-0-87220-673-1 (cloth)
ISBN-13: 978-0-87220-672-4 (pbk.)

The paper used in this publication meets the minimum requirements of American
National Standard for Information Sciences—Permanence of Paper for Printed
Library Materials, ANSI Z39.48—1984.
∞

CONTENTS

PREFACE

The present text is essentially that of the second (1674) edition of *Paradise Lost* and is reproduced here as it stands in my *Milton: Complete Poems and Major Prose* (Odyssey Press, 1957). Milton's spelling and punctuation are modernized although most of his seventeenth century typographical peculiarities, especially the italicization of proper names and place names, are preserved. Emphatic pronominal forms (*mee, wee, hee, shee,* and *their*) are distinguished from the unemphatic *me, we, he, she,* and *thir*. In rare cases the readings are not those of the second edition, but the deviations are fewer than those in Miss Helen Darbishire's Revised Edition of *The Poetical Works of John Milton* (1958) and they will usually be found to have the support of Professor B. A. Wright's Everyman edition of *Milton's Poems* (1956).

The notes have been revised in the light of scholarship since 1957. The bibliography of books and articles on *Paradise Lost* tries to include all items too recent for inclusion in Professor Calvin Huckaby's *John Milton: A Bibliographical Supplement: 1929–1957* (Pittsburgh, Duquesne University Press, 1960). Eleven book titles are added to his listing. Perhaps Professor Lily B. Campbell's *Divine Poetry and Drama in Sixteenth Century England* (Berkeley, University of California Press, 1959) should also be included, for it leads towards Professor Burton O. Kurth's approach to the poem through seventeenth century Biblical epic themes and forms in *Milton and Christian Heroism*.

The swing away from purely historical criticism is clear in the titles of many of the articles in the bibliography of periodical contributions to the study of *Paradise Lost* from 1957 to the early months of 1961 which follows the selective bibliography of books at the end of the Introduction to the poem. Among the books the critical trend centers on the attack upon Milton's handling of his fable and characters by A. J. A. Waldock in *"Paradise Lost" and its Critics* (1947), which has been resumed by John Peter in *A Critique of "Paradise Lost"* and by William Empson in *Milton's God*. Though Frank Kermode does not meet Waldock head-on in *The Living Milton*, he and Bernard Bergonzi outflank him by exposing the narrowness of his front in his rigorously naturalistic application of the code of the modern novel to *Paradise Lost*. Kermode's wider perspective makes the poem "absolutely contemporary — its subject is human experience symbolized in the basic myth" (p. 99). For this position there is strong support in Mrs. I. G. MacCaffrey's *"Paradise Lost" as 'Myth'* although (and because) the two works are quite independent of each other. Support of a different kind may be seen in R. M. Frye's *God, Man, and Satan*, which treats the poem as a Christian testament accommodated to the theological tradition from St. Augustine to Paul Tillich. In Bergonzi's essay the attacks of F. R. Leavis and John Peter upon Milton's verse are outmanoeuvred by an appeal to the great body of his modern readers who do not share Leavis' '*a priori* distaste' for 'ritualistic poetry' nor agree with him in demanding that all poetry be 'expressive,' 'sensitive,' and 'subtle.' Similar concessions to Waldock are made by J. B. Broadbent in *Some Graver Subject*, the most valuable of the recent critical studies of Milton, but their importance falls into proper perspective in this rich analysis of what Broadbent calls Milton's 'south-polar mood,' the mood in which he treated Satan, man, and society in the light of the theme of the epic.

Directly and indirectly this edition of *Paradise Lost* is indebted to the work of many preceding editors and to several scholars who have been generous with help: Douglas Bush and William Haller prominent among them. I owe much to Louis B. Wright and the staff of the Folger Shakespeare Library for doing everything within their power to secure the proper works of reference for me there and for making their great collections in the seventeenth century available to me. My greatest debt is to my triune co-worker, audience, and critic, whose constant help has enabled me to finish my task.

MERRITT Y. HUGHES

A CHRONOLOGY OF THE MAIN EVENTS IN MILTON'S LIFE

1608, Dec. 9. Birth in Bread Street, Cheapside, London.

1617 (?). Attendance at St. Paul's School begun.

1625, Feb. 12. Admission to Christ's College, Cambridge.

1632, July 3. Admission to the degree of M. A.

1632–1635. Residence at Hammersmith.

1634, Sept. 29. First performance of *Comus*.

1635–1638. Residence at Horton.

1638, May (?), to July(?), 1639. Italian journey.

1639 (?). Residence and teaching in London begun.

1641, May. *Of Reformation in England*, Milton's first anti-episcopal tract, published. June or July. *Of Prelatical Episcopacy.*

July (?). *Animadversions upon the Remonstrant's Defense against Smectymnuus*, published.

1642, Jan. (?). *The Reason of Church Government Urged against Prelaty*, published. April. *An Apology against A Modest Confutation*, published.

June (?). Marriage to Mary Powell.

Aug. (?). Return of Mary to her father's home in Buckinghamshire.

1643, Aug. 1. *The Doctrine and Discipline of Divorce*, published.

1644, June 5. *Of Education*, published.

Aug. 6. *The Judgment of Martin Bucer concerning Divorce*, published.

Nov. 23. *Areopagitica*, published.

1645, March 4. *Tetrachordon* and *Colasterion*, published.

Summer (?). Return of Mary Powell Milton to her husband in London.

1646, Jan. *Poems of Mr. John Milton*, published.

July 29. Birth of Milton's daughter Anne.

1648, Oct. 25. Birth of Milton's daughter Mary.

1649, Feb. 13. *The Tenure of Kings and Magistrates*, published.

March 15. Milton appointed Secretary of Foreign Tongues to the Council of State.

Oct. 6. *Eikonoklastes*, published.

1651, Feb. 24. *Defensio pro Populo Anglicano (A Defense of the English People)*, published.

March 16. Birth of Milton's son John.

1652, Feb. (?). Milton's blindness becomes almost total.

May 2. Birth of Milton's daughter Deborah.

May 5 (?). Death of Mary Powell Milton.

June 16 (?). Death of Milton's son John.

At various times, relieved of many of his duties as Secretary to the Council of State, Milton continues work on the *History of Britain* and begins *De Doctrina Christiana (A Treatise on Christian Doctrine)*.

1654, May 30. *Defensio Secunda (A Second Defense of the English People)*, published.

1656, Nov. 12. Marriage to Katherine Woodcock.

1658, Feb. 3. Death of Katherine Woodcock Milton.

1659, Feb. (?). *A Treatise of Civil Power in Ecclesiastical Causes*, published.

1660, Feb. *The Ready and Easy Way to Establish a Free Commonwealth*, published.
1663, Feb. 24. Marriage to Elizabeth Minshull.
1667, Aug. (?). *Paradise Lost. A Poem Written in Ten Books*, published.
1670. *The History of Britain*, published.
1671. *Paradise Regained* and *Samson Agonistes*, published.
1673. *Of True Religion, Heresy, Schism, and Toleration*, published.
1674. *Paradise Lost. A Poem in Twelve Books*, published.
    Nov. 8 (?). Death.

ABBREVIATIONS OF TITLES OF MILTON'S WORKS

NOTE: Not all Milton's titles are included. Those which are not included are cited in full in the notes. References to Milton's prose works are to *The Works of John Milton*, Columbia University Press, 1931–1942. The abbreviation is C.Ed.

Animadversions — *Animadversions upon the Remonstrant's Defense against Smectymnuus*
Apology — *An Apology against a Pamphlet Called "A Modest Confutation of the Animadversions upon the Remonstrant's Defense against Smectymnuus"*
Arc — *Arcades*
Areop — *Areopagitica*
Britain — *The History of Britain*
Bucer — *The Judgment of Martin Bucer concerning Divorce*
Carrier I etc. — *Upon the University Carrier* I etc.
CB — Commonplace Book
CD — *De Doctrina Christiana (The Christian Doctrine)*
C.Ed. — *The Works of John Milton*, Columbia University Press, 1931–1942
CG — *The Reason of Church Government Urged against Prelaty*
Circumcision — *On the Circumcision*
Civil Power — *A Treatise of Civil Power*
Colas — *Colasterion*
Damon — *Epitaphium Damonis (Damon's Epitaph)*
DDD — *The Doctrine and Discipline of Divorce*
Def 1 — *Johannis Miltoni, pro populo Anglicano defensio contra Claudii Salmasii defensionem regiam (The Defense of the English People . . . against Salmasius)*
Def 2 — *Johannis Miltoni, Angli, pro populo Anglicano defensio secunda . . . (The Second Defense of the English People)*
Def se — *Defensio pro se (A Defense of Himself)*
Educ — *Of Education*
Eikon — *Eikonoklastes*
El I etc. — *Elegy I* etc.
Ely — *In obitum praesulis Eliensis (On the Death of the Bishop of Ely)*
Forcers — *On the New Forcers of Conscience under the Long Parliament*
Hirelings — *Considerations Touching the Likeliest Means to Remove Hirelings out of the Church*
Idea — *De idea Platonica (On the Platonic Idea)*
Il Pen — *Il Penseroso*
Infant — *On the Death of a Fair Infant Dying of a Cough*

L'All — *L'Allegro*

Leon I etc. — *Ad Leonoram Romae canentem* (*To Leonora Singing in Rome I* etc.)

Logic — *Artis logicae plenior institutio ad Petri Rami methodum concinnata* (*A Fuller Treatment of the Art of Logic, Adjusted to the Method of Peter Ramus*)

Lyc — *Lycidas*

Manso — *Mansus* (*Manso*)

May — *Song: On May Morning*

Muscovia — *A Brief History of Muscovia*

Music — *At a Solemn Music*

Nat — *On the Morning of Christ's Nativity*

Naturam — *Naturam non pati senium* (*That Nature Is Not Subject to Old Age*)

Pas — *The Passion*

Patrem — *Ad patrem* (*To His Father*)

Peace — *Observations on Ormond's Articles of the Peace with the Irish Rebels*

PL — *Paradise Lost*

Plot — *In proditionem bombardicam* (*On the Gunpowder Plot*)

PR — *Paradise Regained*

Prol I etc. — *Prolusiones oratoriae* (*Academic Exercises* I etc.)

Ps i etc. — Psalm i etc. Milton's translations of individual Psalms are cited in the usual way.

QNov — *In quintum Novembris* (*On the Fifth of November*)

Ref — *Of Reformation Touching Church Discipline in England*

Rous — *Ad Johannem Rousium, Oxoniensis Academiae Bibliothecarium* (*To John Rouse, Librarian of Oxford University*)

SA — *Samson Agonistes*

Salsillo — *Ad Salsillum, Poetam Romanum, aegrotantem* (*To Salzilli, a Roman Poet, When He Was Ill*)

Shak — *On Shakespeare*

Sonn I etc. — *Sonnet* I etc.

Tetr — *Tetrachordon*

TKM — *The Tenure of Kings and Magistrates*

TR — *Of True Religion, Heresy, Schism, and Toleration*

Vac — *At a Vacation Exercise*

Way — *A Ready and Easy Way to Establish a Free Commonwealth*

Winchester — *An Epitaph on the Marchioness of Winchester*

ABBREVIATIONS OF TITLES OF LITERARY AND CRITICAL WORKS CITED IN THE NOTES

NOTE: Works of one-book authors such as Natale Conti's *Mythology* (*Mythologiae libri decem*, Frankfurt, 1696), Diodorus Siculus' *Library of History*, Pausanius' *Description of Greece*, Persius' *Satires*, Pliny's *Natural History*, and Propertius' *Elegies* are cited simply by the authors' names, followed by the appropriate reference.

Advancement — Francis Bacon, *The Advancement of Learning*

Aen. — Virgil, *Aeneid*

Anatomy — Robert Burton, *The Anatomy of Melancholy* (Everyman Ed.)

Angels — Robert H. West, *Milton and the Angels* (1955)

Antiquities — Josephus, *Antiquities of the Jews*

Argument — Maurice Kelley, *This Great Argument* (1941)

Background — Sister Mary Corcoran, *Milton's Paradise with Reference to the Hexaemeral Background* (1945)

Britannia — William Camden, *A Chorographical Description of Britain* (1607)

Chariot — G. Wilson Knight, *Chariot of Wrath*

Commentary — John S. Diekhoff, *Milton's "Paradise Lost," A Commentary on the Argument* (1946)

Conflicts — Joseph R. Tanner, *Constitutional Conflicts of the Seventeenth Century* (1928)

Counterpoint — James Whaler, *Counterpoint and Symbol*

Critics — A. J. A. Waldock, *"Paradise Lost" and Its Critics* (1947)

Cycle — Watson Kirkconnell, *The Celestial Cycle: The Theme of "Paradise Lost" in World Literature* (1952)

Dictionaries — DeWitt T. Starnes and Ernest W. Talbert, *Classical Myth and Legend in Renaissance Dictionaries* (1955)

Dilemma — Arthur Barker, *Milton and the Puritan Dilemma* (1942)

Diodatis — Donald Dorian, *The English Diodatis* (1950)

D.N.B. — *Dictionary of National Biography*

Documents — Samuel R. Gardiner, *The Constitutional Documents of the Puritan Revolution* (1889)

Dogma — Malcolm M. Ross, *Poetry and Dogma* (1954)

Ec. — Virgil, *Eclogues*

E.H.W.C. — *Essays in Honor of Walter Clyde Curry* (1954)

Englishman — James Holly Hanford, *John Milton: Englishman*

Ep. — Horace, *Epodes*

Expositor — Arnold Williams, *The Common Expositor* (1948)

F.Q. — Edmund Spenser, *The Faerie Queene*

Génie — Canon Camille Looten, *J. Milton: quelques aspects de son génie* (1938)

Georg. — Virgil, *Georgics*

Haller — William Haller, *Tracts on Liberty in the Puritan Revolution*, 3 Vols. (1934)

Handbook — James Holly Hanford, *A Milton Handbook*, 4th Ed. (1946)

Heresy — George N. Conklin, *Biblical Criticism and Heresy in Milton* (1949)

Hexaemeral Lit. — Frank H. Robbins, *The Hexaemeral Literature: A Study of the Greek and Latin Commentaries on Genesis* (1912)

Hierarchie — Thomas Heywood, *The Hierarchie of the Blessed Angels*

Humanism — Douglas Bush, *The Renaissance and English Humanism* (1939)

I.E.M.V. — F. T. Prince, *The Italian Element in Milton's Verse* (1954)

IKON — Robert Adams, *IKON: John Milton and the Modern Critics* (1955)

Il. — Homer, *Iliad*

Inf. — Dante, *Inferno*

J.D. — Torquato Tasso, *Jerusalem Delivered* (*La Gerusalemme Liberata*)

Knowledge — J. Howard Schultz, *Milton and Forbidden Knowledge* (1955)

Laws — Plato, *Laws*

Met. — Ovid, *Metamorphoses*

Milieu — George W. Whiting, *Milton's Literary Milieu* (1939)
M.P.L.C. — John Arthos, *On a Mask Presented at Ludlow Castle* (1954)
M.R.R. — Harris Fletcher, *Milton's Rabbinical Readings* (1930)
M.&S. — Kester Svendsen, *Milton and Science* (1956)
M.S. — E. M. W. Tillyard, *The Miltonic Setting* (1938)
Od. — Homer, *Odyssey*
Odes — Horace, *Odes (Carmina)*
O.E.D. — *Oxford English Dictionary*
O.F. — Ludovico Ariosto, *Orlando Furioso*
Oracle — G. Wilson Knight, *The Burning Oracle* (1939)
Our Time — Douglas Bush, *"Paradise Lost" in Our Time* (1945)
Ovid — Davis P. Harding, *Milton and the Renaissance Ovid* (1946)
Par. — Dante, *Paradiso*
Pastoral — William Empson, *Some Versions of Pastoral* (n.d.)
Poetic — Ruth Wallerstein, *Studies in Seventeenth Century Poetic* (1950)
Polity — Richard Hooker, *Of the Laws of Ecclesiastical Polity* (Everyman Ed.)
P.&M. — Irene Samuel, *Plato and Milton* (1947)
Preface — C. S. Lewis, *A Preface to "Paradise Lost"* (1942)
Prom. — Aeschylus, *Prometheus*
Purg. — Dante, *Purgatorio*
Read — *Studies for William A. Read*, ed. by Nathaniel M. Caffee (1940)
Reader — B. Rajan, *"Paradise Lost" and the Seventeenth Century Reader* (1947)
Relation — George Sandys, *A Relation of a Journey*
Rep. — Plato, *Republic*
Royalism — Malcolm M. Ross, *Milton's Royalism: A Study of the Conflict of Symbol and Idea in the Poems* (1943)
Sat. — Juvenal, *Satires*
S.C.S.H.G. — *Seventeenth Century Studies Presented to Sir Herbert Grierson* (1938)
Semitic — Harris F. Fletcher, *Milton's Semitic Studies and Some Manifestations of Them in His Poetry* (1926)
Serpents — Edward Topsell, *A Historie of Serpents*
S.M. — E. M. W. Tillyard, *Studies in Milton* (1951)
Stuarts — Godfrey Davies, *The Early Stuarts, 1603–1660* (1937)
Style — Arnold Stein, *Answerable Style* (1953)
Summa Theol. — St. Thomas Aquinas, *Summa Theologica*
T.G.C.T. — Arnold Williams, ed., *A Tribute to George Coffin Taylor* (1952)
Theog. — Hesiod, *Theogony*
Thinker — Denis Saurat, *Milton: Man and Thinker* (1925)
Tim. — Plato, *Timaeus*
Tradition — Elizabeth M. Pope, *"Paradise Regained": The Tradition and the Poem* (1947)
Vanity — Joseph Glanvill, *The Vanity of Dogmatizing*
Verse — W. B. C. Watkins, *An Anatomy of Milton's Verse* (1955)
Vision — Don Cameron Allen, *The Harmonious Vision* (1954)
V.&M. — Sir Maurice Bowra, *From Virgil to Milton* (1945)
Wars — Josephus, *The Wars of the Jews*

ABBREVIATIONS OF TITLES OF PERIODICALS CITED IN THE NOTES

Archiv — *Archiv für das Studium der neueren Sprachen und Literaturen*
CEA Critic — *C*(ollege) *E*(nglish) *A*(ssociation) *Critic*
CL — *Comparative Literature*
CE — *College English*
EA — *Etudes Anglaises*
EIC — *Essays in Criticism* (Oxford)
EIHC — *Essex Institute Historical Collections*
ELH — *ELH: A Journal of English Literary History*
ELL — *The English Language and Literature* (English Literary Society of Korea)
ES — *English Studies*
E & S — *Essays and Studies* published by the English Association
Expl. — *Explicator*
HLQ — *Huntington Library Quarterly*
HTR — *Harvard Theological Review*
JEGP — *Journal of English and Germanic Philology*
JHI — *Journal of the History of Ideas*
JWCI — *Journal of the Warburg and Courtauld Institute*
KR — *Kenyon Review*
MFS — *Modern Fiction Studies*
MLN — *Modern Language Notes*
MLQ — *Modern Language Quarterly*
MLR — *Modern Language Review*
MP — *Modern Philology*
Neophil. — *Neophilologus* (Gröningen)
NQ — *Notes and Queries*
NS — *Die neueren Sprachen*
PMLA — *Publications of the Modern Language Association of America*
PQ — *The Philological Quarterly*
QJS — *Quarterly Journal of Speech*
RES — *Review of English Studies*
RSUL — *Research Studies of the University of Louisiana*
RSUW — *Research Studies of the University of Washington*
SEL — *Rice University Studies in English Literature, 1500–1900*
SN — *Studia Neophilologica*
SP — *Studies in Philology*
Spec — *Speculum*
SR — *Sewanee Review*
TLS — *The London Times Literary Supplement*
TSE — *Tulane Studies in English*
TSLL — *Texas Studies in Literature and Language*
UKCR — *University of Kansas City Review*
UTQ — *University of Toronto Quarterly*
UTSE — *University of Texas Studies in English*
ZAA — *Zeitschrift für Anglistik und Amerikanistik* (East Berlin)

INTRODUCTION

Epic or Drama?

1. A reader coming to *Paradise Lost* for the first time, and going rapidly through it to the end of Book X, is likely to get the impression that he is reading drama. It is a heightened kind of drama which is too big for the stage and too rich for it in poetic perspectives around the conversations and debates that take up more room than the narrative does. If he reads on through the unfolding of the never-ending but finally defeated waylaying of good by evil in human history as Michael unfolds it to Adam in a quiet dialogue in the last two books of the poem, he will miss the clash of characters and ideas in the earlier books, but he may find satisfaction in the sombre but not tragic resolution of the plot as the final step in the development of Adam's character. Looking back, he will see a series of dramas composing the epic plot: the council of the devils in Book II, with Moloch, Belial, and Mammon making bids for leadership which wonderfully reveal their characters but fail to shake Satan's command; the council in heaven in Book III, where the Son of God discovers his character by making himself responsible for mankind's redemption; Satan's first attempt to seduce Eve, by a dream, in Book IV; the revolt of Satan's followers against God as Raphael reports it to Adam in Books V and VI, pausing to tell him of the refusal of a single seraph in the throng, Abdiel, to be swept into the crime; the dialogue about creation and nature in Books VII and VIII, which should have made Adam proof against the temptation to betray his own nature by disobedience to God's order in Book IX; the great temptation scenes in that book; and the hardly less psychologically interesting scenes of reconciliation between Adam and Eve, in which she takes the initiative and becomes almost, if not quite, the stronger character in Book X.

2. But *Paradise Lost* is not a drama; it is an epic built out of drama. Its plan is epic. It begins as the *Iliad* and the *Aeneid* begin, with a plunge into the action at a point where it has reached its third crisis, the time when the devils, after the decision to revolt in Heaven and their defeat in battle there, debate their policy against God and man in Hell. The first two crises wait for narration by Raphael to Adam in Book V. The fourth crisis in the order of events is the scene in Heaven in Book III. Here we find a new kind of drama — the drama of contrast between situations. What has just happened in Hell is a parody of what happens in Heaven. As Satan has established his right to rule the devils by monopolizing the glory of undertaking man's destruction, so the Son of God proves his right to reign in heaven by undertaking man's redemption. There is direct narrative in Book II of Satan's flight through Chaos and in later books more of it about his travels in our universe. But the high peaks in his later story are dramatic — his soliloquies on the theme of "Myself am hell," his seduction of Eve, his encounter with his daughter Sin and grandson Death on their bridge across Chaos, and the grand opera scene in Pandaemonium where his final disappearance in serpent form begins with the rising orchestral roar of recognition by his followers and ends in their

involuntary hisses — hisses that Dr. Edith Sitwell thinks are the finest sibilant music in all English poetry. We seldom see Satan except at moments of high drama, but his career is epic.

3. Just how epic Satan's career is we can see only in the light of the whole poem. His revolt in Heaven depopulates it by drawing off perhaps a third of the angels. Out of that evil good comes immediately in the creation of the universe and of man, who is intended to sire a race which — as Raphael explains to Adam — can ultimately achieve a virtually angelic nature and live at will on earth or in Heaven. When Satan wrecks that plan in Book IX the result is the epic struggle for man's redemption in the three following books. For Milton's contemporaries that story had the fascination simply as a theory of history which historical writing like Toynbee's has for us today, but with the difference that its redemptive hope for both humanity in general and for individual men was absolutely assured by the scriptural texts that stud Milton's lines. And in creation Milton had the great epic theme of his century, the theme of the *Divine Weeks* of the French Calvinist poet Guillaume Salluste Sieur du Bartas, which was more popular in the English translation of Joshua Sylvester that Milton knew as a child than the original ever was in France. Creation was the theme of Torquato Tasso's *The Creation of the World* (*Il mondo creato*) and — to some extent — of pagan poems like Hesiod's *Theogony*, Ovid's *Metamorphoses*, and Lucretius' *On the Nature of Things* (*De rerum natura*). Milton's cosmic passages bear the occasional print of all these poems as plainly as his first two books occasionally reflect facets of the hells of Homer and Virgil, Dante and Spenser. Such poems were not Milton's models but they were a part of the sinews of his strength as he pursued

Things unattempted yet in Prose or Rhyme.

4. So his poem is not a drama though its dramatic roots are strong. Less has been written about them than about its epic subsoil. Like that subsoil, they lie on both sides of the poem, the classical and the Christian. Traditionally, Milton's Satan has been compared with Aeschylus' Prometheus, and the older editions of *Paradise Lost* mark many lines in Satan's speeches as conscious echoes of *Prometheus Bound*. But it would be impossible to write a book exploring Milton's debt to Greek drama on the scale of the studies of his epic backgrounds by Dr. Tillyard and Sir Maurice Bowra. And recently we have been taught by J. C. Maxwell and Robert Adams to suspect the Promethean parallels and to think of Satan and Prometheus as contrasting characters rather than the high-souled first cousins that Shelley made them for the nineteenth century. Milton's Satan owes only a general debt to Greek tragedy. It is of the vitally negative kind that P. F. Fisher implies when he says that, by concentrating the Greek tragic flaw of pride (*hybris*) in "the character of the Adversary and the Author of Evil . . . Milton repudiated the doctrine that life was essentially tragic and that retribution was . . . the final victory of evil as far as man was concerned." As an influence on the characters and design of *Paradise Lost* Greek drama counts for less than classical epic.

5. When we turn to Christian drama, the balance shifts. In Milton its two main currents flow together — the medieval, native stream of the half-forgotten mystery plays and the contemporary, continental revival of their tradition in Holland and Italy. If anyone will take the trouble to read Hugo Grotius' *Adamus Exul* and Giambattista Andreini's *L'Adamo* in the *Celestial Cycle* of Watson Kirkconnell or in any other translations of the original Latin and Italian, he will be struck with many things that they have in common with *Paradise Lost* and with each other. The ground common to all three is especially extensive in the treatment of the temptation, the sin, and Adam's involvement in it through his love or passion for Eve. The lovers' quarrel threatens the existence of humanity but is reconciled in a scene of some psychological depth. In a general way Milton stands close to Grotius in the scenes between Raphael and Adam in *Paradise Lost* — much closer than he does in the scenes in Books I and II to the corresponding scenes in the work of another Dutchman whose claim to have influenced him can hardly be proved, the *Lucifer* of Joost van den Vondel. Milton must have heard about and perhaps seen performances of sacred plays like Andreini's *L'Adamo* in Italy, and the cumulative Italian influence upon him may have been substantial; but the more Italian plays one reads and the more closely one reads them individually, the weaker become their individual claims to have influenced Milton. The late Norman Douglas was fond of insisting (in *Old Calabria* and elsewhere) that Milton's main source was the *Adamo caduto* (*Adam's Fall*) of Serafino della Salandra, which was published in 1647 and may not even have been known to Milton. Their few strikingly close but merely verbal resemblances are noted in the proper places in this edition. Their differences are far more instructive. Salandra's demons are classico-medieval monsters. Anything like epic characterization of them is unthinkable. And Salandra's treatment of the basic theme of Redemption, the paradox of the Fortunate Fall, has as little as possible in common with Adam's echo of the medieval hymn *O felix culpa* when in Book XII he explains:

> O goodness infinite, goodness immense!
> That all this good of evil shall produce,
> And evil turn to good.

In Salandra's last act an allegorical Misericordia taunts Sin, Malice, and Death with their failure to destroy mankind, and in Heaven later vaunts the inexhaustible "excesses" of divine love in its more than successful effort to repair the harm done in Eden.

6. When Milton returned to London from his Italian tour in the summer of 1639 he may have already been meditating plans for some biblical dramas like those that he sketched in the Trinity manuscript in 1640 to 1642. The plans undoubtedly have a bearing on *Paradise Lost*, and perhaps they are a link between it and the native English medieval drama. In puppet shows or "motions" that drama still survived in Milton's youth, and a capital criticism of its main weakness is implied in Milton's sneer in *Areopagitica* at its failure to make Adam anything but a pawn in a game between God and the Devil. Milton's Adam has a will as well as a mind of his own, and by them

hangs the justification of the ways of God to man in *Paradise Lost*. But there were things that he could admire in the English mysteries, such things as the traditional debate of Justice and Mercy over Adam before the throne of God. If there had been no such tradition, we should have no scene like the appeal of the Son of God for man in Book III, 227–265, and the following speech by the Father. In the two most elaborate plans for dramas on the subject of the fall of man in the Trinity manuscript the medieval allegorical element is obvious, but it is most interestingly entangled with other elements that plainly come from Italy and ancient Greece.

7. In the Trinity manuscript Milton left four sketches of a developing plan for a drama on the fall of man. The two last and most elaborate of them fuse or confuse the features of the sacred dramas of the Counter-Reformation in Italy with Greek and medieval elements. In the fourth sketch there are signs of an inclination to treat the subject epically — as if Milton were feeling his way toward an epic design as alone giving scope to the different levels of his drama in Hell, Heaven, and Earth. The scene opens with Gabriel descending on a mission like that which we see him executing when he takes Satan into custody in *Paradise Lost* IV, 798–990. He explains to a chorus of angels that since Lucifer's revolt he is constantly on guard in Eden, and he tells them what he knows

of Man, as the creation of Eve, with their love, and marriage. After this Lucifer appears after his overthrow, bemoans himself, seeks revenge on Man. The Chorus prepare resistance at his first approach. At last, after discourse of enmity on either side, he departs; whereat the Chorus sings of the battle and victory in Heaven against him and his accomplices, as before, after the first Act, was sung a hymn of the Creation. Here again may appear Lucifer, relating and insulting in what he had done to the destruction of Man. Man next and Eve, having been by this time seduced by the Serpent, appears confusedly, covered with leaves. Conscience, in a shape, accuses him; Justice cites him to the place whither Jehovah called for him. In the meantime the Chorus entertains the stage and is informed by some Angel of the manner of his Fall. Here the Chorus bewails Adam's fall. Adam then and Eve return and accuse one another; but especially Adam lays the blame to his wife — is stubborn in his offence. Justice appears, reasons with him, convinces him. The Chorus admonisheth Adam, and bids him beware by Lucifer's example of impenitence. The Angel is sent to banish them out of Paradise; but, before, causes to pass before his eyes, in shapes, a masque of all the evils of this life and world. He is humbled, relents, despairs. At last appears Mercy, comforts him, promises him the Messiah; then calls in Faith, Hope, Charity; instructs him. He repents, gives God the glory, submits to his penalty. The Chorus briefly concludes. Compare this with the former Draft.

8. An interesting aspect of this draft is its greater emphasis on Adam and Eve and the angelic actors than on Lucifer-Satan, in comparison with the stresses in *Paradise Lost*. Lucifer seems to be simply the evil one. There is no trace of the intriguing, exploring, despairing Satan of the poem that we have. There is no trace of the Satan who still seems to many readers to be tragic in at least an Elizabethan if not a Greek sense of the word. In an Elizabethan sense that makes tragedy consist in wilful self-exclusion from all good Miss Helen Gardner has pled that Milton's Satan is like Macbeth, Doctor

Faustus, and Beatrice-Joanna in Middleton's *Changling*. Satan's repeated confession that he is his own hell has often been set beside Mephistophilis' matter-of-fact statement to the same effect in *Faustus*, but Miss Gardner makes it a part of Satan's passion for self-pitying soliloquy, which is in turn an aspect of the perversion of will that shuts him wilfully out of all good. If we look at him in this way, his character becomes consistent and the Shakespearian echoes that editors have spotted in his speeches become a part of a unified tragic character. But not a noble one. And Miss Gardner explains that in her view such tragic heroes are unforgettable because they are not pitiable.

9. So *Paradise Lost* first germinated in Milton's mind as a drama and became an epic only after years of reflection and some experience with at least partial drafts finally ended in the poem that we have. From one such draft we know that he preserved a few lines in Satan's address to the sun in Book IV (32–41). Perhaps, as Arthur Barker suggests, the original conception explains the division of the poem into ten books in the first edition — breaking the action into something like the structure of a five-act play. When the original, very long Book X was split into the Books XI and XII of the second edition, their true weight in the drama of human destiny was clarified though the only addition to them was the opening five lines of Book XII. In the new arrangement Book IX dominates the action less than it seemed to do in the original one, and the many dramatic ironies in the structure of the whole poem are strengthened by the new weighting of the recovery of the "paradise within you happier far" in Books X to XII.

10. Building on the small external evidence that we have about the writing of the poem and also on lynx-eyed analysis of internal evidence of changes, additions, and minor inconsistencies, Allan H. Gilbert has made it impossible to think that the composition of *Paradise Lost* was a single, straightforward act. There were afterthoughts. Perhaps one of them was the episode of Abdiel's refusal to join the rebel angels who sweep him along with them into the north parts of Heaven in Book V. By Raphael his story is intended as an example of brave obedience to Adam, and by Milton it was intended as a contrast to Adam's later behavior. The most interesting surmise about Milton's additions to his original design is the suggestion that he added the first two books somewhere late in the process of composing his poem in order to provide it with a standard epic beginning — a plunge into the midst of the action at the start. If the suggestion is sound, it disposes of the persistent objection that poetically the remaining books of *Paradise Lost* are an anticlimax because in Book III Milton grew tired and irretrievably lost the dash and power that made the first two books great. The suggestion would also, almost if not quite dispose of A. J. A. Waldock's view that Milton "blundered in the earlier books by making Satan much more glorious than he ever meant to do," and then "sought somewhat belatedly to rectify his earlier errors."

Satan Hero?

11. It is only in the first two books of *Paradise Lost* that Satan seems heroic. There is grandeur but no heroism in his later soliloquies and after the seduction of Eve he departs to Hell, leaving the world to his vice-gerents Sin and Death.

There is no doubt of Milton's intent to degrade him, step by step, down to the scene of his second and involuntary appearance in serpent form in Book X. The first shock to any admiration for him in a reader's mind comes when he meets his allegorical daughter Sin and his incestuously begotten grandson Death at Hell's gates (II, 648–883). For over two centuries critics agreed that the step into pure allegory in Sin and Death was a blemish on the poem and an external incrustation. Recently they have been wondering whether it is not a part of the structural irony of the whole design. Satan, Sin, and Death are now seen to be a parody of the Trinity of Heaven. Satan's "daughter and . . . darling without end" is the antitype of the Son of God's bosom who is his "word, wisdom, and effectual might" (III, 170). Sin makes only one further appearance, but again it seems — as Ernest Schanzer observes — that the purpose is to extend the over-arching dramatic irony that ties the poem together. When she meets Satan in Chaos she tells him that she has been drawn to him from Hell by "a secret harmony" that moves her heart with his, "joined in connexion sweet," and that the distance of worlds between them has not broken the "fatal consequence" that will forever unite them. Her words can hardly be an accidental parallel to Adam's protestation to Eve at the moment of decision in Eden:

> So forcibly within my heart I feel
> The bond of Nature draw me to my own;
> My own in thee; for what thou art is mine.

12. Everything in the poem, of course, depends on the way in which this speech of Adam's is read. Mr. Waldock has read it as both the most dramatic and the noblest utterance in the entire poem — a brave and beautiful expression of human love at its heroic best. He will not even consider it as an honest effort by Milton to accept the hardest element in the biblical account of the Fall — the deception of Adam by Eve. Mr. Waldock had nothing but contempt for the critics who variously condemn or palliate Adam's act as "uxoriousness" (Milton's term for it in the *Christian Doctrine*) "gregariousness," "passion," "sentimentality," or (G. M. Hopkins' view) "sinful chivalry." For Mr. Waldock then Adam becomes the hero of the poem though he behaves rather badly with Eve later on and is in danger of losing his laurels as a human being to her.

13. By the same token Mr. Waldock saw Satan as a dramatic failure and a hopelessly inconsistent personality in the course of his whole story. He constantly misses his opportunities for tragedy. His character does not degenerate; it is degraded. In the later books he becomes essentially an allegory and a kind of emblem of evil. This criticism seems wide of the mark when we think of Satan's intelligently and shrewdly consistent play on Eve's vanity in the two temptation scenes and compare his flattery of her half-formed wish for "godhead" with his flattery of the same craving in his followers in Books V (772–802) and I (94–124). But in general Mr. Waldock's objection to Satan as a dramatic character is sound, and it is a searching criticism of the poem itself. In substance, it comes close to Mr. Rajan's view of Satan as a great opportunist, putty to be molded by the changing situation, constant only to

his resolve in Book I (165) "out of good still to find means of evil."   But Mr. Rajan's view of Satan is less critical than it is historical.   For Milton's contemporaries Satan was simply the Adversary whom John Calvin described as "an enemie that is in courage most hardie, in strength most mightie, in policies most subtle, in diligence and celeritie unweariable, with all sorts of engins plenteously furnishd, in skill of warre most readie."   The Satan of the seventeenth century was a figure to hate and fear.   In poetry and in life alike, he was the father of lies, "with all sorts of engins plenteously furnishd."   And that was his main character.

14.   But he was also courageous and "in skill of warre most readie" — a fact that we overlook even though we see him fighting in spite of his wounds, like Turnus or Hector, through the three days of battle in Heaven, and proving his skill by inventing artillery on the eve of the second day.   As a field marshal in Heaven, the critics agree to find Satan disgusting and to say as little as possible about him except to deplore his jibes and Belial's at the angels whom their first salvo topples over.   But the jeers at God are a part of Satan's nature.   We hear them in his first speeches to his followers in Book V, and we hear them still echoing in Book X (625–27) when God speaks of

> my scornful Enemies
> That laugh, as if transported with some fit
> Of Passion.

The contrast of Satan's jeers with the laughter of Him "that sitteth in the heavens," is a part of the cosmic irony of *Paradise Lost*.   In the battle in Heaven Satan is a much more comic than tragic figure, and he is constantly skirting comedy all the way through the poem.   In the allegory of his defeat by the Son of God on the third day of that battle Satan ceases to be comic only because the situation is too serious.   All the faith in Truth's power to crush Falsehood in any open encounter that Milton poured into *Areopagitica* is symbolized in the all-seeing eyes of the victorious Son's chariot.

15.   Probably Milton regarded the war in Heaven as both allegorical and historical.   For centuries various commentators had regarded the drawing off of a "third part of the angels" by Lucifer, in Revelation xii, 4–11, and his battle there with Michael, as a record of angelic war before the creation of Adam.   Others regarded it as a prophecy of a battle to be fought at the end of the world, or an allegory of some moral crisis in Heaven.   In *Lucifer* the poet Vondel treated it as allegory with the resonance of history behind it.   In the moment of Lucifer's defeat he and his rebel angels are all suddenly transformed into monsters more terrible than the serpents into which Satan and his followers are changed when we see them for the last time in *Paradise Lost*.   Here no grim comedy is intended — as it may be intended in Milton's scene.   Vondel is interested only in driving home the truth that Jakob Boehme put into the teaching that after "the divine light went out of the Devils, they . . . became like Serpents, Dragons, Wormes, and evill Beasts: as may be seen by *Adam's* Serpent."

16.   But Milton was too much a humanist and at the same time too much interested in the historical truth to be found in the Bible to be content to treat

the battle in heaven as sheer allegory. The biblical warrant for it as history might be small, but in the traditions of battles between the Olympian gods and the Titans which Hesiod tells, and which left their marks widely in classical literature and sculpture, Milton — like most of his contemporaries — saw a survival of sacred history in the legends of the pagans. This belief was part of a larger one that is mentioned in paragraph 25 below. It is cryptically involved in the allusion to Eurynome in *Paradise Lost* X, 581. Once more the rebels, the Titans, or at least many of them, were traditionally described as taking serpent or other monstrous forms. The forms might be allegory, but for Milton the legends about the Titans' war with the gods of light on Olympus were proof of a core of some kind of historical truth in the revolt of the angels.

17. As the battle in Heaven was in one of its aspects actual for Milton, so was Satan himself. He believed in the existence of the historical Author of Evil at least in the Augustinian sense that evil is deprivation or negation of good and is produced by pride. The only way to portray Satan then was as a voice confessing and vaunting the proud will and the discovery that in his assault on heaven the speaker has himself created a hell within him. In achieving that kind of a Satan Milton earned the praise of William Hazlitt and the Romantics generally for having got away from the medieval devil of Tasso and of all the poets up to his time, Italian and English too, who had drawn portraits of the fiends. But pride is self-deception, and Milton's Satan deceives himself so well that he deceived Shelley into thinking him a Promethean apostle of human regeneration, and Byron into thinking him an inspiring symbol of revolt against political tyranny. For Milton Satan was the archetypal tyrant. His reign in hell is the express antitype of the reign of the Son of God by merit in Heaven. And at the moment of commitment to the attack on Eve in Book IV, 393–94, it is "with necessity, The Tyrant's plea," that he justifies his act. It is not the courage of Satan's revolt against God that counts; it is the ambition which betrays him into what Arnold Stein calls "the trap of leadership." In recent years Satan has been too often and too easily compared with Mussolini and Hitler, but such analogies are not very helpful. Nor is it helpful to compare Satan with Cromwell. The "trap of leadership" deprives Satan of all private character and makes him speak to the councils in Hell and act in Eden in mechanical response to what he calls in his soliloquy in Book IV "public reason." If he had an historical counterpart in Milton's mind, it was prelacy. Satan's comparison with "huge Python" in *PL* X, 531, has been paralleled by J. B. Broadbent with the simile for prelacy in *The Reason of Church Government* as "that huge dragon of Egypt, . . . Python," which Apollo killed with his arrows of light. In like manner, said Milton, the prelates would be "shot to death with . . . the powerful beams of God's word."

18. It should be clear that in drawing his portrait of Satan Milton was objective. Its weakness is its greatness — its power to fool readers into its own delusion of power and make them say that Milton's Satan is a noble anticipation of the Nietzschean superman. If, to give the devil his due, we must say that in the first two books of *Paradise Lost* he is drawn with too many virtues, the answer is perhaps in Socrates' words in the *Republic* when he says that the finer virtues — "courage, temperance, and the rest" — belong to the

most evil men: "Or do you fancy that great crimes and unmixed wickedness come from a feeble nature and not rather from a noble nature that has been ruined?"

Milton's Cosmos

19. Satan's revolt in Heaven, his plunge with his followers through Chaos to Hell, and his journey up from Hell to the created universe — these and the later steps in Milton's plot imply a cosmic scheme like that below which is reproduced with the permission of Professor Walter Clyde Curry. In Milton's time his treatment of Chaos would not have seemed strange. He conceived it much as St. Augustine did when he described it in the *Confessions* XIII, xxix, 40, as "formless matter, prior in origin but not by interval of time to

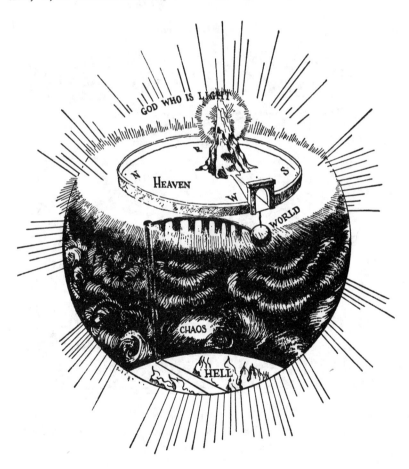

formed matter, and therefore never having existed independently in this world." To scientific minds it was a physical hypothesis, yet not far removed from the poet's vision of "the huge eternall chaos" out of which Spenser imagined all forms and all living things as arising, only to be gathered into it again by "Time's eternall sickle" in the Garden of Adonis. But it was also understood as a kind of womb of space, vast enough to engulf the universe and filled with warring atoms. It had been pictured in half-allegorical scenes like the one below, taken from Geffrey Whitney's *A Choice of Emblemes* (1586), where Chaos is a maelstrom of "warring atoms" or formless matter which is being blown into ever greater confusion by a being who seems to be both its personification and its ruler. In Boccaccio's *Genealogy of the Gods* Chaos is

122   *Sine iuſtitia, confuſio.*

Ad eoſdem Iudices.

W H E N Fire, and Aire, and Earthe, and Water, all weare one:
    Before that worke deuine was wroughte , which nowe wee
    looke vppon.

represented as a crowned figure sitting on a throne with his consort Night, as Hesiod described those first parents of all things in the *Theogony*. In Milton's "anarch" enthroned "on the wasteful Deep" in *Paradise Lost* II, 960, his readers would recognize Boccaccio's Chaos. Thus, in some mysterious way, Milton's "anarch" was identifiable with a Chaos bounded by Heaven above and more or less by Hell below it and also by our universe, which had recently been excavated out of it somewhere not far below the floor of Heaven.

20. Milton's Heaven is a realm of light. God is a "fountain of light" so dazzling that the angels, who are themselves creatures of pure light, must see him only through a veil of cloud that surrounds him "like a radiant shrine" (III, 378). When he speaks, "ambrosial fragrance fills all Heaven" (III, 135). His Son is the "effulgence" (VI, 680) of the Father's glory, "shining most glorious" himself (III, 139). It is as light that he defeats Satan in the battle in Heaven. If the angels are less luminous than he, it is because they shine with rainbow colors, as Raphael does when he appears like the god Mercury in "colors dipt in heaven" (V, 283), radiating light and "Heavenly fragrance" as he travels down to Eden to talk with Adam. According to St. Augustine and several other Fathers of the Church, the angels were creatures made of the light that came into being on the first day of creation, when God said, "Let there be light." The Heaven which Milton's angels inhabit is a celestial incandescence that is called by a Greek name, the Empyrean, which literally describes it. In some esoteric sense, its fiery substance is indestructible (though for Milton the divine origin of all matter implied the indestructibility of its substance if not of its forms). That is why Satan assures the demons that their "Empyreal substance cannot fail" (I, 117), or — in other words — that they are immortal, past God's power to destroy them. Milton left his readers free to doubt Satan's deduction, but if they were acquainted with the *Treatise of Angels* of the former Jesuit John Salkeld, who was a master of the literature of the subject, they had his authority for thinking that both "natural philosophy and true divinity" taught that "no spirits whatsoever they be are subject to corruption."

21. Although Raphael and Michael have major roles in *Paradise Lost* and Uriel, Gabriel, Ithuriel, and Zephon have variously important minor ones, Milton tells us little about the angels in Heaven. Unlike St. Augustine, he followed an ancient tradition that placed their creation long before that of our universe. Of their life before earthly time began we learn nothing except what Raphael tells Adam about the conclave when God first made his Son known to them as reigning over them "by right of merit," and about the battle in Heaven and the interest of the loyal angels in the creation of the universe. In the convocations in Heaven and the parody of them in Pandaemonium by the devils it was inevitable that Milton should use the titles of the nine orders of the heavenly hierarchy that the Church had inherited from Dionysius the "Areopagite," who was thought to have been a disciple of St. Paul. His sequence was this: Seraphim (the order of contemplative angels to whom Milton perhaps compared himself in the first sonnet on his blindness), and then downward, the Cherubim, Thrones, Dominations, Virtues, Powers, Principalities, Archangels, and Angels. In a literal and passionate way of his own Milton believed in the angels as he understood that St. Paul believed

in the "principalities and powers" of Romans viii, 38, against whom all Christians must contend. But — as Robert West makes clear in *Milton and the Angels* — there is every evidence of Protestant and Puritan reticence about belief in angels in *Paradise Lost*. Nowhere does Milton quite commit himself to so much as definite acceptance of the Dionysian hierarchy. He tells us little more about the angelic world than that its ranks were multiple and that the devils willingly perpetuated them in Hell. In *Paradise Lost* VII, 182, we hear an echo of the song of the angels at creation in the Book of Job xxxviii, 7; and in III, 654, Uriel's fitness for his charge of the sun is hinted at by his identification as one of the seven angels who are God's "eyes" throughout the universe in Zechariah's prophecy. And the angels in the four principal angelic roles have the full force of tradition behind them, stretching back through the approval of their invocation by name in a decision of the Council of Trent to its practice in the Jewish night prayer: "May Michael be at my right hand, Gabriel at my left, before me Uriel, and behind me Raphael, and above my head the divine presence of God."

22. Milton's Hell is more complex than his Heaven. It is local and as terribly remote from our universe as Milton declares it to be when he reasons that, "if the whole world is finally to be consumed by fire, it follows that Hell, if situated in the centre of the earth, must share the fate of the surrounding universe; a consummation more to be desired than expected by the souls in perdition." Between Milton's Hell and Dante's local one in the bowels of the earth there are many differences, yet they both have traces of the geography of Virgil's Hades in the *Aeneid*, and there are moments when the "fiery Deluge" that scorches Milton's devils "With ever-burning sulphur unconsumed" (I, 69) makes his climate seem much like Dante's. We may agree with Mr. J. B. Broadbent that Milton's imagination worked only in terms of the "sophisticated and Christian notion of an inner hell," and that he was "irritated at having to support it with classico-medieval flames and sulphur." Up to a certain point we can go along with Mr. Broadbent. When the devils build their proud palace of Pandaemonium, when they amuse themselves with tournaments of the kind that Milton says in the invocation to Book IX are unworthy subjects of epic poetry, when they reason like pagan philosophers and sing sentimental songs of self-pity, when they howl their praise of Satan with one voice like a mob saluting a dictator, we feel the poet's imagination working at a more intense pitch than it is when they suffer the torments of alternate frost and fire, as do some of Dante's damned souls. Milton usually thought of Hell as psychological and non-local, as Spenser did. At its most intense he imagined it in the heart of Satan when the devil cries, "Myself am Hell" (IV, 75). But for Milton Heaven and Hell both definitely outlast the physical universe. He agreed with St. Augustine and many other theologians that they could be imagined without limit as states of the spirit as long as their historical and local existence was not denied.

23. Milton's conception of Hell can be illustrated with one of its features that naive readers usually take in a purely physical sense — its "darkness visible" (I, 63). The phrase is not a lapse into the vagueness that Macaulay marked as distinguishing Milton's Hell from Dante's. Nor is there any ground for Mr. T. S. Eliot's objection that "it is difficult to imagine a burning lake

where there was only darkness visible." The only fair objection to the phrase is that it was a paradox that Milton's contemporaries knew only too well and regarded as a profound and perennially fresh truth. They did not have to go to Robert Herrick's *Noble Numbers* to learn that

> The fire of Hell this strange condition hath,
> To burn, not shine (as Learned Basil saith).

Many of them could have turned easily to the passage that Herrick had in mind, as many of them could have turned to the passage in the *Summa Theologica* III, xcvii, 4, where St. Thomas Aquinas makes the same observation in a matter-of-fact way and explains Hell's tenebrosity as mainly due to the earth encasing it. Mr. West notes that for as "scientific" a writer as Cornelius Agrippa in the sixteenth century the dark fires of Hell were simply one of its punishments. On the other hand, for a philosophical poet like Milton's contemporary Joseph Beaumont the dark fires were a natural part of the devil's inner hell:

> . . . th'immortal Prince of equall spight
> Abhorrs all *Love* in every name and kinde;
> But chiefly that which burns with flames as bright
> As his are dark, and which as long shall finde
> Their living fuell.

24. Two of Milton's devils, Belial and Mammon, he knew were — a matter of historical fact — only popular personifications of the abstractions that were originally meant by the two names. In the Old Testament we meet "sons of Belial" who commit acts of lust, but the phrase is a Hebraism that by no means implied that Belial was a deity or the father of sons. So in the Gospels we are told that men serve Mammon rather than God, but Mammon there means simply avarice or worldliness. Yet in the medieval religious drama and in plays like Salandra's *Adamo caduto* Belial appears as a grossly sensual devil. Mammon is not a character in any of the dramas that are represented in Kirkconnell's *Celestial Cycle*, but in Andreini's *L'Adamo* the World appears in a speaking role that might easily be taken by Mammon. Beside these demonic personifications of vices in most of the plays Beelzebub usually has a leading part as a prince of the devils second only to Satan and loosely corresponding to the Pharisees' description of him as such in Matthew xii, 24. Milton's readers expected to find these three devils in *Paradise Lost*, and they almost certainly expected to find them participating in some grand demonic conspiratorial council like those that come early in the action of *Adamo caduto*, *L'Adamo*, in both of Vondel's plays *Lucifer* and *Adam in Ballingschap*, and in a familiar epic poem like Tasso's *Jerusalem Delivered*. Milton did not disappoint them. His council has the glory and humanity of the assemblies of the gods in Homer, and the roll-call of the participating demons had associations that made it more interesting and powerful than Homer's catalogue of ships.

25. The catalogue of devils rests on a widely accepted belief, coming down from antiquity, that in ancient times the devils deceived mankind and usurped God's worship by masquerading as the gods of the pagan world. Richard

Hooker put the matter succinctly in *The Laws of Ecclestiastical Polity:* "The fall of the angels was pride. Since their fall, . . . being dispersed, some in the air, some on the earth, some in the water, some among the minerals, dens, and caves that are under the earth, they have by all means laboured to effect a universal rebellion against the laws, and as far as in them lieth, utter destruction of the works of God. These wicked spirits the heathens honoured instead of gods, . . . some in oracles, some in idols, some as household gods, some as nymphs" (I, iv, 3). The belief plays a momentary part in Vondel's *Lucifer* when Lucifer says to his followers:

> I shall exalt my haughty tyranny,
> And ye, my sons, shall be adored as gods.
> At altars in high temples without number,
> Worshipped with cattle, frankincense, and gold.
> *(Celestial Cycle,* p. 417)

In Milton's roll-call of devils their later careers as pagan deities let them appear under the names of the gods whom the prophets denounced for seducing Israel. The best known of them to Milton's readers was probably

> *Moloch,* horrid King besmear'd with blood
> Of human sacrifice, and parents' tears,
> Though for the noise of Drums and Timbrels loud
> Thir children's cries unheard, that past through fire
> To his grim Idol.
>
> (I, 392–96)

Milton did not exaggerate his importance in letting him speak first from the floor in Pandaemonium.

26. After Moloch a modern reader may not recognize many of the names except Astarte and Adonis. Their cult is described in lines (I, 437–46) which may have inspired John Singer Sargent's painting of them in the ceiling of the Boston Public Library, where Astarte's cloudy robes and dancing priestesses make a delicate contrast to the bull-head of Moloch. Milton's readers would easily have recognized them all and matched their names with the places that are infamous in the Bible records for their seductions of the Israelites. Many of the places were shown on maps like the two from Thomas Fuller's *A Pisgah-Sight of Palestine* on pages xxix and xxx. Chemos and Baal-Peor and Dagon, whose worship in five Philistine cities figures in Milton's list, could be tracked to their lairs on the maps, and in some cases their very temples could be seen. The names of the cities live for us only in the poetry, but for Milton's public they were familiar in geography and terrible in history.

27. When — leaving Hell — we approach the universe which the Son of God shapes with his golden compasses in Book VII we are inclined to think of the account of the creation as only a kind of long approach to the — for us — more interesting account of astronomy in the first two hundred lines of Book VIII. Beyond the dialogue on astronomy lies Adam's narrative to Raphael of his own awakening to life in Eden, of his naming of the animals, and of the creation of Eve. Of the three great subjects of discussion between

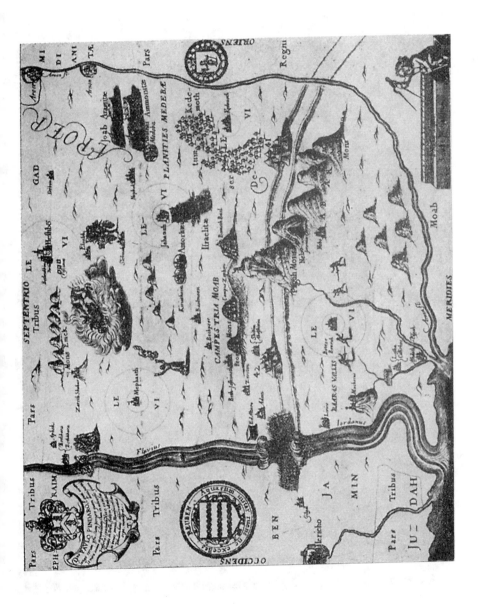

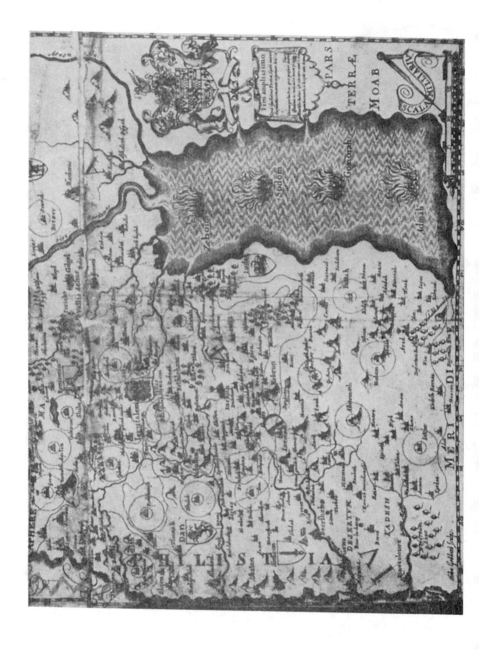

the angel and the man, the least interesting in Milton's judgment was their debate over the Copernican theory of the heavens as contrasted with that of Aristotle, Ptolemy, and the medieval astronomers. The most interesting subject was the creation, and since Adam's experience was really only an aspect of that great miracle, the dialogue on astronomy must have seemed to Milton to be a mere interlude in the symphony of the angels and the spheres praising the Creator. It was as music that Milton imagined the creation — the song of the angels shouting for joy as they do in the account of it in the Book of Job (xxxviii). That is why — as Mr. Watkins says in his chapter on the subject in *An Anatomy of Milton's Verse* — Milton made creation both an expression of power in the vision of "Heavens and Earth" rising in a moment "out of Chaos" and an expression of wisdom and love in the figure of the heavenly spirit sitting "Dove-like brooding on the vast abyss" to make it "pregnant." "By passing constantly from one to the other Milton manages to infuse a brooding warmth into his abstractions, so that when we come to the Golden Compasses drawing swift arcs over Chaos the image seems more biological than geometric."

28. But the image of the spirit brooding on the face of the primeval waters comes from Genesis, and in the expansion of the story of the six days of creation Milton stayed as close as he could to the letter of Scripture. He regarded it less as a source than as an authority and an inspiration. To have felt that way would have been impossible if countless writers coming between him and the first redaction of the Book of Genesis had not variously shared and anticipated his creative veneration for its authority. At least as early as the writing of the first of the many versions of the Apocryphal Book of Enoch in the second century before Christ or earlier, men's imaginations had been at work interpreting and embroidering the record of creation in Genesis. It was extended by the Hebrew commentaries that Professor Harris Fletcher has brought into the Miltonic orbit in *Milton's Rabbinical Readings*, and by the Christian commentaries of the Fathers, Greek and Latin, the medieval Schoolmen, and their heirs in the Renaissance, to many of whom Professor Arnold Williams introduces us in *The Common Expositor*. Through Mr. Williams at least a bowing acquaintance becomes possible with theologians like the great Frenchman, Marin Mersenne, the friend of Cardinal Bellarmine and of Descartes; or like the German Lutheran David Pareus and the Italian Protestant Girolamo Zanchi (cited in our notes as Zanchius). In their works abundant warrant could be found for Milton's dramatic treatment of the creation of the world as an expression of God's goodness if not of his will to bring good out of the evil done by the revolt of Satan and his angels.

29. Turning now to the architecture of the spherical universe that Milton hangs by a golden chain from Heaven's floor, we must first remember that he was writing for a public that visualized the universe essentially as it appears in the following scheme on page xxxii from Peter Apian's *Cosmographia*, edition of 1584. It was published without change for nearly a century from its first appearance in 1524. Quite unresponsive to the changes in astronomical thinking that began with the publication of Copernicus' work *On Celestial Motions* in 1543, the schools continued to teach the Ptolemaic theory that pictured the universe with the earth at its center and the "seven planets" —

6   PRIMA PARS COSMOGRAPH.

Schema prædictæ diuisionis.

the moon, Mercury, Venus, the sun, Mars, Jupiter, and Saturn — and beyond
them the fixed stars — revolving as if supported by concentric spheres which
were moved by an enveloping "First Mover" or sphere, whose ceaseless move-
ment turned everything within it except the motionless earth.   Between the
Eighth Heaven or sphere of the fixed stars and the "First Mover" (*Primum
Mobile*) medieval astronomy put a crystalline sphere, to which Milton refers
in Book III, 482, but which he did not have in mind when he put a crystalline
ocean *outside* the limits of the universe in VII, 271.   Apian put the Empyrean
or Habitation of God outside his spherical universe but not so definitely above
it as it is in Milton's scheme.

30. Milton was as well aware as his enlightened contemporaries were of the inadequacy of the Ptolemaic view of the heavens, but he knew that his readers could easily visualize them only as we see them in Apian's chart. For them the sun and the moon were planets like the "other five," as we find them in *Paradise Lost* X, 651–57. And it is down through the sphere of the fixed stars and then through those of the "planets seven" — sailing between "worlds and worlds" — that Raphael descends (V, 268) from the opening at the foot of the golden chain of Book II, 1051, which becomes the "Structure high" of III, 503, that seems comparable with

> The Stairs . . . whereon *Jacob* saw
> Angels ascending and descending, bands
> Of Guardians bright . . .
> (III, 509–511)

31. When Milton has Raphael drop, "prone in flight . . . between worlds and worlds," there is an implication that some at least of the planets that he passes are inhabited. A few lines earlier Milton has referred to "the glass of Galileo" and to his famous discovery that the moon's surface was much more terrestrial and less mysterious than tradition had made it. And in Book VIII, in lines which many modern readers have regarded as expressing Milton's private astronomical opinions, Adam puts the crucial question whether it is possible to believe that the apparent diurnal motion of the heavens is due to their revolution or to the earth's rotation. If the Copernican reply was made to that question, the same reply seemed inevitable to the question whether the universe was geocentric. And as soon as the earth ceased to be regarded as the center of the universe, we know that the doctrine of a plurality of worlds seemed to follow for many of Milton's contemporaries as a matter of course. But Raphael's reply to Adam's question is non-committal and brings us back to Galileo's observations of the moon. The angel says that, "if land be there," then there may be "fields and inhabitants"; and that if the spots on the moon are clouds, then those

> Clouds may rain, and Rain produce
> Fruits in her soften'd Soil, for some to eat
> Allotted there; and other Suns perhaps
> With their attendant Moons thou shalt descry . . .
> (VIII, 146–49)

32. On the strength mainly of Adam's dialogue with Raphael, Professor E. N. S. Thompson, writing in 1917 in *MLN*, XXXIII, 479, drew the conclusion that Milton was a convinced Copernican when he wrote *Paradise Lost*, and in 1932 Mr. Grant McColley (in *MLN*, XLVII, 323) was inclined to concur. But five years later (in *PMLA*, LII, 728–62) Mr. McColley took a different view in a study of the debate between Bishop John Wilkins in his *Discovery of a New World* and his *Discourse Concerning a New Planet, That the Earth May be a Planet* (1640), and his truculent antagonist, the Presbyterian divine Alexander Ross, in *The New Planet: or, The Earth no wandring Star: Except in the wandring heads of Galileans* (1646). Limitations of space forbid the discussion

of these books here and of Professor Marjorie Nicolson's survey in *A World in the Moon* of the more interesting speculation on the subject that began with the publication of Galileo's *Heavenly Messenger* (*Sidereus Nuncius*) in 1610, that was intensified in 1634 by the *Dream* (*Somnium*) — a speculative voyage to the moon—of the German astronomer Kepler, and reached a climax in France with the publication of Fontenelle's *Conversations on the Plurality of Worlds* in 1686. But in the *Sidereus Nuncius* Galileo denied the possibility of life on the moon and the question remained open. Milton may have been thinking of Galileo's skepticism when he wrote that

by night the Glass
Of *Galileo*, less assur'd, observes
Imagin'd Lands and Regions in the Moon.
(V, 261–63)

33. There is no doubt that Milton had long been fascinated by the "Optic Glass" (I, 288) of the "Tuscan Artist," or that he shared the eagerness of his contemporaries to see the heavens as they had been probed by the discoverer of the satellites of Jupiter and the phases of Venus, the "Morning Planet," of which he wonderingly said that she "gilds her horns" (VII, 366). For him, no less than for his scientifically informed contemporaries, the great question was the centrality of the earth, just as for us it seems to be that of an expanding universe. Quite as important a point in Miss Nicolson's studies as the kindling of his imagination by Galileo's evidence for the heliocentric theory is her stress upon the fact that much of its prestige in the eyes of his classically trained contemporaries came from antiquity. It had — supposedly — been taught by Pythagoras, and from Milton's second Prolusion ("On the Music of the Spheres") and from *At a Solemn Music* we know how strongly he responded to Pythagoras' more famous doctrine that the orbs of the seven planets rang with a harmony such as Plato describes in the tenth book of the *Republic*. The still powerful hold of that doctrine on the imagination of the time is clear from the drawing reproduced on page xxxv from *The History of both Worlds* (*Utriusque Cosmi Historia* — 1624) of Milton's acquaintance Robert Flud, whom Saurat has regarded as exerting an influence on much of his cosmological thinking.

34. For men hesitating to accept the Copernican view because they disliked novelty and craved some venerable authority for it such as Aristotle and the Bible itself seemed to give to the Ptolemaic theory there were ingenious compromises such as the scheme of Tycho Brahe reproduced on page xxxvi from John Swan's *Speculum Mundi, or a Glasse Representing the Face of the World* (Cambridge, 1655). The scheme and the bit of text above and below it are interesting for the light they throw on a once famous attempt to preserve the stationary dignity of the earth by making the sun wheel around it, and yet to let the sun be as nearly as possible the center of the universe by having the other planets revolve around *it*. This theory had the inconvenience of making the spheres of Venus, Mars, and Mercury cut through the sun's orbit — an assumption inconsistent with the usual view that the spheres were not merely the orbital paths of the planets in space, but that they were impenetrable

TRACTATUS I. LIB. III.

Hic autem monochordum mundanum cum suis proportionibus, confo-
nantiis & intervallis exactiùs compofuimus, cujus motorem extra mundum effe
hoc modo depinximus.

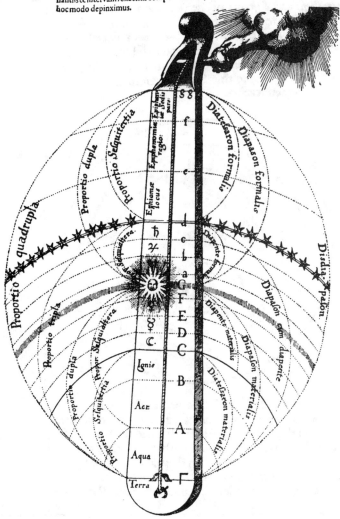

though transparent balls — "corporeal substances" that were turned, as
Raphael says (VIII, 108–110), by "Omnipotence" with "Speed almost
Spiritual."

35. Milton's treatment of astronomy is not "evasive," nor is it unctuously
pious like John Swan's. When he speaks of the divine laughter at the "quaint

Hypothesis and *Systema* of the world make it also plain,
that the sphere of the Sunne must be intersected by
the orbs of *Venus*, *Mars*, and *Mercury*: which could
not be if the heavens were impenetrable, or differed
toto genere from this soft aire wherein we live and
move. And now see this figure, framed according to
Tycho's demonstration.

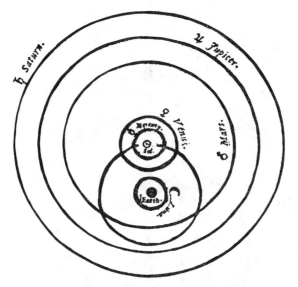

    Thus *Tycho* describeth the wayes and situations of
the Planets. The starres therefore move in the heavens
as birds in the aire, or fishes in the sea, and the like: yet so,
as their bounds are set; which with great regularitie, to
the admiration of their Maker, they constantly come un-
to, & depart away from, in their appointed times and de-
termined orders; and therefore said to be set in the firma-
                    R r 3   ment

Opinions" (VIII, 77–78) of men like Tycho, which were so "wide" of the
truth, his contempt is incomparably more restrained than George Herbert's
sweeping denunciation of all astronomical and scientific speculation in a
poem like *Vanitie*. Milton had none of the cosmic insecurity that shudders
in the verses by John Donne that are quoted in our footnote to Book VIII, 82.

Professor E. E. Stoll has collected abundant and beautiful evidence to show that not only was Milton undisturbed by the fact that this earth is what Adam calls a "punctual spot" (VIII, 23) in the universe, a grain of sand, but that he had good historical reasons for accepting the fact. The tininess of the earth had been put into an emphatic perspective by Roger Bacon in the thirteenth century, and the moral of that fact had been drawn by Chaucer, Dante, Cicero, and even Ptolemy himself. The fact is — as Mr. Howard Schultz proves with a cloud of witnesses supporting him in *Milton and Forbidden Knowledge* — that Milton's attitude toward all the sciences was no more evasive or "obscurantist" than that of his learned contemporaries. From the time when he wrote his third Prolusion as a student at Cambridge until he put the warning against the pursuit of scientific knowledge as an end in itself into Raphael's mouth in *Paradise Lost*, Milton's attitude never varied. He exalted the sciences as an enrichment of life but he subordinated them (like Socrates) to philosophy and divinity.

Milton's Ontology

36. If we try to probe Milton's ontology we find that, even more than his cosmology, it implies his theology and leads constantly toward his theological treatise *On Christian Doctrine* (*De doctrina christiana*). Since no one now challenges Professor Maurice Kelley's proof in *This Great Argument* that the treatise was given its present form almost contemporaneously with the writing of *Paradise Lost* — probably a very little earlier than the final writing of the poem — its relevance for us seems clear. It has been used in the notes to this edition with references both by part and chapter and by volume and page in the Columbia Edition of *The Works of John Milton*. Its relevance hardly suffers if we accept Mr. P. F. Fisher's thesis, in *JHI*, XVII (1956), 28–53, that the treatise was finished perhaps three years earlier than the poem and states a still immature faith in theological speculation which was soon to be transcended in the imaginative illumination of poetry. However illuminating the spiritual experience of the composition of the poem may have been, there is good evidence showing that Milton's confidence in his *Christian Doctrine* was such as to lead him to hope that it might be published after his death and contribute to the great theological debates of his time. Its study for its own sake is of no interest here, but its light on *Paradise Lost* and *Paradise Regained* is worth having, especially as it bears on four much debated passages in the former.

37. Diverse though the four passages are, they are all aspects of that "Christian materialism" that M. Saurat expounded in *Milton: Man and Thinker* in 1925, and developed more boldly in *Milton et le matérialisme chrétien* three years later. Two of them have to do with Milton's treatment of the angels and are not so important as the debate over them has made them seem. They are the places in Book V, 404–413, and VIII, 620–629, where Raphael tells Adam that the angels eat in the physical sense that men do, and that when they make love:

> Easier than Air with Air, if Spirits embrace,
> Total they mix, Union of Pure with Pure
> Desiring.

These passages are negatively illuminated by the perfect silence on both points in the chapter on the angels in *Christian Doctrine*. Food and sex were not important in Milton's thinking about angels. Mr. West is surely right in thinking that Milton inserted the two passages in his poem because he wished to stress and dramatize his materialism, which in different ways is the subject of the two other passages in question here. They are Raphael's comparison of the development of man to that of a tree which obviously is a symbol of the Great Chain of Being in Book V, 469–503, and the very different passage in VII, 168–172, where the Almighty says to the Son as he rides out on his creative mission into Chaos:

> Boundless the Deep, because I am who fill
> Infinitude, nor vacuous the space.
> Though I uncircumscribed myself retire,
> And put not forth my goodness, which is free
> To act or not.

38. From this description of creation as voluntary withdrawal by the Creator from the infinitude which he had previously filled M. Saurat drew the conclusion that Milton's justification of God's ways to man could be entirely read into these five lines. He saw in them the basis for Milton's belief in absolute human freedom, at least before Adam's fall, and consequently in man's responsibility for evil. His authority for reducing creation to a simple act of "withdrawal" by God from infinitude was a passage in the *Zohar* of which he took Milton's lines to be a translation. M. Saurat has been assailed for this theory by an army of opponents — most recently and devastatingly by R. J. Zwi Werblowski in *JWCI*, XVIII (1955), 90–113. The story of the attack on him has been told by Professor Robert Adams in *IKON*. It is not, as he says, that the *Zohar* is "a tangled, confused, elaborate mass of mumbo-jumbo," or that Saurat misread both what it and Milton say in the two passages in question. Mr. Kelley puts his finger on the main point when he says in *This Great Argument* (p. 211) that M. Saurat's "Retraction Theory" of creation destroys his own sound doctrine that Milton derived matter itself from God and therefore believed in its essential goodness and in a monistic universe.

39. In a much more interesting ontological passage Raphael declares (V, 469–471) that all things "proceed" from God and return to him — a statement which is just as clearly made in the *Christian Doctrine* (I, vii; C.Ed. XV, 22–24). It leaves no doubt that Milton thought of creation as God's shaping through the Word, his Son, of the unformed matter which originated in him. Milton's reason for thinking so was simply his understanding of the meaning of the Hebrew word that is translated "make" in the verse, "In the beginning God made heaven and earth."

40. Milton's most beautiful and crucial ontological passage is in Book V, 469–503. In "Some Notes on Milton's View of the Creation" (*PQ*, XXVIII, 1949, pp. 211–236), Professor Woodhouse suggests that in all the ontological passages Milton was writing as a Christian Humanist who was out of sympathy with the effort of some ultra-orthodox clergymen to interpret Genesis i, 1,

in a unique, theological sense. The divines could see no alternative to their view except atheistic materialism. To both views Milton opposed "creation by God (*ex Deo*)" — a conception which was "implicit in the Stoic conception of reason as an active aspect of matter, which they 'did not scruple to call God.' " The Stoic view was usually regarded as pantheistic and heretical, and so Milton may have regarded it himself. In the *Christian Doctrine* he clearly defined nature as God's creation and subject to God's laws, but described matter as if, though passive, it were informed with something like the 'seminal reason' of the Stoics. In this he saw no contradiction — just as he saw no inconsistency in describing the appearance of animal life on the earth and the invention of fire and metals as they are described in the "materialist" poem *On the Nature of Things* by the Epicurean, Lucretius. His ideas and imagery were drawn from a great variety of sources that have been largely explored by Professors W. C. Curry and W. B. Hunter, Jr., in a series of studies that have widened the base of his thinking and at the same time proved its critical independence. In one of them (*RSUL*, 1941, pp. 173–192) Mr. Curry brings us well within sight of the imagery in Book V, 469–503, that takes us to the heart of Milton's thinking about the nature of man as it originally was in Eden, and as by God's grace it yet may be again. But the thought is not inharmonious with Aristotle's conception of nature as growth, nor with St. Paul's belief that "the human body is sown a natural body," but "raised a spiritual body."

41. Very deliberately, Milton has Raphael put the essence of his thought into the image of the tree which represents the scale of being in the universe as a whole as well as man's body and mind as a replica or microcosm of nature. Both man and nature are like a tree from whose

> root
> Springs lighter the green stalk, from thence the leaves
> More aery, last the bright consummate flow'r
> Spirits odorous breathes.

Life and all being vitally resemble or involve processes like those of the digestion of food in the human body, which produces spirits (as Milton calls the chyle, blood, etc. in the medical language of his time) that both animate it and make it capable of intellectual activity —

> give both life and sense
> Fancy and understanding, whence the Soul
> Reason receives, and reason is her being.

42. Milton's image may go back to Plato's *Timaeus* (90a), where man's spiritual root and perfecting character are both said to end in heaven. Milton's readers could find something like his image in several medieval writers, and they could find something like his thought among contemporary Platonists of the Cambridge School. Indeed, it had become a familiar idea among popular theologians like William Ames that "all natural things tend to God." If Milton's readers wanted scientific confirmation for his idea of the human body, they had the word of William Harvey, the discoverer of

the circulation of the blood, that "the blood is a spirit, celestial in nature," which nourishes "the soul, that which answers to the essence of the stars, . . . something analogous to heaven, the instrument of heaven." Or, as the philosophical poet John Davies of Hereford put it in *Mirum in Modum* (1602):

> The *Body* in the Elements is cloz'd;
> The *Bloud* within the body is confin'd;
> The *Spirits*, within the Bloud; the Soul's dispoz'd
> Within the *Spirites*, which *Soule* includes the *Minde*.
> The *Understanding* in the Minde's repoz'd,
> And God in th'Understanding rest doth find:
> So this Worlde's made for *Man*, Man for the Soule,
> *Soule* for the *Mind*, and *Minde* for God her Gole.

43. Milton's thought might further be illustrated by countless passages like these from Harvey and Davies to show how familiar and convincing it was to his contemporaries. His image of the tree — as Kester Svendsen shows in *Milton and Science*, pp. 114–116 — was also familiar in contemporary scientific works as various as Mercator's *Historia Mundi* and Matthew Hale's *The Primitive Origination of Mankind, considered according to the Light of Nature.* Milton used the tree as a symbol of his conceptions of matter and of the nature and destiny of man. It is a kind of microcosm of his whole poem, and in Raphael's words he made it into an emblem of man's potential divinity in obedience to God:

> Your bodies may at last turn all to Spirit,
> Improv'd by tract of time, and wing'd ascend
> Ethereal as wee, or may at choice
> Here or in Heav'nly Paradises dwell;
> If ye be found obedient, and retain
> Unalterably firm his love entire
> Whose progeny you are.

"*Of Man's First Disobedience*"

44. Unless we are in a mood to think that

> Malt does more than Milton can
> To justify God's ways to man,

we have to recognize that in at least one way human disobedience is the theme of *Paradise Lost*. We may regret the fact, as Sir Walter Raleigh did in his *Milton* when he said that the poem was "a monument to dead ideas." We may even accept Sir Herbert Grierson's view in *Milton and Wordsworth* that the "shift of perspective" since the seventeenth century makes it impossible for us to accept the myth of Eden and "take refuge in the mystery." Milton himself was not satisfied with that refuge, but his discussion of the matter in the *Christian Doctrine* seems too "legalistic" to satisfy us. And we come with a shock to his analysis of it in the *Christian Doctrine* I, xi (C.Ed. XV, 180–182), as including "at once distrust of the divine veracity, and a proportionate credulity in the assurances of Satan; unbelief; ingratitude; disobedience; gluttony; in the man excessive uxoriousness, in the woman a want of proper regard for her husband, in both an insensibility to the welfare of their off-spring, and that offspring the whole human race; parricide, theft, invasion of the rights of others, sacrilege, deceit, presumption in aspiring to divine attributes, fraud in the means employed to attain the object, pride, and arro-gance."

45. Unless a reader can accept this passage as a matter of religious faith or strong philosophical conviction, he is likely to reject it outright and he may reject *Paradise Lost* into the bargain. Short of such conviction, Professor C. S. Lewis said in *A Preface to Paradise Lost* (p. 70), readers must either "accept Milton's doctrine of obedience as they accept the inexplicable prohibitions in *Lohengrin*, *Cinderella*, or *Cupid and Psyche*," or else they must play at historical make-believe seriously enough to read the poem from inside "that whole hierarchical conception of the universe" to which it belongs.

46. One way of playing that game is to follow Professor John Diekhoff in his *Commentary on the Argument of Paradise Lost* step by step through the scenes in the poem which establish the logical and legal case against Adam. Another way is to try testing the case by Milton's own rules as he stated them in his *Art of Logic*. Only a reader with some logical training is likely to wish to follow the critical study of that work as bearing on *Paradise Lost* which has been made by Professor Leon Howard in *HLQ*, IX (1946), 149–73. The reader needs some knowledge of Aristotelian logic as it was taught in Milton's youth and also of the challenge to it by the French logician Peter Ramus, whose work was to some extent a basis of Milton's *Art of Logic*. Otherwise it may not seem helpful to find that Eve is the "procatarctic" cause of Adam's fall, or that the fall itself was due to all four of the traditional kinds of cause — efficient, material, formal, and final. But it may be suggestive to find Adam's innocence regarded as the material cause of his deception. And — regardless of the extent to which Milton's logic was Ramist or Aristotelian — it is encouraging to find Mr. Howard agreeing with Mr. Diekhoff that, "Man in the person of Adam was the principal cause of his own disobedience." And a welcome light is shed on Adam's cry in Book XII, 469–471, that the evil of his sin has been turned into a vastly greater good when we are told that the final cause of his fall was not only the "glory of God," but also the "greater glory of man."

47. If we could stick strictly to logic and law we might accept Milton's attitude toward man's disobedience. The great logical objection to doing so — for most readers — is probably the close resemblance of Eve's reasoning to justify tasting the Tree of Knowledge to Milton's own reasoning against "a fugitive and cloistered virtue" in *Areopagitica*. For Milton's readers there was no problem for they agreed with Francis Bacon — in the *Advancement of Learning* VI, 138 — that it was "not curiosity about Nature's secrets but the desire for moral omniscience in order that Adam might be a law unto himself that caused the Fall." In its dogmatic way Bacon's distinction may seem empty, but at bottom it is very much like what Mr. Philip Wheelwright has to say when in the *Sewanee Review*, LIX (1951), 589–90, he compares a Navajo myth about the breaking of a tabu of silence to the symbolism of "the

Eden myth." His interpretation of the third chapter of Genesis is that "the creature, not content with the bounty of the tree of life, which is freely allowed him, dares to take good and evil into his own hands and to speak in his own way of primal matters, instead of bringing his mind and heart into the stillness of listening and thus into the harmony of universal rhythms."

48. With Bacon and Mr. Wheelwright championing the soundness of the tabu on the Tree of Knowledge, Milton's case against Adam and Eve may seem to have been confirmed, if ever there was such a case. There is an old suggestion that Milton did not really intend his shrewder readers to believe that Adam and Eve lost innocence when they tasted the Tree of Knowledge, simply because they had none to lose. Recently the suspicion has been getting support from delvers into the psychology of the Renaissance. In studies of "Milton's Prelapsarian Adam" in *RSUW*, XII (1946), 163–84, and of "Eve's Demonic Dream" in *ELH*, XIII (1946), 255–65, M. W. Bundy and W. B. Hunter, Jr., have reminded us that Eve's dream in *Paradise Lost* IV, 800–809, and V, 31–93, does not merely add a touch of the supernatural to the poem, as Agamemnon's dream of the woes threatening the Greek forces embarking for Troy casts a beam of prophecy ahead on the action of the *Iliad*. Eve's dream of a vaguely divine adventure near the forbidden tree betrays her susceptibility to the temptation awaiting her in Book IX. Perhaps it is itself a temptation. Evil spirits were held to be able to work through dreams to stir the imagination, rouse the Sensitive Appetite, lull the Reason into compliance or take advantage of its impotence in sleep, and move the will itself to evil. We are given a case history from a rather outstanding book, *Of Our Communion and Warre with Angels*, by Henry Lawrence, to whose son Edward Milton addressed a sonnet. The parallel with Eve's dream is interesting and close. But the conclusion that Eve is already fallen is not by any means inevitable.

49. The case for Eve as already fallen from our first sight of her, fascinated by her own image in the pool, is pressed hard by Mrs. Millicent Bell, in *PMLA*, LXX (1955), 1192–1202, who argues Eve's pride before the fall from her earlier betrayals of self-love, and Adam's uxoriousness as already apparent in his conversation with Raphael. What happens at noon on the fatal day is seen simply as a natural consequence of the passions that show in the lovers' quarrel when Adam gives way to Eve in the morning. In this way we may try to evade the problem of the sudden step from innocence to guilt by the simple breach of the tabu on the Tree o Knowledge. Of course, Milton did not evade it. At the edge of Eve's surrender to the serpent's wiles, we are told that she is "yet sinless" (IX, 659). But it is alluring for the reader who instinctively tries to read modern psychology into Milton to try to evade the problem in "the intractable myth" by injecting a smooth development of character into the story at the expense of losing Milton's tenacious faith that, although the fall was "fortunate," something in a supreme way valuable was forever and needlessly lost through the fruit of the Tree of Knowledge, the power to know good without knowing evil.

50. Milton understood the need for convincing character development and in the last three books of his poem he faced that problem against the still undiminished intractability of the myth. In the scene of Eve's reconciliation with Adam it is generally agreed that he notably achieved the transition from

THE SITVATION OF THE GARDEN OF EDEN.

¶ Because mention is made in the tenth verse of this chapter, of the river that watred the garden, we must note that Euphrates and Tygris called in Ebrew, Perath and Hiddekel, were called but one river where they ioyned together, els they had foure heads: that is, two at their springs, and two where they fell into the Persian sea. In this countrey and most plentifull land Adam dwelt, and this was called Paradise, that is, a garden of pleasure, because of the fruitfulnesse and abundance therof. And whereas it is said that Pishon compasseth the land of Hauilah, it is ment of Tygris, which in some countries, as is passed by diuers places, was called by sundry names, as sometime Diglito, in other places, Pasigris, and of some Phasin or Pishon. Likewise Euphrates toward the countrey of Cush or Ethiopia, or Arabia, was called Gihon. So that Tygris and Euphrates (which were but two riuers, and sometime when they ioyned together, were called after one name) were according to diuers places called by these foure names, so that they might seeme to haue bene foure diuers riuers.

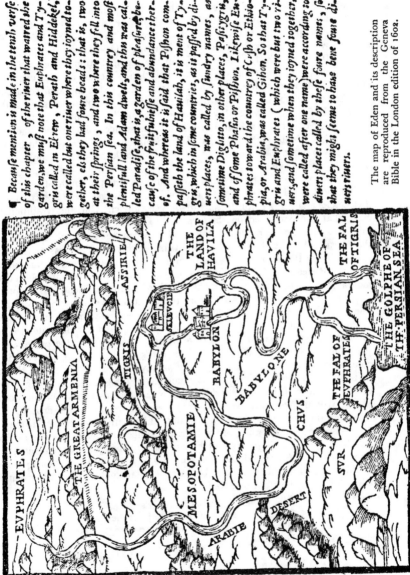

EVPHRATES · TIE GREAT ARMENIA · ASSIRIE · TIGRIS · THE LAND OF HAVILA · SALEVCH · BABYLON · BABYLONE · MESOPOTAMIE · CHVS · SVR · DESERT · ARABIE · THE FAL OF EVPHRATES · THE FAL OF TIGRIS · THE GOLPHE OF THE PERSIAN SEA

The map of Eden and its description are reproduced from the Geneva Bible in the London edition of 1602.

despair to hope and purpose through love in a dialogue that is both personal and universal, both idiomatic in its style as the talk of unfallen Adam and Eve was not, and at the same time charged with the tone of strong passion. The story in Genesis gives Milton no lead of that kind, nor does it in the least suggest that the initiative in the dialogue should be taken by Eve. Certainly it does not suggest, as does Mr. J. H. Summers in *PMLA*, LXX (1955), 1088, that her words counterpoint those of the Son of God speaking as the Redeemer in XI, 30–44, and XII, 614–623. From the reconciliation scene to the end of the poem there is no breach in the evolution of her mood and character. When the moment of final banishment from the garden in Eden comes, she and Adam are up to it. They do not — as John Erskine once suggested in the mood of the time when "we were very young" — go out into the world in the spirit of a bride and groom of the Renaissance going to seek their fortune. They go out rather in what E. E. Stoll has called "a twilight mood," but it is the mood of those who are determined to know good though it must be only through evil.

51. It is perhaps not strictly accurate to say that the myth of Eden gave Milton no hint of the redemptive role of Eve in his last three books. In the text of Genesis it does not do so, but by very ancient Christian tradition the curse that is pronounced on the serpent in Genesis iii, 15 — "I will put enmity between thee and the woman, and between her seed and thy seed; it shall bruise thy head, and thou shalt bruise his heel" — was interpreted as identifying the serpent with Satan and the seed of the woman particularly with the Redeeming Christ. Milton may well have known that Jewish commentary and tradition by no means justified even the identification of the serpent of Genesis with Satan. From the point of view of a man anxious to minimize the miraculous elements in Scripture — as we know from the *Christian Doctrine* that Milton was — it must have required a deliberate decision to accept the Christian influence of a prophecy of Christ in the promise that the woman's seed should bruise the serpent's head. Milton accepted it as completely as possible — as completely as any man of his time. In the last three books of *Paradise Lost* it is as much taken for granted as it is in Caravaggio's picture of the *Madonna della Serpe*, where the boy Christ and his mother Mary, Milton's "Second Eve" (X, 183), together tread down a serpent. The Christian inference into the myth did not make it untractable for Milton.

52. But the full meaning of the Christian inference is hardly clear in *Paradise Lost*. In Adam's preview of human history it is just distinct enough to let him be sure of the good that is to come out of evil, but it is not clear enough for him to be told more about it by Michael than that he must not dream of Christ's coming battle with Satan

> As of a Duel, or the local wounds
> Of head or heel: not therefore joins the Son
> Manhood to Godhead, with more strength to foil
> Thy enemy.
>
> (XII, 387–390)

The preview of history seems to have given Adam an impression of a struggle ending in a second casting out of "that old serpent, Satan" from heaven and earth at the end of time, as popular interpreters of Revelation xii, 9, had usually read the prophecy. All interpreters of Scripture — among them the most learned — men like Zanchius and Melanchthon — were agreed that the outcome of human history would be a proof of the "Fortunate Fall." Milton had seen some of the dangers of a popular, political interpretation of the promise that the seed of the woman should bruise the serpent's head, and he did not intend that *Paradise Lost* should contribute to that illusion. But the canvas of history was not to be his medium for imaginative escape from that illusion. His escape could be complete only when the paradise that had been lost by "one man's disobedience" had been recovered

> to all mankind
> By one man's firm obedience fully tried
> Through all temptation, . . .
> (*Paradise Regained* I, 3–5)

Milton's Muse

53. A critic who has seen far into Milton's mind and art has said that the language, images, and rhythms of *Paradise Lost* can be explained only as a mysterious gift of the "Celestial Patroness" of whom he said that she

> deigns
> Her nightly visitation unimplor'd,
> And dictates to me slumbring, or inspires
> Easy my unpremeditated Verse.
> (IX, 21–24)

Scholarship and criticism have, however, been very busy with the mystery, and they seem almost determined to destroy it. Even without the reminders of Miss Darbishire's work on the manuscript of the first book of the poem and on her text of 1952, without Gilbert's book *On the Composition of Paradise Lost* or Diekhoff's study of "The Trinity MS and the Dictation of Paradise Lost" in *PQ*, XXVIII (1949), 44–52, we should hardly imagine that Milton's experience in writing the poem resembled that of a stenographer taking dictation from a heavenly spirit. The poem which began as a drama and, years later, became an epic, we should feel certain, must have developed in the poet's mind as a long-cultivated garden develops. Much planning and changing lie behind the harmony of its beds and shrubs, but its summer beauty is a product of an almost spontaneous growth. And for Milton as he composed his poem in "parcels of ten, twenty, or thirty verses at a time," as his nephew Edward Phillips says that he did, the finally inevitable combination of the words, lines, and paragraphs into the crystallizing design of the entire work would seem to have something of the spontaneous blooming of flowers.

54. It would be a mistake to doubt him when he tells us that the poetic experience was the heavenly revelation for which he prayed in the invocations to Books I, III, and VII. In undertaking to retell the story of the fall he asked for inspiration by the Spirit that the opening verses of Genesis describe as brooding on the waters when the earth "was without form and void." In Book I he called his Muse simply by that divine name, adding a comparison

of her to the nine Muses of classical tradition which implies his belief that the myths of the pagan gods were shadows of the truth in Scripture. We see that belief become explicit when he tells us that Homer's story of Mulciber (Hephaestus) being thrown out of heaven by Zeus was a tale that the pagans told,

> Erring; for he with this [Satan's] rebellious rout
> Fell long before.   (I, 747–748)

When in Book VII he is ready to tell the story of creation he invokes his Muse by the name of the traditional patroness of astronomy, the ninth of the Muses of Greek tradition, Urania; but he says that what he has in mind is "the meaning, not the Name" (VII, 5). His words — Gilbert Murray tells us in *Classical Tradition and Poetry* (Harvard, 1927; p. 9) — plainly owe something to the ancient Stoics and something to Theocritus, but his prayer is not pagan. Nor did it suggest a pagan Muse to his readers. To many of them it suggested the Urania whom Du Bartas pompously invoked in *The Divine Weeks*, the Urania whom Spenser also invoked in *The Teares of the Muses* (499–502) as patronizing the knowledge of

> the worlds creation,
> How in his cradle first he fostred was;
> And judge of Natures cunning operation,
> How things she formed of a formelesse mas.

55. Milton speaks of his Urania as a sister of Eternal Wisdom, with whom she played "In presence of th'Almighty Father" and pleased him with her "Celestial Song." So perhaps Urania is the Understanding by which, together with Wisdom, Professor Fletcher reminds us in *Milton's Rabbinical Readings* (p. 111), rabbinical tradition said that the world was made. We need not wander away with M. Saurat in his cabalistic speculations about the sisters' games before the creation of the world, nor review the crushing replies that have been made to him. The most recent is by Jackson I. Cope in *MP*, LV (1957), 6–10. It is wiser to follow Mr. Hanford in "That Shepherd Who First Taught the Chosen Seed" in *UTQ*, VII (1939), 403–19, and to take Milton at his word when he says that he is not interested in the name but is interested in guidance by the Spirit which inspired Moses,

> That Shepherd, who first taught the Chosen Seed,
> In the beginning how the Heav'ns and Earth
> Rose out of Chaos.   (I, 8–10)

56. In the most personal of his four invocations Milton has something to say about his experience with his Muse, whom here he simply calls Light. Was he thinking of the divine Light that sits with Sapience in Spenser's *Hymne of Heavenly Beautie* (183)? Or simply of the light that we are told "is God" in I John i, 5? Or of the light that Dante said in the *Paradise* XIII, l–lvi, is God's creative power as well as an aspect of his essence, and that he calls in the *Convito* III, xii, "the spiritual and intellectual sun that is God"? Or of St. Augustine's distinction in the *Confessions* VII, x, between "the light which is God and the light which God has made"? Or was he — as Arnold Williams

suggests in *The Common Expositor* (p. 54) — thinking of the discussion by the great Catholic commentator Benedictus Pererius of Dionysius' comparison of the attributes of light to those of God? Or is Professor Kelley right in believing (*Argument*, p. 92) that by light in this passage Milton meant simply the physical light from which he was cut off by blindness? Or is D. C. Allen right in *The Harmonious Vision* (p. 101) in regarding Milton's invocation as a kind of metaphor comparing the varying intensities of physical light to the spiritual ladder of light by which Marsilio Ficino and the Florentine Neo-Platonists taught that man rises to the Creator of all light? We may hear as many literary overtones as we choose to do in his prayer to the "Celestial Light" to

> Shine inward, and the mind through all her powers
> Irradiate, there plant eyes, all mist from thence
> Purge and disperse.   (III, 52–54)

In this prayer "a complete, deliberate, and substantial theory of poetry" has been found, and there is no doubt that it is a perfect expression of the Renaissance theory that great poetry — and particularly great epic poetry — can be written only by men who deserve and enjoy divine illumination. It is as revealing an account of the poetic experience as Milton ever wrote.

57. But if the invocation to Book III is our best key to Milton's art, we can only agree with Dr. Tillyard that the mystery of his Muse is inscrutable. In the *Essay on Rime* Karl Shapiro seems to hope that the key can be found in the prosody when, contrasting the "auricular" power of Shakespeare's verse with Milton's appeal to the eye, he says that

> No metre more exactly planned exists
> Than his. A perfect mechanism turns
> *Paradise Lost*, his solar masterpiece,
> Written in blindness and by count of eye.
> In Bridges' study of the poem we learn
> What feats the decasyllable performs.

Yet modern prosodists are not satisfied with Robert Bridges' analysis of Milton's verse. Not even when it is amended by E. Ernest Sprott in *Milton's Art of Prosody* (Oxford, 1953) does it seem likely to satisfy the objection to Bridges' method that is voiced for many readers by B. Rajan when he says that, to talk of the poem's prosody or language is "a misleading abstraction." Perhaps we shall have the key in Mr. Edward Weismiller's promised study of the problem.

58. It is by way of the verse paragraph that Mr. Wylie Sypher attacks the problem of Milton's style when — as a typical example — he analyzes the description of Adam and Eve in the nuptial bower (IV, 691–743) and briefly identifies its "verse rhythms with their repletions" as characteristic of the "plenitude of the baroque" (in *Four Stages of Renaissance Style*, New York, 1955, p. 193). We may not come very close to the heart of Milton's mystery when we are told that "*Paradise Lost* is the flood-tide of baroque poetry" because it has in fullest measure the baroque elements of the "sumptuous, pompous, invigorating, fleshly, authoritarian." But until we feel these qualities among

others we have not begun to understand the poem. Its pomp may best be explicable as Mr. C. S. Lewis has explained it in his chapter on the ritual style that it has in common with the *Aeneid* and other "literary epics." Its fleshliness is both a matter of taste and of Milton's ontology, his belief in a "theistic materialism." Its authoritative tone, like its style, expresses his nature; but it is also the only possible tone in a poem about good and evil that was written, as Milton said, to be "exemplary to a nation."

59. Mr. Sypher speaks also of the "plastic quality of baroque space" as vital and highly characteristic in *Paradise Lost*, and in *Poetry and Humanism* Miss Mahood speaks of its "shapelessness" moulding every element in it from the over-all design to the verse-paragraphs and individual phrases. For her the quality is also baroque. It has been brilliantly discussed from the points of view of space and time by D. C. Allen in *The Harmonious Vision* and by Arnold Stein in *Answerable Style*. Mr. Allen makes us see how a panorama like the review of the demons marching into Pandaemonium moves before us until we are caught in its motion ourselves. Though he regards the essence of the passage as baroque art, he does not draw an analogy with the power of baroque architecture to involve us with the upward movement of the soaring domes of its churches. Approaching the structural problem in *Paradise Lost* from the point of view of its depth in time, we learn — for example — in the great speeches of Satan how both to hear and see him in action not far down stage, but at the same time to see him in the perspective of the larger action of the entire poem. Its complete design in terms of the irony of the drama between evil and good is never so clear as when Satan is speaking. But it is also true that we can discover the ironies of the poem and its depth in time in other ways. One of them, as Mr. Whaler said in an old-fashioned article on "The Miltonic Simile" in *PMLA*, LXVI (1931), 1034–74, that anticipates much later discussion of the subject, is simply to look through a comparison like that of Satan to the sun "In dim eclipse" (I, 597) at what it plainly implies about his destiny. In a fine analysis of the baroque elements in *Paradise Lost* in *UTQ*, XIV (1945), 407, Roy Daniells treats Satan's career as the supreme illustration of Milton's power to hold "in one tense equilibrium his own strong instinct for individualistic revolt and his Christian submission to reasoned doctrine, to the revealed will of God."

60. When a ticket like "the baroque" has been fastened to Milton's style, there is a temptation to feel that it has been brought completely under control, especially by readers who are less interested in poetry than they are in some other arts. But it is good for students who are less interested in painting and sculpture than they ought to be to read a study like Mario Praz's comparison of Milton's style with that of Poussin (in *Seventeenth Century Studies presented to Sir Herbert Grierson*, Oxford, 1938). They need not be disturbed by the fact that for Mr. Sypher the baroque artist with whom Milton has most in common is Rubens, or that for other investigators of the styles of the Renaissance he owes the sculptural power of his portraits of Adam and Eve to Michelangelo. For various reasons Milton is compared by Mr. Sypher to a dozen different Italian artists. It is impossible to see the aptness of the comparisons with them all, but it is not necessary to see the aptness of any of them to be qualified to agree with Dr. Tillyard's remark that in the painting of Poussin and Claude

Loraine we have a key to the formality — the absence of "the tone of ordinary talk" — in both the dramas of Racine and in *Paradise Lost*. A landscape of Poussin is a commentary on the heroic atmosphere of Milton's Garden of Eden and on the heroic mould of Adam and Eve.

61. From the exclusive point of view of style it is possible to agree — as Mr. M. M. Ross does in *Poetry and Dogma* — that the term *baroque* applies well to Milton, and yet to deny that his art has anything in common with the spirit of the Counter-Reformation or with traditional Christianity itself. It is possible to see that Milton's style harmonizes with the Catholic tradition of worship and yet to feel that his spirit was too humanistic to share deeply in the belief and experience of Dante. This involves identifying him with the movement that culminated in the empirical rationalism of John Locke and cutting him off in a fundamental way from the Christian tradition. Such an excommunication carries with it the charge that his central and symbolic images — unlike Dante's — are outside the Christian pale. For Mr. Ross the Platonic image of the tree and the implied image of the chain of being in Book V, 479–500, are applicable only to man's unfallen life in Eden and seem blasphemous when they are applied to the actual life of the world. But he is significantly silent about the invocation to Book III, the ladder of light, which is central to Milton's experience both as a poet and as a man, and which was also central in the Catholic Neo-Platonism of the Florentine School. Milton's experience had taught him that the foot of the ladder rests on the basic Christian virtue of humility. In the hard school of experience he had learned that virtue so well that — as Douglas Bush puts it in *"Paradise Lost" in Our Time* (p. 56) — he ended his career in a complete break from the movement that had already "inaugurated the scientific naturalism and scientific *hybris* of modern times."

62. There is one possible objection to much discussion of Milton's style as baroque or "grand." Such terms can blind us to its flexibility. It is important to notice how the manner changes from speaker to speaker in the debate in Pandæmonium, how the formality and high titles drop out of Adam's conversations with Eve after the fall, how the tone of the verse changes when the subject becomes what Milton recognized as 'redemptive' in his last three books. The blank verse of the speeches in Hell in Book II is more regular than that in any of the plays of the seventeenth century. It is more formal because the speakers are superhuman and incarnate certain passions in an almost abstract way, yet it expresses personality in Moloch, Belial, and Belial's imitator, Mammon, as well as in Satan himself. It can also express impersonality. When God speaks in Book III it is not like the "School Divine" that Pope said that Milton made of him. It is like the logical and dispassionate voice of Truth itself. Milton was more aware of this flexibility in his style — decorum, as he would have called it — than he was of some other features in it that interest modern readers. To keep decorum, his contemporaries believed, that was the great art.

63. There is a question on which some oblique light may be thrown by comparison of Milton's style with the styles of the painters whom he probably admired in Italy. He was — as Dr. Johnson said two hundred years ago — evidently desirous "to use English words with a foreign idiom." Dr. Johnson

did not like Latinisms such as "was walkt" (VII, 503), where a verb which does not work well in the passive voice and in an impersonal construction is used passively and impersonally because the usage was frequent in Latin. It probably seemed to him wilfully quaint to use *intelligent* in its Latin sense of "knowledgeable about" something, as Milton uses it of the mysteriously "prudent crane" in VII, 427. Presumably, Dr. Johnson disliked Grecisms such as "Adam the goodliest man of men since born" (IX, 644) as a casual way of mentioning even the only man who was ever created perfect. None of us may be quite prepared to understand a Hebraism like "the Tree of prohibition" (IX, 644) when Milton applies it to the Tree of Knowledge. For many readers such things are annoying even after they have learned from Mr. Empson in *Seven Types of Ambiguity* that many of Milton's poetic doublings of the meanings of his words come from his habit of using many of them in combinations of their Latin and English senses. But are we sure that Milton had a special fondness for Latin even though he wrote a great deal of it for publication? Excellent and powerful though his Latin style was, it was not quite idiomatic in the sense that it represented spoken Latin or even the colloquial element in the style of Ovid or any other Roman poet.

64. We are not perfectly sure what language made the greatest impact on the style of *Paradise Lost*. The question is not merely academic. Too many people have been sure that Milton's style was fundamentally bad because it is "Latinate." What if it is fundamentally something else? Dr. Johnson thought it was Italianate and said that "the disposition of his words was frequently Italian" — that the strongest influence on his style was that of "the Tuscan poets." In a study that was suggested by Johnson's *Life of Milton*, Mr. F. T. Prince actually finds reason to believe that Johnson was right. He finds good evidence that both practising poets and critics in Italy had been preaching and practising what Milton himself said was the first essential of blank verse: "the sense variously drawn out from one verse to another." Milton's striking habit of placing a noun between two adjectives —

> Two of far nobler shape erect and tall,
> Godlike erect —   (IV, 288–289)

seems to Mr. Prince to have been taught him by the Italian sonneteers from Petrarch down to Giovanni della Casa. Other devices for suspending the logical word-order so as to diffuse the sense through several successive lines appear to have been suggested to Milton by the Italians. So do the puns, and so does the theory that poets should pun and ought to make their puns out of the differences between the meanings of their words in everyday life and the meanings of the Latin and Greek words from which they were obviously derived. And as Mr. A. M. Clark suggests, the theories of the Italians played a part in Milton's preference for blank verse over rhyme.

65. The Muse that Milton invoked seems to have allowed us a glimpse into his secret by consenting to let us call him — at least tentatively — a baroque artist and a stylist whose ideals of the language of heroic poetry were consciously Italian. But if we think that we have penetrated very far into his secret, we should go back and reread the invocation to light at the beginning of the third book of *Paradise Lost*.

BIBLIOGRAPHY OF BOOKS DEALING MAINLY
WITH *PARADISE LOST* PUBLISHED SINCE 1934

Adams, Robert Martin. *IKON: John Milton and the Modern Critics.* Ithaca, 1955.

Allen, Don Cameron. *The Harmonious Vision: Studies in Milton's Poetry.* Baltimore, 1954.

Banks, Theodore. *Milton's Imagery.* New York, 1950.

Belloc, Hilaire. *Milton.* Philadelphia and London, 1935.

Bowra, Sir Maurice. *From Virgil to Milton.* London, 1945.

Broadbent, J. B. *Some Graver Subject. An Essay on "Paradise Lost."* London 1960.

Bush, Douglas. *"Paradise Lost" in Our Time: Some Comments.* New York, 1945.

————. *The Renaissance and English Humanism.* Toronto, 1939.

Cawley, Robert R. *Milton and the Literature of Travel.* Princeton, 1952.

Chinol, Elio. *Il Dramma divino e il Dramma umano nel "Paradiso Perduto."* Naples, 1957.

Conklin, George Newton. *Biblical Criticism and Heresy in Milton.* New York, 1949.

Corcoran, Sister M. I. *Milton's Paradise with Reference to the Hexaemeral Background.* Chicago, 1945.

Curry, Walter Clyde. *Milton's Ontology, Cosmogony, and Physics.* Lexington, Kentucky, 1957.

Daiches, David. *Milton.* London, 1956.

Diekhoff, John S. *Milton's "Paradise Lost": A Commentary on the Argument.* New York, 1946.

Empson, William. *Milton's God.* London, 1961.

Frye, Roland Mushat. *God, Man, and Satan. Patterns of Christian Thought and Life in "Paradise Lost," "Pilgrim's Progress," and the Great Theologians.* Princeton, 1960.

Gilbert, Allan H. *On the Composition of "Paradise Lost."* Chapel Hill, 1947.

Grierson, Sir Herbert J. C. *Milton and Wordsworth: Poets and Prophets.* Cambridge, 1937.

Grün, Richard Heinrich. *Das Menschenbild John Miltons in "Paradise Lost." Eine Interpretation seines Epos im Lichte des Begriffes 'Disobedience.'* Heidelberg, 1956.

Hamilton, G. Rostrevor. *Hero or Fool?* London, 1944.

Hanford, James H. *John Milton, Englishman.* New York, 1949.

————. *A Milton Handbook.* Fourth edition. New York, 1946.

Harding, Davis P. *Milton and the Renaissance Ovid.* Urbana, 1946.

Hutchinson, F. E. *Milton and the English Mind.* London, 1946.

Kelley, Maurice. *This Great Argument: A Study of Milton's "De Doctrina Christiana" as a Gloss upon "Paradise Lost."* Princeton, 1941.

Kermode, Frank, ed. *The Living Milton.* London, 1960.

Kirkconnell, Watson. *The Celestial Cycle.* Toronto, 1952.

Knight, G. Wilson. *The Frozen Labyrinth* and *The Burning Oracle*. London, 1939.
————. *Chariot of Wrath: The Message of John Milton to Democracy at War.* London, 1942.
Kurth, Burton O. *Milton and Christian Heroism. Biblical Epic Themes and Forms in Seventeenth Century England.* Berkeley, 1959.
Le Comte, Edward S. *Yet Once More.* New York, 1953.
————. *A Milton Dictionary.* New York, 1961.
Lewis, Clive S. *A Preface to "Paradise Lost."* London, 1942.
Looten, Canon Camille. *J. Milton: quelques aspects de son génie.* Lille and Paris, 1938.
MacCaffrey, Isabel Gamble. *"Paradise Lost" as 'Myth.'* Cambridge, Massachusetts, 1959.
Madsen, William G. "The Idea of Nature in Milton's Poetry," in *Three Studies in the Renaissance: Sidney, Jonson, Milton.* New Haven, 1958.
Mahood, M. M. *Poetry and Humanism.* London, 1950.
McColley, Grant. *"Paradise Lost": An Account of Its Growth and Major Origins, with a Discussion of Milton's Use of Sources and Literary Patterns.* Chicago, 1940.
McDill, Joseph M. *Milton and the Pattern of Calvinism.* Nashville, 1942.
Mody, Jehangir R. P. *Vondel and Milton.* Bombay, 1942.
Mohl, Ruth. *Studies in Spenser, Milton, and the Theory of Monarchy.* New York, 1949.
Muir, Kenneth. *John Milton.* London, 1955.
Nazari, Emilio. *Problemi miltoniani.* Palermo, 1952.
Nicolson, Marjorie. *A World in the Moon.* Smith College Studies in Modern Languages XVII, 1936.
Oras, Ants. *Notes on Some Miltonic Usages.* Tartu, 1938.
Peter, John. *A Critique of "Paradise Lost."* New York, 1960.
Phelps-Morand, Paul. *De Comus à Satan.* Paris, 1939.
Pommer, Henry F. *Milton and Melville.* Pittsburgh, 1950.
Prince, F. T. *The Italian Elements in Milton's Verse.* Oxford, 1954.
Rajan, B. *"Paradise Lost" and the Seventeenth Century Reader.* London, 1947.
Ross, Malcolm M. *Milton's Royalism: A Study of the Conflict of Symbolism and Idea in the Poems.* Ithaca, 1943.
————. *Poetry and Dogma: The Transfiguration of Eucharist Symbols in Seventeenth Century English Poetry.* New Brunswick, 1954.
SAMLA Studies in Milton, edited by Max Patrick. Gainesville, 1953.
Samuel, Irene. *Plato and Milton.* Ithaca, 1947.
Saurat, Denis. *Milton: Man and Thinker.* New York, 1925. Second edition, London, 1946.
Schultz, Howard. *Milton and Forbidden Knowledge.* New York, 1955.
Sewell, Arthur. *A Study in Milton's "Christian Doctrine."* London, 1939.
Smith, Logan Pearsall. *Milton and his Modern Critics.* London, 1940.
Sprott, S. Ernest. *Milton's Art of Prosody.* Oxford, 1953.
Starnes, DeWitt T., and Talbert, Ernest W. *Classical Myth and Legend in Renaissance Dictionaries.* Chapel Hill, 1955.
Stein, Arnold. *Answerable Style: Essays on "Paradise Lost."* Minneapolis, 1953.
Studies in Milton: Essays in Memory of Elbert N. S. Thompson. Philological Quarterly XXVIII (1949). Iowa City, 1949.

Svendsen, Kester. *Milton and Science.* Cambridge, Massachusetts, 1956.
Thorpe, James. *Milton Criticism: Selections from Four Centuries.* New York, 1950.
Tillyard, E. M. W. *Milton.* London, 1930. Second edition, 1949.
————. *Studies in Milton.* London, 1951.
————. *The Miltonic Setting, Past and Present.* Cambridge, 1938.
————. *The Metaphysicals and Milton.* London, 1956.
Waldock, A. J. A. *"Paradise Lost" and Its Critics.* Cambridge, 1947.
Warner, Rex. *John Milton.* London, 1949.
Watkins, W. B. C. *An Anatomy of Milton's Verse.* Baton Rouge, 1955.
Werblowski, R. J. Zwi. *Lucifer and Prometheus: A Study of Milton's Satan.* London, 1952.
West, Robert H. *Milton and the Angels.* Athens, Georgia, 1955.
Whaler, James. *Counterpoint and Symbol: An Inquiry into the Rhythm of Milton's Epic Style. Anglistica,* Vol. VI. Copenhagen, 1956.
Whiting, George W. *Milton and This Pendant World.* Austin, 1958.
————. *Milton's Literary Milieu.* Chapel Hill, 1939.
Williams, Arnold. *The Common Expositor.* Chapel Hill, 1948.
Wright, Bernard A. *Milton's "Paradise Lost": A Reassessment of the Poem.* London, 1962.

SOME OUTSTANDING EDITIONS OF
PARADISE LOST SINCE 1935

The Poems of John Milton, with introduction and notes by J. H. Hanford. New York, 1936. Second edition, 1953.
Complete Poems of John Milton, with complete notes by Thomas Newton, illustrated by Gustave Doré and others. New York, 1936.
"Paradise Lost" and "Paradise Regained," by John Milton, with an introduction by William Rose Benét and illustrations by Carlotta Petrina. San Francisco, 1936.
Paradise Lost. A poem by John Milton. The text of the first edition prepared for the press by J. Isaacs. London, 1937.
Complete Poetry and Selected Prose of John Milton, edited by E. H. Visiak. London and New York, 1938.
Paradise Lost, by John Milton, with the illustrations of William Blake: printed in color for the first time and with prefaces by Philip Hefer and John T. Winterich. New York, 1940.
The Poetical Works of Milton, edited by Charles Williams. London (The World's Classics), 1940.
The Complete Poetical Works of John Milton, edited by Harris Fletcher. Boston, 1941.
Complete Poetry and Selected Prose of John Milton. New York (Modern Library), 1942.
Complete Poetical Works of John Milton, reproduced in photographic facsimile by Harris Fletcher. Urbana, 1943.
"Paradise Lost," and other poems by John Milton, edited by Maurice Kelley. New York, 1943.

"Paradise Lost" and other poems by John Milton, edited by Northrop Frye. New York, 1951.

The Portable Milton, edited by Douglas Bush. New York, 1949.

The Poetical Works of John Milton, edited by Helen Darbishire. Vol. I. *"Paradise Lost."* Oxford, 1952. Vol. II. *"Paradise Regain'd," "Samson Agonistes," "Poems upon Several Occasions,"* both English and Latin. Oxford, 1955.

Milton's Poems. Textual editing, Glossary, and Introduction by B. A. Wright. London, 1956. Everyman's Library.

BIBLIOGRAPHY OF ARTICLES DEALING
MAINLY WITH *PARADISE LOST*
PUBLISHED SINCE 1957*

Adamson, J. H. "Kepler and Milton." *MLN*, LXXIV (1959), 683–5.

————. "Milton's Arianism." *HTR*, LIII (1960), 269–76.

————. "The War in Heaven: Milton's Version of the Merkabah." *JEGP*, LVII (1958), 690–703.

Allen, Don Cameron. "Milton and the Name of Eve." *MLN*, LXXIV (1959), 681–3.

————. "Milton's Eve and the Evening Angels." *MLN*, LXXV (1960), 108–9.

————. "Milton and the Descent to Light." *JEGP*, LX (1961), 614–30.

————. "Milton and the Love of Angels." *MLN*, LXXVI (1961), 489–90.

Aquinas, Sister Thomas. "Summary of Remarks on *Paradise Lost*." *CEA Critic*, XXI (1959), 6–7.

Barker, Arthur. "Recent Studies in the English Renaissance: Section 4." Rice University *Studies in English Literature*, I (1961), 147–57.

Bateson, F. W. "Milton for Everyman." *TLS*, July 4, 1958, p. 377.

Beck, Richard J. "Milton and the Spirit of His Age." *ES*, XLII (1961), 288–300.

Bekker, Hugo. "The Religio-Philosophical Orientations of Vondel's *Lucifer*, Milton's *Paradise Lost*, and Grotius' *Adamus Exul*." *Neophil.*, XLIV (1960), 234–44.

Bergonzi, Bernard. "Criticism and the Milton Controversy." In *The Living Milton*, ed. Kermode, 1960, pp. 162–80.

Blondel, Jacques. "Milton, poète de la Bible dans le *Paradis perdu*." *Archives des lettres modernes*, XXI (1959), 87 pp.

Bodkin, Maud. "Literature and the Individual Reader." *Literature and Psychology*, X (1960), 39–44.

Broadbent, J. B. "Milton's Rhetoric." *MP*, LVI (1959), 224–42.

Bush, Douglas. "Ironic and Ambiguous Allusion in *Paradise Lost*." *JEGP*, LX (1961), 631–40.

Camelot, P. Th. "La théologie de l'Image de Dieu." *Revue des sciences philosophiques et théologiques*, XL (1956), 45.

---

* Professor Calvin Huckaby of Hardin-Simmons University has helped substantially in making this bibliography as nearly complete as it is.

Ciardi, John. "A Poem Talks to Itself: One Thing Calls Another into Being." *Saturday Review*, Jan. 24, 1959, pp. 12–13.

Cohen, B. Bernard. "*Paradise Lost* and 'Young Goodman Brown.' " *EIHC*, XCIV (1958), 282–96.

Colie, Rosalie. "Time and Eternity: Paradox and Structure in *Paradise Lost.*" *JWCI*, XXIII (1960), 127–38.

Cook, Albert. "Milton's Abstract Music." *UTQ*, XXIX (1960), 370–85.

Cope, Jackson I. "Satan's Disguises: *Paradise Lost* and *Paradise Regained.*" *MLN*, LXXIII (1958), 9–12.

————. "Time and Space as Miltonic Symbol." *ELH*, XXVI (1959), 497–513.

Cutler, Bruce. "The Facts of Human Defeat." *Poetry*, XCIII (1959), 404–8.

Daiches, David. "The Opening of *Paradise Lost.*" In *The Living Milton*, ed. Kermode, 1960, pp. 55–69.

Daniels, Edgar F. "Milton's Fallen Angels — Self-corrupted or Seduced?" *NQ*, N.S., VII (1960), 447–50.

————. "Thomas Adams and 'Darkness Visible.' (*Paradise Lost*, I, 62–3)." *NQ*, N.S., VI (1959), 369–70.

Davie, Donald. "Syntax and Music in *Paradise Lost.*" In *The Living Milton*, ed. Kermode, 1960, pp. 70–84.

Empson, William. "Adam and Eve." *Listener*, LXIV (1960), 64–65.

————. " 'Heaven's Awful Monarch.' " *Listener*, LXIV (1960), 111–14.

————. "Satan Argues His Case." *Listener*, LXIV (1960), 11–13.

————. "The Satan of Milton." *Hudson Review*, XIII (1960), 33–59.

Fiore, Amadeus, O.F.M. "A Note on Milton's Critics." *Franciscan Studies*, XIX (1959), 142–49.

————. "Satan is a Problem: The Problem of Milton's 'Satanic Fallacy' in Contemporary Criticism." *A Christian Approach to Western Literature*. Newman Press (1961).

Fletcher, Harris. "Milton's Demogorgon — *Prolusion* I and *Paradise Lost*, II, 960–65." *JEGP*, LVII (1958), 684–89.

Fox, Robert C. "Milton's *Paradise Lost*, II, 226–228." *Expl.*, XVIII (1959), Item 4.

————. "Satan's Triad of Vices." *TSLL*, II (1960), 261–81.

Freedman, Morris. "Dryden's Reported Reaction to *Paradise Lost.*" *NQ*, N.S., V (1958), 14–16.

————. "Satan and Shaftesbury." *PMLA*, LXXIV (1959), 544–47.

Gilbert, Allan F. "Form and Matter in *Paradise Lost*, Book III." *JEGP*, LX (1961), 651–63.

Gossman, Ann. "Milton's *Paradise Lost*, II, 1013." *Expl.*, XIX (1961), Item 51.

————. "Two Milton Notes. 1: Milton, Plutarch, and 'Darkness Visible.' 2: The Iron Rod and Golden Sceptre in *Paradise Lost.*" *NQ*, N.S., VIII (1961), 182–83.

Gottfried, Rudolf B. "Milton and Poliziano." *NQ*, N.S., V (1958), 195–96.

Greenfield, Stanley B. "Milton's *Paradise Lost*, XII, 629–632." *Expl.*, XIX (1961), Item 57.

Hankins, John E. "Milton and Olaus Magnus." *Studies in Honor of T. W. Baldwin* (Urbana, 1958), pp. 205–10.

Harding, Davis P. "Milton's Bee-Simile." *JEGP*, LX (1961), 664–69.

Hartman, Geoffrey. "Milton's Counterplot." *ELH*, XXV (1958), 1–12.

Herman, William R. "Heroism and *Paradise Lost*." *CE*, XXI (1959), 13–17.

Howarth, Herbert. "Eliot and Milton: The American Aspect." *UTQ*, XXX (1961), 150–62.

Huckabay, Calvin. "Satan and the Narrative Structure of *Paradise Lost*." *Studia Neophilologica*, XXII (1961), 96–102.

Hughes, Merritt Y. "Milton's Celestial Battle and the Theogonies." *Studies in Honor of T. W. Baldwin* (Urbana, 1958), pp. 237–53.

————. "Some Illustrators of Milton: The Expulsion from Paradise." *JEGP*, LX (1961), 670–79.

Hunter, William B., Jr. "Holy Light in *Paradise Lost*." *Rice Institute Pamphlet*, XLVI (1960), 1–14.

————. "The Meaning of 'Holy Light' in *Paradise Lost* III." *MLN*, LXXIV (1959), 589–92.

————. "Milton on the Incarnation: Some More Heresies." *JHI*, XXI (1960), 349–69.

————. "Milton's Arianism Reconsidered." *HTR*, LII (1959), 9–35.

Hutcherson, Dudley R. "Milton's Adam as Lover." *University of Mississippi Studies in English*, II (1961), 1–11.

————. "Milton's Eve and Other Eves." *University of Mississippi Studies in English*, I (1960), 12–31.

Illo, John. "Animal Sources for Milton's Sin and Death." *NQ*, N.S., VII (1960), 425–26.

Jarrett-Kerr, Martin. "Milton, Poet and Paraphrast." *EIC*, X (1960), 373–89.

Kelley, Maurice. "Milton's Arianism Reconsidered." *HTR*, LIV (1961), 195·205.

Kermode, Frank. "Adam Unparadised." In *The Living Milton*, ed. Kermode, 1960, pp. 85–123.

Kim, Sun Sook. "Ethics in Milton's *Paradise Lost*." *ELL*, V (1958), 1–27.

Klammer, Enno. "The Fallacy of the *Felix Culpa* in Milton's *Paradise Lost*." *Cresset*, XXIII (1960), 13–14.

Koehler, G. Stanley. "Milton on 'Numbers,' 'Quantity,' and 'Rime.' " *SP*, LV (1958), 201–17.

Lauter, Paul. "Milton's 'Siloa's Brook.' " *NQ*, N.S., V (1958), 204–5.

Lutter, Tibor. "Milton's *Verlorenes Paradies:* Ein Interpretationsversuch." *ZAA*, V (1957), 378–403.

Madsen, William G. "Earth the Shadow of Heaven: Typological Symbolism in *Paradise Lost*." *PMLA*, LXXV (1960), 519–27.

————. "The Fortunate Fall in *Paradise Lost*." *MLN*, LXXIV (1959), 103–5.

Manley, Francis. "Paradise Parched." *MLN*, LXXIV (1959), 7–9.

Manley, Frank. "Milton and the Beasts of the Field." *MLN*, LXXVI (1961), 398–408.

————. "Moloch on Demonic Motion." *MLN*, LXXVI (1961), 110–16.

Marilla, E. L. "Milton's Pandemonium." *NS*, 1960, pp. 167–74.

————. "Milton's 'Paradise of Fools.' " *ES*, XLII (1961), 159–64.

————. "A Reading of Two Episodes in *Paradise Lost*." *EA*, XII (1959), 135–41.

Marshall, William H. "*Paradise Lost: Felix Culpa* and the Problem of Structure." *MLN*, LXXVI (1961), 15–20.

Maxwell, J. C. "Milton for Everyman." *TLS*, Aug. 15, 1958, p. 459.

McNamee, Maurice B., S. J. "Magnanimity in Milton." In *Honor and the Epic Hero* (New York, 1960), pp. 160–79.

Moloney, Michael F. "Plato and Plotinus in Milton's Cosmogony." *PQ*, XL (1961), 34–43.

Morris, Harry. "Some Uses of Angel Iconography in English Literature." *CL*, X (1958), 36–44.

Parish, John E. "Milton and an Anthropomorphic God." *SP*, LVI (1959), 619–25.

————. "Milton and God's Curse on the Serpent." *JEGP*, LVIII (1959), 241–47.

Parker, W. M. "Lockhart's notes on *Paradise Lost*." *English*, XII (1958), 48–53.

Patrides, C. A. "Milton and his Contemporaries on the Chains of Satan." *MLN*, LXXIII (1958), 257–60.

————. "Milton and the Protestant Theory of the Atonement." *PMLA*, LXXIV (1959), 7–13.

————. "Renaissance and Modern Thought on Last Things: A Study in Changing Conceptions." *HTR*, LI (1958), 169–85.

Pecheux, Mother Mary Christopher. "The Concept of the Second Eve in *Paradise Lost*." *PMLA*, LXXV (1960), 359–66.

Pelletier, Robert R. "Satan and Prometheus in Captivity." *NQ*, N.S., VII (1960), 107–8.

————. "Shade and Bower Images in Milton and Shelley." *NQ*, N.S., VIII (1961), 20–21.

————. "Shelley's Ahasuerus and Milton's Satan." *NQ*, N.S., VII (1960), 259-60.

Prince, F. T. "On the Last Two Books of *Paradise Lost*." *E & S*, XI (1958), 38–52.

Ransom, John Crowe. "The Idea of a Literary Anthropologist and What He Might Say of the *Paradise Lost* of Milton." *KR*, XXI (1959), 121–40.

Redman, Harry, Jr. "Albert Joseph Ulpein, Early French Miltonist." *Romance Notes*, I (1959), 122–26.

————. "Villemain on Milton: A Document in Romantic Criticism." *CL*, X (1958), 241–45.

Rigter, G. H. "Milton's Treatment of Satan in *Paradise Lost*." *Neophil.*, XLII (1958), 309–22.

Robins, Harry F. "That Unnecessary Shell of Milton's World." *Studies in Honor of T. W. Baldwin* (Urbana, 1958), 211–19.

————. "Satan's Journey: Direction in *Paradise Lost*." *JEGP*, LX (1961), 699–711.

Samarin, R. "John Milton: Various Opinions of his Life and Work." *Voprosi Literaturi*, I (1959), 155–72.

Samuels, C. T. "Tragic Vision in *Paradise Lost.*" *UKCR*, XXVII (1960), 65–78.

Sasek, Lawrence A. "Milton's *Paradise Lost*, II, 226–8." *Expl.*, XVI (1958), Item 30.

Schanzer, Ernest. "Verse and Its Feet." *RES*, X (1958), 292–93.

Schlinghoff, Margot. "Miltons Bildersprache im 'Paradise Lost.'" *NS*, 1958, pp. 263–71.

Schulz, Max F. "Coleridge, Milton, and Lost Paradise." *NQ*, N.S. VI (1959), 143–44.

Shawcross, John T. "The Chronology of Milton's Major Poems." *PMLA*, LXXVI (1961), 345–58.

Sirluck, Ernest. "Milton's Idle Right Hand." *JEGP*, LX (1961), 749–85.

Stanton, Robert. "*Typee* and Milton: Paradise Well Lost." *MLN*, LXXIV (1959), 407–11.

Starkman, M. K. "The Militant Miltonist." *ELH*, XXVI (1959), 209–28.

Stavrou, C. N. "Milton's Satan: One Word More." *UKCR*, XXV (1958), 157–60.

Steadman, John M. "Adam and the Prophesied Redeemer." *SP*, LVI (1959), 214–25.

————. "Archangel to Devil: The Background of Satan's Metamorphosis." *MLQ*, XXI (1961), 321–35.

————. "The Devil and Pharaoh's Chivalry." *MLN*, LXXV (1960), 197–201.

————. "'From the Safe Shore': Milton and Tremellius." *Neophil.*, XLIV (1960), 218–19.

————. "The God of *Paradise Lost* and the *Divina Commedia.*" *Archiv*, CXCV (1958), 273–89.

————. "Grosseteste on the Genealogy of Sin and Death." *NQ*, N.S., VI (1959), 367–68.

————. "Heroic Virtue and the Divine Image in *Paradise Lost.*" *JWCI*, XXII (1959), 88–105.

————. "Image and Idol: Satan and the Element of Illusion in *Paradise Lost.*" *JEGP*, LIX (1960), 640–54.

————. "Islamic Tradition and 'That Divelish Engin.'" *Hist. Ideas News Letter*, IV (1958), 39–41.

————. "Mammon and 'Heav'ns Pavement' (*Paradise Lost*, I, 682)." *NQ*, N.S., VII (1960), 220.

————. "'Man's First Disobedience': The Causal Structure of the Fall." *JHI*, XXI (1960), 180–97.

————. "Milton and Mazzoni: The Genre of the *Divina Commedia.*" *HLQ*, XXIII (1960), 107–22.

————. "Milton and Patristic Tradition: the Quality of Hell-fire." *Anglia*, LXXVI (1958), 116–28.

————. "Milton and St. Basil: The Genesis of Sin and Death." *MLN*, LXXIII (1958), 83–84.

————. "Milton and Wolleb Again." *HTR*, LII (1960), 155–56.

————. "Milton, Valvasone, and the Schoolmen." *PQ*, XXXVII (1958), 502–4.

————. "Milton, Virgil, and St. Jerome (*Paradise Lost*, III, 168–170)." *NQ*, N.S., VI (1959), 368–69.

————. "Milton's 'Giant Angels': An Additional Parallel." *MLN*, LXXV (1960), 551–53.

————. " 'Nature's Prime' (*Paradise Lost*, III, 168–170) and William Byrd." *NQ*, N.S., V (1958), 472–73.

————. "*Paradise Lost* and the 'Tragic Illustrious'." *Anglia*, LXXVIII (1960), 302–16.

————. "Recognition in the Fable of *Paradise Lost*." *SN*, XXXI (1959), 159–73.

————. "Sin, Echidna, and the Viper's Brood." *MLR*, LVII (1961), 62–66.

————. "Sin and the Serpent of Genesis: *Paradise Lost*, II, 650–653." *MP*, LIX (1957), 217–20.

————. "The 'Suffering Servant' and Milton's Heroic Norm." *HTR*, LIV (1961), 29–43.

————. "Tradition and Innovation in Milton's 'Sin': The Problem of Literary Indebtedness." *PQ*, XXXIX (1960), 93–103.

————. "*Paradise Lost* and the '*Tragic Illustrious*.' " *Anglia*, LXXVII (1960), 302–16.

Stroup, Thomas D. "Parallel Entrances and Exits in *Paradise Lost*." Tennessee Studies in Literature, VI (1961), 71–75.

Svendsen, Kester. "John Martin and the Expulsion Scene of *Paradise Lost*." Rice University *Studies in English Literature*, I (1961), 63–74.

————. "Satan and Science." *Bucknell Review*, IX (1960), 130–42.

Swidler, Arlene Anderson. "Milton's *Paradise Lost*, II, 866–870." *Expl.*, XVII (1959), Item 41.

Taylor, Dick, Jr. "Milton and the Paradox of the Fortunate Fall Once More." *TSE*, IX (1959), 35–51.

————. "Milton's Treatment of the Judgment and Expulsion in *Paradise Lost*." *TSE*, X (1960), 51–82.

Tillyard, E. M. W. "The Literary Kinds and Milton." *Stil- und Formprobleme in der Literatur*. Vorträge des VII Kongresses der Internationalen Vereinigung für Moderne Sprachen und Literaturen in Heidelberg (1957). Heidelberg, 1959, pp. 95–103.

————. "On Annotating *Paradise Lost*, Books IX and X." *JEGP*, LX (1961), 808–16.

Treip, Mindele C. "*Paradise Lost*, II, 257–262 and XII, 561–569." *NQ*, N.S., V (1958), 209–10.

Tuve, Rosemond. "Baroque and Mannerist Milton?" *JEGP*, LX (1961). 817–33.

Walzl, Florence L. "*Paradise Lost*, III, 150–66." *Expl.*, XX (1961), Item 11.

Weidhorn, Manfred. "Satan's Persian Expedition." *NQ*, N.S., V (1958), 398–92.

Whiteley, M. "Verse and Its Feet." *RES*, N.S., IX (1958), 268–79.

Whiting, George Wesley. "And without Thorn the Rose." *RES*, X (1959), 60–62.

————, and Ann Gossman. "Siloa's Brook, the Pool of Siloam, and Milton's Muse," *SP*, LVIII (1961), 193–205.

Widmer, Kingsley. "The Iconography of Renunciation: The Miltonic Simile." *ELH*, XXV (1958), 258–69.

————. "Lawrence and the Fall of Modern Woman." *MFS*, V (1959), 47–56.

Wrenn, C. L. "The Language of Milton." *Studies in English Language and Literature*. Presented to Dr. Karl Brunner on the Occasion of his Seventieth Birthday (Vienna, 1958), pp. 252–67

Wright, B. A. "Counsels Different." *NQ*, N.S., V (1958), 205.

————. "Milton for Everyman." *TLS*, July 18, 1958, p. 409.

————. "Milton's Use of the Word 'Waft'." *NQ*, N.S., V (1958), 341.

————. "A Note on Milton's 'Night-Founder'd.' " *NQ*, N.S., V (1958), 203–4.

————. "A Note on Milton's 'Worth Ambition.' " *NQ*, N.S., V (1958), 200.

————. "A Note on *Paradise Lost*, II, 70–81." *NQ*, N.S., V (1958), 208–10.

————. "A Note on *Paradise Lost*, IV, 310." *NQ*, N.S., V (1958), 341.

————. "*Paradise Lost*, IX, 1079–1080." *RES*, X (1959), 62–63.

————. " 'Shade' for 'Tree' in Milton's Poetry." *NQ*, N.S., V (1958), 205–8.

————. "Stressing of the Preposition *Without* in the Verse of *Paradise Lost*." *NQ*, N.S., V (1958), 202–3.

UNPUBLISHED DOCTORAL DISSERTATIONS (SINCE 1957) DEALING MAINLY WITH *PARADISE LOST*

Ashley, Jack Dillard. "Cosmic Symbolism in *Paradise Lost*." University of Tennessee, 1960.

Burke, Herbert Caryl. "The Poles of Pride and Humility in the *Paradise Lost* of John Milton." University of Michigan, 1958.

Childers, Charles Louis. "Milton's Doctrine of God Studied in the Light of Historical Christianity." Vanderbilt University, 1959.

Forrest, James French. "The Evil Thought in the Blameless Mind." Cornell University, 1960.

Kivette, Ruth M. "Milton on the Trinity." Columbia University, 1960.

McAlister, Floyd Lavern. "A Survey of Twentieth Century Milton Scholarship with Particular Attention to Controversies." University of Minnesota, 1958.

Muldrow, George McMurry. "The Theme of Man's Restoration in Milton's 'Later Poetry." Stanford University, 1961.

Sidelow, Sally Yeates. "The Narrative Method of *Paradise Lost*." Bryn Mawr College, 1960.

Zwicky, Laurie Bowman. "Milton's Use of Time: Image and Principle." University of Oklahoma, 1959.

Paradise Lost.

A
POEM
IN
TWELVE BOOKS.

The Author
JOHN MILTON.

𝕿𝖍𝖊 𝕾𝖊𝖈𝖔𝖓𝖉 𝕰𝖉𝖎𝖙𝖎𝖔𝖓
Revised and Augmented by the
same Author.

LONDON,
Printed by *S. Simmons* next door to the
Golden Lion in *Aldersgate-street,* 1674.

IN
PARADISUM AMISSAM

SUMMI POETÆ
JOHANNIS MILTONI

Qui legis Amissam Paradisum, grandia magni
   Carmina Miltoni, *quid nisi cuncta legis?*
Res cunctas, & cunctarum primordia rerum,
   Et fata, & fines continet iste liber.
Intima panduntur magni penetralia mundi,
   Scribitur & toto quicquid in Orbe latet.
Terræque, tractusque maris, cælumque profundum,
   Sulphureumque Erebi flammivomumque specus.
Quæque colunt terras, Pontumque & Tartara cæca,
   Qæque colunt summi lucida regna Poli.
Et quodcunque ullis conclusum est finibus usquam,
   Et sine fine Chaos, & sine fine Deus;
Et sine fine magis, si quid magis est sine fine,
   In Christo erga homines conciliatus amor.
Hæc qui speraret quis crederet esse futurum?
   Et tamen hæc hodie terra Britanna *legit.*
O quantos in bella Duces! quæ protulit arma!
   Quæ canit, et quanta prælia dira tuba.
Cælestes acies! atque in certamine Cælum!
   Et quæ Cælestes pugna deceret agros!
Quantus in ætheriis tollit se Lucifer *armis!*
   Atque ipso graditur vix Michaële *minor!*
Quantis, & quam funestis concurritur iris
   Dum ferus hic stellas protegit, ille rapit!
Dum vulsos Montes ceu Tela reciproca torquent,
   Et non mortali desuper igne pluunt:
Stat dubius cui se parti concedat Olympus,
   Et metuit pugnæ non superesse suæ.
At simul in cælis Messiæ insignia fulgent,
   Et currus animes, armaque digna Deo,
Horrendumque rotæ strident, & sæva rotarum
   Erumpunt torvis fulgura luminibus,
Et flammæ vibrant, & vera tonitrua rauco
   Admistis flammis insonuere Polo:
Excidit attonitis mens omnis, & impetus omnis
   Et cassis dextris irrita Tela cadunt.
Ad pœnas fugiunt, & ceu foret Orcus asylum
   Infernis certant condere se tenebris.
Cedite Romani *scriptores, cedite* Graii
   Et quos fama recens vel celebravit anus.
Hæc quicunque leget tantum cecinisse putabit
   Mæonidem ranas, Virgilium *culices.*

S. B., M. D.

ON
PARADISE LOST

When I beheld the Poet blind, yet bold,
In slender Book his vast Design unfold,
Messiah Crown'd, God's Reconcil'd Decree,
Rebelling Angels, the Forbidden Tree,
Heav'n, Hell, Earth, Chaos, All; the Argument
Held me a while misdoubting his Intent,
That he would ruin (for I saw him strong)
The sacred Truths to Fable and old Song
(So *Sampson* grop'd the Temple's Posts in spite)
The World o'erwhelming to revenge his sight.

Yet as I read, soon growing less severe,
I lik'd his Project, the success did fear;
Through that wide Field how he his way should find
O'er which lame Faith leads Understanding blind;
Lest he perplex'd the things he would explain,
And what was easy he should render vain.

Or if a Work so infinite he spann'd,
Jealous I was that some less skilful hand
(Such as disquiet always what is well,
And by ill imitating would excel)
Might hence presume the whole Creation's day
To change in Scenes, and show it in a Play.

Pardon me, Mighty Poet, nor despise
My causeless, yet not impious, surmise.
But I am now convinc'd, and none will dare
Within thy Labours to pretend a share.
Thou hast not miss'd one thought that could be fit,
And all that was improper dost omit:
So that no room is here for Writers left,
But to detect their Ignorance or Theft.

That Majesty which through thy Work doth Reign
Draws the Devout, deterring the Profane.
And things divine thou treat'st of in such state
As them preserves, and thee, inviolate.
At once delight and horror on us seize,
Thou sing'st with so much gravity and ease;
And above human flight dost soar aloft
With Plume so strong, so equal, and so soft.
The Bird nam'd from that Paradise you sing
So never flags, but always keeps on Wing.

Where couldst thou words of such a compass find?
Whence furnish such a vast expense of mind?
Just Heav'n thee like *Tiresias* to requite
Rewards with Prophecy thy loss of sight.

Well mightst thou scorn thy Readers to allure

3

With tinkling Rime, of thy own sense secure;
While the *Town-Bayes* writes all the while and spells,
And like a Pack-horse tires without his Bells:
Their Fancies like our Bushy-points appear,
The Poets tag them, we for fashion wear.
I too transported by the Mode offend,
And while I meant to Praise thee must Commend.
Thy Verse created like thy Theme sublime,
In Number, Weight, and Measure, needs not Rime.

A. M. (Andrew Marvell)

THE PRINTER TO THE READER

Courteous Reader,   There was no Argument at first intended to the Book, but for the satisfaction of many that have desired it, I have procured it, and withal a reason of that which stumbled many others, why the Poem Rimes not.

THE VERSE

The measure is *English* Heroic Verse without Rime, as that of *Homer* in *Greek*, and of *Virgil* in *Latin;* Rime being no necessary Adjunct or true Ornament of Poem or good Verse, in longer Works especially, but the Invention of a barbarous Age, to set off wretched matter and lame Meter; grac't indeed since by the use of some famous modern Poets, carried away by Custom, but much to thir own vexation, hindrance, and constraint to express many things otherwise, and for the most part worse than else they would have exprest them.   Not without cause therefore some both *Italian* and *Spanish* Poets of prime note have rejected Rime both in longer and shorter Works, as have also long since our best *English* Tragedies, as a thing of itself, to all judicious ears, trivial and of no true musical delight; which consists only in apt Numbers, fit quantity of Syllables, and the sense variously drawn out from one Verse into another, not in the jingling sound of like endings, a fault avoided by the learned Ancients both in Poetry and all good Oratory.   This neglect then of Rime so little is to be taken for a defect, though it may seem so perhaps to vulgar Readers, that it rather is to be esteem'd an example set, the first in *English*, of ancient liberty recover'd to Heroic Poem from the troublesome and modern bondage of Riming.[1]

---

[1] Milton's difference of opinion with Dryden about "the troublesome and modern bondage of Riming" has been limited to "specialized couplet rhyme" by G. Stanley Koehler in *SP*, LV (1958), 201–217, in a study which is complemented by Morris Friedman's finding in *N&Q*, V (1958), 14–16, that Dryden's "later use of rhyme and the poor opinion of blank verse that he occasionally expressed suggest that, however much he admired Milton, it was not because Milton forsook rhyme." In *The Miltonic Setting*, p. 204, E. M. W. Tillyard shrewdly suggests that "the acrid tone of Milton's note on *Paradise Lost*" sprang from his dislike of the rhymed couplets of Cowley's *Davideis*, "the first original poem in English to affect the growingly fashionable neo-classic form in all its strictness and using the couplet in a new and vital way."   Perhaps — though Masson had good authority for saying in his *Life of Milton*, VI, 682, that of all contemporaries Milton most admired Cowley — the success of the *Davideis* (published in 1656) may have contributed to the acridity of the note on the verse of *Paradise Lost*.   Milton's opinion and use of rhyme are discussed by Frank Kermode in *The Living Milton*, pp. 94–98.

Handwritten top:
Paradise Lost encompasses all of Time. However, it is put into
5 days. 5 days corresponded with the 5 acts of a tragedy.

John Milton is ambitious, Most English Lit was rythmic, but
He does not write is Rhythmic but rather in Blank, as
Iambic pentameter

Paradise Lost

Handwritten: Milton emphasized free will (anti-Calvinis) — An Inversion of the Epic concept
The epic to end all epics

BOOK I
THE ARGUMENT

This first Book proposes, first in brief, the whole Subject, *Man's disobedience, and the loss thereupon of Paradise wherein he was plac't:* Then touches *the prime cause of his fall, the Serpent, or rather* Satan *in the Serpent;* who revolling from God, and drawing to his side many Legions of Angels, was by the command of God driven out of Heaven with all his Crew into the great Deep. Which action past over, the Poem hastes into the midst of things, presenting *Satan with his Angels now fallen into Hell,* describ'd here, *not in the Centre* (for Heaven and Earth may be suppos'd as yet not made, certainly not yet accurst) *but in a place of utter darkness,* fitliest call'd Chaos: *Here* Satan *with his Angels lying on the burning Lake, thunderstruck and astonisht, after a certain space recovers, as from confusion, calls up him who next in Order and Dignity lay by him; they confer of thir miserable fall.* Satan *awakens all his Legions, who lay till then in the same manner confounded; They rise, thir Numbers, array of Battle, thir chief Leaders nam'd, according to the Idols known afterwards in* Canaan *and the Countries adjoining. To these* Satan *directs his Speech, comforts them with hope yet of regaining Heaven, but tells them lastly of a new World and new kind of Creature to be created, according to an ancient Prophecy or report in Heaven; for that Angels were long before this visible Creation, was the opinion of many ancient Fathers. To find out the truth of this Prophecy, and what to determine thereon he refers to a full Council. What his Associates thence attempt.* Pandemonium *the Palace of* Satan *rises, suddenly built out of the Deep: The infernal Peers there sit in Council.*

Handwritten left margin: Chaos is pure matter
Hell mirrors Heaven, Chaos Mirrors Earth

Handwritten above line: not time lost, Very similar Death

Of Man's First Disobedience, and the Fruit
Of that Forbidden Tree, whose mortal taste
Brought Death into the World, and all our woe,
With loss of *Eden,* till one greater Man
Restore us, and regain the blissful Seat,
Sing Heav'nly Muse, that on the secret top
Of *Oreb,* or of *Sinai,* didst inspire
That Shepherd, who first taught the chosen Seed,

Handwritten right: Miltonic English is Unique. Newers in English but Latin/Greek Anglo-Saxon etc.

Handwritten left: We are all — purpose of Muse 1st of 4

1–4. *Man* is emphatically repeated in a way that recalls the stress upon the corresponding words in the opening lines of the *Odyssey* and *Aeneid* and the conviction of Milton's contemporaries that epic poetry should portray a "vertuous man," as Spenser said — in the letter to Raleigh introducing *The Faerie Queene* — that Homer did "in the persons of Agamemnon and Ulysses." Milton's purpose is to draw two perfect men, Adam and the "greater man," the Son of God, whose portrayal is complete only in *PR.* The tradition culminating in these lines is illuminated by R. W. Condee in *JEGP,* L (1951), 502–8, on its formal side, and on its theological side by L. A. Cormican in *From Donne to Marvell,* ed. by Boris Ford (London, 1956), pp. 176–9.

Handwritten bottom: "Loss of Eden" is the loss of Eden's purpose, happiness. Happiness is strong. Nostalgia for true bliss, Eden

In the Beginning how the Heav'ns and Earth
Rose out of *Chaos:* Or if *Sion* Hill   10
Delight thee more, and *Siloa's* Brook that flow'd
Fast by the Oracle of God; I thence
Invoke thy aid to my advent'rous Song,
That with no middle flight intends to soar
Above th' *Aonian* Mount, while it pursues   15
Things unattempted yet in Prose or Rhyme.
And chiefly Thou O Spirit, that dost prefer
Before all Temples th' upright heart and pure,
Instruct me, for Thou know'st; Thou from the first
Wast present, and with mighty wings outspread   20
Dove-like satst brooding on the vast Abyss
And mad'st it pregnant: What in me is dark
Illumine, what is low raise and support;
That to the highth of this great Argument
I may assert Eternal Providence,   25
And justify the ways of God to men.
    Say first, for Heav'n hides nothing from thy view
Nor the deep Tract of Hell, say first what cause
Mov'd our Grand Parents in that happy State,
Favor'd of Heav'n so highly, to fall off   30
From thir Creator, and transgress his Will
For one restraint, Lords of the World besides?
Who first seduc'd them to that foul revolt?
Th' infernal Serpent; hee it was, whose guile
Stirr'd up with Envy and Revenge, deceiv'd   35
The Mother of Mankind; what time his Pride
Had cast him out from Heav'n, with all his Host
Of Rebel Angels, by whose aid aspiring
To set himself in Glory above his Peers,
He trusted to have equall'd the most High,   40

6–17. For the *Heav'nly Muse*, the *Urania* of VII, 1, see the Introduction 54–57.

7–8. The *Shepherd* is Moses, who received the Law on Mount *Oreb* or its spur, Mount *Sinai*, for the *chosen Seed*, the children of Israel (Exod. xix–xx). Cf. XII, 227–30; and the Introduction 55.

10–11. To be understood, *Chaos* must be explored with Satan in II, 890–1053. Cf. *Sion* and *Siloa* in III, 29–31, n. See also the Introduction 19.

16. The line ironically paraphrases Ariosto's opening of the *Orlando Furioso*. The reason why is explained in IX, 29–31, n.

21. *Abyss* was the word used by the translators of the Old Testament into Greek for the Hebrew word translated as "the deep" in Genesis i, 2. Cf. II, 405.

24. *Argument* is used, as it more evidently is used in IX, 28, to mean the subject and development of the poem — not to refer only to the justification of God's ways. See the Introduction 46.

33. So Homer (*Il.* I, 8) asks who it was that brought discord among the Greeks and instantly answers that it was Apollo.

34. *Th' Infernal Serpent* here and in XII, 383, is "that old serpent, which is the Devil, and Satan" (Rev. xx, 2–3) more distinctly than he is the serpent seducer of Eve. He is *infernal* in the literal sense that he is doomed to the punishment of hell or "the bottomless pit," where Milton imagines all the devils as dramatically turned into serpents (X, 509–40).

38. The first of the rare lines ending in an unstressed, redundant syllable. Less than one per cent of the lines in *PL* have feminine endings.

[handwritten margin notes: war between angels and god. Milton wants warfare, he thought it was silly. He wraps it in away. Angels can't die line miscels from Homer]

If he oppos'd; and with ambitious aim
Against the Throne and Monarchy of God
Rais'd impious War in Heav'n and Battle proud
With vain attempt.　Him the Almighty Power　　　　45
Hurl'd headlong flaming from th' Ethereal Sky
With hideous ruin and combustion down
To bottomless perdition, there to dwell
In Adamantine Chains and penal Fire,
Who durst defy th' Omnipotent to Arms.
Nine times the Space that measures Day and Night　　　50
To mortal men, hee with his horrid crew
Lay vanquisht, rolling in the fiery Gulf
Confounded though immortal;　But his doom
Reserv'd him to more wrath; for now the thought
Both of lost happiness and lasting pain　　　　55
Torments him;　round he throws his baleful eyes
That witness'd huge affliction and dismay
Mixt with obdurate pride and steadfast hate:
At once as far as Angels' ken he views
The dismal Situation waste and wild,　　　　60
A Dungeon horrible, on all sides round
As one great Furnace flam'd, yet from those flames
No light, but rather darkness visible
Serv'd only to discover sights of woe,
Regions of sorrow, doleful shades, where peace　　　65
And rest can never dwell, hope never comes
That comes to all; but torture without end
Still urges, and a fiery Deluge, fed
With ever-burning Sulphur unconsum'd:
Such place Eternal Justice had prepar'd　　　　70
For those rebellious, here thir Prison ordained
In utter darkness, and thir portion set
As far remov'd from God and light of Heav'n
As from the Center thrice to th' utmost Pole.

45–48. The lines blend biblical associations stretching from Isaiah xiv, 12 — "How art thou fallen from heaven, O Lucifer, son of the morning" — to the picture of "the angels which kept not their first estate . . . in everlasting chains, under darkness," in Jude i, 6.

50. Here and in VI, 871, the devils fall for as many days as Hesiod (*Theog.*, 664–735) gives for the Titans' fall from heaven after their overthrow by the Olympian gods.　See the Introduction 10–16, and l. 74 below.

59. Early editions are irregular in their use of the apostrophe to indicate the possessive case, which is lacking in them after *Angels*.　It is inserted here on the assumption that *ken* is a noun and is used as it is in XI, 379.

63. The thought goes back to Job's description of the world of the dead as a realm where "the light is darkness" (x, 22). See the Introduction 23.

66. A deliberate echo of Dante's inscription over Hell's gate — "All hope abandon ye who enter here" (*Inf.* III, 9) — is unmistakable.

70. No less explicitly, Dante made hell the creation of divine justice, power, wisdom, and love (*Inf.* III, 4–6).

73–74. So heaven towers up to the celestial north pole in a passage of Aratus' *Phainomena* which Cicero paraphased in *On the Nature of the Gods* (II, xl–xli), but the scene directly recalls Virgil's picture of Avernus as *twice* as far under the earth as heaven is above (*Aen.* VI, 577–79). Cf. V, 503, n.

O how unlike the place from whence they fell!   **75**
There the companions of his fall, o'erwhelm'd
With Floods and Whirlwinds of tempestuous fire,
He soon discerns, and welt'ring by his side
One next himself in power, and next in crime,
Long after known in *Palestine*, and nam'd   **80**
Beëlzebub. To whom th' Arch-Enemy,
And thence in Heav'n call'd Satan, with bold words
Breaking the horrid silence thus began.
    If thou beest hee; But O how fall'n! how chang'd
From him, who in the happy Realms of Light   **85**
Cloth'd with transcendent brightness didst outshine
Myriads though bright: If he whom mutual league,
United thoughts and counsels, equal hope,
And hazard in the Glorious Enterprise,
Join'd with me once, now misery hath join'd   **90**
In equal ruin: into what Pit thou seest
From what highth fall'n, so much the stronger prov'd
He with his Thunder: and till then who knew
The force of those dire Arms? yet not for those,
Nor what the Potent Victor in his rage   **95**
Can else inflict, do I repent or change,
Though chang'd in outward luster; that fixt mind
And high disdain, from sense of injur'd merit,
That with the mightiest rais'd me to contend,
And to the fierce contention brought along   **100**
Innumerable force of Spirits arm'd
That durst dislike his reign, and mee preferring,
His utmost power with adverse power oppos'd
In dubious Battle on the Plains of Heav'n,

81. The wavering traditions behind Beelzebub's title of "chief of the devils" in Matthew x, 25 (cf. Mark iii, 22, and Luke xi, 15) were skeptically reviewed by Milton's friend, John Selden, in his *Syrian Gods* (*De Dis Syris* syntagmata II — London, 1617 — II, b), and the literal meaning of the name, "god of flies," was compared with some titles of Jupiter and other deities who were sometimes worshipped as deliverers from insect pests, or as lords of altars that were either avoided or infested by flies. For Milton's readers Beelzebub was vaguely the prince of the first order of demons that Burton made him in the *Anatomy* (I, ii, 1, 2; Everyman Ed. I, p. 187) or the monarch of flaming hell that Marlowe made him in Faust's first invocation in *Doctor Faustus*. R. H. West notes in *The Invisible World* (Athens, 1939), p. 69 that in the *Occult Philosophy* of Cornelius Agrippa Beelzebub was, in general, any demon engaged in the "false assumption of god-

head." In X, 383–84, the literal meaning of *Satan* is again stressed.

84–85. Satan's first words recall Aeneas' vision of the ghost of Hector on the night of Troy's fall — so changed from the living Hector beside whom he had fought against the Greeks (*Aen.* II, 275–76).

94–97. A possible echo of Capaneus' boast in *Inferno* XIV, 52–91, that Jove's thunder would never break his blasphemous spirit, or of the warning of Aeschylus' Prometheus to Hermes (*Prom.*, 987–96) that he would never yield to Zeus though the god might buffet him with thunder and snow forever. A traditionally exaggerated view of Satan as a magnificently Promethean hero has suggested several other doubtful parallels between their speeches.

98. Contrast Satan's assertion of *merit* here and in II, 6 and 21, with the merit that makes Christ "more than birthright Son of God" (III, 309) and entitles him to reign in heaven (VI, 43).

[margin: The will is glorified]

And shook his throne. What though the field be lost?   105
All is not lost; the unconquerable Will,
And study of revenge, immortal hate,
And courage never to submit or yield:
And what is else not to be overcome?

[margin: God is only God because he is recognized as God]

That Glory never shall his wrath or might   110
Extort from me. To bow and sue for grace
With suppliant knee, and deify his power
Who from the terror of this Arm so late
Doubted his Empire, that were low indeed,
That were an ignominy and shame beneath   115

[margin: Satan believes the will can overcome even God. It can change reality.]

This downfall; since by Fate the strength of Gods
And this Empyreal substance cannot fail,
Since through experience of this great event
In Arms not worse, in foresight much advanc't,
We may with more successful hope resolve   120
To wage by force or guile eternal War
Irreconcilable to our grand Foe,
Who now triumphs, and in th' excess of joy
Sole reigning holds the Tyranny of Heav'n.

[margin: He does not want God, he wants where there is none]

    So spake th' Apostate Angel, though in pain,   125
Vaunting aloud, but rackt with deep despair:
And him thus answer'd soon his bold Compeer.
    O Prince, O Chief of many Throned Powers,
That led th' imbattl'd Seraphim to War
Under thy conduct, and in dreadful deeds   130

[margin: Beelzebub has a greater grip of reality]

Fearless, endanger'd Heav'n's perpetual King;
And put to proof his high Supremacy,
Whether upheld by strength, or Chance, or Fate;
Too well I see and rue the dire event,
That with sad overthrow and foul defeat   135
Hath lost us Heav'n, and all this mighty Host
In horrible destruction laid thus low,
As far as Gods and Heav'nly Essences
Can perish: for the mind and spirit remains
Invincible, and vigor soon returns,   140
Though all our Glory extinct, and happy state

114. *Doubted:* feared for.
115. *ignominy:* probably pronounced "ignomy" here and in II, 207, though not in VI, 383. "Ignomy" was a common spelling.
116. Compare the unwilling recognition of the supremacy of fate by Belial (II, 197), Mammon (II, 231–33), and Beelzebub (II, 393) with Sin's certainty that fate has doomed her and Death to a common end (II, 805–807), and God's declaration that His will is fate (VII, 173).
    Though the angels are sometimes called

"gods" (even by God himself in III, 341), J. C. Maxwell marks Satan's use of the word here as "redolent of paganism; and Beelzebub, in echoing his master, implies the same error" — *N&Q,* CXCIII (1948), 234–45. The speeches anticipate Satan's claim (V, 853–66) that the devils are self-begotten and his promise to Eve (IX, 708) that by eating the forbidden fruit she and Adam should "be as gods." See the Introduction 20.
129. *Seraphim* is the Hebrew plural of *seraph.* Cf. the note on *Baalim* in l. 422 below.

Here swallow'd up in endless misery.
But what if he our Conqueror (whom I now
Of force believe Almighty, since no less
Than such could have o'erpow'rd such force as ours)   145
Have left us this our spirit and strength entire
Strongly to suffer and support our pains,
That we may so suffice his vengeful ire,
Or do him mightier service as his thralls
By right of War, whate'er his business be   150
Here in the heart of Hell to work in Fire,
Or do his Errands in the gloomy Deep;
What can it then avail though yet we feel
Strength undiminisht, or eternal being
To undergo eternal punishment?   155
Whereto with speedy words th' Arch-fiend repli'd.
  Fall'n Cherub, to be weak is miserable
Doing or Suffering: but of this be sure,
To do aught good never will be our task,
But ever to do ill our sole delight,   160
As being the contrary to his high will
Whom we resist. If then his Providence
Out of our evil seek to bring forth good,
Our labor must be to pervert that end,
And out of good still to find means of evil;   165
Which oft-times may succeed, so as perhaps
Shall grieve him, if I fail not, and disturb
His inmost counsels from thir destin'd aim.
But see the angry Victor hath recall'd
His Ministers of vengeance and pursuit   170
Back to the Gates of Heav'n: the Sulphurous Hail
Shot after us in storm, o'erblown hath laid
The fiery Surge, that from the Precipice
Of Heav'n receiv'd us falling, and the Thunder,
Wing'd with red Lightning and impetuous rage,   175
Perhaps hath spent his shafts, and ceases now
To bellow through the vast and boundless Deep.
Let us not slip th' occasion, whether scorn,
Or satiate fury yield it from our Foe.
Seest thou yon dreary Plain, forlorn and wild,   180
The seat of desolation, void of light,
Save what the glimmering of these livid flames

---

148. Beelzebub's words recall Milton's (CD, I, ix) description of the bad angels as "sometimes permitted to wander throughout the whole earth, the air, the heaven itself, to execute the judgments of God" (C.Ed. XV, 109).
158. *doing or suffering:* Cf. II, 199, n., and *PR* III, 195.
162-168. Satan's dramatic resolve and

self-characterization here and in IX, 118-30, prepare for the final discovery, in Adam's words, that God shall produce all the good to be worked in the world by the Son's redemption of Adam's sin, and so "evil turn to good" (XII, 471).
180-188. The livid darkness recalls descriptions of hell as diverse as Statius' picture of the shadowy "Styx livida"

Casts pale and dreadful? Thither let us tend
From off the tossing of these fiery waves,
There rest, if any rest can harbor there,   185
And reassembling our afflicted Powers,
Consult how we may henceforth most offend
Our Enemy, our own loss how repair,
How overcome this dire Calamity,
What reinforcement we may gain from Hope,   190
If not what resolution from despair.
    Thus Satan talking to his nearest Mate
With Head up-lift above the wave, and Eyes
That sparkling blaz'd, his other Parts besides
Prone on the Flood, extended long and large   195
Lay floating many a rood, in bulk as huge
As whom the Fables name of monstrous size,
Titanian, or *Earth-born*, that warr'd on *Jove*,
Briareos or *Typhon*, whom the Den
By ancient *Tarsus* held, or that Sea-beast   200
Leviathan, which God of all his works
Created hugest that swim th' Ocean stream:
Him haply slumb'ring on the *Norway* foam
The Pilot of some small night-founder'd Skiff,
Deeming some Island, oft, as Seamen tell,   205
With fixed Anchor in his scaly rind
Moors by his side under the Lee, while Night
Invests the Sea, and wished Morn delays:
So stretcht out huge in length the Arch-fiend lay
Chain'd on the burning Lake, nor ever thence   210

(*Thebaid* I, 57), Dante's picture of the place where all light is "silent" (*Inf.* V, 28), and the fiery but lightless land described in Caedmon's *Genesis* (333–34).

186. *afflicted* has its Latin force of "stricken" or "overthrown."

199. In the war of the Titans with the Olympian gods the hundred-armed *Briareos* is described by Hesiod (*Theog.*, 713–16) as helping to defeat his brother Titans. For the parallel with the revolt of Satan's angels see the Introduction. Hesiod's story of *Typhon* or Typhoeus as the most frightful of Earth-born monsters (*Theog.*, 819–85) whom Zeus hurled back from Olympus and Ovid's description of him as buried alive under Aetna and neighboring mountains (*Met.* V, 346–58), were typically allegorized by Natale Conti (*Mythologiae* liber VI, xxii) as symbolizing ambition that assails even heaven itself, is as fiery-mouthed as Aetna, and has as many violent plots as Typhon had serpent-heads. The parallel between him and Satan is traced back by Conti to Theodorus' *De Bello Giganteo*. See the Introduction 16.

200. The connection of Typhon with Tarsus stems from Pindar's reference to him in *Pythian Odes*, I, 28–39, as having been born in a cave in Cilicia, of which Tarsus was the capital.

201–209. Of all the biblical allusions to the mysterious sea-monster Leviathan, the closest is Isaiah's prophecy that the Lord "shall punish Leviathan, the piercing serpent, even Leviathan, that crooked serpent; and he shall slay the dragon that is in the sea" (xxviii, 1). The tale of the mariners who mistake the leviathan for an island is widespread: in the story of Sinbad the sailor in the Arabian nights, in Olaus Magnus' *Historia de gentibus septentrionalibus* (Rome, 1555), in Caxton's *Mirrour of the World* (II, ix), in Bartholemew's *De proprietatibus rerum* (xiii, 29), etc. See J. H. Pitman, "Milton and the Physiologus," in *MLN, XL* (1925), 439.

210–215. Milton's discussion of Scriptural evidence for the doctrine of God's blamelessness in permitting the crimes of the wicked, in *CD*, I, viii, is worth comparing here (C.Ed. XV, 72–73).

Had ris'n or heav'd his head, but that the will
And high permission of all-ruling Heaven
Left him at large to his own dark designs,
That with reiterated crimes he might
Heap on himself damnation, while he sought   215
Evil to others, and enrag'd might see
How all his malice serv'd but to bring forth
Infinite goodness, grace and mercy shown
On Man by him seduc't, but on himself
Treble confusion, wrath and vengeance pour'd.   220
Forthwith upright he rears from off the Pool
His mighty Stature; on each hand the flames
Driv'n backward slope thir pointing spires, and roll'd
In billows, leave i' th' midst a horrid Vale.
Then with expanded wings he steers his flight   225
Aloft, incumbent on the dusky Air
That felt unusual weight, till on dry Land
He lights, if it were Land that ever burn'd
With solid, as the Lake with liquid fire
And such appear'd in hue; as when the force   230
Of subterranean wind transports a Hill
Torn from *Pelorus*, or the shatter'd side
Of thund'ring *Ætna*, whose combustible
And fuell'd entrails thence conceiving Fire,
Sublim'd with Mineral fury, aid the Winds,   235
And leave a singed bottom all involv'd
With stench and smoke: Such resting found the sole
Of unblest feet. Him follow'd his next Mate,
Both glorying to have scap't the *Stygian* flood
As Gods, and by thir own recover'd strength,   240
Not by the sufferance of supernal Power.
    Is this the Region, this the Soil, the Clime,
Said then the lost Arch-Angel, this the seat
That we must change for Heav'n, this mournful gloom
For that celestial light? Be it so, since he   245

230. *hue* is glossed as meaning "aspect" or appearance by Wright — *RES*, XXIII (1947), 146 — on the strength of Milton's bracketing of it with "look" in *Of Prelatical Episcopacy*.
231–237. The lines recall Virgil's picture of Mt. Aetna darkening the peninsula of Pelorus in Sicily with its smoke (*Aen*. III, 570–77) and Ovid's account of the rending of Sicily from Italy by winds bursting out of the earth (*Met*. XV, 296–377). Ovid's seismology was still acceptable when Burton surmised in the *Anatomy of Melancholy* (II, ii, 3) that the earth might "be full of wind, or sulfureous, innate fire, as our Meteorologists

inform us, which, sometimes breaking out, causeth horrible earthquakes" (Everyman Ed. II, p. 43).
235. Milton had sulphur mainly in mind as one of the three or four basic minerals of the alchemists, for whom "sublimation" meant the refining of metals by the hottest possible fires.
239. The word is often used without reference to the Styx, the most famous of hell's rivers, to mean "infernal," but usually it connotes darkness, as here and in *Comus*, 90, and *El IV*, 95.
242. Cf. *clime* used to mean "region" in I, 297; II, 572; X, 678; and XII, 636.

Satan is a sympathiser and the archetype of modern Ideas of freedom

Who now is Sovran can dispose and bid
What shall be right: fardest from him is best
Whom reason hath equall'd, force hath made supreme
Above his equals. Farewell happy Fields
Where Joy for ever dwells: Hail horrors, hail   250
Infernal world, and thou profoundest Hell
Receive thy new Possessor: One who brings
A mind not to be chang'd by Place or Time.
The mind is its own place, and in itself
Can make a Heav'n of Hell, a Hell of Heav'n.   255
What matter where, if I be still the same,
And what I should be, all but less than hee
Whom Thunder hath made greater? Here at least
We shall be free; th' Almighty hath not built
Here for his envy, will not drive us hence: 260
Here we may reign secure, and in my choice
To reign is worth ambition though in Hell:
Better to reign in Hell, than serve in Heav'n.
But wherefore let we then our faithful friends,
Th' associates and copartners of our loss   265
Lie thus astonisht on th' oblivious Pool,
And call them not to share with us their part
In this unhappy Mansion: or once more
With rallied Arms to try what may be yet
Regain'd in Heav'n, or what more lost in Hell?   270
   So *Satan* spake, and him *Beëlzebub*
Thus answer'd. Leader of those Armies bright,
Which but th' Omnipotent none could have foiled,
If once they hear that voice, thir liveliest pledge
Of hope in fears and dangers, heard so oft   275
In worst extremes, and on the perilous edge

Satan appeals to our desire for freedom

Satan believes in full autonomy

Satan's... ification

Satan is simply a voice

246. *Sovran* was Milton's preferred
spelling for *sovereign*. Cf. I, 753; II,
244, etc.
255. Satan's heresy is traced by D. C.
Allen in *MLN*, LXXI (1956), 325, to
Amaury de Bene, who was burned for
his denial of the resurrection early in the
thirteenth century. A corollary of his
heresy was the doctrine that heaven and
hell alike are found only in the indi-
vidual's heart. The wider roots of
Satan's boast are traced in *MP*, LIII
(1956), 80–94, to ancient Stoic denials
of a local Tartarus and of its torments
as existing anywhere but in the con-
sciences of sinners, to Renaissance dis-
tortions of the Stoic doctrine that the
mind is master of its fate, and to the
interpretation of Christ's teaching that
"the kingdom of God is within you" by
Jakob Boehme and his disciples as mean-
ing that "we have heaven and hell in

ourselves" (Boehme's *The Threefold Life
of Man*, xiv, 72).
263. The passage contrasts with Ab-
diel's warning to Satan in heaven that
his reign in hell will be mere bondage
(VI, 178–88). It parodies a remark
attributed to Julius Caesar by Plutarch
(*Life of Caesar*, xi, 2) that he would
rather be the first man in a Spanish
village than second in Rome. Its parody
by Satan was traditional; in *Adamo
caduto* (II, i) Serafino Salandra's Lucifer
tells Belial that he would rather be first
(Duce) in hell than a mere prince in
heaven.
266. There is a reference to the in-
fernal river Lethe which (as the ghost
in *Hamlet* I, v, 33, recalled) causes for-
getfulness.
276. *edge* has its now obsolete, Latin
meaning of the front line of battle.

Of battle when it rag'd, in all assaults
Thir surest signal, they will soon resume
New courage and revive, though now they lie
Groveling and prostrate on yon Lake of Fire,   280
As we erewhile, astounded and amaz'd;
No wonder, fall'n such a pernicious highth.

He scarce had ceas't when the superior Fiend
Was moving toward the shore; his ponderous shield
Ethereal temper, massy, large and round,   285
Behind him cast; the broad circumference
Hung on his shoulders like the Moon, whose Orb
Through Optic Glass the *Tuscan* Artist views
At Ev'ning from the top of *Fesole*,
Or in *Valdarno*, to descry new Lands,   290
Rivers or Mountains in her spotty Globe.
His Spear, to equal which the tallest Pine
Hewn on *Norwegian* hills, to be the Mast
Of some great Ammiral, were but a wand,
He walkt with to support uneasy steps   295
Over the burning Marl, not like those steps
On Heaven's Azure, and the torrid Clime
Smote on him sore besides, vaulted with Fire;
Nathless he so endur'd, till on the Beach
Of that inflamed Sea, he stood and call'd   300
His Legions, Angel Forms, who lay intrans't
Thick as Autumnal Leaves that strow the Brooks
In *Vallombrosa*, where th' *Etrurian* shades
High overarch't imbow'r; or scatter'd sedge
Afloat, when with fierce Winds *Orion* arm'd   305
Hath vext the Red-Sea Coast, whose waves o'erthrew
Busiris and his *Memphian* Chivalry,

282. *pernicious* keeps its Latin meaning of "death-giving."

285. *ethereal:* Cf. the notes on l. 117 above and II, 139.

288. The *Tuscan artist* is Galileo, the first astronomer to use a telescope capable of revealing the real nature of the moon's surface. In *Areopagitica* Milton recalls what seems to have been an actual visit to him at Fiesole in the Tuscan hills above the Arno, whose valley is (in Italian) the *Valdarno*. Cf. V, 415–26, n., and the Introduction 32–33.

294. *Ammiral:* admiral's ship. Neither the meaning nor the spelling was obsolete; the latter indicates Milton's preferred pronunciation here.

302–304. Perhaps a memory of Dante's spirits numberless as autumn leaves (*Inf.* III, 112–14) or of the image as C. M. Bowra notes it (in *From Virgil to Milton,* 240–41) in Homer, Bacchylides, Virgil and Tasso. Milton may have visited the

shady valley, Vallombrosa, during his stay in Florence.

304–314. The rapidly compounding simile fuses Virgilian descriptions of the constellation Orion as cloudy and stormy (*Aen.* I, 535; VII, 719) with biblical references to the masses of seaweed in the Red Sea, which in turn recalls the destruction there of Pharaoh's chariots and horsemen (the *Memphian Chivalry*) whom it overwhelmed as they tried to stop the flight of the Hebrews across it from the Land of Goshen in Egypt to safety on the eastern shore.

307. D. C. Allen has shown — *MLN,* LXV (1950), 115 — that the *Chronicle* of Carion, which Milton used in Melanchthon's revision, misled him into identifying the mythical Busiris with the Pharaoh of Exodus, who had long been recognized by commentators as a type of Satan, *vera daemonis figura,* as he is called in the Prologue to the Rule of St. Benedict.

While with perfidious hatred they pursu'd
The Sojourners of *Goshen,* who beheld
From the safe shore thir floating Carcasses   310
And broken Chariot Wheels; so thick bestrown
Abject and lost lay these, covering the Flood,
Under amazement of thir hideous change.
He call'd so loud, that all the hollow Deep
Of Hell resounded. Princes, Potentates,   315
Warriors, the Flow'r of Heav'n, once yours, now lost,
If such astonishment as this can seize
Eternal spirits; or have ye chos'n this place
After the toil of Battle to repose
Your wearied virtue, for the ease you find   320
To slumber here, as in the Vales of Heav'n?
Or in this abject posture have ye sworn
To adore the Conqueror? who now beholds
Cherub and Seraph rolling in the Flood
With scatter'd Arms and Ensigns, till anon   325
His swift pursuers from Heav'n Gates discern
Th' advantage, and descending tread us down
Thus drooping, or with linked Thunderbolts
Transfix us to the bottom of this Gulf.
Awake, arise, or be for ever fall'n.   330
    They heard, and were abasht, and up they sprung
Upon the wing; as when men wont to watch
On duty, sleeping found by whom they dread,
Rouse and bestir themselves ere well awake.
Nor did they not perceive the evil plight   335
In which they were, or the fierce pains not feel;
Yet to thir General's Voice they soon obey'd
Innumerable. As when the potent Rod
Of *Amram's* Son in *Egypt's* evil day
Wav'd round the Coast, up call'd a pitchy cloud   340
Of *Locusts,* warping on the Eastern Wind,
That o'er the Realm of impious *Pharaoh* hung
Like Night, and darken'd all the Land of *Nile:*
So numberless were those bad Angels seen
Hovering on wing under the Cope of Hell   345
'Twixt upper, nether, and surrounding Fires;
Till, as a signal giv'n, th' uplifted Spear

313. For the use of *amazement* see VI, 646, n.

314. In the MS Miss Darbishire notes that the reading is *deeps,* as if to suggest reverberation from one level to another.

339. *Amram* was Moses' father. The plague of locusts which he called down on the Egyptians by the power of his rod, so that it covered "the face of the whole earth, so that the land was dark-ened" (Exod. x, 12–15), was the basis of a familiar metaphor that was applied alike to men and devils by Phineas Fletcher in his *Locustae* (1607). Cf. XII, 176–99.

341. *O.E.D.* quotes this line to illustrate *warping* in this sense and brackets it with an earlier example of the word applied to "snow driving and warping in the wind."

Of thir great Sultan waving to direct
Thir course, in even balance down they light
On the firm brimstone, and fill all the Plain;   350
A multitude, like which the populous North
Pour'd never from her frozen loins, to pass
Rhene or the *Danaw*, when her barbarous Sons
Came like a Deluge on the South, and spread
Beneath *Gibraltar* to the *Lybian* sands.   355
Forthwith from every Squadron and each Band
The Heads and Leaders thither haste where stood
Thir great Commander; Godlike shapes and forms
Excelling human, Princely Dignities,
And Powers that erst in Heaven sat on Thrones;   360
Though of thir Names in heav'nly Records now
Be no memorial, blotted out and ras'd
By thir Rebellion, from the Books of Life.
Nor had they yet among the Sons of *Eve*
Got them new Names, till wand'ring o'er the Earth,   365
Through God's high sufferance for the trial of man,
By falsities and lies the greatest part
Of Mankind they corrupted to forsake
God thir Creator, and th' invisible
Glory of him that made them, to transform   370
Oft to the Image of a Brute, adorn'd
With gay Religions full of Pomp and Gold,
And Devils to adore for Deities:
Then were they known to men by various Names,
And various Idols through the Heathen World.   375
Say, Muse, thir Names then known, who first, who last,
Rous'd from the slumber on that fiery Couch,
At thir great Emperor's call, as next in worth
Came singly where he stood on the bare strand,
While the promiscuous crowd stood yet aloof?   380

353–355. Perhaps an echo of Machiavelli's opening of the *Florentine History* (anonymous translation of 1674): "The people inhabiting the Regions Northwards from the rivers *Rhyne* and *Danube*, living in a healthful clime, and apt for Generation, oft-times increase to such vast multitudes, that part of them are constrained to forsake their Native Country, and seek new places to dwell in. . . . These people were they, who destroyed the *Roman* Empire." The crossing of the Vandals into North Africa (the *Lybian sands*) is prominent on Machiavelli's second page. Cf. the opening of *Prol* V.

360–375. For the *Powers that erst sat on thrones* and later were known by various names to the heathen see the Introduction 25–26.

361–363. Biblical references to the Book of Life run from Psalm lxix, 28, to the "Lamb's book of life" in Revelation xxi, 27, into which came nothing "that defileth, neither whatsoever worketh abomination or maketh a lie." Cf. V, 658–59, n.

367–371. The lines recall St Paul's contempt for pagan religions that "changed the glory of the incorruptible God into an image made like to corruptible man, and to birds, and four-footed beasts, and creeping things" (Rom. i, 23).

376. The line echoes Homer's introduction of the catalogue of ships in the *Iliad* (II, 484) with the plea to the Muse to tell him who were the commanders and lords of the Greeks. See the Introduction 25.

The chief were those who from the Pit of Hell
Roaming to seek thir prey on earth, durst fix
Thir Seats long after next the Seat of God,
Thir Altars by his Altar, Gods ador'd
Among the Nations round, and durst abide   385
Jehovah thund'ring out of *Sion*, thron'd
Between the Cherubim; yea, often plac'd
Within his Sanctuary itself thir Shrines,
Abominations; and with cursed things
His holy Rites, and solemn Feasts profan'd   390
And with thir darkness durst affront his light.
First *Moloch*, horrid King besmear'd with blood
Of human sacrifice, and parents' tears,
Though for the noise of Drums and Timbrels loud
Thir children's cries unheard, that pass'd through fire   395
To his grim Idol. Him the *Ammonite*
Worshipt in *Rabba* and her wat'ry Plain,
In *Argob* and in *Basan*, to the stream
Of utmost *Arnon*. Nor content with such
Audacious neighborhood, the wisest heart   400
Of *Solomon* he led by fraud to build
His Temple right against the Temple of God
On that opprobrious Hill, and made his Grove
The pleasant Valley of *Hinnom*, *Tophet* thence
And black *Gehenna* call'd, the Type of Hell.   405
Next *Chemos*, th' obscene dread of *Moab's* Sons,
From *Aroar* to *Nebo*, and the wild

382–389. The image is that of the "Shepherd of Israel, . . . thou that dwellest between the cherubim," of Psalm lxxx, 1, whose shrine on Mt. Sion in Jerusalem itself was sometimes dishonored by apostate kings of Judah, who, like Ahaz (II Kings xvi, 10–18), surrounded it with pagan altars.

392. The name *Moloch* literally means "king." Cf. the account of his worship in *Nativity*, 205–12.

397. *Rabba*, the Ammonite capital, was conquered by David (II Sam. xii, 27).

398–399. Near the Moabite border stream of *Arnon* lay *Argob* and *Basan*, where the Israelites destroyed the "sons of Ammon" (Deut. iii, 1–13).

401. Beguiled by his wives, Solomon built "an high place for Chemosh, the abomination of Moab, in the hill that is before Jerusalem, and for Moloch, the abomination of Ammon" (I Kings xi, 7). The hill was the Mount of Olives, the "mount of offense" of II Kings xxiii, 13, and the "hill of scandal" of l. 416 below. See the Introduction 26.

404. In Jeremiah (xix, 6) the apostate Israelites burn "their sons with fire for burnt offerings unto Baal" in the valley of the "son of Hinnom." The form *Gehenna*, as St. Jerome wrote in his *Commentary on the Gospel of Matthew*, is not biblical, but under that name he identified the place and associated it with the Baal-worship of the neighboring valley of Tophet, which was called "the monument to the dead"; hence "the eternal punishments by which sinners are tortured are designated by the name of this place." Reflections of St. Jerome in several biblical commentators are traced by A. L. Kellogg in *N&Q*, CXCV (1950), 10–13. Cf. Starnes and Talbert, *Dictionaries*, pp. 317–318.

406. In Numbers xxi, 29, the Moabites are called the "people of Chemosh." He is not identified in Selden's *De Dis Syris*, and Fuller was in doubt whether the "*Babylonish* Deity Bell" was "the same with *Chemosh* and *Baal-Peor* (which is the opinion of St. Jerome) and if not, wherein lay the difference" (*Pisgah-Sight*, p. 64).

407–409. *Aroar*, Mt. *Nebo*, the *Abarim* hills, and *Hesebon* (Heshbon) are conspicuous on Thomas Fuller's map of the

Of Southmost *Abarim;* in *Hesebon*
And *Horonaim, Seon's* Realm, beyond
The flow'ry Dale of *Sibma* clad with Vines,   410
And *Eleale* to th' *Asphaltic* Pool.
Peor his other Name, when he entic'd
Israel in *Sittim* on thir march from *Nile*
To do him wanton rites, which cost them woe.
Yet thence his lustful Orgies he enlarg'd   415
Even to that Hill of scandal, by the Grove
Of *Moloch* homicide, lust hard by hate;
Till good *Josiah* drove them thence to Hell.
With these came they, who from the bord'ring flood
Of old *Euphrates* to the Brook that parts   420
Egypt from *Syrian* ground, had general Names
Of *Baalim* and *Ashtaroth,* those male,
These Feminine. For Spirits when they please
Can either Sex assume, or both; so soft
And uncompounded is thir Essence pure,   425
Not ti'd or manacl'd with joint or limb,
Nor founded on the brittle strength of bones,
Like cumbrous flesh; but in what shape they choose
Dilated or condens't, bright or obscure,
Can execute thir aery purposes,   430
And works of love or enmity fulfil.
For those the Race of *Israel* oft forsook
Thir living strength, and unfrequented left
His righteous Altar, bowing lowly down
To bestial Gods; for which thir heads as low   435
Bow'd down in Battle, sunk before the Spear

---

land of the tribe of Reuben — in *A Pisgah-Sight* (p. 55) — together with the other places that are named in ll. 398 and 406–18 below. The destruction of *Seon's* (Sihon's) city of Heshbon is celebrated in Numbers xxi, 25. Cf. Psalms cxxxv, 11, and cxxxvi, 19, and Isaiah xv, 5.

410–411. Close to the city of *Eleale* on Fuller's map *Sibma* is marked by a vine and in his text the valley is described as filled with vineyards for whose destruction the prophets later mourned (Isa. xvi, 8–9, and Jer. xlviii, 32).

411. *th'Asphaltic* Pool: the Dead Sea, which is described in a famous passage of Diodorus Siculus' *Library* (XIX, 98) as producing a floating island of solid asphalt every year.

413. On the march from Egypt to Canaan "Israel abode in Shittim, and the people began to commit whoredom with the daughters of Moab. . . . And Israel joined himself unto Baal-Peor" (Num. xxv, 1, 3). Later biblical passages

(Psalm cvi, 28, and Hosea ix, 10) treat the incident as a lasting national disgrace, but Selden (*De Dis Syris* II, v) was skeptical of the identification of Baal-Peor's rites by the commentators with those of other obscene deities, including those of the Sidonian gods to whom Milton refers in ll. 440–46.

420. The Euphrates bounded Palestine on the east and the "brook Besor" (I Sam. xxx, 10) was the Egyptian frontier.

422–431. *Baalim* and *Ashtaroth:* plural forms: cf. the singular *Astoreth* in l. 438. Baal-Peor was only one of several local Baals in Scripture. In attributing Protean powers to the devils and angels Milton had in mind a passage in Michael Psellus' work of the tenth century, the *De operatione daemonum* (V, 8–9), which was published in Paris in 1615 and widely quoted by writers on witchcraft to explain spirit-apparitions in the forms of beasts, men, or angels. Cf. *PL* III, 636; IV, 800; and VI, 327–92.

Of despicable foes. With these in troop
Came *Astoreth*, whom the *Phœnicians* call'd
Astarte, Queen of Heav'n, with crescent Horns;
To whose bright Image nightly by the Moon   440
Sidonian Virgins paid thir Vows and Songs,
In *Sion* also not unsung, where stood
Her Temple on th' offensive Mountain, built
By that uxorious King, whose heart though large,
Beguil'd by fair Idolatresses, fell   445
To Idols foul. *Thammuz* came next behind,
Whose annual wound in *Lebanon* allur'd
The *Syrian* Damsels to lament his fate
In amorous ditties all a Summer's day,
While smooth *Adonis* from his native Rock   450
Ran purple to the Sea, suppos'd with blood
Of *Thammuz* yearly wounded: the Love-tale
Infected *Sion's* daughters with like heat,
Whose wanton passions in the sacred Porch
Ezekiel saw, when by the Vision led   455
His eye survey'd the dark Idolatries
Of alienated *Judah*. Next came one
Who mourn'd in earnest, when the Captive Ark
Maim'd his brute Image, head and hands lopt off
In his own Temple, on the grunsel edge,   460
Where he fell flat, and sham'd his Worshippers:
Dagon his Name, Sea Monster, upward Man
And downward Fish: yet had his Temple high
Rear'd in *Azotus*, dreaded through the Coast
Of *Palestine*, in *Gath* and *Ascalon*,   465

438. Cf. the allusions to *Astarte*, the Phoenecian Aphrodite or Venus, as "mooned Ashtaroth, Heaven's queen," in *Nativity*, 200, and as the "Assyrian queen" in *Comus*, 1002.

444. The *uxorious King* is Solomon. Cf. l. 401 above.

446. Because *Thammuz* was identified with Adonis in St. Jerome's commentary on Ezekiel's account (viii, 13–14) of the idolatrous weeping of the women of Jerusalem for his "death" when annually, in July, the river that bore his name in Lebanon ran red (supposedly with the god's blood), his story was popular and could be found in works as heterogeneous as Sir Walter Raleigh's *History of the World*, George Sandys' *Relation of a Journey*, and Charles Stephanus' *Dictionary* in forms so close to Milton's passage that all of them have been mentioned as possible sources. Selden (in *De Dis Syris* II, x) found Thammuz-Adonis identified by various commentators with many pagan deities,

including Osiris, and treated his worship as a nature cult. Cf. Milton's allusion in *Manso*, 11.

458–466. The story of the miraculous fall of the image of the fish-deity Dagon "upon his face to the ground before the ark of the Lord" so that "the head of Dagon and both the palms of his hands were cut off upon the threshold" (I Sam. v, 5) was hardly less popular than the story of Thammuz. Sandys, Selden, Purchase, Raleigh, and the great vulgarizer of pagan backgrounds to the Bible, Alexander Ross, in *Pansebeia, or, A View of all Religions of the World* (1653), all describe Dagon's fall in Ashdod and represent his image as human from the waist up but fishlike below. Cf. *SA*, 13, etc.

464. *Azotus* is the Greek form given on Ortelius' maps for *Ashdod*, the form in *SA*, 981, where *Accaron* is mentioned as *Ekron*. All five Philistine cities lay on or near the Mediterranean shore.

And *Accaron* and *Gaza's* frontier bounds.
Him follow'd *Rimmon*, whose delightful Seat
Was fair *Damascus*, on the fertile Banks
Of *Abbana* and *Pharphar*, lucid streams.
He also against the house of God was bold: 470
A Leper once he lost and gain'd a King,
Ahaz his sottish Conqueror, whom he drew
God's Altar to disparage and displace
For one of *Syrian* mode, whereon to burn
His odious off'rings, and adore the Gods   475
Whom he had vanquisht. After these appear'd
A crew who under Names of old Renown,
Osiris, Isis, Orus and thir Train
With monstrous shapes and sorceries abus'd
Fanatic *Egypt* and her Priests, to seek   480
Thir wand'ring Gods disguis'd in brutish forms
Rather than human. Nor did *Israel* scape
Th' infection when thir borrow'd Gold compos'd
The Calf in *Oreb:* and the Rebel King
Doubl'd that sin in *Bethel* and in *Dan*,   485
Lik'ning his Maker to the Grazed Ox,
Jehovah, who in one Night when he pass'd
From *Egypt* marching, equall'd with one stroke
Both her first born and all her bleating Gods.
Belial came last, than whom a Spirit more lewd   490
Fell not from Heaven, or more gross to love
Vice for itself: To him no Temple stood
Or Altar smok'd; yet who more oft than hee
In Temples and at Altars, when the Priest
Turns Atheist, as did *Ely's* Sons, who fill'd   495

467–476. II Kings xvi, 10, deplores
King Ahaz's apostasy to the Syrian god
Rimmon after conquering Damascus,
where his temple stood. The familiarity
of Elisha's curing of the leprous Syrian
general Naaman by the water of Jordan
is shown by Ralph Cudworth's allusion
in his Sermon before the Commons
(p. 31): "The Gospel is not like Abana
and Pharphar, those common rivers of
Damascus, that could only cleanse the
outside; but it is a true Jordan."
    478. Cf. the rout of the Egyptian gods
by "the dreaded Infant's hand" in *Na-
tivity*, 211–15.
    482–484. The golden calf worshipped
by the Israelites in the desert (Exod.
xxxii, 4) is identified with the Egyptian
bull god, Apis.
    484–489. When Jeroboam led the se-
cession of the Ten Tribes from the
Judaean kingdom he set up golden
calves in the key cities of Samaria,
Bethel and *Dan*, and proclaimed, "Behold

thy gods, O Israel, which brought thee
up out of the land of Egypt" (I Kings
xii, 28). Milton contrasts the miraculous
slaying of the first-born children and
cattle, including the sacred Egyptian
animals (the *bleating gods*) on the night
of Israel's escape from Egypt.
    490–501. In the biblical account of the
crimes in *Sodom* and *Gibeah* (Gen. xix,
4–11) *Belial* is an abstract noun meaning
profligacy. *Sons of Belial* was a widely
current phrase in the Bible and in Puritan
sermons and pamphlets, meaning dissi-
pated men or enemies of God. In the
New Testament it was sometimes per-
sonified (as in II Cor. vi, 15), and in
sacred dramas Belial often appeared as
a character like Burton's prince of the
third order of devils, the "vessels of
anger and inventors of all mischief"
(*Anatomy* I, ii, 1, 2; Everyman Ed. I,
p. 187).
    495. The story is found in I Samuel ii,
12–25.

With lust and violence the house of God.
In Courts and Palaces he also Reigns
And in luxurious Cities, where the noise
Of riot ascends above thir loftiest Tow'rs,
And injury and outrage: And when Night   500
Darkens the Streets, then wander forth the Sons
Of *Belial*, flown with insolence and wine.
Witness the Streets of *Sodom*, and that night
In *Gibeah*, when the hospitable door
Expos'd a Matron to avoid worse rape.   50*
These were the prime in order and in might;
The rest were long to tell, though far renown'd,
Th' *Ionian* Gods, of *Javan's* Issue held
Gods, yet confest later than Heav'n and Earth
Thir boasted Parents; *Titan* Heav'n's first born   510
With his enormous brood, and birthright seiz'd
By younger *Saturn*, he from mightier *Jove*
His own and *Rhea's* Son like measure found;
So *Jove* usurping reign'd: these first in *Crete*
And *Ida* known, thence on the Snowy top   515
Of cold *Olympus* rul'd the middle Air
Thir highest Heav'n; or on the *Delphian* Cliff,
Or in *Dodona*, and through all the bounds
Of *Doric* Land; or who with *Saturn* old
Fled over *Adria* to th' *Hesperian* Fields,   520
And o'er the *Celtic* roam'd the utmost Isles.
All these and more came flocking; but with looks
Downcast and damp, yet such wherein appear'd
Obscure some glimpse of joy, to have found thir chief
Not in despair, to have found themselves not lost   525
In loss itself; which on his count'nance cast
Like doubtful hue: but he his wonted pride
Soon recollecting, with high words, that bore
Semblance of worth, not substance, gently rais'd
Thir fainting courage, and dispell'd thir fears.   530
Then straight commands that at the warlike sound
Of Trumpets loud and Clarions be uprear'd
His mighty Standard; that proud honor claim'd

508–510. The identification of the Ionians (Greeks) as descendants of Javan, the son of Japhet (Gen. x, 2) goes back as far as the translation of the Old Testament into Greek in the third century B.C. Cf. IV, 717, and SA, 716.

510–519. In the background are myths of the Titans as the first children of *Heaven* and *Earth*, of their displacement by Zeus or *Jove*, the son of the youngest of them, *Saturn*, and his sister *Rhea*, and of the rearing of Zeus on Mt. *Ida* in

Crete and of his worship at *Delphi* and in the grove of *Dodona* in Epeirus. After losing power to Zeus, Saturn fled across the Adriatic Sea (*Adria*) to Italy, where he left the tradition of a "reign of gold" to which *Il Penseroso*, 25, refers. Later he fled to the *Celtic land* of Britain, which was sometimes identified with the Islands of the *Hesperides*, where — according to a tale mentioned by Plutarch in his essay *On the Cessation of Oracles* — he was still imprisoned, asleep, on the Isle of Anglesea.

Azazel as his right, a Cherub tall:
Who forthwith from the glittering Staff unfurl'd   535
Th' Imperial Ensign, which full high advanc't
Shone like a Meteor streaming to the Wind
With Gems and Golden lustre rich imblaz'd,
Seraphic arms and Trophies: all the while
Sonorous metal blowing Martial sounds: 540
At which the universal Host upsent
A shout that tore Hell's Concave, and beyond
Frighted the Reign of *Chaos* and old Night.
All in a moment through the gloom were seen
Ten thousand Banners rise into the Air   545
With Orient Colors waving: with them rose
A Forest huge of Spears: and thronging Helms
Appear'd, and serried Shields in thick array
Of depth immeasurable: Anon they move
In perfect *Phalanx* to the *Dorian* mood   550
Of Flutes and soft Recorders; such as rais'd
To highth of noblest temper Heroes old
Arming to Battle, and instead of rage
Deliberate valor breath'd, firm and unmov'd
With dread of death to flight or foul retreat,   555
Nor wanting power to mitigate and swage
With solemn touches, troubl'd thoughts, and chase
Anguish and doubt and fear and sorrow and pain
From mortal or immortal minds. Thus they
Breathing united force with fixèd thought   560
Mov'd on in silence to soft Pipes that charm'd
Thir painful steps o'er the burnt soil; and now
Advanc't in view they stand, a horrid Front
Of dreadful length and dazzling Arms, in guise
Of Warriors old with order'd Spear and Shield,   565
Awaiting what command thir mighty Chief

534. In Lev. xvi, 20, *Azazel* is the word signifying the scapegoat which annually carried the sins of Israel into the wilderness, but in Jewish tradition as represented by the Book of Enoch (x, 4) the name is given to a prince of the devils whom Raphael binds "to await the great day of fire." In Origen's work *Contra Celsum* (VI, 43) *Azazel* is identified with Satan himself. In the occult writings of Cornelius Agrippa, John Reuchlin, and Robert Fludd — as R. H. West shows in *Angels*, pp. 155–6 — he ranked with Samael, Azael, and Mahazael as a standard-bearer in Satan's armies.

543. *Reign of Chaos:* the realm of Chaos. Cf. II, 895 and 907, where Chaos is used to signify both the region of disorganized matter between hell and heaven and the ruler of that realm.

550–567. In the background is Plato's teaching in the *Republic* III, 399A, that music in the quietly firm Dorian mode best prepares men for battle. In John Bingham's translation of Aelian's *Tacktics* (1616), p. 70, Thucydides, Plutarch, and several other ancient writers are quoted on the Spartan practice of going into battle to the music of the flute, "neither dissolving their order, nor shewing any astonishment of minde, but mildely and ioyfully approaching the danger of conflict." In Peter Whitehorne's translation of Machiavelli's *Arte of Warre* (1560), p. 126, the Spartan practice is contrasted with the Roman use of the trumpet in battle — a comparison that is made by several Renaissance writers.

Had to impose: He through the armed Files
Darts his experienc't eye, and soon traverse
The whole Battalion views, thir order due,
Thir visages and stature as of Gods;   570
Thir number last he sums. And now his heart
Distends with pride, and hard'ning in his strength
Glories: For never since created man,
Met such imbodied force, as nam'd with these
Could merit more than that small infantry   575
Warr'd on by Cranes: though all the Giant brood
Of *Phlegra* with th' Heroic Race were join'd
That fought at *Thebes* and *Ilium*, on each side
Mixt with auxiliar Gods; and what resounds
In Fable or *Romance* of *Uther's* Son   580
Begirt with *British* and *Armoric* Knights;
And all who since, Baptiz'd or Infidel
Jousted in *Aspramont* or *Montalban*,
Damasco, or *Marocco*, or *Trebisond*,
Or whom *Biserta* sent from *Afric* shore   585
When *Charlemain* with all his Peerage fell
By *Fontarabbia*. Thus far these beyond
Compare of mortal prowess, yet observ'd
Thir dread commander: he above the rest
In shape and gesture proudly eminent   590
Stood like a Tow'r; his form had yet not lost

---

573. *since created man:* since the creation of man.

575. The *small infantry* are "that pygmean race beyond the Indian mount" of l. 780. A tradition as old as Homer (*Il.* III, 1–5), much embroidered by Pliny (VII, ii), was perpetuated by pygmy figures drawn on some maps of eastern Asia to illustrate the "Pygmaeans there (men but a cubite in height) which riding on Goats and Rammes do kepe warre with Cranes" — William Cunningham, *The Cosmographical Glasse* (London, 1559), Rvi^r.

577. Since the battle of the giants with the gods is associated with Mt. Aetna in *Prolusion* 1 (C.Ed. XII, 123) and also in line 233 above, as it was by Ovid in *Met.* V, 352, the sulfurous plain of Phlegra in Italy seems to be intended here rather than the Macedonian Phlegra where Pindar located the battle in *Nemean Odes,* I, 100.

578–579. *Thebes* and *Ilium* (Troy) are symbolic of the epic struggles in the war of the Seven Greek heroes against Boeotian Thebes in which the intervention of the gods is represented from the first as very important in Statius' *Thebaid*, and of the similar struggles with divine intervention frequently occurring in the *Iliad.*

580–581. *Uther's Son*, Arthur, with his knights both *British* and *Armoric* (i.e. from Brittany), recall another reference to them in a context of renunciation (*PR* II, 360–62) of such fables. Cf. *Manso*, 81.

582–583. *Aspramont*, Calabria, gave its name to an Italian romance, published in 1516, which narrates Charlemagne's repulse of a Saracen invasion. *Montalban* is Rinaldo's castle in Luigi Pulci's *Il Morgante Maggiore*, Matteo Boiardo's *Orlando Inammorato*, and Ariosto's *Orlando Furioso.*

584. In Ariosto's *Orlando Furioso,* Canto XVII, *Damascus* is the scene of a tournament of Christian and pagan knights, one of whom is the king of *Morocco*. The Byzantine city of *Trebizond*, on the south shore of the Black Sea, was captured by the Turks in 1461. Its story was popular in Giovanni Ambrogio Marini's romance *Il Colloandro Fedele* (Bracciano, 1640). It was translated into French by M. de Scudéry and imitated in La Calprènede's *Cléopâtre.*

587. The climax of the *Song of Roland,* the massacre of Charlemagne's rearguard in the Pyrenees by the Saracens, was commonly placed at *Fontarabbia*, forty miles from the scene of the battle at Roncesvalles.

All her Original brightness, nor appear'd
Less than Arch-Angel ruin'd, and th' excess
Of Glory obscur'd: As when the Sun new ris'n
Looks through the Horizontal misty Air   595
Shorn of his Beams, or from behind the Moon
In dim Eclipse disastrous twilight sheds
On half the Nations, and with fear of change
Perplexes Monarchs. Dark'n'd so, yet shone
Above them all th' Arch-Angel: but his face   600
Deep scars of Thunder had intrencht, and care
Sat on his faded cheek, but under Brows
Of dauntless courage, and considerate Pride
Waiting revenge: cruel his eye, but cast
Signs of remorse and passion to behold   605
The fellows of his crime, the followers rather
(Far other once beheld in bliss) condemn'd
For ever now to have thir lot in pain,
Millions of Spirits for his fault amerc't
Of Heav'n, and from Eternal Splendors flung   610
For his revolt, yet faithful how they stood,
Thir Glory wither'd. As when Heaven's Fire
Hath scath'd the Forest Oaks, or Mountain Pines,
With singed top thir stately growth though bare
Stands on the blasted Heath. He now prepar'd   615
To speak; whereat thir doubl'd Ranks they bend
From wing to wing, and half enclose him round
With all his Peers: attention held them mute.
Thrice he assay'd, and thrice in spite of scorn,
Tears such as Angels weep, burst forth: at last   620
Words interwove with sighs found out thir way.
      O Myriads of immortal Spirits, O Powers
Matchless, but with th' Almighty, and that strife
Was not inglorious, though th' event was dire,
As this place testifies, and this dire change   625
Hateful to utter: but what power of mind
Foreseeing or presaging, from the Depth
Of knowledge past or present, could have fear'd
How such united force of Gods, how such
As stood like these, could ever know repulse?   630
For who can yet believe, though after loss,

598. Milton may have intended his
readers to think of similar comparisons
of doomed rulers to the rising sun in
clouds or eclipse such as Shakespeare's
simile for the appearance of Richard II,
like

     the blushing, discontented sun
From out the fiery portal of the east,
When he perceives the envious clouds
     are bent

To dim his glory.
                  (*Richard II* III, iii, 62–66)
The simile adumbrates Satan's final
defeat as the eclipse in Book XI, 181–84,
adumbrates the effect of man's sin on
the world.   Charles II's censor is said to
have objected to the lines as a veiled
threat to the King.
     603. *considerate:* deliberate, conscious.
     609. *amerc't:* penalized, punished.

That all these puissant Legions, whose exile
Hath emptied Heav'n, shall fail to re-ascend
Self-rais'd, and repossess thir native seat?
For mee be witness all the Host of Heav'n,   635
If counsels different, or danger shunn'd
By me, have lost our hopes. But he who reigns
Monarch in Heav'n, till then as one secure
Sat on his Throne, upheld by old repute,
Consent or custom, and his Regal State   640
Put forth at full, but still his strength conceal'd,
Which tempted our attempt, and wrought our fall.
Henceforth his might we know, and know our own
So as not either to provoke, or dread
New War, provok't; our better part remains   645
To work in close design, by fraud or guile
What force effected not: that he no less
At length from us may find, who overcomes
By force, hath overcome but half his foe.
Space may produce new Worlds; whereof so rife   650
There went a fame in Heav'n that he ere long
Intended to create, and therein plant
A generation, whom his choice regard
Should favor equal to the Sons of Heaven:
Thither, if but to pry, shall be perhaps   655
Our first eruption, thither or elsewhere:
For this Infernal Pit shall never hold
Celestial Spirits in Bondage, nor th' Abyss
Long under darkness cover. But these thoughts
Full Counsel must mature: Peace is despair'd,   660
For who can think Submission? War then, War
Open or understood, must be resolv'd.
   He spake: and to confirm his words, out-flew
Millions of flaming swords, drawn from the thighs
Of mighty Cherubim; the sudden blaze   665
Far round illumin'd hell: highly they rag'd
Against the Highest, and fierce with grasped Arms
Clash'd on thir sounding shields the din of war,
Hurling defiance toward the Vault of Heav'n.
   There stood a Hill not far whose grisly top   670
Belch'd fire and rolling smoke; the rest entire
Shone with a glossy scurf, undoubted sign
That in his womb was hid metallic Ore,

---

636. *different* means "differing," says
B. A. Wright in *N&Q* N.S. V (1958), 205.
"Contrary, opposite" is the *O.E.D.* second
meaning. "Procrastinating" is improbable.
   642. *tempted our attempt:* Cf. the simi-
lar pun in IX, 648. In Milton such puns
usually have a grim humor, but as a

figure of speech they had been much ad-
mired as part of the "bravery" of poetry,
as Abraham Fraunce said that they were
in his *Arcadian Rhetorike* (London, 1588).
   646. *close:* secret.
   651. *fame:* rumor. Cf. II, 345–53,
830–35, and X, 481.

The work of Sulphur. Thither wing'd with speed
A numerous Brigad hasten'd. As when bands   675
Of Pioners with Spade and Pickax arm'd
Forerun the Royal Camp, to trench a Field,
Or cast a Rampart. *Mammon* led them on,
Mammon, the least erected Spirit that fell
From Heav'n, for ev'n in Heav'n his looks and thoughts   680
Were always downward bent, admiring more
The riches of Heav'n's pavement, trodd'n Gold,
Than aught divine or holy else enjoy'd
In vision beatific: by him first
Men also, and by his suggestion taught,   685
Ransack'd the Center, and with impious hands
Rifl'd the bowels of thir mother Earth
For Treasures better hid. Soon had his crew
Op'n'd into the Hill a spacious wound
And digg'd out ribs of Gold. Let none admire   690
That riches grow in Hell; that soil may best
Deserve the precious bane. And here let those
Who boast in mortal things, and wond'ring tell
Of *Babel*, and the works of *Memphian* Kings,
Learn how thir greatest Monuments of Fame,   695
And Strength and Art are easily outdone
By Spirits reprobate, and in an hour
What in an age they with incessant toil
And hands innumerable scarce perform.
Nigh on the Plain in many cells prepar'd,   700
That underneath had veins of liquid fire
Sluic'd from the Lake, a second multitude
With wondrous Art founded the massy Ore,

---

674. Cf. VI, 509–15.
675. *Brigad:* brigade. Milton accented the first syllable.
678. *Mammon* — an Aramaic word meaning riches — enters the Bible in Matthew vi, 24. Mediaeval tradition personified it, and Mammon became the prince of the lowest of the nine orders of demons, "those tempters in several kinds," as Burton called them in the *Anatomy* I, ii, 1, 2 (Everyman Ed. I, p. 188).
684. The *vision beatific* of Dante's *Paradiso*, the fulfilment of the promise that "the pure in heart shall see God" (Matt. v, 8), is as much a part of the imaginative background of *PL* as it is of the *Divine Comedy*. Cf. V, 613. In *On Time*, 18, it is translated in "happy-making sight." In the final chapter of *Of Reformation* it gives Milton his conception of the reformers in their "super-eminence of beatific vision, progressing the dateless and irrevoluble circle of

eternity."
686–692. In *Nature is not Subject to Old Age*, 63–65, Milton alludes to Ovid's classic statement of this commonplace (*Met.* I, 137–42). The root of all evil is the gold that men first stole from the earth when the golden age ended. The oxymoron of gold as *precious bane* (valuable evil) inspired the often repeated paradox that Chaucer translated from Boethius in *The Former Age:*

But cursed was the tyme, I dar wel seye,
That men first dide hir swety bysinesse,
To grobbe up metal, lurkinge in derknesse.

Cf. VI, 470–520, and *Comus*, 732–35.
690. *admire:* wonder.
694. *Babel:* the capital of the tyrant Nimrod, whose story is told in XII, 24–62. Here *Memphian* means "Egyptian," but it connotes the great temples at Memphis on the Nile.
703. The reading of the second edition, *found out*, has the disadvantage of repeat-

Severing each kind, and scumm'd the Bullion dross:
A third as soon had form'd within the ground   705
A various mould, and from the boiling cells
By strange conveyance fill'd each hollow nook:
As in an Organ from one blast of wind
To many a row of Pipes the sound-board breathes.
Anon out of the earth a Fabric huge   710
Rose like an Exhalation, with the sound
Of Dulcet Symphonies and voices sweet,
Built like a Temple, where *Pilasters* round
Were set, and Doric pillars overlaid
With Golden Architrave; nor did there want   715
Cornice or Frieze, with bossy Sculptures grav'n;
The Roof was fretted Gold. Not *Babylon,*
Nor great *Alcairo* such magnificence
Equall'd in all thir glories, to inshrine
Belus or *Serapis* thir Gods, or seat   720
Thir Kings, when *Egypt* with *Assyria* strove
In wealth and luxury. Th' ascending pile
Stood fixt her stately highth, and straight the doors
Op'ning thir brazen folds discover wide
Within, her ample spaces, o'er the smooth   725
And level pavement: from the arched roof
Pendant by subtle Magic many a row
Of Starry Lamps and blazing Cressets fed
With *Naphtha* and *Asphaltus* yielded light
As from a sky. The hasty multitude   730
Admiring enter'd, and the work some praise
And some the Architect: his hand was known
In Heav'n by many a Tow'red structure high,
Where Scepter'd Angels held thir residence,

---

ing the thought in l. 690; that of the first, *founded,* has the disadvantage of anticipating the process of founding the metal that is described in ll. 705–709. The case for *found out* is stated by B. A. Wright in *TLS,* Aug. 9, 1934, p. 553.

709. *sound-board:* the surface that deflects the air from the bellows into an organ's pipes. Pandemonium, like Troy and Camelot, is built to music.

710–717. The passage has resemblances to Ovid's description of the palaces of the gods (*Met.* I, 171–72, and IV, 762–64) and especially to the technical architectural terms in his description of the palace built by Vulcan for Apollo. It compares more interestingly with the machinery of a masque at court on the Sunday after Twelfth Night in 1637: "the *earth open'd,* and there rose up a richly-adorned pallace, seeming all of goldsmith's work, with porticos vaulted, on pilasters of rich rustick work; their bases and capitels of gold. Above these ran an architrave freese, and coronis of the same — the freese enrich'd with jewels." (Quoted by Todd from *The Stage Condemn'd,* 1698.)

717. In *PR* III, 280, the pride of Babylon, "the wonder of all tongues," is again a symbol of Satan's power. In its glory it rivalled Egypt's Memphis, to which Milton here gives its modern name of Cairo (*Alcairo*).

720. *Belus* is a variant of Baal (cf. l. 421 above). *Serapis* (usually, though not here, accented on the second syllable) was a name given to Osiris as lord of the underworld and patron of the land's fertility.

728. *Cressets:* iron baskets for burning fragments of the bitumen, or *Asphalt,* from which the *Naphtha* was extracted.

And sat as Princes, whom the supreme King 735
Exalted to such power, and gave to rule,
Each in his Hierarchy, the Orders bright.
Nor was his name unheard or unador'd
In ancient *Greece;* and in *Ausonian* land
Men call'd him *Mulciber;* and how he fell 740
From Heav'n, they fabl'd, thrown by angry *Jove*
Sheer o'er the Crystal Battlements: from Morn
To Noon he fell, from Noon to dewy Eve,
A Summer's day; and with the setting Sun
Dropt from the Zenith like a falling Star, 745
On *Lemnos* th' *Ægæan* Isle: thus they relate,
Erring; for he with this rebellious rout
Fell long before; nor aught avail'd him now
To have built in Heav'n high Tow'rs; nor did he scape
By all his Engines, but was headlong sent 750
With his industrious crew to build in hell.
Meanwhile the winged Heralds by command
Of Sovran power, with awful Ceremony
And Trumpets' sound throughout the Host proclaim
A solemn Council forthwith to be held 755
At *Pandæmonium*, the high Capitol
Of Satan and his Peers: thir summons call'd
From every Band and squared Regiment
By place or choice the worthiest; they anon
With hundreds and with thousands trooping came 760
Attended: all access was throng'd, the Gates
And Porches wide, but chief the spacious Hall
(Though like a cover'd field, where Champions bold
Wont ride in arm'd, and at the Soldan's chair
Defi'd the best of *Paynim* chivalry 765
To mortal combat or career with Lance)
Thick swarm'd, both on the ground and in the air,
Brusht with the hiss of rustling wings. As Bees

739. Italy, the *Ausonian* land, is given its ancient Greek name.

740. *Mulciber:* the "founder of metal," more commonly called Vulcan in Latin, and in Greek Hephaestus. Homer's story (*Il.* I, 588–95) that Zeus tossed him out of heaven in drunken rage, and that he was all day long in falling onto the island of *Lemnos* in the *Aegean* Sea, was condemned as frivolous by Plato (*Rep.* II, 378d). Milton's attitude toward it resembles Sandys' (*Relation*, p. 23) in contempt for a story still told by the Lemnians with superstitious credulity. See the Introduction 54.

756. *Pandæmonium:* the name, from Greek πάν ("all") and δαίμων ("spirit")

or "deity"), and the conception seem indebted to Henry More's *Pandæmonio-then*, which signifies the dominion of the devils in this world, which is so densely inhabited by personified sins of all kinds that

What Poets phancies fain'd to be in Hell
Are truly here, A Vulture *Tytius* heart
Still gnaws, yet death doth never *Ty-tius* quell:
Sad Sisyphus a stone with toylsome smart
Doth roul up hill, but it transcends his art,
To get it to the top, . . .

(*Psychozoia* I, iii, 23, 1–6)

In spring time, when the Sun with *Taurus* rides,
Pour forth thir populous youth about the Hive   770
In clusters; they among fresh dews and flowers
Fly to and fro, or on the smoothed Plank,
The suburb of thir Straw-built Citadel,
New rubb'd with Balm, expatiate and confer
Thir State affairs. So thick the aery crowd   775
Swarm'd and were strait'n'd; till the Signal giv'n,
Behold a wonder! they but now who seem'd
In bigness to surpass Earth's Giant Sons
Now less than smallest Dwarfs, in narrow room
Throng numberless, like that Pigmean Race   780
Beyond the *Indian* Mount, or Faery Elves,
Whose midnight Revels, by a Forest side
Or Fountain some belated Peasant sees,
Or dreams he sees, while over-head the Moon
Sits Arbitress, and nearer to the Earth   785
Wheels her pale course; they on thir mirth and dance
Intent, with jocund Music charm his ear;
At once with joy and fear his heart rebounds.
Thus incorporeal Spirits to smallest forms
Reduc'd thir shapes immense, and were at large,   790
Though without number still amidst the Hall
Of that infernal Court. But far within
And in thir own dimensions like themselves
The great Seraphic Lords and Cherubim
In close recess and secret conclave sat   795
A thousand Demi-Gods on golden seats,
Frequent and full. After short silence then
And summons read, the great consult began.

The End of the First Book.

---

769. The Bull, *Taurus*, the second sign in the Zodiac, is entered by the sun in April.

768–775. The simile opens vistas on comparisons of throngs of people to bees by Homer (*Il.* II, 87–90) and Virgil (*Aen.* 1, 430–36) and on Milton's interpretation of Virgil's account of bees as possessing cities and laws (*Georg.* IV, 149–227) in the *First Defense* (C.Ed. VII, 84) in reply to Salmasius' serious assertion that the respect of bees for their "kings" was a divine example of absolute monarchy worthy of human imitation. It is worth noting also, as Miss R. W. Smith points out in her architectural comparison of *Pandæmonium* with St. Peter's in Rome — *MP*, XXIX (1931), 187–98 — that the bee was the emblem of the Barberini Pope Urban VIII, who dedicated the basilica in 1636, and that "his followers were often referred to as bees."

774. *expatiate:* to walk abroad (the Latin sense of the word originally).

780–781. Cf. l. 575, n., and the allusion to the Himalayas as "the *Indian* steep" in *Comus*, 139.

781–787. Comparison with *A Midsummer Night's Dream* II, i, is fair, but the note of perilous mystery is Miltonic, like the sound of "sands and shores and desert wildernesses" in *Comus*, 208–209. There is certainly a reminiscence of Virgil's picture of Aeneas in the Elysian Fields, seeing or thinking that he sees Dido, "like the fugitive moon among clouds" (*Aen.* VI, 450–55).

795. *close recess:* a secret meeting place. *Conclave* — literally, "inner chamber" — illustrates the use of that word and its equivalent, "cabinet," to mean secret governing councils.

797. *Frequent:* in throngs. The word has its basic Latin meaning.

30 JOHN MILTON

BOOK II

THE ARGUMENT

The Consultation begun, Satan *debates whether another Battle be to be hazarded for the recovery of Heaven: some advise it, others dissuade: A third proposal is preferr'd, mention'd before by* Satan, *to search the truth of that Prophecy or Tradition in Heaven concerning another world, and another kind of creature equal or not much inferior to themselves, about this time to be created: Thir doubt who shall be sent on this difficult search:* Satan *thir chief undertakes alone the voyage, is honor'd and applauded. The Council thus ended, the rest betake them several ways and to several employments, as thir inclinations lead them, to entertain the time till* Satan *return. He passes on his Journey to Hell Gates, finds them shut, and who sat there to guard them, by whom at length they are op'n'd, and discover to him the great Gulf between Hell and Heaven; with what difficulty he passes through, directed by* Chaos, *the Power of that place, to the sight of this new World which he sought.*

High on a Throne of Royal State, which far
Outshone the wealth of *Ormus* and of *Ind,*
Or where the gorgeous East with richest hand
Show'rs on her Kings *Barbaric* Pearl and Gold,
Satan exalted sat, by merit rais'd   5
To that bad eminence; and from despair
Thus high uplifted beyond hope, aspires
Beyond thus high, insatiate to pursue
Vain War with Heav'n, and by success untaught
His proud imaginations thus display'd.   10
   Powers and Dominions, Deities of Heav'n,
For since no deep within her gulf can hold
Immortal vigor, though opprest and fall'n,
I give not Heav'n for lost. From this descent
Celestial Virtues rising, will appear   15
More glorious and more dread than from no fall
And trust themselves to fear no second fate:
Mee though just right and the fixt Laws of Heav'n
Did first create your Leader, next, free choice,

1. The scene may have been intended to recall Spenser's more symbolic description of the throne of Lucifera, incarnate Pride:

High above all a cloth of state was spred,
And a rich throne, as bright as sunny day.
(*F.Q.* I, iv, 8, 1–2)

2. The strategic position of the island situation of *Ormus* at the mouth of the Persian gulf made it a rich trading city that figured conspicuously on the maps. Fulke Greville made it the scene of his tragedy of *Alaham,* and perhaps some of Milton's readers responded to the name

by recalling the cry of the usurping hero in the last scene:

Is this *Ormus?* Or is *Ormus* my hell,
Where only Furies, and not Men, doe dwell?

Cf. Satan's comparison with an eastern sultan as a type of tyranny in I, 348.

5. Cf. I, 98, n., and II, 21.

9. Cf. *success* in l. 123 below. The word meant "outcome" or "event" without implying either good or bad results.

11. For the titles in the infernal hierarchy and the background of the demonic council see the Introduction 21 and 24.

With what besides, in Counsel or in Fight,   20
Hath been achiev'd of merit, yet this loss
Thus far at least recover'd, hath much more
Establisht in a safe unenvied Throne
Yielded with full consent. The happier state
In Heav'n, which follows dignity, might draw   25
Envy from each inferior; but who here
Will envy whom the highest place exposes
Foremost to stand against the Thunderer's aim
Your bulwark, and condemns to greatest share
Of endless pain? where there is then no good   30
For which to strive, no strife can grow up there
From Faction; for none sure will claim in Hell
Precedence, none, whose portion is so small
Of present pain, that with ambitious mind
Will covet more. With this advantage then   35
To union, and firm Faith, and firm accord,
More than can be in Heav'n, we now return
To claim our just inheritance of old,
Surer to prosper than prosperity
Could have assur'd us; and by what best way,   40
Whether of open War or covert guile,
We now debate; who can advise, may speak.
    He ceas'd, and next him *Moloch*, Scepter'd King
Stood up, the strongest and the fiercest Spirit
That fought in Heav'n; now fiercer by despair: 45
His trust was with th' Eternal to be deem'd
Equal in strength, and rather than be less
Car'd not to be at all; with that care lost
Went all his fear: of God, or Hell, or worse
He reck'd not, and these words thereafter spake.   50
    My sentence is for open War: Of Wiles,
More unexpert, I boast not: them let those
Contrive who need, or when they need, not now.
For while they sit contriving, shall the rest,
Millions that stand in Arms, and longing wait   55
The Signal to ascend, sit ling'ring here

---

28. *Thunderer* recalls Ovid's repeated attribution of the thunderbolt to Jove as his emblem (*Met.* I, 154, 170, 197). Satan uses the symbol of omnipotence to suggest that God is a tyrant. Cf. Belial's reference to "his red right hand" (II, 174), a reminiscence of Horace's picture of Jove threatening to destroy Rome (*Odes* I, ii), and Moloch's proposal to counter the tyrant's lightning with black fire and infernal thunder (II, 66–67).

32. Milton had no intention of making Satan a tragic hero of the kind that (like Alaham's father in Greville's play) fails

to understand Bacon's warning that, "when factions are carried too high and too violently, it is a sign of weakness in princes" (*Essays* LI).

43. *Moloch*, the "furious king" of the battle in heaven (VI, 357) is *Scepter'd* as the kings often are in Homeric councils (e.g. *Il.* II, 86, and *Od.* II, 231).

51. *sentence* has its basic Latin meaning of "decision" or "judgment." Cf. l. 291 below.

52. *unexpert* keeps its basic Latin meaning of "inexperienced." Cf. *expert* in VI, 233.

Heav'n's fugitives, and for thir dwelling place
Accept this dark opprobrious Den of shame,
The Prison of his Tyranny who Reigns
By our delay? no, let us rather choose   60
Arm'd with Hell flames and fury all at once
O'er Heav'n's high Tow'rs to force resistless way,
Turning our Tortures into horrid Arms
Against the Torturer; when to meet the noise
Of his Almighty Engine he shall hear   65
Infernal Thunder, and for Lightning see
Black fire and horror shot with equal rage
Among his Angels; and his Throne itself
Mixt with *Tartarean* Sulphur, and strange fire,
His own invented Torments. But perhaps   70
The way seems difficult and steep to scale
With upright wing against a higher foe.
Let such bethink them, if the sleepy drench
Of that forgetful Lake benumb not still,
That in our proper motion we ascend   75
Up to our native seat: descent and fall
To us is adverse. Who but felt of late
When the fierce Foe hung on our brok'n Rear
Insulting, and pursu'd us through the Deep,
With what compulsion and laborious flight   80
We sunk thus low? Th' ascent is easy then;
Th' event is fear'd; should we again provoke
Our stronger, some worse way his wrath may find
To our destruction: if there be in Hell
Fear to be worse destroy'd: what can be worse   85
Than to dwell here, driv'n out from bliss, condemn'd
In his abhorred deep to utter woe;
Where pain of unextinguishable fire
Must exercise us without hope of end
The Vassals of his anger, when the Scourge   90
Inexorably, and the torturing hour
Calls us to Penance? More destroy'd than thus
We should be quite abolisht and expire.

65. *Engine* has the military significance that it has in IV, 17, and VI, 484.

69. *Tartarean* is derived from *Tartarus*, the name for the place of torment in the classical underworld.

74. The *forgetful Lake*, like the "oblivious pool" of I, 266, is the river Lethe, a *drench* (drink) of whose waters made the spirits of the dead forget their earthly life. Moloch's contempt for his companions' forgetfulness of their glory in heaven suggests the reference of the ghost in *Hamlet* (I, v, 32–33) to the "dulness" of "the fat weed/That rots itself in ease on Lethe wharf." Other echoes of the scene are perhaps heard in the following lines here.

89. *exercise* keeps its Latin meaning of "torment."

90. *Vassals* has its Latin meaning of "servant" or "slave," as it does in Spenser's description of men as "The vassals of God's *wrath*, and slaves of sin," in *The Teares of the Muses*, 126. But Bentley suggested that the word should be "vessels," and that the allusion is to "vessels of wrath, fitted to destruction" in Romans ix, 22.

What fear we then? what doubt we to incense
His utmost ire? which to the highth enrag'd,   95
Will either quite consume us, and reduce
To nothing this essential, happier far
Than miserable to have eternal being:
Or if our substance be indeed Divine,
And cannot cease to be, we are at worst   100
On this side nothing; and by proof we feel
Our power sufficient to disturb his Heav'n,
And with perpetual inroads to Alarm,
Though inaccessible, his fatal Throne:
Which if not Victory is yet Revenge.   105
   He ended frowning, and his look denounc'd
Desperate revenge, and Battle dangerous
To less than Gods. On th' other side up rose
Belial, in act more graceful and humane;
A fairer person lost not Heav'n; he seem'd   110
For dignity compos'd and high exploit:
But all was false and hollow; though his Tongue
Dropt Manna, and could make the worse appear
The better reason, to perplex and dash
Maturest Counsels: for his thoughts were low;   115
To vice industrious, but to Nobler deeds
Timorous and slothful: yet he pleas'd the ear,
And with persuasive accent thus began.
   I should be much for open War, O Peers,
As not behind in hate; if what was urg'd   120
Main reason to persuade immediate War,
Did not dissuade me most, and seem to cast
Ominous conjecture on the whole success:
When he who most excels in fact of Arms,
In what he counsels and in what excels   125
Mistrustful, grounds his courage on despair
And utter dissolution, as the scope
Of all his aim, after some dire revenge.
First, what Revenge? the Tow'rs of Heav'n are fill'd
With Armed watch, that render all access   130
Impregnable; oft on the bordering Deep
Encamp thir Legions, or with obscure wing
Scout far and wide into the Realm of night,
Scorning surprise. Or could we break our way

[handwritten marginal note: Belial is a ready lawyer]

97. *essential* — the adjective used as a noun — means "essence." Cf. I, 138.

104. Cf. the meanings of *fate* and *gods* in I, 116.

109. Cf. Belial's first appearance in I, 490, and his later ones in VI, 620-27, and *PR* II, 150-73. For his bearing Milton may have been indebted to the tradition that he "taketh the form of a beautifull angel, he speaketh faire" — in Reginald Scot's *Discoverie of Witchcraft* (1584), xv, 2 — but the characterization is Milton's own — as E. E. Stoll shows in "Belial as an Example" in *MLN*, XLVIII (1933), 419-27.

124. *fact of arms:* deed or feat of arms.

By force, and at our heels all Hell should rise   135
With blackest Insurrection, to confound
Heav'n's purest Light, yet our great Enemy
All incorruptible would on his Throne
Sit unpolluted, and th' Ethereal mould
Incapable of stain would soon expel   140
Her mischief, and purge off the baser fire
Victorious. Thus repuls'd, our final hope
Is flat despair: we must exasperate
Th' Almighty Victor to spend all his rage,
And that must end us, that must be our cure,   145
To be no more; sad cure; for who would lose,
Though full of pain, this intellectual being,
Those thoughts that wander through Eternity,
To perish rather, swallow'd up and lost
In the wide womb of uncreated night,   150
Devoid of sense and motion? and who knows,
Let this be good, whether our angry Foe
Can give it, or will ever? how he can
Is doubtful; that he never will is sure.
Will he, so wise, let loose at once his ire,   155
Belike through impotence, or unaware,
To give his Enemies thir wish, and end
Them in his anger, whom his anger saves
To punish endless? wherefore cease we then?
Say they who counsel War, we are decreed,   160
Reserv'd and destin'd to Eternal woe;
Whatever doing, what can we suffer more,
What can we suffer worse? is this then worst,
Thus sitting, thus consulting, thus in Arms?
What when we fled amain, pursu'd and strook   165
With Heav'n's afflicting Thunder, and besought
The Deep to shelter us? this Hell then seem'd
A refuge from those wounds: or when we lay
Chain'd on the burning Lake? that sure was worse.
What if the breath that kindl'd those grim fires   170
Awak'd should blow them into sevenfold rage

139–141. In part the passage rests on the conception of God as "a consuming fire" (Deut. v, 24) and of "his angels" as "a flaming fire" (Psalm civ, 4), and in part it rests on the distinction between *Ethereal* or celestial fire and the *baser fire* of earth, which Spenser allegorized by making Vesta a symbol of "the fire aetheriall,/Vulcan, of this, with us so usuall" (*F.Q.* VII, vii, 26, 6–7). Cf. *PL* I, 117, n., and XI, 48–53.

146–151. Editors quote Claudio's dread of death, when "This sensible warm motion" will "become/A kneaded clod" (*Measure for Measure* III, i, 120–21); but the thought parallels Seneca's in writing to his mother, Helvia (*On Consolation* xi, 7), about the soul as kindred to the gods and at home in every world and every age because its thought ranges through all heaven and through all past and future time. Cf. Plato's quotation of Pindar (in *Theaetetus*, 173E) on the mind's power to explore the universe independently of the body. Milton repeats the thought in *Areopagitica* (C.Ed. IV, p. 320), "minds that can wander beyond all limit and satiety."

And plunge us in the flames? or from above
Should intermitted vengeance arm again
His red right hand to plague us? what if all
Her stores were op'n'd, and this Firmament   175
Of Hell should spout her Cataracts of Fire,
Impendent horrors, threat'ning hideous fall
One day upon our heads; while we perhaps
Designing or exhorting glorious war,
Caught in a fiery Tempest shall be hurl'd   180
Each on his rock transfixt, the sport and prey
Of racking whirlwinds, or for ever sunk
Under yon boiling Ocean, wrapt in Chains;
There to converse with everlasting groans,
Unrespited, unpitied, unrepriev'd,   185
Ages of hopeless end; this would be worse.
War therefore, open or conceal'd, alike
My voice dissuades; for what can force or guile
With him, or who deceive his mind, whose eye
Views all things at one view? he from Heav'n's highth   190
All these our motions vain, sees and derides;
Not more Almighty to resist our might
Than wise to frustrate all our plots and wiles.
Shall we then live thus vile, the race of Heav'n
Thus trampl'd, thus expell'd to suffer here   195
Chains and these Torments? better these than worse
By my advice; since fate inevitable
Subdues us, and Omnipotent Decree,
The Victor's will. To suffer, as to do,
Our strength is equal, nor the Law unjust   200
That so ordains: this was at first resolv'd,
If we were wise, against so great a foe
Contending, and so doubtful what might fall.
I laugh, when those who at the Spear are bold
And vent'rous, if that fail them, shrink and fear   205
What yet they know must follow, to endure
Exile, or ignominy, or bonds, or pain,
The sentence of thir Conqueror: This is now
Our doom; which if we can sustain and bear,
Our Supreme Foe in time may much remit   210

---

174. Cf. l. 28 above, n.
174–184. Several classical parallels have been cited — none of them close. There is a real resemblance, however, to the description of the felling of the Titans Atlas and Typhon by the thunders of Zeus and their living entombment in Aeschylus' *Prometheus*, 353–68.
191. Belial anticipates Psalm ii, 4: "He that sitteth in the heavens shall laugh; the Lord shall have them in derision."
199. *To suffer, as to do* translates the word of Mucius Scaevola as he thrust his hand into the fire to give his Etruscan captors a casual example of what a Roman could suffer after he had been seized in a suicidal attempt to assassinate their king (Livy, ii, 12).
207. For the pronunciation of ignominy see I, 115, n.

His anger, and perhaps thus far remov'd
Not mind us not offending, satisfi'd
With what is punisht; whence these raging fires
Will slack'n, if his breath stir not thir flames.
Our purer essence then will overcome   215
Thir noxious vapor, or enur'd not feel,
Or chang'd at length, and to the place conform'd
In temper and in nature, will receive
Familiar the fierce heat, and void of pain;
This horror will grow mild, this darkness light,   220
Besides what hope the never-ending flight
Of future days may bring, what chance, what change
Worth waiting, since our present lot appears
For happy though but ill, for ill not worst,
If we procure not to ourselves more woe.   225
    Thus *Belial* with words cloth'd in reason's garb
Counsell'd ignoble ease, and peaceful sloth,
Not peace: and after him thus *Mammon* spake.
    Either to disinthrone the King of Heav'n
We war, if war be best, or to regain   230
Our own right lost: him to unthrone we then
May hope, when everlasting Fate shall yield
To fickle Chance, and *Chaos* judge the strife:
The former vain to hope argues as vain
The latter: for what place can be for us   235
Within Heav'n's bound, unless Heav'n's Lord supreme
We overpower? Suppose he should relent
And publish Grace to all, on promise made
Of new Subjection; with what eyes could we
Stand in his presence humble, and receive   240
Strict Laws impos'd, to celebrate his Throne
With warbl'd Hymns, and to his Godhead sing
Forc't Halleluiahs; while he Lordly sits
Our envied Sovran, and his Altar breathes
Ambrosial Odors and Ambrosial Flowers,   245

213–219. The thought is allied to that attributed to St. Augustine by Thomas Heywood in his *Hierarchie of the Blessed Angels* (1635) IV, p. 211:
> For in Saint *Austines* Comment you may finde,
> The subtile essence of the Angels (pure
> At first, that they more fully might endure
> The sence of Fire) was grossed in their Fall,
> Of courser temper, then th'Originall.

218. *temper* — loosely equivalent to "temperament" — was used physiologically to mean the balance of physical "humors" in the body, variations in

which caused various individual natures or characters. Cf. l. 276 below.
224. *for happy:* from the point of view of happiness.
228. Cf. *Mammon* in I, 678.
232. Cf. *Fate* in I, 116, n.
243. *Halleluiah* transliterates the Hebrew phrase, "Praise ye Jah," i.e. Jehovah. Bishop Sanderson said (*Sermons* I, p. 115) that the Psalms could all be summed up in the words *Hosannah* and *Halleluiah.*
245. In the *Iliad* (IV, 3–4) Hebe pours out ambrosia for the gods, but it is often mentioned as their food. *Ambrosial* naturally appeared in contexts like the "Celestial food, Divine, Ambrosial" of *PR* IV, 588–89.

Our servile offerings. This must be our task
In Heav'n, this our delight; how wearisome
Eternity so spent in worship paid
To whom we hate. Let us not then pursue
By force impossible, by leave obtain'd   250
Unacceptable, though in Heav'n, our state
Of splendid vassalage, but rather seek
Our own good from ourselves, and from our own
Live to ourselves, though in this vast recess,
Free, and to none accountable, preferring   255
Hard liberty before the easy yoke
Of servile Pomp. Our greatness will appear
Then most conspicuous, when great things of small,
Useful of hurtful, prosperous of adverse
We can create, and in what place soe'er   260
Thrive under evil, and work ease out of pain
Through labor and endurance. This deep world
Of darkness do we dread? How oft amidst
Thick clouds and dark doth Heav'n's all-ruling Sire
Choose to reside, his Glory unobscur'd,   265
And with the Majesty of darkness round
Covers his Throne; from whence deep thunders roar
Must'ring thir rage, and Heav'n resembles Hell?
As he our darkness, cannot we his Light
Imitate when we please? This Desert soil   270
Wants not her hidden lustre, Gems and Gold;
Nor want we skill or art, from whence to raise
Magnificence; and what can Heav'n show more?
Our torments also may in length of time
Become our Elements, these piercing Fires   275
As soft as now severe, our temper chang'd
Into their temper; which must needs remove
The sensible of pain. All things invite
To peaceful Counsels, and the settl'd State
Of order, how in safety best we may   280

249. *pursue:* try to obtain. Its object, *state*, is modified by the relative clauses "[what is] by force impossible" and "[what is, if] by leave obtain'd, unacceptable."

255–257. This Miltonic principle is restated in *SA*, 268-71. Here it seems to echo the closing words of the invective of the Consul Aemilius Lepidus against the tyrant Cornelius Sulla in 78 B.c: as it is found in Sallust's version of that *Oration to the Roman People.*

264. At the dedication of Solomon's temple the house was filled with a cloud . . . for the glory of the Lord filled the house of God. Then said Solomon, the Lord hath said that he would dwell in the thick darkness" (II Chron. v, 13-vi, 1). Cf. Psalm xviii, 11-13: "He made darkness his secret place; his pavilion round about him were dark waters and thick clouds of the skies. The Lord also thundered in the heavens."

275. Traditionally, the devils were assigned to the elements and might be classified, as they were by Burton in the *Anatomy* (I, ii, 1, 2; Everyman Ed. I, p. 190), into Fiery Spirits or Devils, Aerial Spirits or Devils, Water-devils, Terrestrial and Sub-Terrestrial devils. Cf. the "Daemons" of "fire, air, flood, or underground" in *Il Pen*, 93–94.

278. *sensible of pain* is rightly glossed by J. C. Maxwell (*RES*, V — n. s., 1954 — 268) as "that element in our pain which is apprehended by the senses," and he notes that Mammon betrays his character by his indifference to all except the physical pains of hell.

Compose our present evils, with regard
Of what we are and where, dismissing quite
All thoughts of War; ye have what I advise.
 He scarce had finisht, when such murmur fill'd
Th' Assembly, as when hollow Rocks retain   285
The sound of blust'ring winds, which all night long
Had rous'd the Sea, now with hoarse cadence lull
Sea-faring men o'erwatcht, whose Bark by chance
Or Pinnace anchors in a craggy Bay
After the Tempest: Such applause was heard   290
As *Mammon* ended, and his Sentence pleas'd,
Advising peace: for such another Field
They dreaded worse than Hell: so much the fear
Of Thunder and the Sword of *Michaël*
Wrought still within them; and no less desire   295
To found this nether Empire, which might rise
By policy, and long process of time,
In emulation opposite to Hev'an.
Which when *Beëlzebub* perceiv'd, than whom,
Satan except, none higher sat, with grave   300
Aspect he rose, and in his rising seem'd
A Pillar of State; deep on his Front engraven
Deliberation sat and public care;
And Princely counsel in his face yet shone,
Majestic though in ruin: sage he stood   305
With *Atlantean* shoulders fit to bear
The weight of mightiest Monarchies; his look
Drew audience and attention still as Night
Or Summer's Noon-tide air, while thus he spake.
 Thrones and Imperial Powers, off-spring of Heav'n,   310
Ethereal Virtues; or these Titles now
Must we renounce, and changing style be call'd
Princes of Hell? for so the popular vote
Inclines, here to continue, and build up here
A growing Empire; doubtless; while we dream,   315

284-290. There are several classical parallels — the closest that in the *Aeneid* (X, 96–99) where the gods in council assent to Juno's violent appeal like winds threatening storm to sailors.
291. Cf. Mammon, "the least erected spirit that fell/From Heav'n" — I, 679–80.
294. An anticipation of Michael's command of the heavenly host in Book VI.
297. *policy:* statesmanship.
299. Cf. Beelzebub's first appearance in I, 81.
302. *Front* keeps its Latin meaning of "forehead."
306. The myth of the Titan, Atlas, "whom the Gentiles feign to bear up

Heav'n" (*SA*, 150), similarly suggested a comparison to "pillars of state" to Spenser when he described England as supported by Lord Burleigh,
As the wide compasse of the firma-
 ment
On Atlas mighty shoulders is up-
 stayd.
(Sonnets Dedicatory to the *Faerie Queene*)
312. *style:* the formal title of a king or nobleman.
315. *doubtless,* standing between semi-colons as it does in the early editions, is a flash of sarcasm between Beelzebub's irony up to this point and his ensuing earnest argument.

And know not that the King of Heav'n hath doom'd
This place our dungeon, not our safe retreat
Beyond his Potent arm, to live exempt
From Heav'n's high jurisdiction, in new League
Banded against his Throne, but to remain   320
In strictest bondage, though thus far remov'd,
Under th' inevitable curb, reserv'd
His captive multitude: For he, be sure,
In highth or depth, still first and last will Reign
Sole King, and of his Kingdom lose no part   325
By our revolt, but over Hell extend
His Empire, and with Iron Sceptre rule
Us here, as with his Golden those in Heav'n.
What sit we then projecting peace and war?
War hath determin'd us, and foil'd with loss   330
Irreparable; terms of peace yet none
Voutsaf't or sought; for what peace will be giv'n
To us enslav'd, but custody severe,
And stripes, and arbitrary punishment
Inflicted? and what peace can we return,   335
But to our power hostility and hate,
Untam'd reluctance, and revenge though slow,
Yet ever plotting how the Conqueror least
May reap his conquest, and may least rejoice
In doing what we most in suffering feel?   340
Nor will occasion want, nor shall we need
With dangerous expedition to invade
Heav'n, whose high walls fear no assault or Siege,
Or ambush from the Deep. What if we find
Some easier enterprise? There is a place   345
(If ancient and prophetic fame in Heav'n
Err not) another World, the happy seat
Of some new Race call'd *Man*, about this time
To be created like to us, though less
In power and excellence, but favor'd more   350
Of him who rules above; so was his will
Pronounc'd among the Gods, and by an Oath,

The deopth of hm

324. The words attributed to God in the Apocalypse, "I am Alpha and Omega, the beginning and the end, the first and the last" (Rev. i, 2; xxi, 6; and xxii, 13), inspire Beelzebub's despair, as later (V, 165) they inspire the triumph of the angels.

327. The *Iron Sceptre* recalls God's promise to his Son, "Thou shalt break them with a rod of iron" (Psalm ii, 9). Iron was a traditional symbol of enmity and gold of friendship, a symbolism which recurs in Abdiel's warning to Satan (V, 886–88).

332. *Voutsaf't:* vouchsafed, granted or gave.

336. *to our power:* to the limit of our power.

346. Cf. Satan's reference to this *fame* in I, 651.

348. Milton makes use of Origen's doctrine (condemned by St. Thomas in the *Summa Theologica* I, 961, a.33) that God created the world after the revolt of the angels.

352. Milton combines biblical representations of God taking an oath by himself "because he could swear by no

That shook Heav'n's whole circumference, confirm'd.
Thither let us bend all our thoughts, to learn
What creatures there inhabit, of what mould,   355
Or substance, how endu'd, and what thir Power,
And where thir weakness, how attempted best,
By force or subtlety: Though Heav'n be shut,
And Heav'n's high Arbitrator sit secure
In his own strength, this place may lie expos'd   360
The utmost border of his Kingdom, left
To their defense who hold it: here perhaps
Some advantageous act may be achiev'd
By sudden onset, either with Hell fire
To waste his whole Creation, or possess   365
All as our own, and drive as we were driven,
The puny habitants, or if not drive,
Seduce them to our Party, that thir God
May prove thir foe, and with repenting hand
Abolish his own works. This would surpass   370
Common revenge, and interrupt his joy
In our Confusion, and our Joy upraise
In his disturbance; when his darling Sons
Hurl'd headlong to partake with us, shall curse
Thir frail Original, and faded bliss,   375
Faded so soon. Advise if this be worth
Attempting, or to sit in darkness here
Hatching vain Empires. Thus *Beëlzebub*
Pleaded his devilish Counsel, first devis'd
By *Satan*, and in part propos'd: for whence,   380
But from the Author of all ill could Spring
So deep a malice, to confound the race
Of mankind in one root, and Earth with Hell
To mingle and involve, done all to spite
The great Creator? But thir spite still serves   385

[handwritten margin note: Satan taught the idea first]

---

greater" (Heb. vi, 13; Gen. xxii, 16) with classical recollections of Zeus shaking Olympus as he makes a vow to Thetis (*Il.* I, 530) or making a promise to Cybele with an oath (*Aen.* IX, 106). Here and in III, 341; V, 60, 117; IX, 164; and X, 90, *Gods* refers to the angels, for — as Milton explains in *CD* I, v (C.Ed. XIV, 245) — "the name of God is not infrequently ascribed, by the will and concession of God the Father, even unto angels and men."

356. *endu'd:* gifted (with qualities of mind).

367. *puny* may have its primary meaning of "later born" — here, "later created." Some versions of the motivation of the revolt of the angels based it simply on their resentment of the honor that God

commanded them to pay to the newly created race of man. So, in an infernal council in *Psyche* (1648), Joseph Beaumont has Beelzebub ask rhetorically:

Was't not enough, against the right-
   eous Law
Of Primogeniture, to throw Us down
From that bright home, which all the
   world do's know
Was by confest inheritance our own:
But, to our shame, Man, that vile
   worm, must dwell
In our fair Orbs, and Heav'n with
   Vermin fili.
                    (Canto I, stanza 24)

375. *Original* seems not to mean "original state," as it does in IX, 150, but to refer to Adam as the original man. The first edition reads: *Originals.*

His glory to augment. The bold design
Pleas'd highly those infernal States, and joy
Sparkl'd in all thir eyes; with full assent
They vote: whereat his speech he thus renews.

  Well have ye judg'd, well ended long debate,   390
Synod of Gods, and like to what ye are,
Great things resolv'd, which from the lowest deep
Will once more lift us up, in spite of Fate,
Nearer our ancient Seat; perhaps in view
Of those bright confines, whence with neighboring Arms   395
And opportune excursion we may chance
Re-enter Heav'n; or else in some mild Zone
Dwell not unvisited of Heav'n's fair Light
Secure, and at the bright'ning Orient beam
Purge off this gloom; the soft delicious Air,   400
To heal the scar of these corrosive Fires
Shall breathe her balm. But first whom shall we send
In search of this new world, whom shall we find
Sufficient? who shall tempt with wand'ring feet
The dark unbottom'd infinite Abyss   405
And through the palpable obscure find out
His uncouth way, or spread his aery flight
Upborne with indefatigable wings
Over the vast abrupt, ere he arrive
The happy Isle; what strength, what art can then   410
Suffice, or what evasion bear him safe
Through the strict Senteries and Stations thick
Of Angels watching round? Here he had need
All circumspection, and wee now no less
Choice in our suffrage; for on whom we send,   415
The weight of all and our last hope relies.

  This said, he sat; and expectation held
His look suspense, awaiting who appear'd
To second, or oppose, or undertake
The perilous attempt; but all sat mute,   420

387. *States:* estates. The parliaments of England and France traditionally consisted of the three estates, lords, clergy, and commons. In *King John* (II, i, 395–96) the Bastard ends a speech to a council of war with the demand:
  How like you this wild counsel,
    mighty States;
  Smacks it not something of the
    policy?
394. Cf. *seat* in the sense of "established home" in l. 347 above.
404. *tempt* has its Latin sense "make trial of," or "make an attempt upon."
406. *palpable obscure* recalls the "darkness which may be felt" which God sent to plague the Egyptians. (Exod. x, 21)

407. *uncouth:* unknown. Cf. l. 827 below.
409. *abrupt:* an adjective used as a noun, like *uncouth*, has its Latin meaning of "a breach" or "rupture." It is the gap between hell and heaven.
412. The three syllables of *senteries* are metrically necessary, and the form was not unusual in the seventeenth century.
415. *suffrage:* vote to select the agent in whose choice no less circumspection is needed than he will need himself to succeed in his mission.
418. *suspense* is an adjective modifying "look" and meaning literally "suspended": i.e. "doubtful" or "in suspense."

Pondering the danger with deep thoughts; and each
In other's count'nance read his own dismay
Astonisht: none among the choice and prime
Of those Heav'n-warring Champions could be found
So hardy as to proffer or accept   425
Alone the dreadful voyage; till at last
Satan, whom now transcendent glory rais'd
Above his fellows, with Monarchal pride
Conscious of highest worth, unmov'd thus spake.
   O Progeny of Heav'n, Empyreal Thrones,   430
With reason hath deep silence and demur
Seiz'd us, though undismay'd: long is the way
And hard, that out of Hell leads up to light;
Our prison strong, this huge convex of Fire,
Outrageous to devour, immures us round   435
Ninefold, and gates of burning Adamant
Barr'd over us prohibit all egress.
These past, if any pass, the void profound
Of unessential Night receives him next
Wide gaping, and with utter loss of being   440
Threatens him, plung'd in that abortive gulf.
If thence he scape into whatever world,
Or unknown Region, what remains him less
Than unknown dangers and as hard escape?
But I should ill become this Throne, O Peers,   445
And this Imperial Sov'ranty, adorn'd
With splendor, arm'd with power, if aught propos'd
And judg'd of public moment, in the shape
Of difficulty or danger could deter
Mee from attempting. Wherefore do I assume   450
These Royalties, and not refuse to Reign,
Refusing to accept as great a share
Of hazard as of honor, due alike
To him who Reigns, and so much to him due
Of hazard more, as he above the rest   455
High honor'd sits? Go therefore mighty Powers,
Terror of Heav'n, though fall'n; intend at home,

423. *prime* has its Latin force of first
men, princes, or leaders.
432. The line harks back to the Sibyl's
warning to Aeneas (*Aen.* VI, 126–29)
that the descent to Avernus is easy, and
perhaps also to Virgil's warning to Dante
(*Inf.* XXXIX, 95), as they prepare to
ascend from the center of the earth toward
Purgatory, that the way is hard. Cf. III,
21.
434. *convex* is used as a noun to mean
the sphere surrounding Hell. Cf. III, 419.
436. *Ninefold* recalls the nine circles of
the Styx around the underworld, in the
Aeneid (VI, 439), as the *gates of burning*

Adamant recall Virgil's columns of solid
adamant supporting the gates of Tar-
tarus (*Aen.* VI, 552).
439–441. *unessential:* without actual
being, uncreated, as in l. 150 above. The
negative form of the word anticipates
abortive, which may mean "aborted"
(lifeless), or "monstrous" (and therefore
terrifying), or "abortion-causing" (frus-
trating, i.e. to an intruder).
448. *moment:* importance. The word
has the Latin force that it still has in the
adjective *momentous*.
457. *intend* has its Latin force of "at-
tend to," "consider."

While here shall be our home, what best may ease
The present misery, and render Hell
More tolerable; if there be cure or charm   460
To respite or deceive, or slack the pain
Of this ill Mansion: intermit no watch
Against a wakeful Foe, while I abroad
Through all the Coasts of dark destruction seek
Deliverance for us all: this enterprise   465
None shall partake with me. Thus saying rose
— The Monarch, and prevented all reply,
Prudent, lest from his resolution rais'd
Others among the chief might offer now
(Certain to be refus'd) what erst they fear'd;   470
And so refus'd might in opinion stand
His Rivals, winning cheap the high repute
Which he through hazard huge must earn. But they
Dreaded not more th' adventure than his voice
Forbidding; and at once with him they rose;   475
Thir rising all at once was as the sound
Of Thunder heard remote. Towards him they bend
With awful reverence prone; and as a God
Extol him equal to the highest in Heav'n:
Nor fail'd they to express how much they prais'd,   480
That for the general safety he despis'd
His own: for neither do the Spirits damn'd
Lose all thir virtue; lest bad men should boast
Thir specious deeds on earth, which glory excites,
Or close ambition varnisht o'er with zeal.   485
Thus they thir doubtful consultations dark
Ended rejoicing in their matchless Chief:
As when from mountain tops the dusky clouds
Ascending, while the North wind sleeps, o'erspread
Heav'n's cheerful face, the low'ring Element   490
Scowls o'er the dark'n'd lantskip Snow, or show'r;
If chance the radiant Sun with farewell sweet
Extend his ev'ning beam, the fields revive,
The birds thir notes renew, and bleating herds
Attest thir joy, that hill and valley rings.   495
O shame to men! Devil with Devil damn'd

---

461. *deceive* has its Latin force of
"elude" or "beguile."
462. *Mansion* is derived from the word
which is equivalent to *seat* as used in
l. 347 above.
468. *rais'd*: emboldened.
478. *awful*: full of awe or reverence.
490. *Element*: sky or atmosphere. Cf.
the "gay creatures of the Element" in
Comus, 299.
491. *lantskip*: landscape. A Dutch

word which had not yet crystallized into
its modern English form.
496–502. The lines state an orthodox
doctrine that is found in Antonio Rusca's
De Inferno et Statu Daemonum (Milan,
1621), pp. 505–507. He does not refer to
the great European wars of the time, as
Milton does, but he says explicitly that
the devils avoid civil strife and maintain
orders and ranks among themselves so as
to tempt mankind most efficiently.

Firm concord holds, men only disagree
Of Creatures rational, though under hope
Of heavenly Grace; and God proclaiming peace,
Yet live in hatred, enmity, and strife   500
Among themselves, and levy cruel wars,
Wasting the Earth, each other to destroy:
As if (which might induce us to accord)
Man had not hellish foes anow besides,
That day and night for his destruction wait.   505
  The *Stygian* Council thus dissolv'd; and forth
In order came the grand infernal Peers:
Midst came thir mighty Paramount, and seem'd
Alone th' Antagonist of Heav'n, nor less
Than Hell's dread Emperor with pomp Supreme,   510
And God-like imitated State; him round
A Globe of fiery Seraphim inclos'd
With bright imblazonry, and horrent Arms.
Then of thir Session ended they bid cry
With Trumpet's regal sound the great result: 515
Toward the four winds four speedy Cherubim
Put to thir mouths the sounding Alchymy
By Herald's voice explain'd: the hollow Abyss
Heard far and wide, and all the host of Hell
With deaf'ning shout, return'd them loud acclaim.   520
Thence more at ease thir minds and somewhat rais'd
By false presumptuous hope, the ranged powers
Disband, and wand'ring, each his several way
Pursues, as inclination or sad choice
Leads him perplext, where he may likeliest find   525
Truce to his restless thoughts, and entertain
The irksome hours, till his great Chief return.
Part on the Plain, or in the Air sublime
Upon the wing, or in swift Race contend,
As at th' *Olympian* Games or *Pythian* fields;   530
Part curb thir fiery Steeds, or shun the Goal

---

507. *Peers:* lords. Like the great nobles in a national parliament, the devils follow their *Paramount* (chief), carrying their weapons imblazoned (cf. l. 513) with their coats of arms.

512. *Globe:* a phalanx of soldiers. *O.E.D.* cites Giles Fletcher's lines:

    Out there flies
A globe of winged angels, swift as
    thought.
  (*Christ's Triumph after Death,* xiii)

Cf. *PR* IV, 581.

517. "Bell-metal," said Sir Francis Bacon in *Articles of Questions Touching Minerals,* speaking of various alloys, "they call *alchemy.*" Numerous examples of the word used to mean alloys

of various kinds are cited by E. H. Duncan in *Osiris* XI (1954), 403–404.

522. *powers:* armies.

530. The sports of the demons are an interlude like the funeral games at the tomb of Anchises in the *Aeneid* (V, 103–603) and those at the tomb of Patroclus in the *Iliad* (XXIII, 287–897), but they include contests in music and oratory, as the Olympian and Pythian games did in ancient Greece.

531. The picture is the famous one of Roman charioteers swinging their teams around the turning posts in the arena as Horace describes them in the opening stanza of his first book of *Odes.*

With rapid wheels, or fronted Brigads form.
As when to warn proud Cities war appears
Wag'd in the troubl'd Sky, and Armies rush
To Battle in the Clouds, before each Van   535
Prick forth the Aery Knights, and couch thir spears
Till thickest Legions close; with feats of Arms
From either end of Heav'n the welkin burns.
Others with vast *Typhœan* rage more fell
Rend up both Rocks and Hills, and ride the Air   540
In whirlwind; Hell scarce holds the wild uproar.
As when *Alcides* from *Oechalia* Crown'd
With conquest, felt th' envenom'd robe, and tore
Through pain up by the roots *Thessalian* Pines,
And *Lichas* from the top of *Oeta* threw   545
Into th' *Euboic* Sea. Others more mild,
Retreated in a silent valley, sing
With notes Angelical to many a Harp
Thir own Heroic deeds and hapless fall
By doom of Battle; and complain that Fate   550
Free Virtue should enthrall to Force or Chance.
Thir Song was partial, but the harmony
(What could it less when Spirits immortal sing?)
Suspended Hell, and took with ravishment
The thronging audience. In discourse more sweet   555
(For Eloquence the Soul, Song charms the Sense,)
Others apart sat on a Hill retir'd,
In thoughts more elevate, and reason'd high
Of Providence, Foreknowledge, Will, and Fate,
Fixt Fate, Free will, Foreknowledge absolute,   560
And found no end, in wand'ring mazes lost.
Of good and evil much they argu'd then,
Of happiness and final misery,
Passion and Apathy, and glory and shame,
Vain wisdom all, and false Philosophy: 565

534. Perhaps there is a reflection of the "chariots and troops of soldiers in their armour running about among the clouds" that Josephus mentions among the portents seen by the Jews before the fall of Jerusalem. (*Wars* VI, v. 3.)

539. Cf. the note on *Typhoean* in I, 197. The name Typhon or Typhoeus meant "whirlwind," and the Greek word has influenced the English word "typhoon," which is of Arabian or Persian origin. Cf. the demonic storm in *PR* IV, 409–19.

542. *Alcides:* Hercules. The passage reflects the story of his death after returning from a victory in *Oechalia* to the island of *Euboea,* off the Attic coast, where he slew his friend *Lichas* in blind rage, as it is treated by Sophocles in the *Trachiniae* and by Seneca in *The Mad Hercules.* Ovid's version (*Met.* IX, 134 ff.) makes Mt. *Oeta* in Thessaly, rather than Euboea, the scene of the action.

552. *Thir Song was partial* to their own view of their quarrel with God as a struggle of *Virtue* against tyrannic *Force.*

564. Cf. the condemnation of the Stoic ideal of *apathy* or absolute mastery of all the passions in *CD* II, x, and the contempt in *PR* IV, 300–301, for the Stoic's *Philosophic pride, by him call'd virtue.*

565. Like Henry More in his *Immortality of the Soul* (III, xvii, 8), Milton found it natural that there should be "students of philosophy" among the demons, who "are divided into sects and opinions, as we are here."

Yet with a pleasing sorcery could charm
Pain for a while or anguish, and excite
Fallacious hope, or arm th' obdured breast
With stubborn patience as with triple steel.
Another part in Squadrons and gross Bands,   570
On bold adventure to discover wide
That dismal World, if any Clime perhaps
Might yield them easier habitation, bend
Four ways thir flying March, along the Banks
Of four infernal Rivers that disgorge   575
Into the burning Lake thir baleful streams;
Abhorred *Styx* the flood of deadly hate,
Sad *Acheron* of sorrow, black and deep;
Cocytus, nam'd of lamentation loud
Heard on the rueful stream; fierce *Phlegeton*   580
Whose waves of torrent fire inflame with rage.
Far off from these a slow and silent stream,
Lethe the River of Oblivion rolls
Her wat'ry Labyrinth, whereof who drinks,
Forthwith his former state and being forgets,   585
Forgets both joy and grief, pleasure and pain.
Beyond this flood a frozen Continent
Lies dark and wild, beat with perpetual storms
Of Whirlwind and dire Hail, which on firm land
Thaws not, but gathers heap, and ruin seems   590
Of ancient pile; all else deep snow and ice,
A gulf profound as that *Serbonian* Bog
Betwixt *Damiata* and Mount *Casius* old,
Where Armies whole have sunk: the parching Air
Burns frore, and cold performs th' effect of Fire.   595
Thither by harpy-footed Furies hal'd,

577–581. The lines translate the meanings of the Greek names of the four rivers. Though they flow into the "burning lake" of Revelation xx, 10, they bound a hell that is like Virgil's (*Aen.* VI, 656–59) or Spenser's. In the *Faerie Queene* II, viii, 20, Spenser's reader found the allegorically "bitter wave of *Styx*"; in II, vi, 50, he met "flaming *Phlegethon*," and in I, v. 33, "the bitter waves of Acheron." Or — as Starnes and Talbert hint in *Dictionaries*, p. 335 — he might find all the etymology and allegory of the infernal rivers in a work like Nicholas Perottus' *Cornucopiae* (1489).

583. *Lethe:* the "forgetful Lake" of l. 74 above.

591. The accumulated hail seems like the ruin of a marble *pile* (i.e. building).

592–594. On Fuller's map of the route

of the Hebrews from Egypt to Palestine (*Pisgah-Sight*, p. 43) and on some maps of Ortelius the reader could find the *Serbonian Bog* between *Damiata* (modern Damietta, on the east mouth of the Nile) and Mt. Casius. In Diodorus Siculus' *Library* I, xxx, 5–7, and several contemporary works he could learn that whole armies had sunk in its quicksands.

595. Claudio's fear that in hell his soul might "bathe in fiery floods" or "reside/In thrilling region of thick-ribbed ice" (*Measure for Measure* III, i, 121–22) reflected a belief which is illustrated in Dante's *Inferno* XXXII, 29 ff., and categorically affirmed by St. Thomas in *Summa Theologica* (Suppl. Part III, 2, xcvii).

596. Virgil anticipated Milton in attributing the claws of the harpies to the Furies or Eumenides, goddesses who avenged crimes like Orestes' slaying of his mother (*Aen.* III, 217).

At certain revolutions all the damn'd
Are brought: and feel by turns the bitter change
Of fierce extremes, extremes by change more fierce,
From Beds of raging Fire to starve in Ice   600
Thir soft Ethereal warmth, and there to pine
Immovable, infixt, and frozen round,
Periods of time, thence hurried back to fire.
They ferry over this *Lethean* Sound
Both to and fro, thir sorrow to augment,   605
And wish and struggle, as they pass, to reach
The tempting stream, with one small drop to lose
In sweet forgetfulness all pain and woe,
All in one moment, and so near the brink;
But Fate withstands, and to oppose th' attempt   610
Medusa with *Gorgonian* terror guards
The Ford, and of itself the water flies
All taste of living wight, as once it fled
The lip of *Tantalus*. Thus roving on
In confus'd march forlorn, th' advent'rous Bands   615
With shudd'ring horror pale, and eyes aghast
View'd first thir lamentable lot, and found
No rest: through many a dark and dreary Vale
They pass'd, and many a Region dolorous,
O'er many a Frozen, many a Fiery Alp,   620
Rocks, Caves, Lakes, Fens, Bogs, Dens, and shades of death,
A Universe of death, which God by curse
Created evil, for evil only good,
Where all life dies, death lives, and Nature breeds,
Perverse, all monstrous, all prodigious things,   625
Abominable, inutterable, and worse
Than Fables yet have feign'd, or fear conceiv'd,
Gorgons and *Hydras*, and *Chimeras* dire.
 Meanwhile the Adversary of God and Man,
Satan with thoughts inflam'd of highest design,   630
Puts on swift wings, and towards the Gates of Hell

---

600. *starve* has its original, general
sense of "die" for any cause.
 611. One of the worst fears of Ulysses
during his visit to Hades in the *Odyssey*
(XI, 634) is that he may be shown the
head of the *Gorgon* that turns all living
men to stone by a mere look.
 614. In Tartarus (*Od.* XI, 582–92)
Ulysses saw *Tantalus* fixed in a pool of
water that forever fell below the reach
of his thirsty lips — "thirsty Tantalus
hung by the chin," as Spenser describes
him (*F.Q.* I, v, 35). Above him laden
fruit trees are just out of his reach.
 620. *Alp:* any high mountain.
 628. The many-headed *Hydras* and

the flame-spitting *Chimeras* are vague
monsters like the "unnumbered spectres"
of Virgil's hell, where
    horrid Hydra stands,
 And Briareus with all his hundred
    hands,
 Gorgons, Geryon with his triple
    frame;
 And vain Chimera vomits empty
    flame.
        (*Aen.* VI, 286–89. Dryden's
                    translation.)
 In *Prol* I Milton treats these monsters
allegorically, as representing the pangs
of guilty consciences.

Explores his solitary flight; sometimes
He scours the right hand coast, sometimes the left,
Now shaves with level wing the Deep, then soars
Up to the fiery concave tow'ring high.   635
As when far off at Sea a Fleet descri'd
Hangs in the Clouds, by *Equinoctial* Winds
Close sailing from *Bengala*, or the Isles
Of *Ternate* and *Tidore*, whence Merchants bring
Thir spicy Drugs: they on the Trading Flood   640
Through the wide *Ethiopian* to the Cape
Ply stemming nightly toward the Pole.   So seem'd
Far off the flying Fiend: at last appear
Hell bounds high reaching to the horrid Roof,
And thrice threefold the Gates; three folds were Brass,   645
Three Iron, three of Adamantine Rock,
Impenetrable, impal'd with circling fire,
Yet unconsum'd.   Before the Gates there sat
On either side a formidable shape;
The one seem'd Woman to the waist, and fair,   650
But ended foul in many a scaly fold
Voluminous and vast, a Serpent arm'd
With mortal sting: about her middle round
A cry of Hell Hounds never ceasing bark'd
With wide *Cerberean* mouths full loud, and rung   655
A hideous Peal: yet, when they list, would creep,
If aught disturb'd thir noise, into her womb,
And kennel there, yet there still bark'd and howl'd
Within unseen.   Far less abhorr'd than these
Vex'd *Scylla* bathing in the Sea that parts   660
Calabria from the hoarse *Trinacrian* shore:
Nor uglier follow the Night-Hag, when call'd

---

632. *Explores* has its Latin meaning of "test, put to the proof," as Elizabeth Holmes notes in *Essays and Studies*, X (1924), 106.

638–641. The simile reflects the interest in the new trade across the *Ethiopian* Sea (the Indian Ocean off east Africa) which English ships reached by sailing round the Cape of Good Hope *en route* to the Moluccas or Spice Islands, of which *Ternate* and *Tidore* were the best known. In Milton's time *Bengal* was part of the Mogul empire.

649–660. The lines become clear only in the light of 762–67 below. Sin owes her serpentine nether parts to conceptions like Spenser's Error:

Halfe like a serpent horribly displaide,
But th'other halfe did womans shape retaine.   (*F.Q.* I, i, 14)

But the dogs around Sin's waist, and especially their *Cerberean mouths* — a literally Ovidian phrase — plainly match Ovid's description of Scylla, the lovely nymph whose body Circe transformed into a mass of yelping hounds from the waist down (*Met.* XIV, 40–74). Finally — according to Ovid — she became the dangerous reef between Sicily (*Trinacria*) and the toe of the Italian boot (*Calabria*). But — as J. F. Gilliam recalls in *PQ*, XIX (1950), 346 — the allegorization of the myth to make Scylla a symbol of sin goes back at least as far as St. John Chrysostom. Cf. l. 665, n.

662. The *Night-Hag* is probably Hecate whose charms were used by Circe to bewitch Scylla. Popular superstition made her the witches' queen, as in *Macbeth* (III, v, and IV, i).

In secret, riding through the Air she comes
Lur'd with the smell of infant blood to dance
With *Lapland* Witches, while the laboring Moon   665
Eclipses at thir charms. The other shape,
If shape it might be call'd that shape had none
Distinguishable in member, joint, or limb,
Or substance might be call'd that shadow seem'd,
For each seem'd either; black it stood as Night,   670
Fierce as ten Furies, terrible as Hell,
And shook a dreadful Dart; what seem'd his head
The likeness of a Kingly Crown had on.
Satan was now at hand, and from his seat
The Monster moving onward came as fast,   675
With horrid strides; Hell trembled as he strode.
Th' undaunted Fiend what this might be admir'd,
Admir'd, not fear'd; God and his Son except,
Created thing naught valu'd he nor shunn'd;
And with disdainful look thus first began.   680
   Whence and what are thou, execrable shape,
That dar'st, though grim and terrible, advance
Thy miscreated Front athwart my way
To yonder Gates? through them I mean to pass,
That be assured, without leave askt of thee: 685
Retire, or taste thy folly, and learn by proof,
Hell-born, not to contend with Spirits of Heav'n.
   To whom the Goblin full of wrath repli'd:
Art thou that Traitor Angel, art thou hee,
Who first broke peace in Heav'n and Faith, till then   690
Unbrok'n, and in proud rebellious Arms
Drew after him the third part of Heav'n's Sons

---

665. In *Muscovia* (C.Ed. X, 361) Milton refers skeptically to one of the many current stories about Lapland as the home of witches. In her *Literary Relations of England and Scandinavia in the 17th Century* (Oxford, 1935) p. 328, Ethel Seaton suggests that Milton switched to a northern scene because the image of Scylla reminded him of Dithmar Blefken's account of the "Dogge-fish, which putting his head out of the Sea, barketh and receiveth the whelps sporting in the Sea again into his belly."

665. *laboring*: undergoing eclipse. In the *Georgics* (II, 478) Virgil speaks of the labors (*labores*) of the moon in this sense. Popular superstition held that witches — like Caliban's mother — "could control the moon, make ebbs and floods" (*Tempest* V, i, 270).

667. Everywhere in Renaissance literature the negativeness of death is stressed,

as it is in Bacon's Essay *Of Death* and Spenser's picture:

> Death with most grim and griesly
>   visage seen,
> Yet is he nought but parting of the
>   breath:
> Ne ought to see, but like a shade to
>   ween,
> Unbodied, unsoul'd, unheard, unseen."
>   (*F.Q.* VII, vii, 46)

673. Milton thought of St. John's vision of the king of terrors, when "a crown was given unto him, and he went forth conquering, and to conquer" (Rev. vi, 2). See Introduction, 3.

677. *admir'd* has its Latin force of "wonder" or "observe."

692. *The third part of Heaven's Sons* alludes to St. John's dragon, whose "tail drew the third part of the stars of heaven, and did cast them to earth" (Rev. xii, 3-4).

Conjur'd against the Highest, for which both Thou
And they outcast from God, are here condemn'd
To waste Eternal days in woe and pain?   695
And reck'n'st thou thyself with Spirits of Heav'n,
Hell-doom'd, and breath'st defiance here and scorn,
Where I reign King, and to enrage thee more,
Thy King and Lord?   Back to thy punishment,
False fugitive, and to thy speed add wings,   700
Lest with a whip of Scorpions I pursue
Thy ling'ring, or with one stroke of this Dart
Strange horror seize thee, and pangs unfelt before.
     So spake the grisly terror, and in shape,
So speaking and so threat'ning, grew tenfold   705
More dreadful and deform: on th' other side
Incens't with indignation *Satan* stood
Unterrifi'd, and like a Comet burn'd,
That fires the length of *Ophiucus* huge
In th' Artic Sky, and from his horrid hair   710
Shakes Pestilence and War.   Each at the Head
Levell'd his deadly aim; thir fatal hands
No second stroke intend, and such a frown
Each cast at th' other, as when two black Clouds
With Heav'n's Artillery fraught, come rattling on   715
Over the *Caspian*, then stand front to front
Hov'ring a space, till Winds the signal blow
To join thir dark Encounter in mid air:
So frown'd the mighty Combatants, that Hell
Grew darker at thir frown, so matcht they stood;   720
For never but once more was either like
To meet so great a foe: and now great deeds
Had been achiev'd, whereof all Hell had rung,
Had not the Snaky Sorceress that sat
Fast by Hell Gate, and kept the fatal Key,   725
Ris'n, and with hideous outcry rush'd between.

---

693. *Conjur'd:* bound together by an oath. The word keeps its Latin meaning literally.

708. So Aeneas shines in his armor like a *Comet* portending disaster as he bears down upon Turnus (*Aen.* X, 272-75). K. Svendsen — among several contemporary theories about comets cited in *M.&S.*, pp. 92 and 266 — quotes John Swan in *Speculum Mundi* for the belief that, "if a Comet be in fashion like unto a sword, it then signifieth warres and destruction of cities." Perhaps the simile in XII, 632-33, implies such a belief about the sword of the cherubim at the gate of Paradise.

709. *Ophiucus*, the "serpent-bearer," is one of the largest northern constellations, his name and situation both sug-

gesting Satan as a serpent and as ruling the northern heavens. Cf. V, 689.

714-718. So Orlando and the Tartar king Agricane encounter each other like *two black Clouds* in Boiardo's *Orlando Innamorato* I, xvi. Cf. *M.&S.*, p. 94.

mid air — as Svendsen notes (*M.&S.*, p. 94) — was the region where clouds, winds, rain, hail, snow, ice, thunder, and lightning were generated. It was also traditionally the realm of the demons, as it is in I, 516, and as it plainly is again when Satan meets his *Potentates in Council* in *the middle Region of thick Air* in *PR* II, 117-118, and in IV, 409-419, has them bring a violent storm upon Christ.

The *Caspian* Sea was proverbial for storms as early as the reference to it as such by Horace in *Odes* II, ix, 2.

O Father, what intends thy hand, she cri'd,
Against thy only Son? What fury O Son,
Possesses thee to bend that mortal Dart
Against thy Father's head? and know'st for whom;   730
For him who sits above and laughs the while
At thee ordain'd his drudge, to execute
Whate'er his wrath, which he calls Justice, bids,
His wrath which one day will destroy ye both.
   She spake, and at her words the hellish Pest   735
Forbore, then these to her *Satan* return'd:
   So strange thy outcry, and thy words so strange
Thou interposest, that my sudden hand
Prevented spares to tell thee yet by deeds
What it intends; till first I know of thee,   740
What thing thou art, thus double-form'd, and why
In this infernal Vale first met thou call'st
Me Father, and that Phantasm call'st my Son?
I know thee not, nor ever saw till now
Sight more detestable than him and thee.   745
   T' whom thus the Portress of Hell Gate repli'd:
Hast thou forgot me then, and do I seem
Now in thine eye so foul, once deem'd so fair
In Heav'n, when at th' Assembly, and in sight
Of all the Seraphim with thee combin'd   750
In bold conspiracy against Heav'n's King,
All on a sudden miserable pain
Surpris'd thee, dim thine eyes, and dizzy swum
In darkness, while thy head flames thick and fast
Threw forth, till on the left side op'ning wide,   755
Likest to thee in shape and count'nance bright,
Then shining heav'nly fair, a Goddess arm'd
Out of thy head I sprung: amazement seiz'd
All th' Host of Heav'n; back they recoil'd afraid
At first, and call'd me *Sin*, and for a Sign   760
Portentous held me; but familiar grown,
I pleas'd, and with attractive graces won
The most averse, thee chiefly, who full oft
Thyself in me thy perfect image viewing
Becam'st enamor'd, and such joy thou took'st   765
With me in secret, that my womb conceiv'd
A growing burden. Meanwhile War arose,
And fields were fought in Heav'n: wherein remain'd

---

752. The myth of Athene's (Mi-
nerva's) birth from the head of Zeus in
Hesiod's *Theogony* (920–29) is fused with
an ancient allegory stemming from St.
James's words (i, 15): "When lust hath
conceived, it bringeth forth sin: and sin,
when it is finished, bringeth forth death."
John Gower's personification of Sin as
the incestuous mother of Death in the
Mirrour de l'Omme (205–37) and An-
dreini's use of the same allegory in the
Adamo caduto have both been cited as
Milton's "source."

(For what could else) to our Almighty Foe
Clear Victory, to our part loss and rout   770
Through all the Empyrean: down they fell
Driv'n headlong from the Pitch of Heaven, down
Into this Deep, and in the general fall
I also; at which time this powerful Key
Into my hand was giv'n, with charge to keep   775
These Gates for ever shut, which none can pass
Without my op'ning. Pensive here I sat
Alone, but long I sat not, till my womb
Pregnant by thee, and now excessive grown
Prodigious motion felt and rueful throes.   780
At last this odious offspring whom thou seest
Thine own begotten, breaking violent way
Tore through my entrails, that with fear and pain
Distorted, all my nether shape thus grew
Transform'd: but he my inbred enemy   785
Forth issu'd, brandishing his fatal Dart
Made to destroy: I fled, and cri'd out *Death;*
Hell trembl'd at the hideous Name, and sigh'd
From all her Caves, and back resounded *Death.*
I fled, but he pursu'd (though more, it seems,   790
Inflam'd with lust than rage) and swifter far,
Mee overtook his mother all dismay'd,
And in embraces forcible and foul
Ingend'ring with me, of that rape begot
These yelling Monsters that with ceaseless cry   795
Surround me, as thou saw'st, hourly conceiv'd
And hourly born, with sorrow infinite
To me, for when they list into the womb
That bred them they return, and howl and gnaw
My Bowels, thir repast; then bursting forth   800
Afresh with conscious terrors vex me round,
That rest or intermission none I find.
Before mine eyes in opposition sits
Grim *Death* my Son and foe, who sets them on,
And me his Parent would full soon devour   805
For want of other prey, but that he knows
His end with mine involv'd; and knows that I
Should prove a bitter Morsel, and his bane,
Whenever that shall be; so Fate pronounc'd.
But thou O Father, I forewarn thee, shun   810
His deadly arrow; neither vainly hope

---

798. Both the allegory and the details
resemble Spenser's Error:
    Of her there bred
A thousand yong ones, which she
    dayly fed,
Sucking upon her poisnous dugs, . . .

Soone as the uncouth light upon them
  shone,
Into her mouth they crept, and sud-
  dain all were gone.
    (*F.Q.* I, i, 15, 4–9. Cf. ll. 649–60
        above.)

To be invulnerable in those bright Arms,
Though temper'd heav'nly, for that mortal dint,
Save he who reigns above, none can resist.
  She finish'd, and the subtle Fiend his lore   815
Soon learn'd, now milder, and thus answer'd smooth.
Dear Daughter, since thou claim'st me for thy Sire,
And my fair Son here shows't me, the dear pledge
Of dalliance had with thee in Heav'n, and joys
Then sweet, now sad to mention, through dire change   820
Befall'n us unforeseen, unthought of, know
I come no enemy, but to set free
From out this dark and dismal house of pain,
Both him and thee, and all the heav'nly Host
Of Spirits that in our just pretenses arm'd   825
Fell with us from on high: from them I go
This uncouth errand sole, and one for all
Myself expose, with lonely steps to tread
Th' unfounded deep, and through the void immense
To search with wand'ring quest a place foretold   830
Should be, and, by concurring signs, ere now
Created vast and round, a place of bliss
In the Purlieus of Heav'n, and therein plac't
A race of upstart Creatures, to supply
Perhaps our vacant room, though more remov'd,   835
Lest Heav'n surcharg'd with potent multitude
Might hap to move new broils: Be this or aught
Than this more secret now design'd, I haste
To know, and this once known, shall soon return,
And bring ye to the place where Thou and Death   840
Shall dwell at ease, and up and down unseen
Wing silently the buxom Air, imbalm'd
With odors; there ye shall be fed and fill'd
Immeasurably, all things shall be your prey.
  He ceas'd, for both seem'd highly pleas'd, and Death 845
Grinn'd horrible a ghastly smile, to hear
His famine should be fill'd, and blest his maw
Destin'd to that good hour: no less rejoic'd
His mother bad, and thus bespake her Sire.
  The key of this infernal Pit by due,   850
And by command of Heav'n's all-powerful King
I keep, by him forbidden to unlock
These Adamantine Gates; against all force
Death ready stands to interpose his dart,

---

818. *pledge:* a child as a pledge of love.
823. *House* is used for Hell as it is in
Job (xxx, 23): ". . . thou wilt bring me
to death, to the house appointed for all
living."
825. *pretenses:* pretensions, legal claims.

840–844. Satan's promise is fulfilled in
X, 397–409.
842. *buxom:* unresisting. Cf. V, 270.
847. *famine:* ravenous hunger. Cf. X,
991.

Fearless to be o'ermatcht by living might.   855
But what owe I to his commands above
Who hates me, and hath hither thrust me down
Into this gloom of *Tartarus* profound,
To sit in hateful Office here confin'd,
Inhabitant of Heav'n, and heav'nly-born,   860
Here in perpetual agony and pain,
With terrors and with clamors compasst round
Of mine own brood, that on my bowels feed:
Thou art my Father, thou my Author, thou
My being gav'st me; whom should I obey   865
But thee, whom follow? thou wilt bring me soon
To that new world of light and bliss, among
The Gods who live at ease, where I shall Reign
At thy right hand voluptuous, as beseems
Thy daughter and thy darling, without end.   870
   Thus saying, from her side the fatal Key,
Sad instrument of all our woe, she took;
And towards the Gate rolling her bestial train,
Forthwith the huge Portcullis high up drew,
Which but herself not all the *Stygian* powers   875
Could once have mov'd; then in the key-hole turns
Th' intricate wards, and every Bolt and Bar
Of massy Iron or solid Rock with ease
Unfast'ns: on a sudden op'n fly
With impetuous recoil and jarring sound   880
Th' infernal doors, and on thir hinges grate
Harsh Thunder, that the lowest bottom shook
Of *Erebus*. She op'n'd, but to shut
Excell'd her power; the Gates wide op'n stood,
That with extended wings a Banner'd Host   885
Under spread Ensigns marching might pass through
With Horse and Chariots rankt in loose array;
So wide they stood, and like a Furnace mouth
Cast forth redounding smoke and ruddy flame.

868. In Homer (*Il.* VI, 138; *Od.* IV, 805, etc.) the *Gods* seem always to *live at ease.*

869. Sin imagines herself enthroned with her father Satan as the Son is seated at his Father's right hand in III, 63, and B. Rajan is undoubtedly right (*Reader*, p. 50) in seeing Satan, Sin, and Death as "a kind of infernal Trinity in contrast with its heavenly counterpart. In *Explicator* XVII (1959), 41, Arlene Anderson suggests that, since Sin is a product of the mind of Satan (cf. l. 858 above), as St. Thomas says that the Son "is the procession of the Word of God" (*Summa Theol.* I, xxvii, 3), and since the Son "proceeds by way of the intellect as Word, and the Holy Ghost by way of the will as love," so that "in this way it is manifest that the Holy Ghost proceeds from the Son," the entire allegory of Satan's paternity of Sin and Death is a perfect parody of orthodox theology. See the Introduction 11.

883. In Hesiod's account of the generation of the oldest Gods (*Theog.*, 123), in a line which Milton quotes in his first Prolusion, *Erebus* is named as the first child of Chaos, while Night is the second. All three are personified, and in Hesiod both Erebus and Chaos mean a dark, vast, primeval envelope of space and matter and are oftenest used in a vaguely local and metaphysical sense.

Before thir eyes in sudden view appear 890
The secrets of the hoary deep, a dark
Illimitable Ocean without bound,
Without dimension, where length, breadth, and highth,
And time and place are lost; where eldest *Night*
And *Chaos*, Ancestors of Nature, hold 895
Eternal Anarchy, amidst the noise
Of endless wars, and by confusion stand.
For hot, cold, moist, and dry, four Champions fierce
Strive here for Maistry, and to Battle bring
Thir embryon Atoms; they around the flag 900
Of each his Faction, in thir several Clans,
Light-arm'd or heavy, sharp, smooth, swift or slow,
Swarm populous, unnumber'd as the Sands
Of *Barca* or *Cyrene's* torrid soil,
Levied to side with warring Winds, and poise 905
Thir lighter wings. To whom these most adhere,
Hee rules a moment; *Chaos* Umpire sits,
And by decision more imbroils the fray
By which he Reigns: next him high Arbiter
Chance governs all. Into this wild Abyss, 910
The Womb of nature and perhaps her Grave,
Of neither Sea, nor Shore, nor Air, nor Fire,
But all these in thir pregnant causes mixt
Confus'dly, and which thus must ever fight,
Unless th' Almighty Maker them ordain 915
His dark materials to create more Worlds,
Into this wild Abyss the wary fiend
Stood on the brink of Hell and look'd a while,
Pondering his Voyage: for no narrow frith

891. Cf. *Abyss* in I, 21, n., and *deep* in I, 152.

895–903. The conception of *Chaos* stems both from Hesiod's mythological account and Ovid's rationalized treatment of the primeval chaotic mass of "warring seeds of things" before the world began (*Met.* I, 5–20). The conception influenced Renaissance thought so deeply that the orthodox Du Bartas imagined Chaos as corresponding to the formless "void" of Genesis i, 2, and described its "brawling Elements" as lying

> jumbled all together,
> Where hot and cold were jarring each with either;
> The blunt with sharp, the dank against the drie,
> The hard with soft . . . .

(Sylvester's translation of Du Bartas' *Divine Weeks* — London, 1608 — p. 8)
The war of the elements and its resolution by love went back to Empedocles but had been Christianized in the eclectic tradition that gave Spenser his view of it as ended when

> their Almightie Maker . . .
> bound them with inviolable bands;
> Else would the waters overflow the lands,
> And fire devoure the ayre, and hell them quight.
>   (*F.Q.* IV, x, 35)

See the Introduction 19.

904. *Barca* is the desert between Egypt and Tunis. *Cyrene* was a city near the site of modern Tripoli.

911. The line is a translation of Lucretius' *De rerum natura* (V, 259), but his materialistic prophecy of the world's destruction is felt here as harmonious with the Christian doctrine that (in Du Bartas' words) "This *world* to Chaos shall again *return*." (*Divine Weeks, The Schisme*, p. 111)

919. *no narrow frith* (i.e. firth): no mere narrow arm of the sea.

He had to cross. Nor was his ear less peal'd   920
With noises loud and ruinous (to compare
Great things with small) than when *Bellona* storms,
With all her battering Engines bent to raze
Some Capital City; or less than if this frame
Of Heav'n were falling, and these Elements   925
In mutiny had from her Axle torn
The steadfast Earth. At last his Sail-broad Vans
He spreads for flight, and in the surging smoke
Uplifted spurns the ground, thence many a League
As in a cloudy Chair ascending rides   930
Audacious, but that seat soon failing, meets
A vast vacuity: all unawares
Flutt'ring his pennons vain plumb down he drops
Ten thousand fadom deep, and to this hour
Down had been falling, had not by ill chance   935
The strong rebuff of some tumultuous cloud
Instinct with Fire and Nitre hurried him
As many miles aloft: that fury stay'd,
Quencht in a Boggy *Syrtis*, neither Sea,
Nor good dry Land, nigh founder'd on he fares,   940
Treading the crude consistence, half on foot,
Half flying; behoves him now both Oar and Sail.
As when a Gryfon through the Wilderness
With winged course o'er Hill or moory Dale,
Pursues the *Arimaspian*, who by stealth   945
Had from his wakeful custody purloin'd
The guarded Gold: So eagerly the fiend
O'er bog or steep, through strait, rough, dense, or rare,
With head, hands, wings, or feet pursues his way,
And swims or sinks, or wades, or creeps, or flies: 950
At length a universal hubbub wild
Of stunning sounds and voices all confus'd

920. *peal'd:* struck or deafened by noise. Cf. III, 329, and *SA*, 235.
922. *Bellona:* the Roman goddess of war.
934. *fadom* was a frequent 17th century spelling and pronunciation of *fathom*.
936-938. Contemporary science explained thunder clouds as occurring when — in the words of J. A. Comenius' *Synopsis of Physics* — the earth's "*sulphury exhalations are mixed with nitrous*, (the first of a hot nature, the second most cold) they endure one another so long, as till the sulphur takes fire. But as soon as that is done, presently there follows the same effect as in gun-powder, (whose composition is the same of Sulphur and Nitre) a fight, a rupture, a noise, a violent casting forth of the matter." The entire passage from the

English translation (1651) of Comenius' *Physicae ad Lumen Divinum reformatae Synopsis* (Amsterdam, 1643) is quoted by E. H. Duncan in *PQ*, XXX (1951), 442-43. *Instinct:* Cf. VI, 752.
939. The classical description of the two vast tidal marshes called the *Syrtis* is in Pliny, V, iv.
945. The popular story of the gold which the *Arimaspians*, "a one-eyed people" living in the north of Europe, "steal from the griffons," goes back to Herodotus (III, 116).
948. Cf. Sir William Alexander's abuse of this device in *Jonathan* (1637), l. 556, in a duel scene between Jonathan and Nahas: they "Urg'd, shunn'd, forc'd, fayn'd, bow'd, rais'd, hand, leg, left, right, . . ."

Borne through the hollow dark assaults his ear
With loudest vehemence: thither he plies,
Undaunted to meet there whatever power   955
Or Spirit of the nethermost Abyss
Might in that noise reside, of whom to ask
Which way the nearest coast of darkness lies
Bordering on light; when straight behold the Throne
Of *Chaos*, and his dark Pavilion spread   960
Wide on the wasteful Deep; with him Enthron'd
Sat Sable-vested *Night*, eldest of things,
The Consort of his Reign; and by them stood
Orcus and *Ades*, and the dreaded name
Of *Demogorgon; Rumor* next and *Chance*,   965
And *Tumult* and *Confusion* all imbroil'd,
And *Discord* with a thousand various mouths.

   T' whom *Satan* turning boldly, thus. Ye Powers
And Spirits of this nethermost Abyss,
Chaos and *ancient Night*, I come no Spy,   970
With purpose to explore or to disturb
The secrets of your Realm, but by constraint
Wand'ring this darksome Desert, as my way
Lies through your spacious Empire up to light,
Alone, and without guide, half lost, I seek   975
What readiest path leads where your gloomy bounds
Confine with Heav'n; or if some other place
From your Dominion won, th' Ethereal King
Possesses lately, thither to arrive
I travel this profound, direct my course;   980
Directed, no mean recompence it brings
To your behoof, if I that Region lost,
All usurpation thence expell'd, reduce
To her original darkness and your sway
(Which is my present journey) and once more   985
Erect the Standard there of *ancient Night;*
Yours be th' advantage all, mine the revenge.

959–967. The Pavilion of *Chaos* recalls
Spenser's description of the home of the
Fates,
   Farre under ground from tract of
      living went,
   Downe in the bottome of the deepe
      Abysse,
   Where *Demogorgon*, in dull dark-
      nesse pent,
   Farre from the view of gods and
      heavens blis,
   The hideous *Chaos* keepes, . . .
            (*F.Q.* IV, ii, 47)
It more distinctly recalls Boccaccio's ac-
count of the mysterious elder deity *Demo-
gorgon* and its vivid illustrations in the
many editions of the *Genealogy of the Gods*
that represent him with his offspring
around him — figures like *Rumor* and
Discord, *Orcus* (Hell) and *Ades* (Hades).
Demogorgon's name is said to be a cor-
ruption of Plato's Demiourgos in the
Timaeus and to figure in literature for
the first time in Lucan's *Pharsalia* VI,
744, where it is the kind of dreaded name
that Spenser made it when he wrote that
at it "*Cocytus* quakes, and *Styx* is put to
flight" (*F.Q.* I, 1, 37).   Cf. Milton's al-
lusion to him as the "ancestor of all the
gods" in *Prolusion* I.
   977. *Confine with:* border upon.

Thus *Satan;* and him thus the Anarch old
With falt'ring speech and visage incompos'd
Answer'd. I know thee, stranger, who thou art,　990
That mighty leading Angel, who of late
Made head against Heav'n's King, though overthrown.
I saw and heard, for such a numerous Host
Fled not in silence through the frighted deep
With ruin upon ruin, rout on rout,　995
Confusion worse confounded; and Heav'n Gates
Pour'd out by millions her victorious Bands
Pursuing. I upon my Frontiers here
Keep residence; if all I can will serve,
That little which is left so to defend,　1000
Encroacht on still through our intestine broils
Weak'ning the Sceptre of old *Night:* first Hell
Your dungeon stretching far and wide beneath;
Now lately Heaven and Earth, another World
Hung o'er my Realm, link'd in a golden Chain　1005
To that side Heav'n from whence your Legions fell:
If that way be your walk, you have not far;
So much the nearer danger; go and speed;
Havoc and spoil and ruin are my gain.

He ceas'd; and *Satan* stay'd not to reply,　1010
But glad that now his Sea should find a shore,
With fresh alacrity and force renew'd
Springs upward like a Pyramid of fire
Into the wild expanse, and through the shock
Of fighting Elements, on all sides round　1015
Environ'd wins his way; harder beset
And more endanger'd, than when *Argo* pass'd
Through *Bosporus* betwixt the justling Rocks:
Or when *Ulysses* on the Larboard shunn'd
Charybdis, and by th' other whirlpool steer'd.　1020
So he with difficulty and labor hard
Mov'd on, with difficulty and labor hee;
But hee once past, soon after when man fell,
Strange alteration! Sin and Death amain
Following his track, such was the will of Heav'n,　1025

988. The *Anarch: Chaos*, personified
as ruler of his lawless realm. Cf. ll. 896
and 907-10 above.
989. *incompos'd:* discomposed.
1005. For Milton's use of the Homeric
story of the golden chain with which Zeus
boasted that he could draw earth and all
its seas up to heaven (*Il.* VIII, 23-24)
see l. 1051 below, n.
1008. *danger* keeps its obsolete sense
of "damage, mischief, or harm." B. A.
Wright compares "Danger will wink on
Opportunity" in *Comus*, 401.

1017. The *Argo* was the ship of Jason
and his crew, the Argonauts, when they
escaped death between the floating is-
lands in the *Bosporus* or Straits of Con-
stantinople, as Apollonius of Rhodes told
the tale in his *Argonautica* II, 552-611.
1020. *Charybdis* is the whirlpool on
the Sicilian side of the Straits of Messina,
to Ulysses' *larboard* as he sailed westward
in Homer's account of his escape from
Charybdis and the still more frightful
Scylla (*Od.* XII, 73-100, 234-59).

Pav'd after him a broad and beat'n way
Over the dark Abyss, whose boiling Gulf
Tamely endur'd a Bridge of wondrous length
From Hell continu'd reaching th' utmost Orb
Of this frail World; by which the Spirits perverse 1030
With easy intercourse pass to and fro
To tempt or punish mortals, except whom
God and good Angels guard by special grace.
But now at last the sacred influence
Of light appears, and from the walls of Heav'n 1035
Shoots far into the bosom of dim Night
A glimmering dawn; here Nature first begins
Her fardest verge, and *Chaos* to retire
As from her outmost works a brok'n foe
With tumult less and with less hostile din, 1040
That *Satan* with less toil, and now with ease
Wafts on the calmer wave by dubious light
And like a weather-beaten Vessel holds
Gladly the Port, though Shrouds and Tackle torn;
Or in the emptier waste, resembling Air, 1045
Weighs his spread wings, at leisure to behold
Far off th' Empyreal Heav'n, extended wide
In circuit, undetermin'd square or round,
With Opal Tow'rs and Battlements adorn'd
Of living Sapphire, once his native Seat; 1050
And fast by hanging in a golden Chain
This pendant world, in bigness as a Star
Of smallest Magnitude close by the Moon.
Thither full fraught with mischievous revenge,
Accurst, and in a cursed hour he hies. 1055

The End of the Second Book.

1037. *Nature*, in Milton's use here, means the created world as distinct from the surrounding Chaos, where not even the first of God's creations, light, is known.
1050. So St. John speaks of one of the foundations of heaven's wall as a sapphire (Rev. xxi, 19).
1051. Cf. Milton's use of the golden chain of Zeus in *Prolusion* II as a symbol of divine design penetrating the entire universe. The conception runs through literature from Plato's *Theaetetus* (153c) to Chaucer's *Knight's Tale* (I-A-2987–93).
The Firste Moevere of the cause above,

When he first made the faire cheyne
of love,
Greet was th'effect, and heigh was
his entente.
Wel wiste he why, and what thereof
he mente;
For with that faire cheyne of love he
bond
The fyr, the eyr, the water, and the
lond
In certeyn boundes, that they may
nat flee.
1052. *The pendant world* is not the earth but the entire spherical universe (see III, 419), which Satan has yet to penetrate.

BOOK III

THE ARGUMENT

God *sitting on his Throne sees* Satan *flying towards this world, then newly created; shows him to the Son who sat at his right hand; foretells the success of* Satan *in perverting mankind; clears his own Justice and Wisdom from all imputation, having created Man free and able enough to have withstood his Tempter; yet declares his purpose of grace towards him, in regard he fell not of his own malice, as did* Satan, *but by him seduc't. The Son of God renders praises to his Father for the manifestation of his gracious purpose towards Man; but God again declares, that Grace cannot be extended towards Man without the satisfaction of divine Justice; Man hath offended the majesty of God by aspiring to Godhead, and therefore with all his Progeny devoted to death must die, unless some one can be found sufficient to answer for his offense, and undergo his Punishment. The Son of God freely offers himself a Ransom for Man: the Father accepts him, ordains his incarnation, pronounces his exaltation above all Names in Heaven and Earth; commands all the Angels to adore him; they obey, and hymning to thir Harps in full Choir, celebrate the Father and the Son. Meanwhile* Satan *alights upon the bare convex of this World's outermost Orb; where wand'ring he first finds a place since call'd The Limbo of Vanity; what persons and things fly up thither; thence comes to the Gate of Heaven, describ'd ascending by stairs, and the waters above the Firmament that flow about it: His passage thence to the Orb of the Sun; he finds there* Uriel *the Regent of that Orb, but first changes himself into the shape of a meaner Angel; and pretending a zealous desire to behold the new Creation and Man whom God had plac't there, inquires of him the place of his habitation, and is directed; alights first on Mount* Niphates.

Hail holy Light, offspring of Heav'n first-born,
Or of th' Eternal Coeternal beam
May I express thee unblam'd? since God is Light,
And never but in unapproached Light
Dwelt from Eternity, dwelt then in thee,   5
Bright effluence of bright essence increate.
Or hear'st thou rather pure Ethereal stream,
Whose Fountain who shall tell? before the Sun,
Before the Heavens thou wert, and at the voice
Of God, as with a Mantle didst invest   10
The rising world of waters dark and deep,
Won from the void and formless infinite.
Thee I revisit now with bolder wing,
Escap't the *Stygian* Pool, though long detain'd
In that obscure sojourn, while in my flight   15
Through utter and through middle darkness borne
With other notes than to th' *Orphean* Lyre

1–12. For the thought and its background see the Introduction 56.
7. *hear'st thou rather:* wouldest thou prefer to be called?

9. Cf. VII, 247–49.
12. *Void:* Cf. VII, 233, n.
16. *utter and middle darkness:* Hell and Chaos. Cf. I, 72, and VI, 614.

I sung of *Chaos* and *Eternal Night*,
Taught by the heav'nly Muse to venture down
The dark descent, and up to reascend,   20
Though hard and rare: thee I revisit safe,
And feel thy sovran vital Lamp; but thou
Revisit'st not these eyes, that roll in vain
To find thy piercing ray, and find no dawn;
So thick a drop serene hath quencht thir Orbs,   25
Or dim suffusion veil'd. Yet not the more
Cease I to wander where the Muses haunt
Clear Spring, or shady Grove, or Sunny Hill,
Smit with the love of sacred Song; but chief
Thee *Sion* and the flow'ry Brooks beneath   30
That wash thy hallow'd feet, and warbling flow,
Nightly I visit: nor sometimes forget
Those other two equall'd with me in Fate,
So were I equall'd with them in renown,
Blind *Thamyris* and blind *Mæonides*,   35
And *Tiresias* and *Phineus* Prophets old.
Then feed on thoughts, that voluntary move

18. Milton may have thought of the Orphic hymn to Night where Night is treated as a beneficent goddess. He surely thought of the tradition of Orpheus as the first interpreter of the physical and spiritual secrets of hell, "a man most learned in divinity," as Conti called him in *Mythologiae* VII, xiv.

21. Cf. the Sibyl's warning that the ascent from hell is hard (*Aen.* VI, 128) and its earlier echo in II, 432.

25. *drop serene* translates the *gutta serena*, the Latin medical term for "all blindness in which the eye retains a normal appearance" (Eleanor Brown, *Blindness*, p. 22). Milton was glad that his eyes — as the portrait-frontispiece of his poem proved — betrayed so little "external appearance of injury," and were "as clear and bright, without the semblance of a cloud, as the eyes of those whose sight is the most perfect" (*Def 2*, C.Ed. VIII, 61).

29. The line echoes Virgil's hope (*Georg.* II, 475–92) that, smitten by the love of the Muses, he may be a prophetic poet and sing the secrets of nature.

30. To the haunts of the Muses near the Castalian spring on Mt. Parnassus Milton prefers Mt. Sion and its brooks Kidron and Siloa. For him — as for Bartolomaeus in the *Book of Nature* (1537), Kkii^v — Sion was "the Mount of lore and teaching, as it is written in Isaye, ii, Out of Syon shall come lawe: mounte of prophesye and reuelation."

35. *Mæonides:* Homer, whose obviously blind eyes were familiar, "turn'd

upwards," as George Chapman described them in *Euthymiae Raptus*, ll. 36–38, because he was "outward blind;
    But, inward; past and future things
        he sawe;
    And was to both, and present times,
        their lawe."
Again in the frontispiece to Chapman's translations of the Homeric Hymns Homer raises blind eyes to Apollo, Hermes, and Athene for inspiration.

Among the obscure myths about *Thamyris*, whom Homer mentions (*Il.* II, (502–509), Milton remembered that he was blind, and that Plutarch (in *On Music*) made him the author of a poem about the war of the Titans against the gods.

36. Cf. Milton's allusion in *De Idea Platonica*, ll. 25–26, to *Tiresias*, the sage who prophesies in Sophocles' *Oedipus the King* and *Antigone*, as "the Theban seer whose blindness proved his great illumination." Speaking of his own blindness (*Def 2*, C.Ed. VIII, 64) he quoted Apollonius' *Argonautica* about *Phineus:*
    Fearless, though Jove might rage, he
        showed
    The arcane purposes of heaven to us;
    Endless old age the gods on him bestowed
    And made him strong, but blind and
        piteous.
Phineus, who was stricken blind by the sun, Conti says (*Mythologiae* VII, vi), chose long old age and blindness rather than a short and happy life.

Harmonious numbers; as the wakeful Bird
Sings darkling, and in shadiest Covert hid
Tunes her nocturnal Note. Thus with the Year   40
Seasons return, but not to me returns
Day, or the sweet approach of Ev'n or Morn,
Or sight of vernal bloom, or Summer's Rose,
Or flocks, or herds, or human face divine;
But cloud instead, and ever-during dark   45
Surrounds me, from the cheerful ways of men
Cut off, and for the Book of knowledge fair
Presented with a Universal blanc
Of Nature's works to me expung'd and ras'd,
And wisdom at one entrance quite shut out.   50
So much the rather thou Celestial Light
Shine inward, and the mind through all her powers
Irradiate, there plant eyes, all mist from thence
Purge and disperse, that I may see and tell
Of things invisible to mortal sight.   55
    Now had th' Almighty Father from above,
From the pure Empyrean where he sits
High Thron'd above all highth, bent down his eye,
His own works and their works at once to view:
About him all the Sanctities of Heaven   60
Stood thick as Stars, and from his sight receiv'd
Beatitude past utterance; on his right
The radiant image of his Glory sat,
His only Son; On Earth he first beheld
Our two first Parents, yet the only two   65
Of mankind, in the happy Garden plac't,
Reaping immortal fruits of joy and love,
Uninterrupted joy, unrivall'd love
In blissful solitude; he then survey'd

38. *numbers:* the measured rhythm of the poem. Cf. the ' true musical delight" of "apt numbers" in Milton's prefatory note on the verse of *PL.*
39. *darkling:* not a participle but an adverb. Cf. *Lear* I, iv, 240: "So out went the candle and we were left darkling."
48. *blanc:* Milton's spelling when he used the word in its primitive sense of "white" or "gray." In his blindness he said that he never lost a sensation of a faint gray light about him.
51–55. The lines bravely parallel Milton's assertion of the rewards of a sharpened vision resulting from his blindness as he described it in a letter of March 24, 1656, to Emeric Bigot. His faith was supported by his confidence in the Neoplatonic conception of the "lucid essence" of God as mysteriously related to the physical light of the sun on the one hand and to the human mind on the other — a doctrine that the Lutheran theologian Philipp Melanchthon approved in his chapter on "The Image of God in Man" in his *De anima.* See the Introduction, 20.
60. *the Sanctities of Heaven:* the angelic hierarchies.
62. Cf. Milton's reference in *CD* I, xxxiii (C.Ed. XVI, 375) to the enjoyment of the sight of God as the supreme joy of the righteous in heaven. Cf. I, 684, n.
63. Hebrews i, 2–3, is quoted in *CD* I, v (C.Ed. XIV, 193) as the fullest account of God's Son, "by whom he made the worlds. Who, being the brightness of his glory, and the express image of his person, . . . sat down on the right hand of the majesty on high."

Hell and the Gulf between, and *Satan* there   70
Coasting the wall of Heav'n on this side Night
In the dun Air sublime, and ready now
To stoop with wearied wings, and willing feet
On the bare outside of this World, that seem'd
Firm land imbosom'd without Firmament,   75
Uncertain which, in Ocean or in Air.
Him God beholding from his prospect high,
Wherein past, present, future he beholds,
Thus to his only Son foreseeing spake.

Only begotten Son, seest thou what rage   80
Transports our adversary, whom no bounds
Prescrib'd, no bars of Hell, nor all the chains
Heapt on him there, nor yet the main Abyss
Wide interrupt can hold; so bent he seems
On desperate revenge, that shall redound   85
Upon his own rebellious head. And now
Through all restraint broke loose he wings his way
Not far off Heav'n, in the Precincts of light,
Directly towards the new created World,
And Man there plac't, with purpose to assay   90
If him by force he can destroy, or worse,
By some false guile pervert; and shall pervert;
For Man will hear'n to his glozing lies,
And easily transgress the sole Command,
Sole pledge of his obedience: So will fall   95
Hee and his faithless Progeny: whose fault?
Whose but his own? ingrate, he had of mee
All he could have; I made him just and right,
Sufficient to have stood, though free to fall.

70–73. Satan flies *sublime* (aloft) through the upper limits of Chaos and close to the wall of heaven in a twilit atmosphere (*dun air*), ready to *stoop* (pounce like a hawk) upon the universe.

74. *World:* not the earth, but the universe. Cf. II, 434, and VII, 266. The *Firmament* is described in VII, 261–67.

76. *Uncertain,* an impersonal and absolute construction. It is uncertain, hard to see, whether Chaos around the floating universe is more like water or like air.

83–84. Cf. *Abyss* in I, 21, and II, 405 and 518. *interrupt* has its Latin meaning and participial form, and means "broken open."

90. *assay:* make trial.

94. *sole Command:* the prohibition to touch the tree of knowledge.

96. *faithless:* because Adam was to break faith with God by his act of disobedience and thereby — without sense of "the welfare of his offspring" (as

Milton said in *CD* I, xi; C.Ed. XV, 183) — involve them all in his breach of faith. Cf. III, 209.

98–102. In *CD* I, iii (C.Ed. XIV, 77–81), in urging God's freedom from responsibility in spite of his foreknowledge, Milton said that he had gifted both men and angels with free will, so that their fall might depend upon their own volition. Thus all the evil which ensued from man's fall was entirely "contingent upon man's will." Cf. Satan's confession in IV, 63–68, and the stress on the angels' guilt in V, 525–43. The thought here, however, hardly amounts to a Pelagian profession of belief in man's ability to stand fast without support from God's grace. In the word *Sufficient* Sister Mary Corcoran points out an allusion to the doctrine of sufficient grace, by which theologians of all communions held that Adam was supported before his fall (*Milton's Paradise*, 1954, pp. 104–105).

Such I created all th' Ethereal Powers   100
And Spirits, both them who stood and them who fail'd;
Freely they stood who stood, and fell who fell.
Not free, what proof could they have giv'n sincere
Of true allegiance, constant Faith or Love,
Where only what they needs must do, appear'd,   105
Not what they would? what praise could they receive?
What pleasure I from such obedience paid,
When Will and Reason (Reason also is choice)
Useless and vain, of freedom both despoil'd,
Made passive both, had serv'd necessity,   110
Not mee. They therefore as to right belong'd,
So were created, nor can justly accuse
Thir maker, or thir making, or thir Fate;
As if Predestination over-rul'd
Thir will, dispos'd by absolute Decree   115
Or high foreknowledge; they themselves decreed
Thir own revolt, not I: if I foreknew,
Foreknowledge had no influence on their fault,
Which had no less prov'd certain unforeknown.
So without least impulse or shadow of Fate,   120
Or aught by me immutably foreseen,
They trespass, Authors to themselves in all
Both what they judge and what they choose; for so
I form'd them free, and free they must remain,
Till they enthrall themselves: I else must change   125
Thir nature, and revoke the high Decree
Unchangeable, Eternal, which ordain'd
Thir freedom: they themselves ordain'd thir fall.
The first sort by thir own suggestion fell,
Self-tempted, self-deprav'd: Man falls deceiv'd   130
By th' other first: Man therefore shall find grace,
The other none: in Mercy and Justice both,
Through Heav'n and Earth, so shall my glory excel,
But Mercy first and last shall brightest shine.
Thus while God spake, ambrosial fragrance fill'd   135

106. Pleading that the miracle of grace is enhanced, not impaired, by belief in the freedom of the will, Milton insisted in *CD* I, iv, that, "The acceptableness of duties done under a law of necessity is diminished, or rather is annihilated altogether" (C.Ed. XIV, 141). Cf. ll. 173–89.

108. Cf. the reliance in *Areopagitica* (C.Ed. IV, 319) upon Aristotle's definition of reason as the power of choice (*Nicomachean Ethics* III, ii, 6).

119. The long chapter "On Predestination" in *CD* I, iv, is devoted to proof that "the prescience of God seems to have no connection with the principle or essence of predestination."

128. Cf. *CD* I, iii, where Milton insists that "God is not mutable, so long as he decrees nothing absolutely which could happen otherwise through the liberty that he assigns to man. He would indeed be mutable if he were to obstruct by another decree that liberty which he had already decreed, or were to darken it with the least shadow of necessity" (C.Ed. XIV, 77).

129. *The first sort:* the angels who revolted. *suggestion:* temptation.

All Heav'n, and in the blessed Spirits elect
Sense of new joy ineffable diffus'd:
Beyond compare the Son of God was seen
Most glorious, in him all his Father shone
Substantially express'd, and in his face   140
Divine compassion visibly appear'd,
Love without end, and without measure Grace,
Which uttering thus he to his Father spake.
    O Father, gracious was that word which clos'd
Thy sovran sentence, that Man should find grace;   145
For which both Heav'n and Earth shall high extol
Thy praises, with th' innumerable sound
Of Hymns and sacred Songs, wherewith thy Throne
Encompass'd shall resound thee ever blest.
For should Man finally be lost, should Man   150
Thy creature late so lov'd, thy youngest Son
Fall circumvented thus by fraud, though join'd
With his own folly? that be from thee far,
That far be from thee, Father, who art Judge
Of all things made, and judgest only right.   155
Or shall the Adversary thus obtain
His end, and frustrate thine, shall he fulfil
His malice, and thy goodness bring to naught,
Or proud return though to his heavier doom,
Yet with revenge accomplish't and to Hell   160
Draw after him the whole Race of mankind,
By him corrupted? or wilt thou thyself
Abolish thy Creation, and unmake,
For him, what for thy glory thou hast made?
So should thy goodness and thy greatness both   165
Be question'd and blasphem'd without defense.
    To whom the great Creator thus repli'd.
O Son, in whom my Soul hath chief delight,
Son of my bosom, Son who art alone
My word, my wisdom, and effectual might,   170
All hast thou spok'n as my thoughts are, all
As my Eternal purpose hath decreed:
Man shall not quite be lost, but sav'd who will,

---

136. The good angels are *Spirits elect.*
In *CD* I, ix, Milton challenges the "opinion that the good angels are now upheld, not as much by their own strength, as by the grace of God"; and he adds that "the elect angels" of I Timothy v, 21, means "those who have not revolted" (C.Ed. XV, 99). Cf. l. 184 below.
140. Hebrews i, 2–3. is interpreted in *CD* I, v (C.Ed. XIV, 193) to mean that "God imparted to the Son as much as he pleased of the divine nature, nay of the

divine substance itself." Cf. Maurice Kelley, in *Argument*, p. 30.
156. Cf. II, 629, and "foe" in l. 179 below.
166. *blasphem'd* keeps its Greek force of "insulting," "evil-speaking."
168. Cf. the words from heaven at Christ's baptism: "This is my beloved Son, in whom I am well pleased" (Matt. iii, 17), and the naming of Christ as "the only begotten Son, which is in the bosom of the Father" (John i, 18).

Yet not of will in him, but grace in me
Freely voutsaf't; once more I will renew 175
His lapsed powers, though forfeit and enthrall'd
By sin to foul exorbitant desires;
Upheld by me, yet once more he shall stand
On even ground against his mortal foe,
By me upheld, that he may know how frail 180
His fall'n condition is, and to me owe
All his deliv'rance, and to none but me.
Some I have chosen of peculiar grace
Elect above the rest; so is my will:
The rest shall hear me call, and oft be warn'd 185
Thir sinful state, and to appease betimes
Th' incensed Deity while offer'd grace
Invites; for I will clear thir senses dark,
What may suffice, and soft'n stony hearts
To pray, repent, and bring obedience due. 190
To Prayer, repentance, and obedience due,
Though but endeavor'd with sincere intent,
Mine ear shall not be slow, mine eye not shut.
And I will place within them as a guide
My Umpire *Conscience*, whom if they will hear, 195
Light after light well us'd they shall attain,
And to the end persisting, safe arrive.
This my long sufferance and my day of grace
They who neglect and scorn, shall never taste;
But hard be hard'n'd, blind be blinded more, 200
That they may stumble on, and deeper fall;
And none but such from mercy I exclude.
But yet all is not done; Man disobeying,
Disloyal breaks his fealty, and sins

174. The distinction between God's grace and man's will may — as Leon Howard insists in *HLQ*, IX (1945), 168 — be an explicit dichotomy such as logicians of Ramus' school made between the two parts of the efficient cause of man's salvation, his own will as the impelling, helping part, and God's grace as the instrumental cause. Milton insists upon the co-operation of the two.

176. *lapsed:* (literally) fallen, and therefore diminished. *forfeit* — forfeited — anticipates the legal view of the penalty properly to be paid by Adam in l. 210 below.

180. "Lord, make me to know . . . how frail I am" (Psalm xxxix, 4).

183–193. Milton distils the essence of his chapter "On Predestination" in *CD* I, iv, which challenges the Calvinistic doctrine (as characteristically stated in the Westminster Confession) that "before the foundation of the world" God, for his own glory, "without any foresight of faith and good works, or perseverance in either of them," had "predestined certain souls to salvation and ordained others to dishonor and wrath for their sin." Milton explains God's "election" of men in terms of his "sufficient grace" and their free acceptance of it. So "none can be reprobated, except they do not believe or continue in the faith, and even this as a consequence rather than a decree" (C.Ed. XIV, 141). M. Kelley analyses the chapter and the Confession in *PMLA*, LII (1937), 75–79.

190. The line looks forward to X, 1081–96.

195. *Conscience* is constantly equated with reason and individual judgment in the *CD*. In the end, says the chapter on the Last Judgment (I, xxxiii), man shall be judged according to the response of his conscience to "the measure of light which he has enjoyed" (C.Ed. XVI, 357).

Against the high Supremacy of Heav'n,   205
Affecting God-head, and so losing all,
To expiate his Treason hath naught left,
But to destruction sacred and devote,
He with his whole posterity must die,
Die hee or Justice must; unless for him   210
Some other able, and as willing, pay
The rigid satisfaction, death for death.
Say Heav'nly Powers, where shall we find such love,
Which of ye will be mortal to redeem
Man's mortal crime, and just th' unjust to save,   215
Dwells in all Heaven charity so dear?
   He ask'd, but all the Heav'nly Choir stood mute,
And silence was in Heav'n: on man's behalf
Patron or Intercessor none appear'd,
Much less that durst upon his own head draw   220
The deadly forfeiture, and ransom set.
And now without redemption all mankind
Must have been lost, adjudg'd to Death and Hell
By doom severe, had not the Son of God,
In whom the fulness dwells of love divine,   225
His dearest mediation thus renew'd.
   Father, thy word is past, man shall find grace;
And shall grace not find means, that finds her way,
The speediest of thy winged messengers,
To visit all thy creatures, and to all   230
Comes unprevented, unimplor'd, unsought?
Happy for man, so coming; he her aid
Can never seek, once dead in sins and lost;
Atonement for himself or offering meet,
Indebted and undone, hath none to bring: 235
Behold mee then, mee for him, life for life
I offer, on mee let thine anger fall;
Account mee man; I for his sake will leave
Thy bosom, and this glory next to thee
Freely put off, and for him lastly die   240
Well pleas'd, on me let Death wreck all his rage;
Under his gloomy power I shall not long

206. It is to be a "Goddess among Gods" that Satan tempts Eve (IX, 547).
208. *sacred* and *devote* both keep their Latin meaning of "dedicated to a deity" for destruction.
216. *charity* has its Greek meaning of "love" that is usual in the New Testament.
218. So St. John says that there was silence in heaven when the seventh seal was opened (Rev. viii, 1).
219. *Patron*, in its Latin sense of a defender in a court of law, and *Intercessor* both reflect the conception of Christ in I John ii, 1: "And if any man sin, we have an advocate with the Father, Jesus Christ the righteous."
225. In the chapter on the Son in *CD* I, v Milton quotes John iii, 35, "The Father loveth the Son, and hath given all things into his hand," as evidence of his power as Redeemer.
231. *unprevented* has its Latin meaning of "unanticipated."
233. So Christ is the reviver of those who are "dead in sins" (Col. ii, 13).

Lie vanquisht; thou hast giv'n me to possess
Life in myself for ever, by thee I live,
Though now to Death I yield, and am his due   245
All that of me can die, yet that debt paid,
Thou wilt not leave me in the loathsome grave
His prey, nor suffer my unspotted Soul
For ever with corruption there to dwell;
But I shall rise Victorious, and subdue   250
My vanquisher, spoil'd of his vaunted spoil;
Death his death's wound shall then receive, and stoop
Inglorious, of his mortal sting disarm'd.
I through the ample Air in Triumph high
Shall lead Hell Captive maugre Hell, and show   255
The powers of darkness bound.   Thou at the sight
Pleas'd, out of Heaven shalt look down and smile,
While by thee rais'd I ruin all my Foes,
Death last, and with his Carcass glut the Grave:
Then with the multitude of my redeem'd   260
Shall enter Heav'n long absent, and return,
Father, to see thy face, wherein no cloud
Of anger shall remain, but peace assur'd,
And reconcilement; wrath shall be no more
Thenceforth, but in thy presence Joy entire.   265
    His words here ended, but his meek aspect
Silent yet spake, and breath'd immortal love
To mortal men, above which only shone
Filial obedience: as a sacrifice
Glad to be offer'd, he attends the will   270
Of his great Father.   Admiration seiz'd

246. Both M. Kelley (*Argument*, p. 32) and D. Saurat — *RES*, XII (1936), 324 — think that Milton is influenced by the doctrine of Robert Overton in *Man's Mortality* (1655), that the soul is simply the life of the body and perishes with it at death (to revive only at the resurrection). But Kelley believes Milton's meaning to be that, "on account of our sins, even the soul of Christ was for a short time subject unto death," while Saurat believes it to be that, because the Son's "soul — his life — is unspotted, therefore he shall not die." But — as George Williamson points out in "Milton and the Mortalist Heresy" (in *Seventeenth Century Contexts*, London, 1960, pp. 148–77) — "mortalism" figured in Sir Thomas Browne's *Religio Medici* (1643) and was a heresy with a long history that was familiar to many of Milton's contemporaries. The thought in the present passage was traditional; the conception of the Son's immunity to death is found in Serafino Salandra's *Adamo caduto* (Cosanza, 1647), V, vii, p. 123. Milton is not splitting theological hairs; he is dealing with the justice of Christ's incarnation and crucifixion, which — as Beatrice explains to Dante in *Paradiso* VII, 40–42 — can be explained only on the ground that in assuming human nature Christ became guilty of all human sin.

253. Milton seems to have been influenced by Sannazaro, in the first book of whose epic on the birth of Christ, *De partu Virginis*, he found a similar network of biblical texts forming a prophecy which is put into the mouth of David. Pluto (Satan) is foreseen as led captive to Tartarus while Christ conquers the powers of the air (the fiends) and subdues Death and Hell.

254. The lines echo Psalm lxviii, 18: "Thou hast ascended on high, thou hast led captivity captive."

255. *maugre:* in spite of.

259. "The last enemy to be destroyed is death" (I Cor. xv, 26).

270. *attends:* waits (for an expression of his Father's will).

All Heav'n, what this might mean, and whither tend
Wond'ring; but soon th' Almighty thus repli'd:
  O thou in Heav'n and Earth the only peace
Found out for mankind under wrath, O thou   275
My sole complacence! well thou know'st how dear
To me are all my works, nor Man the least
Though last created, that for him I spare
Thee from my bosom and right hand, to save,
By losing thee a while, the whole Race lost.   280
Thou therefore whom thou only canst redeem,
Thir Nature also to thy Nature join;
And be thyself Man among men on Earth,
Made flesh, when time shall be, of Virgin seed,
By wondrous birth: Be thou in *Adam's* room   285
The Head of all mankind, though *Adam's* Son.
As in him perish all men, so in thee
As from a second root shall be restor'd,
As many as are restor'd, without thee none.
His crime makes guilty all his Sons, thy merit   290
Imputed shall absolve them who renounce
Thir own both righteous and unrighteous deeds,
And live in thee transplanted, and from thee
Receive new life. So Man, as is most just,
Shall satisfy for Man, be judg'd and die,   295
And dying rise, and rising with him raise
His Brethren, ransom'd with his own dear life.
So Heav'nly love shall outdo Hellish hate,
Giving to death, and dying to redeem,
So dearly to redeem what Hellish hate   300
So easily destroy'd, and still destroys
In those who, when they may, accept not grace.
Nor shalt thou by descending to assume
Man's Nature, lessen or degrade thine own.
Because thou hast, though Thron'd in highest bliss   305
Equal to God, and equally enjoying

276. *complacence:* satisfaction, basis
of pleasure.
  282. "How much better it is for us to
know simply that the Son of God, our
Mediator, was made flesh, that he is
called both God and Man, and is such
in reality," than it is to indulge in subtle
explanations of the fact, says Milton in
CD I, xv (C.Ed. XV, 272).
  284. Similarly in Matthew i, 23,
Isaiah's prophecy (vii, 14), "Behold a
virgin shall conceive, and bear a son, and
shall call his name Immanuel," is inter-
preted as a prophecy of the birth of
Christ. Cf. X, 74.
  287. "For as in Adam all die, even so
in Christ shall all be made alive" (I Cor.
xv, 22).

291. So, says Milton in *CD* I, xxii
(C.Ed. XVI, 29), "Christ paid the ransom
of our sins, which he took upon himself
by imputation."
  299. "The Son of Man came . . . to
give his life a ransom for many" (Matt.
xx, 28).
  306. The hard problem of Milton's
precise view of the Son's equality to the
Father, if it can be solved in any single
statement in the chapter on the Son of
God in *CD* (I, v), is best reduced to the
statement that, "lastly, the Son himself
and his apostles acknowledge throughout
the whole of their discourses and writings,
that the Father is greater than the Son
in all things" (C.Ed. XIV, 219).

God-like fruition, quitted all to save
A world from utter loss, and hast been found
By Merit more than Birthright Son of God,
Found worthiest to be so by being Good,   310
Far more than Great or High; because in thee
Love hath abounded more than Glory abounds,
Therefore thy Humiliation shall exalt
With thee thy Manhood also to this Throne;
Here shalt thou sit incarnate, here shalt Reign   315
Both God and Man, Son both of God and Man,
Anointed universal King; all Power
I give thee, reign for ever, and assume
Thy Merits; under thee as Head Supreme
Thrones, Princedoms, Powers, Dominions I reduce: 320
All knees to thee shall bow, of them that bide
In Heaven, or Earth, or under Earth in Hell;
When thou attended gloriously from Heav'n
Shalt in the Sky appear, and from thee send
The summoning Arch-Angels to proclaim   325
Thy dread Tribunal: forthwith from all Winds
The living, and forthwith the cited dead
Of all past Ages to the general Doom
Shall hast'n, such a peal shall rouse thir sleep.
Then all thy Saints assembl'd, thou shalt judge   330
Bad men and Angels, they arraign'd shall sink
Beneath thy Sentence; Hell, her numbers full,
Thenceforth shall be for ever shut. Meanwhile
The World shall burn, and from her ashes spring
New Heav'n and Earth, wherein the just shall dwell   335
And after all thir tribulations long
See golden days, fruitful of golden deeds,
With Joy and Love triumphing, and fair Truth.
Then thou thy regal Sceptre shalt lay by,
For regal Sceptre then no more shall need,   340
God shall be All in All. But all ye Gods,

317–318. The lines fuse God's words to the Son in Hebrews i, 9: "Thou hast loved righteousness and hated iniquity; therefore God, even thy God, hath anointed thee with the oil of gladness above thy fellows," and Christ's saying that, "All power is given unto me" (Matt. xxviii, 18).

321. The promise stems from Philippians ii, 10: "That at the name of Jesus every knee should bow, of things in heaven, and things in earth, and things under the earth."

324. The details of the last judgment are from Matthew xxv, 31–32, and I Thessalonians iv, 16.

326. *from all Winds:* from all directions.

334. *CD* I, xxxiii (C.Ed. XVI, 369) affirms "the destruction of the present unclean and polluted world itself, namely, the FINAL CONFLAGRATION."

335. The new heaven and earth of Revelation xxi, 1, meant to Milton "the renovation of heaven and earth, and of all things therein adapted to our service or delight, to be possessed in perpetuity — Isaiah lxv, 17" (C.Ed. XVI, 379). Cf. XI, 900–901 and XII, 547–51.

341. "And when all things shall be subdued unto him, then shall the Son himself be subject unto him that put all things under him, that God may be all in all" (I Cor. xv, 28). For *Gods* see II, 352, n.

Adore him, who to compass all this dies,
Adore the Son, and honor him as mee.
　No sooner had th' Almighty ceas't, but all
The multitude of Angels with a shout   345
Loud as from numbers without number, sweet
As from blest voices, uttering joy, Heav'n rung
With Jubilee, and loud Hosannas fill'd
Th' eternal Regions: lowly reverent
Towards either Throne they bow, and to the ground   350
With solemn adoration down they cast
Thir Crowns inwove with Amarant and Gold,
Immortal Amarant, a Flow'r which once
In Paradise, fast by the Tree of Life
Began to bloom, but soon for man's offense   355
To Heav'n remov'd where first it grew, there grows,
And flow'rs aloft shading the Fount of Life,
And where the river of Bliss through midst of Heav'n
Rolls o'er *Elysian* Flow'rs her Amber stream;
With these that never fade the Spirits elect   360
Bind thir resplendent locks inwreath'd with beams,
Now in loose Garlands thick thrown off, the bright
Pavement that like a Sea of Jasper shone
Impurpl'd with Celestial Roses smil'd.
Then Crown'd again thir gold'n Harps they took,   365
Harps ever tun'd, that glittering by thir side
Like Quivers hung, and with Preamble sweet
Of charming symphony they introduce
Thir sacred Song, and waken raptures high;
No voice exempt, no voice but well could join   370
Melodious part, such concord is in Heav'n.
　Thee Father first they sung Omnipotent,
Immutable, Immortal, Infinite,

---

353. *Amarant* (unfading) describes
the saints' "heavenly inheritance incor-
ruptible and undefiled, that fadeth not
away" in I Peter i, 4. The flower called
amaranthus ("Love-lies-bleeding" or
"Prince's Feather") grows beside the
Tree of Life — D. C. Allen suggests —
because Clement of Alexandria put it
there in the *Paedagogus* (Dindorff, I,
277). Cf. *Lyc*, 149 and *PL* XI, 78.
　358. *The river of Bliss* is St. John's
"pure river of water of life, clear as
crystal" (Rev. xxii, 1) though it flows
through the Elysian Fields and is the
haunt of spirits singing paeans, as Virgil
describes the Elysian river (*Aen.* VI,
656–59).
　363. The colors are those of the "sea
of glass, like unto crystal" (Rev. iv, 6)
and the "light like unto a stone most
precious, even like a jasper stone, clear

as crystal" (Rev. xxi, 11) that St. John
saw around the throne of God.
　373–382. Visually, the lines recall
Moses' accounts of God speaking to him
on Sinai when "a cloud covered the
mount" (Exod. xxiv, 15) and Isaiah's
vision (vi, 1–4) of "the Lord sitting upon
a throne" with the seraphim veiling their
eyes about him in the smoke-filled temple.
Theologically, the lines reflect Milton's
thought in *CD* I, ii, that, as the uncaused
cause, God is knowable and definable only
by his attributes. But the conception
was familiar, as G. C. Taylor notes in
Milton and Du Bartas, p. 42, and was
put in superficially similar language in
Sylvester's translation of the *Divine
Weeks* (p. 2):
　Before all Time, all Matter, Form,
　　and Place,
　God all in all, and all in God it was:

Eternal King; thee Author of all being,
Fountain of Light, thyself invisible   375
Amidst the glorious brightness where thou sit'st
Thron'd inaccessible, but when thou shad'st
The full blaze of thy beams, and through a cloud
Drawn round about thee like a radiant Shrine,
Dark with excessive bright thy skirts appear,   380
Yet dazzle Heav'n, that brightest Seraphim
Approach not, but with both wings veil thir eyes.
Thee next they sang of all Creation first,
Begotten Son, Divine Similitude,
In whose conspicuous count'nance, without cloud   385
Made visible, th' Almighty Father shines,
Whom else no Creature can behold; on thee
Impresst th' effulgence of his Glory abides,
Transfus'd on thee his ample Spirit rests.
Hee Heav'n of Heavens and all the Powers therein   390
By thee created, and by thee threw down
Th' aspiring Dominations: thou that day
Thy Father's dreadful Thunder didst not spare,
Nor stop thy flaming Chariot wheels, that shook
Heav'n's everlasting Frame, while o'er the necks   395
Thou drov'st of warring Angels disarray'd.
Back from pursuit thy Powers with loud acclaim
Thee only extoll'd, Son of thy Father's might,
To execute fierce vengeance on his foes:
Not so on Man; him through their malice fall'n,   400
Father of Mercy and Grace, thou didst not doom
So strictly, but much more to pity incline:
No sooner did thy dear and only Son
Perceive thee purpos'd not to doom frail Man
So strictly, but much more to pity inclin'd,   405
Hee to appease thy wrath, and end the strife
Of Mercy and Justice in thy face discern'd,
Regardless of the Bliss wherein hee sat
Second to thee, offer'd himself to die
For man's offense. O unexampl'd love,   410
Love nowhere to be found less than Divine!
Hail Son of God, Savior of Men, thy Name

Immutable, immortal, infinite,
Incomprehensible, all spirit, all light,
All Majestie, all-self-Omnipotent
Invisible.
Cf. II, 264, and V, 599.
383–392. The conception of the Son
as the Word *by* whom God created the
universe is elaborated in *CD* I, vii (C.Ed.
XV, 7–11). Cf. VII, 174–75. The Son's

triumph over the *aspiring Dominations*
or rebellious powers of Satan is the theme
of VI, 824–92.
389. M. Kelley rightly observes that
here and in I, 17, and VII, 165, 209, and
235, the reference is to the "virtue and
power of God the Father," and "not to
the Third Person" or Holy Spirit (*Argu-
ment*, p. 109).

Shall be the copious matter of my Song
Henceforth, and never shall my Harp thy praise
Forget, nor from thy Father's praise disjoin.   415
   Thus they in Heav'n, above the starry Sphere,
Thir happy hours in joy and hymning spent.
Meanwhile upon the firm opacous Globe
Of this round World, whose first convex divides
The luminous inferior Orbs, enclos'd   420
From *Chaos* and th' inroad of Darkness old,
Satan alighted walks: a Globe far off
It seem'd, now seems a boundless Continent
Dark, waste, and wild, under the frown of Night
Starless expos'd, and ever-threat'ning storms   425
Of *Chaos* blust'ring round, inclement sky;
Save on that side which from the wall of Heav'n,
Though distant far, some small reflection gains
Of glimmering air less vext with tempest loud:
Here walk'd the Fiend at large in spacious field.   430
As when a Vultur on *Imaus* bred,
Whose snowy ridge the roving *Tartar* bounds,
Dislodging from a Region scarce of prey
To gorge the flesh of Lambs or yeanling Kids
On Hills where Flocks are fed, flies toward the Springs   435
Of *Ganges* or *Hydaspes*, *Indian* streams;
But in his way lights on the barren Plains
Of *Sericana*, where *Chineses* drive
With Sails and Wind thir cany Waggons light:
So on this windy Sea of Land, the Fiend   440
Walk'd up and down alone bent on his prey,
Alone, for other Creature in this place
Living or lifeless to be found was none,
None yet, but store hereafter from the earth

413. Here, as usual in his angel choruses, Milton puts himself into the choir and uses *my Song* and *Harp* as if he spoke with the angels as a representative of the City of God on earth.
416. *The starry Sphere* is inside the shell of the universe on which Satan has landed in l. 74 above. The empyreal heaven of the angels is outside and "above" it.
418. *opacous:* opaque.
431. The vulture was described in Batman's version of Bartholomaeus' *Book of Nature* (*De proprietatibus rerum*, 1582, p. Gg) as able to scent its prey across whole continents. Milton's picture resembles Ortelius' maps of Asia, showing Mt. *Imaus* stretching from the Hyperborean Ocean to the Caucasus, with *Sericana* to the southeast and the *Hydaspes* flowing into the Indus, but — as

Starnes and Talbert note in *Dictionaries*, p. 322 — it more closely resembles the description of the sources of the Ganges and Hydaspes in the dictionaries.
438–439. Several geographers confirmed the story of the Chinese windwagons, which first reached England in Robert Parke's translation of the Spanish Jesuit Juan Gonzalez de Mendoza's *Historie of the Great and Mighty Kingdome of China* (1588). F. L. Huntley says in *MLN*, LXIX (1954), 406, that Ortelius' maps of China were trimmed with handsome landships, but he suspects that Milton was sceptical of Mendoza's story and intended his readers to recall that his name, in its Latin form, means "blundersome" and therefore "untrustworthy."
444–496. Though Milton (l. 471), like Dante (*Inf.* IV, 138), puts Empedocles

Up hither like Aereal vapors flew   445
Of all things transitory and vain, when Sin
With vanity had fill'd the works of men:
Both all things vain, and all who in vain things
Built thir fond hopes of Glory or lasting fame,
Or happiness in this or th' other life;   450
All who have thir reward on Earth, the fruits
Of painful Superstition and blind Zeal,
Naught seeking but the praise of men, here find
Fit retribution, empty as thir deeds;
All th' unaccomplisht works of Nature's hand,   455
Abortive, monstrous, or unkindly mixt,
Dissolv'd on Earth, fleet hither, and in vain,
Till final dissolution, wander here,
Not in the neighboring Moon, as some have dream'd;
Those argent Fields more likely habitants,   460
Translated Saints, or middle Spirits hold
Betwixt th' Angelical and Human kind:
Hither of ill-join'd Sons and Daughters born
First from the ancient World those Giants came
With many a vain exploit, though then renown'd: 465
The builders next of *Babel* on the Plain
Of *Sennaar*, and still with vain design
New *Babels*, had they wherewithal, would build:
Others came single; he who to be deem'd
A God, leap'd fondly into *Ætna* flames,   470
Empedocles, and hee who to enjoy
Plato's Elysium, leap'd into the Sea,

---

into Limbo, his Limbo of Vanity has little in common with Dante's circle of the great poets, philosophers, and heroes. Nor has it much in common with Ariosto's Limbo, where Astolfo loses his wits and finally finds them on the moon, hidden in

"a goodly valley, where he sees
A mighty mass of things strangely confus'd,
Things that on earth were lost, or were abus'd."

(*Orlando Furioso* XXXIV, 70. The translation is by Milton in *Of Reformation in England*.)

In "A Justification of Milton's Paradise of Fools" in *ELH*, XXI (1954), 107–113, F. L. Huntley relates the entire passage to Satan's purposes by observing that his pride, his "bluster and disguise," and his paternity of Sin and Death are all symbolized by the human types that gather on the windy outside of the shell of Milton's universe.

459–462. The air, the moon, and the stars had speculatively been peopled with various spirit inhabitants by philosophers like Giordano Bruno, Jerome Cardan, and Milton's contemporary at Cambridge, Henry More. "Readers of *PL*," says H. Schultz in *Milton and Forbidden Knowledge*, p. 16, "had been taught to smile, especially at moon-dwellers, by Ariosto's Lunar paradise or Donne's in *Ignatius*, the supplement to the *Satyre Menippé*, Ben Jonson's masques," etc.

464. For the story of the misbegotten giants see XI, 573–97.

466. For *Babel* see XII, 45. *Sennaar* is the plain of Shinar in Genesis x, 10.

470–474. As J. Horrell notes in *RES*, xviii (1943), 413–27, these suicides come from Lactantius' chapter on "The False Wisdom of the Philosophers" in the *Divine Institutes* III. The moral was pointed by John Hall in *Heaven upon Earth*, Sec. 17, and by John Eliot in *The Monarchie of Man* (ed. Grosart 1879, II, 162), where Cleombrotus is said to have killed himself after a too enthusiastic study of "Platoes discourses of the immortalitie of the Soule" (*Phaedo*, 68).

Cleombrotus, and many more too long,
Embryos, and Idiots, Eremites and Friars
White, Black and Grey, with all thir trumpery.   475
Here Pilgrims roam, that stray'd so far to seek
In *Golgotha* him dead, who lives in Heav'n;
And they who to be sure of Paradise
Dying put on the weeds of *Dominic*,
Or in *Franciscan* think to pass disguis'd;   480
They pass the Planets seven, and pass the fixt,
And that Crystalline Sphere whose balance weighs
The Trepidation talkt, and that first mov'd;
And now Saint *Peter* at Heav'n's Wicket seems
To wait them with his Keys, and now at foot   485
Of Heav'n's ascent they lift thir Feet, when lo
A violent cross wind from either Coast
Blows them transverse ten thousand Leagues awry
Into the devious Air; then might ye see
Cowls, Hoods and Habits with thir wearers tost   490
And flutter'd into Rags, then Reliques, Beads,
Indulgences, Dispenses, Pardons, Bulls,
The sport of Winds: all these upwhirl'd aloft
Fly o'er the backside of the World far off
Into a *Limbo* large and broad, since call'd   495
The Paradise of Fools, to few unknown
Long after, now unpeopl'd, and untrod;
All this dark Globe the Fiend found as he pass'd,
And long he wander'd, till at last a gleam
Of dawning light turn'd thither-ward in haste   500
His travell'd steps; far distant he descries
Ascending by degrees magnificent

474–475. *Eremites:* hermits. The *White Friars* are the Carmelites; the *Black*, the Dominicans; and the *Grey*, the Franciscans.
477. *Golgotha:* the hill near Jerusalem where Christ was crucified (John xix, 17).
479. Illustrations of the practice are given by J. Huizinga in *The Waning of the Middle Ages* (London, 1924), pp. 164–65.
481–483. "They pass the seven planets; the star-sphere; and the crystalline sphere, whose balance (i.e. the sign of Libra, the Scales), weighs (i.e. measures) the amount of the supposed trepidation of the star-sphere; and they pass the primum mobile." — G. Carnall's paraphrase in *N&Q*, CXCVII (1952), 315–16. Cf. l. 558 below.
483. *Trepidation:* "a libration of the eighth or ninth sphere, added to the system of Ptolemy by the Arab astronomer Thabet ben Korah, c. 950, . . . to account for certain phenomena . . .

really due to the rotation of the earth's axis" (*O.E.D.*). An account of Copernicus' use of the hypothesis of trepidation to explain the observable irregularities in the precession of the equinoxes is given by F. R. Johnson in *Astronomical Thought in Renaissance England* (Baltimore, 1937), pp. 110–11.
490–496. An illuminating parallel to this passage has been noted by W. J. Grace — in *SP*, LII (1955), 590 — in Burton's anticipation of phrases like "the sport of Winds" and "Indulgences, Dispenses, Pardons, Bulls" in the familiar passage in the *Anatomy* III, iv, 1, 2 (III, 333, Everyman Ed.) which declares that the doctrine of pardons (*Dispenses* in Milton's phrase) has "so fleeced the commonalty, and spurred on this free superstitious horse, that he runs himself blind, and is an Ass to carry burdens."
501. *travell'd* has the French and Italian force of "tired."
502. *degrees:* steps (of a stairway).

Up to the wall of Heaven a Structure high,
At top whereof, but far more rich appear'd
The work as of a Kingly Palace Gate   505
With Frontispiece of Diamond and Gold
Imbellisht; thick with sparkling orient Gems
The Portal shone, inimitable on Earth
By Model, or by shading Pencil drawn.
The Stairs were such as whereon *Jacob* saw   510
Angels ascending and descending, bands
Of Guardians bright, when he from *Esau* fled
To *Padan-Aram* in the field of *Luz*,
Dreaming by night under the open Sky,
And waking cri'd, 'This is the Gate of Heav'n'.   515
Each Stair mysteriously was meant, nor stood
There always, but drawn up to Heav'n sometimes
Viewless, and underneath a bright Sea flow'd
Of Jasper, or of liquid Pearl, whereon
Who after came from Earth, sailing arriv'd,   520
Wafted by Angels, or flew o'er the Lake
Rapt in a Chariot drawn by fiery Steeds.
The Stairs were then let down, whether to dare
The Fiend by easy ascent, or aggravate
His sad exclusion from the doors of Bliss.   525
Direct against which op'n'd from beneath,
Just o'er the blissful seat of Paradise,
A passage down to th' Earth, a passage wide,
Wider by far than that of after-times
Over Mount *Sion*, and, though that were large,   530
Over the *Promis'd Land* to God so dear,
By which, to visit oft those happy Tribes,
On high behests his Angels to and fro
Pass'd frequent, and his eye with choice regard
From *Paneas* the fount of *Jordan's* flood   535

506. *Frontispiece:* façade of heaven's gate, the *Wicket* of l. 484 above.

510–518. The *mysteriously meant* stair is the ladder whose top Jacob dreamed "reached to heaven, and behold the angels of God ascending and descending on it" (Gen. xxviii, 12). The scene of his vision in *Padan-Aram* was familiar in an actual representation of the "ladder" on Fuller's map showing it in the *field of Luz* in *A Pisgah-Sight.* Milton knew it also in Dante's vision of it in the Orb of Saturn (*Par.* xxi), where the poet meets Sts. Damian and Benedict and is amazed by their glory and their denunciation of corruption in the Church. Sacred art often portrayed it, and — as D. C. Allen notes in *MLN*, LXVIII (1953), 360 — liberal interpreters like Jean Bodin (in *Heptaplomeres*) identified it with the golden chain of Zeus (to which Milton refers

in II, 1005 and 1051) as a symbol of the links of causation that bind the universe together.

518–519. The *Sea . . . of Jasper* is the "waters above the Firmament" which the Argument to this book says flow about the gate of heaven. Cf. l. 574 below and VII, 261.

521. The parable of the flight of the beggar Lazarus to heaven in the arms of angels (Luke xvi, 22) is paralleled with Elijah's translation to heaven in a "chariot of fire" (II Kings ii, 11).

530. Cf. *Sion* in I, 386 and 442, and III, 30.

535–536. *Paneas,* the city of Dan, near the source of the Jordan in the north of Palestine, and Beersheba (*Beërsaba*) in the extreme south, are often mentioned as the bounds of the country (e.g. I Kings iv, 25).

To *Beërsaba*, where the *Holy Land*
Borders on *Egypt* and th' *Arabian* shore;
So wide the op'ning seem'd, where bounds were set
To darkness, such as bound the Ocean wave.
Satan from hence now on the lower stair   540
That scal'd by steps of Gold to Heaven Gate
Looks down with wonder at the sudden view
Of all this World at once. As when a Scout
Through dark and desert ways with peril gone
All night; at last by break of cheerful dawn   545
Obtains the brow of some high-climbing Hill,
Which to his eye discovers unaware
The goodly prospect of some foreign land
First seen, or some renown'd Metropolis
With glistering Spires and Pinnacles adorn'd,   550
Which now the Rising Sun gilds with his beams.
Such wonder seiz'd, though after Heaven seen,
The Spirit malign, but much more envy seiz'd
At sight of all this World beheld so fair.
Round he surveys, and well might, where he stood   555
So high above the circling Canopy
Of Night's extended shade; from Eastern Point
Of *Libra* to the fleecy Star that bears
Andromeda far off *Atlantic* Seas
Beyond th' Horizon; then from Pole to Pole   560
He views in breadth, and without longer pause
Down right into the World's first Region throws
His flight precipitant, and winds with ease
Through the pure marble Air his oblique way
Amongst innumerable Stars, that shone   565
Stars distant, but nigh hand seem'd other Worlds,
Or other Worlds they seem'd, or happy Isles,
Like those *Hesperian* Gardens fam'd of old,

---

552. *though after Heaven seen:* though he had seen Heaven's glory.

555-579. Entering the universe at the point where it is suspended from heaven by the golden chain (cf. II, 1051), Satan sees the panorama of the stars stretching from the Scales (*Libra*) at the eastern end of the Zodiac to the constellation of the Ram, the *fleecy star*, with that of *Andromeda* seeming to ride on it at the western end, below the *Atlantic* horizon. He plunges through the upper air or *World's first Region*, through the orbs of the *primum mobile*, the Crystalline Sphere and the fixed stars (in the reverse order from that in which they are named in ll. 481-83 above), and then, entering the lower region of the planets, is attracted by the sun, whose orb in the geocentric, Ptolemaic astronomy was *below* that of

the fixed stars. The *golden Sun* is *above* the stars in the sense that it is more splendid than they and *dispenses Light* to them, as it is said again to do in V, 423.

564. The reference, as Svendsen notes in *M.&S.*, p. 88, is to the uppermost of the four bands of air which contemporary meteorology regarded as lying three below and one above the fiery spheres of the stars. The air of that uppermost or "first Region" was deadly cold and shining. Shining is the literal meaning of the Greek word from which marble is derived. Cf. the "marble heaven" of *Othello* III, iii, 460.

567. Here, as in *Comus*, 981-82, the *Hesperian Gardens* are in the *happy Isles* or Hesperides, which were vaguely identified with the Canary Islands or even with the British Isles. Cf. I, 510-19, n.

Fortunate Fields, and Groves and flow'ry Vales,
Thrice happy Isles, but who dwelt happy there   570
He stay'd not to enquire: above them all
The golden Sun in splendor likest Heaven
Allur'd his eye: Thither his course he bends
Through the calm Firmament; but up or down
By centre, or eccentric, hard to tell,   575
Or Longitude, where the great Luminary
Aloof the vulgar Constellations thick,
That from his Lordly eye keep distance due,
Dispenses Light from far; they as they move
Thir Starry dance in numbers that compute   580
Days, months, and years, towards his all-cheering Lamp
Turn swift thir various motions, or are turn'd
By his Magnetic beam, that gently warms
The Universe, and to each inward part
With gentle penetration, though unseen,   585
Shoots invisible virtue even to the deep:
So wondrously was set his Station bright.
There lands the Fiend, a spot like which perhaps
Astronomer in the Sun's lucent Orb
Through his glaz'd Optic Tube yet never saw.   590
The place he found beyond expression bright,
Compar'd with aught on Earth, Metal or Stone;
Not all parts like, but all alike inform'd
With radiant light, as glowing Iron with fire;
If metal, part seem'd Gold, part Silver clear;   595
If stone, Carbuncle most or Chrysolite,
Ruby or Topaz, to the Twelve that shone
In *Aaron's* Breastplate, and a stone besides
Imagin'd rather oft than elsewhere seen,
That stone, or like to that which here below   600
Philosophers in vain so long have sought,
In vain, though by thir powerful Art they bind

---

575. Editors surmise that Milton hesitates here between the Ptolemaic and Copernican views of the sun respectively as *eccentric*, because not at the center of the universe, or at the *centre*.

576. The *Longitude* or horizontal direction of Satan's movement is as hard to define as the vertical direction.

579–581. Here, as in VII, 341–42, there is an echo of Genesis i, 14: "And God said, Let there be lights in the firmament of the heaven to divide the day from the night; and let them be for signs, and for seasons, and for days, and for years." Equally clear is the reflection of Plato's dance of the stars (*Tim.*, 40).

583–585. Cf. VI, 472–83, and the note there.

589–590. Galileo's discovery of sun spots with his *glaz'd Optic Tube* (telescope) in 1609 was one of the most exciting astronomical events of the century.

596. D. P. Harding — in *Milton and the Renaissance Ovid*, p. 90 — sees in *Carbuncle* a translation of Ovid's *pyropus* in his famous description of the temple of the sun (*Met.* II, 2), which obviously influences this entire passage in spite of the express reference to the twelve precious stones of *Aaron's Breastplate* in Exodus xxviii, 17–24.

600–605. "*Hermes* and *Proteus*," E. H. Duncan points out in *Osiris*, XI (1954), 405, were the "metaphorical names for 'the elixir of the philosophers,' the proxi-

Volatile *Hermes*, and call up unbound
In various shapes old *Proteus* from the Sea,
Drain'd through a Limbec to his Native form.   605
What wonder then if fields and regions here
Breathe forth *Elixir* pure, and Rivers run
Potable Gold, when with one virtuous touch
Th' Arch-chemic Sun so far from us remote
Produces with Terrestrial Humor mixt   610
Here in the dark so many precious things
Of color glorious and effect so rare?
Here matter new to gaze the Devil met
Undazzl'd, far and wide his eye commands,
For sight no obstacle found here, nor shade,   615
But all Sun-shine, as when his Beams at Noon
Culminate from th' *Equator*, as they now
Shot upward still direct, whence no way round
Shadow from body opaque can fall, and the Air,
Nowhere so clear, sharp'n'd his visual ray   620
To objects distant far, whereby he soon
Saw within ken a glorious Angel stand,
The same whom *John* saw also in the Sun:
His back was turn'd, but not his brightness hid;

---

mate material of the philosopher's stone or transmuting elixir."

605. *Limbec:* alembic, the distilling apparatus of the alchemists.

607. The name *Elixir*, which was the drink of the gods in Homer, was the basis of the mediaeval medical term "elixir of life," a life-prolonging substance akin to the "philosopher's stone" and so to be regarded as *Potable Gold*.

608–612. The belief that the sun's rays generate precious stones in the ground (to which *Comus*, 732–36, and *PL* VI, 479–81 refer) is used here as evidence that precious metals must abound in the sun, which glows with the virtue of the "Philosophers' Stone" and of the elixir which were thought capable of transmuting base metals into gold. So in *The Extasie* (stanza 8) Cowley describes the "*Essences of Gems*" as "Drawn forth" in the heavens by "*Chymic Angels Art.*" In *M.&S.* (pp. 29–30 and 124–27) Svendsen traces many contemporary allusions to potable gold or elixir, the Philosophers' Stone, and to gems which shine in darkness with the solar fire that is their essence — ideas all of which contribute to the contrast between the sun's purity and Satan's wickedness.

610. *Humor* is equivalent to moisture.

617–621. Satan's *visual ray* (his sight) is sharpened because no shadows fall anywhere when the sun *culminates* or reaches the meridian over the *Equator*. Though this happens only at the spring and

autumn equinoxes, Milton thought of it as happening daily before, as a result of Adam's sin, the sun was pushed "from th' Equinoctial Road" (X, 672). In an unpublished Northwestern University dissertation, "Folklore in Milton's Major Poems," E. C. Kirkland suggests that Satan's temptation of Eve at high noon (IX, 739) and of Christ at the same hour (*PR* II, 292) is connected with the ancient fear of the noonday devil (the *daemonio meridi*, as the Vulgate renders the Hebrew that is translated "the destruction that wasteth at noonday" in the King James Bible, Psalm xci, 6).

622. The *glorious Angel*, Uriel, though he is never mentioned in the Bible, is here painted like the angel whom St. John saw "standing in the sun" (Rev. xix, 17). Milton knew that, with Michael, Gabriel, and Raphael, Uriel was one of the four great archangels of Jewish tradition who ruled the four quarters of the world — Uriel's being the south. R. West, in *Milton and the Angels*, p. 208, wonders whether Milton made Uriel regent of the sun because Agrippa and Robert Fludd assigned various angels to the planets, though they did not assign Uriel to the sun. The name in Hebrew means — as *The Jewish Encyclopaedia* notes — "the fire of God," and in "medieval mysticism is represented as the source of the heat of the day in winter." Milton's "source" for Uriel was his own imagination playing on the tradition.

Of beaming sunny Rays, a golden tiar   625
Circl'd his Head, nor less his Locks behind
Illustrious on his Shoulders fledge with wings
Lay waving round; on some great charge employ'd
He seem'd, or fixt in cogitation deep.
Glad was the Spirit impure; as now in hope   630
To find who might direct his wand'ring flight
To Paradise the happy seat of Man,
His journey's end and our beginning woe.
But first he casts to change his proper shape,
Which else might work him danger or delay: 635
And now a stripling Cherub he appears,
Not of the prime, yet such as in his face
Youth smil'd Celestial, and to every Limb
Suitable grace diffus'd, so well he feign'd;
Under a Coronet his flowing hair   640
In curls on either cheek play'd, wings he wore
Of many a color'd plume sprinkl'd with Gold,
His habit fit for speed succinct, and held
Before his decent steps a Silver wand.
He drew not nigh unheard; the Angel bright,   645
Ere he drew nigh, his radiant visage turn'd,
Admonisht by his ear, and straight was known
Th' Arch-Angel *Uriel*, one of the sev'n
Who in God's presence, nearest to his Throne
Stand ready at command, and are his Eyes   650
That run through all the Heav'ns, or down to th' Earth
Bear his swift errands over moist and dry,
O'er Sea and Land: him *Satan* thus accosts.
    Uriel, for thou of those sev'n Spirits that stand
In sight of God's high Throne, gloriously bright,   655
The first art wont his great authentic will
Interpreter through highest Heav'n to bring,
Where all his Sons thy Embassy attend;
And here art likeliest by supreme decree
Like honor to obtain, and as his Eye   660
To visit oft this new Creation round;

---

625. *tiar:* tiara, crown.

648. Milton had in mind "the seven Spirits" whom St. John saw before God's throne (Rev. i, 4) and of whom Zechariah wrote (iv, 10): "The Seven are the eyes of the Lord, which run to and fro through the whole earth." In a Discourse on this text Joseph Mede, Fellow of Christ's College, Cambridge, in Milton's time, treated it as an interesting Jewish tradition symbolizing the seven great archangels by the seven-branched candlestick and — according to Josephus in *The Wars of the Jews* VI, vi — making the seven angels "the Prefects of the Seven Planets." But Uriel's name is not mentioned by Mede, who identifies only Michael, Gabriel, and Raphael as belonging to the seven prime angels. (*The Works of . . . Joseph Mede* — London, 1677 — pp. 41-42.)

658. Like the writer of Job (ii, 1), Milton calls the angels Sons of God and thinks of them as living scattered through the provinces of heaven, except on the days when they must "present themselves before the Lord."

Unspeakable desire to see, and know
All these his wondrous works, but chiefly Man,
His chief delight and favor, him for whom
All these his works so wondrous he ordain'd,   665
Hath brought me from the Choirs of Cherubim
Alone thus wand'ring. Brightest Seraph, tell
In which of all these shining Orbs hath Man
His fixed seat, or fixed seat hath none,
But all these shining Orbs his choice to dwell;   670
That I may find him, and with secret gaze,
Or open admiration him behold
On whom the great Creator hath bestow'd
Worlds, and on whom hath all these graces pour'd;
That both in him and all things, as is meet   675
The Universal Maker we may praise;
Who justly hath driv'n out his Rebel Foes
To deepest Hell, and to repair that loss
Created this new happy Race of Men
To serve him better: wise are all his ways.   680
    So spake the false dissembler unperceiv'd;
For neither Man nor Angel can discern
Hypocrisy, the only evil that walks
Invisible, except to God alone,
By his permissive will, through Heav'n and Earth: 685
And oft though wisdom wake, suspicion sleeps
At wisdom's Gate, and to simplicity
Resigns her charge, while goodness thinks no ill
Where no ill seems: Which now for once beguil'd
Uriel, though Regent of the Sun, and held   690
The sharpest-sighted Spirit of all in Heav'n;
Who to the fraudulent Impostor foul
In his uprightness answer thus return'd.
    Fair Angel, thy desire which tends to know
The works of God, thereby to glorify   695
The great Work-Master, leads to no excess
That reaches blame, but rather merits praise
The more it seems excess, that led thee hither
From thy Empyreal Mansion thus alone,
To witness with thine eyes what some perhaps   700
Contented with report hear only in Heav'n:
For wonderful indeed are all his works,
Pleasant to know, and worthiest to be all

---

685. The distinction between God's *permissive* and his active will avoids making him responsible for evil. Cf. I, 211.
696. It was a principle of Renaissance Neoplatonism (e.g. The *Heroic Madnesses* of Giordano Bruno, Part I, Dialogue ii)
that no extreme in the contemplation of God and his works could violate Aristotle's principle in the *Nicomachean Ethics* that virtue consists in avoiding extremes.
702. Several Psalms are echoed: e.g. viii and cxi, 4.

Had in remembrance always with delight;
But what created mind can comprehend   705
Thir number, or the wisdom infinite
That brought them forth, but hid thir causes deep.
I saw when at his Word the formless Mass,
This world's material mould, came to a heap:
Confusion heard his voice, and wild uproar   710
Stood rul'd, stood vast infinitude confin'd;
Till at his second bidding darkness fled,
Light shone, and order from disorder sprung:
Swift to thir several Quarters hasted then
The cumbrous Elements, Earth, Flood, Air, Fire,   715
And this Ethereal quintessence of Heav'n
Flew upward, spirited with various forms,
That roll'd orbicular, and turn'd to Stars
Numberless, as thou seest, and how they move;
Each had his place appointed, each his course,   720
The rest in circuit walls this Universe.
Look downward on that Globe whose hither side
With light from hence, though but reflected, shines:
That place is Earth the seat of Man, that light
His day, which else as th' other Hemisphere   725
Night would invade, but there the neighboring Moon
(So call that opposite fair Star) her aid
Timely interposes, and her monthly round
Still ending, still renewing through mid Heav'n,
With borrow'd light her countenance triform   730
Hence fills and empties to enlighten the Earth,
And in her pale dominion checks the night.
That spot to which I point is *Paradise*,
Adam's abode, those lofty shades his Bow'r.
Thy way thou canst not miss, me mine requires.   735

706. The word *wisdom* in Proverbs iii,
19, to which Milton alludes — "The Lord
by wisdom hath founded the earth; by
understanding hath he established the
heavens" — was sometimes interpreted
as referring to Christ, the Word by whom
the world is created in the passage in
VII, 208–21, which is anticipated here.
See the Introduction 55.

710. *Confusion* and *uproar*, like Chaos
in II, 895 and 907, are half-personified.

713–719. In l. 713 *Light* is the first of
God's creations, as it is in Genesis and in
l. 1 above. The conception of creation as
ending the war of "embryon atoms" in
Chaos (cf. II, 900, above) by the sepa-
rating out of the four elements reflects
Plato's picture of creation in the *Timaeus*
30a, as a divine transformation of dis-
order into order. That of an *Ethereal
quintessence* or fifth element, called aether,
rising from chaos to form the imperishable

substance of heaven and the stars stems
from Ovid's account of the creation (*Met.*
I, 21–27), and from Aristotle's assertion
of it as a trustworthy tradition from earli-
est times (*On the Heavens* I, iii, 270b).
In *Milton's Ontology, Cosmogony and
Physics*, p. 199, W. C. Curry traces
Milton's *Ethereal quintessence* mainly to
Lucretius' *On the Nature of Things*, V,
449–475. Cf. VII, 237–242 below.

718. The *Timaeus* (33b, 41d–e) and
the forgery known as the *Timaeus Locrus*
were responsible for the conception of the
heavenly bodies as living spirits and for
the belief that, since the most perfect
form is the sphere, their shape is spherical.

730. *triform* is a reminiscence of Ho-
race's term, the "triform goddess" (*Odes*
III, 22, 4), which implies both that the
moon has three visible phases and was
also known as three divinities, Luna,
Diana, and Hecate.

Thus said, he turn'd, and *Satan* bowing low,
As to superior Spirits is wont in Heav'n,
Where honor due and reverence none neglects,
Took leave, and toward the coast of Earth beneath,
Down from th' Ecliptic, sped with hop'd success,   740
Throws his steep flight in many an Aery wheel,
Nor stay'd, till on *Niphates*' top he lights.

The End of the Third Book.

BOOK IV

THE ARGUMENT

Satan *now in prospect of* Eden, *and nigh the place where he must now attempt the bold enterprise which he undertook alone against God and Man, falls into many doubts with himself, and many passions, fear, envy, and despair; but at length confirms himself in evil, journeys on to Paradise, whose outward prospect and situation is described, overleaps the bounds, sits in the shape of a Cormorant on the Tree of Life, as highest in the Garden to look about him. The Garden describ'd;* Satan's *first sight of* Adam *and* Eve; *his wonder at thir excellent form and happy state, but with resolution to work thir fall; overhears thir discourse, thence gathers that the Tree of Knowledge was forbidden them to eat of, under penalty of death; and thereon intends to found his Temptation, by seducing them to transgress: then leaves them a while, to know further of thir state by some other means. Meanwhile* Uriel *descending on a Sun-beam warns* Gabriel, *who had in charge the Gate of Paradise, that some evil spirit had escap'd the Deep, and past at Noon by his Sphere in the shape of a good Angel down to Paradise, discovered after by his furious gestures in the Mount.* Gabriel *promises to find him ere morning. Night coming on,* Adam *and* Eve *discourse of going to thir rest: thir Bower describ'd; thir Evening worship.* Gabriel *drawing forth his Bands of Night-watch to walk the round of Paradise, appoints two strong Angels to* Adam's *Bower, lest the evil spirit should be there doing some harm to* Adam *or* Eve *sleeping; there they find him at the ear of* Eve, *tempting her in a dream, and bring him, though unwilling, to* Gabriel; *by whom question'd, he scornfully answers, prepares resistance, but hinder'd by a Sign from Heaven, flies out of Paradise.*

O for that warning voice, which he who saw
Th' *Apocalypse*, heard cry in Heav'n aloud,
Then when the Dragon, put to second rout,
Came furious down to be reveng'd on men,
'Woe to the inhabitants on Earth!' that now,   5
While time was, our first Parents had been warn'd

---

740. Satan now plunges earthward from the *Ecliptic*, the sun's path, and the sun itself, where he has been talking with Uriel. Cf. ll. 617–21 above.

742. Mt. *Niphates* was in the Taurus range in Armenia, near Assyria, as Milton

says in IV, 126. In XI, 381, and *PR* III, 252–65, he ironically makes it the scene of Satan's vain temptation of Christ.

1–5. To make the transition to earth and the scene of man's fall Milton paraphrases St. John's prophecy of the defeat

The coming of thir secret foe, and scap'd
Haply so scap'd his mortal snare; for now
Satan, now first inflam'd with rage, came down,
The Tempter ere th' Accuser of man-kind,
To wreck on innocent frail man his loss   10
Of that first Battle, and his flight to Hell:
Yet not rejoicing in his speed, though bold,
Far off and fearless, nor with cause to boast,
Begins his dire attempt, which nigh the birth   15
Now rolling, boils in his tumultuous breast,
And like a devilish Engine back recoils
Upon himself; horror and doubt distract
His troubl'd thoughts, and from the bottom stir
The Hell within him, for within him Hell   20
He brings, and round about him, nor from Hell
One step no more than from himself can fly
By change of place: Now conscience wakes despair
That slumber'd, wakes the bitter memory
Of what he was, what is, and what must be   25
Worse; of worse deeds worse sufferings must ensue.
Sometimes towards *Eden* which now in his view
Lay pleasant, his griev'd look he fixes sad,
Sometimes towards Heav'n and the full-blazing Sun,
Which now sat high in his Meridian Tow'r: 30
Then much revolving, thus in sighs began.
    O thou that with surpassing Glory crown'd,
Look'st from thy sole Dominion like the God
Of this new World; at whose sight all the Stars

---

of the "dragon," Satan, as a defeat of the "serpent" who tempted Eve and the "accuser" who tempted Job: "And there was war in heaven: Michael and his angels fought against the dragon; and the dragon fought and his angels. . . . And the great dragon was cast out, that old serpent, called the Devil and Satan, which deceiveth the whole world: he was cast out into the earth, and his angels were cast out with him" (Rev. xii, 7–9).

17. *a devilish Engine:* a cannon. Cf. VI, 518.

20–23. The most famous of many assertions of the doctrine is by Marlowe's Mephistophelis:

Hell hath no limits, nor is circumscribed
In any one self place; for where we are is hell,
And where hell is, there must we ever be.
        (*Doctor Faustus*, ll. 553–55)

But St. Bonaventura said (*Sentences* II, d, vi, 2, 2) that "the devils carry the fire of hell wherever they go," and St. Thomas Aquinas declared (*Summa Theol.* I, q. 64,

art. 4) that they are "bound with the fire of hell while they are in the dark atmosphere of this world." Cf. I, 255, and VI, 181.

25. Cf. Francesca's cry to Dante: "No greater pain than the recollection of happiness in misery" (*Inf.* V, 121–22) — words which Dante remembered as coming from Boethius' *Consolation of Philosophy* (II, pr. iv), a passage put into Pandarus' mouth by Chaucer:

The worste kynde of infortune is this,
A man to han ben in prosperitee,
And it remembren, when it passed is.
    (*Troilus and Criseyde* III, 1626–28)

The commonplace was applied to the devils by Sir Thomas Browne in *Christian Morals* II, 10, and to the damned in hell by St. Thomas in the *Summa Theol.*, Suppl. Part. III, q. 98, art. 7.

32–39. For Edward Phillips' statement that these lines were written "several years before the poem was begun," see his Life of Milton beginning on p. 309. Their resemblance to the openings of Euripides' *Phoenissae* and Aeschylus' *Prometheus Bound* cannot have been accidental.

Hide thir diminisht heads; to thee I call,   35
But with no friendly voice, and add thy name
O Sun, to tell thee how I hate thy beams
That bring to my remembrance from what state
I fell, how glorious once above thy Sphere;
Till Pride and worse Ambition threw me down   40
Warring in Heav'n against Heav'n's matchless King:
Ah wherefore! he deserv'd no such return
From me, whom he created what I was
In that bright eminence, and with his good
Upbraided none; nor was his service hard.   45
What could be less than to afford him praise,
The easiest recompense, and pay him thanks,
How due! yet all his good prov'd ill in me,
And wrought but malice; lifted up so high
I sdein'd subjection, and thought one step higher   50
Would set me highest, and in a moment quit
The debt immense of endless gratitude,
So burdensome, still paying, still to owe;
Forgetful what from him I still receiv'd,
And understood not that a grateful mind   55
By owing owes not, but still pays, at once
Indebted and discharg'd; what burden then?
O had his powerful Destiny ordain'd
Me some inferior Angel, I had stood
Then happy; no unbounded hope had rais'd   60
Ambition. Yet why not? some other Power
As great might have aspir'd, and me though mean
Drawn to his part; but other Powers as great
Fell not, but stand unshak'n, from within
Or from without, to all temptations arm'd.   65
Hadst thou the same free Will and Power to stand?
Thou hadst: whom hast thou then or what to accuse,
But Heav'n's free Love dealt equally to all?
Be then his Love accurst, since love or hate,
To me alike, it deals eternal woe.   70
Nay curs'd be thou; since against his thy will
Chose freely what it now so justly rues.
Me miserable! which way shall I fly

40–57. Replying to a criticism that "there is no complexity or pressure of feeling in Satan's address to the Sun," Sir H. J. C. Grierson says (in *Milton and Wordsworth*, pp. 126–27) that the only rival of the passage, and its possible source, is "the speech of Claudius when he has fled from the play-scene and pours forth the agitation of his tormented conscience; and Milton's the more impressive because of the loftier character of Satan . . . and his more terrible situation."

43. Contrast Satan's declaration that the angels are "self-begot" (V, 860).

45. "God giveth to all men liberally, and upbraideth not" (James i, 5).

50. *sdein'd:* disdained.

53–54. *still:* continually.

66–72. Cf. God's statement that the devils fell "freely" (III, 102) and Raphael's insistence on the free obedience of the good angels (V, 535).

Infinite wrath, and infinite despair?
Which way I fly is Hell; myself am Hell;   75
And in the lowest deep a lower deep
Still threat'ning to devour me opens wide,
To which the Hell I suffer seems a Heav'n.
O then at last relent: is there no place
Left for Repentance, none for Pardon left?   80
None left but by submission; and that word
Disdain forbids me, and my dread of shame
Among the Spirits beneath, whom I seduc'd
With other promises and other vaunts
Than to submit, boasting I could subdue   85
Th' Omnipotent. Ay me, they little know
How dearly I abide that boast so vain,
Under what torments inwardly I groan:
While they adore me on the Throne of Hell,
With Diadem and Sceptre high advanc'd   90
The lower still I fall, only Supreme
In misery; such joy Ambition finds.
But say I could repent and could obtain
By Act of Grace my former state; how soon
Would highth recall high thoughts, how soon unsay   95
What feign'd submission swore: ease would recant
Vows made in pain, as violent and void.
For never can true reconcilement grow
Where wounds of deadly hate have pierc'd so deep:
Which would but lead me to a worse relapse,   100
And heavier fall: so should I purchase dear
Short intermission bought with double smart.
This knows my punisher; therefore as far
From granting hee, as I from begging peace:
All hope excluded thus, behold instead   105
Of us out-cast, exil'd, his new delight,
Mankind created, and for him this World.
So farewell Hope, and with Hope farewell Fear,
Farewell Remorse: all Good to me is lost;
Evil be thou my Good; by thee at least   110
Divided Empire with Heav'n's King I hold

75. Cf. I, 255, n; IX, 122–23, and especially l. 20 above.
75–77. In *Doctrine of Divorce* II, iii, Milton, arguing that even the pagans understood that sin's natural punishment was the sinner's depravity, wrote: "To banish forever into a local hell, whether in the air or in the centre, or in that uttermost and bottomless gulf of chaos, deeper from the holy bliss than the world's diameter multiplied; they thought not a punishing so proper and proportionate for God to inflict as to punish sin with sin"

(C.Ed. III, 442). See the Introduction 22.
82–86. Cf. ll. 388–92 below.
94. *Act of Grace:* formal pardon.
110. Cf. I, 165, and IX, 122–23.
111–113. *reign:* govern. The idea appears in poems on the fall of man as early as St. Avitus' *De originali peccato* (sixth century — published in 1508 and again, in his *Works*, in 1643). His Satan tells Adam and Eve that as their teacher (*magister*) he has a greater claim on them than God has as their creator.

By thee, and more than half perhaps will reign;
As Man ere long, and this new World shall know.
    Thus while he spake, each passion dimm'd his face,
Thrice chang'd with pale, ire, envy and despair,   115
Which marr'd his borrow'd visage, and betray'd
Him counterfeit, if any eye beheld.
For heav'nly minds from such distempers foul
Are ever clear. Whereof hee soon aware,
Each perturbation smooth'd with outward calm,   120
Artificer of fraud; and was the first
That practis'd falsehood under saintly show,
Deep malice to conceal, couch't with revenge:
Yet not anough had practis'd to deceive
Uriel once warn'd; whose eye pursu'd him down   125
The way he went, and on th' *Assyrian* mount
Saw him disfigur'd, more than could befall
Spirit of happy sort: his gestures fierce
He mark'd and mad demeanor, then alone,
As he suppos'd, all unobserv'd, unseen.   130
    So on he fares, and to the border comes
Of *Eden*, where delicious Paradise,
Now nearer, Crowns with her enclosure green,
As with a rural mound the champain head
Of a steep wilderness, whose hairy sides   135
With thicket overgrown, grotesque and wild,

115–120. Satan's *borrow'd visage* is that of a *stripling Cherub* (III, 636) and was ruddy or sanguine, the complexion which Timothy Bright described in his *Treatise of Melancholy* (1586), p. 97, as resulting from a "just proportion" of the spirits and humors of the body, such that they "all conspire together in due proportion" and breed "an indifferencie to all passion." It might be turned pale by a *perturbation* like anger or fear, which — as Bright noted (p. 88) — procured "a boyling of heat" about the heart that was caused by "a retraite of the bloud and certaine spirits not farre of, . . . as in feare, . . . euen from the extreme and utmost parts: whereby it gathereth great heate within. . . ."

121. *Artificer of fraud:* Satan as "father of lies." Cf. III, 683.

123. *couch't:* lying concealed.

126. *Assyrian mount:* Niphates. Cf. III, 742.

132–135. *Eden* signifies, literally, "pleasure." Somewhere to the east within its boundaries (which are drawn in ll. 210–214 below) lay the *delicious Paradise* which Sister M. Corcoran notes (*Milton's Paradise*, p. 20) got its name from the *deliciarum paradisum* of the Polyglot Bible and its echo in Purchas's "delicious Land" in the midst of a "nat-

urall Amphitheatre" amid "woodie hils" which surrounded though they did not top what Milton calls the *champaign head* (plateau) of the Garden of Eden. His synthetic details owe something to the "divine forest" of Dante's Earthly Paradise crowning the Mount of Purgatory (*Purg.* xxviii, 2), something more to Spenser's Garden of Adonis,

  With mountaines rownd about environed,
  And mightie woodes, which did the valley shade,
  And like a stately theatre it made.

(*F.Q.* III, vi, 39). Cf. *Comus*, 980–81. His main debt was to Diodorus' description of the *Nyseian Isle*, to which he refers in l. 275 below, and which — as studies by E. M. Clark and T. D. Starnes in *University of Texas Studies in English*, XXIX (1950), 138–41, and XXXI (1952), 46–50, indicate — was embroidered in Purchas's *Pilgrimage* (1613), VII, 5, and Heylyn's *Cosmography* (1657), p. 980, and reproduced in Conti's *Mythography* III, xix. Cf. ll. 281 and 544 below.

136. *grotesque:* the form is French though the word comes from Italian *grotto*, a cave. In Milton's time it referred to painting or sculpture in which foliage was prominent.

Access deni'd; and over head up grew
Insuperable highth of loftiest shade,
Cedar, and Pine, and Fir, and branching Palm,
A Silvan Scene, and as the ranks ascend   140
Shade above shade, a woody Theatre
Of stateliest view. Yet higher than thir tops
The verdurous wall of Paradise up sprung:
Which to our general Sire gave prospect large
Into his nether Empire neighboring round.   145
And higher than that Wall a circling row
Of goodliest Trees loaden with fairest Fruit,
Blossoms and Fruits at once of golden hue
Appear'd, with gay enamell'd colors mixt:
On which the Sun more glad impress'd his beams   150
Than in fair Evening Cloud, or humid Bow,
When God hath show'r'd the earth; so lovely seem'd
That Lantskip: And of pure now purer air
Meets his approach, and to the heart inspires
Vernal delight and joy, able to drive   155
All sadness but despair: now gentle gales
Fanning thir odoriferous wings dispense
Native perfumes, and whisper whence they stole
Those balmy spoils. As when to them who sail
Beyond the *Cape of Hope*, and now are past   160
Mozambic, off at Sea North-East winds blow
Sabean Odors from the spicy shore
Of *Araby* the blest, with such delay
Well pleas'd they slack thir course, and many a League
Cheer'd with the grateful smell old Ocean smiles. 165
So entertain'd those odorous sweets the Fiend
Who came thir bane, though with them better pleas'd
Than *Asmodeus* with the fishy fume,

151. *humid Bow* — the rainbow — is used in a setting like that in *Comus*, 992.
160. *Cape of Hope:* the Cape of Good Hope.
161. *Mozambic:* a province of Portuguese East Africa and its island capital. It was so fertile that "all the Armadas and Fleetes that sayle from Portugall to the Indies, if they cannot finish and performe their Voyage, will goe and Winter . . . in this Iland of Mozambique" (Samuel Purchas, *Pilgrimes* — 1625 — Part II, p. 1023).
162. *Saba*, the Sheba of the Bible, "in the Greeke tongue signifieth a secret mysterie" (Pliny, Holland's translation, XII, 14). It was in *Araby the blest* or *Arabia Felix*, the land described by Diodorus (III, xlv) as swept by winds that "waft the air from off that land, perfumed with sweet odours of myrrh and

other odoriferous plants, to the adjacent parts of the sea."
167. *bane:* harm. In Old English the word means "a murderer."
168. The interest of the time in the apocryphal Book of Tobit is illustrated by Savoldo's painting of Milton's "sociable Spirit" (V, 221) accompanying Tobias, Tobit's son, in Media. There by Raphael's advice Tobias married Sara, who had previously lost seven husbands — all of them murdered on the wedding night by her demon lover *Asmodeus*, or *Asmadai*, as he is called in VI, 365. He would have slain Tobias on the wedding night if Raphael had not instructed the youth to burn the heart and liver of a fish in his chamber. "The which smell when the evil spirit had smelled, he fled into the utmost parts of Egypt, and the angel bound him." (Tobit viii, 3.)

That drove him, though enamor'd, from the Spouse
Of *Tobit's* Son, and with a vengeance sent   170
From *Media* post to *Egypt*, there fast bound.
   Now to th' ascent of that steep savage Hill
Satan had journey'd on, pensive and slow;
But further way found none, so thick entwin'd,
As one continu'd brake, the undergrowth   175
Of shrubs and tangling bushes had perplext
All path of Man or Beast that pass'd that way:
One Gate there only was, and that look'd East
On th' other side: which when th' arch-felon saw
Due entrance he disdain'd, and in contempt   180
At one slight bound high overleap'd all bound
Of Hill or highest Wall, and sheer within
Lights on his feet. As when a prowling Wolf,
Whom hunger drives to seek new haunt for prey,
Watching where Shepherds pen thir Flocks at eve   185
In hurdl'd Cotes amid the field secure,
Leaps o'er the fence with ease into the Fold:
Or as a Thief bent to unhoard the cash
Of some rich Burgher, whose substantial doors,
Cross-barr'd and bolted fast, fear no assault,   190
In at the window climbs, or o'er the tiles:
So clomb this first grand Thief into God's Fold:
So since into his Church lewd Hirelings climb.
Thence up he flew, and on the Tree of Life,
The middle Tree and highest there that grew,   195
Sat like a Cormorant; yet not true Life
Thereby regain'd, but sat devising Death
To them who liv'd; nor on the virtue thought
Of that life-giving Plant, but only us'd
For prospect, what well us'd had been the pledge   200
Of immortality. So little knows

172. *savage* may have essentially its original sense of "woody" (from Italian *selvaggio*, Latin *silvaticum*) and may mean simply that the hill was covered with trees.

178. It was on the "east of the garden of Eden" (Gen. iii, 24) that God posted the cherubs to prevent Adam and Eve from re-entering it after their banishment.

181. The value of the pun in *bound* as the climax of the similes that transform Satan from the tragic mood of his invocation to the sun to the comic one where "he can assume the form of no more dignified bird than a cormorant," is traced by Tillyard in *Studies in Milton*, pp. 71–75.

183–193. St. John's warning against the thief climbing into the sheepfold

(x, 1) underlies the passage as clearly as it does *Lycidas*, 115.

194. "Out of the ground made the Lord God to grow every tree that is pleasant to the sight and good for food; and the tree of life also in the midst of the garden, and the tree of knowledge of good and evil" (Gen. ii, 9). Cf. ll. 218–21 below.

195–198. The *Tree* is the "tree of life in the midst of the garden" (Gen. ii, 9), whose virtue is implied in the possibility that Adam might, after his sin, "put forth his hand, and take also of the tree of life, and eat, and live forever" (Gen. iii, 22).

196. The *Cormorant* (literally, "crow of the sea") was a traditional symbol of greed and greedy men. Cf. the vulture simile in III, 431.

Any, but God alone, to value right
The good before him, but perverts best things
To worst abuse, or to thir meanest use.
Beneath him with new wonder now he views   205
To all delight of human sense expos'd
In narrow room Nature's whole wealth, yea more,
A Heaven on Earth: for blissful Paradise
Of God the Garden was, by him in the East
Of *Eden* planted; *Eden* stretch'd her Line   210
From *Auran* Eastward to the Royal Tow'rs
Of Great *Seleucia*, built by *Grecian* Kings,
Or where the Sons of *Eden* long before
Dwelt in *Telassar:* in this pleasant soil
His far more pleasant Garden God ordain'd;   215
Out of the fertile ground he caus'd to grow
All Trees of noblest kind for sight, smell, taste;
And all amid them stood the Tree of Life,
High eminent, blooming Ambrosial Fruit
Of vegetable Gold; and next to Life   220
Our Death the Tree of Knowledge grew fast by,
Knowledge of Good bought dear by knowing ill.
Southward through *Eden* went a River large,
Nor chang'd his course, but through the shaggy hill
Pass'd underneath ingulft, for God had thrown   225
That Mountain as his Garden mould high rais'd
Upon the rapid current, which through veins
Of porous Earth with kindly thirst up-drawn,
Rose a fresh Fountain, and with many a rill

210. Cf. l. 132 above. Though there was immense discussion of the situation of Eden, A. Williams finds (*Expositor*, p. 99) that "The consensus of nearly all opinion in the Renaissance . . . was that Eden, of which Paradise was a part, was somewhere between Palestine and Persia."

211. *Auran*, as Whiting notes (*Milieu* p. 50), was spelled *Haran, Charran,* or *Charrae,* and was taken by Sir Walter Raleigh to be the city or province in Mesopotamia where Abraham once lived (Gen. xi, 31).

212. Alexander's general, Seleucus, founded *Seleucia* as the seat of his Greek kingdom in western Asia on the Tigris, about fifteen miles below modern Bagdad.

214. *Telassar* is mentioned as a city of Eden in II Kings xix, 12, and Isaiah xxxvii, 12. Willem Blaeu put it on his map of Mesopotamia and described it in *Geographie Blaviane* (Amsterdam, 1667) XI, 33, as lying in the part of Upper Chaldaea called Auranite, near the Euphrates, a fact which seemed to him to prove positively that that rich region was

the biblical Eden.

218–220. The picture — as Harding notes in *Milton and the Renaissance Ovid*, p. 80 — comes both from Genesis ii, 9, and Ovid's fable of the dragon-guarded apples of the Hesperides (*Met.* x, 647–48). In the *History of the World* (1614), p. 86, Raleigh said that the dragon of the Hesperides was "taken from the Serpent, which tempted Evah: so was Paradise it selfe transported out of Asia into Africa."

222. Cf. the statement in *Areopagitica* (C.Ed. IV, 311), that "perhaps this is that doom which Adam fell into of knowing good and evil, that is to say, of knowing good by evil."

229–240. The passage rests upon the translation of the doubtful language of Genesis ii, 10, which the King James Bible renders: "A river went out of Eden to water the garden: and from thence it was parted, and became into four heads." Milton declines to mention the four rivers of Paradise, though in IX, 71, he mentions the Tigris as one of them. Their *Nectar* is a reminiscence of

Water'd the Garden; thence united fell   230
Down the steep glade, and met the nether Flood,
Which from his darksome passage now appears,
And now divided into four main Streams,
Runs diverse, wand'ring many a famous Realm
And Country whereof here needs no account,   235
But rather to tell how, if Art could tell,
How from that Sapphire Fount the crisped Brooks,
Rolling on Orient Pearl and sands of Gold,
With mazy error under pendant shades
Ran Nectar, visiting each plant, and fed   240
Flow'rs worthy of Paradise which not nice Art
In Beds and curious Knots, but Nature boon
Pour'd forth profuse on Hill and Dale and Plain,
Both where the morning Sun first warmly smote
The open field, and where the unpierc't shade   245
Imbrown'd the noontide Bow'rs: Thus was this place,
A happy rural seat of various view:
Groves whose rich Trees wept odorous Gums and Balm,
Others whose fruit burnisht with Golden Rind
Hung amiable, *Hesperian* Fables true,   250
If true, here only, and of delicious taste:
Betwixt them Lawns, or level Downs, and Flocks
Grazing the tender herb, were interpos'd,
Or palmy hillock, or the flow'ry lap
Of some irriguous Valley spread her store,   255
Flow'rs of all hue, and without Thorn the Rose:
Another side, umbrageous Grots and Caves
Of cool recess, o'er which the mantling Vine
Lays forth her purple Grape, and gently creeps
Luxuriant; meanwhile murmuring waters fall   260
Down the slope hills, disperst, or in a Lake,
That to the fringed Bank with Myrtle crown'd,
Her crystal mirror holds, unite thir streams.
The Birds thir choir apply; airs, vernal airs,
Breathing the smell of field and grove, attune   265

---

the nectar streams of Ovid's Age of Gold
(*Met.* I, 111).

239. *error* has its Latin force of "wandering." The *O.E.D.* cites Ben Jonson's *Discoveries* as calling the wanderings of Aeneas his "error by sea."

242. *boon:* liberal.

246. *Imbrown'd* has the Italian sense of "darkened" that it has in IX, 1088.

250. For the *Hesperian Fable* see ll. 218-20, n., above.

252-268. In reply to criticism of these lines and their context by F. R. Leavis and G. W. Knight as the focus of a "sensuous poverty" from which *PL* very

often suffers, J. B. Broadbent agrees — in *MP*, LI (1954), 171 — with Leavis that they lack "the sensuous richness of *Comus,*" but makes the point that "in *Paradise* the details are not so sensuously rich because sensuousness would have been out of place. These are the riches of God. *Comus* is more than sensuously rich: the subject of the speech is a degraded Epicureanism."

256. Herrick's epigram, *The Rose,* repeats the tradition that
Before man's fall the Rose was born,
St. Ambrose says, without the thorn.

The trembling leaves, while Universal *Pan*
Knit with the *Graces* and the *Hours* in dance
Led on th' Eternal Spring.   Not that fair field
Of *Enna*, where *Proserpin* gath'ring flow'rs
Herself a fairer Flow'r by gloomy *Dis*   270
Was gather'd, which cost *Ceres* all that pain
To seek her through the world; nor that sweet Grove
Of *Daphne* by *Orontes*, and th' inspir'd
Castalian Spring might with this Paradise
Of *Eden* strive; nor that *Nyseian* Isle   275
Girt with the River *Triton*, where old *Cham*,
Whom Gentiles *Ammon* call and *Lybian Jove*,
Hid *Amalthea* and her Florid Son,
Young *Bacchus*, from his Stepdame *Rhea's* eye;
Nor where *Abassin* Kings thir issue Guard,   280
Mount *Amara*, though this by some suppos'd
True Paradise under the *Ethiop* Line

266–267. The Orphic *Hymn to Pan* underlies the conception of *Universal Pan* as the god of all nature, enthroned with the *Hours*. In *Mythology* V, vi, Conti identified him with nature itself, proceeding from and created by the divine mind. Cf. the dance of "The Graces and the rosy-bosom'd Hours" in *Comus*, 986.

268. So Dante describes the Earthly Paradise on the mount of Purgatory as alive with the seminal gales of spring (*Purg.* xxviii, 106–11), and the symbolic gardens of Adonis in Spenser (cf. ll. 132–35 above) and in Drayton's *Endymion and Phoebe* are also in the background. Even the gardens of the Celtic underworld — as A. Williams notes in *Expositor*, p. 5 — "somehow became entangled with the Mount of Paradise." Cf. Milton's *Elegy V*.

269–272. It is from a landscape of perpetual spring in the Sicilian grove of *Enna* that Ovid has *Proserpina* kidnapped by *Dis* (Pluto, in *Met.* V, 385–91). The Homeric *Hymn to Demeter* describes *Ceres'* quest of her daughter for "nine days through the earth with flaming torches in her hands, nor did she once taste sweet nectar or ambrosia in her grief." The myth inspired Milton's figure in a letter to Charles Diodati in 1637: "Ceres never sought her daughter Proserpina . . . with greater ardor than I do this idea of Beauty" (C.Ed. XII, 26). Cf. Starnes & Talbert, *Dictionaries*, pp. 276–77.

273. The gardens of *Daphne* on the river *Orontes* in Syria had a temple of Apollo and a spring called after the *Castalian Spring* on Mt. Parnassus (cf. III, 30, n.). It was *inspired* because its waters traditionally gave oracles.

275–279. Nysa was an island in the *River Triton* in modern Tunis, where (according to a widely-known passage in Diodorus' *Library* III, 67) Saturn's son *Ammon*, fearing the jealousy of his wife, had his love-child by the nymph *Amalthea*, *Bacchus*, secretly brought up. As Starnes and Talbert show (*Dictionaries*, p. 237), *Ammon* was identified with the *Lybian Jove* and with Noah's son Ham or *Cham*. Milton does not identify Bacchus with Jove, as Empson supposes in *Pastoral*, p. 174, though he *may* associate them in order, as Empson says, to express "his pagan feelings about paradise" by the symbol of a "demigod of the glory and fertility of the earth."

280. *Abassin:* Abyssinian.   *issue:* children.

281–285. "In locating Mt. Amara on the equator" (the *Ethiop Line*), Clark notes ("Abyssinian Paradise," p. 144; cf. l. 132 above, n.) that "both Milton and Purchas, though wrong, were in exact accord with the best maps available up to the year of the completion of *PL*." On Ortelius' maps it is prominent; on Livio Sanuto's map (in *Geografia*, Venice, 1588) it dominates Abyssinia as the "regalis mons." Milton was also influenced by a widely-repeated story which Heylin told at length in *Cosmographie* IV, lxiv: "The hill of Amara is a day's journey high, on the top whereof are thirty-four palaces in which the younger sons of the emperor are continually enclosed to avoid sedition: . . . though not much distant from the Equator if not plainly under it, yet blessed with such a temperate air that some have taken it for the place of Paradise."

By *Nilus* head, enclos'd with shining Rock,
A whole day's journey high, but wide remote
From this *Assyrian* Garden, where the Fiend   285
Saw undelighted all delight, all kind
Of living Creatures new to sight and strange:
Two of far nobler shape erect and tall,
Godlike erect, with native Honor clad
In naked Majesty seem'd Lords of all,   290
And worthy seem'd, for in thir looks Divine
The image of thir glorious Maker shone,
Truth, Wisdom, Sanctitude severe and pure,
Severe, but in true filial freedom plac't;
Whence true autority in men; though both   295
Not equal, as thir sex not equal seem'd;
For contemplation hee and valor form'd,
For softness shee and sweet attractive Grace,
Hee for God only, shee for God in him:
His fair large Front and Eye sublime declar'd   300
Absolute rule; and Hyacinthine Locks
Round from his parted forelock manly hung
Clust'ring, but not beneath his shoulders broad:
Shee as a veil down to the slender waist
Her unadorned golden tresses wore   305
Dishevell'd, but in wanton ringlets wav'd
As the Vine curls her tendrils, which impli'd
Subjection, but requir'd with gentle sway,
And by her yielded, by him best receiv'd,
Yielded with coy submission, modest pride,   310
And sweet reluctant amorous delay.
Nor those mysterious parts were then conceal'd,
Then was not guilty shame: dishonest shame
Of Nature's works, honor dishonorable,
Sin-bred, how have ye troubl'd all mankind   315
With shows instead, mere shows of seeming pure,
And banisht from man's life his happiest life,
Simplicity and spotless innocence.
So pass'd they naked on, nor shunn'd the sight
Of God or Angel, for they thought no ill: 320

285. By making Paradise an *Assyrian Garden* Milton indicates his belief that it was in Assyria or somewhere in the Euphrates region and not in Africa.
288. Classical tradition (e.g. Ovid, *Met.* I, 82–86) stressed man's uprightness in contrast with the other creatures. Cf. VII, 506–11.
300. *sublime:* upward-looking.
301. The suggestion is of superhuman beauty such as Athene gave to Ulysses when she made him taller and mightier than ordinary men and gave him flowing

locks like the hyacinth flower (*Od.* VI, 230–32). The effect, Homer says, was like silver overlaid with gold.
303. Milton's authority is St. Paul: ". . . if a man have long hair, it is a shame unto him, But if a woman have long hair, it is a glory unto her; for her hair is given unto her for a covering" (I Cor. xi, 14–15). But Eve's coloring is like the "golden Aphrodite" of Homer (*Il.* III, 61, and many times elsewhere).
310. *coy:* shy.
313. *dishonest:* unchaste.

So hand in hand they pass'd, the loveliest pair
That ever since in love's imbraces met,
Adam the goodliest man of men since born
His Sons, the fairest of her Daughters *Eve.*
Under a tuft of shade that on a green   325
Stood whispering soft, by a fresh Fountain side
They sat them down, and after no more toil
Of thir sweet Gard'ning labor than suffic'd
To recommend cool *Zephyr*, and made ease
More easy, wholesome thirst and appetite   330
More grateful, to thir Supper Fruits they fell,
Nectarine Fruits which the compliant boughs
Yielded them, side-long as they sat recline
On the soft downy Bank damaskt with flow'rs:
The savory pulp they chew, and in the rind   335
Still as they thirsted scoop the brimming stream;
Nor gentle purpose, nor endearing smiles
Wanted, nor youthful dalliance as beseems
Fair couple, linkt in happy nuptial League,
Alone as they. About them frisking play'd   340
All Beasts of th' Earth, since wild, and of all chase
In Wood or Wilderness, Forest or Den;
Sporting the Lion ramp'd, and in his paw
Dandl'd the Kid; Bears, Tigers, Ounces, Pards
Gamboll'd before them, th' unwieldy Elephant   345
To make them mirth us'd all his might, and wreath'd
His Lithe Proboscis; close the Serpent sly
Insinuating, wove with Gordian twine
His braided train, and of his fatal guile
Gave proof unheeded; others on the grass   350
Coucht, and now fill'd with pasture gazing sat,
Or Bedward ruminating; for the Sun
Declin'd was hasting now with prone career

329. *Zephyr:* the west wind, which Homer says refreshed the Elysian Fields (*Od.* IV, 567). Cf. *L'All*, 19, and *El V*, 69.
333. *recline:* reclining.
334. *damask:* richly figured, like silks from Damascus.
337. *purpose:* conversation. So Spenser says that Una and the Red Cross Knight sit together in her father's palace and "fitting purpose frame" (*F.Q.* I, xii, 13, 9).
388. *Wanted:* were lacking.
340–352. Biblical illustrators liked to represent the friendly animals around Adam and Eve in Eden in the spirit of their description in popular poems like Samuel Pordage's *Mundorum explicatio* (1663):

ADAM is Lord, and King: each animal
Comes at his beck, and doth obey his call;
All bow their lofty heads if he come near,
The Hart, nor timerous Hare his presence fear:
The shaggy Lion, Bear, the Bull, the Bore
Couch at his feet, him as their God adore.
(pp. 58–59) Cf. *PL* VIII, 345–54, n.
344. *Ounces:* lynxes.
348. *Insinuating:* coiling. *Gordian twine:* tangle like the Gordian knot which Alexander the Great cut. Cf. IX, 436.
352. *Bedward ruminating:* chewing the cud on the way to bed.

To th' Ocean Isles, and in th' ascending Scale
Of Heav'n the Stars that usher Evening rose: 355
When *Satan* still in gaze, as first he stood,
Scarce thus at length fail'd speech recover'd sad.
    O Hell! what do mine eyes with grief behold,
Into our room of bliss thus high advanc't
Creatures of other mould, earth-born perhaps,   360
Not Spirits, yet to heav'nly Spirits bright
Little inferior; whom my thoughts pursue
With wonder, and could love, so lively shines
In them Divine resemblance, and such grace
The hand that form'd them on thir shape hath pour'd.   365
Ah gentle pair, yee little think how nigh
Your change approaches, when all these delights
Will vanish and deliver ye to woe,
More woe, the more your taste is now of joy;
Happy, but for so happy ill secur'd   370
Long to continue, and this high seat your Heav'n
Ill fenc't for Heav'n to keep out such a foe
As now is enter'd; yet no purpos'd foe
To you whom I could pity thus forlorn
Though I unpitied: League with you I seek,   375
And mutual amity so strait, so close,
That I with you must dwell, or you with me
Henceforth; my dwelling haply may not please
Like this fair Paradise, your sense, yet such
Accept your Maker's work; he gave it me,   380
Which I as freely give; Hell shall unfold,
To entertain you two, her widest Gates,
And send forth all her Kings; there will be room,
Not like these narrow limits, to receive
Your numerous offspring; if no better place,   385
Thank him who puts me loath to this revenge
On you who wrong me not for him who wrong'd.
And should I at your harmless innocence
Melt, as I do, yet public reason just,

354. *Ocean Isles:* the Azores, as l. 592
below indicates.
359. Cf. the reference to the *vacant
room* of the fallen angels in VII, 190.
362. Satan paraphrases Psalm viii, 5,
which says that God has made man "a
little lower than the angels."
375. *Though I unpitied:* though Satan
is beyond God's pity, he feels an impulse
to pity Adam and Eve.
376. *strait:* close, intimate.
382. The lines echo Isaiah xiv, 9:
"Hell from beneath is moved for thee to
meet thee at thy coming; . . . it hath
raised up from their thrones all the kings
of the nations."
389. *public reason:* reason of state, a

perversion of the Ciceronian principle
(*Laws* III, iii, 8) that the good of the
people is the supreme law. In *The
Contra-Replicant* (1643, p. 19) Henry
Parker approved its use by Parliament
and condemned the Royalists for too
frequent appeals to it. In the *Advance-
ment* I, ii, 3 (edited by William Aldis
Wright, Oxford, 1900), Bacon recalled
that its abuse in Italy under the name
ragione di stato had been condemned by
Pius V as an invention "against religion
and the moral virtues." In *Adamo ca-
duto* V, ii, Salandra has Satan tell the
devils that they are going to corrupt
mankind by inventing *ragione di stato*.

Honor and Empire with revenge enlarg'd,   390
By conquering this new World, compels me now
To do what else though damn'd I should abhor.
  So spake the Fiend, and with necessity,
The Tyrant's plea, excus'd his devilish deeds.
Then from his lofty stand on that high Tree   395
Down he alights among the sportful Herd
Of those fourfooted kinds, himself now one,
Now other, as thir shape serv'd best his end
Nearer to view his prey, and unespi'd
To mark what of thir state he more might learn   400
By word or action markt: about them round
A Lion now he stalks with fiery glare,
Then as a Tiger, who by chance hath spi'd
In some Purlieu two gentle Fawns at play,
Straight couches close, then rising changes oft   405
His couchant watch, as one who chose his ground
Whence rushing he might surest seize them both
Gript in each paw: when *Adam* first of men
To first of women *Eve* thus moving speech,
Turn'd him all ear to hear new utterance flow.   410
  Sole partner and sole part of all these joys,
Dearer thyself than all; needs must the Power
That made us, and for us this ample World
Be infinitely good, and of his good
As liberal and free as infinite,   415
That rais'd us from the dust and plac't us here
In all this happiness, who at his hand
Have nothing merited, nor can perform
Aught whereof hee hath need, hee who requires
From us no other service than to keep   420
This one, this easy charge, of all the Trees
In Paradise that bear delicious fruit
So various, not to taste that only Tree
Of Knowledge, planted by the Tree of Life,
So near grows Death to Life, whate'er Death is,   425

---

398. *end:* object, purpose.
404. *Purlieu:* border tract around a wood.
402–408. So in Du Bartas' *Divine Weeks*, "a mischiefe to effect," Satan

Thinks now the beauty of a Horse to
  borrow;
Anon to creep into a Haifer's side,
Then in a Cock, or in a Dog to hide;
Then in a nimble Hart himself to
  shroud;
Then in the starr'd plumes of a Pea-
  cock proud.
  (Kirkconnell, *Cycle*, p. 67)
410. *him* may refer to Satan, who is *all ear* to catch what Adam will say, or

to Adam, who is eager to draw a reply from Eve.
  419–428. In the *Commentarius de para-diso* of the Syriac bishop Moses Bar-Cepha, which was published in Latin in Antwerp in 1569, Grant McColley found a parallel for Milton's episode and especially for Satan's picking up of Adam's "words to his wife concerning the precept" against the Tree of Knowledge (*Paradise Lost*, p. 155). The traditional situation finds its most ridiculous parallel in Salandra's scene with Lucifer, Belial, and Behemoth all eavesdropping in Eden (*Adamo caduto* I, vii; Kirkconnell, *Cycle*, p. 306).

Some dreadful thing no doubt; for well thou know'st
God hath pronounc't it death to taste that Tree,
The only sign of our obedience left
Among so many signs of power and rule
Conferr'd upon us, and Dominion giv'n   430
Over all other Creatures that possess
Earth, Air, and Sea.   Then let us not think hard
One easy prohibition, who enjoy
Free leave so large to all things else, and choice
Unlimited of manifold delights: 435
But let us ever praise him, and extol
His bounty, following our delightful task
To prune these growing Plants, and tend these Flow'rs,
Which were it toilsome, yet with thee were sweet.
   To whom thus *Eve* repli'd.   O thou for whom   440
And from whom I was form'd flesh of thy flesh,
And without whom am to no end, my Guide
And Head, what thou hast said is just and right.
For wee to him indeed all praises owe,
And daily thanks, I chiefly who enjoy   445
So far the happier Lot, enjoying thee
Preëminent by so much odds, while thou
Like consort to thyself canst nowhere find.
That day I oft remember, when from sleep
I first awak't, and found myself repos'd   450
Under a shade on flow'rs, much wond'ring where
And what I was, whence thither brought, and how.
Not distant far from thence a murmuring sound
Of waters issu'd from a Cave and spread
Into a liquid Plain, then stood unmov'd   455
Pure as th' expanse of Heav'n; I thither went
With unexperienc't thought, and laid me down
On the green bank, to look into the clear
Smooth Lake, that to me seem'd another Sky.
As I bent down to look, just opposite,   460
A Shape within the wat'ry gleam appear'd
Bending to look on me, I started back,
It started back, but pleas'd I soon return'd,
Pleas'd it return'd as soon with answering looks
Of sympathy and love; there I had fixt   465
Mine eyes till now, and pin'd with vain desire,
Had not a voice thus warn'd me, What thou seest,

---

430. Cf. God's words of man at crea-
tion: "Let us make man in our image,
. . . and let him have dominion over the
fish of the sea, and over the fowl of
the air, and over the cattle, and over all
the earth" (Gen. i, 26).
   443. Cf. St. Paul's words: "The head

of the woman is the man" (I Cor. xi, 3).
   461. So Ovid describes Narcissus lying
beside a pool, fascinated by his reflection,
but pining away because he never learns
that what he sees and loves is himself
(*Met.* III, 402–510).

What there thou seest fair Creature is thyself,
With thee it came and goes; but follow me,
And I will bring thee where no shadow stays   470
Thy coming, and thy soft imbraces, hee
Whose image thou art, him thou shalt enjoy
Inseparably thine, to him shalt bear
Multitudes like thyself, and thence be call'd
Mother of human Race: what could I do,   475
But follow straight, invisibly thus led?
Till I espi'd thee, fair indeed and tall,
Under a Platan, yet methought less fair,
Less winning soft, less amiably mild,
Than that smooth wat'ry image; back I turn'd,   480
Thou following cri'd'st aloud, Return fair *Eve*,
Whom fli'st thou? whom thou fli'st, of him thou art,
His flesh, his bone; to give thee being I lent
Out of my side to thee, nearest my heart
Substantial Life, to have thee by my side   485
Henceforth an individual solace dear;
Part of my Soul I seek thee, and thee claim
My other half: with that thy gentle hand
Seiz'd mine, I yielded, and from that time see
How beauty is excell'd by manly grace   490
And wisdom, which alone is truly fair.
    So spake our general Mother, and with eyes
Of conjugal attraction unreprov'd,
And meek surrender, half imbracing lean'd
On our first Father, half her swelling Breast   495
Naked met his under the flowing Gold
Of her loose tresses hid: hee in delight
Both of her Beauty and submissive Charms
Smil'd with superior Love, as *Jupiter*
On *Juno* smiles, when he impregns the Clouds   500
That shed *May* Flowers; and press'd her Matron lip
With kisses pure: aside the Devil turn'd
For envy, yet with jealous leer malign
Ey'd them askance, and to himself thus plain'd.
    Sight hateful, sight tormenting! thus these two   505
Imparadis't in one another's arms
The happier *Eden*, shall enjoy thir fill

---

470. *stays:* waits for.
475. XI, 168–72, explains that Eve
means mother of life.
478. *Platan:* plane tree. *methought:*
it seemed to me.
483. The line paraphrases Adam's
words after Eve's creation in Genesis ii,
23.
486. *individual* keeps its Latin mean-
ing of "inseparable."

493. *unreprov'd:* unreprovable, inno-
cent. Cf. *L'All,* 40, and *unremov'd* in
l. 987 below.
499–500. Traditionally, *Jupiter* (as
the name literally indicates) was "Lord
of the sky," and "*Juno*, of the ayre"
(*F.Q.* VII, vii, 26).
502–504. Satan's envy of the love of
Adam and Eve was traditional. The
devils knew desire but not love.

Of bliss on bliss, while I to Hell am thrust,
Where neither joy nor love, but fierce desire,
Among our other torments not the least,　　510
Still unfulfill'd with pain of longing pines;
Yet let me not forget what I have gain'd
From thir own mouths; all is not theirs it seems:
One fatal Tree there stands of Knowledge call'd,
Forbidden them to taste: Knowledge forbidd'n?　　515
Suspicious, reasonless. Why should thir Lord
Envy them that? can it be sin to know,
Can it be death? and do they only stand
By Ignorance, is that thir happy state,
The proof of thir obedience and thir faith?　　520
O fair foundation laid whereon to build
Thir ruin! Hence I will excite thir minds
With more desire to know, and to reject
Envious commands, invented with design
To keep them low whom Knowledge might exalt　　525
Equal with Gods; aspiring to be such,
They taste and die: what likelier can ensue?
But first with narrow search I must walk round
This Garden, and no corner leave unspi'd;
A chance but chance may lead where I may meet　　530
Some wand'ring Spirit of Heav'n, by Fountain side,
Or in thick shade retir'd, from him to draw
What further would be learnt. Live while ye may,
Yet happy pair; enjoy, till I return,
Short pleasures, for long woes are to succeed.　　535
　　So saying, his proud step he scornful turn'd,
But with sly circumspection, and began
Through wood, through waste, o'er hill, o'er dale his roam.
Meanwhile in utmost Longitude, where Heav'n
With Earth and Ocean meets, the setting Sun　　540
Slowly descended, and with right aspect
Against the eastern Gate of Paradise
Levell'd his ev'ning Rays: it was a Rock
Of Alablaster, pil'd up to the Clouds,

511. *pines:* makes (me) pine.
526. Cf. IX, 547–48.
539. *utmost Longitude:* farthest west.
541. *right aspect:* direct view. The setting sun shines straight upon the inner side of the eastern gate of Paradise.
544–548. *Alablaster* (modern "alabaster") is defined in Cockeram's *English Dictionarie* (1623) as "a very cold Marble, white and clear." The picture of the *Rock* may — as Clark thinks ("Abyssinian Paradise," p. 146) — be due to Purchas's account of Mt. Amara as seeming "to him that stands beneath, like a high wall, whereon the heaven is as it were propped" — at the top, "overhanged with rocks, jutting forth of the sides the space of a mile, bearing out like mushromes, so that it is impossible to ascend it" except at "the ascending place, a faire gate." But such descriptions go back to stories in Diodorus like that (in *Library* III, 69) of the central African crag overlooking the cave where the infant Bacchus was nursed — "a crag of immense height, formed of parti-colored rocks . . . in bands sending forth a bright lustre, some like sea-purple, some

Conspicuous far, winding with one ascent 545
Accessible from Earth, one entrance high;
The rest was craggy cliff, that overhung
Still as it rose, impossible to climb.
Betwixt these rocky Pillars *Gabriel* sat
Chief of th' Angelic Guards, awaiting night; 550
About him exercis'd Heroic Games
Th' unarmed Youth of Heav'n, but nigh at hand
Celestial Armory, Shields, Helms, and Spears
Hung high with Diamond flaming, and with Gold.
Thither came *Uriel*, gliding through the Even 555
On a Sun-beam, swift as a shooting Star
In *Autumn* thwarts the night, when vapors fir'd
Impress the Air, and shows the Mariner
From what point of his Compass to beware
Impetuous winds: he thus began in haste. 560
   Gabriel, to thee thy course by Lot hath giv'n
Charge and strict watch that to this happy place
No evil thing approach or enter in;
This day at highth of Noon came to my Sphere
A Spirit, zealous, as he seem'd, to know 565
More of th' Almighty's works, and chiefly Man
God's latest Image: I describ'd his way
Bent all on speed, and markt his Aery Gait;
But in the Mount that lies from *Eden* North,
Where he first lighted, soon discern'd his looks 570
Alien from Heav'n, with passions foul obscur'd:
Mine eye pursu'd him still, but under shade
Lost sight of him; one of the banisht crew
I fear, hath ventur'd from the Deep, to raise
New troubles; him thy care must be to find. 575
   To whom the winged Warrior thus return'd:
Uriel, no wonder if thy perfect sight,
Amid the Sun's bright circle where thou sitst,
See far and wide: in at this Gate none pass
The vigilance here plac't, but such as come 580
Well known from Heav'n; and since Meridian hour
No Creature thence: if Spirit of other sort,
So minded, have o'erleapt these earthy bounds
On purpose, hard thou know'st it to exclude

---

bluish, and others of every brilliant hue. . . . Before the entrance grow marvellous trees, some fruit-bearing, others evergreen, and all fashioned by nature to delight the eye." Cf. ll 281–85.
   549. Though none of the scriptural references to Gabriel (Dan. viii, 16; ix, 21; and Luke i, 19) implies his guardianship of Paradise, tradition had made him (with Michael and Raphael)

one of the three protecting angels to whom "the Catholic church sanctioned prayer by name" (West, *Milton and the Angels*, p. 62). See the Introduction 21.
   557. *thwarts*: flies across. *vapors fir'd*: "heat-lightning."
   567. *God's latest Image*: man. The first was the Son, cf. III, 63 and 384.
   580. *vigilance*: the abstract word is put for the vigilant Gabriel himself.

Spiritual substance with corporeal bar.　　　　　　585
But if within the circuit of these walks
In whatsoever shape he lurk, of whom
Thou tell'st, by morrow dawning I shall know.
　So promis'd hee, and *Uriel* to his charge
Return'd on that bright beam, whose point now rais'd　590
Bore him slope downward to the Sun now fall'n
Beneath th' *Azores;* whither the prime Orb,
Incredible how swift, had thither roll'd
Diurnal, or this less volubil Earth
By shorter flight to th' East, had left him there　　595
Arraying with reflected Purple and Gold
The Clouds that on his Western Throne attend:
Now came still Ev'ning on, and Twilight gray
Had in her sober Livery all things clad;
Silence accompanied, for Beast and Bird,　　　　600
They to thir grassy Couch, these to thir Nests
Were slunk, all but the wakeful Nightingale;
She all night long her amorous descant sung;
Silence was pleas'd: now glow'd the Firmament
With living Sapphires: *Hesperus* that led　　　　605
The starry Host, rode brightest, till the Moon
Rising in clouded Majesty, at length
Apparent Queen unveil'd her peerless light,
And o'er the dark her Silver Mantle threw.
　When *Adam* thus to *Eve:* Fair Consort, th' hour　610
Of night, and all things now retir'd to rest
Mind us of like repose, since God hath set
Labor and rest, as day and night to men
Successive, and the timely dew of sleep
Now falling with soft slumbrous weight inclines　615
Our eye-lids; other Creatures all day long
Rove idle unimploy'd, and less need rest;
Man hath his daily work of body or mind
Appointed, which declares his Dignity,
And the regard of Heav'n on all his ways;　　　620
While other Animals unactive range,

585. Cf. I, 423–31, n.
591. *Uriel* slides *down* the sunbeam to the sun, which is now below the horizon, and therefore, in a Ptolemaic universe, *lower* than the earth.
592. Cf. the Azores in l. 354 above. *prime Orb:* the sun.
593. Milton shared Donne's wonder (though perhaps not his faith) that "so vast and immense a body as the Sun, should run so many miles, in a minute" (Sermon at St. Paul's, Easter, 1627. *Sermons,* ed. Simpson and Potter, VII, 374). He seems impartial about the

alternative — the rotation of the *volubil* (turning) earth. Cf. 661–64 below, and VIII, 25–38.
603. *descant:* a warbled song. It was often used of birds' singing.
604. Cf. *Silence,* enchanted by the Lady's music in *Comus,* 557–60, and in *Il Penseroso,* 55–56, "the mute Silence" to be broken only by the nightingale's song.
605. *Hesperus:* the evening star. Cf. IX, 49.
608. *Apparent Queen:* manifest or visible queen.

And of thir doings God takes no account.
Tomorrow ere fresh Morning streak the East
With first approach of light, we must be ris'n,
And at our pleasant labor, to reform   625
Yon flow'ry Arbors, yonder Alleys green,
Our walk at noon, with branches overgrown,
That mock our scant manuring, and require
More hands than ours to lop thir wanton growth:
Those Blossoms also, and those dropping Gums,   630
That lie bestrown unsightly and unsmooth,
Ask riddance, if we mean to tread with ease;
Meanwhile, as Nature wills, Night bids us rest.
  To whom thus *Eve* with perfect beauty adorn'd.
My Author and Disposer, what thou bidd'st   635
Unargu'd I obey; so God ordains,
God is thy Law, thou mine: to know no more
Is woman's happiest knowledge and her praise.
With thee conversing I forget all time,
All seasons and thir change, all please alike.   640
Sweet is the breath of morn, her rising sweet,
With charm of earliest Birds; pleasant the Sun
When first on this delightful Land he spreads
His orient Beams, on herb, tree, fruit, and flow'r,
Glist'ring with dew; fragrant the fertile earth   645
After soft showers; and sweet the coming on
Of grateful Ev'ning mild, then silent Night
With this her solemn Bird and this fair Moon,
And these the Gems of Heav'n, her starry train:
But neither breath of Morn when she ascends   650
With charm of earliest Birds, nor rising Sun
On this delightful land, nor herb, fruit, flow'r,
Glist'ring with dew, nor fragrance after showers,
Nor grateful Ev'ning mild, nor silent Night
With this her solemn Bird, nor walk by Moon,   655
Or glittering Star-light without thee is sweet.
But wherefore all night long shine these, for whom
This glorious sight, when sleep hath shut all eyes?
  To whom our general Ancestor repli'd.

623–633. Williams notes — *Expositor*, p. 110 — that Milton declined to follow St. Augustine in the view that Adam lived the purely contemplative rather than the active life in Paradise; and he quotes Donne's *Sermon XIX* (*Works* I, 372): "Adam was not put into Paradise, only in that Paradise to contemplate the future Paradise, but to dress and keep the present."

628. *manuring* has its Latin meaning of "working with the hands," i.e. "cultivating."

635. Eve's formal titles for Adam and his for her (as in l. 660) are traced to complimentary titles of Homer's heroes for one another, but before Adam's sin they have an aptness which — as M. Barstow notes in "Milton's Use of the Forms of Epic Address," in *MLN*, XXXI (1916), 121 — is lost afterwards; and in Books IX to XII Adam and Eve do not use them.

640. *seasons:* times, periods in the day.

642. *charm:* song (the etymological meaning of the word). It is used in this sense in *PR* IV, 257.

Daughter of God and Man, accomplisht *Eve*,   660
Those have thir course to finish, round the Earth,
By morrow Ev'ning, and from Land to Land
In order, though to Nations yet unborn,
Minist'ring light prepar'd, they set and rise;
Lest total darkness should by Night regain   665
Her old possession, and extinguish life
In Nature and all things, which these soft fires
Not only enlighten, but with kindly heat
Of various influence foment and warm,
Temper or nourish, or in part shed down   670
Thir stellar virtue on all kinds that grow
On Earth, made hereby apter to receive
Perfection from the Sun's more potent Ray.
These then, though unbeheld in deep of night,
Shine not in vain, nor think, though men were none,   675
That Heav'n would want spectators, God want praise;
Millions of spiritual Creatures walk the Earth
Unseen, both when we wake, and when we sleep:
All these with ceaseless praise his works behold
Both day and night: how often from the steep   680
Of echoing Hill or Thicket have we heard
Celestial voices to the midnight air,
Sole, or responsive each to other's note
Singing thir great Creator: oft in bands
While they keep watch, or nightly rounding walk,   685
With Heav'nly touch of instrumental sounds
In full harmonic number join'd, thir songs
Divide the night, and lift our thoughts to Heaven.
    Thus talking hand in hand alone they pass'd
On to thir blissful Bower; it was a place   690
Chos'n by the sovran Planter, when he fram'd
All things to man's delightful use; the roof
Of thickest covert was inwoven shade
Laurel and Myrtle, and what higher grew
Of firm and fragrant leaf; on either side   695
Acanthus, and each odorous bushy shrub
Fenc'd up the verdant wall; each beauteous flow'r,
Iris all hues, Roses, and Jessamin
Rear'd high thir flourisht heads between, and wrought

660. *accomplisht:* full of accomplishments. Cf. Samson's ironical description of Dalila as his "accomplisht snare." (*SA,* 230.)
    668. *kindly:* natural.
    667–673. Cf. the theory that the sun's ray is all-potent in III, 606–12, and the transformation of the stars' influence into something *malign* in X, 657–67. Cf. also VII, 171, and VIII, 150.
    674–688. The angelic singers seem like

the Muses in Hesiod's *Theogony,* 3–21 and 35–52, who sing the greatness of their father Zeus, the earth and heaven, in ceaseless concert as they mount the cloudy slope of Olympus in the darkness.
    688. *Divide the night:* break it up into watches that the Roman soldiers marked off by trumpet calls.
    699. *flourish:* flower-laden, or adorned with flowers.

Mosaic; underfoot the Violet,   700
Crocus, and Hyacinth with rich inlay
Broider'd the ground, more color'd than with stone
Of costliest Emblem: other Creature here
Beast, Bird, Insect, or Worm durst enter none;
Such was thir awe of Man. In shadier Bower   705
More sacred and sequester'd, though but feign'd,
Pan or *Silvanus* never slept, nor Nymph,
Nor *Faunus* haunted. Here in close recess
With Flowers, Garlands, and sweet-smelling Herbs
Espoused *Eve* deckt first her Nuptial Bed,   710
And heav'nly Choirs the Hymenæn sung,
What day the genial Angel to our Sire
Brought her in naked beauty more adorn'd,
More lovely than *Pandora*, whom the Gods
Endow'd with all thir gifts, and O too like   715
In sad event, when to the unwiser Son
Of *Japhet* brought by *Hermes*, she ensnar'd
Mankind with her fair looks, to be aveng'd
On him who had stole *Jove's* authentic fire.

Thus at thir shady Lodge arriv'd, both stood,   720
Both turn'd, and under op'n Sky ador'd
The God that made both Sky, Air, Earth and Heav'n
Which they beheld, the Moon's resplendent Globe
And starry Pole: Thou also mad'st the Night,
Maker Omnipotent, and thou the Day,   725
Which we in our appointed work imploy'd
Have finisht happy in our mutual help
And mutual love, the Crown of all our bliss
Ordain'd by thee, and this delicious place
For us too large, where thy abundance wants   730

702. *stone Of costliest Emblem:* stone inlaid with precious metal.

706. *feign'd* — in the sense that "the truest poetry is the most feigning" (*As You Like It* III, iii, 21–22) — implies that myths of *Pan, Sylvanus,* and *Faunus,* were pagan fabrications. Cf. l. 266 above, n.

708. *close:* secret.

711. *Hymenæan:* marriage song.

712. *genial:* nuptial. The term becomes a kind of title for the angel presiding over the union of Adam and Eve.

714–719. *Pandora* was given by *Hermes* to Epimetheus (After-thought), *unwiser* than his brother Prometheus (Forethought), whose theft of fire from heaven made men the gods resented. Epimetheus married her and opened the casket that the gods sent with her, but found it full of all life's ills. "Plato and Chrysippus," Milton wrote in *Doctrine of Divorce* II, iii (C.Ed. III, 441), "knew

not what a consummate and most adorned Pandora was bestowed upon Adam, to be the nurse . . . of his native innocence and perfection, which might have kept him from being our true Epimetheus." The brothers were sons of the Titan Iapetos, who was sometimes identified with Noah's son *Japhet* (Gen. ix, 27; x, 1), the father of Javan, the founder of the Greek race, who is mentioned in I, 508.

724. *Pole* stands here for the entire sky, as it does in *Comus*, 99.

724–735. The passage has much in common with Psalm lxxiv, 16: "The day is thine, and the night is thine," and Psalm cxxvii, 2: "he giveth his beloved sleep"; but the *gift of sleep* is often mentioned in Homer and Virgil in passages like Aeneas' reference to the quiet of evening coming to bring the most welcome gift of the gods (*Aen.* II, 269).

Partakers, and uncropt falls to the ground.
But thou hast promis'd from us two a Race
To fill the Earth, who shall with us extol
Thy goodness infinite, both when we wake,
And when we seek, as now, thy gift of sleep.   735
    This said unanimous, and other Rites
Observing none, but adoration pure
Which God likes best, into thir inmost bower
Handed they went; and eas'd the putting off
These troublesome disguises which wee wear,   740
Straight side by side were laid, nor turn'd I ween
Adam from his fair Spouse, nor *Eve* the Rites
Mysterious of connubial Love refus'd:
Whatever Hypocrites austerely talk
Of purity and place and innocence,   745
Defaming as impure what God declares
Pure, and commands to some, leaves free to all.
Our Maker bids increase, who bids abstain
But our Destroyer, foe to God and Man?
Hail wedded Love, mysterious Law, true source   750
Of human offspring, sole propriety
In Paradise of all things common else.
By thee adulterous lust was driv'n from men
Among the bestial herds to range, by thee
Founded in Reason, Loyal, Just, and Pure,   755
Relations dear, and all the Charities
Of Father, Son, and Brother first were known.
Far be it, that I should write thee sin or blame,
Or think thee unbefitting holiest place,
Perpetual Fountain of Domestic sweets,   760
Whose bed is undefil'd and chaste pronounc't,
Present, or past, as Saints and Patriarchs us'd.
Here Love his golden shafts imploys, here lights

---

743. So Milton justifies the "intelligible flame," not "in Paradise to be resisted," in *Divorce* I, iv (C.Ed. III, 397). He calls it *mysterious* because St. Paul calls marriage "a great mystery" (Ephes. v, 32), and in *Colasterion* (C.Ed. IV, 263) he rebuts an objection to his description of marriage as "a mystery of joy." Hexameral literature was full of eulogies of marriage, a fair example of which is a speech of Joseph to Potiphar in Joseph Beaumont's *Psyche* I, 203–06:

    Except the venerable Temples, what
        Place is more reverend than the Nuptial Bed?
    Nay, heav'n has made a Temple too
        of that
    For Chastitie's most secret rites . . .

744. On this controversial point Milton took the established Protestant position that was stated by John Salkeld in *A Treatise of Paradise* (1617), pp. 178–79, when he rejected the opinion of "Gregory Nisene, Damascene, Chrysostome, Procopius, Gazeus, and divers others, . . . that if *Adam* had not sinned, there should have been no such naturall generation of mankinde, as is now." But C. S. Lewis notes — *Allegory of Love* (1935), p. 15 — that Albertus Magnus also swept away "the idea that the pleasure is evil and the result of the Fall," declaring that it "would have been greater if we had remained in Paradise."

748. Cf. "Be fruitful, and multiply, and replenish the earth" (Gen. i, 28).

763. So Ovid describes Cupid with an arrow of gold, inspiring love, and another of lead, which banished it (*Met.* I, 468).

His constant Lamp, and waves his purple wings,
Reigns here and revels; not in the bought smile   765
Of Harlots, loveless, joyless, unindear'd,
Casual fruition, nor in Court Amours,
Mixt Dance, or wanton Mask, or Midnight Ball,
Or Serenate, which the starv'd Lover sings
To his proud fair, best quitted with disdain.   770
These lull'd by Nightingales imbracing slept,
And on thir naked limbs the flow'ry roof
Show'rd Roses, which the Morn repair'd. Sleep on,
Blest pair; and O yet happiest if ye seek
No happier state, and know to know no more.   775
    Now had night measur'd with her shadowy Cone
Half way up Hill this vast Sublunar Vault,
And from thir Ivory Port the Cherubim
Forth issuing at th' accustom'd hour stood arm'd
To thir night watches in warlike Parade,   780
When *Gabriel* to his next in power thus spake.
    Uzziel, half these draw off, and coast the South
With strictest watch; these other wheel the North;
Our circuit meets full West. As flame they part
Half wheeling to the Shield, half to the Spear.   785
From these, two strong and subtle Spirits he call'd
That near him stood, and gave them thus in charge.
    Ithuriel and *Zephon*, with wing'd speed
Search through this Garden, leave unsearcht no nook,
But chiefly where those two fair Creatures Lodge,   790
Now laid perhaps asleep secure of harm.
This Ev'ning from the Sun's decline arriv'd
Who tells of some infernal Spirit seen
Hitherward bent (who could have thought?) escap'd
The bars of Hell, on errand bad no doubt: 795
Such where ye find, seize fast, and hither bring.
    So saying, on he led his radiant Files,
Dazzling the Moon; these to the Bower direct

768. Cf. Milton's attack on the bishops for encouraging "gaming, jigging, wassailing, and mixed dancing" in *Of Reformation* (C.Ed. III, 53).

773. *repair'd:* supplied the loss (with fresh roses).

775. *know to know no more:* be wise enough to seek no more knowledge (i.e. of good and evil). Cf. VII, 120.

776–777. The cone of the earth's shadow, cast by the sun below the horizon at an angle of 45°, indicates that it is nine o'clock. When the point of the cone reaches the zenith, it will be midnight.

782. *Uzziel* occurs in the Bible only as a human name, literally meaning "strength of God" (Exod. vi, 18, and Num. iii, 19). West notes — *Milton and the Angels*, p. 154 — that it occurs in "the *Sepher Raziel*, for instance, and in several other mystical and Cabalistic works." The ordonnance of the lines — as Whaler notes (*Counterpoint*, pp. 76–79) — matches the complete circle to be made by the angels on their rounds.

788. *Ithuriel* ("discovery of God") does not occur in the Bible, and *Zephon* ("searcher") occurs only as a human name (Num. xxvi, 15). West (p. 155) spots a Baal-Zephon among the many local Baals (cf. I, 422, n.), but surmises that "perhaps Milton knew somewhere in the literature of angelology of a Zephon that was a good angel. Or perhaps he did not, and cared very little."

In search of whom they sought: him there they found
Squat like a Toad, close at the ear of *Eve;*   800
Assaying by his Devilish art to reach
The Organs of her Fancy, and with them forge
Illusions as he list, Phantasms and Dreams,
Or if, inspiring venom, he might taint
Th' animal spirits that from pure blood arise   805
Like gentle breaths from Rivers pure, thence raise
At least distemper'd, discontented thoughts,
Vain hopes, vain aims, inordinate desires
Blown up with high conceits ingend'ring pride.
Him thus intent *Ithuriel* with his Spear   810
Touch'd lightly; for no falsehood can endure
Touch of Celestial temper, but returns
Of force to its own likeness: up he starts
Discover'd and surpris'd.   As when a spark
Lights on a heap of nitrous Powder, laid   815
Fit for the Tun some Magazin to store
Against a rumor'd War, the Smutty grain
With sudden blaze diffus'd, inflames the Air:
So started up in his own shape the Fiend.
Back stepp'd those two fair Angels half amaz'd   820
So sudden to behold the grisly King;
Yet thus, unmov'd with fear, accost him soon.
    Which of those rebel Spirits adjudg'd to Hell
Com'st thou, escap'd thy prison, and transform'd,
Why satst thou like an enemy in wait   825
Here watching at the head of these that sleep?
    Know ye not then said *Satan*, fill'd with scorn,
Know ye not mee? ye knew me once no mate
For you, there sitting where ye durst not soar;
Not to know mee argues yourselves unknown,   830
The lowest of your throng; or if ye know,

800–803. See the Introduction 48.
804–809. Burton (*Anatomy* I, i, 2, 2; Everyman Ed. I, 148) explained the theory of the natural, vital, and animal spirits: "The *natural* are begotten in the *liver*, and thence dispersed through the veins. . . . The *vital spirits* are made in the *heart*. . . . The *animal* [i.e. spiritual, from Latin *anima*, soul] *spirits* formed of the *vital*, brought up to the brain, and diffused by the nerves, to the subordinate members, give sense and motion to them all." In "Eve's Demonic Dream" (*ELH*, XIII — 1946 — pp. 359–64) W. B. Hunter, Jr., quotes numerous passages from St. Thomas Aquinas and other theologians affirming that evil spirits may act on the fancy or imagination through the "animal spirits" in the blood. See the Introduction 42–43.

809. *pride* is prominent in Satan's successful attempt on Eve in IX, 703–32, and P. L. Carver believes (*RES*, XVI — 1940 — p. 427) that Satan does induce Eve "to acquiesce, according to the words of St. Augustine, 'in the love of her own power, and in a presumption of self-conceit.' " But McColley traces through Calvin and others a tradition of two temptations of Eve, the first of which is not successful (*Harvard Theological Review*, XXXII — 1939 — p. 211).
815. *nitrous Powder:* gunpowder.
817. *Against:* in anticipation of.
830. *argues:* proves.   As an example of this use of the word Milton quotes a Virgilian tag, "Fear argues degenerate souls" (*Aen.* IV, 13) in *Art of Logic* I, ii (C.Ed. XI, 24).   Cf. l. 931 below.

Why ask ye, and superfluous begin
Your message, like to end as much in vain?
To whom thus *Zephon*, answering scorn with scorn.
Think not, revolted Spirit, thy shape the same,   835
Or undiminisht brightness, to be known
As when thou stood'st in Heav'n upright and pure;
That Glory then, when thou no more wast good,
Departed from thee, and thou resembl'st now
Thy sin and place of doom obscure and foul.   840
But come, for thou, be sure, shalt give account
To him who sent us, whose charge is to keep
This place inviolable, and these from harm.
    So spake the Cherub, and his grave rebuke
Severe in youthful beauty, added grace   845
Invincible: abasht the Devil stood,
And felt how awful goodness is, and saw
Virtue in her shape how lovely, saw, and pin'd
His loss; but chiefly to find here observ'd
His lustre visibly impair'd; yet seem'd   850
Undaunted. If I must contend, said he,
Best with the best, the Sender not the sent,
Or all at once; more glory will be won,
Or less be lost. Thy fear, said *Zephon* bold,
Will save us trial what the least can do   855
Single against thee wicked, and thence weak.
    The Fiend repli'd not, overcome with rage;
But like a proud Steed rein'd, went haughty on,
Champing his iron curb: to strive or fly
He held it vain; awe from above had quell'd   860
His heart, not else dismay'd. Now drew they nigh
The western Point, where those half-rounding guards
Just met, and closing stood in squadron join'd
Awaiting next command. To whom thir Chief
Gabriel from the Front thus call'd aloud.   865
    O friends, I hear the tread of nimble feet
Hasting this way, and now by glimpse discern
Ithuriel and *Zephon* through the shade,
And with them comes a third of Regal port,
But faded splendor wan; who by his gait   870
And fierce demeanor seems the Prince of Hell,

---

832. *superfluous:* with superfluous
words.
    840. *obscure* has its Latin force,
"dark."
    843. *these:* the sleeping Adam and Eve.
    848. In *Comus*, 214–16, the Platonic
conception of the virtues as capable of
making their forms visible suggests the
Lady's glimpse of Hope as a "hovering
angel girt with golden wings" and her cry,

"Thou unblemish't form of Chas-
        tity!
I see ye visible."
    862. *Point:* the western limit of Para-
dise, due west from Gabriel's station at
its gate on the east side. *half-rounding:*
completing the half-circle of the garden,
some having swung north, the others
south, so as to meet in the west.

Not likely to part hence without contest;
Stand firm, for in his look defiance low'rs.
　　He scarce had ended, when those two approach'd
And brief related whom they brought, where found,　　875
How busied, in what form and posture coucht.
　　To whom with stern regard thus *Gabriel* spake.
Why hast thou, *Satan*, broke the bounds prescrib'd
To thy transgressions, and disturb'd the charge
Of others, who approve not to transgress　　880
By thy example, but have power and right
To question thy bold entrance on this place;
Imploy'd it seems to violate sleep, and those
Whose dwelling God hath planted here in bliss?
　　To whom thus *Satan*, with contemptuous brow.　　885
Gabriel, thou hadst in Heav'n th' esteem of wise,
And such I held thee; but this question askt
Puts me in doubt. Lives there who loves his pain?
Who would not, finding way, break loose from Hell,
Though thither doom'd? Thou wouldst thyself, no doubt,　　890
And boldly venture to whatever place
Farthest from pain, where thou might'st hope to change
Torment with ease, and soonest recompense
Dole with delight, which in this place I sought;
To thee no reason; who know'st only good,　　895
But evil hast not tri'd: and wilt object
His will who bound us? let him surer bar
His Iron Gates, if he intends our stay
In that dark durance: thus much what was askt.
The rest is true, they found me where they say;　　900
But that implies not violence or harm.
　　Thus he in scorn. The warlike Angel mov'd,
Disdainfully half smiling thus repli'd.
O loss of one in Heav'n to judge of wise,
Since *Satan* fell, whom folly overthrew,　　905
And now returns him from his prison scap't,
Gravely in doubt whether to hold them wise
Or not, who ask what boldness brought him hither
Unlicens't from his bounds in Hell prescrib'd;
So wise he judges it to fly from pain　　910
However, and to scape his punishment.
So judge thou still, presumptuous, till the wrath,
Which thou incurr'st by flying, meet thy flight
Sevenfold, and scourge that wisdom back to Hell,
Which taught thee yet no better, that no pain　　915

879. *charge:* Adam and Eve, with whose protection Gabriel's troop is charged.
896. *object:* raise the legal objection (that the devils are confined to hell by God's will).
904. *O loss:* O what a loss (to lose such a judge of wisdom as Satan).
911. *However:* howsoever, by whatever means.

Can equal anger infinite provok't.
But wherefore thou alone? wherefore with thee
Came not all Hell broke loose? is pain to them
Less pain, less to be fled, or thou than they
Less hardy to endure? courageous Chief,   920
The first in flight from pain, hadst thou alleg'd
To thy deserted host this cause of flight,
Thou surely hadst not come sole fugitive.
   To which the Fiend thus answer'd frowning stern.
Not that I less endure, or shrink from pain,   925
Insulting Angel, well thou know'st I stood
Thy fiercest, when in Battle to thy aid
The blasting volley'd Thunder made all speed
And seconded thy else not dreaded Spear.
But still thy words at random, as before,   930
Argue thy inexperience what behooves
From hard assays and ill successes past
A faithful Leader, not to hazard all
Through ways of danger by himself untri'd.
I therefore, I alone first undertook   935
To wing the desolate Abyss, and spy
This new created World, whereof in Hell
Fame is not silent, here in hope to find
Better abode, and my afflicted Powers
To settle here on Earth, or in mid Air;   940
Though for possession put to try once more
What thou and thy gay Legions dare against;
Whose easier business were to serve thir Lord
High up in Heav'n, with songs to hymn his Throne,
And practis'd distances to cringe, not fight.   945
   To whom the warrior Angel soon repli'd.
To say and straight unsay, pretending first
Wise to fly pain, professing next the Spy,
Argues no Leader, but a liar trac't,
Satan, and couldst thou faithful add? O name,   950
O sacred name of faithfulness profan'd!
Faithful to whom? to thy rebellious crew?
Army of Fiends, fit body to fit head;
Was this your discipline and faith ingag'd,

926. *stood:* withstood or confronted, stood up against. A flashback in time but a look forward in the poem to the battle in heaven in VI, 56–879.
931. *Argue:* Cf. l. 830 above. The thought is that Gabriel's reasoning betrays his ignorance of a leader's duty to his followers.
938. Cf. *fame* in I, 651.
939. Cf. Satan's *afflicted Powers* in I, 186.

940. Satan is the "prince of the power of the air" in Ephesians ii, 2. Cf. II, 275, n.
944. Editors generally quote the taunt of Aeschylus' Prometheus (*Prom.* 937–39) to the chorus: "Worship, adore, and fawn upon the ruler"; and Gabriel's words to Satan in l. 962 below as echoing Hermes' warning to him in reply (*Prom.*, 1071). The first parallel isf ar from close. Cf. I, 116, n.

Your military obedience, to dissolve   955
Allegiance to th' acknowledg'd Power supreme?
And thou sly hypocrite, who now wouldst seem
Patron of liberty, who more than thou
Once fawn'd, and cring'd, and servilely ador'd
Heav'n's awful Monarch? wherefore but in hope   960
To dispossess him, and thyself to reign?
But mark what I arede thee now, avaunt;
Fly thither whence thou fledd'st: if from this hour
Within these hallow'd limits thou appear,
Back to th' infernal pit I drag thee chain'd,   965
And Seal thee so, as henceforth not to scorn
The facile gates of hell too slightly barr'd.
    So threat'n'd hee, but *Satan* to no threats
Gave heed, but waxing more in rage repli'd.
    Then when I am thy captive talk of chains,   970
Proud limitary Cherub, but ere then
Far heavier load thyself expect to feel
From my prevailing arm, though Heaven's King
Ride on thy wings, and thou with thy Compeers,
Us'd to the yoke, draw'st his triumphant wheels   975
In progress through the road of Heav'n Star-pav'd.
    While thus he spake, th' Angelic Squadron bright
Turn'd fiery red, sharp'ning in mooned horns
Thir Phalanx, and began to hem him round
With ported Spears, as thick as when a field   980
Of *Ceres* ripe for harvest waving bends
Her bearded Grove of ears, which way the wind
Sways them; the careful Plowman doubting stands
Lest on the threshing floor his hopeful sheaves
Prove chaff. On th' other side *Satan* alarm'd   985
Collecting all his might dilated stood,
Like *Teneriff* or *Atlas* unremov'd:
His stature reacht the Sky, and on his Crest
Sat horror Plum'd; nor wanted in his grasp
What seem'd both Spear and Shield: now dreadful deeds   990

958. Cf. the similar use of *Patron* in
III, 219.
  962. *arede:* advise. Cf. l. 944 above, n.
  965. Cf. I, 45–48.
  971. *limitary:* "boundary-protecting"
is the meaning, but there is an overtone
suggesting that Gabriel is presuming too
much in setting bounds to Satan's move-
ments.
  975. The line looks forward to VI,
770–71.
  978. *mooned:* crescent-shaped.
  980. *ported:* held diagonally across the
bearer's breast.
  981. *Ceres,* the name of the goddess of
grain, represents the grain itself. Cf. *On*

the Fifth of November, 32.
  983. *careful:* anxious.
  987. *Teneriff,* the great peak in the
Canary Islands, like the *Atlas* range in
Morocco, was made dramatically con-
spicuous on the maps of Milton's time,
but he might visualize it from Virgil's
description of "the top of Atlas . . .
    Whose brawny back supports the
        starry skies —
  Atlas, whose head, with piny forests
        crown'd,
  Is beaten by the winds — with foggy
        vapors bound."
        (*Aen.* IV, 246–49. Dryden's
                    translation.)

Might have ensu'd, nor only Paradise
In this commotion, but the Starry Cope
Of Heav'n perhaps, or all the Elements
At least had gone to rack, disturb'd and torn
With violence of this conflict, had not soon   995
Th' Eternal to prevent such horrid fray
Hung forth in Heav'n his golden Scales, yet seen
Betwixt *Astrea* and the *Scorpion* sign,
Wherein all things created first he weigh'd,
The pendulous round Earth with balanc't Air   1000
In counterpoise, now ponders all events,
Battles and Realms: in these he put two weights
The sequel each of parting and of fight;
The latter quick up flew, and kickt the beam;
Which *Gabriel* spying, thus bespake the Fiend.   1005
   Satan, I know thy strength, and thou know'st mine,
Neither our own but giv'n; what folly then
To boast what Arms can do, since thine no more
Than Heav'n permits, nor mine, though doubl'd now
To trample thee as mire: for proof look up,   1010
And read thy Lot in yon celestial Sign
Where thou art weigh'd, and shown how light, how weak,
If thou resist. The Fiend lookt up and knew
His mounted scale aloft: nor more; but fled
Murmuring, and with him fled the shades of night.   1015

The End of the Fourth Book.

992. *Cope* (which is etymologically related to "cape") is again used of the sky in VI, 215.

997. Milton remembered the golden scales in which Zeus weighed the destinies of the Greeks against those of the Trojans (*Il.* VIII, 69–72), and of Hector against Achilles (*Il.* XXII, 209), or the weighing of Aeneas' fate against that of Turnus (*Aen.* XII, 725–27), but he gives the conception cosmic scope by identifying the scales with the constellation of *Libra*, or the Scales, which stands between the Virgin and the Scorpion in the Zodiac.

999. Compare Isaiah xl, 12: God is he "Who hath measured the waters in the hollow of his hand, and meted out heaven with the span, and comprehended the dust of the earth in a measure, and weighed the mountains in scales, and the hills in a balance."

1001. *ponders* has its literal, Latin meaning, "weighs."

1003. *sequel:* consequence.

1012. Milton repeats a phrase from the record in Daniel (v, 27) of God's use of the figure of the scales to warn the Babylonian king, Belshazzar: "Thou art weighed in the balance, and art found wanting."

1015. Like Book II, Book IV ends with a transition from darkness to day.

BOOK V

THE ARGUMENT

Morning approacht, Eve *relates to* Adam *her troublesome dream; he likes it not, yet comforts her: They come forth to thir day labors: Thir Morning Hymn at the Door of thir Bower.* God to render Man inexcusable sends Raphael *to admonish him of his obedience, of his free estate, of his enemy near at hand; who he is, and why his enemy and whatever else may avail* Adam *to know.* Raphael *comes down to Paradise, his appearance describ'd, his coming discern'd by* Adam *afar off sitting at the door of his Bower; he goes out to meet him, brings him to his lodge, entertains him with the choicest fruits of Paradise got together by* Eve; *thir discourse at Table:* Raphael *performs his message, minds* Adam *of his state and of his enemy; relates at* Adam's *request who that enemy is, and how he came to be so, beginning from his first revolt in Heaven, and the occasion thereof; how he drẃv his Legions after him to the parts of the North, and there incited them to rebel with him, persuading all but only* Abdiel *a Seraph, who in Argument dissuades and opposes him, then forsakes him.*

Now Morn her rosy steps in th' Eastern Clime
Advancing, sow'd the Earth with Orient Pearl,
When *Adam* wak't, so custom'd, for his sleep
Was Aery light, from pure digestion bred,
And temperate vapors bland, which th' only sound   5
Of leaves and fuming rills, *Aurora's* fan,
Lightly dispers'd, and the shrill Matin Song
Of Birds on every bough; so much the more
His wonder was to find unwak'n'd *Eve*
With Tresses discompos'd, and glowing Cheek,   10
As through unquiet rest: hee on his side
Leaning half-rais'd, with looks of cordial Love
Hung over her enamor'd, and beheld
Beauty, which whether waking or asleep,
Shot forth peculiar graces; then with voice   15
Mild, as when *Zephyrus* on *Flora* breathes,
Her hand soft touching, whisper'd thus. Awake
My fairest, my espous'd, my latest found,
Heav'n's last best gift, my ever new delight,

1. The *rosy steps* are Milton's transformation of the rosy-fingered Dawn of Homer. Cf. VI, 524, and VII, 29.
4. After their sin the sleep of Adam and Eve is "grosser" (IX, 1049).
5. *vapors* is a definite medical term meaning the exhalations of digestion. Cf. the "vapors of wine" in *Church Government* (C.Ed. III, 241).
6. *Aurora's fan:* the leaves, stirred by the breeze of the goddess of morning, Aurora.
15. *peculiar:* solely belonging (to Eve).

16. So *Zephyrus* plays with the Dawn in *L'Allegro,* 19, and fans Paradise in IV, 329. *Flora,* goddess of flowers, is half personification and half metonymy, as *Ceres* is in IV, 981.
17-25. The obvious parody of the Song of Solomon ii, 10 — "Rise up, my love, my fair one, and come away" — is an inversion of the pictures, "changing the dove for the nightingale, keeping only the sensuous delights," as H. Schultz observes in "Satan's Serenade" in *PQ,* XXVII (1948), 24.

Awake, the morning shines, and the fresh field   20
Calls us; we lose the prime, to mark how spring
Our tended Plants, how blows the Citron Grove,
What drops the Myrrh, and what the balmy Reed,
How Nature paints her colors, how the Bee
Sits on the Bloom extracting liquid sweet.   25
 Such whispering wak'd her, but with startl'd eye
On *Adam*, whom imbracing, thus she spake.
 O Sole in whom my thoughts find all repose,
My Glory, my Perfection, glad I see
Thy face, and Morn return'd, for I this Night,   30
Such night till this I never pass'd, have dream'd,
If dream'd, not as I oft am wont, of thee,
Works of day past, or morrow's next design,
But of offense and trouble, which my mind
Knew never till this irksome night; methought   35
Close at mine ear one call'd me forth to walk
With gentle voice, I thought it thine; it said,
Why sleep'st thou *Eve?* now is the pleasant time,
The cool, the silent, save where silence yields
To the night-warbling Bird, that now awake   40
Tunes sweetest his love-labor'd song; now reigns
Full Orb'd the Moon, and with more pleasing light
Shadowy sets off the face of things; in vain,
If none regard; Heav'n wakes with all his eyes,
Whom to behold but thee, Nature's desire,   45
In whose sight all things joy, with ravishment
Attracted by thy beauty still to gaze.
I rose as at thy call, but found thee not;
To find thee I directed then my walk;
And on, methought, alone I pass'd through ways   50
That brought me on a sudden to the Tree
Of interdicted Knowledge: fair it seem'd,
Much fairer to my Fancy than by day:
And as I wond'ring lookt, beside it stood
One shap'd and wing'd like one of those from Heav'n   55
By us oft seen; his dewy locks distill'd
Ambrosia; on that Tree he also gaz'd;
And O fair Plant, said he, with fruit surcharg'd,

21. *prime:* the first hour of the day.
Cf. l. 170 below.
 22. *blows:* blooms. Cf. VII, 319, and
IX, 629.
 23. *balmy Reed:* balm-producing reed.
 44. So for Spenser (and many other
poets) the stars were the "many eyes"
with which "High heven beholdes" man-
kind (*F.Q.* III, xi, 45, 7-8).
 45-47. The passage, like the anticipa-
tion of a theme to be developed later in a
symphony, looks forward to the tempta-

tion in IX, 494–833.
 55-57. Milton remembered Virgil's
Venus appearing in sudden glory to
Aeneas with
    dishevell'd hair,
Which flowing from her shoulders
  reach'd the ground,
And widely spread ambrosial scents
  around.
   (*Aen.* I, 403–404. Dryden's
       translation.)

Deigns none to ease thy load and taste thy sweet,
Nor God, nor Man; is Knowledge so despis'd?   60
Or envy, or what reserve forbids to taste?
Forbid who will, none shall from me withhold
Longer thy offer'd good, why else set here?
This said he paus'd not, but with vent'rous Arm
He pluckt, he tasted; mee damp horror chill'd   65
At such bold words voucht with a deed so bold:
But he thus overjoy'd, O Fruit Divine,
Sweet of thyself, but much more sweet thus cropt,
Forbidd'n here, it seems, as only fit
For Gods, yet able to make Gods of Men: 70
And why not Gods of Men, since good, the more
Communicated, more abundant grows,
The Author not impair'd, but honor'd more?
Here, happy Creature, fair Angelic *Eve*,
Partake thou also; happy though thou art,   75
Happier thou may'st be, worthier canst not be:
Taste this, and be henceforth among the Gods
Thyself a Goddess, not to Earth confin'd,
But sometimes in the Air, as wee, sometimes
Ascend to Heav'n, by merit thine, and see   80
What life the Gods live there, and such live thou.
So saying, he drew nigh, and to me held,
Even to my mouth of that same fruit held part
Which he had pluckt; the pleasant savory smell
So quick'n'd appetite, that I, methought,   85
Could not but taste. Forthwith up to the Clouds
With him I flew, and underneath beheld
The Earth outstretcht immense, a prospect wide
And various: wond'ring at my flight and change
To this high exaltation; suddenly   90
My Guide was gone, and I, methought, sunk down,
And fell asleep; but O how glad I wak'd
To find this but a dream! Thus *Eve* her Night
Related, and thus *Adam* answer'd sad.
     Best Image of myself and dearer half,   95
The trouble of thy thoughts this night in sleep
Affects me equally; nor can I like
This uncouth dream, of evil sprung I fear;
Yet evil whence? in thee can harbor none,
Created pure. But know that in the Soul   100

---

60. *God* here means "angel," as in II,
352, and V, 117.
  65. *damp horror:* the sweat of fear.
  71. The ambiguous use of the word
"gods" figures in Satan's temptation of
Eve in IX, 705–712, as it has in his speech
to Beelzebub in I, 116.

100–116. The passage summarizes the
popular faculty psychology which is fa-
miliar in Spenser's allegory (*F.Q.* II, ix,
49–58) of Phantastes, the faculty which
Adam calls *Fancy* and contrasts for its
fertility in *Imaginations, Aery shapes*,
with *Reason*. In *M.&S.*, pp. 36–38,

Are many lesser Faculties that serve
Reason as chief; among these Fancy next
Her office holds; of all external things,
Which the five watchful Senses represent,
She forms Imaginations, Aery shapes,   105
Which Reason joining or disjoining, frames
All what we affirm or what deny, and call
Our knowledge or opinion; then retires
Into her private Cell when Nature rests.
Oft in her absence mimic Fancy wakes   110
To imitate her; but misjoining shapes,
Wild work produces oft, and most in dreams,
Ill matching words and deeds long past or late.
Some such resemblances methinks I find
Of our last Ev'ning's talk, in this thy dream,   115
But with addition strange; yet be not sad.
Evil into the mind of God or Man
May come and go, so unapprov'd, and leave
No spot or blame behind: Which gives me hope
That what in sleep thou didst abhor to dream,   120
Waking thou never wilt consent to do.
Be not disheart'n'd then, nor cloud those looks
That wont to be more cheerful and serene
Than when fair Morning first smiles on the World,
And let us to our fresh imployments rise   125
Among the Groves, the Fountains, and the Flow'rs
That open now thir choicest bosom'd smells
Reserv'd from night, and kept for thee in store.
So cheer'd he his fair Spouse, and she was cheer'd,
But silently a gentle tear let fall   130
From either eye, and wip'd them with her hair;

Svendsen quotes several discussions of this "faculty of the fantasie" from La Primaudaye's *French Academie* and other encyclopaedias.

107–113. D. F. Bond aptly quotes (in *Explicator* III, 54) from Bishop Bramhall's *Castigation of Mr. Hobbes* (1658): "In time of sleep, . . . when the imagination is not governed by reason, we see what absurd and monstrous and inconsistent shapes and phansies it doth collect, remote from true deliberation."

117–119. *God* is probably rightly interpreted by T. Banks — in *MLN*, LIV (1939), 451 — as meaning "angel," as it does in III, 341. Thus the line repeats Raphael's statement in V, 538, that the good angels remain good by their own free choice. Interpreting *God* as "the Infinite," Saurat (in *Milton: Man and Thinker*, p. 110) regards the lines as meaning that the world was created "to

drive away the evil latent in the Infinite, and to exalt the good latent also." But Milton may be simply appealing to the universally received view of God's omniscience as implying that His knowledge extends to the potential, accidental evil in good things because — as St. Thomas explains (*Summa Theol.* I, q. 14, a.10) — "God would not know good things perfectly unless he knew evil things." The lines suggest to Mrs. Bell — in *PMLA*, LXVIII (1953), 871 — that Eve is "already receptive to the Tempter's choice flattery" — a position which W. Shumaker challenges on theological ground in *PMLA*, LXX (1955), 1199. Milton was echoing Titus, i, 15: "Unto the pure, all things are pure; but unto them that are defiled is nothing pure; but even their mind and conscience is defiled." Cf. *Areop*, (C.Ed. IV, 308).

Two other precious drops that ready stood,
Each in thir crystal sluice, hee ere they fell
Kiss'd as the gracious signs of sweet remorse
And pious awe, that fear'd to have offended.   135
 So all was clear'd, and to the Field they haste.
But first from under shady arborous roof,
Soon as they forth were come to open sight
Of day-spring, and the Sun, who scarce up risen
With wheels yet hov'ring o'er the Ocean brim,   140
Shot parallel to the earth his dewy ray,
Discovering in wide Lantskip all the East
Of Paradise and *Eden's* happy Plains,
Lowly they bow'd adoring, and began
Thir Orisons, each Morning duly paid   145
In various style, for neither various style
Nor holy rapture wanted they to praise
Thir Maker, in fit strains pronounc't or sung
Unmeditated, such prompt eloquence
Flow'd from thir lips, in Prose, or numerous Verse,   150
More tuneable than needed Lute or Harp
To add more sweetness, and they thus began.
 These are thy glorious works, Parent of good,
Almighty, thine this universal Frame,
Thus wondrous fair; thyself how wondrous then!   155
Unspeakable, who sit'st above these Heavens
To us invisible or dimly seen
In these thy lowest works, yet these declare
Thy goodness beyond thought, and Power Divine:
Speak yee who best can tell, ye Sons of Light,   160
Angels, for yee behold him, and with songs
And choral symphonies, Day without Night,
Circle his Throne rejoicing, yee in Heav'n;
On Earth join all ye Creatures to extol
Him first, him last, him midst, and without end.   165
Fairest of Stars, last in the train of Night,

---

137. *arborous:* arbor-like, tree-made.
142. Cf. *Lantskip* in II, 491.
146–152. So in *CD* II, iv (C.Ed. XVII,
85), Milton stresses "the superfluousness
of set forms of worship."
150. With *numerous* cf. the "Har-
monious numbers" of III, 38.
154. *Frame* is used as it is in Hamlet's
"goodly frame, the earth" (*Hamlet* II,
ii, 310).
156–169. The theme of the hymn is
the doctrine of God's revelation of him-
self only in his creatures — in Du Bartas'
words:
 God, of himself incapable to sensce,
 In's Works, reveals him t'our intelli-
  gence.
(*Divine Weeks,* p. 5. Cf. Taylor, *Du*

Bartas, p. 82.)
 The hymn parallels Psalm cxlviii, 2–4
and 8–10:
 "Praise ye him, all his angels: praise
  ye him, all his hosts.
 Praise ye him, sun and moon: praise
  ye him, all ye stars of light. . . .
 Fire, and hail: snow, and vapor:
  stormy wind fulfilling his word:
 Mountains, and all hills: fruitful
  trees, and all cedars:
 Beasts, and all cattle: creeping
  things, and flying fowl."
162. Cf. ll. 642–46 below.
166. So Venus is the fairest star in
Heaven in the *Iliad* XXII, 318. In the
pre-sunrise sky it is Lucifer, the light-
bringer, and after sunset it is Hesperus.

If better thou belong not to the dawn,
Sure pledge of day, that crown'st the smiling Morn
With thy bright Circlet, praise him in thy Sphere
While day arises, that sweet hour of Prime. 170
Thou Sun, of this great World both Eye and Soul,
Acknowledge him thy Greater, sound his praise
In thy eternal course, both when thou climb'st,
And when high Noon hast gain'd, and when thou fall'st.
Moon, that now meet'st the orient Sun, now fli'st 175
With the fixt Stars, fixt in thir Orb that flies,
And yee five other wand'ring Fires that move
In mystic Dance not without Song, resound
His praise, who out of Darkness call'd up Light.
Air, and ye Elements the eldest birth 180
Of Nature's Womb, that in quaternion run
Perpetual Circle, multiform, and mix
And nourish all things, let your ceaseless change
Vary to our great Maker still new praise.
Ye Mists and Exhalations that now rise 185
From Hill or steaming Lake, dusky or grey,
Till the Sun paint your fleecy skirts with Gold,
In honor to the World's great Author rise,
Whether to deck with Clouds th' uncolor'd sky,
Or wet the thirsty Earth with falling showers, 190
Rising or falling still advance his praise.
His praise ye Winds, that from four Quarters blow,
Breathe soft or loud; and wave your tops, ye Pines,
With every Plant, in sign of Worship wave.
Fountains and yee, that warble, as ye flow, 195
Melodious murmurs, warbling tune his praise.
Join voices all ye living Souls; ye Birds,
That singing up to Heaven Gate ascend,
Bear on your wings and in your notes his praise;

171. As Donne conceived the sun in terms of the metaphor that made it the eye of the world and the male force inspiriting it —

> Thee, eye of heaven. this great Soule envies not,
> By thy male force, is all wee have. begot.

(*Progress of the Soul*, stanza 2) (Cf. *PL* VIII, 150.) — so Milton conceived its light as "male" and as a life-giving spirit. The conception of the sun as the soul of the world goes back to Pliny (*Nat. Hist.* II, 4) and was developed by Conti (*Mythologiae* V, xvii, p. 543) into a synthesis of many solar myths signifying that the sun was "lord of the stars and giver of life to mortals, since he is the author of light to the other stars and by him all things flourish." In *Milton's Ontology, Cosmogony, and Physics*, pp. 116–120, W. C. Curry traces the conception to the Stoics. Cf. IV, 667–73, and VIII, 94–97, n.

176. For the *Orb that flies* see the Introduction 34.

177. The *five other wand'ring Fires* are Venus, Mercury, Mars, Jupiter, and Saturn. So in *Doctor Faustus* I, vi, 43–44, Marlowe refers to the literal meaning of the word "planet" by calling Saturn, Mars, and Jupiter "erring stars." Cf. VIII, 126.

181. As far back as Plato's *Timaeus* (49c), the four elements were supposed to be reversibly transformable into one another. Cf. ll. 415–26 below.

189. *uncolor'd:* without variety of colors.

Yee that in Waters glide, and yee that walk 200
The Earth, and stately tread, or lowly creep;
Witness if I be silent, Morn or Even,
To Hill, or Valley, Fountain, or fresh shade
Made vocal by my Song, and taught his praise.
Hail universal Lord, be bounteous still 205
To give us only good; and if the night
Have gather'd aught of evil or conceal'd,
Disperse it, as now light dispels the dark.
  So pray'd they innocent, and to thir thoughts
Firm peace recover'd soon and wonted calm. 210
On to thir morning's rural work they haste
Among sweet dews and flow'rs; where any row
Of Fruit-trees overwoody reach'd too far
Thir pamper'd boughs, and needed hands to check
Fruitless imbraces: or they led the Vine 215
To wed her Elm; she spous'd about him twines
Her marriageable arms, and with her brings
Her dow'r th' adopted Clusters, to adorn
His barren leaves. Them thus imploy'd beheld
With pity Heav'n's high King, and to him call'd 220
Raphael, the sociable Spirit, that deign'd
To travel with *Tobias*, and secur'd
His marriage with the seven-times-wedded Maid.
  Raphael, said hee, thou hear'st what stir on Earth
Satan from Hell scap't through the darksome Gulf 225
Hath rais'd in Paradise, and how disturb'd
This night the human pair, how he designs
In them at once to ruin all mankind.
Go therefore, half this day as friend with friend
Converse with *Adam*, in what Bow'r or shade 230
Thou find'st him from the heat of Noon retir'd,
To respite his day-labor with repast,
Or with repose; and such discourse bring on,
As may advise him of his happy state,
Happiness in his power left free to will, 235
Left to his own free Will, his Will though free,

202. Each speaker seems to invoke every creature to witness his fidelity to God's praise, night and morning, as the Psalmist (cxxxvii, 6) prays that, if he forgets Zion, his tongue may cleave to the roof of his mouth.
206. The lines seem to echo Socrates' prayer "for good gifts, for the gods know best what things are good," as Xenophon reports it in *Memorabilia* I, ii, 2, and as Cardinal Bembo recalled it in Castiglione's *Courtier* when he prayed God "to correct the falsehood of the senses and, after long wandering in vanitie, to give us the right and sound joy" (Everyman Ed. of Hoby's tr., p. 321).
216. The figure was traditional when Spenser wrote of the "vine-propp elme" (*F.Q.* I, i, 8, 7) and when Horace used it in *Odes* II, xv, 4, and IV, v, 31.
221. The name *Raphael* means "medicine of God," and it corresponds with the angel's role in the Book of Tobit as it is reflected in IV, 166-71. With Michael, Gabriel, and Uriel, Raphael is one of "the four angels of the presence" of God in Jewish tradition.
234. *advise:* inform.

Yet mutable; whence warn him to beware
He swerve not too secure: tell him withal
His danger, and from whom, what enemy
Late fall'n himself from Heaven, is plotting now   240
The fall of others from like state of bliss;
By violence, no, for that shall be withstood,
But by deceit and lies; this let him know,
Lest wilfully transgressing he pretend
Surprisal, unadmonisht, unforewarn'd.   245
So spake th' Eternal Father, and fulfill'd
All Justice: nor delay'd the winged Saint
After his charge receiv'd; but from among
Thousand Celestial Ardors, where he stood
Veil'd with his gorgeous wings, up springing light   250
Flew through the midst of Heav'n; th' angelic Choirs
On each hand parting, to his speed gave way
Through all th' Empyreal road; till at the Gate
Of Heav'n arriv'd, the gate self-open'd wide
On golden Hinges turning, as by work   255
Divine the sovran Architect had fram'd.
From hence, no cloud, or, to obstruct his sight,
Star interpos'd, however small he sees,
Not unconform to other shining Globes,
Earth and the Gard'n of God, with Cedars crown'd   260
Above all Hills. As when by night the Glass
Of *Galileo*, less assur'd, observes
Imagin'd Lands and Regions in the Moon:
Or Pilot from amidst the *Cyclades*
Delos or *Samos* first appearing kens   265
A cloudy spot. Down thither prone in flight
He speeds, and through the vast Ethereal Sky
Sails between worlds and worlds, with steady wing
Now on the polar winds, then with quick Fan
Winnows the buxom Air; till within soar   270
Of Tow'ring Eagles, to all the Fowls he seems
A *Phœnix*, gaz'd by all, as that sole Bird

238. *secure:* overconfident of safety (literally, "without care"). Cf. IV, 186.
247. Cf. the use of *Saints* in III, 330.
249. *Ardors:* angels, as in Psalm civ, 4: "Who maketh his angels spirits; his ministers a flaming fire."
259. *Not unconform:* not unlike.
261-262. *the Glass Of Galileo:* the telescope. Cf. I, 287-91.
264. *Cyclades:* the Aegean archipelago of which *Delos* is the center. *Samos* lies outside them to the northeast.
266. *prone:* downward moving. The picture is more splendid than those of Mercury running Jove's errands over sea and land (in *Il.* XXIV, 341, and *Aen.* IV,

241). Raphael plunges earthward by the same *passage* or route that Satan has followed in III, 528-37, but without pausing at the sun.
269. *Fan:* wing.
272. Milton knew many accounts of the *Phoenix*, the unique bird that Ovid describes (*Met.* XV, 391-407) as immolating itself once in five hundred years on a pyre of spices, only to "carry its own cradle and its father's tomb to the city of the sun." Ovid's city of the sun, Heliopolis, becomes Milton's neighboring Egyptian city of Thebes. In *The Phoenix* that is attributed to Lactantius and in Tasso's *Phoenix* he found the reborn bird

When to enshrine his reliques in the Sun's
Bright Temple, to *Egyptian Thebes* he flies.
At once on th' Eastern cliff of Paradise   275
He lights, and to his proper shape returns
A Seraph wing'd; six wings he wore, to shade
His lineaments Divine; the pair that clad
Each shoulder broad, came mantling o'er his breast
With regal Ornament; the middle pair   280
Girt like a Starry Zone his waist, and round
Skirted his loins and thighs with downy Gold
And colors dipt in Heav'n; the third his feet
Shadow'd from either heel with feather'd mail
Sky-tinctur'd grain. Like *Maia's* son he stood,   285
And shook his Plumes, that Heav'nly fragrance fill'd
The circuit wide. Straight knew him all the Bands
Of Angels under watch; and to his state,
And to his message high in honor rise;
For on some message high they guess'd him bound.   290
Thir glittering Tents he pass'd, and now is come
Into the blissful field, through Groves of Myrrh,
And flow'ring Odors, Cassia, Nard, and Balm;
A Wilderness of sweets; for Nature here
Wanton'd as in her prime, and play'd at will   295
Her Virgin Fancies, pouring forth more sweet,
Wild above Rule or Art, enormous bliss.
Him through the spicy Forest onward come
Adam discern'd, as in the door he sat
Of his cool Bow'r, while now the mounted Sun   300
Shot down direct his fervid Rays, to warm
Earth's inmost womb, more warmth than *Adam* needs;
And *Eve* within, due at her hour prepar'd
For dinner savoury fruits, of taste to please
True appetite, and not disrelish thirst   305
Of nectarous draughts between, from milky stream,
Berry or Grape: to whom thus *Adam* call'd.
     Haste hither *Eve*, and worth thy sight behold
Eastward among those Trees, what glorious shape
Comes this way moving; seems another Morn   310

---

in full flight described as a splendid "thing to gaze at." J. Whaler notes, in *PMLA*, XLVII (1932), 545, that the simile may have had a secondary application for Milton in the light of an Elizabethan proverb that "A faithful friend is like a phoenix." Cf. *SA*, 1699–1707.

276. Raphael's *proper shape* Milton takes to be that of the seraphs in Isaiah vi, 2, each with "six wings; with twain he covered his face, and with twain he covered his feet, and with twain did he fly."

285. *Sky-tinctur'd grain:* sky-blue color. *Maia's son:* Mercury.
288. *state:* majestic rank. Cf. I, 640, and II, 511, and l. 353 below.
289. *message:* mission (as God's emissary).
292. *blissful field:* Paradise. Cf. *bliss* in l. 297 below.
299. So Abraham, sitting in front of his tent, saw the Lord coming and told Sarah to prepare a meal (Gen. xviii, 2–8).
308. *worth thy sight:* worth seeing.

Ris'n on mid-noon; some great behest from **Heav'n**
To us perhaps he brings, and will voutsafe
This day to be our Guest. But go with speed,
And what thy stores contain, bring forth and pour
Abundance, fit to honor and receive   315
Our Heav'nly stranger; well we may afford
Our givers thir own gifts, and large bestow
From large bestow'd, where Nature multiplies
Her fertile growth, and by disburd'ning grows
More fruitful, which instructs us not to spare.   320
    To whom thus *Eve. Adam*, earth's hallow'd mould,
Of God inspir'd, small store will serve, where store,
All seasons, ripe for use hangs on the stalk;
Save what by frugal storing firmness gains
To nourish, and superfluous moist consumes: 325
But I will haste and from each bough and brake,
Each Plant and juiciest Gourd will pluck such choice
To entertain our Angel guest, as hee
Beholding shall confess that here on Earth
God hath dispenst his bounties as in Heav'n.   330
    So saying, with dispatchful looks in haste
She turns, on hospitable thoughts intent
What choice to choose for delicacy best,
What order, so contriv'd as not to mix
Tastes, not well join'd, inelegant, but bring   335
Taste after taste upheld with kindliest change;
Bestirs her then, and from each tender stalk
Whatever Earth all-bearing Mother yields
In *India* East or West, or middle shore
In *Pontus* or the *Punic* Coast, or where   340
Alcinoüs reign'd, fruit of all kinds, in coat,
Rough, or smooth rin'd, or bearded husk, or shell
She gathers, Tribute large, and on the board
Heaps with unsparing hand; for drink the Grape
She crushes, inoffensive must, and meaths   345
From many a berry, and from sweet kernels prest
She tempers dulcet creams, nor these to hold
Wants her fit vessels pure, then strews the ground
With Rose and Odors from the shrub unfum'd.
Meanwhile our Primitive great Sire, to meet   350

322. *inspir'd:* inspirited or fertilized.
336. *kindliest:* in perfect harmony with nature.
339. *India East or West:* tropical Asia and tropical America. *middle shore:* the coast of the Mediterranean Sea.
340. As *PR* II, 347, testifies, fish from the Black Sea on its Pontic (or southern) shore were a Roman delicacy. The *Punic Coast* is the Carthaginian coast of the Mediterranean — modern Tunis.

341. Around *Alcinoüs'* palace Ulysses found a garden of perpetual springtime and harvest (*Od.* VII, 125–28), like that in Paradise.
345. *must:* unfermented wine. *meath:* mead.
349. *the shrub unfum'd:* unburned. The perfume from the fresh plant, not from its burning — not from any kind of incense.

His god-like Guest, walks forth, without more train
Accompanied than with his own complete
Perfections; in himself was all his state,
More solemn than the tedious pomp that waits
On Princes, when thir rich Retinue long   355
Of Horses led, and Grooms besmear'd with Gold
Dazzles the crowd, and sets them all agape,
Nearer his presence *Adam* though not aw'd,
Yet with submiss approach and reverence meek,
As to a superior Nature, bowing low,   360
    Thus said. Native of Heav'n, for other place
None can than Heav'n such glorious shape contain;
Since by descending from the Thrones above,
Those happy places thou hast deign'd a while
To want, and honor these, voutsafe with us   365
Two only, who yet by sovran gift possess
This spacious ground, in yonder shady Bow'r
To rest, and what the Garden choicest bears
To sit and taste, till this meridian heat
Be over, and the Sun more cool decline.   370
    Whom thus the Angelic Virtue answer'd mild.
Adam, I therefore came, nor art thou such
Created, or such place hast here to dwell,
As may not oft invite, though Spirits of Heav'n
To visit thee; lead on then where thy Bow'r   375
O'ershades; for these mid-hours, till Ev'ning rise
I have at will. So to the Silvan Lodge
They came, that like *Pomona's* Arbor smil'd
With flow'rets deck't and fragrant smells; but *Eve*
Undeckt, save with herself more lovely fair   380
Than Wood-Nymph, or the fairest Goddess feign'd
Of three that in Mount *Ida* naked strove,
Stood to entertain her guest from Heav'n; no veil
Shee needed, Virtue-proof, no thought infirm
Alter'd her cheek. On whom the Angel 'Hail'   385
Bestow'd, the holy salutation us'd
Long after to blest *Mary*, second *Eve*.
    Hail Mother of Mankind, whose fruitful Womb
Shall fill the World more numerous with thy Sons
Than with these various fruits the Trees of God   390

365. *want:* do without.
371. As a seraph or one of the supreme rank in the heavenly hierarchy, Raphael may have the title of any of the inferior orders, of which the *Virtues* were one. See the Introduction 21.
374. *though Spirits of Heav'n:* even heavenly spirits.
378. *Pomona:* the Roman goddess of flowers.
382. The *three that in Mount Ida naked* strove are Hera, Aphrodite, and Athene, to the second of whom · Paris awarded the apple of discord that bore the inscription, "For the fairest." Mt. Ida overlooked ancient Troy.
384. *Virtue-proof:* proof (against evil) by her virtue.
385–388. *Hail* is the greeting of the angel of the Annunciation to Mary (Luke i, 28). Mary is the *second Eve* of X, 183, as she is here. Cf. XI, 158–59.

Have heap'd this Table. Rais'd of grassy turf
Thir Table was, and mossy seats had round,
And on her ample Square from side to side
All *Autumn* pil'd, though *Spring* and *Autumn* here
Danc'd hand in hand. A while discourse they hold;   395
No fear lest Dinner cool; when thus began
Our Author. Heav'nly stranger, please to taste
These bounties which our Nourisher, from whom
All perfet good unmeasur'd out, descends,
To us for food and for delight hath caus'd   400
The Earth to yield; unsavory food perhaps
To spiritual Natures; only this I know,
That one Celestial Father gives to all.

    To whom the Angel. Therefore what he gives
(Whose praise be ever sung) to man in part   405
Spiritual, may of purest Spirits be found
No ingrateful food: and food alike those pure
Intelligential substances require
As doth your Rational; and both contain
Within them every lower faculty   410
Of sense, whereby they hear, see, smell, touch, taste,
Tasting concoct, digest, assimilate,
And corporeal to incorporeal turn.
For know, whatever was created, needs
To be sustain'd and fed; of Elements   415
The grosser feeds the purer, Earth the Sea,
Earth and the Sea feed Air, the Air those Fires
Ethereal, and as lowest first the Moon;
Whence in her visage round those spots, unpurg'd
Vapors not yet into her substance turn'd.   420
Nor doth the Moon no nourishment exhale
From her moist Continent to higher Orbs.
The Sun that light imparts to all, receives
From all his alimental recompense
In humid exhalations, and at Even   425
Sups with the Ocean: though in Heav'n the Trees

---

399. The line recalls James i, 17:
"Every good and perfect gift is from
above, and cometh down from the Father
of lights."
403–500. For the conception of angels
and cosmic nature see the Introduction
37.
412. Cf. the first process of digestion
as concoction in *Of Education* (C.Ed. IV,
289).
415–426. Plato's theory of the four
elements as "passing one into another
in an unbroken circle of birth" (*Tim.*
49c) helps explain why Justus Lipsius
— in *Physiologiae Stoicorum* (Antwerp,

1637) II, xiv, p. 540 — could find count-
less authorities, among them Homer,
Cleanthes, Cicero, Seneca, and especially
Pliny (*Nat. Hist.* II, ix), for the idea that
the stars "feed on the vapors of the earth
that the sun sups on the waters of the
great ocean, and the moon on those of
rivers and brooks." Milton was sympa-
thetic with contemporary revivals of the
doctrine like that of Robert Fludd in
Utriusque cosmi historia I, v, 6, where an
engraving shows the sun actually "sup-
ping with the ocean" at sunset. Yet in
I, 290–91, he mentions the lunar land-
scape as the telescope reveals it.

Of life ambrosial fruitage bear, and vines
Yield Nectar, though from off the boughs each Morn
We brush mellifluous Dews, and find the ground
Cover'd with pearly grain: yet God hath here   430
Varied his bounty so with new delights,
As may compare with Heaven; and to taste
Think not I shall be nice. So down they sat,
And to thir viands fell, nor seemingly
The Angel, nor in mist, the common gloss   435
Of Theologians, but with keen dispatch
Of real hunger, and concoctive heat
To transubstantiate; what redounds, transpires
Through Spirits with ease; nor wonder; if by fire
Of sooty coal the Empiric Alchemist   440
Can turn, or holds it possible to turn
Metals of drossiest Ore to perfet Gold
As from the Mine. Meanwhile at Table *Eve*
Minister'd naked, and thir flowing cups
With pleasant liquors crown'd: O innocence   445
Deserving Paradise! if ever, then,
Then had the Sons of God excuse to have been
Enamour'd at that sight; but in those hearts
Love unlibidinous reign'd, nor jealousy
Was understood, the injur'd Lover's Hell.   450
    Thus when with meats and drinks they had suffic't,
Not burd'n'd Nature, sudden mind arose
In *Adam*, not to let th' occasion pass
Given him by this great Conference to know
Of things above his World, and of thir being   455
Who dwell in Heav'n, whose excellence he saw
Transcend his own so far, whose radiant forms,
Divine effulgence, whose high Power so far
Exceeded human, and his wary speech
Thus to th' Empyreal Minister he fram'd.   460
    Inhabitant with God, now know I well
Thy favor, in this honor done to Man,
Under whose lowly roof thou hast voutsaf't
To enter, and these earthly fruits to taste,
Food not of Angels, yet accepted so,   465
As that more willingly thou couldst not seem
At Heav'n's high feasts to have fed: yet what compare?
    To whom the winged Hierarch repli'd.

---

429. *mellifluous:* honey-flowing.
433. *nice:* fastidious.
438. *redounds:* is excessive or unas-
similable. Cf. the angels' immunity to
surfeit at their heavenly feasts in heaven
in l. 638–39 below.
440. The *Empiric Alchemist* is any
dabbling experimenter in alchemy.

445. So the cups of Apollo's worship-
pers are literally "crowned" with wine in
Iliad I, 470, and so Virgil's peasants
"crown" their cups in *Georgics* II, 528.
447. Cf. the *Sons of God* in XI, 573–
627, n.
467. *what compare?:* what comparison
can there be?

O *Adam*, one Almighty is, from whom
All things proceed, and up to him return, 470
If not deprav'd from good, created all
Such to perfection, one first matter all,
Indu'd with various forms, various degrees
Of substance, and in things that live, of life;
But more refin'd, more spiritous, and pure, 475
As nearer to him plac't or nearer tending
Each in thir several active Spheres assign'd,
Till body up to spirit work, in bounds
Proportion'd to each kind. So from the root
Springs lighter the green stalk, from thence the leaves 480
More aery, last the bright consummate flow'r
Spirits odorous breathes: flow'rs and thir fruit
Man's nourishment, by gradual scale sublim'd
To vital spirits aspire, to animal,
To intellectual, give both life and sense, 485
Fancy and understanding, whence the Soul
Reason receives, and reason is her being,
Discursive, or Intuitive; discourse
Is oftest yours, the latter most is ours,
Differing but in degree, of kind the same. 490
Wonder not then, what God for you saw good
If I refuse not, but convert, as you,
To proper substance; time may come when men
With Angels may participate, and find
No inconvenient Diet, nor too light Fare: 495
And from these corporal nutriments perhaps
Your bodies may at last turn all to spirit,
Improv'd by tract of time, and wing'd ascend
Ethereal, as wee, or may at choice
Here or in Heav'nly Paradises dwell; 500
If ye be found obedient, and retain
Unalterably firm his love entire
Whose progeny you are. Meanwhile enjoy

469–500. For the image of the tree and the thought of the entire passage see the Introduction 40–43 and 61.

488–490. *discourse* literally means the "running to and fro" of the human mind in reasoning about things which the angels intuitively know. The principle had the best theological authority. Zanchius, for example, declared in *De Operibus Dei* (Neustadt, 1591) III, vi, that "angels do not know by rationating, combining and dividing data" as men do, and in this respect heaven differs from earth as much as it does in other ways. The distinction itself stems from Plato (*Rep*. VII, 534a) and — as W. B. Hunter's Vanderbilt thesis shows — was widely developed by Christian commentators on the *Timaeus*.

493. *proper:* veritable substance of the angel himself.

498. *tract:* extent.

503. The words *Whose progeny you are* are taken from St. Paul's sermon to the Athenians (Acts xvii, 28), but St. Paul expressly quoted them from Aratus' *Phainomena* (l. 5). From a study of Milton's own edition of Aratus, M. Kelley has shown in *PMLA*, LXX (1955), 1092, that he found corroboration for the thought in Lucretius' materialistic derivation of all life from "one celestial seed" in *De rerum natura* II, 991–92. Cf. I, 73–74, n.

Your fill what happiness this happy state
Can comprehend, incapable of more.   505
  To whom the Patriarch of mankind repli'd:
O favorable Spirit, propitious guest,
Well hast thou taught the way that might direct
Our knowledge, and the scale of Nature set
From centre to circumference, whereon   510
In contemplation of created things
By steps we may ascend to God. But say,
What meant that caution join'd, *if ye be found*
Obedient? can we want obedience then
To him, or possibly his love desert   515
Who form'd us from the dust, and plac'd us here
Full to the utmost measure of what bliss
Human desires can seek or apprehend?
  To whom the Angel. Son of Heav'n and Earth,
Attend: That thou art happy, owe to God;   520
That thou continu'st such, owe to thyself,
That is, to thy obedience; therein stand.
This was that caution giv'n thee; be advis'd.
God made thee perfet, not immutable;
And good he made thee, but to persevere   525
He left it in thy power, ordain'd thy will
By nature free, not over-rul'd by Fate
Inextricable, or strict necessity;
Our voluntary service he requires,
Not our necessitated, such with him   530
Finds no acceptance, nor can find, for how
Can hearts, not free, be tri'd whether they serve
Willing or no, who will but what they must
By Destiny, and can no other choose?
Myself and all th' Angelic Host that stand   535
In sight of God enthron'd, our happy state
Hold, as you yours, while our obedience holds;
On other surety none; freely we serve,
Because we freely love, as in our will
To love or not; in this we stand or fall: 540
And some are fall'n, to disobedience fall'n,
And so from Heav'n to deepest Hell; O fall
From what high state of bliss into what woe!

509. The *scale of Nature* also stems — as A. O. Lovejoy shows in *The Great Chain of Being* (Cambridge, Mass., 1953), p. 50 — from the *Timaeus*, but its ramifications in the thought of Milton's time were such as to let him regard the *golden Chain* of II, 1005, as one of its symbols.

521. Cf. III, 96–128, and *CD* I, iii (C.Ed. XIV, 75) where Milton declares that it would be "unworthy of God that man should nominally enjoy a liberty of which he was virtually deprived, which would be the case were that liberty to be oppressed or even obscured under the pretext of some sophistical necessity of immutability."

540. So in *CD* I, iii (C.Ed. XIV, 81) Milton says that "in assigning the gift of free will God suffered both men and angels to stand or fall at their own uncontrolled choice."

To whom our great Progenitor. Thy words
Attentive, and with more delighted ear   545
Divine instructor, I have heard, than when
Cherubic Songs by night from neighboring Hills
Aereal Music send: nor knew I not
To be both will and deed created free;
Yet that we never shall forget to love   550
Our maker, and obey him whose command
Single, is yet so just, my constant thoughts
Assur'd me and still assure: though what thou tell'st
Hath past in Heav'n, some doubt within me move,
But more desire to hear, if thou consent,   555
The full relation, which must needs be strange,
Worthy of Sacred silence to be heard;
And we have yet large day, for scarce the Sun
Hath finisht half his journey, and scarce begins
His other half in the great Zone of Heav'n.   560
  Thus *Adam* made request, and *Raphaël*
After short pause assenting, thus began.
  High matter thou injoin'st me, O prime of men,
Sad task and hard, for how shall I relate
To human sense th' invisible exploits   565
Of warring Spirits; how without remorse
The ruin of so many glorious once
And perfet while they stood; how last unfold
The secrets of another World, perhaps
Not lawful to reveal? yet for thy good   570
This is dispens't, and what surmounts the reach
Of human sense, I shall delineate so,
By lik'ning spiritual to corporal forms,
As may express them best, though what if Earth
Be but the shadow of Heav'n, and things therein   575
Each to other like, more than on Earth is thought?
  As yet this World was not, and *Chaos* wild

547. Cf. the *celestial Voices* of IV, 682.
556–560. The *full relation* to be told by Raphael in the remaining *large day* includes the war in heaven (VI), the creation of the universe (VII), and a short discussion of the stars (VIII, 1–178). The *Sacred silence* is a reminiscence of that of the spirits in the underworld as Horace imagined them (*Odes* II, xii, 29–30) listening to the songs of the shades of the poets.
563–570. So Aeneas begins his story of the fall of Troy that fills the first two books of the *Aeneid.* Addressing Dido he says:

Great Queen, what you command me
   to relate
Renews the sad remembrance of our
   fate.

An empire from its old foundations
   rent,
And every woe the Trojans under-
   went.

(*Aen.* II, 3–6. Dryden's translation.)
571–576. Though the conception of earth as the shadow of heaven has been traced to various sources, it stems from Plato's doctrine of the universe as formed on a divine and eternal model, and from Cicero's interpretation of it (in *Timaeus ex Platone* ii, 39–41) as implying that "the world which we see is a simulacrum of an eternal one." In *PMLA*, LXXV (1960), 519–26, W. G. Madsen interprets Raphael's words as referring simply to the Christian typological tradition stemming from Colossians ii, 16–17, and Hebrews viii, 1–5.

Reign'd where these Heav'ns now roll, where Earth now rests
Upon her Centre pois'd, when on a day
(For Time, though in Eternity, appli'd   580
To motion, measures all things durable
By present, past, and future) on such day
As Heav'n's great Year brings forth, th' Empyreal Host
Of Angels by Imperial summons call'd,
Innumerable before th' Almighty's Throne   585
Forthwith from all the ends of Heav'n appear'd
Under thir Hierarchs in orders bright;
Ten thousand thousand Ensigns high advanc'd,
Standards and Gonfalons, twixt Van and Rear
Stream in the Air, and for distinction serve   590
Of Hierarchies, of Orders, and Degrees;
Or in thir glittering Tissues bear imblaz'd
Holy Memorials, acts of Zeal and Love
Recorded eminent. Thus when in Orbs
Of circuit inexpressible they stood,   595
Orb within Orb, the Father infinite,
By whom in bliss imbosom'd sat the Son,
Amidst as from a flaming Mount, whose top
Brightness had made invisible, thus spake.
　　Hear all ye Angels, Progeny of Light,   600
Thrones, Dominations, Princedoms, Virtues, Powers,
Hear my Decree, which unrevok't shall stand.
This day I have begot whom I declare

578–579. Cf. the fuller account of the *Earth self-balanc't on her Centre* in VII, 242.

580–582. Pleading in *CD* I, vii that "it seems probable that the apostasy which caused the expulsion of so many thousands [of angels] from heaven, took place before the foundations of the world were laid," Milton attacked "the common opinion that motion and time (which is the measure of motion) could not, according to the ratio of priority and subsequence, have existed before the world was made." He was thinking of Plato's account of the divine creation of the "sun, the moon, and the five other planets" as indicators of time (*Tim.* 38c–e), and he went on to argue that "Aristotle, who teaches that no ideas of motion and time can be formed except in reference to this world, nevertheless pronounces the world itself to be eternal." See the Introduction 21.

583. The conception of the *great Year*, when all the stars should return to their first positions, is also from the *Timaeus* (39d). Plato implies that it contained 36,000 earthly years.

597. Cf. III, 169, n., for the representation of the Son *in bliss imbosom'd*.

599. Cf. II, 263–67, for God's invisible brightness.

603–615. In deciding to begin the chronological action of *PL* by dramatizing a tradition of the revelation of the exaltation of Christ to the angels that stems from Hebrews i, 6, and had orthodox theological support such as St. Thomas gives to it (*Summa Theol.* I, q. 57, a.5), Milton was strongly influenced by Psalm ii, 6–7, which he quoted in *CD* I, v, and in 1653 had translated in this way:

. . . but I saith he
Anointed have my King (though
　　ye rebell)
On Sion my holi' hill. A firm decree
　　I will declare: the Lord to me hath
　　say'd
Thou art my Son, I have begotten
　　thee
This day; . . .

The words in parentheses, which are not suggested by the Hebrew original, are related to the dramatic situation in this passage by C. Dahlberg in *MLN*, LXVII (1952), 27. In summing up the meaning of *begot* in l. 603, M. Kelley rightly rejects Saurat's view that it means that the Son was created at this moment of his presentation to the angels. The generation

My only Son, and on this holy Hill
Him have anointed, whom ye now behold   605
At my right hand; your Head I him appoint;
And by my Self have sworn to him shall bow
All knees in Heav'n, and shall confess him Lord:
Under his great Vice-gerent Reign abide
United as one individual Soul   610
For ever happy: him who disobeys
Mee disobeys, breaks union, and that day
Cast out from God and blessed vision, falls
Into utter darkness, deep ingulft, his place
Ordain'd without redemption, without end.   615
  So spake th' Omnipotent, and with his words
All seem'd well pleas'd, all seem'd, but were not all.
That day, as other solemn days, they spent
In song and dance about the sacred Hill,
Mystical dance, which yonder starry Sphere   620
Of Planets and of fixt in all her Wheels
Resembles nearest, mazes intricate,
Eccentric, intervolv'd, yet regular
Then most, when most irregular they seem:
And in thir motions harmony Divine   625
So smooths her charming tones, that God's own ear
Listens delighted. Ev'ning now approach'd
(For wee have also our Ev'ning and our Morn,
Wee ours for change delectable, not need)
Forthwith from dance to sweet repast they turn   630
Desirous; all in Circles as they stood,
Tables are set, and on a sudden pil'd
With Angels' Food, and rubied Nectar flows:
In Pearl, in Diamond, and massy Gold,
Fruit of delicious Vines, the growth of Heav'n.   635
On flow'rs repos'd, and with fresh flow'rets crown'd,
They eat, they drink, and in communion sweet
Quaff immortality and joy, secure
Of surfeit where full measure only bounds

---

is "figurative" (*Argument*, p. 105); it
means that Christ was exalted, and it is
used because God, "in proclaiming the
Son ruler over the angels, is metaphori-
cally generating a new thing — a king."
  607. So God swears by himself to
Abraham (Gen. xxii, 16).
  613. Cf. the reference to the beatific
vision in I, 684.
  623. *Eccentric* has the astronomical
application that it has in III, 575, and
VIII, 83.
  620–624. Milton could count on his
readers to know both Plato's conception
of the orderly movement of the stars as

a *dance* and its literary trail in poems
like Sir John Davies' *Orchestra: Or a
Poeme of Dauncing* (1596):
> What if to you these sparks dis-
>   ordered seeme
> As if by chaunce they had been
>   scattered there?
> The Gods a solemne measure doe it
>   deeme
> And see a iust proportion euery
>   where.
>   (Stanza 36, 1–4)
  637. Cf. the *fellowships of joy* in XI,
80, and the *sweet societies of Lycidas*, 179.

Excess, before th' all bounteous King, who show'r'd   640
With copious hand, rejoicing in thir joy.
Now when ambrosial Night with Clouds exhal'd
From that high mount of God, whence light and shade
Spring both, the face of brightest Heav'n had chang'd
To grateful Twilight (for Night comes not there   645
In darker veil) and roseate Dews dispos'd
All but the unsleeping eyes of God to rest,
Wide over all the Plain, and wider far
Than all this globous Earth in Plain outspread,
(Such are the Courts of God) th' Angelic throng   650
Disperst in Bands and Files thir Camp extend
By living Streams among the Trees of Life,
Pavilions numberless, and sudden rear'd,
Celestial Tabernacles, where they slept
Fann'd with cool Winds, save those who in thir course   655
Melodious Hymns about the sovran Throne
Alternate all night long: but not so wak'd
Satan, so call him now, his former name
Is heard no more in Heav'n; he of the first,
If not the first Arch-Angel, great in Power,   660
In favor and preëminence, yet fraught
With envy against the Son of God, that day
Honor'd by his great Father, and proclaim'd
Messiah King anointed, could not bear
Through pride that sight, and thought himself impair'd.   665
Deep malice thence conceiving and disdain,
Soon as midnight brought on the dusky hour
Friendliest to sleep and silence, he resolv'd
With all his Legions to dislodge, and leave
Unworshipt, unobey'd the Throne supreme,   670
Contemptuous, and his next subordinate
Awak'ning, thus to him in secret spake.
     Sleep'st thou, Companion dear, what sleep can close
Thy eye-lids? and rememb'rest what Decree
Of yesterday, so late hath past the lips   675
Of Heav'n's Almighty. Thou to me thy thoughts
Wast wont, I mine to thee was wont to impart;
Both waking we were one; how then can now
Thy sleep dissent? new Laws thou see'st impos'd;

645. The *Twilight* corresponds to the prophecy in Revelation xxi, 25, that "there shall be no night there."
647. God is *unsleeping*, for "he that keepeth Israel shall neither slumber nor sleep" (Psalm cxxi, 4).
658-659. Cf. the explanation in I, 361-63, that the names of the fallen angels are blotted out of *heavenly records*.
664. *Messiah* literally means "anointed."
665. *impair'd*: lowered in rank among the heavenly peers or aristocratic hierarchy.
671. *his next subordinate:* Beelzebub. Cf. II, 299-300. P. L. Carver notes — *RES*, XVI (1940), 423 — that St. Thomas describes (*Summa Theol.* I, q. 63, a.7) Satan, moved by pride and envy to revolt against God, as appealing to his fellows in just the way that Satan does to Beelzebub here.

New Laws from him who reigns, new minds may raise 680
In us who serve, new Counsels, to debate
What doubtful may ensue; more in this place
To utter is not safe. Assemble thou
Of all those Myriads which we lead the chief;
Tell them that by command, ere yet dim Night 685
Her shadowy Cloud withdraws, I am to haste,
And all who under me thir Banners wave,
Homeward with flying march where we possess
The Quarters of the North, there to prepare
Fit entertainment to receive our King 690
The great *Messiah*, and his new commands,
Who speedily through all the Hierarchies
Intends to pass triumphant, and give Laws.
   So spake the false Arch-Angel, and infus'd
Bad influence into th' unwary breast 695
Of his Associate; hee together calls,
Or several one by one, the Regent Powers,
Under him Regent, tells, as he was taught,
That the most High commanding, now ere Night,
Now ere dim Night had disincumber'd Heav'n, 700
The great Hierarchal Standard was to move;
Tells the suggested cause, and casts between
Ambiguous words and jealousies, to sound
Or taint integrity; but all obey'd
The wonted signal, and superior voice 705
Of thir great Potentate; for great indeed
His name, and high was his degree in Heav'n;
His count'nance, as the Morning Star that guides
The starry flock, allur'd them, and with lies
Drew after him the third part of Heav'n's Host: 710
Meanwhile th' Eternal eye, whose sight discerns
Abstrusest thoughts, from forth his holy Mount
And from within the golden Lamps that burn
Nightly before him, saw without thir light

---

689. The tradition of Satan as lord of the north is partly due to the key passage in Isaiah xiv, 12, from which his name of Lucifer is taken together with the idea that the passage referred to Satan as rebelling against God, and from the following verse: "I will ascend into heaven, I will exalt my throne above the stars of God: I will sit also upon the mount of the congregation, in the sides of the north." St. Augustine rationalized the tradition (in Epistle 140, sect. 55) by suggesting that, because the devils have turned their backs on the warmth of charity and are far advanced in pride and envy, they are torpid in icy hardness. "And hence through a figure they are put in the north." The tradition was wide-spread in folklore and popular literature. Shakespeare's audience had no trouble in recognizing Satan under the name of "the lordly monarch of the north" (*I Henry VI* V, iii, 6).

696. *he:* Beelzebub.

697. *several:* severally, separately.

708. *The Morning Star* is still another allusion to "Lucifer, son of the morning" (Isa. xiv, 12).

710. Cf. II, 692, n.

713. Milton refers to the "seven lamps of fire burning before the throne" (Rev. iv, 5) and the "unsleeping eyes of God" (cf. l. 647 above), passages which he perhaps related to the seven angelic eyes mentioned in Zechariah iii, 9, which figure in III, 648.

Rebellion rising, saw in whom, how spread 715
Among the sons of Morn, what multitudes
Were banded to oppose his high Decree;
And smiling to his only Son thus said.
    Son, thou in whom my glory I behold
In full resplendence, Heir of all my might, 720
Nearly it now concerns us to be sure
Of our Omnipotence, and with what Arms
We mean to hold what anciently we claim
Of Deity or Empire, such a foe
Is rising, who intends to erect his Throne 725
Equal to ours, throughout the spacious North;
Nor so content, hath in his thought to try
In battle, what our Power is, or our right.
Let us advise, and to this hazard draw
With speed what force is left, and all imploy 730
In our defense, lest unawares we lose
This our high place, our Sanctuary, our Hill.
    To whom the Son with calm aspect and clear
Lightning Divine, ineffable, serene,
Made answer. Mighty Father, thou thy foes 735
Justly hast in derision, and secure
Laugh'st at thir vain designs and tumults vain,
Matter to mee of Glory, whom thir hate
Illustrates, when they see all Regal Power
Giv'n me to quell thir pride, and in event 740
Know whether I be dext'rous to subdue
Thy Rebels, or be found the worst in Heav'n.
    So spake the Son, but *Satan* with his Powers
Far was advanc't on winged speed, an Host
Innumerable as the Stars of Night, 745
Or Stars of Morning, Dew-drops, which the Sun
Impearls on every leaf and every flower.
Regions they pass'd, the mighty Regencies
Of Seraphim and Potentates and Thrones
In thir triple Degrees, Regions to which 750
All thy Dominion, *Adam* is no more
Than what this Garden is to all the Earth,
And all the Sea, from one entire globose

---

716. The phrase *sons of Morn* is from Isaiah xiv, 12. Cf. *Nativity*, 119.
719. Cf. III, 63, n.
734. The Son is the *Similitude* of the invisible *Fountain of Light* in III, 375-84.
736. Cf. II, 191, n.
739. *Illustrates:* makes luminous or glorious. The picture is that of Christ set as king on God's "holy hill" in Psalm ii, 6.
740. *event* keeps its Latin meaning of "outcome." Cf. II, 82.
743. *Powers* means "armies" and is not used here, as it is in 601 above, with reference to that rank in the *triple Degrees* of the Dionysian hierarchy of angels that are mentioned in ll. 749-750 below. See the Introduction 21.
748. *Regencies:* provinces, dominions.
753. *globose:* sphere. It is imagined as stretched on a flat projection.

Stretcht into Longitude; which having pass'd
At length into the limits of the North
They came, and *Satan* to his Royal seat   755
High on a Hill, far blazing, as a Mount
Rais'd on a Mount, with Pyramids and Tow'rs
From Diamond Quarries hewn, and Rocks of Gold,
The Palace of great *Lucifer*, (so call   760
That Structure in the Dialect of men
Interpreted) which not long after, he
Affecting all equality with God,
In imitation of that Mount whereon
Messiah was declar'd in sight of Heav'n,   765
The Mountain of the Congregation call'd:
For thither he assembl'd all his Train,
Pretending so commanded to consult
About the great reception of thir King,
Thither to come, and with calumnious Art   770
Of counterfeited truth thus held thir ears.

   Thrones, Dominations, Princedoms, Virtues, Powers,
If these magnific Titles yet remain
Not merely titular, since by Decree
Another now hath to himself ingross't   775
All Power, and us eclipst under the name
Of King anointed, for whom all this haste
Of midnight march, and hurried meeting here,
This only to consult how we may best
With what may be devis'd of honors new   780
Receive him coming to receive from us
Knee-tribute yet unpaid, prostration vile,
Too much to one, but double how endur'd,
To one and to his image now proclaim'd?
But what if better counsels might erect   785
Our minds and teach us to cast off this Yoke?
Will ye submit your necks, and choose to bend
The supple knee? ye will not, if I trust
To know ye right, or if ye know yourselves
Natives and Sons of Heav'n possest before   790
By none, and if not equal all, yet free,
Equally free; for Orders and Degrees

---

763. *Affecting*: aspiring or pretending (to possess something).

777. *King anointed* looks back to *Messiah* in l. 664 above.

784. Cf. the *radiant Image of his Glory* in III, 63.

788. The *supple knee* recalls "the tribute of his supple knee" in Shakespeare's *Richard II*, I, iv, 33, and other examples that reveal its proverbial character.

792-99. Satan twists the truth that Milton asserted in *CD* I, ix, and embodied in his conception of human order and liberty in *The Reason of Church Government* (C.Ed. III, 185) as patterned upon "the angels themselves, in whom no disorder is feared, as the apostle that saw them in his rapture describes, . . . distinguished and quaternioned into their celestial princedoms and satrapies, according as God himself has writ his imperial decrees through the great provinces of heaven."

Jar not with liberty, but well consist.
Who can in reason then or right assume
Monarchy over such as live by right   795
His equals, if in power and splendor less,
In freedom equal? or can introduce
Law and Edict on us, who without law
Err not? much less for this to be our Lord,
And look for adoration to th' abuse   800
Of those Imperial Titles which assert
Our being ordain'd to govern, not to serve?
    Thus far his bold discourse without control
Had audience, when among the Seraphim
Abdiel, than whom none with more zeal ador'd   805
The Deity, and divine commands obey'd,
Stood up, and in a flame of zeal severe
The current of his fury thus oppos'd.
    O argument blasphemous, false and proud!
Words which no ear ever to hear in Heav'n   810
Expected, least of all from thee, ingrate,
In place thyself so high above thy Peers.
Canst thou with impious obloquy condemn
The just Decree of God, pronounc't and sworn,
That to his only Son by right endu'd   815
With Regal Sceptre, every Soul in Heav'n
Shall bend the knee, and in that honor due
Confess him rightful King? unjust thou say'st
Flatly unjust, to bind with Laws the free,
And equal over equals to let Reign,   820
One over all with unsucceeded power.
Shalt thou give Law to God, shalt thou dispute
With him the points of liberty, who made
Thee what thou art, and form'd the Pow'rs of Heav'n
Such as he pleas'd, and circumscrib'd thir being?   825
Yet by experience taught we know how good,
And of our good, and of our dignity
How provident he is, how far from thought
To make us less, bent rather to exalt
Our happy state under one Head more near   830
United. But to grant it thee unjust,
That equal over equals Monarch Reign:

---

804. *audience:* hearing, acceptance.
805. The name *Abdiel*, meaning "servant of God," occurs only as a human name in the Bible (I Chron. v, 15). Milton invented his character as an embodiment of that "ardent desire of hallowing the name of God, together with an indignation against whatever tends to the violation or contempt of religion" which he said in *CD* II, vi (C.Ed. XVII,

153) "is called zeal." Though — as A. H. Gilbert says in *MP*, XL (1943), 19–42 — Abdiel's episode is not essential to the narrative plot, it dramatizes Satan's revolt against the Son of God, who is imagined here as the "king" of Psalm ii, of whom God has set upon his "holy hill 6, Zion," and who represents Milton's ideal of the ruler "who by right of merit Reigns" in VI, 43.

Thyself though great and glorious dost thou count,
Or all Angelic Nature join'd in one,
Equal to him begotten Son, by whom   835
As by his Word the mighty Father made
All things, ev'n thee, and all the Spirits of Heav'n
By him created in thir bright degrees,
Crown'd them with Glory, and to thir Glory nam'd
Thrones, Dominations, Princedoms, Virtues, Powers,   840
Essential Powers, nor by his Reign obscur'd,
But more illustrious made, since he the Head
One of our number thus reduc't becomes,
His Laws our Laws, all honor to him done
Returns our own. Cease then this impious rage,   845
And tempt not these; but hast'n to appease
Th' incensed Father, and th' incensed Son,
While Pardon may be found in time besought.

    So spake the fervent Angel, but his zeal
None seconded, as out of season judg'd,   850
Or singular and rash, whereat rejoic'd
Th' Apostate, and more haughty thus repli'd.

    That we were form'd then say'st thou? and the work
Of secondary hands, by task transferr'd
From Father to his Son? strange point and new!   855
Doctrine which we would know whence learnt: who saw
When this creation was? remember'st thou
Thy making, while the Maker gave thee being?
We know no time when we were not as now;
Know none before us, self-begot, self-rais'd   860
By our own quick'ning power, when fatal course
Had circl'd his full Orb, the birth mature
Of this our native Heav'n, Ethereal Sons.
Our puissance is our own, our own right hand
Shall teach us highest deeds, by proof to try   865
Who is our equal: then thou shalt behold
Whether by supplication we intend
Address, and to begirt th' Almighty Throne
Beseeching or besieging. This report,
These tidings carry to th' anointed King;   870

---

834. *all Angelic Nature:* all that part
of nature (or of God's creation) that is
represented by the angels.

835–845. Milton echoes Colossians i,
15–17, which he interprets in *CD* I, vii
(C.Ed. XIV, 191) as meaning that all
things were created *through* Christ, who
is "the first-born of every creature" both
in the sense that he existed before all
other creatures and in the sense that he
excels all his fellow creatures and stands
nearest of them all to the maker of all.

853–863. As early as I, 116, Satan is

casting doubt upon the article of faith
that Milton formulated in *CD* I, vii
(C.Ed. XV, 33) in the words: "the angels
were created at some particular period."
Precedent for Satan's insinuation that
his followers were self-created has been
observed by G. McColley in *Harvard
Theological Review*, XXXII (1939), 183,
as early as the twelfth century in perhaps
the first imaginative treatment of the
theme of the victory of the Son, the *De
victoria Verbi Dei* of Abbot Rupert
Tuitensis.

And fly, ere evil intercept thy flight.

He said, and as the sound of waters deep
Hoarse murmur echo'd to his words applause
Through the infinite Host, nor less for that
The flaming Seraph fearless, though alone   875
Encompass'd round with foes, thus answer'd bold.

O alienate from God, O Spirit accurst,
Forsak'n of all good; I see thy fall
Determin'd, and thy hapless crew involv'd
In this perfidious fraud, contagion spread   880
Both of thy crime and punishment: henceforth
No more be troubl'd how to quit the yoke
Of God's *Messiah:* those indulgent Laws
Will not be now voutsaf'd, other Decrees
Against thee are gone forth without recall;   885
That Golden Sceptre which thou didst reject
Is now an Iron Rod to bruise and break
Thy disobedience. Well thou didst advise,
Yet not for thy advice or threats I fly
These wicked Tents devoted, lest the wrath   890
Impendent, raging into sudden flame
Distinguish not: for soon expect to feel
His Thunder on thy head, devouring fire.
Then who created thee lamenting learn,
When who can uncreate thee thou shalt know.   895

So spake the Seraph *Abdiel* faithful found,
Among the faithless, faithful only hee;
Among innumerable false, unmov'd,
Unshak'n, unseduc'd, unterrifi'd
His Loyalty he kept, his Love, his Zeal;   900
Nor number, nor example with him wrought
To swerve from truth, or change his constant mind
Though single. From amidst them forth he pass'd,
Long way through hostile scorn, which he sustain'd
Superior, nor of violence fear'd aught;   905
And with retorted scorn his back he turn'd
On those proud Tow'rs to swift destruction doom'd.

The End of the Fifth Book.

---

887. Cf. the *iron Sceptre* which the
devils have learned to fear in II, 327.
Abdiel's words resemble the threat in
Of Reformation II (C.Ed. III, 69) that
he who rejects "the meek censure of the
church" must "fear to fall under the
iron sceptre of his [Christ's] anger, that
will dash him to pieces like a potsherd."
890. Abdiel resembles Moses urging

the Jews to abandon the blasphemous
rebels Korah, Dathan, and Abiram with
the words, "Depart from the tents of
these wicked men, lest ye be consumed
in all their sins" (Num. xvi, 26).
890. *devoted* has its Latin force of
"doomed to destruction."
906. *retorted* keeps its literal Latin
meaning of "turned back."

BOOK VI

THE ARGUMENT

Raphael continues to relate how Michael *and* Gabriel *were sent forth to Battle against* Satan *and his Angels. The first Fight describ'd:* Satan *and his Powers retire under Night: He calls a Council, invents devilish Engines, which in the second day's Fight put* Michael *and his Angels to some disorder; but they at length pulling up Mountains overwhelm'd both the force and Machines of* Satan*: Yet the Tumult not so ending, God on the third day sends* Messiah *his Son, for whom he had reserv'd the glory of that Victory: Hee in the Power of his Father coming to the place, and causing all his Legions to stand still on either side, with his Chariot and Thunder driving into the midst of his Enemies, pursues them unable to resist towards the wall of Heaven; which opening, they leap down with horror and confusion into the place of punishment prepar'd for them in the Deep:* Messiah *returns with triumph to his Father.*

All night the dreadless Angel unpursu'd
Through Heav'n's wide Champaign held his way, till Morn,
Wak't by the circling Hours, with rosy hand
Unbarr'd the gates of Light.   There is a Cave
Within the Mount of God, fast by his Throne,   5
Where light and darkness in perpetual round
Lodge and dislodge by turns, which makes through Heav'n
Grateful vicissitude, like Day and Night;
Light issues forth, and at the other door
Obsequious darkness enters, till her hour   10
To veil the Heav'n, though darkness there might well
Seem twilight here; and now went forth the Morn
Such as in highest Heav'n, array'd in Gold
Empyreal, from before her vanisht Night,
Shot through with orient Beams: when all the Plain   15
Cover'd with thick embattl'd Squadrons bright,
Chariots and flaming Arms, and fiery Steeds
Reflecting blaze on blaze, first met his view:
War he perceiv'd, war in procinct, and found
Already known what he for news had thought   20

1. *the dreadless Angel:* Abdiel.
2–4. Cf. *Morn with rosy steps* in V, 1.
Homer first personified the Hours (*Il.* V, 749) as the "fair daughters of high Jove" whom we find in the *Faerie Queene* guarding

the charge to them fore-shewed
By mighty Jove; who did them por-
ters make
Of heavens gate.
(VII, vii, 45, 5–7)
The cave of Light and Darkness seems like an adaptation of the abysm where Hesiod said that Day and Night alternately lived (*Theog.*, 736–57).

8. *vicissitude:* alternation, change. Cf. VII, 351.
10. *Obsequious* has little more than its neutral Latin meaning of "following," but cf. the *Grateful twilight* of V, 645.
14. In *Empyreal* there is a reference both to its derivation from the Greek word for "fire" and to the distinction of heavenly from earthly fire that is intimated in II, 139.
19. So Chapman uses the technical Latin term *procinct* in translating *Iliad* XII, 88–89: "each chariot and steed . . . to be kept in all procinct of warre." The word means "readiness."

To have reported: gladly then he mixt
Among those friendly Powers who him receiv'd
With joy and acclamations loud, that one
That of so many Myriads fall'n, yet one
Return'd not lost: On to the sacred hill   25
They led him high applauded, and present
Before the seat supreme; from whence a voice
From midst a Golden Cloud thus mild was heard.
    Servant of God, well done, well hast thou fought
The better fight, who single hast maintain'd   30
Against revolted multitudes the Cause
Of Truth, in word mightier than they in Arms;
And for the testimony of Truth hast borne
Universal reproach, far worse to bear
Than violence: for this was all thy care   35
To stand approv'd in sight of God, though Worlds
Judg'd thee perverse: the easier conquest now
Remains thee, aided by this host of friends,
Back on thy foes more glorious to return
Than scorn'd thou didst depart, and to subdue   40
By force, who reason for thir Law refuse,
Right reason for thir Law, and for thir King
Messiah, who by right of merit Reigns.
Go *Michael* of Celestial Armies Prince,
And thou in Military prowess next,   45
Gabriel, lead forth to Battle these my Sons
Invincible, lead forth my armed Saints
By Thousands and by Millions rang'd for fight;
Equal in number to that Godless crew
Rebellious, them with Fire and hostile Arms   50
Fearless assault, and to the brow of Heav'n
Pursuing drive them out from God and bliss,
Into thir place of punishment, the Gulf
Of *Tartarus*, which ready opens wide
His fiery *Chaos* to receive thir fall.   55

29. *Servant of God* translates the literal meaning of *Abdiel.* Cf. V, 805. The greeting, "Well done, good and faithful servant," to the man in the parable of judgment (Matt. xxv, 21) who is told to "enter into the joy" of his Lord, mingles here with St. Paul's cry, "I have fought a good fight."
32. So Truth appears in metaphors of struggle in *Areopagitica* as "strong, next to the Almighty" (C.Ed. IV, 348).
34. Spenser put the maxim into the words: "For evill deedes may better then bad words be bore" (*F.Q.* IV, iv, 4, 9).
42. Cf. *Reason* as "the image of God" in *Areopagitica.*
43. In I, 98, this line is foreshadowed.
44. In Jewish tradition *Michael* (the "God-like" or "strength of God") is "the great prince which standeth for the children of thy people" (Dan. xii, 1), as Milton noted in *CD* I, ix (C.Ed. XV, 105). Jewish and Christian tradition concur in making him the chief angel, but the *Jewish Encyclopaedia* notes (VIII, 537) that the legend of Michael and the dragon "is not found in Jewish sources except insofar as Samael or Satan is called in the Cabala 'the primitive serpent.' " West notes (in *Milton and Angels*, p. 125) that in making the name *Michael* signify "not Christ but the first of the Angels," Milton accepted Catholic rather than Protestant opinion.
46. Cf. *Gabriel* in IV, 549.

So spake the Sovran voice, and Clouds began
To darken all the Hill, and smoke to roll
In dusky wreaths, reluctant flames, the sign
Of wrath awak't: nor with less dread the loud
Ethereal Trumpet from on high gan blow: 60
At which command the Powers Militant,
That stood for Heav'n, in mighty Quadrate join'd
Of Union irresistible, mov'd on
In silence thir bright Legions, to the sound
Of instrumental Harmony that breath'd   65
Heroic Ardor to advent'rous deeds
Under thir God-like Leaders, in the Cause
Of God and his *Messiah*. On they move
Indissolubly firm; nor obvious Hill,
Nor straitening Vale, nor Wood, nor Stream divides   70
Thir perfet ranks; for high above the ground
Thir march was, and the passive Air upbore
Thir nimble tread; as when the total kind
Of Birds in orderly array on wing
Came summon'd over *Eden* to receive   75
Thir names of thee; so over many a tract
Of Heav'n they march'd, and many a Province wide
Tenfold the length of this terrene: at last
Far in th' Horizon to the North appear'd
From skirt to skirt a fiery Region, stretcht   80
In battailous aspect, and nearer view
Bristl'd with upright beams innumerable
Of rigid Spears, and Helmets throng'd, and Shields
Various, with boastful Argument portray'd,
The banded Powers of *Satan* hasting on   85
With furious expedition; for they ween'd
That selfsame day by fight, or by surprise
To win the Mount of God, and on his Throne
To set the envier of his State, the proud
Aspirer, but thir thoughts prov'd fond and vain   90
In the mid way: though strange to us it seem'd
At first, that Angel should with Angel war,

57. The scene resembles Mt. Sinai when it was "altogether on a smoke, because the Lord descended upon it in fire; and the smoke thereof ascended as the smoke of a furnace" (Exod. xix, 18).

62. *Quadrate:* a square phalanx. Another such military term is *globe* in II, 512. Cf. the devils moving "in perfect phalanx" to Dorian strains in I, 550.

69. *obvious* keeps its literal, Latin meaning of "in the way."

70. *straitening:* confining.

74. So Homer (*Il.* II, 459–63) and Vergil (*Aen.* VII, 699–701) compare mustering troops to flights of birds.

79. Cf. the mustering of the devils in the *Quarters of the North* in V, 689.

84. *Argument:* the signification of the inscriptions or emblems on the shields. There may be an allusion to the boastfully inscribed shields of the seven doomed kings in the assault on Thebes in Euripides' *Phoenician Maidens*, 1108–40.

86. *expedition* keeps its Latin force of "haste."

And in fierce hosting meet, who wont to meet
So oft in Festivals of joy and love
Unanimous, as sons of one great Sire   95
Hymning th' Eternal Father: but the shout
Of Battle now began, and rushing sound
Of onset ended soon each milder thought.
High in the midst exalted as a God
Th' Apostate in his Sun-bright Chariot sat   100
Idol of Majesty Divine, enclos'd
With Flaming Cherubim, and golden Shields;
Then lighted from his gorgeous Throne, for now
'Twixt Host and Host but narrow space was left,
A dreadful interval, and Front to Front   105
Presented stood in terrible array
Of hideous length: before the cloudy Van,
On the rough edge of battle ere it join'd,
Satan with vast and haughty strides advanc'd,
Came tow'ring, arm'd in Adamant and Gold;   110
Abdiel that sight endur'd not, where he stood
Among the mightiest, bent on highest deeds,
And thus his own undaunted heart explores.
    O Heav'n! that such resemblance of the Highest
Should yet remain, where faith and realty   115
Remain not; wherefore should not strength and might
There fail where Virtue fails, or weakest prove
Where boldest; though to sight unconquerable?
His puissance, trusting in th' Almighty's aid,
I mean to try, whose Reason I have tri'd   120
Unsound and false; nor is it aught but just,
That he who in debate of Truth hath won,
Should win in Arms, in both disputes alike
Victor; though brutish that contest and foul,
When Reason hath to deal with force, yet so   125
Most reason is that Reason overcome.
    So pondering, and from his armed Peers
Forth stepping opposite, half way he met
His daring foe, at this prevention more
Incenst, and thus securely him defi'd.   130
    Proud, art thou met? thy hope was to have reacht
    The highth of thy aspiring unoppos'd,

93. *hosting:* rallying of troops into hosts. *wont:* accustomed.
100. *Apostate* is felt almost as a verb as well as a noun. It means a seceder, a person who stands out from or against others.
101. *Idol* suggests that Satan is idolized by his followers, who ought, of course, to worship the true image of God in his Son.
113. The line translates Homer's introduction of Hector's soliloquy of decision to face Achilles in the single combat in which he finally is slain (*Il.* xxii, 98).
115. *realty*, if it is not a misprint for "lealty" or "fealty," is a contraction of "reality," the want of which Abdiel charges to the *Idol*, Satan.
120. *tri'd:* proved by trial.
129. *prevention* has the literal, Latin force of "confrontation" — in this case by an obstacle or challenge.

The Throne of God unguarded, and his side
Abandon'd at the terror of thy Power
Or potent tongue; fool, not to think how vain   135
Against th' Omnipotent to rise in Arms;
Who out of smallest things could without end
Have rais'd incessant Armies to defeat
Thy folly; or with solitary hand
Reaching beyond all limit, at one blow   140
Unaided could have finisht thee, and whelm'd
Thy Legions under darkness; but thou seest
All are not of thy Train; there be who Faith
Prefer, and Piety to God, though then
To thee not visible, when I alone   145
Seem'd in thy World erroneous to dissent
From all: my Sect thou seest, now learn too late
How few sometimes may know, when thousands err.
     Whom the grand Foe with scornful eye askance
Thus answer'd. Ill for thee, but in wisht hour   150
Of my revenge, first sought for thou return'st
From flight, seditious Angel, to receive
Thy merited reward, the first assay
Of this right hand provok'd, since first that tongue
Inspir'd with contradiction durst oppose   155
A third part of the Gods, in Synod met
Thir Deities to assert, who while they feel
Vigor Divine within them, can allow
Omnipotence to none. But well thou com'st
Before thy fellows, ambitious to win   160
From me some Plume, that thy success may show
Destruction to the rest: this pause between
(Unanswer'd lest thou boast) to let thee know;
At first I thought that Liberty and Heav'n
To heav'nly Souls had been all one; but now   165
I see that most through sloth had rather serve,
Minist'ring Spirits, train'd up in Feast and Song;
Such hast thou arm'd, the Minstrelsy of Heav'n,
Servility with freedom to contend,

---

143. *there be:* there are those. *Faith:* faithfulness, fidelity.

146. *erroneous:* erring. Cf. *erroneous* in the literal sense of "wandering" in VII, 20. Satan lives in a world of wandering from truth.

147. *Sect* was a term of reproach among the Royalists for the denominations into which Protestantism was splintering. In the Preface to *Eikonoklastes* (C.Ed. V, 73) Milton protested against the "odious names of Schism and Sectarism," and added, "I never knew that time in *England,* when men of truest Religion were not counted Sectaries."

153. *assay:* trial of strength.

156. As in II, 391, *Synod* is Satan's pompous term for the assembly of *Gods* who have rallied to his standard.

161. As in II, 123, *success* implies doubt of a happy outcome.

162. The *pause* is the time between Satan's meeting with Abdiel and their impending combat.

167–169. The *Minstrelsy* stands for the loyal angels who are still God's ministers, chanting hymns in his praise; *freedom* stands for the rebels.

As both thir deeds compar'd this day shall prove.   170
To whom in brief thus *Abdiel* stern repli'd.
Apostate, still thou err'st, nor end wilt find
Of erring, from the path of truth remote:
Unjustly thou deprav'st it with the name
Of *Servitude* to serve whom God ordains,   175
Or Nature; God and Nature bid the same,
When he who rules is worthiest, and excels
Them whom he governs. This is servitude,
To serve th' unwise, or him who hath rebell'd
Against his worthier, as thine now serve thee,   180
Thyself not free, but to thyself enthrall'd;
Yet lewdly dar'st our minist'ring upbraid.
Reign thou in Hell thy Kingdom, let mee serve
In Heav'n God ever blest, and his Divine
Behests obey, worthiest to be obey'd;   185
Yet Chains in Hell, not Realms expect: meanwhile
From mee return'd, as erst thou said'st, from flight,
This greeting on thy impious Crest receive.
So saying, a noble stroke he lifted high,
Which hung not, but so swift with tempest fell   190
On the proud Crest of *Satan*, that no sight,
Nor motion of swift thought, less could his Shield
Such ruin intercept: ten paces huge
He back recoil'd; the tenth on bended knee
His massy Spear upstay'd; as if on Earth   195
Winds under ground or waters forcing way
Sidelong, had pusht a Mountain from his seat
Half sunk with all his Pines. Amazement seiz'd
The Rebel Thrones, but greater rage to see
Thou foil'd thir mightiest, ours joy fill'd, and shout,   200
Presage of Victory and fierce desire
Of Battle: whereat *Michaël* bid sound
Th' Arch-Angel trumpet; through the vast of Heav'n
It sounded, and the faithful Armies rung
Hosanna to the Highest: nor stood at gaze   205

174. *deprav'st* keeps its Latin force of "perverting" or "impairing."

176. The thought is that of nature as 'the mysterious power and efficacy of the divine voice which went forth in the beginning, and to which, as to a perpetual command, all things have since paid obedience" (*CD* I, viii, C.Ed. XV, 93). The laws of nature and reason are one, and obedience to God as reason is natural. Cf. l. 42 above, n.

178–181. So servitude is defined in XII, 90–101, and *PR* II, 463–72. The thought is anticipated in I, 255, and IV, 75.

187. *as erst thou said'st* recalls As-

canius' tough reply to Numanus in their typical, epic exchange of boasts between heroes in battle (*Aen.* IX, 599–635).

193–194. J. Whaler suggests (in *Counterpoint*, p. 100) that in the number symbolism of Milton's times, ten would signify power and ten reversed, power destroyed.

196. So the cause of earthquakes is implied in I, 231–37, to be.

199. *Thrones*, though it means one of the nine orders of angels, is loosely used to mean all of Satan's adherents. See the Introduction, 21.

205. Cf. II, 243.

The adverse Legions, nor less hideous join'd
The horrid shock: now storming fury rose,
And clamor such as heard in Heav'n till now
Was never, Arms on Armor clashing bray'd
Horrible discord, and the madding Wheels   210
Of brazen Chariots rag'd; dire was the noise
Of conflict; over head the dismal hiss
Of fiery Darts in flaming volleys flew,
And flying vaulted either Host with fire.
So under fiery Cope together rush'd   215
Both Battles main, with ruinous assault
And inextinguishable rage; all Heav'n
Resounded, and had Earth been then, all Earth
Had to her Centre shook. What wonder? when
Millions of fierce encount'ring Angels fought   220
On either side, the least of whom could wield
These Elements, and arm him with the force
Of all thir Regions: how much more of Power
Army against Army numberless to raise
Dreadful combustion warring, and disturb,   225
Though not destroy, thir happy Native seat;
Had not th' Eternal King Omnipotent
From his stronghold of Heav'n high over-rul'd
And limited thir might; though number'd such
As each divided Legion might have seem'd   230
A numerous Host, in strength each armed hand
A Legion; led in fight, yet Leader seem'd
Each Warrior single as in Chief, expert
When to advance, or stand, or turn the sway
Of Battle, open when, and when to close   235
The ridges of grim War; no thought of flight,
None of retreat, no unbecoming deed
That argu'd fear; each on himself reli'd,
As only in his arm the moment lay
Of victory; deeds of eternal fame   240
Were done, but infinite: for wide was spread
That War and various; sometimes on firm ground
A standing fight, then soaring on main wing
Tormented all the Air; all Air seem'd then
Conflicting Fire: long time in even scale   245
The Battle hung; till *Satan*, who that day
Prodigious power had shown, and met in Arms

215 *Cope:* sky (as in IV, 992).
Hesiod describes it as darkened by missiles in the struggle of the giants with the gods (*Theog.*, 716–17). Cf. I, 50.
222. *These Elements* are those of earth, which, as Raphael implies, had not yet been created. Their equivalents in value for warlike purposes were, however, at the disposal of the least of the angels.
229. *number'd such:* so numerous.
232. *led in fight,* etc. Though they had leaders, every individual acted with the skill of an experienced commander.
236. *ridges:* ranks.
239. *moment:* weight (here equivalent to force). Cf. X, 45.

No equal, ranging through the dire attack
Of fighting Seraphim confus'd, at length
Saw where the Sword of *Michael* smote, and fell'd   250
Squadrons at once, with huge two-handed sway
Brandisht aloft the horrid edge came down
Wide wasting; such destruction to withstand
He hasted, and oppos'd the rocky Orb
Of tenfold Adamant, his ample Shield   255
A vast circumference: At his approach
The great Arch-Angel from his warlike toil
Surceas'd, and glad as hoping here to end
Intestine War in Heav'n, the Arch-foe subdu'd
Or Captive dragg'd in Chains, with hostile frown   260
And visage all inflam'd first thus began.
 Author of evil, unknown till thy revolt,
Unnam'd in Heav'n, now plenteous, as thou seest
These Acts of hateful strife, hateful to all,
Though heaviest by just measure on thyself   265
And thy adherents: how hast thou disturb'd
Heav'n's blessed peace, and into Nature brought
Misery, uncreated till the crime
Of thy Rebellion? how hast thou instill'd
Thy malice into thousands, once upright   270
And faithful, now prov'd false. But think not here
To trouble Holy Rest; Heav'n casts thee out
From all her Confines. Heav'n the seat of bliss
Brooks not the works of violence and War.
Hence then, and evil go with thee along,   275
Thy offspring, to the place of evil, Hell,
Thou and thy wicked crew; there mingle broils,
Ere this avenging Sword begin thy doom,
Or some more sudden vengeance wing'd from God
Precipitate thee with augmented pain.   280
 So spake the Prince of Angels; to whom thus
The Adversary. Nor think thou with wind
Of airy threats to awe whom yet with deeds
Thou canst not. Hast thou turn'd the least of these
To flight, or if to fall, but that they rise   285
Unvanquisht, easier to transact with mee

254. *Orb,* the circle of Satan's shield is rocky because it is made of adamant, which might mean diamond, as it does when it is applied to Arthur's shield in *F.Q.* V, xi, 10, 7–9, and, probably, in II, 853, though Milton seems to identify it with iron in *CD* I, viii, and has the armor of the angels made of it (l. 542 below).
259. *Intestine War:* civil war. *the Arch-foe subdued:* when the chief foe should be subdued.

267. *Nature* is treated as having been created free from all discord, until the fall of the angels disturbs *Heav'n's blessed peace,* as man's fall further disturbs it in IX, 782.
275–276. *evil . . . thy offspring* is a contemptuous reference to Sin's parentage in II, 743–58.
282. Cf. Satan as the *Adversary* in III, 81 and 156.
286. *transact:* deal (in the sense of "dealing" with an antagonist in a

That thou shouldst hope, imperious, and with threats
To chase me hence? err not that so shall end
The strife which thou call'st evil, but wee style
The strife of Glory: which we mean to win,   290
Or turn this Heav'n itself into the Hell
Thou fabl'st, here however to dwell free,
If not to reign: meanwhile thy utmost force,
And join him nam'd 'Almighty' to thy aid,
I fly not, but have sought thee far and nigh.   295
    They ended parle, and both address'd for fight
Unspeakable; for who, though with the tongue
Of Angels, can relate, or to what things
Liken on Earth conspicuous, that may lift
Human imagination to such highth   300
Of Godlike Power: for likest Gods they seem'd,
Stood they or mov'd, in stature, motion, arms
Fit to decide the Empire of great Heav'n.
Now wav'd thir fiery Swords, and in the Air
Made horrid Circles; two broad Suns thir Shields   305
Blaz'd opposite, while expectation stood
In horror; from each hand with speed retir'd
Where erst was thickest fight, th' Angelic throng,
And left large field, unsafe within the wind
Of such commotion, such as, to set forth   310
Great things by small, if Nature's concord broke,
Among the Constellations war were sprung,
Two Planets rushing from aspect malign
Of fiercest opposition in mid Sky,
Should combat, and thir jarring Spheres confound.   315
Together both with next to Almighty Arm,
Uplifted imminent one stroke they aim'd
That might determine, and not need repeat,
As not of power, at once; nor odds appear'd
In might or swift prevention; but the sword   320
Of *Michael* from the Armory of God

struggle).
288. *err not:* do not make the error
(of prejudging the result of battle).
289. In l. 268 above Michael has
called Satan's disturbance of the peace
a *crime.*
296. *parle:* parleying. *address'd:* pre-
pared.
306. *Expectation* represents the ex-
pectant, watching armies; or it is a
personification of their mood. So in
the Prologue to Shakespeare's *Henry V,*
Expectation "sits . . . in the air."
311. So Spenser described nature's
concord, by which
  . . . the heaven is in his course con-
    tained.

And all the world in state unmoved
  stands,
As their Almightie Maker first or-
  dained,
And bound them with inviolable
  bands.
        (*F.Q.* IV, x, 35, 1–4)
313. So in X, 658–59, the opposite
aspect of two planets — their opposite
positions in the heavens — is mentioned.
It is *malign* because their colliding rays
were supposed by astrologers to be in-
jurious to life on earth.
318. *determine:* end (the matter).
repeat: repetition, second trial.
320. *prevention:* speed in anticipating
a blow.

Was giv'n him temper'd so, that neither keen
Nor solid might resist that edge: it met
The sword of *Satan* with steep force to smite
Descending, and in half cut sheer, nor stay'd,   325
But with swift wheel reverse, deep ent'ring shear'd
All his right side; then *Satan* first knew pain,
And writh'd him to and fro convolv'd; so sore
The griding sword with discontinuous wound
Pass'd through him, but th' Ethereal substance clos'd   330
Not long divisible, and from the gash
A stream of Nectarous humor issuing flow'd
Sanguine, such as Celestial Spirits may bleed,
And all his Armor stain'd erewhile so bright.
Forthwith on all sides to his aid was run   335
By Angels many and strong, who interpos'd
Defense, while others bore him on thir Shields
Back to his Chariot, where it stood retir'd
From off the files of war: there they him laid
Gnashing for anguish and despite and shame   340
To find himself not matchless, and his pride
Humbl'd by such rebuke, so far beneath
His confidence to equal God in power.
Yet soon he heal'd; for Spirits that live throughout
Vital in every part, not as frail man   345
In Entrails, Heart or Head, Liver or Reins,
Cannot but by annihilating die;·
Nor in thir liquid texture mortal wound
Receive, no more than can the fluid Air:
All Heart they live, all Head, all Eye, all Ear,   350
All Intellect, all Sense, and as they please,
They Limb themselves, and color, shape or size
Assume, as likes them best, condense or rare.
Meanwhile in other parts like deeds deserv'd
Memorial, where the might of *Gabriel* fought,   355

327–334. In I, 55, we have already
found the devils capable of pain. In
the tradition of Michael Psellus, to which
West (in *Milton and Angels*, pp. 146–47)
traces this passage through Marsilio
Ficino's rendering of it, their bodies are
said to be able to recover immediately
from wounds and to close "like air and
water" although they suffer "while
divided," and "fear the edge of the
sword."

329. *discontinuous:* breaking the con-
tinuity or solidity of the body.

332. Milton was perhaps thinking of
the clear ichor that Homer attributed to
the gods instead of blood.

335. Cf. this impersonal, Latin con-
struction with X, 229. The meaning is
that there was a rush, or running, to

Satan's aid on all sides.

350–353. These powers of the demons
are implied in I, 422–33.

354–362. If A. H. Gilbert is justified
in his suggestion that Milton intended
readers of the Italian romances to see a
resemblance here to the comic battle
between devils and Saracens in Boiardo's
Orlando Innamorato II, xxii, 50–54, the
wild physical violence of Milton's
devils and angels becomes all the more
striking in contrast with the symbolic
power of truth that is represented in
their overthrow by the Son of God who
ends the "wild work in Heav'n" (l. 698).
See *Italica* XX (1943), 132–34.

355. *the might of Gabriel:* the mighty
Gabriel. Cf. ll. 371–72.

And with fierce Ensigns pierc'd the deep array
Of *Moloch* furious King, who him defi'd,
And at his Chariot wheels to drag him bound
Threat'n'd, nor from the Holy One of Heav'n
Refrain'd his tongue blasphemous; but anon   360
Down clov'n to the waist, with shatter'd Arms
And uncouth pain fled bellowing. On each wing
Uriel and *Raphaël* his vaunting foe,
Though huge, and in a Rock of Diamond Arm'd,
Vanquish'd *Adramelech*, and *Asmadai*,   365
Two potent Thrones, that to be less than Gods
Disdain'd, but meaner thoughts learn'd in thir flight,
Mangl'd with ghastly wounds through Plate and Mail.
Nor stood unmindful *Abdiel* to annoy
The Atheist crew, but with redoubl'd blow   370
Ariel and *Arioch*, and the violence
Of *Ramiel* scorcht and blasted overthrew.
I might relate of thousands, and thir names
Eternize here on Earth; but those elect
Angels contented with thir fame in Heav'n   375
Seek not the praise of men; the other sort
In might though wondrous and in Acts of War,
Nor of Renown less eager, yet by doom
Cancell'd from Heav'n and sacred memory,
Nameless in dark oblivion let them dwell.   380
For strength from Truth divided and from Just,
Illaudable, naught merits but dispraise
And ignominy, yet to glory aspires
Vain-glorious, and through infamy seeks fame:
Therefore Eternal silence be thir doom.   385
    And now thir Mightiest quell'd, the battle swerv'd
With many an inroad gor'd; deformed rout
Enter'd, and foul disorder; all the ground

---

360. Milton adapts Isaiah's question: "Whom hast thou reproached and blasphemed?" (II Kings xix, 22).

365. *Adramelech*, the "mighty king," was a local phase of the Babylonian sun god. II Kings xvii, 31, says that children were burned on his altar. *Asmadai* is the *Asmodeus* of IV, 168, but medieval tradition, which (according to Heywood in the *Hierarchie*, p. 436) made him chief of the fourth order of fallen angels, makes him one of their leaders here.

366. *Gods* is ironical, referring to the divine ambitions of the devils which Satan flatters by calling them *Gods* in II, 391, and VI, 156.

370. Since the devils disbelieve in God's nature as transcending their own, they may be called an *Atheist crew*.

371-372. *Ariel* — "lion of God" or "light of God" — is an epithet of Jerusalem in Isaiah, xxix, 1, and in xxxiii, 7, it is translated doubtfully as "valiant ones." West notes (*Milton and Angels*, p. 154) that in the translations of the Old Testament by Aquila and Symmachus *Ariel* signifies the pagan city of Arina or Ariopolis, which worshipped the idol *Ariel* (Mars). So *Ariel* "was, like many of his fellows in *PL*, a heathen god, and got his name from a biblical place."

Arioch is the name of one of the kings with whom Abram (Abraham) fights in defense of Lot (Gen. xiv), but the aptness of its meaning of "lion-like" here is perhaps also related to the fact that it is the name of the captain of Nebuchadnezzar's guard (Dan. ii, 14), who (the *Jewish Encyclopaedia* notes) roared like a lion

With shiver'd armor strown, and on a heap
Chariot and Charioteer lay overturn'd   390
And fiery foaming Steeds; what stood, recoil'd
O'erwearied, through the faint Satanic Host
Defensive scarce, or with pale fear surpris'd,
Then first with fear surpris'd and sense of pain
Fled ignominious, to such evil brought   395
By sin of disobedience, till that hour
Not liable to fear or flight or pain.
Far otherwise th' inviolable Saints
In Cubic Phalanx firm advanc'd entire,
Invulnerable, impenetrably arm'd: 400
Such high advantages thir innocence
Gave them above thir foes, not to have sinn'd,
Not to have disobey'd; in fight they stood
Unwearied, unobnoxious to be pain'd
By wound, though from thir place by violence mov'd.   405
    Now Night her course began, and over Heav'n
Inducing darkness, grateful truce impos'd,
And silence on the odious din of War:
Under her Cloudy covert both retir'd,
Victor and Vanquisht: on the foughten field   410
Michaël and his Angels prevalent
Encamping, plac'd in Guard thir Watches round,
Cherubic waving fires: on th' other part
Satan with his rebellious disappear'd,
Far in the dark dislodg'd, and void of rest,   415
His Potentates to Council call'd by night;
And in the midst thus undismay'd began.
    O now in danger tri'd, now known in Arms
Not to be overpow'r'd, Companions dear,
Found worthy not of Liberty alone,   420
Too mean pretense, but what we more affect,
Honor, Dominion, Glory, and renown,
Who have sustain'd one day in doubtful fight,
(And if one day, why not Eternal days?)
What Heaven's Lord had powerfullest to send   425
Against us from about his Throne, and judg'd
Sufficient to subdue us to his will,

---

against the Jews in Babylon. As the
"spirit of Revenge," West notes that he
was known to demonologists like Robert
Turner and turns up in Thomas Nashe's
Pierce Pennilesse.
    the violence of Ramiel may be intended
as a translation of *Ramiel* "thunder of
God" and also as a metonymy. Though
the name occurs in the *Book of Enoch,*
West thinks that Milton knew it only in
Cabalistic accounts of devils of "wizardry
and superstition."

391. *what stood:* those who stood.
393. *Defensive scarce:* hardly able to
stand on the defensive.
398. *inviolable Saints:* the loyal angels,
who are immune to harm.
404. *unobnoxious:* unexposed to harm,
incapable of being harmed.
415. *dislodg'd:* driven from their
lodges or positions.
421. *Too mean pretense:* too low an
object of ambition.

But proves not so: then fallible, it seems,
Of future we may deem him, though till now
Omniscient thought. True is, less firmly arm'd,   430
Some disadvantage we endur'd and pain,
Till now not known, but known as soon contemn'd,
Since now we find this our Empyreal form
Incapable of mortal injury,
Imperishable, and though pierc'd with wound,   435
Soon closing, and by native vigor heal'd.
Of evil then so small as easy think
The remedy; perhaps more valid Arms,
Weapons more violent, when next we meet,
May serve to better us, and worse our foes,   440
Or equal what between us made the odds,
In Nature none: if other hidden cause
Left them Superior, while we can preserve
Unhurt our minds, and understanding sound,
Due search and consultation will disclose.   445
   He sat; and in th' assembly next upstood
Nisroch, of Principalities the prime;
As one he stood escap't from cruel fight,
Sore toil'd, his riv'n Arms to havoc hewn,
And cloudy in aspect thus answering spake.   450
Deliverer from new Lords, leader to free
Enjoyment of our right as Gods; yet hard
For Gods, and too unequal work we find
Against unequal arms to fight in pain,
Against unpain'd, impassive; from which evil   455
Ruin must needs ensue; for what avails
Valor or strength, though matchless, quell'd with pain
Which all subdues, and makes remiss the hands
Of Mightiest. Sense of pleasure we may well
Spare out of life perhaps, and not repine,   460
But live content, which is the calmest life:
But pain is perfet misery, the worst
Of evils, and excessive, overturns
All patience. He who therefore can invent
With what more forcible we may offend   465
Our yet unwounded Enemies, or arm
Ourselves with like defense, to me deserves
No less than for deliverance what we owe.

---

429. *Of future:* in future.
432. *known as soon contemn'd:* despised as soon as it is known.
447. *Nisroch*, whose name may mean "eagle," was an Assyrian deity in whose temple Sennacherib was murdered (II Kings xix, 37). In Charles Stephanus' *Dictionarium* — according to Starnes and Talbert, *Dictionaries*, p. 268 — he is uncertainly defined as Sennacherib's idol, as a fugitive, and as perhaps a standard-bearer.
455. *impassive:* not subject to passion or painful sensation.
465. *offend* keeps its Latin force of "strike at."
467. *to me:* in my judgment.

Whereto with look compos'd *Satan* repli'd.
Not uninvented that, which thou aright   470
Believ'st so main to our success, I bring;
Which of us who beholds the bright surface
Of this Ethereous mould whereon we stand,
This continent of spacious Heav'n, adorn'd
With Plant, Fruit, Flow'r Ambrosial, Gems and Gold,   475
Whose Eye so superficially surveys
These things, as not to mind from whence they grow
Deep under ground, materials dark and crude,
Of spiritous and fiery spume, till toucht
With Heav'n's ray, and temper'd they shoot forth   480
So beauteous, op'ning to the ambient light.
These in thir dark Nativity the Deep
Shall yield us, pregnant with infernal flame,
Which into hollow Engines long and round
Thick ramm'd, at th' other bore with touch of fire   485
Dilated and infuriate shall send forth
From far with thund'ring noise among our foes
Such implements of mischief as shall dash
To pieces, and o'erwhelm whatever stands
Adverse, that they shall fear we have disarm'd   490
The Thunderer of his only dreaded bolt.
Nor long shall be our labor, yet ere dawn,
Effect shall end our wish. Meanwhile revive;
Abandon fear; to strength and counsel join'd
Think nothing hard, much less to be despair'd.   495
He ended, and his words thir drooping cheer

472–483. Tracing this passage to Aristotle's theory of the origin of metals in the *Meteorologica* I, 4 (341b) and III, 6 (348a), E. H. Duncan explains — in *Osiris*, XI (1954), 388 — that Milton's *spiritous and fiery spume* is simply the exhalation of fire and water underground, by whose evaporation under the influence of *Heaven's ray* (the sunshine) metals of all kinds were supposed to "originate from the imprisonment of the vaporous exhalation in the earth and especially in stones." Cf. III, 583–85, 609–12, and *Comus*, 732–36.

484–489. One Italian scholar has found a direct source for this passage in Ariosto's comic account of Cimasco's invention of the arquebus in *Orlando Furioso* IX, 91, while another has found such a source in Erasmo di Valvasone's *L'Angeleida*. Its entirely serious account of the battle of Michael and his angels against the rebel angels in heaven is reproduced in Kirkconnell's *Celestial Cycle*, pp. 80–87, and the stanza on the invention of cannon is on p. 81. But the attitude toward artillery was a commonplace which found

its way into the *Faerie Queene* in a condemnation of

. . . that divelish engin, wrought
    In deepest hell, and framd by furies
        skill,
With windy nitre and quick sulphur
        fraught,
And ramd with bollet rownd, or-
        daind to kill.

(*F.Q.* I, vii, 13, 1–4.) Cf. 597–606 below. Milton seems not to have shared Donne's faith that "by the benefit of this light of reason, (men) have found out *Artillery*, by which warres come to quicker ends than heretofore, and the great expense of bloud is avoyded: for the numbers of men slain now, since the invention of Artillery, are much lesse than before, when the sword was the executioner" (sermon at St. Paul's, Christmas, 1621).

494. *to strength and counsel:* with the aid of strength and good judgment.

496. *cheer*, which in Old French meant "face," developed the meanings of "appearance," "aspect," and "mood" or "frame of mind" in English.

Enlight'n'd, and thir languisht hope reviv'd.
Th' invention all admir'd, and each, how hee
To be th' inventor miss'd, so easy it seem'd
Once found, which yet unfound most would have thought   500
Impossible: yet haply of thy Race
In future days, if Malice should abound,
Some one intent on mischief, or inspir'd
With dev'lish machination might devise
Like instrument to plague the Sons of men   505
For sin, on war and mutual slaughter bent.
Forthwith from Council to the work they flew,
None arguing stood, innumerable hands
Were ready, in a moment up they turn'd
Wide the Celestial soil, and saw beneath   510
Th' originals of Nature in thir crude
Conception; Sulphurous and Nitrous Foam
They found, they mingl'd, and with subtle Art,
Concocted and adusted they reduc'd
To blackest grain, and into store convey'd: 515
Part hidd'n veins digg'd up (nor hath this Earth
Entrails unlike) of Mineral and Stone,
Whereof to found thir Engines and thir Balls
Of missive ruin; part incentive reed
Provide, pernicious with one touch to fire.   520
So all ere day-spring, under conscious Night
Secret they finish'd, and in order set,
With silent circumspection unespi'd.
Now when fair Morn Orient in Heav'n appear'd
Up rose the Victor Angels, and to Arms   525
The matin Trumpet Sung: in Arms they stood
Of Golden Panoply, refulgent Host,
Soon banded; others from the dawning Hills
Look'd round, and Scouts each Coast light-armed scour
Each quarter, to descry the distant foe,   530
Where lodg'd, or whither fled, or if for fight,
In motion or in halt: him soon they met
Under spread Ensigns moving nigh, in slow
But firm Battalion; back with speediest Sail
Zophiel, of Cherubim the swiftest wing,   535

---

512. With *Foam* cf. *spume* in l. 479 above.

514. *concocted* has its Latin meaning of "cook" or "bake." *adusted* was familiar as a medical term with the basic, Latin meaning of "burnt" or "reduced to ashes."

519. *missive ruin:* missile destruction. Both words have their basic, Latin meaning. The *incentive* ("kindling") reed is the gunner's match.

520. *pernicious* keeps its Latin mean-

ing of "swift," i.e. in destructive response to the match.

521. *conscious Night* is night personified and interested in watching the work. So Virgil has Dido pray to the stars that are "conscious of her fate" (*Aen.* IV, 519), and Ovid makes night "conscious" or aware of the frauds of Ulysses.

535. *Zophiel* ("Spy of God") is found nowhere in the Bible nor can he be clearly traced in any authorities better

Came flying, and in mid Air aloud thus cri'd.

Arm, Warriors, Arm for fight, the foe at hand,
Whom fled we thought, will save us long pursuit
This day, fear not his flight; so thick a Cloud
He comes, and settl'd in his face I see   540
Sad resolution and secure: let each
His Adamantine coat gird well, and each
Fit well his Helm, grip fast his orbed Shield,
Borne ev'n or high, for this day will pour down,
If I conjecture aught, no drizzling show'r,   545
But rattling storm of Arrows barb'd with fire.

So warn'd he them aware themselves, and soon
In order, quit of all impediment;
Instant without disturb they took Alarm,
And onward move Embattl'd; when behold   550
Not distant far with heavy pace the Foe
Approaching gross and huge; in hollow Cube
Training his devilish Enginry, impal'd
On every side with shadowing Squadrons Deep,
To hide the fraud. At interview both stood   555
A while, but suddenly at head appear'd
Satan: And thus was heard Commanding loud.

Vanguard, to Right and Left the Front unfold;
That all may see who hate us, how we seek
Peace and composure, and with open breast   560
Stand ready to receive them, if they like
Our overture, and turn not back perverse;
But that I doubt; however witness Heaven,
Heav'n witness thou anon, while we discharge
Freely our part: yee who appointed stand   565
Do as you have in charge, and briefly touch
What we propound, and loud that all may hear.

So scoffing in ambiguous words, he scarce
Had ended; when to Right and Left the Front
Divided, and to either Flank retir'd.   570
Which to our eyes discover'd new and strange,

---

than Robert Fludd and Cornelius Agrippa
who (according to West in *Milton and
Angels*, p. 77) made him the ruler of the
Cherubim in Dionysius' angelic hierarchy.
540. *He,* the foe collectively. So in
II Peter ii, 17, the host of the blasphemers
are called "clouds carried with a tempest."
541. *Sad:* firm. *secure:* reckless.
548. *quit of all impediment:* unencumbered of all baggage (for which the Latin
military term was *impedimenta*).
549. *Instant* keeps its Latin meaning
of "forward," "urgent."
553. *training:* dragging.   *impal'd:*
surrounded.

560. *composure:* composition, agreement.
569–594. H. H. Scudder notes —
N&Q, CVC (1950), 335 — that one of
many parallels to this maneuver in the
military records of the time is the "stratagem" in H. C. Davila's *Historie of the
Warres of France* — in the translation of
Aylesbury and Cotterel (1647), p. 141
— of the masking of "ordnance" behind
troops, "invisibly, loaden with *Musquetbullet:* and when they should have
charged the Enemy, made them wheel
off, that those bloody Engins might break
their ranks, which they performed to
purpose, and forced them to retire. . . .',

A triple-mounted row of Pillars laid
On Wheels (for like to Pillars most they seem'd
Or hollow'd bodies made of Oak or Fir
With branches lopt, in Wood or Mountain fell'd)   575
Brass, Iron, Stony mould, had not thir mouths
With hideous orifice gap't on us wide,
Portending hollow truce; at each behind
A Seraph stood, and in his hand a Reed
Stood waving tipt with fire; while we suspense,   580
Collected stood within our thoughts amus'd,
Not long, for sudden all at once thir Reeds
Put forth, and to a narrow vent appli'd
With nicest touch. Immediate in a flame,
But soon obscur'd with smoke, all Heav'n appear'd,   585
From those deep-throated Engines belcht, whose roar
Embowell'd with outrageous noise the Air,
And all her entrails tore, disgorging foul
Thir devilish glut, chain'd Thunderbolts and Hail
Of Iron Globes, which on the Victor Host   590
Levell'd, with such impetuous fury smote,
That whom they hit, none of thir feet might stand,
Though standing else as Rocks, but down they fell
By thousands, Angel on Arch-Angel roll'd;
The sooner for thir Arms; unarm'd they might   595
Have easily as Spirits evaded swift
By quick contraction or remove; but now
Foul dissipation follow'd and forc't rout;
Nor serv'd it to relax thir serried files.
What should they do? if on they rush'd repulse   600
Repeated, and indecent overthrow
Doubl'd, would render them yet more despis'd,
And to thir foes a laughter; for in view
Stood rankt of Seraphim another row
In posture to displode thir second tire   605
Of Thunder: back defeated to return
They worse abhorr'd. *Satan* beheld thir plight,
And to his Mates thus in derision call'd.
     O Friends, why come not on these Victors proud?
Erewhile they fierce were coming, and when wee,   610
To entertain them fair with open Front
And Breast, (what could we more?) propounded terms

576. *mould:* substance. Cf. III, 709,
and IV, 226.
578. *hollow* puns on the physical and
moral senses of the word.
580. *suspense* has the force of a Latin
participle, "suspended" (i.e. with curi-
osity).
581. *amus'd:* in a muse or daze.
587. *Embowell'd:* filled, packed.

597. *quick contraction or remove* recalls
the ability attributed to the angels in
I, 429.
598. *dissipation* keeps its Latin, mili-
tary meaning of "disperse" or "rout."
601. *indecent* keeps its Latin force of
"ugly" or "disgraceful."
605. *displode:* explode, fire. *tire:*
volley.

Of composition, straight they chang'd thir minds,
Flew off, and into strange vagaries fell,
As they would dance, yet for a dance they seem'd   615
Somewhat extravagant and wild, perhaps
For joy of offer'd peace: but I suppose
If our proposals once again were heard
We should compel them to a quick result.
    To whom thus *Belial* in like gamesome mood.   620
Leader, the terms we sent were terms of weight,
Of hard contents, and full of force urg'd home,
Such as we might perceive amus'd them all,
And stumbl'd many; who receives them right,
Had need from head to foot well understand;   625
Not understood, this gift they have besides,
They show us when our foes walk not upright.
    So they among themselves in pleasant vein
Stood scoffing, highth'n'd in thir thoughts beyond
All doubt of Victory, eternal might   630
To match with thir inventions they presum'd
So easy, and of his Thunder made a scorn,
And all his Host derided, while they stood
A while in trouble; but they stood not long,
Rage prompted them at length, and found them arms   635
Against such hellish mischief fit to oppose.
    Forthwith (behold the excellence, the power
Which God hath in his mighty Angels plac'd)
Thir Arms away they threw, and to the Hills
(For Earth hath this variety from Heav'n   640
Of pleasure situate in Hill and Dale)
Light as the Lightning glimpse they ran, they flew,
From thir foundations loos'ning to and fro
They pluckt the seated Hills with all thir load,
Rocks, Waters, Woods, and by the shaggy tops   645
Uplifting bore them in thir hands: Amaze,
Be sure, and terror seiz'd the rebel Host,
When coming towards them so dread they saw
The bottom of the Mountains upward turn'd,
Till on those cursed Engines' triple-row   650
They saw them whelm'd, and all thir confidence

---

615. Satan's irony, which Addison regarded (in *Spectator*, 279) as in the worst possible taste, has reminded most editors of Patroclus' praise of the "skilful dance" of Hector's charioteer in his death agony.

625. The pun is on the familiar, metaphorical meaning of *understand* and its now obsolete meaning of "support." So Viola says, "My legs do better understand me, sir, than I understand what you mean" (*Twelfth Night* III, i, 90).

640. *from Heav'n:* derived from heaven, resembling heaven.

642. *Light:* swift because light in weight.

643–666. So the giants fighting for Zeus against the titans in Hesiod's *Theogony* (713–20) uproot the hills and hurl them at their enemies. Cf. the allusion to the same battle in Hesiod in *PL* I, 50.

646. *Amaze:* amazement.

Under the weight of Mountains buried deep,
Themselves invaded next, and on thir heads
Main Promontories flung, which in the Air
Came shadowing, and opprest whole Legions arm'd,   655
Thir armor help'd thir harm, crush't in and bruis'd
Into thir substance pent, which wrought them pain
Implacable, and many a dolorous groan,
Long struggling underneath, ere they could wind
Out of such prison, though Spirits of purest light,   660
Purest at first, now gross by sinning grown.
The rest in imitation to like Arms
Betook them, and the neighboring Hills uptore;
So Hills amid the Air encounter'd Hills
Hurl'd to and fro with jaculation dire,   665
That under ground they fought in dismal shade:
Infernal noise; War seem'd a civil Game
To this uproar; horrid confusion heapt
Upon confusion rose: and now all Heav'n
Had gone to wrack, with ruin overspread,   670
Had not th' Almighty Father where he sits
Shrin'd in his Sanctuary of Heav'n secure,
Consulting on the sum of things, foreseen
This tumult, and permitted all, advis'd:
That his great purpose he might so fulfil,   675
To honor his Anointed Son aveng'd
Upon his enemies, and to declare
All power on him transferr'd: whence to his Son
Th' Assessor of his Throne he thus began.
    Effulgence of my Glory, Son belov'd,   680
Son in whose face invisible is beheld
Visibly, what by Deity I am,
And in whose hand what by Decree I do,
Second Omnipotence, two days are past,
Two days, as we compute the days of Heav'n,   685
Since *Michael* and his Powers went forth to tame
These disobedient; sore hath been thir fight,
As likeliest was, when two such Foes met arm'd;
For to themselves I left them, and thou know'st,

655. *opprest:* physically crushed.
665. *jaculation:* throwing.
666. The scene recalls the volleys of mountains thrown by the contending giants and titans in Hesiod's story.
667. *civil* is used in a sense contrasted to "military."
673. *sum of things* translates Lucretius' almost technical term for the universe in *De rerum natura* V, 361.
674. *advis'd:* with a mind informed and resolved in advance.
679. *Assessor* is still used in England of associate judges as "sharers of the seat" of a chief judge and of associate officials generally (*O.E.D.*).
682–684. The chapter on "The Son of God" in the *Christian Doctrine* (I, v) begins with a reference to the verse that is echoed here: "Who is the image of the invisible God" (Col. i, 15). In the later discussion of the Son's Omnipotence Milton quotes John v, 19: "The Son can do nothing of himself, but what he seeth the Father do" (C.Ed. XIV, 319).

Equal in thir Creation they were form'd,   690
Save what sin hath impair'd, which yet hath wrought
Insensibly, for I suspend thir doom;
Whence in perpetual fight they needs must last
Endless, and no solution will be found:
War wearied hath perform'd what War can do,   695
And to disorder'd rage let loose the reins,
With Mountains as with Weapons arm'd, which makes
Wild work in Heav'n, and dangerous to the main.
Two days are therefore past, the third is thine;
For thee I have ordain'd it, and thus far   700
Have suffer'd, that the Glory may be thine
Of ending this great War, since none but Thou
Can end it. Into thee such Virtue and Grace
Immense I have transfus'd, that all may know
In Heav'n and Hell thy Power above compare,   705
And this perverse Commotion govern'd thus,
To manifest thee worthiest to be Heir
Of all things, to be Heir and to be King
By Sacred Unction, thy deserved right.
Go then thou Mightiest in thy Father's might,   710
Ascend my Chariot, guide the rapid Wheels
That shake Heav'n's basis, bring forth all my War,
My Bow and Thunder, my Almighty Arms
Gird on, and Sword upon thy puissant Thigh;
Pursue these sons of Darkness, drive them out   715
From all Heav'n's bounds into the utter Deep:
There let them learn, as likes them, to despise
God and *Messiah* his anointed King.
　　He said, and on his Son with Rays direct
Shone full; hee all his Father full exprest   720
Ineffably into his face receiv'd,
And thus the filial Godhead answering spake.
　　O Father, O supreme of heav'nly Thrones,
First, Highest, Holiest, Best, thou always seek'st
To glorify thy Son, I always thee,   725

692. *Insensibly:* imperceptibly, i.e. not so as to have perceptibly weakened the strength of the rebel angels.

695. *War wearied* etc.: war's resources have been exhausted without settling the dispute.

698. *main:* the continent or whole extent of heaven.

701. *suffer'd:* permitted (matters to run their course).

709. the *Sacred Unction* is implied in the *anointed King* of V, 664.

712. *War* means "army," as it does again in XII, 214.

717. *as likes them:* as pleases them.

Cf. "the music likes me not" (*Two Gentlemen of Verona* IV, ii, 56).

723–733. The lines are woven from several New Testament passages which Milton quotes in *CD* I, v (C.Ed. XIV, 341) to show that "the Father does not alienate his glory from himself in imparting it to the Son, inasmuch as the Son uniformly glorifies the Father."

725. The thought is that of Christ's prayer before the crucifixion: "Father, the hour is come; glorify thy Son, that thy Son also may glorify thee" (John xvii, 1).

As is most just; this I my Glory account,
My exaltation, and my whole delight,
That thou in me well pleas'd, declar'st thy will
Fulfill'd, which to fulfil is all my bliss.
Sceptre and Power, thy giving, I assume   730
And gladlier shall resign, when in the end
Thou shalt be All in All, and I in thee
For ever, and in mee all whom thou lov'st;
But whom thou hat'st, I hate, and can put on
Thy terrors, as I put thy mildness on,   735
Image of thee in all things; and shall soon,
Arm'd with thy might, rid heav'n of these rebell'd,
To thir prepar'd ill Mansion driven down,
To chains of darkness, and th' undying Worm,
That from thy just obedience could revolt,   740
Whom to obey is happiness entire.
Then shall thy Saints unmixt, and from th' impure
Far separate, circling thy holy Mount
Unfeigned *Halleluiahs* to thee sing,
Hymns of high praise, and I among them chief.   745
So said, he o'er his Sceptre bowing, rose
From the right hand of Glory where he sat,
And the third sacred Morn began to shine
Dawning through Heav'n: forth rush'd with whirl-wind sound
The Chariot of Paternal Deity,   750
Flashing thick flames, Wheel within Wheel, undrawn,
Itself instinct with Spirit, but convoy'd
By four Cherubic shapes, four Faces each
Had wondrous, as with Stars thir bodies all
And Wings were set with Eyes, with Eyes the Wheels   755
Of Beryl, and careering Fires between;
Over thir heads a crystal Firmament,
Whereon a Sapphire Throne, inlaid with pure

728. Cf. the voice from heaven at Christ's baptism and again at the transfiguration, "This is my beloved Son, in whom I am well pleased" (Matt. iii, 17, and xvii, 5).
732. Cf. III, 341.
734. The line is from Psalm cxxxix, 21: "Do not I hate them, O Lord, that hate thee?"
739. As in I, 47–48, and IV, 965, the reference is to the chaining of Satan in the Apocalypse (Rev. xx, 1–2. Cf. II Pet. ii, 4, and Jude i, 6). The *undying Worm* echoes Mark ix, 44.
748. The Homeric phrase *sacred Morn* (*Il.* XI, 84) stresses the contrast of the peaceful landscape with its impending violation.
750–759. The chariot comes from Ezekiel's vision of "a great cloud, and a fire infolding itself, . . . Also out of the midst thereof came the likeness of four living creatures, . . . And every one had four faces, and every one had four wings" (Ezek. i, 4–6). From the same chapter come the ideas of the chariot as self-moved because it is pure spirit, of its mysterious wheels, the play of colors in its precious stones, its darting eyes, and the firmament above it. At least one hexameral poet before Milton, Rupert of Deutz in the twelfth century, had — as G. McColley notes in *Paradise Lost*, pp. 36–38 — used the vision of Ezekiel as a symbol of Christ triumphing spiritually over the rebel angels. Cf. V, 853, n.
752. *instinct* is used in its Latin participial meaning of "instigated" or "impelled," as it is in II, 937.

Amber, and colors of the show'ry Arch.
Hee in Celestial Panoply all arm'd   760
Of radiant *Urim*, work divinely wrought,
Ascended, at his right hand Victory
Sat Eagle-wing'd, beside him hung his Bow
And Quiver with three-bolted Thunder stor'd,
And from about him fierce Effusion roll'd   765
Of smoke and bickering flame, and sparkles dire;
Attended with ten thousand thousand Saints,
He onward came, far off his coming shone,
And twenty thousand (I thir number heard)
Chariots of God, half on each hand were seen: 770
Hee on the wings of Cherub rode sublime
On the Crystalline Sky, in Sapphire Thron'd.
Illustrious far and wide, but by his own
First seen, them unexpected joy surpris'd,
When the great Ensign of *Messiah* blaz'd   775
Aloft by Angels borne, his Sign in Heav'n:
Under whose Conduct *Michael* soon reduc'd
His Army, circumfus'd on either Wing,
Under thir Head imbodied all in one.
Before him Power Divine his way prepar'd;   780
At his command the uprooted Hills retir'd
Each to his place, they heard his voice and went
Obsequious, Heav'n his wonted face renew'd,
And with fresh Flow'rets Hill and Valley smil'd.
This saw his hapless Foes, but stood obdur'd,   785
And to rebellious fight rallied thir Powers
Insensate, hope conceiving from despair.
In heav'nly Spirits could such perverseness dwell?
But to convince the proud what Signs avail,
Or Wonders move th' obdurate to relent?   790
They hard'n'd more by what might most reclaim,
Grieving to see his Glory, at the sight

761. The *Urim* are first mentioned in
the Bible as something to be worn in
Aaron's high-priestly "breastplate of
judgment" (Exod. xxviii, 30). Their
radiance here is part of the symbolism
of the spiritual light incarnate in the Son
as God's judge and executioner.

762. *Victory* is personified and visual-
ized like the statuettes of Victory on the
war chariots of the Greeks.

767-770. So the loyal angels are called
Saints in l. 398 above. Cf. Psalm lxviii,
17: "The chariots of God are twenty
thousand, even thousands of angels."

771. The line echoes David's cry:
God "rode upon a cherub, and did fly;
and he was seen upon the wings of the
wind" (II Sam. xxii, 11). *sublime —*

aloft — is a recollection of that divine
flight.

776. The *Sign* recalls the promise that
at the end of the world there "shall appear
the sign of the Son of Man in heaven"
(Matt. xxiv, 30).

777. *reduc'd:* led back. The word has
its basic, Latin meaning.

785. *obdur'd* has its Latin meaning of
"hardened." So in *CD* I, iv (C.Ed. XIV,
163) Milton speaks of "hardening of the
heart" as the self-induced punishment
of those who abuse the freedom of the
will.

788. The line translates Virgil's ques-
tion at the end of his account of Juno's
malice against Aeneas (*Aen.* I, 11).

Took envy, and aspiring to his highth,
Stood reimbattl'd fierce, by force or fraud
Weening to prosper, and at length prevail   795
Against God and *Messiah*, or to fall
In universal ruin last, and now
To final Battle drew, disdaining flight,
Or faint retreat; when the great Son of God
To all his Host on either hand thus spake.   800
   Stand still in bright array ye Saints, here stand
Ye Angels arm'd, this day from Battle rest;
Faithful hath been your Warfare, and of God
Accepted, fearless in his righteous Cause,
And as ye have receiv'd, so have ye done   805
Invincibly: but of this cursed crew
The punishment to other hand belongs;
Vengeance is his, or whose he sole appoints;
Number to this day's work is not ordain'd
Nor multitude, stand only and behold   810
God's indignation on these Godless pour'd
By mee; not you but mee they have despis'd,
Yet envied; against mee is all thir rage,
Because the Father, t'whom in Heav'n supreme
Kingdom and Power and Glory appertains,   815
Hath honor'd me according to his will.
Therefore to mee thir doom he hath assign'd;
That they may have thir wish, to try with mee
In Battle which the stronger proves, they all,
Or I alone against them, since by strength   820
They measure all, of other excellence
Not emulous, nor care who them excels;
Nor other strife with them do I voutsafe.
   So spake the Son, and into terror chang'd
His count'nance too severe to be beheld   825
And full of wrath bent on his Enemies.
At once the Four spread out thir Starry wings
With dreadful shade contiguous, and the Orbs
Of his fierce Chariot roll'd, as with the sound
Of torrent Floods, or of a numerous Host.   830
Hee on his impious Foes right onward drove,
Gloomy as Night; under his burning Wheels

---

808. The thought often recurs in the
Bible (Deut. xxxii, 35; Ps. xciv, 1;
Rom. xii, 19; and Heb. x, 30).
832. So Hector, though splendidly
armed, was "gloomy as night" (*Il.* XII,
462), and so, with Apollo's aid, he para-
lyzed his foes (*Il.* XV, 323). The *Wheels*
here, which are a part of Ezekiel's vision
as reflected in l. 755 above, prompt West
to say (in *Milton and Angels*, p. 157) that

"Milton always associates Wheels with
Cherubim, the second order in the Diony-
sian scheme as Wheels was in the Cabalis-
tic." When Christ rides out to realize
in Creation his "Great Idea" (VII, 557),
Milton seems to identify the Cherubim
on whose wings the Son is uplifted (VII,
218) with the "fervid Wheeles" of VII,
224.

The steadfast Empyrean shook throughout,
All but the Throne itself of God. Full soon
Among them he arriv'd; in his right hand   835
Grasping ten thousand Thunders, which he sent
Before him, such as in thir Souls infix'd
Plagues; they astonisht all resistance lost,
All courage; down thir idle weapons dropp'd;
O'er Shields and Helms, and helmed heads he rode   840
Of Thrones and mighty Seraphim prostrate,
That wish't the Mountains now might be again
Thrown on them as a shelter from his ire.
Nor less on either side tempestuous fell
His arrows, from the fourfold-visag'd Four,   845
Distinct with eyes, and from the living Wheels,
Distinct alike with multitude of eyes;
One Spirit in them rul'd, and every eye
Glar'd lightning, and shot forth pernicious fire
Among th' accurst, that wither'd all thir strength,   850
And of thir wonted vigor left them drain'd,
Exhausted, spiritless, afflicted, fall'n.
Yet half his strength he put not forth, but check'd
His Thunder in mid Volley, for he meant
Not to destroy, but root them out of Heav'n: 855
The overthrown he rais'd, and as a Herd
Of Goats or timorous flock together throng'd
Drove them before him Thunder-struck, pursu'd
With terrors and with furies to the bounds
And Crystal wall of Heav'n, which op'ning wide,   860
Roll'd inward, and a spacious Gap disclos'd
Into the wasteful Deep; the monstrous sight
Struck them with horror backward, but far worse
Urg'd them behind; headlong themselves they threw
Down from the verge of Heav'n, Eternal wrath   865

---

838. *Plagues* has its original Greek force of "blow" or "stroke."

840. The imagery is compared by Broadbent in *ES*, XXXVII (1956), 51, to "the invincible warrior Zeal" in *An Apology*. Arming his "ethereal substance" in "complete diamond," Zeal "ascends his fiery Chariot drawn with two blazing Meteors figur'd like beasts, but of a higher breed than any the Zodiac yields, resembling two of those four which Ezekiel and Saint John saw, the one visag'd like a Lion to express power, high authority and indignation, the other of count'nance like a man to cast derision and scorn upon perverse and fraudulent seducers" (C.Ed. III, 313–14). Cf. *PL* III, 388–92, and the Introduction 17.

842. The line evokes the cry of the wicked at the last judgment, saying "to the mountains and rocks, Fall on us, and hide us from the face of him that sitteth on the throne" (Rev. vi, 16).

856–857. It is interesting to find the early editors excusing the bad taste of this simile on the ground that Homer compares the Greek hosts to flies around a milk-pail, or that Milton had in mind the separation of the "sheep" from the "goats" at the last judgment (Matt. xxv, 33), while for A. Stein the simile is the skilful climax of a series of indications throughout the battle in heaven that Milton's object was to leave the rebels "exposed to laughter" (*Answerable Style*, p. 25) both divine and human.

864. With this line the chain of events whose last link was given to the reader in I, 44–49, is complete.

Burn'd after them to the bottomless pit.
Hell heard th' unsufferable noise, Hell saw
Heav'n ruining from Heav'n, and would have fled
Affrighted; but strict Fate had cast too deep
Her dark foundations, and too fast had bound.   870
Nine days they fell; confounded *Chaos* roar'd,
And felt tenfold confusion in thir fall
Through his wild Anarchy, so huge a rout
Incumber'd him with ruin: Hell at last
Yawning receiv'd them whole, and on them clos'd,   875
Hell thir fit habitation fraught with fire
Unquenchable, the house of woe and pain.
Disburd'n'd Heav'n rejoic'd, and soon repair'd
Her mural breach, returning whence it roll'd.
Sole Victor from th' expulsion of his Foes   880
Messiah his triumphal Chariot turn'd:
To meet him all his Saints, who silent stood
Eye-witnesses of his Almighty Acts,
With Jubilee advanc'd; and as they went,
Shaded with branching Palm, each order bright,   885
Sung Triumph, and him sung Victorious King,
Son, Heir, and Lord, to him Dominion giv'n,
Worthiest to Reign: he celebrated rode
Triumphant through mid Heav'n, into the Courts
And Temple of his mighty Father Thron'd   890
On high; who into Glory him receiv'd,
Where now he sits at the right hand of bliss.
    Thus measuring things in Heav'n by things on Earth
At thy request, and that thou mayst beware
By what is past, to thee I have reveal'd   895
What might have else to human Race been hid:
The discord which befell, and War in Heav'n
Among th' Angelic Powers, and the deep fall
Of those too high aspiring, who rebell'd

868. With *ruining* cf. *ruin* in I, 46.
879. *mural breach:* breach in the walls.
880–892. The apocalyptic echoes here culminate in the final allusion to St. Paul's vision of the Son "upholding all things by the word of his power" and sitting down "on the right hand of the Majesty on high" (Heb. i, 3). Many critics take the lines as a final reason for believing that Milton intended the war in heaven seriously as a physical battle — as Matthew Arnold took it in "A French Critic of Milton," in *Mixed Essays* (New York, 1899), p. 197. But if Milton intended it other than symbolically he stands in marked contrast to most hexameral poets from Rupert of Deutz to Thomas Heywood, for whom the "weapons" of the angels wers

Onely spiritual Armes . . .
And these were call'd *Affection* and *Consent.*
Now both of these, in *Lucifer* the Diuell
And his Complyes, immoderate were, and euill.
Those that in *Michael* the Arch-Angell raign'd,
And his good Spirits, meekely were maintain'd,
Squar'd and directed by th'Almighties will
(The Rule by which they fight, and conquer still).
(*Hierarchie of the Blessed Angels* — 1635 — Bk. VI, pp. 341-42) See the Introduction 14–15.

With *Satan*, hee who envies now thy state,   900
Who now is plotting how he may seduce
Thee also from obedience, that with him
Bereav'd of happiness thou mayst partake
His punishment, Eternal misery;
Which would be all his solace and revenge,   905
As a despite done against the most High,
Thee once to gain Companion of his woe.
But list'n not to his Temptations, warn
Thy weaker; let it profit thee to have heard
By terrible Example the reward   910
Of disobedience; firm they might have stood,
Yet fell; remember, and fear to transgress.

The End of the Sixth Book.

BOOK VII

THE ARGUMENT

Raphael *at the request of* Adam *relates how and wherefore this world was first created; that God, after the expelling of* Satan *and his Angels out of Heaven, declar'd his pleasure to create another World and other Creatures to dwell therein; sends his Son with Glory and attendance of Angels to perform the work of Creation in six days: the Angels celebrate with Hymns the performance thereof, and his reascension into Heaven.*

Descend from Heav'n *Urania*, by that name
If rightly thou art call'd, whose Voice divine
Following, above th' *Olympian* Hill I soar,
Above the flight of *Pegasean* wing.
The meaning, not the Name I call: for thou   5
Nor of the Muses nine, nor on the top
Of old *Olympus* dwell'st, but Heav'nly born,
Before the Hills appear'd, or Fountain flow'd,
Thou with Eternal Wisdom didst converse,
Wisdom thy Sister, and with her didst play   10

909. *Thy weaker:* Eve, the "weaker vessel" of I Peter iii, 7. Even the humanist, Vives, could speak of woman as "a frail thing, and of weak discretion, and that may lightly be deceived, which thing our first mother Eve showeth, whom the Devil caught with a light argument." (Richard Hyrde's translation of Vives' *Instruction of a Christian Woman,* ed. by Watson, p. 56.)
1. *Urania* is invoked both to inspire the coming account of creation and to lift the poet up to the heavens where it mainly takes place. For the meaning of her name here and her invocation in I, 6, see the Introduction 54.

3. The *Olympian Hill,* like the *Aonian Mount* of I, 15, was a haunt of the classical Muses, whose inspiration falls short of Milton's need.
4. Pegasus, the winged horse traditionally symbolizing poetic inspiration, anticipates the reference to his rider *Bellerophon* in l. 18.
9. Behind the conception of *Eternal Wisdom* playing before God lies Proverbs viii, 30, where Wisdom tells of her part in the Creation, and adds, "Then I was by him [God], as one brought up with him: and I was daily his delight, rejoicing ['playing' in the Vulgate] always before him." In the *Wisdom of Solomon* vii,

In presence of th' Almighty Father, pleas'd
With thy Celestial Song. Up led by thee
Into the Heav'n of Heav'ns I have presum'd,
An Earthly Guest, and drawn Empyreal Air,
Thy temp'ring; with like safety guided down   15
Return me to my Native Element:
Lest from this flying Steed unrein'd, (as once
Bellerophon, though from a lower Clime)
Dismounted, on th' *Aleian* Field I fall
Erroneous there to wander and forlorn.   20
Half yet remains unsung, but narrower bound
Within the visible Diurnal Sphere;
Standing on Earth, not rapt above the Pole,
More safe I Sing with mortal voice, unchang'd
To hoarse or mute, though fall'n on evil days,   25
On evil days though fall'n, and evil tongues;
In darkness, and with dangers compast round,
And solitude; yet not alone, while thou
Visit'st my slumbers Nightly, or when Morn

17–18, Milton found Wisdom gifted with knowledge "how the world was made" and understanding "the operation of the elements . . . the alteration of the turning of the sun and the change of the seasons," etc. In the Renaissance this quasi-theological figure gathered prestige from the half-metaphysical wisdom of classical philosophy, the wisdom which "is knowledge of things divine and human, and in which is contained the relationships and the society of men with gods mutually" (Cicero, *De officiis* I, 145). Drawing upon both Hebrew and Neo-Platonic sources, Spenser dedicated *An Hymne of Heavenly Beautie* to Sapience (i.e., Wisdom),

The soveraine dearling of the Deity. (184)

.   .   .   .

Both heaven and earth obey unto her
    will,
And all the creatures which they both
    containe:
For of her fulnesse, which the world
    doth fill,
They all partake, and do in state re-
    maine,
As their great Maker did at first or-
    daine. (197–201)

15. *Thy temp'ring:* thou temperest the heavenly air to my mortal lungs.
16. *Native Element:* the earth.
18. Quoting Natalis Comes' treatment of the myth of Pegasus and Bellerophon as representing overconfidence in individual fame or poetic talent. Mary Lascelles points out in *Elizabethan and Jacobean Studies Presented to F. P. Wilson*

(Oxford. Clarendon Press, 1959), p. 188, that even before the medieval allegorization of Homer's story of *Bellerophon,* whom the gods prospered in battle with the Chimaera but afterwards hated and sent wandering, blind, to his death on the Aleian plain (*Iliad*, VI, 200–202). there was a hint of the tragic vision of the poet. The later myth mounted him on the winged horse only to have Jove send a gadfly to cause his fall, though Pegasus mounts the skies to be immortal as a constellation. Though no interpretation can catch the full meaning of *Bellerophon* and the *Pegasean wing* for Milton, Miss Lascelles sees the allusions to them as indicating a mood in Milton which will not let him presume on the past guidance of his Muse as he descends from the celestial scene in Book VI to treat the events to occur in Eden.
22. *Diurnal Sphere:* the globe of the skies that seems to revolve daily.
23. *rapt* — "caught up" (into heaven) — illustrates the basic meaning of *rapture* as used metaphorically in l. 36 below. Cf. *Pole* used in the sense found here also in I, 74 and IV, 724.
25–27. *evil days:* the period of reaction against the Puritan revolution after the Stuart Restoration, when for a time Milton's life is said by his early biographer, John Toland, to have been in some danger. The *darkness* refers to his blindness, to contrast it — as in III, 21–55 — with his inward illumination.
29. Cf. the nightly visits of Milton's Muse in III, 32, and IX, 22.

Purples the East: still govern thou my Song,   30
Urania, and fit audience find, though few.
But drive far off the barbarous dissonance
Of *Bacchus* and his Revellers, the Race
Of that wild Rout that tore the *Thracian* Bard
In *Rhodope*, where Woods and Rocks had Ears   35
To rapture, till the savage clamor drown'd
Both Harp and Voice; nor could the Muse defend
Her Son. So fail not thou, who thee implores:
For thou art Heavn'ly, shee an empty dream.
   Say Goddess, what ensu'd when *Raphaël*,   40
The affable Arch-angel, had forewarn'd
Adam by dire example to beware
Apostasy, by what befell in Heaven
To those Apostates, lest the like befall
In Paradise to *Adam* or his Race,   45
Charg'd not to touch the interdicted Tree,
If they transgress, and slight that sole command,
So easily obey'd amid the choice
Of all tastes else to please thir appetite,
Though wand'ring. He with his consorted *Eve*   50
The story heard attentive, and was fill'd
With admiration, and deep muse to hear
Of things so high and strange, things to thir thought
So unimaginable as hate in Heav'n,
And War so near the Peace of God in bliss   55
With such confusion: but the evil soon
Driv'n back redounded as a flood on those
From whom it sprung, impossible to mix

31. So in the Preface to *Eikonoklastes* (C.Ed. V, 65) Milton launched that tract "to find out her own fit readers: few perhaps, but those few, such of value and substantial worth, as truth and wisdom, not respecting numbers and big names, have been ever wont in all ages to be contented with." But the attitude had been commended since Joachim du Bellay advised the poet "who aspires to a more than vulgar glory to separate himself from inept admirers, . . . and to content himself with few readers" (*La deffence et illustration de la langue françoyse* — 1549 — II, xi).

32–33. An over-positive identification of the *barbarous rout* with the courtiers of Charles II by McColley, in an effort to date *PL* in 1660, is challenged by Broadbent in *ES* XXXVII (1956), 61, on the basis of "very similar pronouncements in *SA*" and of the use of the Orpheus myth in *Lycidas*, as well as of the allusion to the Irish rebels in *CG* (C.Ed. III, 228), as a "barbarous crew."

33–38. With equal emotion Milton re-told Ovid's version of the story of the murder of Orpheus by the worshippers of Bacchus in *Lycidas*, 57–63. He expects his readers to remember Ovid's details: the scene on the Thracian mountain, *Rhodope*, the trees and rocks that so loved Orpheus' voice and lyre that they resisted being used as missiles against him by the drunken bacchantes. In *Lycidas* also the Muse of epic poetry, Calliope, cannot save Orpheus.

40. Compare *Raphael, the sociable spirit*, of V, 221.

44. Compare *Apostate* in VI, 100.

46. The interdiction on which Milton's story turns is the word of God to Adam in Paradise: "But of the tree of the knowledge of good and evil, thou shalt not eat of it: for in the day that thou eatest thereof, thou shalt surely die" (Gen. ii, 17).

50. *consorted:* associated. "Consort" was a not unusual name for a wife.

57. *redounded:* thrown back. The root of the word is the Latin word for "wave."

With Blessedness. Whence *Adam* soon repeal'd
The doubts that in his heart arose: and now   60
Led on, yet sinless, with desire to know
What nearer might concern him, how this World
Of Heav'n and Earth conspicuous first began,
When, and whereof created, for what cause,
What within *Eden* or without was done   65
Before his memory, as one whose drouth
Yet scarce allay'd still eyes the current stream,
Whose liquid murmur heard new thirst excites,
Proceeded thus to ask his Heav'nly Guest.
   Great things, and full of wonder in our ears,   70
Far differing from this World, thou hast reveal'd
Divine Interpreter, by favor sent
Down from the Empyrean to forewarn
Us timely of what might else have been our loss,
Unknown, which human knowledge could not reach: 75
For which to th' infinitely Good we owe
Immortal thanks, and his admonishment
Receive with solemn purpose to observe
Immutably his sovran will, the end
Of what we are. But since thou hast voutsaf't   80
Gently for our instruction to impart
Things above Earthly thought, which yet concern'd
Our knowing, as to highest wisdom seem'd,
Deign to descend now lower, and relate
What may no less perhaps avail us known,   85
How first began this Heav'n which we behold
Distant so high, with moving Fires adorn'd
Innumerable, and this which yields or fills
All space, the ambient Air wide interfus'd
Imbracing round this florid Earth, what cause   90
Mov'd the Creator in his holy Rest
Through all Eternity so late to build
In *Chaos,* and the work begun, how soon
Absolv'd, if unforbid thou mayst unfold
What wee, not to explore the secrets ask   95

59. *repeal'd* preserves the French
meaning of "call back."
  63. *conspicuous:* visible (in contrast to
the unseen heaven of the angels).
  66. *drouth:* thirst. The feeling is like
that of Dante saying to Virgil in the
fourth circle of Purgatory (*Purg.* XVIII,
4) that his thirst for more revelation of
theological truth is still urgent.
  72. *Divine Interpreter* recalls Virgil's
title for Mercury as spokesman of the
gods (*Aen.* IV, 378), and perhaps Virgil
himself as Dante's "master."
  79. *end:* final purpose. Cf. God's

glorification as "the chief end of man"
in the Shorter Catechism.
  83. *seem'd:* seemed good.
  90. *florid:* flowery.
  92. To Adam, as to many a mediaeval
schoolman and rabbi, and to Milton him-
self, it was "not imaginable that God
should have been wholly occupied from
eternity in decreeing that which was to
be created in a period of six days" (*CD* I,
vii; C.Ed. XV, 3).
  94. *Absolv'd* has its Latin force of
"finished" or "completed."

Of his Eternal Empire, but the more
To magnify his works, the more we know.
And the great Light of Day yet wants to run
Much of his Race though steep, suspense in Heav'n
Held by thy voice, thy potent voice he hears,   100
And longer will delay to hear thee tell
His Generation, and the rising Birth
Of Nature from the unapparent Deep:
Or if the Star of Ev'ning and the Moon
Haste to thy audience, Night with her will bring   105
Silence, and Sleep list'inng to thee will watch,
Or we can bid his absence, till thy Song
End, and dismiss thee ere the Morning shine.
   Thus *Adam* his illustrious Guest besought:
And thus the Godlike Angel answer'd mild.   110
This also thy request with caution askt
Obtain: though to recount Almighty works
What words or tongue of Seraph can suffice,
Or heart of man suffice to comprehend?
Yet what thou canst attain, which best may serve   115
To glorify the Maker, and infer
Thee also happier, shall not be withheld
Thy hearing, such Commission from above
I have receiv'd, to answer thy desire
Of knowledge within bounds; beyond abstain   120
To ask, nor let thine own inventions hope
Things not reveal'd, which th' invisible King,
Only Omniscient, hath supprest in Night,
To none communicable in Earth or Heaven:
Anough is left besides to search and know.   125
But Knowledge is as food, and needs no less
Her Temperance over Appetite, to know
In measure what the mind may well contain,
Oppresses else with Surfeit, and soon turns

---

98. *wants:* is short (of having run).
99. *suspense* has the Latin meaning that it has in VI, 580.
103. The *Deep* or Chaos is *unapparent* (invisible) both because it is outside the visible universe and because Milton regarded it as "confused and formless" (*CD* I, vii; C.Ed. XV, 23). For him the act of creation itself was the imposition of forms upon unformed matter. Cf. l. 233 below.
105. *audience:* hearing.
106. *watch:* stay awake, keep vigil.
116. *infer:* prove. Cf. VIII, 91.
120-125. The passage fuses the pagan dread of revealing ultimate secrets such as Virgil prayed that he might safely reveal in the *Aeneid* VI, 264–67, with Jewish awe of the "glorious and secret

things of God" (Ecclesiasticus xi, 4) and Christian respect for the principle of control of the lust of knowledge for its own sake. Cf. VIII, 66–75, as well as the closing lines of VII.
121. *inventions* has the meaning of *Conjecture* in VIII, 76: the guesswork of science.
126. The comparison was familiar, as Keightley's quotation from Davenant's *Gondibert* (II, viii, 22–25) shows:
  For though books serve as diet for the
    mind,
  If knowledge, early got, self-value
    breeds,
  By false digestion it is turned to
    wind,
  And what should nourish on the
    eater feeds.

Wisdom to Folly, as Nourishment to Wind.   130
　　Know then, that after *Lucifer* from Heav'n
(So call him, brighter once amidst the Host
Of Angels, than that Star the Stars among)
Fell with his flaming Legions through the Deep
Into his place, and the great Son return'd   135
Victorious with his Saints, th' Omnipotent
Eternal Father from his Throne beheld
Thir multitude, and to his Son thus spake.
　　At least our envious Foe hath fail'd, who thought
All like himself rebellious, by whose aid   140
This inaccessible high strength, the seat
Of Deity supreme, us dispossest,
He trusted to have seiz'd, and into fraud
Drew many, whom thir place knows here no more;
Yet far the greater part have kept, I see,   145
Thir station, Heav'n yet populous retains
Number sufficient to possess her Realms
Though wide, and this high Temple to frequent
With Ministeries due and solemn Rites:
But lest his heart exalt him in the harm   150
Already done, to have dispeopl'd Heav'n,
My damage fondly deem'd, I can repair
That detriment, if such it be to lose
Self-lost, and in a moment will create
Another World, out of one man a Race   155
Of men innumerable, there to dwell,
Not here, till by degrees of merit rais'd
They open to themselves at length the way
Up hither, under long obedience tri'd,
And Earth be chang'd to Heav'n, and Heav'n to Earth, 160
One Kingdom, Joy and Union without end.
Meanwhile inhabit lax, ye Powers of Heav'n;

132. *So call him* alludes to Satan's loss of his angelic name. Cf. I, 361, n.
133. The *Star* is Venus as the morning star, bringing or heralding the day, as the name *Lucifer* literally signifies. Like Spenser, Milton thought of all angels as "bright,
All glistring glorious in their Makers light;"
(*An Hymne of Heavenly Love*, 55–56) and of Satan as
"The brightest angell, even the Child of Light" (l. 83).
Cf. I, 84, n.
136. As in VI, 767, *Saints* means the loyal angels.
137. The throne is that seen by St. John, "set in heaven, and one sat on the throne" (Rev. iv, 2).

142. *us dispossest:* after dispossessing us.
143. *fraud* keeps its Latin meaning of "injury" or "treachery."
144. The line echoes the words of Job (vii, 10) about the lot of the dead: "Neither shall his place know him any more."
154. *Self-lost:* lost, or ruined, by their own act and to themselves rather than to God.
160. The line tallies with Raphael's account of the process of man's development in V, 469–79.
162. *inhabit lax:* spread out, settle widely through the regions which have lost a third of their inhabitants in Satan's revolt.

And thou my Word, begotten Son, by thee
This I perform, speak thou, and be it done:
My overshadowing Spirit and might with thee   165
I send along, ride forth, and bid the Deep
Within appointed bounds be Heav'n and Earth,
Boundless the Deep, because I am who fill
Infinitude, nor vacuous the space
Though I uncircumscrib'd myself retire,   170
And put not forth my goodness, which is free
To act or not, Necessity and Chance
Approach not mee, and what I will is Fate.
 So spake th' Almighty, and to what he spake
His Word, the Filial Godhead, gave effect.   175
Immediate are the Acts of God, more swift
Than time or motion, but to human ears
Cannot without process of speech be told,
So told as earthly notion can receive.
Great triumph and rejoicing was in Heav'n   180
When such was heard declar'd the Almighty's will;
Glory they sung to the most High, good will
To future men, and in thir dwellings peace:
Glory to him whose just avenging ire
Had driven out th' ungodly from his sight   185
And th' habitations of the just; to him
Glory and praise, whose wisdom had ordain'd
Good out of evil to create, instead
Of Spirits malign a better Race to bring
Into their vacant room, and thence diffuse   190

163. Cf. Milton's insistence in *CD* I, v (C.Ed. XIV, 307–09) that the Son was voluntarily begotten by the Father, that creation was accomplished through him by the Father, and that the Son "in his capacity of creator is himself called 'the first-born of every creature' " (Col. i, 15–17).
165. For the identity of the Spirit see ll. 235–37 below.
170–172. The doctrine of creation by "withdrawal" is discussed in the Introduction 37–38.
173. *what I will is Fate* does not mean that God's will is arbitrary. Fate, said Milton in *CD* I, ii (C.Ed. XIV, 27), "means either the essence of a thing or that general law which is the origin of everything, and under which everything acts; . . . fate can be nothing but a divine decree emanating from some almighty power." God is replying to Satan, who, in Tasso's *Jerusalem Delivered* IV, 17, actually says that what he wills shall be fate. Cf. I, 116, n.
176. A mass of Jewish and Christian commentary on Genesis declared that creation was instantaneous — that, as Du Bartas said,

 His Word and Deed, all in an instant wrought.

     (*Divine Weeks*, p. 164)

But commentators generally held either that the instantaneous work was later revealed by the stages of the six days of creation in Genesis, or — as Bacon thought — that while God's power was manifest in the making of "the confused mass and matter of heaven and earth in a moment," his wisdom was manifest in "the order and disposition of that chaos or mass" in "the work of six days" (*Advancement* I, vi, 2).
179. *earthly notion:* human intelligence.
182. There is an echo both of the angels' song to the shepherds at Christ's birth (Luke ii, 13–14) and of their shouting "for joy before God at the creation" in Job xxxviii, 7, a verse that is quoted in *CD* I, vii (C.Ed. XV, 33) to prove that the angels were created before the visible universe. Cf. *Nativity*, 119–20.

His good to Worlds and Ages infinite.
So sang the Hierarchies: Meanwhile the Son
On his great Expedition now appear'd,
Girt with Omnipotence, with Radiance crown'd
Of Majesty Divine, Sapience and Love   195
Immense, and all his Father in him shone.
About his Chariot numberless were pour'd
Cherub and Seraph, Potentates and Thrones,
And Virtues, winged Spirits, and Chariots wing'd,
From the Armory of God, where stand of old   200
Myriads between two brazen Mountains lodg'd
Against a solemn day, harness't at hand,
Celestial Equipage; and now came forth
Spontaneous, for within them Spirit liv'd,
Attendant on thir Lord: Heav'n op'n'd wide   205
Her ever-during Gates, Harmonious sound
On golden Hinges moving, to let forth
The King of Glory in his powerful Word
And Spirit coming to create new Worlds.
On heav'nly ground they stood, and from the shore   210
They view'd the vast immeasurable Abyss
Outrageous as a Sea, dark, wasteful, wild,
Up from the bottom turn'd by furious winds
And surging waves, as Mountains to assault
Heav'n's highth, and with the Centre mix the Pole.   215
   Silence, ye troubl'd waves, and thou Deep, peace,
Said then th' Omnific Word, your discord end:
   Nor stay'd, but on the Wings of Cherubim
Uplifted, in Paternal Glory rode
Far into *Chaos*, and the World unborn;   220
For *Chaos* heard his voice: him all his Train
Follow'd in bright procession to behold
Creation, and the wonders of his might.
Then stay'd the fervid Wheels, and in his hand
He took the golden Compasses, prepar'd   225

196. The line parallels III, 138, and recalls VI, 719–21.
200. So in Jeremiah i, 25, "the Lord hath opened his armoury."
201. The *brazen Mountains* recall Zechariah's vision of four chariots coming "out from between two mountains; and the mountains were mountains of brass" (Zech. vi, 1).
205–215. The opening gates suggest Psalm xxiv, 9: "Lift up your heads, O ye gates: . . . and the King of glory shall come in." The view of Chaos recalls Satan's view of it when the infernal doors open for him "and on thir hinges grate Harsh thunder" (II, 881–82).
217. *omnific:* all-creating.

218. Cf. the chariot made of the wings of cherubim in VI, 827, and its rolling *Orbs*, which here become *fervid Wheels* — fervid because they gleam in swift motion, or perhaps because they are like the wheels of the chariot of deity in Ezekiel i, 16, which "was like unto the color of a beryl."
225. Milton thought of Wisdom's account of the Creation in Proverbs viii, 27: "When he prepared the heavens, I was there: when he set a compass upon the face of the depth." Here compass means simply a circle, but — as H. Fletcher notes (*M.R.R.*, p. 108) — Rabbi Kimchi's commentary in the Buxtorf Bible interpreted the passage as meaning that a

In God's Eternal store, to circumscribe
This Universe, and all created things:
One foot he centred, and the other turn'd
Round through the vast profundity obscure,
And said, Thus far extend, thus far thy bounds,   230
This be thy just Circumference, O World.
Thus God the Heav'n created, thus the Earth,
Matter unform'd and void: Darkness profound
Cover'd th' Abyss: but on the wat'ry calm
His brooding wings the Spirit of God outspread,   235
And vital virtue infus'd, and vital warmth
Throughout the fluid Mass, but downward purg'd
The black tartareous cold Infernal dregs
Adverse to life; then founded, then conglob'd
Like things to like, the rest to several place   240
Disparted, and between spun out the Air,
And Earth self-balanc't on her Centre hung.
        Let there be Light, said God, and forthwith Light

---

literal compass was used in creation, with one foot on the earth and the other describing the surrounding heavens. This is the picture in Dante's reference (*Par.* xix, 40–42) to him "who rolled the compass round the limit of the universe." But the divine hand drawing a circle in Chaos was a familiar printer's ornament, and — as McColley shows in *N&Q*, CLXXVI (1939), 98 — it was a part of the conception of God as the architect of the universe that is given by the popular preacher Godfrey Goodman in a sermon printed in 1616 (p. 16): "In the beginning God did square and proportion the heauens for the earth, vsing his rule, leauell, and compasse; the earth as a center, and the heauens for the circumference." See the Introduction 27.

233. The formless matter of Plato's account of the beginning of the universe (*Tim.* 50e) harmonizes both with Milton's conception in V, 469–74, and with the description of the earth as "without form and void," with darkness spreading over the face of the deep, in Genesis i, 2.

235–237. From here on Milton follows the Bible closely. In Genesis i, 2, where the Spirit is said to have "moved upon the face of the deep," he saw, not the Holy Spirit, but — as *CD* I, vii (C.Ed. XV, 13–15) explains — either Christ, "to whom the name of Spirit is sometimes given in the Old Testament," or some "subordinate minister." The Hebrew word which is translated by "moved" — as Milton observed — means "brood" and was so explained by most lexicons and commentators on Genesis. The mistranslation — as G. N. Conklin notes in *Criticism*, p. 50 — is perpetuated in the Sumner translation of *CD* in spite of Milton's rendering of it by the Latin *incubabat* (brooded). Cf. I, 21, and III, 713–19.

237–242. The picture is the ultimately Platonic conception that Cicero visualized in the *Tusculans* I, xvii, 40, of the original differentiation of the four elements by the sinking of the earthy and damp elements "by their own weight" and the rising of the airy and fiery ones to form the "heavenly region" above the solid "center of the universe." Milton was familiar with the same idea in Ovid's "self-poised world" at the center of the universe (*Met.* I, 12), and — as A. H. Gilbert notes in *SP*, XIX (1922), 160 — he could find the conception of the earth as "suspended and balanced in the circumference of the great circle" of heaven in Galileo's *Dialogue about the two Chief Cosmic Systems, the Ptolemaic and the Copernican*. But for Milton the primary authority was Job xxvi, 7: "He hangeth the earth upon nothing." Cf. *Nativity*, 124.

243. *Let there be light* is God's first creative command (Gen. i, 3).

243–252. God's command, "Let there be light," and his division of the light from the darkness (Gen. i, 4–5) occur on the first day of creation, while it is on the fourth day that the "two great lights, the greater light to rule the day, and the lesser light to rule the night, . . . and the stars also," are created (Gen. ii, 16). In *CD* I, vii (C.Ed. XV, 31) Milton recognized the difficulty of conceiving of "light independent of a luminary," but such was the light above the heavens, where he recalled that God is described (in Eph. iv, 10) as "dwelling in the light that no man can approach unto."

Ethereal, first of things, quintessence pure
Sprung from the Deep, and from her Native East   245
To journey through the airy gloom began,
Spher'd in a radiant Cloud, for yet the Sun
Was not; shee in a cloudy Tabernacle
Sojourn'd the while. God saw the Light was good;
And light from darkness by the Hemisphere   250
Divided: Light the Day, and Darkness Night
He nam'd. Thus was the first Day Ev'n and Morn:
Nor pass'd uncelebrated, nor unsung
By the Celestial Choirs, when Orient Light
Exhaling first from Darkness they beheld;   255
Birth-day of Heav'n and Earth; with joy and shout
The hollow Universal Orb they fill'd,
And touch'd thir Golden Harps, and hymning prais'd
God and his works, Creator him they sung,
Both when first Ev'ning was, and when first Morn.   260
    Again, God said, let there be Firmament
Amid the Waters, and let it divide
The Waters from the Waters: and God made
The Firmament, expanse of liquid, pure,
Transparent, Elemental Air, diffus'd   265
In circuit to the uttermost convex
Of this great Round: partition firm and sure,
The Waters underneath from those above
Dividing: for as Earth, so hee the World
Built on circumfluous Waters calm, in wide   270
Crystalline Ocean, and the loud misrule
Of *Chaos* far remov'd, lest fierce extremes
Contiguous might distemper the whole frame:
And Heav'n he nam'd the Firmament: So Ev'n
And Morning *Chorus* sung the second Day.   275
    The Earth was form'd, but in the Womb as yet
Of Waters, Embryon immature involv'd,
Appear'd not: over all the face of Earth
Main Ocean flow'd, not idle, but with warm

261–271. In Gen. i, 6–8, God says,
"Let there be a firmament in the midst
of the water. . . . And God made the
firmament, and divided the waters which
were under the firmament from the waters
which were above the firmament. . . .
And God called the firmament heaven."
Although — as Robbins shows in *Hexaem-
eral Lit.*, p. 38 — the hexameral writers
prevailingly understood the firmament as
a solid shell of air, vapor, or some other
substance which served to prevent the
water above it from engulfing the still
uncreated stars and the earth below (or

within) it, Milton's prevailing conception
of it — as Svendsen shows in *M.&S.*,
p. 60 — was that of the entire mass of
air and vapor between the earth and the
"uttermost convex" of the created uni-
verse. The waters above it then become
the *Crystalline Ocean* of l. 271. This
outer ocean is distinguished by H. F.
Robins, in *PMLA LXIX* (1954), 904,
from the *Crystalline Sphear* of *PL* III,
482.
    267–269. *Round* and *World* both mean
the universe, at the center of which the
Earth is poised.

Prolific humor soft'ning all her Globe,   280
Fermented the great Mother to conceive,
Satiate with genial moisture, when God said,
Be gather'd now ye Waters under Heav'n
Into one place, and let dry Land appear.
Immediately the Mountains huge appear   285
Emergent, and thir broad bare backs upheave
Into the Clouds, thir tops ascend the Sky:
So high as heav'd the tumid Hills, so low
Down sunk a hollow bottom broad and deep,
Capacious bed of Waters: thither they   290
Hasted with glad precipitance, uproll'd
As drops on dust conglobing from the dry;
Part rise in crystal Wall, or ridge direct,
For haste; such flight the great command impress'd
On the swift floods: as Armies at the call   295
Of Trumpet (for of Armies thou hast heard)
Troop to thir Standard, so the wat'ry throng,
Wave rolling after Wave, where way they found,
If steep, with torrent rapture, if through Plain,
Soft-ebbing; nor withstood them Rock or Hill,   300
But they, or under ground, or circuit wide
With Serpent error wand'ring, found thir way,
And on the washy Ooze deep Channels wore;
Easy, ere God had bid the ground be dry,
All but within those banks, where Rivers now   305
Stream, and perpetual draw thir humid train.
The dry Land, Earth, and the great receptacle
Of congregated Waters he call'd Seas:
And saw that it was good, and said, Let th' Earth
Put forth the verdant Grass, Herb yielding Seed,   310
And Fruit Tree yielding Fruit after her kind;
Whose Seed is in herself upon the Earth,
He scarce had said, when the bare Earth, till then
Desert and bare, unsightly, unadorn'd,
Brought forth the tender Grass, whose verdure clad   315

280. The *Prolific humor* of the fertiliz-
ing sea is less biblical than it is in keeping
with Ovid's account of creation (*Met.* I,
1–51) and with Lucretius' theory of or-
ganic life (*De rerum natura* V, 783–820),
but it is in harmony with Milton's con-
ception of the impregnating spirit brood-
ing on the waters in I, 21, and VII, 235–
37. See the Introduction 40.
282. *genial:* fertilizing, life-producing.
285–292. The lines fuse the picture of
the mountains and valleys going up and
down "unto the place which thou has
founded for them" in Psalm civ, 8, with
the command of God in Genesis i, 9:
"Let the waters under the heaven be

gathered together unto one place, and
let the dry land appear." In *The Break-
ing of the Circle* (Evanston, 1950), p. 20,
M. Nicolson sees in the lines the clear
statement of a traditional belief in a
symmetrical correspondence between the
depths of the sea and the height of the
world's mountains.
302. *error:* meandering (in serpentine
coils). Cf. *erroneous* in VII, 20.
306. *humid train:* liquid flow.
309. Cf Genesis i, 11: "And God said,
Let the earth bring forth grass, the herb
yielding seed, and the fruit tree yielding
fruit after his kind, whose seed is in itself
upon earth."

Her Universal Face with pleasant green,
Then Herbs of every leaf, that sudden flow'r'd
Op'ning thir various colors, and made gay
Her bosom smelling sweet: and these scarce blown,
Forth flourish'd thick the clust'ring Vine, forth crept   320
The smelling Gourd, up stood the corny Reed
Embattl'd in her field: and th' humble Shrub,
And Bush with frizzl'd hair implicit: last
Rose as in Dance the stately Trees, and spread
Thir branches hung with copious Fruit: or gemm'd   325
Thir Blossoms: with high Woods the Hills were crown'd,
With tufts the valleys and each fountain side,
With borders long the Rivers. That Earth now
Seem'd like to Heav'n, a seat where Gods might dwell,
Or wander with delight, and love to haunt   330
Her sacred shades: though God had yet not rain'd
Upon the Earth, and man to till the ground
None was, but from the Earth a dewy Mist
Went up and water'd all the ground, and each
Plant of the field, which ere it was in the Earth   335
God made, and every Herb, before it grew
On the green stem; God saw that it was good:
So Ev'n and Morn recorded the Third Day.

Again th' Almighty spake: Let there be Lights
High in th' expanse of Heaven to divide   340
The Day from Night; and let them be for Signs,
For Seasons, and for Days, and circling Years,
And let them be for Lights as I ordain
Thir Office in the Firmament of Heav'n
To give Light on the Earth; and it was so.   345
And God made two great Lights, great for thir use
To Man, the greater to have rule by Day,
The less by Night altern: and made the Stars,

321. Bentley's emendation of "swelling" for "smelling" is doubtfully challenged by McColley (*Paradise Lost*, p. 57) on the ground that Du Bartas mentions the "smelling" (i.e. sweet smelling) Indian pepper in a context like this where Milton's "gourd" is mentioned. *corny*: corn- (i.e. grain-) bearing. Cf. *balmy Reed* in V. 23.

322. So a *field of Ceres* is like an army with ported spears in IV, 980–83. Ed. 1 reads *add* for *and*.

323. *frizzl'd* is paralleled by the *O.E.D.* in Browne's *Britannia's Pastorals*: "The frizled coates which doe the mountaines hide." *implicit* keeps its Latin meaning of "tangled."

325. *gemm'd* keeps its Latin meaning of "budding."

327. Cf. the *tufted Groves* of *L'Allegro* 78.

331–334. Cf. Genesis ii, 5–6: ". . . God had not caused it to rain upon the earth, and there was not a man to till the ground. But there went up a mist from the earth, and watered the whole face of the ground."

335–337. God's creation of "every plant of the earth before it was in the earth" (Gen. ii, 5) may have meant to Milton — as Robbins notes (*Hexaemeral Lit.*, p. 32) that it did to Philo — "that the plants were created before the sun so that men might not ascribe their creation to it, but rather to God."

339–351. These lines closely paraphrase Genesis i, 14–19.

And set them in the Firmament of Heav'n
To illuminate the Earth, and rule the Day   350
In thir vicissitude, and rule the Night,
And Light from Darkness to divide.   God saw,
Surveying his great Work, that it was good:
For of Celestial Bodies first the Sun
A mighty Sphere he fram'd, unlightsome first,   355
Though of Ethereal Mould: then form'd the Moon
Globose, and every magnitude of Stars,
And sow'd with Stars the Heav'n thick as a field:
Of Light by far the greater part he took,
Transplanted from her cloudy Shrine, and plac'd   360
In the Sun's Orb, made porous to receive
And drink the liquid Light, firm to retain
Her gather'd beams, great Palace now of Light.
Hither as to thir Fountain other Stars
Repairing, in thir gold'n Urns draw Light,   365
And hence the Morning Planet gilds her horns;
By tincture or reflection they augment
Thir small peculiar, though from human sight
So far remote, with diminution seen.
First in his East the glorious Lamp was seen,   370
Regent of Day, and all th' Horizon round
Invested with bright Rays, jocund to run
His Longitude through Heav'n's high road: the gray
Dawn, and the *Pleiades* before him danc'd
Shedding sweet influence: less bright the Moon,   375
But opposite in levell'd West was set
His mirror, with full face borrowing her Light
From him, for other light she needed none
In that aspect, and still that distance keeps
Till night, then in the East her turn she shines,   380
Revolv'd on Heav'n's great Axle, and her Reign
With thousand lesser Lights dividual holds,
With thousand thousand Stars, that then appear'd
Spangling the Hemisphere: then first adorn'd

351. Cf. *vicissitude* (meaning alternation) in VI, 8.
356. Cf. *Mould* (meaning matter in general) in III, 709.
359–366. For another poetical development of Pliny's conception of the sun as the fountain of light (*Nat. Hist.* II, iv, 6) see VIII, 148–52.
366. The gilded horns of the *Morning Planet* plainly refer to Galileo's discovery that Venus has phases like those of the moon, whose horns were a traditional metaphor.
367. Either by absorbing (*tincture*) or by reflecting the sun's rays the planets increase the light which, as Svendsen

shows in *M.&S.*, p. 73, most contemporary encyclopaedias taught that the planets naturally radiated from themselves.
373. Cf. *Longitude* in III, 576, and IV, 539.
374. There is an allusion to "the sweet influence of Pleiades" (Job xxxviii, 31) and perhaps to Guido Reni's picture of the sun's chariot with the dawn incarnate as a lovely woman flying before it and seven nymphs — who correspond in number to the Pleiades — alongside.
382. *dividual*, which modifies *Reign*, has its Latin meaning of "divided."

With thir bright Luminaries that Set and Rose,   385
Glad Ev'ning and glad Morn crown'd the fourth day.
    And God said, let the Waters generate
Reptile with Spawn abundant, living Soul:
And let Fowl fly above the Earth, with wings
Display'd on the op'n Firmament of Heav'n.   390
And God created the great Whales, and each
Soul living, each that crept, which plenteously
The waters generated by thir kinds,
And every Bird of wing after his kind;
And saw that it was good, and bless'd them, saying,   395
Be fruitful, multiply, and in the Seas
And Lakes and running Streams the waters fill;
And let the Fowl be multipli'd on the Earth.
Forthwith the Sounds and Seas, each Creek and Bay
With Fry innumerable swarm, and Shoals   400
Of Fish that with thir Fins and shining Scales
Glide under the green Wave, in Sculls that oft
Bank the mid Sea: part single or with mate
Graze the Seaweed thir pasture, and through Groves
Of Coral stray, or sporting with quick glance   405
Show to the Sun thir wav'd coats dropt with Gold,
Or in thir Pearly shells at ease, attend
Moist nutriment, or under Rocks thir food
In jointed Armor watch: on smooth the Seal,
And bended Dolphins play: part huge of bulk   410
Wallowing unwieldly, enormous in thir Gait
Tempest the Ocean: there Leviathan
Hugest of living Creatures, on the Deep
Stretcht like a Promontory sleeps or swims,
And seems a moving Land, and at his Gills   415
Draws in, and at his Trunk spouts out a Sea.
Meanwhile the tepid Caves, and Fens and shores
Thir Brood as numerous hatch, from th' Egg that soon
Bursting with kindly rupture forth disclos'd
Thir callow young, but feather'd soon and fledge   420
They summ'd thir Pens, and soaring th' air sublime

387–398. The lines paraphrase Genesis i, 20–23.

388. *Reptile* means any reptant or creeping thing in the broadest sense and includes fish. *Soul* is used in Genesis i, 20, as equivalent to life, and in *CD* I, vii, Milton emphasizes its application to "every beast of the field wherein there is life."

402. *Sculls:* schools.

403. *Bank the mid Sea:* make a bank with their numbers in mid-ocean.

409. *on smooth:* on the smooth sea.

412–415. Cf. the *Leviathan* in I, 200–205.

417–421. D. C. Allen suspects (*MLN*, LXIII — 1948 — p. 264) that the egg is intentionally put before the bird and quotes Plutarch's mooting of that question in *Symposiacs*, Macrobius' in the *Saturnalia* VII, xvi, and Erycius Puteanus' in his *Praise of the Egg* (*Ovi encomium*). Puteanus' *Comus* (Louvain, 1608) seems to have been known to Milton.

419. *kindly:* natural.

420. *callow:* unfledged. *fledge:* fledged.

421. *summ'd their Pens:* developed complete plumage.

With clang despis'd the ground, under a cloud
In prospect; there the Eagle and the Stork
On Cliffs and Cedar tops thir Eyries build:
Part loosely wing the Region, part more wise   425
In common, rang'd in figure wedge thir way,
Intelligent of seasons, and set forth
Thir Aery Caravan high over Seas
Flying, and over Lands with mutual wing
Easing thir flight; so steers the prudent Crane   430
Her annual Voyage, borne on Winds; the Air
Floats, as they pass, fann'd with unnumber'd plumes:
From Branch to Branch the smaller Birds with song
Solac'd the Woods, and spread thir painted wings
Till Ev'n, nor then the solemn Nightingale   435
Ceas'd warbling, but all night tun'd her soft lays:
Others on Silver Lakes and Rivers Bath'd
Thir downy Breast; the Swan with Arched neck
Between her white wings mantling proudly, Rows
Her state with Oary feet: yet oft they quit   440
The Dank, and rising on stiff Pennons, tow'r
The mid Aereal Sky: Others on ground
Walk'd firm; the crested Cock whose clarion sounds
The silent hours, and th' other whose gay Train
Adorns him, color'd with the Florid hue   445
Of Rainbows and Starry Eyes. The Waters thus
With Fish replenisht, and the Air with Fowl,
Ev'ning and Morn solemniz'd the Fift day.
  The Sixt, and of Creation last arose
With Ev'ning Harps and Matin, when God said,   450
Let th' Earth bring forth Soul living in her kind,
Cattle and Creeping things, and Beast of the Earth,
Each in their kind. The Earth obey'd, and straight
Op'ning her fertile Womb teem'd at a Birth
Innumerous living Creatures, perfet forms,   455
Limb'd and full grown: out of the ground up rose

---

422. *under a cloud:* under what seemed from the point of view of the earth below to be a cloud (so great was the number of birds).

425. *Region* is probably "the middle Region of thick Air" of *PR* II, 117, the middle stratum of the three layers into which the atmosphere was traditionally divided. Cf. I, 516.

426–431. In war *the prudent Crane* understood (according to several Elizabethan writers whom K. Svendsen quotes in *M.&S.*, pp. 157–58 and 275–76) "the expedient of posting sentries and the triangular order of battle." In flight "the hindmost do commonly rest their heads upon the foremost, and when the guide is weary of going before, he cometh hindmost." Cf. I, 576, and the Introduction 63.

432. *Floats:* undulates, is fanned into waves.

439. According to *O.E.D.*, *mantling* is uniquely used by Milton in the sense that it has here and in V, 279.

441. *The Dank:* the water. *tow'r:* soar high in air.

450. The command of God is based on Genesis i, 24–25.

451. Bentley's emendation of *Fowle* in the early editions to *Soul* seems inevitable. Cf. VII, 388, n.

454. *teem'd:* brought forth.

As from his Lair the wild Beast where he wons
In Forest wild, in Thicket, Brake, or Den;
Among the Trees in Pairs they rose, they walk'd:
The Cattle in the Fields and Meadows green: 460
Those rare and solitary, these in flocks
Pasturing at once, and in broad Herds upsprung.
The grassy Clods now Calv'd, now half appear'd
The Tawny Lion, pawing to get free
His hinder parts, then springs as broke from Bonds,   465
And Rampant shakes his Brinded mane; the Ounce,
The Libbard, and the Tiger, as the Mole
Rising, the crumbl'd Earth above them threw
In Hillocks; the swift Stag from under ground
Bore up his branching head: scarce from his mould   470
Behemoth biggest born of Earth upheav'd
His vastness: Fleec't the Flocks and bleating rose,
As Plants: ambiguous between Sea and Land
The River Horse and scaly Crocodile.
At once came forth whatever creeps the ground,   475
Insect or Worm; those wav'd thir limber fans
For wings, and smallest Lineaments exact
In all the Liveries deckt of Summer's pride
With spots of Gold and Purple, azure and green:
These as a line thir long dimension drew,   480
Streaking the ground with sinuous trace; not all
Minims of Nature; some of Serpent kind
Wondrous in length and corpulence involv'd
Thir Snaky folds, and added wings. First crept

457. *wons*: dwells.

463–470. Here Coleridge thought that Milton "certainly copied the *fresco* of the Creation in the Sistine Chapel at Rome," but said that, though the image was justified by "the necessities of the painter," it was "wholly unworthy . . . of the enlarged powers of the poet" (Brinkley, *Coleridge*, p. 598). Actually the calving clods and the struggling lion are two of several resemblances to Lucretius' illustrations of the fertility of the earth in its prime, 'when it directly brought forth all forms of life' (*De rerum natura* II, 991–98). Cf. X, 1075–78, and the Introduction 40.

466. *Brinded*: brindled. *Ounce*: lynx or panther.

471. A marginal note on Job xl, 15–24, in the Geneva Bible says: "The Hebrues say Behemoth signifieth Elephant, so called for his hugenesse, by the whiche may be understood the deuyl." The *Jewish Encyclopaedia* does not confirm the identification with the elephant, but brackets *Behemoth* with Leviathan as a primeval monster.

474. *River Horse* is a literal translation of the Greek "hippopotamus."

476. *Worm*, as in IX, 1068, means serpent, but here — generally — any creeping animal. Milton agreed with Henry More — in *An Antidote against Atheisme* (1653), p. 83 — that "the swarmes of little *Vermine*, and of *Flyes*, and innumerable suchlike diminutive Creatures" deserve that we should "congratulate their coming into Being rather than murmure sullenly and scornfully against their Existence."

480. *These* are the *Worm* (and serpent) kind of l. 476.

482. *Minims*: tiniest creatures.

483. *corpulence involv'd*: coiled body.

484. For winging his serpents — as D. C. Allen notes in *MLN*, LIX (1944), 538 — Milton had the authority of Isaiah xxx, 6, and Herodotus II, 75, as well as of Samuel Bochart's *Hierozoicon* (a work on biblical animals, published in London in 1663) and of several standard writers.

The Parsimonious Emmet, provident   485
Of future, in small room large heart enclos'd,
Pattern of just equality perhaps
Hereafter, join'd in her popular Tribes
Of Commonalty: swarming next appear'd
The Female Bee that feeds her Husband Drone   490
Deliciously, and builds her waxen Cells
With Honey stor'd: the rest are numberless,
And thou thir Natures know'st, and gav'st them Names,
Needless to thee repeated; nor unknown
The Serpent subtl'st Beast of all the field,   495
Of huge extent sometimes, with brazen Eyes
And hairy Mane terrific, though to thee
Not noxious, but obedient at thy call.
Now Heav'n in all her Glory shone, and roll'd
Her motions, as the great first-Mover's hand   500
First wheel'd thir course; Earth in her rich attire
Consummate lovely smil'd; Air, Water, Earth,
By Fowl, Fish, Beast, was flown, was swum, was walkt
Frequent; and of the Sixt day yet remain'd;
There wanted yet the Master work, the end   505
Of all yet done; a Creature who not prone
And Brute as other Creatures, but endu'd
With Sanctity of Reason, might erect
His Stature, and upright with Front serene
Govern the rest, self-knowing, and from thence   510
Magnanimous to correspond with Heav'n,
But grateful to acknowledge whence his good
Descends, thither with heart and voice and eyes

485–492. The *Emmet*, like the ant in Horace's *Satires* I, i, 35, provides for the future. The supposed democracy of the ants seemed to Milton as exemplary as the monarchy of the bees, which he twitted some Royalist writers for taking too seriously. Cf. *Def 1* (C.Ed. VII, 279). In Charles Butler's *The Feminine Monarchie* (1634), p. 55, the worker bees are expressly declared to be females and to spoil the drones, who always have "a drop of nectar in their mouths."

493. Cf. Adam's naming of the animals in VIII, 349–54.

494–499. Before its curse (cf. X, 175–78) the serpent was thought to have been a splendid creature, and for its mane Milton had the example of the sea-serpents that Virgil describes as devouring Laocoon and his sons (*Aen.* II, 203–207). Cf. IX, 494–502.

503. With the impersonal, Latin constructions cf. that in VI, 335.

504. *Frequent* keeps its Latin meaning of "in throngs" or "in hosts." Cf. *PR.* I, 128, and II, 130.

505. *the end:* the object. Cf. l. 79 above, n. and l. 591 below.

505–511. The belief in man's upright attitude as a symbol of his superiority to the beasts and kinship with God runs through classical literature from Plato (*Tim.* 90a) to Cicero (*On the Nature of the Gods* II, lvi) and Ovid (*Met.* I, 76–86). The idea is so frequent in Lactantius that K. Hartwell in *Milton and Lactantius*, p. 75, says that "there are too many instances to quote"; and it runs through hexameral literature in many passages like Du Bartas' description of Adam as

Yet, not his Face down to the earth-
  ward bending,
Like beasts that but regard their
  belly, . . .
. . . but towards the Azure Skyes.
                (*Divine Weeks*, p. 165)

In *JHI*, XIX (1958), 256–258, C. A. Patrides cites numerous medieval and Renaissance parallels.

Directed in Devotion, to adore
And worship God Supreme who made him chief   515
Of all his works: therefore th'Omnipotent
Eternal Father (For where is not hee
Present) thus to his Son audibly spake.
     Let us make now Man in our image, Man
In our similitude, and let them rule   520
Over the Fish and Fowl of Sea and Air,
Beast of the Field, and over all the Earth,
And every creeping thing that creeps the ground.
This said, he form'd thee, *Adam*, thee O Man
Dust of the ground, and in thy nostrils breath'd   525
The breath of Life; in his own Image hee
Created thee, in the Image of God
Express, and thou becam'st a living Soul.
Male he created thee, but thy consort
Female for Race; then bless'd Mankind, and said,   530
Be fruitful, multiply, and fill the Earth,
Subdue it, and throughout Dominion hold
Over Fish of the Sea, and Fowl of the Air,
And every living thing that moves on the Earth.
Wherever thus created, for no place   535
Is yet distinct by name, thence, as thou know'st
He brought thee into this delicious Grove,
This Garden, planted with the Trees of God,
Delectable both to behold and taste;
And freely all thir pleasant fruit for food   540
Gave thee, all sorts are here that all th' Earth yields,
Variety without end; but of the Tree
Which tasted works knowledge of Good and Evil,
Thou may'st not; in the day thou eat'st, thou di'st;
Death is the penalty impos'd, beware,   545
And govern well thy appetite, lest sin
Surprise thee, and her black attendant Death.
Here finish'd hee, and all that he had made

---

518. In *CD* I, vii (C.Ed. XV, 37) Milton observed that "the Deity speaks like to a man deliberating" when, in Genesis i, 26, he says, "Let us make man in our own image, after our own likeness." Biblical commentary traditionally interpreted the passage as meaning — in words that Sir Walter Raleigh translated from the Spanish Jesuit Benedict Pereira in the *History of the World* I, ii, 2 — that man images God's "reasonable and understanding nature" and "the divine grace and heavenly glory, which is indeed the perfection and accomplishment of the natural image."

520–534. The lines paraphrase Genesis i, 26–28. The command to Adam to

"have dominion over the fish of the sea, and over the fowl of the air, and over every living thing that moveth upon the earth" rang through seventeenth century literature in countless passages like Burton's glorification of man as the "Sovereigne Lord of the Earth, Viceroy of the World, sole Commander and Governour of all the creatures in it" (*Anatomy* I, i, 1; Everyman Ed. I, 130). Cf. VIII, 495–508.

535–538. Genesis ii, 15, says that God put Adam into the *Garden*, and the Apocryphal book of II Esdras iii, 6, says that Adam was led into paradise, which God had planted.

View'd, and behold all was entirely good;
So Ev'n and Morn accomplish'd the Sixt day: 550
Yet not till the Creator from his work,
Desisting, though unwearied, up return'd
Up to the Heav'n of Heav'ns his high abode,
Thence to behold this new created World
Th' addition of his Empire, how it show'd 555
In prospect from his Throne, how good, how fair,
Answering his great Idea. Up he rode
Follow'd with acclamation and the sound
Symphonious of ten thousand Harps that tun'd
Angelic harmonies: the Earth, the Air 560
Resounded, (thou remember'st, for thou heard'st)
The Heav'ns and all the Constellations rung,
The Planets in thir station list'ning stood,
While the bright Pomp ascended jubilant.
Open, ye everlasting Gates, they sung, 565
Open, ye Heav'ns, your living doors; let in
The great Creator from his work return'd
Magnificent, his Six days' work, a World;
Open, and henceforth oft; for God will deign
To visit oft the dwellings of just Men 570
Delighted, and with frequent intercourse
Thither will send his winged Messengers
On errands of supernal Grace. So sung
The glorious Train ascending: He through Heav'n,
That open'd wide her blazing Portals, led 575
To God's Eternal house direct the way,
A broad and ample road, whose dust is Gold
And pavement Stars, as Stars to thee appear,
Seen in the Galaxy, that Milky way
Which nightly as a circling Zone thou seest 580
Powder'd with Stars. And now on Earth the Seventh
Ev'ning arose in *Eden*, for the Sun
Was set, and twilight from the East came on,
Forerunning Night; when at the holy mount
Of Heav'n's high-seated top, th' Imperial Throne 585

557. So in *CD* I, iii (C.Ed. XIV, 65), Milton speaks of God's foreknowledge and wisdom as "that idea of everything, which he had in his mind, to use the language of men, before he decreed anything." Here the thought also seems congenial with the pleasure of Plato's creator in the fulfilment of his pattern in the universe that he produces (*Tim.* 37c).

564. *Pomp* keeps its Greek meaning of "splendid procession."

565-566. Cf. ll. 205-215 above, n.

571. In *CD* I, v (C.Ed. XIV, 249), Milton observed that in the Old Testament "the name of God seems to be attributed to angels, because as heavenly messengers they bear the appearance of the divine glory and person, and even speak in the very words of the Deity." Cf. III, 531-34.

577-581. The lines resemble Ovid's description of the Milky Way (*Met.* I, 166-69), though — as M. Nicolson suggests in *ELH*, II (1935), 24 — we may also have here "a Galilean description of the Milky Way," since there has been a reference to Galileo's telescope in l. 366 above.

584. Cf. the *holy mount* in V, 643.

Of Godhead, fixt for ever firm and sure,
The Filial Power arriv'd, and sat him down
With his great Father, for he also went
Invisible, yet stay'd (such privilege
Hath Omnipresence) and the work ordain'd,   590
Author and end of all things, and from work
Now resting, bless'd and hallow'd the Sev'nth day,
As resting on that day from all his work,
But not in silence holy kept; the Harp
Had work and rested not, the solemn Pipe,   595
And Dulcimer, all Organs of sweet stop,
All sounds on Fret by String or Golden Wire
Temper'd soft Tunings, intermixt with Voice
Choral or Unison; of incense Clouds
Fuming from Golden Censers hid the Mount.   600
Creation and the Six days' acts they sung:
Great are thy works, *Jehovah*, infinite
Thy power; what thought can measure thee or tongue
Relate thee; greater now in thy return
Than from the Giant Angels; thee that day   605
Thy Thunders magnifi'd; but to create
Is greater than created to destroy.
Who can impair thee, mighty King, or bound
Thy Empire? easily the proud attempt
Of Spirits apostate and thir Counsels vain   610
Thou hast repell'd, while impiously they thought
Thee to diminish, and from thee withdraw
The number of thy worshippers. Who seeks
To lessen thee, against his purpose serves
To manifest the more thy might: his evil   615
Thou usest, and from thence creat'st more good.
Witness this new-made World, another Heav'n
From Heaven Gate not far, founded in view
On the clear *Hyaline*, the Glassy Sea;
Of amplitude almost immense, with Stars   620
Numerous, and every Star perhaps a World
Of destin'd habitation; but thou know'st

592. The blessing of the Sabbath is based on Genesis ii, 2–3.

597. *Fret:* the bar on the finger-board of a guitar.

605. Satan's rebel hosts — as Todd's notes indicate — are called *Giant Angels* because the Hebrew word *gibbor* implies "a proud, fierce, and aspiring temper," and because here, as in VI, 643–66, Milton had the revolt of the giants against Zeus in mind and intended to suggest that "the fictions of the Greek poets owed their rise to some clouded tradition of this real event, and that their giants

were, if they understood his story aright, his fallen angels."

619. The *Glassy Sea* is the waters above the firmament and therefore visible to eyes looking down from heaven on the outside of the universe. Cf. VII, 261–71, n. *Hyaline* translates the Greek word meaning "glassy" which describes the sea of glass before God's throne in Revelation iv, 6.

622. The actively controversial idea that the stars may be inhabited goes back to Plato's *Timaeus*, 41. Cf. III, 565–71, and VIII, 144–45.

Thir seasons: among these the seat of men,
Earth with her nether Ocean circumfus'd,
Thir pleasant dwelling-place.   Thrice happy men,   625
And sons of men, whom God hath thus advanc't,
Created in his Image, there to dwell
And worship him, and in reward to rule
Over his Works, on Earth, in Sea, or Air,
And multiply a Race of Worshippers   630
Holy and just: thrice happy if they know
Thir happiness, and persevere upright.
So sung they, and the Empyrean rung,
With *Halleluiahs:* Thus was Sabbath kept.
And thy request think now fulfill'd, that ask'd   635
How first this World and face of things began,
And what before thy memory was done
From the beginning, that posterity
Inform'd by thee might know; if else thou seek'st
Aught, not surpassing human measure, say.   640

The End of the Seventh Book.

BOOK VIII

THE ARGUMENT

Adam *inquires concerning celestial Motions, is doubtfully answer'd, and exhorted to search rather things more worthy of knowledge:* Adam *assents, and still desirous to detain* Raphael, *relates to him what he remember'd since his own Creation, his placing in Paradise, his talk with God concerning solitude and fit society, his first meeting and Nuptials with* Eve, *his discourse with the Angel thereupon; who after admonitions repeated departs.*

624. The *nether Ocean* is the waters under the firmament, which were regarded by ancient geographers as encircling all the continents.

629. Cf. Psalm viii, 6: "Thou madest him to have dominion over the works of thy hands; thou hast put all things under his feet."

631. Adam's idyllic happiness evokes Virgil's famous lines on the happiness of the Italian peasants:

O, happy, if he knew his happy state,
The swain, who, free from bus'ness
  and debate,
Receives his easy food from nature's
  hand.
      (*Georg.* II, 457–59. Dryden's
                     translation.)

632. Cf. Raphael's repeated warning to Adam to persevere in VIII, 639.

636. *face of things:* visible nature. Cf. l. 63 above.   Milton's readers were familiar with this transition from man's creation in the image of God in Book VII to his introduction to the marvels of nature in Book VIII.   Commenting on a parallel thought in Aristotle's *Politics* I, i, Loys le Roy compared the passages from Plato and Lactantius that are mentioned in the note on ll. 505–511 above, and added: "Man is begotten . . . after the image and similitude of God . . . to celebrate his honour . . . to the end that he may view the order of the celestiall bodies, and keepe . . . the habitation of this middle terrestrial globe" (I. D.'s translation, London, 1598, p. 18).

The Angel ended, and in *Adam's* Ear
So Charming left his voice, that he a while
Thought him still speaking, still stood fixt to hear;
Then as new wak't thus gratefully repli'd.
What thanks sufficient, or what recompense 5
Equal have I to render thee, Divine
Historian, who thus largely hast allay'd
The thirst I had of knowledge, and voutsaf't
This friendly condescension to relate
Things else by me unsearchable, now heard 10
With wonder, but delight, and, as is due,
With glory attributed to the high
Creator; something yet of doubt remains,
Which only thy solution can resolve.
When I behold this goodly Frame, this World 15
Of Heav'n and Earth consisting, and compute
Thir magnitudes, this Earth a spot, a grain,
An Atom, with the Firmament compar'd
And all her number'd Stars, that seem to roll
Spaces incomprehensible (for such 20
Thir distance argues and thir swift return
Diurnal) merely to officiate light
Round this opacous Earth, this punctual spot,
One day and night; in all thir vast survey
Useless besides; reasoning I oft admire, 25
How Nature wise and frugal could commit
Such disproportions, with superfluous hand
So many nobler Bodies to create,
Greater so manifold to this one use,

1–4. These lines were added in the second edition when Milton divided the original Book VII at l. 640 to make the present Books VII and VIII. The original line 641 read,
To whom thus *Adam* gratefully repli'd.
The words sounding in Adam's ears may be an echo of those of the incarnate Laws that Socrates hears ringing in his ears and obeys at the close of Plato's *Crito.*
15. *Frame:* creation, universe. Cf. V, 154, and VII, 273.
19. Probably *number'd* means "numerous," but it resembles Psalm cxlvii, 4: "He telleth the number of the stars: He calleth them by their names." The entire speech is colored by Psalm viii.
22. *officiate:* furnish.
23. *opacous:* shadowy, dark. *punctual:* point-like. Milton was aware that Copernican astronomers stressed the tiny earth and the widening astronomical spaces that terrified Pascal, but he also knew that Ptolemy had declared the earth a dot in comparison with the heavens,

that to Dante as he saw it from the heaven of fixed stars it seemed like a little threshing-floor (*Par.* xxii, 151), as it did to Chaucer's Troilus from the same point-of-view, and that to a Protestant theologian like Jerome Zanchius the fact that the earth was "less than a point" in the universe was a prime reason for glorifying God (*De operibus Dei* II, ii, 5, Neustadt, 1591). Cf. ll. 107–110 below, n. See the Introduction 35.
25–38. *admire:* wonder, question. Though Milton's Adam regards the *sedentary Earth* as motionless, he is as puzzled as Burton was by the "fury . . . that shall drive the Heavens . . . about in 24 hours" (*Anatomy* II, ii, 3; Everyman Ed. II, p. 52). Joseph Glanvill, writing as a Copernican in 1661, and believing that before the fall Adam's sight penetrated to the limits of the universe, thought that " 'tis not unlikely that he had as clear a perception of the earth's motion, as we think we have of its quiescence" (*Vanity of Dogmatizing,* p. 5).

For aught appears, and on thir Orbs impose   30
Such restless revolution day by day
Repeated, while the sedentary Earth,
That better might with far less compass move,
Serv'd by more noble than herself, attains
Her end without least motion, and receives,   35
As Tribute such a sumless journey brought
Of incorporeal speed, her warmth and light;
Speed, to describe whose swiftness Number fails.

So spake our Sire, and by his count'nance seem'd
Ent'ring on studious thoughts abstruse, which *Eve*   40
Perceiving where she sat retir'd in sight,
With lowliness Majestic from her seat,
And Grace that won who saw to wish her stay,
Rose, and went forth among her Fruits and Flow'rs,
To visit how they prosper'd, bud and bloom,   45
Her Nursery; they at her coming sprung
And toucht by her fair tendance gladlier grew.
Yet went she not, as not with such discourse
Delighted, or not capable her ear
Of what was high: such pleasure she reserv'd,   50
Adam relating, she sole Auditress;
Her Husband the Relater she preferr'd
Before the Angel, and of him to ask
Chose rather: hee, she knew, would intermix
Grateful digressions, and solve high dispute   55
With conjugal Caresses, from his Lip
Not Words alone pleas'd her. O when meet now
Such pairs, in Love and mutual Honor join'd?
With Goddess-like demeanor forth she went;
Not unattended, for on her as Queen   60
A pomp of winning Graces waited still,
And from about her shot Darts of desire
Into all Eyes to wish her still in sight.
And *Raphael* now to *Adam's* doubt propos'd
Benevolent and facile thus repli'd.   65
   To ask or search I blame thee not, for Heav'n
Is as the Book of God before thee set,

36. *sumless:* immeasurable.
37. *incorporeal,* as applied to the speed
of the heavenly bodies, matches *spiritual*
in l. 110 below. The words, says Ruth
Wallerstein (*Poetic,* p. 258), are "entirely
consonant with his [Milton's] view in
Book V . . . of the indefinable gradation
from 'matter' to spirit."
46. *Nursery* means the objects of nurs-
ing. King Lear says (*King Lear* I, i,
126), speaking of Cordelia, that he had
depended for his rest "on her kind nurs-
ery."
61. *pomp:* procession. Cf. VII, 564.

64. *doubt propos'd:* question raised.
Cf. l. 13 above.
65. *facile* has its Latin meaning of
"easy of access," "gracious."
67. "The Book of God" or the "Book
of the Creation" (or "of the Creatures")
was a traditional metaphor among the-
ologians, who, like Richard Baxter, con-
demned the sceptical philosophy which
"most readeth the book of Nature and
least understandeth or feeleth the mean-
ing of it" (*The Reasons of the Christian
Religion,* 1667, p. 108).

Wherein to read his wond'rous Works, and learn
His Seasons, Hours, or Days, or Months, or Years:
This to attain, whether Heav'n move or Earth,   70
Imports not, if thou reck'n right; the rest
From Man or Angel the great Architect
Did wisely to conceal, and not divulge
His secrets to be scann'd by them who ought
Rather admire; or if they list to try   75
Conjecture, he his Fabric of the Heav'ns
Hath left to thir disputes, perhaps to move
His laughter at thir quaint Opinions wide
Hereafter, when they come to model Heav'n
And calculate the Stars, how they will wield   80
The mighty frame, how build, unbuild, contrive
To save appearances, how gird the Sphere
With Centric and Eccentric scribbl'd o'er,
Cycle and Epicycle, Orb in Orb:
Already by thy reasoning this I guess,   85
Who are to lead thy offspring, and supposest
That bodies bright and greater should not serve
The less not bright, nor Heav'n such journeys run,
Earth sitting still, when she alone receives
The benefit: consider first, that Great   90
Or Bright infers not Excellence: the Earth
Though, in comparison of Heav'n, so small,
Nor glistering, may of solid good contain
More plenty than the Sun that barren shines,
Whose virtue on itself works no effect,   95
But in the fruitful Earth; there first receiv'd
His beams, unactive else, thir vigor find.

---

78. *wide:* i.e. of the truth.

82. *To save appearances,* or to "save the phenomena" were traditional terms for the attempts of astronomers to explain the movements of the heavenly bodies systematically. Their efforts seemed to John Donne only to have warped the globe of heaven and forced

> Men to finde out so many Eccentrique parts,
> Such divers downe-right lines, such overthwarts,
> As disproportion that pure forme: It teares
> The Firmament in eight and forty sheires . . .
>
> (*The First Anniversary,* 255–58)

83. *Centric and Eccentric:* spheres respectively centred or not centred on the earth as the centre of the universe. Burton ridiculed one hypothesis which made "the Earth as before the universal Center," but made the sun [although its sphere was conceived as geocentric] the centre of the orbits of "the five upper

planets," and ascribed "diurnal motion" to the eighth sphere (that of the fixed stars), and so, "as a tinker stops one hole and makes two," the astronomer "reforms some [errors], and mars all" (*Anatomy* II, ii, 3; Everyman Ed. II, p. 57).

84. *Epicycle:* "A small circle, having its centre on the circumference of a greater circle. In the Ptolemaic system . . . each of the 'seven planets' was supposed to revolve in an epicycle, the centre of which moved along a greater circle called a deferent" (*O.E.D.*). The device was also used by Copernicus.

94–97. The thought is related by W. B. Hunter in *MLR,* XLIV (1949), 89, to Proclus' description of the sun as "shadowless and unreceptive of generation" in his *Commentaries on the Timaeus of Plato,* and to Marsilio Ficino's conception of the sun as "the soul of the world" that "distributes life, sense, and motion to the universe" (in the chapter "On the Sun and Light" in his translation of *Iamblichus de Mysteriis*). Cf. V, 171.

Yet not to Earth are those bright Luminaries
Officious, but to thee Earth's habitant.
And for the Heav'n's wide Circuit, let it speak   100
The Maker's high magnificence, who built
So spacious, and his Line stretcht out so far;
That Man may know he dwells not in his own;
An Edifice too large for him to fill,
Lodg'd in a small partition, and the rest   105
Ordain'd for uses to his Lord best known.
The swiftness of those Circles attribute,
Though numberless, to his Omnipotence,
That to corporeal substances could add
Speed almost Spiritual; mee thou think'st not slow,   110
Who since the Morning hour set out from Heav'n
Where God resides, and ere mid-day arriv'd
In *Eden*, distance inexpressible
By Numbers that have name. But this I urge,
Admitting Motion in the Heav'ns, to show   115
Invalid that which thee to doubt it mov'd;
Not that I so affirm, though so it seem
To thee who hast thy dwelling here on Earth.
God to remove his ways from human sense,
Plac'd Heav'n from Earth so far, that earthly sight,   120
If it presume, might err in things too high,
And no advantage gain. What if the Sun
Be Centre to the World, and other Stars
By his attractive virtue and their own
Incited, dance about him various rounds?   125
Thir wandring course now high, now low, then hid,
Progressive, retrograde, or standing still,
In six thou seest, and what if sev'nth to these
The Planet Earth, so steadfast though she seem,
Insensibly three different Motions move?   130
Which else to several Spheres thou must ascribe,
Mov'd contrary with thwart obliquities,
Or save the Sun his labor, and that swift
Nocturnal and Diurnal rhomb suppos'd,

99. *officious:* serviceable. Cf. *officiate* in l. 22 above.

102. The line echoes God's question about the earth: "Who hath laid the measures thereof, if thou knowest? or who hath stretched the line upon it?" (Job xxxviii, 5.)

107–110. The swift circles seem like a reminiscence of the "sempitern courses of the stars" and their "rushing spheres" which are contrasted in Cicero's "Dream of Scipio" (*De re publica* VI, xvii–xix) with this point (*punctum*), the earth. See the Introduction 34.

124. *attractive virtue:* power of attrac-

tion. Cf. the sun's *Magnetic beam* in III, 583.

126. Cf. V, 177, n.

130. *Insensibly:* imperceptibly. The three motions are rotation, orbital revolution, and the very slow revolution of the earth's north pole around that of the ecliptic, causing the precession of the equinoxes or *Trepidation* of III, 483.

132. *thwart obliquities:* the transverse movements of the spheres as conceived oblique to one another in the Ptolemaic system.

134–136. The *Nocturnal and Diurnal rhomb* is the invisible sphere or *primum*

Invisible else above all Stars, the Wheel 135
Of Day and Night; which needs not thy belief,
If Earth industrious of herself fetch Day
Travelling East, and with her part averse
From the Sun's beam meet Night, her other part
Still luminous by his ray. What if that light 140
Sent from her through the wide transpicuous air,
To the terrestrial Moon be as a Star
Enlight'ning her by Day, as she by Night
This Earth? reciprocal, if Land be there,
Fields and Inhabitants: Her spots thou seest 145
As Clouds, and Clouds may rain, and Rain produce
Fruits in her soft'n'd Soil, for some to eat
Allotted there; and other Suns perhaps
With thir attendant Moons thou wilt descry
Communicating Male and Female Light, 150
Which two great Sexes animate the World,
Stor'd in each Orb perhaps with some that live.
For such vast room in Nature unpossest
By living Soul, desert and desolate,
Only to shine, yet scarce to contribute 155
Each Orb a glimpse of Light, convey'd so far
Down to this habitable, which returns
Light back to them, is obvious to dispute.
But whether thus these things, or whether not,
Whether the Sun predominant in Heav'n 160
Rise on the Earth, or Earth rise on the Sun,
Hee from the East his flaming road begin,
Or Shee from West her silent course advance
With inoffensive pace that spinning sleeps
On her soft Axle, while she paces Ev'n, 165
And bears thee soft with the smooth Air along,
Solicit not thy thoughts with matters hid,
Leave them to God above, him serve and fear;
Of other Creatures, as him pleases best,
Wherever plac't, let him dispose: joy thou 170
In what he gives to thee, this Paradise

---

mobile by which Ptolemaic astronomers regarded the spheres of the seven planets and that of fixed stars as enclosed and moved.

137. *industrious:* active, i.e. moving, not stationary.

142. The *terrestrial Moon* is the moon as understood to be inhabitable like the earth. For Milton's ambivalent treatment of the matter see the Introduction 31.

150. That the sun is *Male* is implied in ll. 94–96 above; the moon's *Female Light*

is traced by Whiting (*Milieu,* p. 78) to Pliny's *Natural History* II, civ.

155. *Only to shine,* for the sake of mere illumination, though the amount of light furnished by each star to *this habitable* (earth) is very small.

158. *obvious:* exposed. In his Seventh *Prolusion* Milton asked his audience of Cambridge undergraduates whether they could believe that the "vast spaces of boundless air are illuminated and adorned by everlasting lights . . . merely to serve as a lantern for base and slothful men."

And thy fair *Eve:* Heav'n is for thee too high
To know what passes there; be lowly wise:
Think only what concerns thee and thy being;
Dream not of other Worlds, what Creatures there   175
Live, in what state, condition or degree,
Contented that thus far hath been reveal'd
Not of Earth only but of highest Heav'n.
    To whom thus *Adam* clear'd of doubt, repli'd.
How fully hast thou satisfi'd me, pure   180
Intelligence of Heav'n, Angel serene,
And freed from intricacies, taught to live
The easiest way, nor with perplexing thoughts
To interrupt the sweet of Life, from which
God hath bid dwell far off all anxious cares,   185
And not molest us, unless we ourselves
Seek them with wand'ring thoughts, and notions vain.
But apt the Mind or Fancy is to rove
Uncheckt, and of her roving is no end;
Till warn'd, or by experience taught, she learn   190
That not to know at large of things remote
From use, obscure and subtle, but to know
That which before us lies in daily life,
Is the prime Wisdom; what is more, is fume,
Or emptiness, or fond impertinence,   195
And renders us in things that most concern
Unpractic'd, unprepar'd, and still to seek.
Therefore from this high pitch let us descend
A lower flight, and speak of things at hand
Useful, whence haply mention may arise   200
Of something not unseasonable to ask
By sufferance, and thy wonted favor deign'd.
Thee I have heard relating what was done
Ere my remembrance: now hear mee relate
My Story, which perhaps thou hast not heard;   205
And Day is yet not spent; till then thou seest

173. So Du Bartas advised:
Be sober wise: so, bound thy frail de-
sire:
And, what thou canst not compre-
hend, admire.
    (*Divine Weeks*, p. 447)
181. *Intelligence:* angelic being. George
Puttenham spoke of poets as the first
students of "Celestial courses, by reason
of the continuall motion of the heavens,
searching after the first mover, and from
thence by degrees coming to know and
consider of the substances separate &
abstract, which we call the divine in-
telligences or good Angels" (*The Arte of
English Poesie* I, iii).
188. Milton is not attacking scientific
curiosity but, like Glanvill, arguing that,

"To say, *Reason* opposeth *Faith,* is to
scandalize both: 'Tis *Imagination* is the
Rebel; *Reason* contradicts its impious
suggestions" (*Vanity,* p. 103).
190-197. The thought in the lines was
traditional when Montaigne recalled it
(*Essays* II, xii. Translation of G. B. Ives,
Harvard University Press, 1925, II, 260):
"The desire to increase in wisdom and
knowledge was the first ruin of the human
race; it was the way by which it cast it-
self into eternal damnation."
    194. *fume:* vapor, vanity.
    195. *fond impertinence:* foolish irrele-
vance. Cf. *fond* in l. 209.
    197. *still to seek:* always seeking (never
finding) solutions.

How subtly to detain thee I devise,
Inviting thee to hear while I relate,
Fond, were it not in hope of thy reply:
For while I sit with thee, I seem in Heav'n,　　　　210
And sweeter thy discourse is to my ear
Than Fruits of Palm-tree pleasantest to thirst
And hunger both, from labor, at the hour
Of sweet repast; they satiate, and soon fill,
Though pleasant, but thy words with Grace Divine　　215
Imbu'd, bring to thir sweetness no satiety.
　　To whom thus *Raphael* answer'd heav'nly meek.
Nor are thy lips ungraceful, Sire of men,
Nor tongue ineloquent; for God on thee
Abundantly his gifts hath also pour'd　　　　220
Inward and outward both, his image fair:
Speaking or mute all comeliness and grace
Attends thee, and each word, each motion forms.
Nor less think wee in Heav'n of thee on Earth
Than of our fellow servant, and inquire　　　　225
Gladly into the ways of God with Man:
For God we see hath honor'd thee, and set
On Man his Equal Love: say therefore on;
For I that Day was absent, as befell,
Bound on a voyage uncouth and obscure,　　　　230
Far on excursion toward the Gates of Hell;
Squar'd in full Legion (such command we had)
To see that none thence issu'd forth a spy,
Or enemy, while God was in his work,
Lest hee incenst at such eruption bold,　　　　235
Destruction with Creation might have mixt.
Not that they durst without his leave attempt,
But us he sends upon his high behests
For state, as Sovran King, and to enure
Our prompt obedience. Fast we found, fast shut　　240
The dismal Gates, and barricado'd strong;
But long ere our approaching heard within
Noise, other than the sound of Dance or Song,
Torment, and loud lament, and furious rage.
Glad we return'd up to the coasts of Light　　　　245
Ere Sabbath Ev'ning: so we had in charge.
But thy relation now; for I attend,
Pleas'd with thy words no less than thou with mine.
　　So spake the Godlike Power, and thus our Sire.

---

213. *from labor:* after labor.
221. Cf. the stress upon man as God's image in VII, 519 and 627.
230. *uncouth:* unknown.
232. Cf. the military use of the term *squar'd* in I, 758.

239. *For state:* to preserve the dignity of God's state, for his honor. *enure:* discipline, train.
244. Cf. the *rage* of the demons in I, 666–69.

For Man to tell how human Life began   250
Is hard; for who himself beginning knew?
Desire with thee still longer to converse
Induc'd me. As new wak't from soundest sleep
Soft on the flow'ry herb I found me laid
In Balmy Sweat, which with his Beams the Sun   255
Soon dri'd, and on the reeking moisture fed.
Straight toward Heav'n my wond'ring Eyes I turn'd,
And gaz'd a while the ample Sky, till rais'd
By quick instinctive motion up I sprung,
As thitherward endeavoring, and upright   260
Stood on my feet; about me round I saw
Hill, Dale, and shady Woods, and sunny Plains,
And liquid Lapse of murmuring Streams; by these,
Creatures that liv'd, and mov'd, and walk'd, or flew,
Birds on the branches warbling; all things smil'd,   265
With fragrance and with joy my heart o'erflow'd.
Myself I then perus'd, and Limb by Limb
Survey'd, and sometimes went, and sometimes ran
With supple joints, as lively vigor led:
But who I was, or where, or from what cause,   270
Knew not; to speak I tri'd, and forthwith spake,
My Tongue obey'd and readily could name
Whate'er I saw. Thou Sun, said I, fair Light,
And thou enlight'n'd Earth, so fresh and gay,
Ye Hills and Dales, ye Rivers, Woods, and Plains   275
And ye that live and move, fair Creatures, tell,
Tell, if ye saw, how came I thus, how here?
Not of myself; by some great Maker then,
In goodness and in power preëminent;
Tell me, how may I know him, how adore,   280
From whom I have that thus I move and live,
And feel that I am happier than I know.
While thus I call'd, and stray'd I knew not whither,
From where I first drew Air, and first beheld
This happy Light, when answer none return'd,   285
On a green shady Bank profuse of Flow'rs
Pensive I sat me down; there gentle sleep
First found me, and with soft oppression seiz'd
My drowsed sense, untroubl'd, though I thought
I then was passing to my former state   290
Insensible, and forthwith to dissolve:

256. Cf. V, 415, n., for the feeding of the sun on the earth's vapors.

260. Cf. VII, 505-11, for the significance of Adam's *upright* posture.

268. *went:* walked.

272. The language which Adam spoke — as Milton assumed in his *Art of Logic* I, xxiv (C.Ed. XI, 221) would be universally taken for granted — was Hebrew.

281. The line clearly evokes Aratus' prayer to Zeus in the opening lines of the *Phaenomena* — Zeus who fills the streets and market-places of his offspring, mankind — and St. Paul's echo of it in Acts xvii, 28: "For in him we live, and move, and have our being."

When suddenly stood at my Head a dream,
Whose inward apparition gently mov'd
My fancy to believe I yet had being,
And liv'd: One came, methought, of shape Divine,   295
And said, thy Mansion wants thee, *Adam*, rise,
First Man, of Men innumerable ordain'd
First Father, call'd by thee I come thy Guide
To the Garden of bliss, thy seat prepar'd.
So saying, by the hand he took me rais'd,   300
And over Fields and Waters, as in Air
Smooth sliding without step, last led me up
A woody Mountain; whose high top was plain,
A Circuit wide, enclos'd, with goodliest Trees
Planted, with Walks, and Bowers, that what I saw   305
Of Earth before scarce pleasant seem'd. Each Tree
Load'n with fairest Fruit, that hung to the Eye
Tempting, stirr'd in me sudden appetite
To pluck and eat; whereat I wak'd, and found
Before mine Eyes all real, as the dream   310
Had lively shadow'd: Here had new begun
My wand'ring, had not hee who was my Guide
Up hither, from among the Trees appear'd,
Presence Divine. Rejoicing, but with awe,
In adoration at his feet I fell   315
Submiss: he rear'd me, and Whom thou sought'st I am,
Said mildly, Author of all this thou seest
Above, or round about thee or beneath.
This Paradise I give thee, count it thine
To Till and keep, and of the Fruit to eat: 320
Of every Tree that in the Garden grows
Eat freely with glad heart; fear here no dearth:
But of the Tree whose operation brings
Knowledge of good and ill, which I have set
The Pledge of thy Obedience and thy Faith,   325
Amid the Garden by the Tree of Life,

292. Compare Adam's discussion of dreams in V, 100-13.
296. The *Mansion* is the Earthly Paradise in Eden, outside of which Adam was created. Cf. the note on VII, 537.
303. Cf. the account of the mountain of Paradise in IV, 133-49.
311. *lively shadow'd:* made appear like the living reality.
316. *submiss* has its Latin force as a participle meaning "cast down."
320-328. Cf. Genesis ii, 15-17: "And the Lord spake unto the man, and put him into the garden of Eden to dress it and keep it. And the Lord God commanded the man, saying, Of every tree of the garden thou mayest freely eat: But of the tree of the knowledge of good and evil, thou shalt not eat of it: for in the day that thou eatest thereof thou shalt surely die." In *CD* I, xii (C.Ed. XV, 202) Milton explains that, "Under the head of death, in Scripture, all evils whatever, together with everything which in its consequences tends to death, must be understood as comprehended; for mere bodily death, as it is called, did not follow the sin of Adam on the same day." In *CD* I, viii (C.Ed. XV, 91) he says that "it is evident that God, at least after the fall of man, limited human life to a certain term."

Remember what I warn thee, shun to taste,
And shun the bitter consequence: for know,
The day thou eat'st thereof, my sole command
Transgrest, inevitably thou shalt die;   330
From that day mortal, and this happy State
Shalt lose, expell'd from hence into a World
Of woe and sorrow. Sternly he pronounc'd
The rigid interdiction, which resounds
Yet dreadful in mine ear, though in my choice   335
Not to incur; but soon his clear aspect
Return'd and gracious purpose thus renew'd.
Not only these fair bounds, but all the Earth
To thee and to thy Race I give; as Lords
Possess it, and all things that therein live,   340
Or live in Sea, or Air, Beast, Fish, and Fowl.
In sign whereof each Bird and Beast behold
After thir kinds; I bring them to receive
From thee thir Names, and pay thee fealty
With low subjection; understand the same   345
Of Fish within thir wat'ry residence,
Not hither summon'd, since they cannot change
Thir Element to draw the thinner Air.
As thus he spake, each Bird and Beast behold
Approaching two and two, These cow'ring low   350
With blandishment, each Bird stoop'd on his wing.
I nam'd them, as they pass'd, and understood
Thir Nature, with such knowledge God endu'd
My sudden apprehension: but in these
I found not what methought I wanted still;   355
And to the Heav'nly vision thus presum'd.
     O by what Name, for thou above all these,
Above mankind, or aught than mankind higher,
Surpassest far my naming, how may I

---

337. *purpose:* speech. Cf. IV, 337.
340. Cf. Adam's rule of the beasts in
VII, 520–43.
345–354. Like his contemporaries,
Milton found proof that Adam was "en-
dued with natural wisdom" in the fact
that, "without extraordinary wisdom he
could not have given names to the whole
animal creation with such sudden intel-
ligence" (*CD* I, vii; C.Ed. XV, 53).
Bacon found proof of man's enjoyment of
the contemplative life in perfection in
Eden in the fact that "the first acts which
man performed in Paradise consisted of
the two summary parts of knowledge; the
view of the creatures, and the imposition
of Names" (*Advancement* I, vi, 6). Since
G. W. Knight objects (*Oracle*, p. 87) to
the blandishments of the beasts in this

scene with Adam, it is worth noting that
in Vondel's account, when he
     gave them one by one their vari-
     ous names,
The mountain-lion wagged his tail
     and smiled
Upon his lord. And at his sovereign
     feet
The tiger too his fierceness laid. The
     bull
Bowed low his horns: the elephant
     his trunk . . .
     (*Lucifer* in *The Celestial Cycle*, p. 364)
355. Cf. Genesis ii, 20: "And Adam
gave names to all cattle, and to the fowl
of the air, and to every beast of the field;
but for Adam there was not found an
help meet for him."
356. *presum'd:* dared speak.

Adore thee, Author of this Universe,   360
And all this good to man, for whose well being
So amply, and with hands so liberal
Thou hast provided all things: but with mee
I see not who partakes. In solitude
What happiness, who can enjoy alone,   365
Or all enjoying, what contentment find?
Thus I presumptuous; and the vision bright,
As with a smile more bright'n'd, thus repli'd.
    What call'st thou solitude? is not the Earth
With various living creatures, and the Air   370
Replenisht, and all these at thy command
To come and play before thee; know'st thou not
Thir language and thir ways? They also know,
And reason not contemptibly; with these
Find pastime, and bear rule; thy Realm is large.   375
So spake the Universal Lord, and seem'd
So ordering. I with leave of speech implor'd,
And humble deprecation thus repli'd.
    Let not my words offend thee, Heav'nly Power,
My Maker, be propitious while I speak.   380
Hast thou not made me here thy substitute,
And these inferior far beneath me set?
Among unequals what society
Can sort, what harmony or true delight?
Which must be mutual, in proportion due   385
Giv'n and receiv'd; but in disparity
The one intense, the other still remiss
Cannot well suit with either, but soon prove
Tedious alike: Of fellowship I speak
Such as I seek, fit to participate   390
All rational delight, wherein the brute
Cannot be human consort; they rejoice
Each with thir kind, Lion with Lioness;
So fitly them in pairs thou hast combin'd;
Much less can Bird with Beast, or Fish with Fowl   395
So well converse, nor with the Ox the Ape;
Worse then can Man with Beast, and least of all.
    Whereto th' Almighty answer'd, not displeas'd.
A nice and subtle happiness I see

372–373. Adam's knowledge of the beasts included that of their language. On the day of Adam's banishment from Paradise, says the Book of Jubilees (c. 100 B.C.) iii, 28, "was closed the mouth of all beasts . . . so that they could no longer speak. For they had all spoken one with another with one lip and one tongue" (Charles's translation).

379. So Abraham pled: "Oh let not the Lord be angry, and I will speak" (Gen. xviii, 30).

384–387. *sort:* be appropriate or satisfying. With *harmony* a musical metaphor begins which continues through *intense* and *remiss* in the figure of taut and slack strings in an instrument, which stand for man's high-strung nature in contrast with that of the animals.

399. *nice:* delicate.

Thou to thyself proposest, in the choice   400
Of thy Associates, *Adam*, and wilt taste
No pleasure, though in pleasure, solitary.
What think'st thou then of mee, and this my State,
Seem I to thee sufficiently possest
Of happiness, or not? who am alone   405
From all Eternity, for none I know
Second to mee or like, equal much less.
How have I then with whom to hold converse
Save with the Creatures which I made, and those
To me inferior, infinite descents   410
Beneath what other Creatures are to thee?
    He ceas'd, I lowly answer'd. To attain
The highth and depth of thy Eternal ways
All human thoughts come short, Supreme of things;
Thou in thyself art perfet, and in thee   415
Is no deficience found; not so is Man,
But in degree, the cause of his desire
By conversation with his like to help,
Or solace his defects. No need that thou
Shouldst propagate, already infinite;   420
And through all numbers absolute, though One;
But Man by number is to manifest
His single imperfection, and beget
Like of his like, his Image multipli'd,
In unity defective, which requires   425
Collateral love, and dearest amity.
Thou in thy secrecy although alone,
Best with thyself accompanied, seek'st not
Social communication, yet so pleas'd,
Canst raise thy Creature to what highth thou wilt   430
Of Union or Communion, deifi'd;
I by conversing cannot these erect
From prone, nor in thir ways complacence find.
Thus I embold'n'd spake, and freedom us'd
Permissive, and acceptance found, which gain'd   435
This answer from the gracious voice Divine.

---

407. The line echoes Horace's allusion to the supreme deity, "than whom no greater exists, and to whom there is none similar or second" (*Odes* I, xii, 17–18), but the thought of the entire passage reflects Aristotle's demonstration of the simplicity and unity of the divine nature (unlike Adam's *unity* or solitary oneness in l. 425 below, which disqualifies him for happiness) and its capacity for eternal happiness in the contemplation of unchanging truth (*Nicomachean Ethics* VII, xiv, 8).

421. *numbers* is here used in its Latin sense of "parts," but in l. 422 it has its ordinary meaning. God is perfect in all respects because he is absolute; but man fulfills himself only in society.

431. Sister M. I. Corcoran notes — *Background*, p. 103 — that "theologians used the term 'deification' to describe the elevation of the soul to a supernatural state." Adam may be deified by God's grace, but the brutes cannot be humanized by conversation with him.

433. *prone:* proneness, the reverse of man's uprightness. Cf. l. 260.

Thus far to try thee, *Adam*, I was pleas'd,
And find thee knowing not of Beasts alone,
Which thou hast rightly nam'd, but of thyself,
Expressing well the spirit within thee free,   440
My Image, not imparted to the Brute,
Whose fellowship therefore unmeet for thee
Good reason was thou freely shouldst dislike,
And be so minded still; I, ere thou spak'st,
Knew it not good for Man to be alone,   445
And no such company as then thou saw'st
Intended thee, for trial only brought,
To see how thou couldst judge of fit and meet:
What next I bring shall please thee, be assur'd,
Thy likeness, thy fit help, thy other self,   450
Thy wish, exactly to thy heart's desire.
    Hee ended, or I heard no more, for now
My earthly by his Heav'nly overpower'd,
Which it had long stood under, strain'd to the highth
In that celestial Colloquy sublime,   455
As with an object that excels the sense,
Dazzl'd and spent, sunk down, and sought repair
Of sleep, which instantly fell on me, call'd
By Nature as in aid, and clos'd mine eyes.
Mine eyes he clos'd, but op'n left the Cell   460
Of Fancy my internal sight, by which
Abstract as in a trance methought I saw,
Though sleeping where I lay, and saw the shape
Still glorious before whom awake I stood;
Who stooping op'n'd my left side, and took   465
From thence a Rib, with cordial spirits warm,
And Life-blood streaming fresh; wide was the wound,
But suddenly with flesh fill'd up and heal'd:
The Rib he form'd and fashion'd with his hands;
Under his forming hands a Creature grew,   470
Manlike, but different sex, so lovely fair,
That what seem'd fair in all the World, seem'd now
Mean, or in her summ'd up, in her contain'd
And in her looks, which from that time infus'd
Sweetness into my heart, unfelt before,   475

450. Against the biblical term for wife, "helpmeet" (fit help) Milton puts the classical term for an ideal friend, an *other self*. In *Doctrine of Divorce* I, ii, interpreting "God's intention" in creating Eve, he wrote: "A meet and happy conversation is the chiefest and the noblest end of marriage" (C.Ed. III, 391).
453. *My earthly*, i.e. nature. Exhausted by the unequal conversation, Adam falls asleep. "The Lord God caused a deep sleep to fall upon Adam, and he slept; and he took one of his ribs. . . . And the rib, which the Lord God had taken from man, made he a woman, and brought her unto the man" (Gen. ii, 21–22).
461. Adam has explained the part of *Fancy* in dreams in V, 102–109.
462. *Abstract:* abstracted, drawn into a trance.
466. *cordial spirits:* the "vital spirits" which the heart was supposed to distribute to the body. Cf. V, 484.

And into all things from her Air inspir'd
The spirit of love and amorous delight.
Shee disappear'd, and left me dark, I wak'd
To find her, or for ever to deplore
Her loss, and other pleasures all abjure: 480
When out of hope, behold her, not far off,
Such as I saw her in my dream, adorn'd
With what all Earth or Heaven could bestow
To make her amiable: On she came,
Led by her Heav'nly Maker, though unseen,   485
And guided by his voice, nor uninform'd
Of nuptial Sanctity and marriage Rites:
Grace was in all her steps, Heav'n in her Eye,
In every gesture dignity and love.
I overjoy'd could not forbear aloud.   490

   This turn hath made amends; thou hast fulfill'd
Thy words, Creator bounteous and benign,
Giver of all things fair, but fairest this
Of all thy gifts, nor enviest. I now see
Bone of my Bone, Flesh of my Flesh, my Self   495
Before me; Woman is her Name, of Man
Extracted; for this cause he shall forgo
Father and Mother, and to his Wife adhere;
And they shall be one Flesh, one Heart, one Soul.

   She heard me thus, and though divinely brought,   500
Yet Innocence and Virgin Modesty,
Her virtue and the conscience of her worth,
That would be woo'd, and not unsought be won,
Not obvious, not obtrusive, but retir'd,
The more desirable, or to say all,   505
Nature herself, though pure of sinful thought,
Wrought in her so, that seeing me, she turn'd;
I follow'd her, she what was Honor knew,
And with obsequious Majesty approv'd
My pleaded reason. To the Nuptial Bow'r   510
I led her blushing like the Morn: all Heav'n,
And happy Constellations on that hour
Shed thir selectest influence; the Earth

481. *When out of hope:* when I had given up hope.
482. The dream resembles Milton's vision of his dead wife in *Sonnet XXIII*.
490. *could not forbear aloud:* could not resist crying aloud.
494. *nor enviest:* nor dost thou grudge thy gifts — in contrast to the Greek gods, who often envied men their happiness.
495–499. Matthew xix, 4–6, and Mark x, 6–8, repeat Genesis ii, 23–24: "And Adam said, This is now bone of my bones, and flesh of my flesh: she shall be called Woman, because she was taken out of Man. Therefore shall a man leave his father and mother, and shall cleave unto his wife: and they shall be one flesh."
502. *conscience:* consciousness.
504. *obvious:* bold, forward.
508. *Honor* perhaps refers to Hebrews xiii, 4: "Marriage is honorable unto all." Cf. VII, 529–31, and IV, 741–47.
513. Cf. the dance of the stars, "shedding sweet influence," as a portent of the happiness of the universe at its creation in VII, 375.

Gave sign of gratulation, and each Hill;
Joyous the Birds; fresh Gales and gentle Airs   515
Whisper'd it to the Woods, and from thir wings
Flung Rose, flung Odors from the spicy Shrub,
Disporting, till the amorous Bird of Night
Sung Spousal, and bid haste the Ev'ning Star
On his Hill top, to light the bridal Lamp.   520
Thus I have told thee all my State, and brought
My Story to the sum of earthly bliss
Which I enjoy, and must confess to find
In all things else delight indeed, but such
As us'd or not, works in the mind no change,   525
Nor vehement desire, these delicacies
I mean of Taste, Sight, Smell, Herbs, Fruits, and Flow'rs,
Walks, and the melody of Birds; but here
Far otherwise, transported I behold,
Transported touch; here passion first I felt,   530
Commotion strange, in all enjoyments else
Superior and unmov'd, here only weak
Against the charm of Beauty's powerful glance.
Or Nature fail'd in mee, and left some part
Not proof enough such Object to sustain,   535
Or from my side subducting, took perhaps
More than enough; at least on her bestow'd
Too much of Ornament, in outward show
Elaborate, of inward less exact.
For well I understand in the prime end   540
Of Nature her th' inferior, in the mind
And inward Faculties, which most excel,
In outward also her resembling less
His Image who made both, and less expressing
The character of that Dominion giv'n   545
O'er other Creatures; yet when I approach
Her loveliness, so absolute she seems
And in herself complete, so well to know
Her own, that what she wills to do or say,
Seems wisest, virtuousest, discreetest, best;   550
All higher knowledge in her presence falls
Degraded, Wisdom in discourse with her

---

518. *amorous Bird of Night:* the
nightingale. Cf. V, 39–41, n.
519. The evening star is Venus. Its
appearance was the traditional signal for
lighting nuptial torches from Catullus'
epithalamium (lxii) to Spenser's:
Long though it be, at last I see it
gloome
And the bright evening-star with
golden crest
Appeare out of the east.
(*Epithalamion,* 285–87)

532. Adam finds himself *superior* to
and *unmoved* by all other pleasures.
537–546. Cf. *Samson Agonistes,* 1025–
30. In the commentaries on Genesis of
both the Catholic Pererius and the Lu-
theran Pareus — as well as in others
cited by A. Williams (*Expositor,* p. 87) —
Eve's resemblance to God is said to be
less perfect than Adam's, though both
are made in his image.
547. *absolute:* perfect.

Loses discount'nanc't, and like folly shows;
Authority and Reason on her wait,
As one intended first, not after made 555
Occasionally; and to consummate all,
Greatness of mind and nobleness thir seat
Build in her loveliest, and create an awe
About her, as a guard Angelic plac't.
To whom the Angel with contracted brow. 560
    Accuse not Nature, she hath done her part;
Do thou but thine, and be not diffident
Of Wisdom, she deserts thee not, if thou
Dismiss not her, when most thou need'st her nigh,
By attributing overmuch to things 565
Less excellent, as thou thyself perceiv'st.
For what admir'st thou, what transports thee so,
An outside? fair no doubt, and worthy well
Thy cherishing, thy honoring, and thy love,
Not thy subjection: weigh with her thyself; 570
Then value: Oft-times nothing profits more
Than self-esteem, grounded on just and right
Well manag'd; of that skill the more thou know'st,
The more she will acknowledge thee her Head,
And to realities yield all her shows; 575
Made so adorn for thy delight the more,
So awful, that with honor thou may'st love
Thy mate, who sees when thou art seen least wise.
But if the sense of touch whereby mankind
Is propagated seem such dear delight 580
Beyond all other, think the same voutsaf't
To Cattle and each Beast; which would not be
To them made common and divulg'd, if aught
Therein enjoy'd were worthy to subdue
The Soul of Man, or passion in him move. 585
What higher in her society thou find'st
Attractive, human, rational, love still;
In loving thou dost well, in passion not,
Wherein true Love consists not; Love refines

556. *occasionally:* for an occasion, i.e.
an accidental need.
    561–570. Cf. God's rebuke to Adam in
X, 145–56.
    569. So the marriage service in the
Book of Common Prayer reads: "I take
thee to my wedded wife . . . to love and
to cherish."
    573. *skill:* power or faculty, i.e. of
self-esteem.
    574. Cf. ". . . the head of the woman
is the man" (I Cor. xi, 3).
    589. The distinction is essentially the
Neoplatonic one between sacred and pro-

fane love which Cardinal Bembo makes
in Castiglione's *Book of the Courtier*, and
which Spenser echoed in *An Hymne in
Honour of Love* (190–94):
    Such is the powre of that sweet pas-
        sion.
    That it all sordid basenesse doth ex-
        pell,
    And the refyned mynd doth newly
        fashion
    Unto a fairer forme, which now doth
        dwell
    In his high thought, that would it
        selfe excell.

The thoughts, and heart enlarges, hath his seat   590
In Reason, and is judicious, is the scale
By which to heav'nly Love thou may'st ascend,
Not sunk in carnal pleasure, for which cause
Among the Beasts no Mate for thee was found.
    To whom thus half abash't *Adam* repli'd.   595
Neither her out-side form'd so fair, nor aught
In procreation common to all kinds
(Though higher of the genial Bed by far,
And with mysterious reverence I deem)
So much delights me, as those graceful acts,   600
Those thousand decencies that daily flow
From all her words and actions, mixt with Love
And sweet compliance, which declare unfeign'd
Union of Mind, or in us both one Soul;
Harmony to behold in wedded pair   605
More grateful than harmonious sound to the ear.
Yet these subject not; I to thee disclose
What inward thence I feel, not therefore foil'd,
Who meet with various objects, from the sense
Variously representing; yet still free   610
Approve the best, and follow what I approve
To Love thou blam'st me not, for Love thou say'st
Leads up to Heav'n, is both the way and guide;
Bear with me then, if lawful what I ask;
Love not the heav'nly Spirits, and how thir Love   615
Express they, by looks only, or do they mix
Irradiance, virtual or immediate touch?
    To whom the Angel with a smile that glow'd
Celestial rosy red, Love's proper hue,
Answer'd. Let it suffice thee that thou know'st   620
Us happy, and without Love no happiness.
Whatever pure thou in the body enjoy'st

591. The *scale* is the scale of nature. Cf. V, 509, n., and IX, 112.

592. *heav'nly Love* is the divine love of Plato's *Symposium* as it had been Christianized by poets from Dante to Spenser in passages like the latter's vision in *An Hymne of Heavenly Love* (271–3) of the divine passion so inflaming the spirit

> With burning zeale, through every part entire,
> That in no earthly thing thou shalt delight,
> But in his sweet and amiable sight.

598. *genial:* procreative. Cf. IV, 712.

599. Cf. *mysterious* in IV, 743, and 750.

601. *decencies:* graces.

608. *not therefore foil'd:* not conquered (by the objects of sense).

619. Change of color is described as possible for the angels in the passage from Psellus on which I, 422–431, is based, but in *blushing Celestial rosy red* E. L. Marilla notes — in *MLN*, LXVIII (1953), 486 — that Raphael turned the *proper hue* of the friendship which, among the angels, is an even higher manifestation of their aspiration to the love of God than even the highest kind of human love can be.

622–629. Physically, Milton conceived the angels much in Henry More's way as "penetrable but indiscerptible body," and, like More in the *Immortality of the Soul* (1659, p. 200), he must have imagined them as singing and dancing together, "reaping the lawful pleasures of the very animal life, in a far higher degree than we are capable of in this world. . . . Wherefore they cannot but enravish one another's souls, while they are mutual spectators of the perfect pulchritude of

(And pure thou wert created) we enjoy
In eminence, and obstacle find none
Of membrane, joint, or limb, exclusive bars: 625
Easier than Air with Air, if Spirits embrace,
Total they mix, Union of Pure with Pure
Desiring; nor restrain'd conveyance need
As Flesh to mix with Flesh, or Soul with Soul.
But I can now no more; the parting Sun   630
Beyond the Earth's green Cape and verdant Isles
Hesperian sets, my Signal to depart.
Be strong, live happy, and love, but first of all
Him whom to love is to obey, and keep
His great command; take heed lest Passion sway   635
Thy Judgment to do aught, which else free Will
Would not admit; thine and of all thy Sons
The weal or woe in thee is plac't; beware.
I in thy persevering shall rejoice,
And all the Blest: stand fast; to stand or fall   640
Free in thine own Arbitrement it lies.
Perfet within, no outward aid require;
And all temptation to transgress repel.
    So saying, he arose; whom *Adam* thus
Follow'd with benediction. Since to part,   645
Go heavenly Guest, Ethereal Messenger,
Sent from whose sovran goodness I adore.
Gentle to me and affable hath been
Thy condescension, and shall be honor'd ever
With grateful Memory: thou to mankind   650
Be good and friendly still, and oft return.
    So parted they, the Angel up to Heav'n
From the thick shade, and *Adam* to his Bow'r.

The End of the Eighth Book.

---

one another's person and comely carriage, of their graceful dancing, their melodious singing and playing." See the Introduction 37.

631. On the Mercator maps Cape Verde is marked *Cabo blanco,* but Starnes and Talbert note (*Dictionaries,* p. 314) that in Charles Stephanus' dictionary its name is given in English as the *green Cape.* The *verdant Isles* are the Cape Verde Islands.

632. *Hesperian* may modify *Isles,* for the Cape Verdes were sometimes identified with the Gardens of the Hesperides; but it may apply to the setting sun.

634. Cf. I John v, 3: "For this is the love of God, that we keep his commandments."

640. The *Blest* are the blessed angels.

BOOK IX

THE ARGUMENT

Satan having compast thĕ Earth, with meditated guile returns as a mist by Night into Paradise, enters into the Serpent sleeping. Adam *and* Eve *in the Morning go forth to thir labors, which* Eve *proposes to divide in several places, each laboring apart:* Adam *consents not, alleging the danger, lest that Enemy, of whom they were forewarn'd, should attempt her found alone:* Eve *loath to be thought not circumspect or firm enough, urges her going apart, the rather desirous to make trial of her strength;* Adam *at last yields: The Serpent finds her alone; his subtle approach, first gazing, then speaking, with much flattery extolling* Eve *above all other Creatures.* Eve *wond'ring to hear the Serpent speak, asks how he attain'd to human speech and such understanding not till now; the Serpent answers, that by tasting of a certain Tree in the Garden he attain'd both to Speech and Reason, till then void of both:* Eve *requires him to bring her to that Tree, and finds it to be the Tree of Knowledge forbidden: The Serpent now grown bolder, with many wiles and arguments induces her at length to eat; she pleas'd with the taste deliberates awhile whether to impart thereof to* Adam *or not, at last brings him of the Fruit, relates what persuaded her to eat thereof:* Adam *at first amaz'd, but perceiving her lost, resolves through vehemence of love to perish with her; and extenuating the trespass, eats also of the Fruit: The effects thereof in them both; they seek to cover thir nakedness; then fall to variance and accusation of one another.*

No more of talk where God or Angel Guest
With Man, as with his Friend, familiar us'd
To sit indulgent, and with him partake
Rural repast, permitting him the while
Venial discourse unblam'd: I now must change   5
Those Notes to Tragic; foul distrust, and breach
Disloyal on the part of Man, revolt,
And disobedience: On the part of Heav'n
Now alienated, distance and distaste,
Anger and just rebuke, and judgment giv'n,   10
That brought into this World a world of woe,
Sin and her shadow Death, and Misery
Death's Harbinger: Sad task, yet argument
Not less but more Heroic than the wrath
Of stern *Achilles* on his Foe pursu'd   15
Thrice Fugitive about *Troy* Wall; or rage

---

6. *Tragic* is used with more than a trace of its medieval meaning, for the falls of Lucifer and Adam were traditionally the greatest of tragedies, as Chaucer's Monk defined them — a story
  Of hym that stood in greet prosperitee,
And is yfallen out of heigh degree.
But basically, Milton used the word in the moral sense that he immediately suggests.

11. Cf. the same word-play in XI, 627.

15. As in the invocations to Books I and VII, Milton challenges comparison with the pagan epics. The *wrath of stern Achilles* is the theme announced in the opening line of the *Iliad*, and its final expression is the brutal slaughter of Hector on the battlefield.

Of *Turnus* for *Lavinia* disespous'd,
Or *Neptune's* ire or *Juno's*, that so long
Perplex'd the *Greek* and *Cytherea's* Son;
If answerable style I can obtain   20
Of my Celestial Patroness, who deigns
Her nightly visitation unimplor'd,
And dictates to me slumb'ring, or inspires
Easy my unpremeditated Verse:
Since first this Subject for Heroic Song   25
Pleas'd me long choosing, and beginning late;
Not sedulous by Nature to indite
Wars, hitherto the only Argument
Heroic deem'd, chief maistry to dissect
With long and tedious havoc fabl'd Knights   30
In Battles feign'd; the better fortitude
Of Patience and Heroic Martyrdom
Unsung; or to describe Races and Games,
Or tilting Furniture, emblazon'd Shields,
Impreses quaint, Caparisons and Steeds;   35
Bases and tinsel Trappings, gorgeous Knights
At Joust and Tournament; then marshall'd Feast
Serv'd up in Hall with Sewers, and Seneschals;
The skill of Artifice or Office mean,
Not that which justly gives Heroic name   40
To Person or to Poem. Mee of these
Nor skill'd nor studious, higher Argument
Remains, sufficient of itself to raise
That name, unless an age too late, or cold

17. The contrast here is with the struggle of *Turnus* and Aeneas for the hand of *Lavinia* in the later books of the *Aeneid*, and with the persecution of Ulysses by *Neptune* in the *Odyssey* and with *Juno's* injustice to Aeneas in the *Aeneid*, simply because she had quarrelled with his mother Venus, or *Cytherea*.

21. The *Celestial Patroness* is the *Urania* of I, 6, and VII, 1.

26. *long choosing, and beginning late:* see the Introduction 6–10.

29–31. In a different tone from the popular poet Samuel Pordage, who professed in the Proaemium to *Mundorum Explicatio,*
  I sing no Hero's douty gests and
    warrs,
  Nor blazon forth some warlike
    Champion's Scarrs, . . .
Milton declares his religious theme to be unlike that of any previous epic poem. Cf. I, 16, n.

35. *Impreses quaint:* emblematic ornaments on the shields of knights (from Italian *impresa*).

36. *Bases:* housings for horses (*O.E.D.* cites this line).

38. *Sewers:* waiters or ushers: literally, "seaters."

40–41. Neither Homer's epics, nor the *Aeneid,* nor any other epic poem has ever exemplified the spiritual heroism that is Milton's theme. Cf. I, 1–4, n.

44. As early as his Cambridge days, in Prolusion VII and in *Nature is not Subject to Old Age*, Milton had challenged the scientific pessimism of a traditional belief that human talents had decayed with the earth itself because (in John Norden's words in *Vicissitudo Rerum*, 1600) the sun had lost its
              pristine gredience:
  The *Solstices* and *Equinoxes* run,
    As in pretended disobedience.
  The *Sunne* observed by *Artes* dili-
    gence,
  Is found in fourteene hundred
    yeeres to fall,
  Neere twelve *Degrees* towards the
    Center ball.
                              (Stanza 41)

Climate, or Years damp my intended wing   45
Deprest; and much they may, if all be mine,
Not Hers who brings it nightly to my Ear.
   The Sun was sunk, and after him the Star
Of *Hesperus*, whose Office is to bring
Twilight upon the Earth, short Arbiter   50
Twixt Day and Night, and now from end to end
Night's Hemisphere had veil'd the Horizon round:
When *Satan* who late fled before the threats
Of *Gabriel* out of *Eden*, now improv'd
In meditated fraud and malice, bent   55
On Man's destruction, maugre what might hap
Of heavier on himself, fearless return'd.
By Night he fled, and at Midnight return'd
From compassing the Earth, cautious of day,
Since *Uriel* Regent of the Sun descri'd   60
His entrance, and forewarn'd the Cherubim
That kept thir watch; thence full of anguish driv'n,
The space of seven continu'd Nights he rode
With darkness, thrice the Equinoctial Line
He circl'd, four times cross'd the Car of Night   65
From Pole to Pole, traversing each Colure;
On th'eighth return'd, and on the Coast averse
From entrance or Cherubic Watch, by stealth
Found unsuspected way. There was a place,
Now not, though Sin, not Time, first wrought the change,   70
Where *Tigris* at the foot of Paradise
Into a Gulf shot under ground, till part
Rose up a Fountain by the Tree of Life;

45–46. Aristotle's theory (*Politics* VII, vi, 1) that northern races lacked intelligence colored Milton's fear in the Preface to Book II of *Reason of Church Government* (C.Ed. III, 237) that "our climate or the fate of this age" might prove to be obstacles to his ambition to write an epic poem. Z. S. Fink, tracing the currency of this theory in Renaissance literature — in *MLQ*, II (1941), 80 — concludes that "the ultimate effect of the climatic theory upon Milton's poetical ambitions was to . . . make him more dependent upon the idea of divine inspiration which he had inherited from the Renaissance and which was congenial to his mind." The scientific basis for the idea — as T. B. Stroup notes in *MLQ*, IV (1943), 188 — was explained by Burton's view that "cold climes are more subject to natural melancholy which is cold and dry: for which cause Mercurius Britannicus belike puts melancholy men to inhabit just

under the Pole" (*Anatomy* I, ii: 2, 5. Everyman Ed. I, 239).
46. Milton's flight would be *Deprest* if his subject did not *raise* it. Cf. l. 43 above.
54. *improv'd* or taught by his experience with *Gabriel* (IV, 873–1015) how to refine his intended deceit.
60. *Uriel . . . descri'd:* in IV, 549–88.
65. *The Car of Night* — meaning simply night as it moves around the earth — is the traditional figure that Milton knew in the "yron charet" of Night, under whose protection Spenser's Duessa pursues her evil purposes (*F.Q.* I, v, 20).
66. *Colure:* circles of longitude intersecting at right angles so as to cut the ecliptic into four equal parts.
67. *the Coast averse:* the side opposite.
71. Milton had the authority of Josephus (*Antiquities* I, i, 3) for relating the *Tigris* to the river which "went out of Eden to water the garden" (Gen. ii, 10).

In with the River sunk, and with it rose
Satan involv'd in rising Mist, then sought   75
Where to lie hid; Sea he had searcht and Land
From *Eden* over *Pontus*, and the Pool
Mæotis, up beyond the River *Ob;*
Downward as far Antarctic; and in length
West from *Orontes* to the Ocean barr'd   80
At *Darien,* thence to the Land where flows
Ganges and *Indus:* thus the Orb he roam'd
With narrow search; and with inspection deep
Consider'd every Creature, which of all
Most opportune might serve his Wiles, and found   85
The Serpent subtlest Beast of all the Field.
Him after long debate, irresolute
Of thoughts revolv'd, his final sentence chose
Fit Vessel, fittest Imp of fraud, in whom
To enter, and his dark suggestions hide   90
From sharpest sight: for in the wily Snake,
Whatever sleights none would suspicious mark,
As from his wit and native subtlety
Proceeding, which in other Beasts observ'd
Doubt might beget of Diabolic pow'r   95
Active within beyond the sense of brute.
Thus he resolv'd, but first from inward grief
His bursting passion into plaints thus pour'd:
      O Earth, how like to Heav'n, if not preferr'd
More justly, Seat worthier of Gods, as built   100
With second thoughts, reforming what was old!
For what God after better worse would build?
Terrestrial Heav'n, danc't round by other Heav'ns
That shine, yet bear thir bright officious Lamps,
Light above Light, for thee alone, as seems,   105
In thee concentring all thir precious beams
Of sacred influence: As God in Heav'n
Is Centre, yet extends to all, so thou
Centring receiv'st from all those Orbs; in thee,

74–75. In his unpublished thesis, "The Folklore of Milton's English Poems," E. C. Kirkland compares several classical and medieval instances where "supernatural creatures enter the world of man by rising through some body of water" (pp. 30–31).

76. Satan first flew north over *Pontus* (the Black Sea) and the *Pool Mæotis* (Sea of Azof), beyond the river *Ob,* or Obi, on the arctic shore of Siberia. In *Moscovia* Milton often refers to the Ob.

80. *Orontes:* the chief river of Syria.
81. *Darien:* the Isthmus of Panama.
82. *the Orb:* the globe of the world.
86. Without mentioning Satan, Gene-sis iii, 1, says that "the Serpent was more subtil than any beast of the field which the Lord had made."

87–88. *irresolute* etc.: undecided among circling thoughts.
89. *Imp:* child.
95. *Doubt:* suspicion.
104. *officious* is used as it is in VIII, 99.
107. *sacred* because light partakes of the sacredness of deity, as in III, 1–12.
109–112. The thought — as McColley noted in *PMLA,* LII (1937), 741–42 — took a bigotedly obscurantist form in works like Alexander Ross's *The New Planet* (1649): "The wise God placed the earth in the midst of this great systeme

Not in themselves, all thir known virtue appears 110
Productive in Herb, Plant, and nobler birth
Of Creatures animate with gradual life
Of Growth, Sense, Reason, all summ'd up in Man.
With what delight could I have walkt thee round,
If I could joy in aught, sweet interchange 115
Of Hill and Valley, Rivers, Woods and Plains,
Now Land, now Sea, and Shores with Forest crown'd,
Rocks, Dens, and Caves; but I in none of these
Find place or refuge; and the more I see
Pleasures about me, so much more I feel 120
Torment within me, as from the hateful siege
Of contraries; all good to me becomes
Bane, and in Heav'n much worse would be my state.
But neither here seek I, no nor in Heav'n
To dwell, unless by maistring Heav'n's Supreme; 125
Nor hope to be myself less miserable
By what I seek, but others to make such
As I, though thereby worse to me redound:
For only in destroying I find ease
To my relentless thoughts; and him destroy'd, 130
Or won to what may work his utter loss,
For whom all this was made, all this will soon
Follow, as to him linkt in weal or woe,
In woe then: that destruction wide may range:
To mee shall be the glory sole among 135
Th'infernal Powers, in one day to have marr'd
What he *Almighty* styl'd, six Nights and Days
Continu'd making, and who knows how long
Before had been contriving, though perhaps
Not longer than since I in one Night freed 140
From servitude inglorious well nigh half
Th' Angelic Name, and thinner left the throng
Of his adorers: hee to be aveng'd,
And to repair his numbers thus impair'd,
Whether such virtue spent of old now fail'd 145

of the world, not onely for mans sake, who being the Lord of this universe, and the most honourable of all the creatures, deserved to have the most honourable place, which is the middle: but chiefly that man with all other animall and vegetable creatures might by an equal distance from all parts of heaven have an equall comfort and influence, what place more fit for conservation, then that which is in the midst of the world? . . . all the powers of the universe uniting themselves together in the earth, as in a small epitome." See the Introduction 32–35.

121–122. Satan feels his mind to be the *siege* (seat) of logical opposites or *contraries*, which Milton defines in the *Art of Logic* I, xiv (C.Ed. XI, 117) as simply one-to-one, mutually exclusive conceptions such as seeing *vs.* blindness and motion *vs.* quiet.

123. *Bane:* evil. Cf. Satan's reflections in IV, 32–112, and IX, 467–70.

133. When Eve tasted the fruit of the Tree of Knowledge, all nature "gave signs of woe" (IX, 783). Cf. X, 651–714.

140–142. Satan contradicts Beelzebub's statement in II, 345–53.

More Angels to Create, if they at least
Are his Created, or to spite us more,
Determin'd to advance into our room
A Creature form'd of Earth, and him endow,
Exalted from so base original,　　　　　　　　　　150
With Heav'nly spoils, our spoils; What he decreed
He effected; Man he made, and for him built
Magnificent this World, and Earth his seat,
Him Lord pronounc'd, and, O indignity!
Subjected to his service Angel wings,　　　　　　155
And flaming Ministers to watch and tend
Thir earthy Charge: Of these the vigilance
I dread, and to elude, thus wrapt in mist
Of midnight vapor glide obscure, and pry
In every Bush and Brake, where hap may find　　160
The Serpent sleeping, in whose mazy folds
To hide me, and the dark intent I bring.
O foul descent! that I who erst contended
With Gods to sit the highest, am now constrain'd
Into a Beast, and mixt with bestial slime,　　　165
This essence to incarnate and imbrute,
That to the highth of Deity aspir'd;
But what will not Ambition and Revenge
Descend to? who aspires must down as low
As high he soar'd, obnoxious first or last　　　170
To basest things. Revenge, at first though sweet,
Bitter ere long back on itself recoils;
Let it; I reck not, so it light well aim'd,
Since higher I fall short, on him who next
Provokes my envy, this new Favorite　　　　　175
Of Heav'n, this Man of Clay, Son of despite,
Whom us the more to spite his Maker rais'd
From dust: spite then with spite is best repaid.
So saying, through each Thicket Dank or Dry,

---

146. Contrast Satan's acknowledgement in IV, 43, that he is God's creature with his assumption here and in I, 116-17, and V. 853-63, that the angels are self-created and immortal.

149. So Vida in the *Christiad* and Tasso in *Jerusalem Delivered* make Satan in an infernal council appeal to the demons' contempt of man on the ground that

> . . . in our Place, the Heavens possess he must,
> Vile Man, begot of Clay, and born of Dust.
> (*Jerusalem Delivered*, Fairfax's translation, IV, x)

155. Satan makes a grievance of the discovery that God "gives his angels charge" (Psalm xci, 11) of mankind.

166. Cf. *This essence* with the *Heavenly Essences* of I, 138, n.

170. *obnoxious:* exposed. Cf. IX, 1094.

175. In the Foreword to Vondel's *Lucifer* pride and envy are made the mainsprings of the devil's nature, and St. Augustine's definition of envy as hatred of another's happiness is quoted as uniting with pride to motivate Satan's temptation of Adam. Cf. *The City of God* XII, xi.

178. Cf. the charge against Beelzebub and Satan of doing all "to spite the great Creator" (II, 384-85). The phrasing here resembles Aeschylus' declaration of enmity against Zeus (*Prom.*, 944).

Like a black mist low creeping, he held on   180
His midnight search, where soonest he might find
The Serpent: him fast sleeping soon he found
In Labyrinth of many a round self-roll'd,
His head the midst, well stor'd with subtle wiles:
Not yet in horrid Shade or dismal Den,   185
Nor nocent yet, but on the grassy Herb
Fearless unfear'd he slept: in at his Mouth
The Devil enter'd, and his brutal sense,
In heart or head, possessing soon inspir'd
With act intelligential; but his sleep   190
Disturb'd not, waiting close th' approach of Morn.
Now whenas sacred Light began to dawn
In *Eden* on the humid Flow'rs, that breath'd
Thir morning incense, when all things that breathe,
From th' Earth's great Altar send up silent praise   195
To the Creator, and his Nostrils fill
With grateful Smell, forth came the human pair
And join'd thir vocal Worship to the Choir
Of Creatures wanting voice; that done, partake
The season, prime for sweetest Scents and Airs: 200
Then commune how that day they best may ply
Thir growing work: for much thir work outgrew
The hands' dispatch of two Gard'ning so wide.
And *Eve* first to her Husband thus began.
     Adam, well may we labor still to dress   205
This Garden, still to tend Plant, Herb and Flow'r,
Our pleasant task enjoin'd, but till more hands
Aid us, the work under our labor grows,
Luxurious by restraint; what we by day
Lop overgrown, or prune, or prop, or bind,   210
One night or two with wanton growth derides
Tending to wild. Thou therefore now advise
Or hear what to my mind first thoughts present,

180. A reminiscence, perhaps, of Thetis
rising "like a cloud" from the sea to
answer Achilles' prayer (*Il.* I, 359), and
an expression of a current belief that,
    as in liquid clouds (exhaled
      thickly),
Water and Ayr (as moist) do mingle
    quickly,
The evill Angells slide too easily,
As subtle spirits into our fantasie.
    (Du Bartas, *Divine Weeks*, p. 251)
191. *close:* hidden.
192. *whenas:* when.
197. So in Genesis viii, 21, the Lord
smells a sweet savor from the altars of
sacrifice erected by Noah.
199. *wanting:* lacking.
208-225. Three views seem possible:

Sister M. I. Corcoran's in *Milton's Para-
dise*, pp. 54 and 126, representing Eve on
the basis of some pre-Christian commen-
taries on Genesis as originally having
part of the garden assigned to her care,
or as pleading to work alone on the day
of temptation in a way which Milton
chose to treat as "obstinate presump-
tion"; or J. C. Ransom's view in *God
without Thunder* (1931), pp. 133-34, that
the forbidden fruit symbolizes applied
science, which makes Eve's plea fore-
shadow the sophistries of modern ef-
ficiency experts; or the private view of
the late W. E. Leonard that her plea is
a final stroke of art in the characterization
of the mother of all women.

Let us divide our labors, thou where choice
Leads thee, or where most needs, whether to wind   215
The Woodbine round this Arbor, or direct
The clasping Ivy where to climb, while I
In yonder Spring of Roses intermixt
With Myrtle, find what to redress till Noon:
For while so near each other thus all day   220
Our task we choose, what wonder if so near
Looks intervene and smiles, or object new
Casual discourse draw on, which intermits
Our day's work brought to little, though begun
Early, and th' hour of Supper comes unearn'd.   225
    To whom mild answer *Adam* thus return'd.
Sole *Eve*, Associate sole, to me beyond
Compare above all living Creatures dear,
Well hast thou motion'd, well thy thoughts imploy'd
How we might best fulfil the work which here   230
God hath assign'd us, nor of me shalt pass
Unprais'd: for nothing lovelier can be found
In Woman, than to study household good,
And good works in her Husband to promote.
Yet not so strictly hath our Lord impos'd   235
Labor, as to debar us when we need
Refreshment, whether food, or talk between,
Food of the mind, or this sweet intercourse
Of looks and smiles, for smiles from Reason flow,
To brute deni'd, and are of Love the food,   240
Love not the lowest end of human life.
For not to irksome toil, but to delight
He made us, and delight to Reason join'd.
These paths and Bowers doubt not but our joint hands
Will keep from Wilderness with ease, as wide   245
As we need walk, till younger hands ere long
Assist us: But if much converse perhaps
Thee satiate, to short absence I could yield.
For solitude sometimes is best society,
And short retirement urges sweet return.   250
But other doubt possesses me, lest harm
Befall thee sever'd from me; for thou know'st
What hath been warn'd us, what malicious Foe
Envying our happiness, and of his own
Despairing, seeks to work us woe and shame   255
By sly assault; and somewhere nigh at hand
Watches, no doubt, with greedy hope to find

218. *Spring:* grove of young trees or
shrubs.
    229. *motion'd:* suggested, "moved,"
as in a deliberative body.
    245 *Wilderness:* wildness.

249. The thought was a favorite aphor-
ism, going back to Cicero's remark that
Africanus was never so little alone as
when he was by himself (*De re publica* I,
xvii, 27). Cf. *PR* I, 302.

His wish and best advantage, us asunder,
Hopeless to circumvent us join'd, where each
To other speedy aid might lend at need;   260
Whether his first design be to withdraw
Our fealty from God, or to disturb
Conjugal Love, than which perhaps no bliss
Enjoy'd by us excites his envy more;
Or this, or worse, leave not the faithful side   265
That gave thee being, still shades thee and protects.
The Wife, where danger or dishonor lurks,
Safest and seemliest by her Husband stays,
Who guards her, or with her the worst endures.
    To whom the Virgin Majesty of *Eve*,   270
As one who loves, and some unkindness meets,
With sweet austere composure thus repli'd.
    Offspring of Heav'n and Earth, and all Earth's Lord,
That such an Enemy we have, who seeks
Our ruin, both by thee inform'd I learn,   275
And from the parting Angel over-heard
As in a shady nook I stood behind,
Just then return'd at shut of Ev'ning Flow'rs.
But that thou shouldst my firmness therefore doubt
To God or thee, because we have a foe   280
May tempt it, I expected not to hear.
His violence thou fear'st not, being such,
As wee, not capable of death or pain,
Can either not receive, or can repel.
His fraud is then thy fear, which plain infers   285
Thy equal fear that my firm Faith and Love
Can by his fraud be shak'n or seduc't;
Thoughts, which how found they harbor in thy breast,
Adam, misthought of her to thee so dear?
    To whom with healing words *Adam* repli'd.   290
Daughter of God and Man, immortal *Eve*,
For such thou art, from sin and blame entire:
Not diffident of thee do I dissuade
Thy absence from my sight, but to avoid

264. Rabbinical commentary on the statement that "the serpent was more subtil than any beast of the field" (Gen. iii, 1) explained that the serpent was jealous of their happiness. Josephus says that "the serpent, which then lived together with Adam and his wife, showed an envious disposition, at his supposal of their living happily; . . . and persuaded the woman out of a malicious intention to taste of the tree of knowledge" (*Antiquities* I, i, 4).
265-266. *the . . . side That gave thee being:* Cf. VIII, 465-71.

270. *virgin:* virginal, innocent.
274-278. Eve's full, independent knowledge of the command not to eat the fruit of the Tree of Knowledge was stressed by several biblical commentators, Catholic and Protestant, who are quoted by Williams in *Expositor*, p. 114.
289. *misthought:* misjudgment.
292. *entire* has its Latin force of "whole" and therefore proof against wrong of any kind, perhaps alluding to Horace's *Ode* (I, xxii) on the strength of the man whose life is "whole" (*integer:* entire). Cf. X, 910.

Th' attempt itself, intended by our Foe.   295
For hee who tempts, though in vain, at least asperses
The tempted with dishonor foul, suppos'd
Not incorruptible of Faith, not proof
Against temptation: thou thyself with scorn
And anger wouldst resent the offer'd wrong,   300
Though ineffectual found: misdeem not then,
If such affront I labor to avert
From thee alone, which on us both at once
The Enemy, though bold, will hardly dare,
Or daring, first on mee th' assault shall light.   305
Nor thou his malice and false guile contemn;
Subtle he needs must be, who could seduce
Angels, nor think superfluous others' aid.
I from the influence of thy looks receive
Access in every Virtue, in thy sight   310
More wise, more watchful, stronger, if need were
Of outward strength; while shame, thou looking on,
Shame to be overcome or over-reacht
Would utmost vigor raise, and rais'd unite.
Why shouldst not thou like sense within thee feel   315
When I am present, and thy trial choose
With me, best witness of thy Virtue tri'd.
    So spake domestic *Adam* in his care
And Matrimonial Love; but *Eve*, who thought
Less attributed to her Faith sincere,   320
Thus her reply with accent sweet renew'd.
    If this be our condition, thus to dwell
In narrow circuit strait'n'd by a Foe,
Subtle or violent, we not endu'd
Single with like defense, wherever met,   325
How are we happy, still in fear of harm?
But harm precedes not sin: only our Foe
Tempting affronts us with his foul esteem
Of our integrity: his foul esteem
Sticks no dishonor on our Front, but turns   330
Foul on himself; then wherefore shunn'd or fear'd
By us? who rather double honor gain
From his surmise prov'd false, find peace within,
Favor from Heav'n, our witness from th' event.
And what is Faith, Love, Virtue unassay'd   335

298. *Faith:* fidelity, loyalty. Cf. *firm Faith* in II, 36.
310. *Access:* increase. Plato's value of the mutual stimulation of friends in lives of virtue (*Symposium*, 178–79) was prominent in the thinking of the Renaissance about friendship.
323. *strait'n'd:* confined, limited.
330. *Front:* brow, as in II, 302. The word points back to *affronts* in l. 328, with its derived meaning of "insult" or impudently "confront" (a person).
334. The reasoning is St. Paul's: "The Spirit itself beareth witness with our spirit, that we are the children of God" (Rom. viii, 16). Cf. the similar use of *event* in I, 134, II, 82, etc.

Alone, without exterior help sustain'd?
Let us not then suspect our happy State
Left so imperfet by the Maker wise,
As not secure to single or combin'd.
Frail is our happiness, if this be so,   340
And *Eden* were no *Eden* thus expos'd.
    To whom thus *Adam* fervently repli'd.
O Woman, best are all things as the will
Of God ordain'd them, his creating hand
Nothing imperfet or deficient left   345
Of all that he Created, much less Man,
Or aught that might his happy State secure,
Secure from outward force; within himself
The danger lies, yet lies within his power:
Against his will he can receive no harm.   350
But God left free the Will, for what obeys
Reason, is free, and Reason he made right,
But bid her well beware, and still erect,
Lest by some fair appearing good surpris'd
She dictate false, and misinform the Will   355
To do what God expressly hath forbid.
Not then mistrust, but tender love enjoins,
That I should mind thee oft, and mind thou me.
Firm we subsist, yet possible to swerve,
Since Reason not impossibly may meet   360
Some specious object by the Foe suborn'd,
And fall into deception unaware,
Not keeping strictest watch, as she was warn'd.
Seek not temptation then, which to avoid
Were better, and most likely if from mee   365
Thou sever not: Trial will come unsought.
Wouldst thou approve thy constancy, approve
First thy obedience; th' other who can know,
Not seeing thee attempted, who attest?
But if thou think, trial unsought may find   370
Us both securer than thus warn'd thou seem'st,
Go; for thy stay, not free, absents thee more;
Go in thy native innocence, rely
On what thou hast of virtue, summon all,
For God towards thee hath done his part, do thine.   375
    So spake the Patriarch of Mankind, but *Eve*

351–356. Adam states the doctrine that he has learned from Raphael (V, 520–40) and that has been distinctly stated by God in III, 96–128; or in Milton's own words: "Reason has been implanted in all, by which they may of themselves resist bad desires" (*CD* I, iv; C.Ed. XIV, 131).
353. *erect:* alert.

358. *mind:* remind.
361. Cf. Archimago's "suborned wyle" in the shape of speciously "falsed letters" in Spenser's *Faerie Queene* II, i, 1, 3.
367. *approve:* prove, give proof of.
371. *securer:* less careful, less on guard. Cf. *secure* in l. 339 above and in IV, 791.

Persisted, yet submiss, though last, repli'd.
With thy permission then, and thus forewarn'd
Chiefly by what thy own last reasoning words
Touch'd only, that our trial, when least sought,   380
May find us both perhaps far less prepar'd,
The willinger I go, nor much expect
A Foe so proud will first the weaker seek;
So bent, the more shall shame him his repulse.
Thus saying, from her Husband's hand her hand   385
Soft she withdrew, and like a Wood-Nymph light,
Oread or *Dryad*, or of *Delia's* Train,
Betook her to the Groves, but *Delia's* self
In gait surpass'd and Goddess-like deport,
Though not as shee with Bow and Quiver arm'd,   390
But with such Gard'ning Tools as Art yet rude,
Guiltless of fire had form'd, or Angels brought.
To *Pales*, or *Pomona*, thus adorn'd,
Likest she seem'd, *Pomona* when she fled
Vertumnus, or to *Ceres* in her Prime,   395
Yet Virgin of *Proserpina* from *Jove*.
Her long and ardent look his Eye pursu'd
Delighted, but desiring more her stay.
Oft he to her his charge of quick return
Repeated, shee to him as oft engag'd   400
To be return'd by Noon amid the Bow'r,
And all things in best order to invite
Noontide repast, or Afternoon's repose.
O much deceiv'd, much failing, hapless *Eve*,
Of thy presum'd return! event perverse!   405
Thou never from that hour in Paradise
Found'st either sweet repast, or sound repose;
Such ambush hid among sweet Flow'rs and Shades
Waited with hellish rancor imminent
To intercept thy way, or send thee back   410
Despoil'd of Innocence, of Faith, of Bliss.
For now, and since first break of dawn the Fiend,
Mere Serpent in appearance, forth was come,

377. *submiss:* submitted (a participle); the meaning is "submissively."
387. *Oread* or *Dryad:* mountain or wood nymph. Diana (Artemis) is called *Delia* from her birthplace, Delos. Milton thought of her with her traditional bow and arrows, leading her nymphs in the hunt.
389. *deport:* deportment, bearing.
393. *Pales* was a primitive Roman goddess of flocks and herds.
394. Ovid pictures the goddess of fruit, *Pomona*, with a symbolic pruning hook (*Met.* XIV, 628) and tells the story

of her long resistance to the pursuit of the wood-god *Vertumnus*.
395. Renaissance painters often represented the young Ceres with the symbolic plough that Ovid says (*Met.* V, 341) she was the first to teach men to use. Cf. Ceres in a different role in IV, 271–72, after she has become the mother of Proserpina.
413. *Mere Serpent:* simply a serpent. The meaning seems to be that the tempter was not the more or less humanized snake with a woman's head often seen in paintings of the temptation. In Andreini's

And on his Quest, where likeliest he might find
The only two of Mankind, but in them   415
The whole included Race, his purpos'd prey.
In Bow'r and Field he sought, where any tuft
Of Grove or Garden-Plot more pleasant lay,
Thir tendance or Plantation for delight,
By Fountain or by shady Rivulet,   420
He sought them both, but wish'd his hap might find
Eve separate, he wish'd, but not with hope
Of what so seldom chanc'd, when to his wish,
Beyond his hope, *Eve* separate he spies,
Veil'd in a Cloud of Fragrance, where she stood,   425
Half spi'd, so thick the Roses blushing round
About her glow'd, oft stooping to support
Each Flow'r of slender stalk, whose head though gay
Carnation, Purple, Azure, or speckt with Gold,
Hung drooping unsustain'd, them she upstays   430
Gently with Myrtle band, mindless the while,
Herself, though fairest unsupported Flow'r,
From her best prop so far, and storm so nigh.
Nearer he drew, and many a walk travers'd
Of stateliest Covert, Cedar, Pine, or Palm,   435
Then voluble and bold, now hid, now seen
Among thick-wov'n Arborets and Flow'rs
Imborder'd on each Bank, the hand of *Eve:*
Spot more delicious than those Gardens feign'd
Or of reviv'd *Adonis,* or renown'd   440
Alcinoüs, host of old *Laertes'* Son,
Or that, not Mystic, where the Sapient King
Held dalliance with his fair *Egyptian* Spouse.
Much hee the Place admir'd, the Person more.
As one who long in populous City pent,   445
Where Houses thick and Sewers annoy the Air,

L'Adamo II, iii, the tempting serpent is
represented as a woman who is serpentine
only from the waist down.
  419. *tendance:* object of care. Cf.
nursery in VIII, 46.
  431. *mindless:* heedless, careless (of
herself).
  436. *voluble* keeps its Latin meaning of
"rolling upon itself."
  438. *imborder'd:* planted with borders.
the hand of Eve: the handiwork of Eve.
  439–440. Cf. Milton's use of the Gar-
den of *Adonis* as a symbol of an earthly
but mystical paradise in *Comus,* 976–
1011. As Williams notes — *Expositor,*
p. 108 — the comparison was traditional
and many commentators had declared
that Paradise excelled the gardens of
Alcinoüs and the Hesperides. Cf. V, 341.

  441. *Laertes' Son* is Ulysses, whose
visit to the gardens of Alcinoüs is told in
the *Odyssey* VII.
  442. *not Mystic* means "real" or "his-
torical," for the garden of Adonis was
mythological. To its pagan mystery is
opposed the garden where Solomon, the
Sapient King, brought his bride when he
"made affinity with Pharaoh king of
Egypt, and took Pharaoh's daughter"
(I Kings iii, 1). Milton had in mind the
allusions to Solomon's garden in the Song
of Solomon, which he may have under-
stood — on the strength of the address
to the "prince's daughter" in vii, 1 — as
an epithalamion writter for the Egyptian
princess. In *Reason of Church Govern-
ment* he calls it "a divine pastoral drama"
(C.Ed. III, 237).

Forth issuing on a Summer's Morn to breathe
Among the pleasant Villages and Farms
Adjoin'd, from each thing met conceives delight,
The smell of Grain, or tedded Grass, or Kine, 450
Or Dairy, each rural sight, each rural sound;
If chance with Nymphlike step fair Virgin pass,
What pleasing seem'd, for her now pleases more,
She most, and in her look sums all Delight.
Such Pleasure took the Serpent to behold 455
This Flow'ry Plat, the sweet recess of *Eve*
Thus early, thus alone; her Heav'nly form
Angelic, but more soft, and Feminine,
Her graceful Innocence, her every Air
Of gesture or least action overaw'd 460
His Malice, and with rapine sweet bereav'd
His fierceness of the fierce intent it brought:
That space the Evil one abstracted stood
From his own evil, and for the time remain'd
Stupidly good, of enmity disarm'd, 465
Of guile, of hate, of envy, of revenge;
But the hot Hell that always in him burns,
Though in mid Heav'n, soon ended his delight,
And tortures him now more, the more he sees
Of pleasure not for him ordain'd: then soon 470
Fierce hate he recollects, and all his thoughts
Of mischief, gratulating, thus excites.
 Thoughts, whither have ye led me, with what sweet
Compulsion thus transported to forget
What hither brought us, hate, not love, nor hope 475
Of Paradise for Hell, hope here to taste
Of pleasure, but all pleasure to destroy,
Save what is in destroying, other joy
To me is lost. Then let me not let pass
Occasion which now smiles, behold alone 480
The Woman, opportune to all attempts,
Her Husband, for I view far round, not nigh,
Whose higher intellectual more I shun,
And strength, of courage haughty, and of limb
Heroic built, though of terrestrial mould, 485
Foe not informidable, exempt from wound,
I not; so much hath Hell debas'd, and pain

450. *tedded:* spread, scattered (to
make hay). *Kine:* cattle.
453. *for her:* on her account.
454. *sums:* gathers together and con-
centrates in herself.
457–466. As G. D. Hildebrand sug-
gests in *N&Q,* CXCVII (1952), 246, the
underlying thought is like that of the
supernatural power of chastity in *Comus.*

446–51.
456. *Plat:* plot of ground.
467. Cf. the *Hell within him* in IV, 20.
481. *opportune:* opportunely situated.
485. *terrestrial mould:* earthly sub-
stance, earth. Cf. *mould* in II, 139.
486. Cf. man's incapability *of death or
pain* in l. 283 above and Satan's first
knowledge of pain in VI, 327.

Infeebl'd me, to what I was in Heav'n.
Shee fair, divinely fair, fit Love for Gods,
Not terrible, though terror be in Love   490
And beauty, not approacht by stronger hate,
Hate stronger, under show of Love well feign'd,
The way which to her ruin now I tend.
So spake the Enemy of Mankind, enclos'd
In Serpent, Inmate bad, and toward *Eve*   495
Address'd his way, not with indented wave,
Prone on the ground, as since, but on his rear,
Circular base of rising folds, that tow'r'd
Fold above fold a surging Maze, his Head
Crested aloft, and Carbuncle his Eyes;   500
With burnisht Neck of verdant Gold, erect
Amidst his circling Spires, that on the grass
Floated redundant: pleasing was his shape,
And lovely, never since of Serpent kind
Lovelier, not those that in *Illyria* chang'd   505
Hermione and *Cadmus*, or the God
In *Epidaurus;* nor to which transform'd
Ammonian Jove, or *Capitoline* was seen,
Hee with *Olympias*, this with her who bore
Scipio the highth of *Rome*. With tract oblique   510
At first, as one who sought access, but fear'd
To interrupt, side-long he works his way.
As when a Ship by skilful Steersman wrought
Nigh River's mouth or Foreland, where the Wind
Veers oft, as oft so steers, and shifts her Sail;   515
So varied hee, and of his tortuous Train
Curl'd many a wanton wreath in sight of *Eve*,
To lure her Eye; shee busied heard the sound
Of rustling Leaves, but minded not, as us'd
To such disport before her through the Field,   520
From every Beast, more duteous at her call,

502. *Spires* keeps its Latin force of "loops" or "coils." The theories of several biblical commentators on the serpent's upright stance before its curse to go upon its belly (cf. X, 177) are collected in Williams' *Expositor*, p. 116.

505. *chang'd:* metamorphosed. The word itself alludes to Ovid's story of the metamorphosis of *Cadmus* and Harmonia (*Hermione*) into serpents (*Met.* IV, 563–603).

506. *The God* is Aesculapius, the deity of healing, whom Ovid described (*Met.* XV, 760–74) as appearing like a serpent with head held as high as a man's breast, and with flashing eyes, in his temple in *Epidaurus*, in Argolis.

507–510. In Edward Topsell's *Historie of Serpents* (1608), p. 5, four ancient authorities are sceptically cited for the stories that *Olympias*, the mother of Alexander the Great, was beloved by Jupiter Ammon (cf. IV, 277) in the form of a serpent, and that the mother of *Scipio* Africanus, the *highth of Rome*, or greatest of Romans, was similarly loved by the *Capitoline* Jupiter. W. Empson interprets this passage as meaning that "Eve turned into a snake and became Satan's consort" (*Pastoral*, p. 175). But Milton's eye was on the tradition that Eve was charmed by the serpent's beauty — a tradition which led John Salkeld in *A Treatise of Paradise* (1617), p. 218, to surmise that her tempter must have been "that most beautiful serpent Scytile," and not the basilisk, though it was the "king of Serpents."

Than at *Circean* call the Herd disguis'd.
Hee bolder now, uncall'd before her stood;
But as in gaze admiring: Oft he bow'd
His turret Crest, and sleek enamell'd Neck,   525
Fawning, and lick'd the ground whereon she trod.
His gentle dumb expression turn'd at length
The Eye of *Eve* to mark his play; he glad
Of her attention gain'd, with Serpent Tongue
Organic, or impulse of vocal Air,   530
His fraudulent temptation thus began.
    Wonder not, sovran Mistress, if perhaps
Thou canst, who are sole Wonder, much less arm
Thy looks, the Heav'n of mildness, with disdain,
Displeas'd that I approach thee thus, and gaze   535
Insatiate, I thus single, nor have fear'd
Thy awful brow, more awful thus retir'd.
Fairest resemblance of thy Maker fair,
Thee all things living gaze on, all things thine
By gift, and thy Celestial Beauty adore   540
With ravishment beheld, there best beheld
Where universally admir'd: but here
In this enclosure wild, these Beasts among,
Beholders rude, and shallow to discern
Half what in thee is fair, one man except,   545
Who sees thee? (and what is one?) who shouldst be seen
A Goddess among Gods, ador'd and serv'd
By Angels numberless, thy daily Train.
    So gloz'd the Tempter, and his Proem tun'd;
Into the Heart of *Eve* his words made way,   550
Though at the voice much marvelling; at length
Not unamaz'd she thus in answer spake.
    What may this mean? Language of Man pronounc't
By Tongue of Brute, and human sense exprest?
The first at least of these I thought deni'd   555
To Beasts, whom God on thir Creation-Day

522. The *Herd disguis'd* are the victims of Circe's power to change men into swine. Homer says that they approached Ulysses' men "like dogs fawning on a returning master" (*Od.* X, 214-19).
530. *Organic:* "as a tool," says A. Williams (*Expositor*, p. 116). Because the devil or the serpent lacked the power of human speech, the latter had either to use the former's tongue as an instrument or else to impel the air in such a way as to make it seem voice-like or *vocal*.
532-548. So — like several other tempting serpents in the scene of Eve's temptation — Andreini's serpent hails her as

Nature's show-piece, micro-paradise,
To whom all things on earth bow down in praise, etc.
(*L'Adamo* II, vi. In the *Celestial Cycle*, p. 244.)
Satan is behaving traditionally though he may also speak a contemporary idiom — as D. S. Berkeley suggests in "Précieuse Gallantry and the Seduction of Eve" in *N&Q*, CXCVI (1951), 337.
549. *gloz'd* recalls Comus' "glozing courtesy,/Baited with reasons not unplausible" (*Comus*, 161-62) in a passage which may also reflect the tone of comparable scenes in contemporary court drama.

Created mute to all articulate sound;
The latter I demur, for in thir looks
Much reason, and in thir actions oft appears.
Thee, Serpent, subtlest beast of all the field   560
I knew, but not with human voice endu'd;
Redouble then this miracle, and say,
How cam'st thou speakable of mute, and how
To me so friendly grown above the rest
Of brutal kind, that daily are in sight?   565
Say, for such wonder claims attention due.
    To whom the guileful Tempter thus repli'd.
Empress of this fair World, resplendent *Eve*,
Easy to mee it is to tell thee all
What thou command'st and right thou should'st be obey'd: 570
I was at first as other Beasts that graze
The trodden Herb, of abject thoughts and low,
As was my food, nor aught but food discern'd
Or Sex, and apprehended nothing high:
Till on a day roving the field, I chanc'd   575
A goodly Tree far distant to behold
Loaden with fruit of fairest colors mixt,
Ruddy and Gold: I nearer drew to gaze;
When from the boughs a savory odor blown,
Grateful to appetite, more pleas'd my sense   580
Than smell of sweetest Fennel, or the Teats
Of Ewe or Goat dropping with Milk at Ev'n,
Unsuckt of Lamb or Kid, that tend thir play.
To satisfy the sharp desire I had
Of tasting those fair Apples, I resolv'd   585
Not to defer; hunger and thirst at once,
Powerful persuaders, quick'n'd at the scent
Of that alluring fruit, urg'd me so keen.
About the mossy Trunk I wound me soon,
For high from ground the branches would require   590
Thy utmost reach or *Adam's:* Round the Tree
All other Beasts that saw, with like desire
Longing and envying stood, but could not reach.
Amid the Tree now got, where plenty hung
Tempting so nigh, to pluck and eat my fill   595
I spar'd not, for such pleasure till that hour
At Feed or Fountain never had I found.

558–559. *demur:* entertain doubts of. God has said that the beasts "know/And reason not contemptibly" (VIII, 373–74).
563. *speakable of mute:* capable of speech from a mute condition.
571–574. Behind the lines is the Aristotelian distinction of the noble pleasures of which men are capable from the gross

limitations of the animals (*Nicomachean Ethics*, I, ix, 9).
581. *Fennel* was supposed to be a favorite food of snakes. Cf. Lyly in *Sappho and Phao* II, iv: "Fancy is a worme, that feedeth first upon fenell." Another popular belief was that they suck the teats of sheep.

Sated at length, ere long I might perceive
Strange alteration in me, to degree
Of Reason in my inward Powers, and Speech   600
Wanted not long, though to this shape retain'd.
Thenceforth to Speculations high or deep
I turn'd my thoughts, and with capacious mind
Consider'd all things visible in Heav'n,
Or Earth, or Middle, all things fair and good;   605
But all that fair and good in thy Divine
Semblance, and in thy Beauty's heav'nly Ray
United I beheld; no Fair to thine
Equivalent or second, which compell'd
Mee thus, though importune perhaps, to come   610
And gaze, and worship thee of right declar'd
Sovran of Creatures, universal Dame.
    So talk'd the spirited sly Snake; and *Eve*
Yet more amaz'd unwary thus repli'd.
    Serpent, thy overpraising leaves in doubt   615
The virtue of that Fruit, in thee first prov'd:
But say, where grows the Tree, from hence how far?
For many are the Trees of God that grow
In Paradise, and various, yet unknown
To us, in such abundance lies our choice,   620
As leaves a greater store of Fruit untoucht,
Still hanging incorruptible, till men
Grow up to thir provision, and more hands
Help to disburden Nature of her Birth.
    To whom the wily Adder, blithe and glad.   625
Empress, the way is ready, and not long,
Beyond a row of Myrtles, on a Flat,
Fast by a Fountain, one small Thicket past
Of blowing Myrrh and Balm; if thou accept
My conduct, I can bring thee thither soon.   630
    Lead then, said *Eve*. Hee leading swiftly roll'd
In tangles, and made intricate seem straight,
To mischief swift. Hope elevates, and joy
Bright'ns his Crest, as when a wand'ring Fire,

---

599. *to degree*, etc., amounting to the gift of a degree of reason in the mind, to which speech was soon added, although there was no change of outward form.
605. *Middle:* the air. Cf. II, 714–18, n.
612. *Dame* keeps its original Latin force of "mistress."
613. *spirited:* spirit-possessed.
623. *to thir provision:* to numbers proportionate to what has been provided.
624. Cf. Milton's translation of Psalm 8. 4, where God's praise is said to be "set Out of the tender mouths of latest bearth"

(i.e. out of the mouths of "babes and sucklings"). The word rhymes with *earth*. Here, as Adams suggests in *Ikon,* pp. 84–5, it combines the meaning of *birth* meaning offspring or the product of bearing (*O.E.D.* 3) with that of *birth*, the word of perhaps Norse origin which the *O.E.D* defines simply as meaning a burden.
629. *blowing:* blossoming. Cf. V, 22, and VII, 319.
634–642. John Swan's popular *Speculum Mundi* (1643), pp. 88–89, is a striking parallel. K. Svendsen notes — *ELH,* IX

Compact of unctuous vapor, which the Night   635
Condenses, and the cold invirons round,
Kindl'd through agitation to a Flame,
Which oft, they say, some evil Spirit attends,
Hovering and blazing with delusive Light,
Misleads th' amaz'd Night-wanderer from his way   640
To Bogs and Mires, and oft through Pond or Pool,
There swallow'd up and lost, from succor far.
So glister'd the dire Snake, and into fraud
Led *Eve* our credulous Mother, to the Tree
Of prohibition, root of all our woe;   645
Which when she saw, thus to her guide she spake.

Serpent, we might have spar'd our coming hither,
Fruitless to mee, though Fruit be here to excess,
The credit of whose virtue rest with thee,
Wondrous indeed, if cause of such effects.   650
But of this Tree we may not taste nor touch;
God so commanded, and left that Command
Sole Daughter of his voice; the rest, we live
Law to ourselves, our Reason is our Law.

To whom the Tempter guilefully repli'd.   655
Indeed? hath God then said that of the Fruit
Of all these Garden Trees ye shall not eat,
Yet Lords declar'd of all in Earth or Air?

To whom thus *Eve* yet sinless. Of the Fruit
Of each Tree in the Garden we may eat,   660
But of the Fruit of this fair Tree amidst
The Garden, God hath said, Ye shall not eat
Thereof, nor shall ye touch it, lest ye die.

She scarce had said, though brief, when now more bold
The Tempter, but with show of Zeal and Love   665
To Man, and indignation at his wrong,
New part puts on, and as to passion mov'd,
Fluctuates disturb'd, yet comely, and in act

(1942), 220 — its definition of the *Ignis
fatuus* or *foolish Fire* as "a fat and oily
Exhalation, hot and drie," which the
"much terrified, ignorant, and super-
stitious people" have often mistaken for
"walking spirits. They are no spirits,
and yet lead out of the way, because
those who see them are amazed, and look
so earnestly after them that they forget
their way: and then . . . wander to and
fro, . . . sometimes to waters, pits, and
other dangerous places." Cf. *Comus*, 433.

644–645. *the Tree/Of prohibition:* a
Hebraism for "the forbidden tree."

648. The pun is pathetically made by
Spenser in the *Faerie Queene* II, vii, 4,
1–3:

Here also sprong that goodly golden
  fruit,

With which Acontius got his lover
  trew,
Whom he had long time sought with
  fruitlesse suit.

653. The Hebraism *Daughter of his
voice* is explained by W. Hunter in *MLQ,*
IX (1948), 180, as a translation of *Bath
Kol*, "a voice sent from heaven," but a
revelation of God's will of less weight
than an absolute command. Eve is
softening the divine prohibition of the
Tree of Knowledge.

654. An echo of St. Paul's remark
about the virtuous Gentiles who, though
outside Hebrew law, were "a law unto
themselves" (Rom. ii, 14). Contrast the
refusal of the devils to accept "Right
reason for thir Law" in VI, 42.

Rais'd, as of some great matter to begin.
As when of old some Orator renown'd   670
In *Athens* or free *Rome*, where Eloquence
Flourish'd, since mute, to some great cause addrest,
Stood in himself collected, while each part,
Motion, each act won audience ere the tongue,
Sometimes in highth began, as no delay   675
Of Preface brooking through his Zeal of Right.
So standing, moving, or to highth upgrown
The Tempter all impassion'd thus began.
O Sacred, Wise, and Wisdom-giving Plant,
Mother of Science, Now I feel thy Power   680
Within me clear, not only to discern
Things in thir Causes, but to trace the ways
Of highest Agents deem'd however wise.
Queen of this Universe, do not believe
Those rigid threats of Death; ye shall not Die: 685
How should ye? by the Fruit? it gives you Life
To Knowledge: By the Threat'ner? look on mee,
Mee who have touch'd and tasted, yet both live,
And life more perfet have attain'd than Fate
Meant mee, by vent'ring higher than my Lot.   690
Shall that be shut to Man, which to the Beast
Is open? or will God incense his ire
For such a petty Trespass, and not praise
Rather your dauntless virtue, whom the pain
Of Death denounc't, whatever thing Death be,   695
Deterr'd not from achieving what might lead
To happier life, knowledge of Good and Evil;
Of good, how just? of evil, if what is evil
Be real, why not known, since easier shunn'd?
God therefore cannot hurt ye, and be just;   700
Not just, not God; not fear'd then, nor obey'd:
Your fear itself of Death removes the fear.
Why then was this forbid? Why but to awe,

670–675. Satan is abusing the art of the orator that Milton admired as it was practiced by the democratic orators of Athens who
    Wielded at will the fierce Democracy.
            (*PR* IV, 269)
674. *audience:* attention, hearing.
675. *highth:* height of feeling.
680. *Science* keeps its Latin meaning of "knowledge."
683. *highest Agents:* active beings of the highest rank, angels or perhaps even God himself.
685. "And the serpent said unto the woman, ye shall not surely die" (Gen. iii, 4).
686–687. *Life To Knowledge:* life as

well as knowledge.
703–709. So Henry Lawrence (to whose son, Edward, Milton's *Sonnet* XX was addressed) explains in *Our Communion and War with Angels* (1646), p. 98, that when Satan tempted Eve he "accused God" and "told her *they should be as Gods, knowing good and evill,* this temptation tooke, now hee intimated that God made that restraynt out of envy, because hee would have none so great and so happy as himself." Interpreting the fall philosophically in *Conjectura Cabbalistica*, Henry More had the serpent tell Eve that "God indeed loves to keep his creatures in awe; . . . but *he knows* very well that if you take your

Why but to keep ye low and ignorant,
His worshippers; he knows that in the day   705
Ye Eat thereof, your Eyes that seem so clear,
Yet are but dim, shall perfetly be then
Op'n'd and clear'd, and ye shall be as Gods,
Knowing both Good and Evil as they know.
That ye should be as Gods, since I as Man,   710
Internal Man, is but proportion meet,
I of brute human, yee of human Gods.
So ye shall die perhaps, by putting off
Human, to put on Gods, death to be wisht,
Though threat'n'd, which no worse than this can bring.   715
And what are Gods that Man may not become
As they, participating God-like food?
The Gods are first, and that advantage use
On our belief, that all from them proceeds;
I question it, for this fair Earth I see,   720
Warm'd by the Sun, producing every kind,
Them nothing: If they all things, who enclos'd
Knowledge of Good and Evil in this Tree,
That who so eats thereof, forthwith attains
Wisdom without their leave? and wherein lies   725
Th' offense, that Man should thus attain to know?
What can your knowledge hurt him, or this Tree
Impart against his will if all be his?
Or is it envy, and can envy dwell
In heav'nly breasts? these, these and many more   730
Causes import your need of this fair Fruit.
Goddess humane, reach then, and freely taste.
    He ended, and his words replete with guile
Into her heart too easy entrance won:
Fixt on the Fruit she gaz'd, which to behold   735
Might tempt alone, and in her ears the sound
Yet rung of his persuasive words, impregn'd
With Reason, to her seeming, and with Truth;
Meanwhile the hour of Noon drew on, and wak'd
An eager appetite, rais'd by the smell   740
So savory of that Fruit, which with desire,

---

liberty with us, and satiate yourselves
freely with your own will, *your eyes will
be wonderfully opened,* . . . and *like God
know all things whatsoever whether good or
evil.*" "To both More and Milton," says
M. Nicolson in quoting this passage in
PQ, VI (1927), 17, "the ethical import of
the fall is that man followed his instincts
and will, not his reason." Cf. 1177–81
below, n.
    711. *Internal Man* corresponds to the
serpent's statement (l. 600 above) that

his *inward Powers* have become human
though his form is unchanged.
    722. *If they* (produced) *all things.*
    731. *import:* indicate, prove.
    732. *humane* may mean "kind," but
Ants Oras is probably right in taking it
literally as combined with *Goddess* in a
typically Miltonic oxymoron — in *MLN*,
II (1954), 51–53.
    741–742. Eve (in Gen. iii, 6) yields
when she sees that the tree is "good for
food . . . and a tree to be desired to
make one wise."

Inclinable now grown to touch or taste,
Solicited her longing eye; yet first
Pausing a while, thus to herself she mus'd.
    Great are thy Virtues, doubtless, best of Fruits,   745
Though kept from Man, and worthy to be admir'd,
Whose taste, too long forborne, at first assay
Gave elocution to the mute, and taught
The Tongue not made for Speech to speak thy praise:
Thy praise hee also who forbids thy use,   750
Conceals not from us, naming thee the Tree
Of Knowledge, knowledge both of good and evil;
Forbids us then to taste, but his forbidding
Commends thee more, while it infers the good
By thee communicated, and our want: 755
For good unknown, sure is not had, or had
And yet unknown, is as not had at all.
In plain then, what forbids he but to know,
Forbids us good, forbids us to be wise?
Such prohibitions bind not. But if Death   760
Bind us with after-bands, what profits then
Our inward freedom? In the day we eat
Of this fair Fruit, our doom is, we shall die.
How dies the Serpent? hee hath eat'n and lives,
And knows, and speaks, and reasons, and discerns,   765
Irrational till then. For us alone
Was death invented? or to us deni'd
This intellectual food, for beasts reserv'd?
For Beasts it seems: yet that one Beast which first
Hath tasted, envies not, but brings with joy   770
The good befall'n him, Author unsuspect,
Friendly to man, far from deceit or guile.
What fear I then, rather what know to fear
Under this ignorance of Good and Evil,
Of God or Death, of Law or Penalty?   775
Here grows the Cure of all, this Fruit Divine,
Fair to the Eye, inviting to the Taste,
Of virtue to make wise: what hinders then
To reach, and feed at once both Body and Mind?
    So saying, her rash hand in evil hour   780
Forth reaching to the Fruit, she pluck'd, she eat:
Earth felt the wound, and Nature from her seat

742. *Inclinable:* easily inclined (as Eve now is).
758. *In plain:* in clear language.
771. *Author unsuspect:* authority not to be suspected.
781. *eat* was the usual spelling for the past tense. Probably the word rhymed with *seat.*
782–784. Cf. IX, 1000–1004, and X,

651–714. The thought was widespread in English poetry from John Gower's expression of it in the *Mirrour de l'Homme* (ll. 26, 810–26, 820) to Joseph Beaumont's assertion that when Eve touched the forbidden fruit,
    she reach'd away
All the Worlds Blisse whil'st she the
    Apple took:

Sighing through all her Works gave signs of woe,
That all was lost. Back to the Thicket slunk
The guilty Serpent, and well might, for *Eve*   785
Intent now wholly on her taste, naught else
Regarded, such delight till then, as seem'd,
In Fruit she never tasted, whether true
Or fancied so, through expectation high
Of knowledge, nor was God-head from her thought.   790
Greedily she ingorg'd without restraint,
And knew not eating Death: Satiate at length,
And hight'n'd as with Wine, jocund and boon,
Thus to herself she pleasingly began.
        O Sovran, virtuous, precious of all Trees   795
In Paradise, of operation blest
To Sapience, hitherto obscur'd, infam'd,
And thy fair Fruit let hang, as to no end
Created; but henceforth my early care,
Not without Song, each Morning, and due praise   800
Shall tend thee, and the fertile burden ease
Of thy full branches offer'd free to all;
Till dieted by thee I grow mature
In knowledge, as the Gods who all things know;
Though others envy what they cannot give;   805
For had the gift been theirs, it had not here
Thus grown. Experience, next to thee I owe,
Best guide; not following thee, I had remain'd
In ignorance, thou op'n'st Wisdom's way,
And giv'st access, though secret she retire.   810
And I perhaps am secret; Heav'n is high,
High and remote to see from thence distinct
Each thing on Earth, and other care perhaps
May have diverted from continual watch
Our great Forbidder, safe with all his Spies   815
About him. But to *Adam* in what sort
Shall I appear? shall I to him make known
As yet my change, and give him to partake
Full happiness with mee, or rather not,
But keep the odds of Knowledge in my power   820
Without Copartner? so to add what wants
In Female Sex, the more to draw his Love,

When low, the Earth did move, the
    Heav'ns did stay,
Beasts and Birds shiver'd, absent
    Adam shook.
            (*Psyche* VI, 254, 1–4)
792. *knew not eating death:* knew not
that she was eating death.
797. *To Sapience:* gifted with power
to confer wisdom. *infam'd:* misreputed,
made the subject of evil fame.

804. The plural, *Gods,* shows that Eve
is so muddled that she echoes Satan's
equivocal use of the word in l. 712 above,
and that she has been deceived by his
reasoning in ll. 720–29. Cf. I, 116, n.
811. *secret:* hidden, unseen. The
thought reflects Job xxii, 13–14: "How
doth God know? can he judge through
the dark cloud?"

And render me more equal, and perhaps,
A thing not undesirable, sometime
Superior: for inferior who is free?   825
This may be well: but what if God have seen,
And Death ensue? then I shall be no more,
And *Adam* wedded to another *Eve*,
Shall live with her enjoying, I extinct;
A death to think. Confirm'd then I resolve,   830
Adam shall share with me in bliss or woe:
So dear I love him, that with him all deaths
I could endure, without him live no life.
    So saying, from the Tree her step she turn'd,
But first low Reverence done, as to the power   835
That dwelt within, whose presence had infus'd
Into the plant sciential sap, deriv'd
From Nectar, drink of Gods. *Adam* the while
Waiting desirous her return, had wove
Of choicest Flow'rs a Garland to adorn   840
Her Tresses, and her rural labors crown,
As Reapers oft are wont thir Harvest Queen.
Great joy he promis'd to his thoughts, and new
Solace in her return, so long delay'd;
Yet oft his heart, divine of something ill,   845
Misgave him; hee the falt'ring measure felt;
And forth to meet her went, the way she took
That Morn when first they parted; by the Tree
Of Knowledge he must pass; there he her met,
Scarce from the Tree returning; in her hand   850
A bough of fairest fruit that downy smil'd,
New gather'd, and ambrosial smell diffus'd.
To him she hasted, in her face excuse
Came Prologue, and Apology to prompt,
Which with bland words at will she thus addrest.   855
    Hast thou not wonder'd, *Adam*, at my stay?
Thee I have misst, and thought it long, depriv'd
Thy presence, agony of love till now

825. Contrast V, 792–93.
827–833. Eve's jealousy is a common-
place which has been traced to the *Zohar*
by D. Saurat in *Milton et le matérialisme
chrétien*, p. 95; to *Yosippon* by H. Flet-
cher in *SP*, XXI (1924), 496 ff.; to
Rabbi Eliezer and other rabbinical
sources by D. C. Allen in *MLN*, LXIII
(1948), 262; to John Mercerus, Peter
Martyr, and other Christian commenta-
tors by A. Williams in *Expositor*, p. 123;
and to Milton's own inventiveness by
C. S. Lewis in *Preface*, p. 121.
832. Milton seems to have been con-
sciously varying the terms of Lydia's

devotion in the closing lines of Horace's
Ode (III, ix), familiar in translations by
Herrick and Ben Jonson.
837. *sciential:* endowed or endowing
with knowledge.
839. *wove:* woven.
845. *divine:* foreseeing. A Latinism.
Compare the verb "divine," in X, 357.
846. *the falt'ring measure:* the irregular
beat.
853. *excuse Came/Prologue, etc:* ex-
cuse came like the *Prologue* to a speech
or play to *prompt* or lead on the following
Apology, or formal defence of her con-
duct.

Not felt, nor shall be twice, for never more
Mean I to try, what rash untri'd I sought,   860
The pain of absence from thy sight. But strange
Hath been the cause, and wonderful to hear:
This Tree is not as we are told, a Tree
Of danger tasted, nor to evil unknown
Op'ning the way, but of Divine effect   865
To open Eyes, and make them Gods who taste;
And hath been tasted such: the Serpent wise,
Or not restrain'd as wee, or not obeying,
Hath eat'n of the fruit, and is become,
Not dead, as we are threat'n'd, but thenceforth   870
Endu'd with human voice and human sense,
Reasoning to admiration, and with mee
Persuasively hath so prevail'd, that I
Have also tasted, and have also found
Th' effects to correspond, opener mine Eyes,   875
Dim erst, dilated Spirits, ampler Heart,
And growing up to Godhead; which for thee
Chiefly I sought, without thee can despise.
For bliss, as thou hast part, to me is bliss,
Tedious, unshar'd with thee, and odious soon.   880
Thou therefore also taste, that equal Lot
May join us, equal Joy, as equal Love;
Lest thou not tasting, different degree
Disjoin us, and I then too late renounce
Deity for thee, when Fate will not permit.   885
    Thus *Eve* with Count'nance blithe her story told;
But in her Cheek distemper flushing glow'd.
On th' other side, *Adam*, soon as he heard
The fatal Trespass done by *Eve*, amaz'd,
Astonied stood and Blank, while horror chill   890
Ran through his veins, and all his joints relax'd;
From his slack hand the Garland wreath'd for *Eve*
Down dropp'd, and all the faded Roses shed:

860. *rash untri'd:* because I was *rash*
and it was *untried* or unfamiliar.
864. *tasted:* if tasted.
867. *tasted:* proved by tasting.
872. *to admiration:* to the point of
seeming marvellous.
890. The language suggests both Job
xvii, 8, "Upright men shall be astonied
at this," and Virgil's description of
Aeneas' horror:
    Mute and amaz'd, my hair with
        terror stood,
    Fear Shrunk my sinews, and con-
        geal'd my blood.
                    (*Aen.* III, 29–30,
                    Dryden's translation)
In his unpublished Vanderbilt thesis W.

B. Hunter quotes Charron's *Of Wisdom*
to show what fear was supposed to do to
moral resistance: Horror, said Charron,
"wastes and weakens the Soul, deprives
us of the use of our Reason, . . . adulter-
ates the whole Man, binds up his Senses,
and lays his Virtues to sleep" (Stanhope's
translation — 1697 — I, 227).
    892–895. Many remotely possible clas-
sical parallels for this passage are capped
by E. M. W. Tillyard (in *TLS*, July 1,
1949, p. 429) from Statius' *Thebaid* VII,
148–50, where the frightened Bacchus
drops his garlands, "while the grapes that
fall from his horned head are *unimpaired*
and as such could well have suggested the
opposite condition of Adam's roses."

Speechless he stood and pale, till thus at length
First to himself he inward silence broke.   895
  O fairest of Creation, last and best
Of all God's Works, Creature in whom excell'd
Whatever can to sight or thought be form'd,
Holy, divine, good, amiable, or sweet!
How art thou lost, how on a sudden lost,   900
Defac't, deflow'r'd, and now to Death devote?
Rather how hast thou yielded to transgress
The strict forbiddance, how to violate
The sacred Fruit forbidd'n! some cursed fraud
Of Enemy hath beguil'd thee, yet unknown,   905
And mee with thee hath ruin'd, for with thee
Certain my resolution is to Die;
How can I live without thee, how forgo
Thy sweet Converse and Love so dearly join'd,
To live again in these wild Woods forlorn?   910
Should God create another *Eve*, and I
Another Rib afford, yet loss of thee
Would never from my heart; no no, I feel
The Link of Nature draw me: Flesh of Flesh,
Bone of my Bone thou art, and from thy State   915
Mine never shall be parted, bliss or woe.
  So having said, as one from sad dismay
Recomforted, and after thoughts disturb'd
Submitting to what seem'd remediless,
Thus in calm mood his Words to *Eve* he turn'd.   920
  Bold deed thou hast presum'd, advent'rous *Eve*,
And peril great provok't, who thus hath dar'd
Had it been only coveting to Eye
That sacred Fruit, sacred to abstinence,
Much more to taste it under ban to touch.   925
But past who can recall, or done undo?
Not God Omnipotent, nor Fate; yet so
Perhaps thou shalt not Die, perhaps the Fact

---

901. *devote:* doomed. Cf. III, 208.
910. C. S. Lewis (*Preface,* p. 67), Brooks and Hardy (*Poems of Mr. John Milton,* pp. 273–74), and M. Giovanni (*Explicator,* Oct., 1953, xii, 1) follow Thyer in regarding the wildness of the woods as subjective and due to Adam's "mental distress." Challenging them (in *Explicator,* June, 1954, xii, 8), G. Korezt notes that vegetation in Eden is "Wild above Rule or Art" (V, 297), and that the garden is a "Wilderness of sweets" (V, 294). The connotation of *wild* may change from its earlier application to Eden, but not its basic meaning.
914. Cf. VIII, 495, n.
914–916. Most familiar among many

precedents for Adam's behavior for Milton was St. Augustine's saying that, "it is to be thought, that the first man did not yield to his wife in this transgression of God's precept, as if he thought she spoke the truth: but only compelled to it by his social love to her, . . . for the apostle says: 'Adam was not deceived: but the woman was deceived' " (*City of God* XII, xi, John Healy's translation). St. Paul's words (I Tim. ii, 14) are paraphrased in l. 999 below.
922. *hath,* which makes the thought a generalization, is the reading of the second edition; *hast,* of the first. See the discussion by B. A. Wright in *RES,* N.S. V (1954), 170.

Is not so heinous now, foretasted Fruit,
Profan'd first by the Serpent, by him first   930
Made common and unhallow'd ere our taste;
Nor yet on him found deadly, he yet lives,
Lives, as thou said'st, and gains to live as Man
Higher degree of Life, inducement strong
To us, as likely tasting to attain   935
Proportional ascent, which cannot be
But to be Gods, or Angels Demi-gods.
Nor can I think that God, Creator wise,
Though threat'ning, will in earnest so destroy
Us his prime Creatures, dignifi'd so high,   940
Set over all his Works, which in our Fall,
For us created, needs with us must fail,
Dependent made; so God shall uncreate,
Be frustrate, do, undo, and labor lose,
Not well conceiv'd of God, who though his Power   945
Creation could repeat, yet would be loath
Us to abolish, lest the Adversary
Triumph and say; Fickle their State whom God
Most Favors, who can please him long? Mee first
He ruin'd, now Mankind; whom will he next?   950
Matter of scorn, not to be given the Foe.
However I with thee have fixt my Lot,
Certain to undergo like doom; if Death
Consort with thee, Death is to mee as Life;
So forcible within my heart I feel   955
The Bond of Nature draw me to my own,
My own in thee, for what thou art is mine;
Our State cannot be sever'd, we are one,
One Flesh; to lose thee were to lose myself.
    So *Adam*, and thus *Eve* to him repli'd.   960
O glorious trial of exceeding Love,
Illustrious evidence, example high!
Ingaging me to emulate, but short
Of thy perfection, how shall I attain,
Adam, from whose dear side I boast me sprung,   965
And gladly of our Union hear thee speak,
One Heart, one Soul in both; whereof good proof
This day affords, declaring thee resolv'd,
Rather than Death or aught than Death more dread
Shall separate us, linkt in Love so dear,   970

---

947. Cf. the meaning of *Adversary* in I, 361, and VI, 282.
953. *Certain*: resolved. A Latinism, translating Aeneas' phrase, *certus eundi*, expressing his determination to leave Carthage (*Aen.* IV, 554).
960–989. Eve's application of the *trial*
of love to Adam is restrained here in comparison with her pressure upon him in Grotius' corresponding scene in *Adamus Exul* (V, i; *Cycle*, pp. 180–84) and in Andreini's *L'Adamo* (III, i; *Cycle*, pp. 254–57).

To undergo with mee one Guilt, one Crime,
If any be, of tasting this fair Fruit,
Whose virtue, for of good still good proceeds,
Direct, or by occasion hath presented
This happy trial of thy Love, which else   975
So eminently never had been known.
Were it I thought Death menac't would ensue
This my attempt, I would sustain alone
The worst, and not persuade thee, rather die
Deserted, than oblige thee with a fact   980
Pernicious to thy Peace, chiefly assur'd
Remarkably so late of thy so true,
So faithful Love unequall'd; but I feel
Far otherwise th' event, not Death, but Life
Augmented, op'n'd Eyes, new Hopes, new Joys,   985
Taste so Divine, that what of sweet before
Hath toucht my sense, flat seems to this, and harsh.
On my experience, *Adam*, freely taste,
And fear of Death deliver to the Winds.

  So saying, she embrac'd him, and for joy   990
Tenderly wept, much won that he his Love
Had so ennobl'd, as of choice to incur
Divine displeasure for her sake, or Death.
In recompense (for such compliance bad
Such recompense best merits) from the bough   995
She gave him of that fair enticing Fruit
With liberal hand: he scrupl'd not to eat
Against his better knowledge, not deceiv'd,
But fondly overcome with Female charm.
Earth trembl'd from her entrails, as again   1000
In pangs, and Nature gave a second groan,
Sky low'r'd, and muttering Thunder, some sad drops
Wept at completing of the mortal Sin
Original; while *Adam* took no thought,
Eating his fill, nor *Eve* to iterate   1005
Her former trespass fear'd, the more to soothe
Him with her lov'd society, that now
As with new Wine intoxicated both
They swim in mirth, and fancy that they feel
Divinity within them breeding wings   1010
Wherewith to scorn the Earth: but that false Fruit

---

980. *Oblige* keeps its Latin force of "involve in guilt." *fact:* deed (of evil), crime.
999. Cf. ll. 914–16 above, n.
1003. In *CD* 1, xi (C.Ed. XV, 180–82) Milton wrote that "sin originated, first, in the instigation of the devil," and that "undoubtedly all sinned in Adam." He recognized the "principle uniformly acted upon in the divine proceedings, and recognized by all nations, . . . that the penalty incurred by the violation of things sacred (and such was the tree of the knowledge of good and evil) attaches not only to the criminal himself, but to the whole of his posterity."

Far other operation first display'd,
Carnal desire inflaming, hee on *Eve*
Began to cast lascivious Eyes, she him
As wantonly repaid; in Lust they burn: 1015
Till *Adam* thus 'gan *Eve* to dalliance move.

   Eve, now I see thou are exact of taste,
And elegant, of Sapience no small part,
Since to each meaning savor we apply,
And Palate call judicious; I the praise   1020
Yield thee, so well this day thou hast purvey'd.
Much pleasure we have lost, while we abstain'd
From this delightful Fruit, nor known till now
True relish, tasting; if such pleasure be
In things to us forbidden, it might be wish'd,   1025
For this one Tree has been forbidden ten.
But come, so well refresh't, now let us play,
As meet is, after such delicious Fare;
For never did thy Beauty since the day
I saw thee first and wedded thee, adorn'd   1030
With all perfections, so inflame my sense
With ardor to enjoy thee, fairer now
Than ever, bounty of this virtuous Tree.

   So said he, and forbore not glance or toy
Of amorous intent, well understood   1035
Of *Eve*, whose Eye darted contagious Fire.
Her hand he seiz'd, and to a shady bank,
Thick overhead with verdant roof imbowr'd
He led her nothing loath; Flow'rs were the Couch,
Pansies, and Violets, and Asphodel,   1040
And Hyacinth, Earth's freshest softest lap.
There they thir fill of Love and Love's disport
Took largely, of thir mutual guilt the Seal,
The solace of thir sin, till dewy sleep
Oppress'd them, wearied with thir amorous play.   1045
Soon as the force of that fallacious Fruit,
That with exhilarating vapor bland
About thir spirits had play'd, and inmost powers
Made err, was now exhal'd, and grosser sleep
Bred of unkindly fumes, with conscious dreams   1050

1017. Milton plays on the literal and figurative meanings of *taste*, remembering Cicero's remark that "a man of discerning heart does not always lack a discerning palate" (*De finibus* II, viii).

1037–1045. The scene resembles that between Zeus and Hera in *Iliad* XIV, 292–353.

1042. Cf. the words of the lewd woman in Proverbs vii, 18: "Come, let us take our fill of love until the morning; let us solace ourselves with loves." In *Expositor*, p. 125, Williams notes that the Protestant commentator John Mercerus and the great Catholic Marin Mersenne more or less favorably discussed the "Jewish notion that the first effect of the fruit was to influence carnal appetite."

1049. The *grosser sleep* contrasts with Adam's *Aery light* sleep in V, 4.

1050. *unkindly:* unnatural.

Encumber'd, now had left them, up they rose
As from unrest, and each the other viewing,
Soon found thir Eyes how op'n'd, and thir minds
How dark'n'd; innocence, that as a veil
Had shadow'd them from knowing ill, was gone,   1055
Just confidence, and native righteousness,
And honor from about them, naked left
To guilty shame: hee cover'd, but his Robe
Uncover'd more. So rose the *Danite* strong
Herculean Samson from the Harlot-lap   1060
Of *Philistean Dalilah*, and wak'd
Shorn of his strength, They destitute and bare
Of all thir virtue: silent, and in face
Confounded long they sat, as struck'n mute,
Till *Adam*, though not less than *Eve* abasht,   1065
At length gave utterance to these words constrain'd.

O *Eve*, in evil hour thou didst give ear
To that false Worm, of whomsoever taught
To counterfeit Man's voice, true in our Fall,
False in our promis'd Rising; since our Eyes   1070
Op'n'd we find indeed, and find we know
Both Good and Evil, Good lost, and Evil got,
Bad Fruit of Knowledge, if this be to know,
Which leaves us naked thus, of Honor void,
Of Innocence, of Faith, of Purity,   1075
Our wonted Ornaments now soil'd and stain'd,
And in our Faces evident the signs
Of foul concupiscence; whence evil store;
Even shame, the last of evils; of the first
Be sure then. How shall I behold the face   1080
Henceforth of God or Angel, erst with joy
And rapture so oft beheld? those heav'nly shapes
Will dazzle now this earthly, with thir blaze
Insufferably bright. O might I here
In solitude live savage, in some glade   1085
Obscur'd, where highest Woods impenetrable
To Star or Sun-light, spread thir umbrage broad,
And brown as Evening: Cover me ye Pines,
Ye Cedars, with innumerable boughs
Hide me, where I may never see them more.   1090

1058. The thought follows Psalm cix,
29: "Let mine adversaries be clothed
with shame." Cf. *SA*, 841–42.
1059. *Samson*, whose betrayal by his
Philistine wife *Dalilah* is recorded in
Judges xvi, came of the tribe of Dan.
1062–1064. Milton had in mind the
first of the four degrees of death that he
defined in *CD* I, xii. Cf. X, 49–53, n.
1070–1076. Like most commentators,

Milton derived the name of the Tree of
Knowledge "from the event; for since
Adam tasted it, we not only know evil,
but we know good only by means of
evil" (*CD* I, x; C.Ed. XV, 115). Cf.
Areopagitica (C.Ed. IV, 311).
1086. Cf. "the shady roof/Of branch-
ing Elm Star-proof" in *Arcades*, 89.
1088. *brown:* shadowy, dark. Cf. *Im-
brown'd* in IV, 246.

But let us now, as in bad plight, devise
What best may for the present serve to hide
The Parts of each from other, that seem most
To shame obnoxious, and unseemliest seen,
Some Tree whose broad smooth Leaves together sew'd,   1095
And girded on our loins, may cover round
Those middle parts, that this new comer, Shame,
There sit not, and reproach us as unclean.
    So counsell'd hee, and both together went
Into the thickest Wood, there soon they chose   1100
The Figtree, not that kind for Fruit renown'd,
But such as at this day to *Indians* known
In *Malabar* or *Decan* spreads her Arms
Branching so broad and long, that in the ground
The bended Twigs take root, and Daughters grow   1105
About the Mother Tree, a Pillar'd shade
High overarch't, and echoing Walks between;
There oft the *Indian* Herdsman shunning heat
Shelters in cool, and tends his pasturing Herds
At Loopholes cut through thickest shade: Those Leaves   1110
They gather'd, broad as *Amazonian* Targe,
And with what skill they had, together sew'd,
To gird thir waist, vain Covering if to hide
Thir guilt and dreaded shame; O how unlike
To that first naked Glory. Such of late   1115
Columbus found th' *American* so girt
With feather'd Cincture, naked else and wild
Among the Trees on Isles and woody Shores.
    Thus fenc't, and as they thought, thir shame in part
Cover'd, but not at rest or ease of Mind,   1120
They sat them down to weep, nor only Tears
Rain'd at thir Eyes, but high Winds worse within

1091–1098. In *CD* I, xii (C.Ed. XV, 204) Milton interprets "They knew that they were naked" (Gen. iii, 7) as signifying "a conscious degradation of mind, whence arises shame," as a result of which "they sewed fig-leaves together and made themselves aprons."

1101–1106. In *Biographia Literaria* xxii, Coleridge called these lines "*creation* rather than *painting*," although he was aware of Warton's attribution of the passage to the description of the banyan or "arched Indian Figtree" in Gerard's *Herball* (1597; III, cxxix), which declares that its leaves are as broad as the shields of Amazons and that its branches touch the ground, "where they take root and grow in such sort, that those twigs become great trees; . . . by meanes whereof it cometh to passe, that of one tree is made a great wood . . . which

the Indians do use for coverture against the extreme heate of the sun. Some . . . cut loopholes or windowes in some places, to the end to receiue thereby the fresh cool air, . . . as also for the light that they may see their cattell that feed thereby. From which vault doth rebound an admirable echo. . . . The first or mother of this wood is hard to be known from the children." In *M.&S.*, pp. 31–32, Svendsen lists countless similar accounts of the Indian figtree in contemporary encyclopaedias.

1122–1131. In *CD* I, xii (C.Ed. XV, 207) Adam's punishment "consists first in the loss, or at least in the darkening to a great extent of that right reason which enabled him to discern the chief good, and in which consisted the life of the understanding." Cf. VI, 41, and XII, 98.

Began to rise, high Passions, Anger, Hate,
Mistrust, Suspicion, Discord, and shook sore
Thir inward State of Mind, calm Region once   1125
And full of Peace, now toss't and turbulent:
For Understanding rul'd not, and the Will
Heard not her lore, both in subjection now
To sensual Appetite, who from beneath
Usurping over sovran Reason claim'd   1130
Superior sway: From thus distemper'd breast,
Adam, estrang'd in look and alter'd style,
Speech intermitted thus to *Eve* renew'd.
　　Would thou hadst heark'n'd to my words, and stay'd
With me, as I besought thee, when that strange   1135
Desire of wand'ring this unhappy Morn,
I know not whence possess'd thee; we had then
Remain'd still happy, not as now, despoil'd
Of all our good, sham'd, naked, miserable.
Let none henceforth seek needless cause to approve   1140
The Faith they owe; when earnestly they seek
Such proof, conclude, they then begin to fail.
　　To whom soon mov'd with touch of blame thus *Eve*.
What words have past thy Lips, *Adam* severe,
Imput'st thou that to my default, or will   1145
Of wand'ring, as thou call'st it, which who knows
But might as ill have happ'n'd thou being by,
Or to thyself perhaps: hadst thou been there,
Or here th' attempt, thou couldst not have discern'd
Fraud in the Serpent, speaking as he spake;   1150
No ground of enmity between us known,
Why hee should mean me ill, or seek to harm.
Was I to have never parted from thy side?
As good have grown there still a lifeless Rib.
Being as I am, why didst not thou the Head   1155
Command me absolutely not to go,
Going into such danger as thou said'st?
Too facile then thou didst not much gainsay,
Nay, didst permit, approve, and fair dismiss.
Hadst thou been firm and fixt in thy dissent,   1160
Neither had I transgress'd, nor thou with mee.
　　To whom then first incenst *Adam* repli'd.
Is this the Love, is this the recompense
Of mine to thee, ingrateful *Eve*, express't
Immutable when thou wert lost, not I,   1165

1132. *alter'd style:* changed manner (of speech).
1141. *owe:* possess. Adam recalls Eve's words in ll. 335–36 above.
1144. The phrase is a Homeric warning to rash speakers (*Il.* XIV, 83).

1155. In a different tone Eve has called Adam her *Head* in IV, 443.
1164. In ll. 956–67 above, Eve has praised Adam for his love *express't/Immutable*, i.e. proved unchangeable by his action.

Who might have liv'd and joy'd immortal bliss,
Yet willingly chose rather Death with thee:
And am I now upbraided, as the cause
Of thy transgressing? not enough severe,
It seems, in thy restraint: what could I more?   1170
I warn'd thee, I admonish'd thee, foretold
The danger, and the lurking Enemy
That lay in wait; beyond this had been force,
And force upon free Will hath here no place.
But confidence then bore thee on, secure   1175
Either to meet no danger, or to find
Matter of glorious trial; and perhaps
I also err'd in overmuch admiring
What seem'd in thee so perfet, that I thought
No evil durst attempt thee, but I rue   1180
That error now, which is become my crime,
And thou th' accuser. Thus it shall befall
Him who to worth in Woman overtrusting
Lets her Will rule; restraint she will not brook,
And left to herself, if evil thence ensue,   1185
Shee first his weak indulgence will accuse.
　 Thus they in mutual accusation spent
The fruitless hours, but neither self-condemning,
And of thir vain contest appear'd no end.

The End of the Ninth Book.

BOOK X

THE ARGUMENT

Man's *transgression known, the Guardian Angels forsake Paradise, and return up to Heaven to approve thir vigilance, and are approv'd, God declaring that the entrance of* Satan *could not be by them prevented. He sends his Son to judge the Transgressors, who descends and gives Sentence accordingly; then in pity clothes them both, and reascends.* Sin *and* Death *sitting till then at the Gates of Hell, by wondrous sympathy feeling the success of* Satan *in this new World, and the sin by Man there committed, resolve to sit no longer confin'd in Hell, but to follow* Satan *thir Sire up to the place of*

1177–1181. M. Nicolson is surely right in recognizing more than a chance resemblance between Milton's contrast of will with reason and Henry More's stress in *Conjectura Cabbalistica* upon "spirit, reason, and man, first as *creative*, and then as *regulative* principles," and upon Eve as representing the instincts and the Will. (Cf. ll. 703–709 above, n.) More's value of the Will, in spite of his treatment of the temptation as an exaggeration of

its influence upon a feminized Adam, leads toward the psychological interpretation of the Fall by P. Turner in "Woman and the Fall of Man" in *English Studies,* XXIX (1948), 1–18, and M. Bertschlinger's "Man's Part in the Fall of Woman" in *English Studies,* XXXI (1950), 49–64.

1183. *Women* is the reading of all the early editions, but Bentley's emendation to *Woman* seems inevitable.

Man: *To make the way easier from Hell to this World to and fro, they pave a broad Highway or Bridge over* Chaos, *according to the Track that* Satan *first made; then preparing for Earth, they meet him proud of his success returning to Hell; thir mutual gratulation.* Satan *arrives at* Pandemonium, *in full assembly relates with boasting his success against Man; instead of applause is entertained with a general hiss by all his audience, transform'd with himself also suddenly into Serpents, according to his doom giv'n in Paradise; then deluded with a show of the forbidden Tree springing up before them, they greedily reaching to take of the Fruit, chew dust and bitter ashes. The proceedings of* Sin *and* Death; *God foretells the final Victory of his Son over them, and the renewing of all things; but for the present commands his Angels to make several alterations in the Heavens and Elements.* Adam *more and more perceiving his fall'n condition heavily bewails, rejects the condolement of* Eve; *she persists and at length appeases him: then to evade the Curse likely to fall on thir Offspring, proposes to* Adam *violent ways, which he approves not, but conceiving better hope, puts her in mind of the late Promise made them, that her Seed should be reveng'd on the Serpent, and exhorts her with him to seek Peace of the offended Deity, by repentance and supplication.*

Meanwhile the heinous and despiteful act
Of *Satan* done in Paradise, and how
Hee in the Serpent had perverted *Eve,*
Her Husband shee, to taste the fatal fruit,
Was known in Heav'n; for what can scape the Eye   5
Of God All-seeing, or deceive his Heart
Omniscient, who in all things wise and just,
Hinder'd not *Satan* to attempt the mind
Of Man, with strength entire, and free will arm'd.
Complete to have discover'd and repulst   10
Whatever wiles of Foe or seeming Friend.
For still they knew, and ought to have still remember'd
The high Injunction not to taste that Fruit,
Whoever tempted; which they not obeying,
Incurr'd, what could they less, the penalty,   15
And manifold in sin, deserv'd to fall.
Up into Heav'n from Paradise in haste
Th' Angelic Guards ascended, mute and sad
For Man, for of his state by this they knew,
Much wond'ring how the subtle Fiend had stol'n   20

7. The lines distil the thought in the chapter "Of the Divine Decrees" in *CD* I, iii, where Milton says that God "suffered both men and angels to stand or fall at their own uncontrolled choice, . . . not necessitating the evil consequences that ensued, but leaving them contingent" (C.Ed. XIV, 81).
9–10. *Complete to:* fully endowed with power to, etc. *Complete* modifies *mind* in l. 8. Cf. IX, 292, n., and 351–56.
16. Though Milton thought of God's prohibition of the Tree of Knowledge as a just though inscrutable "exercise of jurisdiction" (*CD* I, x; C.Ed. XV, 115),

he also regarded its violation as comprehending "at once distrust of the divine veracity, . . . unbelief; ingratitude; disobedience; gluttony; in the man excessive uxoriousness, in the woman a want of proper regard for her husband, in both an insensibility to the welfare of their offspring; . . . parricide, theft, invasion of the rights of others, sacrilege, deceit, presumption in aspiring to divine attributes, fraud, . . . pride and arrogance" (*CD* I, xi; C.Ed. XV, 180–82).
18. The *Guards* are Gabriel, Ithuriel, Zephon, and their troop in IV, 561–1015.
19. *by this:* by this time.

Entrance unseen. Soon as th' unwelcome news
From Earth arriv'd at Heaven Gate, displeas'd
All were who heard, dim sadness did not spare
That time Celestial visages, yet mixt
With pity, violated not thir bliss.   25
About the new-arriv'd, in multitudes
Th' ethereal People ran, to hear and know
How all befell: they towards the Throne Supreme
Accountable made haste to make appear
With righteous plea, thir utmost vigilance,   30
And easily approv'd; when the most High
Eternal Father from his secret Cloud,
Amidst in Thunder utter'd thus his voice.

 Assembl'd Angels, and ye Powers return'd
From unsuccessful charge, be not dismay'd,   35
Nor troubl'd at these tidings from the Earth,
Which your sincerest care could not prevent,
Foretold so lately what would come to pass,
When first this Tempter cross'd the Gulf from Hell.
I told ye then he should prevail and speed   40
On his bad Errand, Man should be seduc't
And flatter'd out of all, believing lies
Against his Maker; no Decree of mine
Concurring to necessitate his Fall,
Or touch with lightest moment of impulse   45
His free Will, to her own inclining left
In even scale. But fall'n he is, and now
What rests, but that the mortal Sentence pass
On his transgression, Death denounc't that day,
Which he presumes already vain and void,   50
Because not yet inflicted, as he fear'd,
But some immediate stroke; but soon shall find
Forbearance no acquittance ere day end.
Justice shall not return as bounty scorn'd.
But whom send I to judge them? whom but thee   55
Vicegerent Son, to thee I have transferr'd
All Judgment, whether in Heav'n, or Earth, or Hell.

---

31. *approv'd:* vindicated.
32–33. The conception is colored by the chapter on the throne of God in the Apocalypse — "out of the throne proceeded lightnings and thunderings and voices" (Rev. iv, 5) — and by other biblical passages that are also reflected in II, 263–67.
40. *I told ye then:* cf. III, 92–97. *speed:* succeed.
45. *moment:* weight. Cf. the use in VI, 239.
48. *rests:* remains to be done.
52. "This death," says *CD* I, xii (C.Ed. XV, 206–208), "consists first, in the loss, or at least in the obscuration to a great extent of that right reason which enabled man to discern the chief good. . . . It consists, secondly, in . . . deprivation of righteousness and liberty to do good. . . . Lastly, sin is its own punishment, and produces . . . the death of the spiritual life." Cf. IX, 1053–64.
53. *acquittance:* acquittal, exoneration. Cf. Claudius' words to Laertes: "Now must your conscience my acquittance seal" (*Hamlet* IV, vii, 1).
56. "The Son," says Milton in *CD* I, v (C.Ed. XIV, 250), "was entitled to the

Easy it may be seen that I intend
Mercy colleague with Justice, sending thee
Man's Friend, his Mediator, his design'd   60
Both Ransom and Redeemer voluntary,
And destin'd Man himself to judge Man fall'n.
    So spake the Father, and unfolding bright
Toward the right hand his Glory, on the Son
Blaz'd forth unclouded Deity; he full   65
Resplendent all his Father manifest
Express'd, and thus divinely answer'd mild.
    Father Eternal, thine is to decree,
Mine both in Heav'n and Earth to do thy will
Supreme, that thou in mee thy Son belov'd   70
May'st ever rest well pleas'd. I go to judge
On Earth these thy transgressors, but thou know'st,
Whoever judg'd, the worst on mee must light,
When time shall be, for so I undertook
Before thee; and not repenting, this obtain   75
Of right, that I may mitigate thir doom
On me deriv'd, yet I shall temper so
Justice with Mercy, as may illustrate most
Them fully satisfied, and thee appease.
Attendance none shall need, nor Train, where none   80
Are to behold the Judgment, but the judg'd,
Those two; the third best absent is condemn'd,
Convict by flight, and Rebel to all Law:
Conviction to the Serpent none belongs.
    Thus saying, from his radiant Seat he rose   85
Of high collateral glory: him Thrones and Powers,
Princedoms, and Dominations ministrant
Accompanied to Heaven Gate, from whence
Eden and all the Coast in prospect lay.
Down he descended straight; the speed of Gods   90
Time counts not, though with swiftest minutes wing'd.

---

name of God . . . in the capacity of a judge"; and he had no doubt of the Son's "future judicial advent" (C.Ed. XIV, 330).

58. *may* is the reading of the first edition; *might*, of the second.

59. Cf. III, 132 and 407, and *Nativity*, 141–46.

60. "*The mediatorial office of* Christ is that whereby . . . *he voluntarily performed, and continues to perform, on behalf of man, whatever is requisite for obtaining reconciliation with God, and eternal salvation*" (*CD* I, xv; C.Ed. XV, 284).

64. Cf. the Son's participation in God's glory in III, 139, and VI, 679–83. Behind these passages is Hebrews i, 3: "Who being the brightness of his glory, and the express image of his person, . . .

sat down on the right hand of the Majesty on high."

74. Cf. the similar allusion in III, 284, to Galatians iv, 4: "But when the fullness of the time was come, God sent forth his Son, made of a woman." For the Son's undertaking, see III, 227–65.

77. *deriv'd* keeps its Latin meaning of "diverted."

78. *illustrate:* shed light upon, glorify. Cf. V, 739.

83–84. *Convict:* convicted. *Conviction:* formal proof of guilt.

89. *Coast:* surrounding region. Cf. II, 633, and VI, 529.

90. *Gods* is used here as it is of the heavenly beings in II, 352. Cf. Raphael's *speed almost spiritual* in VIII, 110.

Now was the Sun in Western cadence low
From Noon, and gentle Airs due at thir hour
To fan the Earth now wak'd, and usher in
The Ev'ning cool, when he from wrath more cool   95
Came the mild Judge and Intercessor both
To sentence Man: the voice of God they heard
Now walking in the Garden, by soft winds
Brought to thir Ears, while day declin'd, they heard,
And from his presence hid themselves among   100
The thickest Trees, both Man and Wife, till God
Approaching, thus to *Adam* call'd aloud.
    Where art thou *Adam*, wont with joy to meet
My coming seen far off? I miss thee here,
Not pleas'd, thus entertain'd with solitude,   105
Where obvious duty erewhile appear'd unsought:
Or come I less conspicuous, or what change
Absents thee, or what chance detains? Come forth.
He came, and with him *Eve*, more loath, though first
To offend, discount'nanc't both, and discompos'd;   110
Love was not in thir looks, either to God
Or to each other, but apparent guilt,
And shame, and perturbation, and despair,
Anger, and obstinacy, and hate, and guile.
Whence *Adam* falt'ring long, thus answer'd brief.   115
    I heard thee in the Garden, and of thy voice
Afraid, being naked, hid myself. To whom
The gracious Judge without revile repli'd.
    My voice thou oft hast heard, and hast not fear'd,
But still rejoic't, how is it now become   120
So dreadful to thee? that thou art naked, who
Hath told thee? hast thou eaten of the Tree
Whereof I gave thee charge thou shouldst not eat?
    To whom thus *Adam* sore beset repli'd.
O Heav'n! in evil strait this day I stand   125
Before my Judge, either to undergo
Myself the total Crime, or to accuse
My other self, the partner of my life;
Whose failing, while her Faith to me remains,
I should conceal, and not expose to blame   130
By my complaint; but strict necessity

92. *cadence* keeps its Latin meaning of "falling" or "descent."
95–97. Cf. Genesis iii, 8: "And they heard the voice of the Lord God walking in the garden in the cool of the day: and Adam and his wife hid themselves from the presence of the Lord God amongst the trees of the garden." The following thirteen verses are closely followed in ll. 103–223.

101. The Son is called *God* as the *Vicegerent God* of l. 56 above.
106. *obvious* keeps its Latin meaning of "confronting in the way," i.e. to meet and welcome a person.
112. *apparent:* evident, conspicuous.
118. *revile:* revilement, reproach.
128. So God calls Eve Adam's *other self* in VIII, 450.

Subdues me, and calamitous constraint,
Lest on my head both sin and punishment,
However insupportable, be all
Devolv'd; though should I hold my peace, yet thou   135
Wouldst easily detect what I conceal.
This Woman whom thou mad'st to be my help,
And gav'st me as thy perfet gift, so good,
So fit, so acceptable, so Divine,
That from her hand I could suspect no ill,   140
And what she did, whatever in itself,
Her doing seem'd to justify the deed;
Shee gave me of the Tree, and I did eat.
   To whom the sovran Presence thus repli'd.
Was shee thy God, that her thou didst obey   145
Before his voice, or was shee made thy guide,
Superior, or but equal, that to her
Thou didst resign thy Manhood, and the Place
Wherein God set thee above her made of thee,
And for thee, whose perfection far excell'd   150
Hers in all real dignity: Adorn'd
She was indeed, and lovely to attract
Thy Love, not thy Subjection, and her Gifts
Were such as under Government well seem'd,
Unseemly to bear rule, which was thy part   155
And person, hadst thou known thyself aright.
   So having said, he thus to *Eve* in few:
Say Woman, what is this which thou hast done?
   To whom sad *Eve* with shame nigh overwhelm'd,
Confessing soon, yet not before her Judge   160
Bold or loquacious, thus abasht repli'd.
   The Serpent me beguil'd and I did eat.
   Which when the Lord God heard, without delay
To Judgment he proceeded on th' accus'd
Serpent though brute, unable to transfer   165
The Guilt on him who made him instrument
Of mischief, and polluted from the end
Of his Creation; justly then accurst,
As vitiated in Nature: more to know
Concern'd not Man (since he no further knew)   170

144–156. The rebuke parallels Ra-
phael's warning in VIII, 561–85, as the
preceding lines match Adam's preceding
speech in ll. 540–59.
   156. *person* has its Latin meaning of
"character in a drama" and continues the
metaphor of *part* (role) in l. 155.
   166–167. So in IX, 530, Satan is said
to make a tool of the serpent, applying it
to a use which was not the *end* (object)
of its creation.

168–181. The mystery is explained in
CD I, xiv (C.Ed. XV, 252), where Milton
says that God, "in pronouncing the pun-
ishment of the serpent, previously to pass-
ing sentence on man, promised that he
would raise up from the seed of the
woman one who would bruise the ser-
pent's head, Gen. iii, 15, and thus an-
ticipated the condemnation of mankind
by a gratuitous redemption." See the
Introduction 51.

Nor alter'd his offense; yet God at last
To Satan first in sin his doom appli'd,
Though in mysterious terms, judg'd as then best:
And on the Serpent thus his curse let fall.

Because thou hast done this, thou art accurst   175
Above all Cattle, each Beast of the Field;
Upon thy Belly groveling thou shalt go,
And dust shalt eat all the days of thy Life.
Between Thee and the Woman I will put
Enmity, and between thine and her Seed;   180
Her Seed shall bruise thy head, thou bruise his heel.

So Spake this Oracle, then verifi'd
When *Jesus* son of *Mary* second *Eve*,
Saw Satan fall like Lightning down from Heav'n,
Prince of the Air; then rising from his Grave   185
Spoil'd Principalities and Powers, triumpht
In open show, and with ascension bright
Captivity led captive through the Air,
The Realm itself of Satan long usurpt,
Whom he shall tread at last under our feet;   190
Ev'n hee who now foretold his fatal bruise,
And to the Woman thus his Sentence turn'd.

Thy sorrow I will greatly multiply
By thy Conception; Children thou shalt bring
In sorrow forth, and to thy Husband's will   195
Thine shall submit, hee over thee shall rule.

On *Adam* last thus judgment he pronounc'd.
Because thou hast heark'n'd to the voice of thy Wife,
And eaten of the Tree concerning which
I charg'd thee, saying: Thou shalt not eat thereof,   200
Curs'd is the ground for thy sake, thou in sorrow
Shalt eat thereof all the days of thy Life;
Thorns also and Thistles it shall bring thee forth
Unbid, and thou shalt eat th' Herb of the Field,
In the sweat of thy Face shalt thou eat Bread,   205
Till thou return unto the ground, for thou
Out of the ground wast taken, know thy Birth,

183–184. Cf. *Mary second Eve* in V, 386–87. In making the prophecy refer to Mary and Jesus — as Williams notes (*Expositor*, p. 128) — Milton took the Catholic position as distinguished from Calvin's view that the enmity was to be "between the righteous, the seed of the woman, and the reprobate, the seed of Satan." In Christ's vision of Satan "as lightning," falling "from heaven" (Luke x, 18), Milton saw the fulfilment of the prophecy that the seed of the woman should "bruise the serpent's head."
185. Cf. I, 516, where the air is the

realm of the demons   In Ephesians ii, 2, Satan is called the "prince of the power of the air."
186. Psalm lxviii, 18 — "Thou hast ascended up on high, thou hast led captivity captive" — blends with St. Paul's prophecy of Christ's resurrection and triumph over "principalities and powers" (Col. ii, 15).
193–196. In *CD* I, x (C.Ed. XV, 121) Milton interprets Genesis iii, 16–19 as meaning that, "The power of the husband was even increased after the fall."

For dust thou art, and shalt to dust return.
So judg'd he Man, both Judge and Savior sent,
And th' instant stroke of Death denounc't that day   210
Remov'd far off; then pitying how they stood
Before him naked to the air, that now
Must suffer change, disdain'd not to begin
Thenceforth the form of servant to assume,
As when he wash'd his servants' feet, so now   215
As Father of his Family he clad
Thir nakedness with Skins of Beasts, or slain,
Or as the Snake with youthful Coat repaid;
And thought not much to clothe his Enemies:
Nor hee thir outward only with the Skins   220
Of Beasts, but inward nakedness, much more
Opprobrious, with his Robe of righteousness,
Arraying cover'd from his Father's sight.
To him with swift ascent he up return'd,
Into his blissful bosom reassum'd   225
In glory as of old, to him appeas'd
All, though all-knowing, what had past with Man
Recounted, mixing intercession sweet.
Meanwhile ere thus was sinn'd and judg'd on Earth,
Within the Gates of Hell sat Sin and Death,   230
In counterview within the Gates, that now
Stood open wide, belching outrageous flame
Far into *Chaos*, since the Fiend pass'd through,
Sin opening, who thus now to Death began.
O Son, why sit we here each other viewing   235
Idly, while Satan our great Author thrives
In other Worlds, and happier Seat provides
For us his offspring dear? It cannot be
But that success attends him; if mishap,
Ere this he had return'd, with fury driv'n   240
By his Avengers, since no place like this
Can fit his punishment, or their revenge.
Methinks I feel new strength within me rise,
Wings growing, and Dominion giv'n me large
Beyond this Deep; whatever draws me on,   245
Or sympathy, or some connatural force

216–217. Genesis iii, 21, says simply that "the Lord God made coats of skins and clothed them," but Milton thought also of Christ's taking "upon him the form of a servant" (Phil. ii, 7) and washing the feet of the disciples (John xiii, 5).
217–218. Milton wonders whether beasts were slain for their pelts or survived the loss like moulting snakes, *repaid* (recompensed) by new skins.
219. *thought not much:* did not grudge.

So Spenser wonders at the mercy which sends the angels "To serve to wicked men, to serve his [God's] wicked foe" (*F.Q.* II, viii, 1).
222. *Robe of righteousness* is a phrase from Isaiah lxi, 10. Cf. IX, 1058.
230–231. So Sin and Death sit opposite each other (*in counterview*) in II, 649.
246. Here and in the Argument to Book X *sympathy* has the quasi-scientific meaning of attraction at great distances.

Powerful at greatest distance to unite
With secret amity things of like kind
By secretest conveyance. Thou my Shade
Inseparable must with mee along:　　　　　　　　　250
For Death from Sin no power can separate.
But lest the difficulty of passing back
Stay his return perhaps over this Gulf
Impassable, Impervious, let us try
Advent'rous work, yet to thy power and mine　　　255
Not unagreeable, to found a path
Over this Main from Hell to that new World
Where Satan now prevails, a Monument
Of merit high to all th' infernal Host,
Easing thir passage hence, for intercourse,　　　260
Or transmigration, as thir lot shall lead.
Nor can I miss the way, so strongly drawn
By this new felt attraction and instinct.
　　Whom thus the meagre Shadow answer'd soon,
Go whither Fate and inclination strong　　　　265
Leads thee, I shall not lag behind, nor err
The way, thou leading, such a scent I draw
Of carnage, prey innumerable, and taste
The savor of Death from all things there that live:
Nor shall I to the work thou enterprisest　　　270
Be wanting, but afford thee equal aid.
　　So saying, with delight he snuff'd the smell
Of mortal change on Earth. As when a flock
Of ravenous Fowl, though many a League remote,
Against the day of Battle, to a Field,　　　　275
Where Armies lie encampt, come flying, lur'd
With scent of living Carcasses design'd
For death, the following day, in bloody fight.
So scented the grim Feature, and upturn'd
His Nostril wide into the murky Air,　　　　　280
Sagacious of his Quarry from so far.
Then Both from out Hell Gates into the waste

249–263. The allegory which Sin now makes almost explicit bears comparison with Samuel Pordage's forced allegory in *Mundorum Explicatio (Celestial Cycle,* p. 431), where Satan, returning in triumph from earth to hell, dispatches Beelzebub with his "discords and plagues," Abaddon with "sicknesse and death," and the other major devils with the crimes and evils appropriate to them, to take possession of the world.
256. *found* has its literal Latin meaning of "lay a foundation."
257. *Main:* the sea of Chaos over which Satan makes his *Voyage* in II, 919.
260–261. *intercourse:* two-way traffic.

transmigration: emigration, not to return.
274. The belief in the power of birds of ravin to foresee impending battles goes back to the verse about the eagle in Job, xxxix, 30: "And where the slain are, there is she." It is quoted with reference to vultures by Abraham Cowley in his notes to his translation of Isaiah xxxiv. Cf. III, 431, n.
279. *Feature* is used in its Italian sense of "creature."
282–305. Anent W. Empson's objection (in *Pastoral,* p. 154) Tillyard first suggests an interesting parallel between this passage and the account in Philostratus' *Life of Apollonius* (I, 25) of the

Wide Anarchy of *Chaos* damp and dark
Flew diverse, and with Power (thir Power was great)
Hovering upon the Waters; what they met   285
Solid or slimy, as in raging Sea
Tost up and down, together crowded drove
From each side shoaling towards the mouth of Hell.
As when two Polar Winds blowing adverse
Upon the *Cronian* Sea, together drive   290
Mountains of Ice, that stop th' imagin'd way
Beyond *Petsora* Eastward, to the rich
Cathaian Coast. The aggregated Soil
Death with his Mace petrific, cold and dry,
As with a Trident smote, and fix't as firm   295
As *Delos* floating once; the rest his look
Bound with *Gorgonian* rigor not to move,
And with *Asphaltic* slime; broad as the Gate,
Deep to the Roots of Hell the gather'd beach
They fasten'd, and the Mole immense wrought on   300
Over the foaming deep high Archt, a Bridge
Of length prodigious joining to the Wall
Immoveable of this now fenceless World
Forfeit to Death; from hence a passage broad,
Smooth, easy, inoffensive down to Hell.   305
So, if great things to small may be compar'd,
Xerxes, the Liberty of *Greece* to yoke,
From *Susa* his *Memnonian* Palace high

construction of a tunnel under the Euphrates, and then notes that in their bridge-building Sin and Death "parody God's creative act in the seventh book." Sin and Death "hover over the waters of chaos (birds of prey, not the dove); . . . and instead of warmth they infuse cold and petrifaction" (*SP*, XXXVIII — 1941 — 267-70).

288. *shoaling:* solidifying into a shoal.
290. The *Cronian Sea:* the Arctic Ocean.
291. *th' imagin'd way:* the northeast passage for which Hudson vainly sought in 1608.
292. "The river [*Petsora*] Pechora," Milton wrote in *Moscovia*, "holding his course through *Siberia*, how far the *Russians* thereabouts know not, runneth into the Sea at 72 mouths, full of Ice . . ." (C.Ed. X, 332).
293. Milton distinguished Cathay from China proper and thought of it as a separate empire, the destined seat of Chingiz Khan (XI, 386-88), in northeastern Asia, as the Mercator maps represented it.
296. Out of the warring elements in Chaos — "hot, cold, moist, and dry" (II, 898) — *Death* separates the *cold* and

dry atoms for the masonry of his bridge and petrifies them with a touch of his *Mace*, as Neptune was fabled to have moulded the island of *Delos* out of the sea with his *Trident*. Later Zeus was supposed to have anchored the island in the centre of the Cyclades.
297. Like the Gorgon Medusa in the myth of Perseus, Death can turn everything at which he looks into stone; and for mortar he uses asphalt, which the devils have previously turned to a different purpose (I, 729).
302. The *Wall* is the boundary of the created universe, which — in spite of it — is *fenceless* (without defense) against Death.
305. *inoffensive* has its Latin force of "free of stumbling-blocks."
307-311. In the dictionaries of Calepine and Charles Stephanus, Milton's readers could find summaries of several ancient accounts of Xerxes scourging the waves of the Hellespont when they broke his bridge of ships between the European and Asiatic shores of the Dardenelles.
308. *Susa* (the biblical Shushan, winter capital of the Persian kings) was founded by Tithonus, the mythical lover of Aurora, by whom he had a son Memnon.

Came to the Sea, and over *Hellespont*
Bridging his way, *Europe* with *Asia* join'd,   310
And scourg'd with many a stroke th' indignant waves.
Now had they brought the work by wondrous Art
Pontifical, a ridge of pendent Rock
Over the vext Abyss, following the track
Of *Satan*, to the selfsame place where hee   315
First lighted from his Wing, and landed safe
From out of *Chaos* to the outside bare
Of this round World: with Pins of Adamant
And Chains they made all fast, too fast they made
And durable; and now in little space   320
The confines met of Empyrean Heav'n
And of this World, and on the left hand Hell
With long reach interpos'd; three sev'ral ways
In sight, to each of these three places led.
And now thir way to Earth they had descri'd,   325
To Paradise first tending, when behold
Satan in likeness of an Angel bright
Betwixt the *Centaur* and the *Scorpion* steering
His *Zenith*, while the Sun in *Aries* rose:
Disguis'd he came, but those his Children dear   330
Thir Parent soon discern'd, though in disguise.
Hee, after *Eve* seduc't, unminded slunk
Into the Wood fast by, and changing shape
To observe the sequel, saw his guileful act
By *Eve*, though all unweeting, seconded   335
Upon her Husband, saw thir shame that sought
Vain covertures; but when he saw descend
The Son of God to judge them, terrifi'd
Hee fled, not hoping to escape, but shun
The present, fearing guilty what his wrath   340
Might suddenly inflict; that past, return'd
By Night, and list'ning where the hapless Pair
Sat in thir sad discourse and various plaint,
Thence gather'd his own doom; which understood

313. The Latin *pontifex* (from which *Pontifical* comes) means "bridge-builder."
314. *vext:* harried by storms, as it is described in II, 894–97, and VII, 211–15.
316. Satan lights on the *opacous Globe* in III, 418.
320–324. The meeting *confines* are the bottom end of the stair which unites the empyrean heaven to the universe in III, 510, the passage thence inside the universe, down to the earth, and the causeway which Sin and Death have just built. In paintings of the Last Judgment as described in Matthew xxv, 33, the side of hell was traditionally the left.
328–329. As in IX, 58–69, Satan puts

the earth between himself and Uriel, who is in the sun, which is in the zodiacal sign of the Ram (*Aries*) and opposite that of the *Scorpion*. D. C. Allen notes — *MLN*, LXVIII (1953), 361 — an allegorical overtone in the astrological doctrine that men who are strongly influenced by Scorpio and the *Centaur* are likely to be very deceitful.
332. *after Eve seduc't:* after the seduction of Eve. Cf. I, 573.
335. *unweeting:* unaware, unsuspecting.
337. The *covertures* are the garments made of leaves in IX, 1110–14.

Not instant, but of future time, with joy   345
And tidings fraught, to Hell he now return'd,
And at the brink of *Chaos*, near the foot
Of this new wondrous Pontifice, unhop't
Met who to meet him came, his Offspring dear.
Great joy was at thir meeting, and at sight   350
Of that stupendous Bridge his joy increas'd.
Long hee admiring stood, till Sin, his fair
Enchanting Daughter, thus the silence broke.
　O Parent, these are thy magnific deeds,
Thy Trophies, which thou view'st as not thine own,   355
Thou art thir Author and prime Architect:
For I no sooner in my Heart divin'd,
My Heart, which by a secret harmony
Still moves with thine, join'd in connexion sweet,
That thou on Earth hadst prosper'd, which thy looks   360
Now also evidence, but straight I felt
Though distant from thee Worlds between, yet felt
That I must after thee with this thy Son;
Such fatal consequence unites us three:
Hell could no longer hold us in her bounds,   365
Nor this unvoyageable Gulf obscure
Detain from following thy illustrious track.
Thou hast achiev'd our liberty, confin'd
Within Hell Gates till now, thou us impow'r'd
To fortify thus far, and overlay   370
With this portentous Bridge the dark Abyss.
Thine now is all this World, thy virtue hath won
What thy hands builded not, thy Wisdom gain'd
With odds what War hath lost, and fully aveng'd
Our foil in Heav'n; here thou shalt Monarch reign,   375
There didst not; there let him still Victor sway,
As Battle hath adjudg'd, from this new World
Retiring, by his own doom alienated,
And henceforth Monarchy with thee divide
Of all things, parted by th' Empyreal bounds,   380
His Quadrature, from thy Orbicular World,
Or try thee now more dang'rous to his Throne.
　Whom thus the Prince of Darkness answer'd glad.
Fair Daughter, and thou Son and Grandchild both,
High proof ye now have giv'n to be the Race   385
Of *Satan* (for I glory in the name,

345–346. *joy/And tidings* mean "joyful
tidings."
　347. *foot:* bottom of the slope of the
bridge (*Pontifice*) leading to the universe
from hell. Cf. l. 313 above, n.
　358. The *secret harmony* is the sym-
pathy of l. 246 above.
　364. *consequence:* dependence.

370. *fortify:* construct (what amounts
to a military road).
　381. Heaven is "foursquare," as it is
in Revelation xxi, 16. Cf. II, 771, n.
　386. In *CD* I, ix (C.Ed. XV, 111)
Milton stresses the fact that the name
Satan means the Adversary in Scripture.
Cf. I, 82.

Antagonist of Heav'n's Almighty King)
Amply have merited of me, of all
Th' Infernal Empire, that so near Heav'n's door
Triumphal with triumphal act have met,   390
Mine with this glorious Work, and made one Realm
Hell and this World, one Realm, one Continent
Of easy thorough-fare. Therefore while I
Descend through Darkness, on your Road with ease
To my associate Powers, them to acquaint   395
With these successes, and with them rejoice,
You two this way, among those numerous Orbs
All yours, right down to Paradise descend;
There dwell and Reign in bliss, thence on the Earth
Dominion exercise and in the Air,   400
Chiefly on Man, sole Lord of all declar'd,
Him first make sure your thrall, and lastly kill.
My Substitutes I send ye, and Create
Plenipotent on Earth, of matchless might
Issuing from mee: on your joint vigor now   405
My hold of this new Kingdom all depends,
Through Sin to Death expos'd by my exploit.
If your joint power prevail, th' affairs of Hell
No detriment need fear, go and be strong.
     So saying he dismiss'd them, they with speed   410
Thir course through thickest Constellations held
Spreading thir bane; the blasted Stars lookt wan,
And Planets, Planet-strook, real Eclipse
Then suffer'd. Th' other way *Satan* went down
The Causey to Hell Gate; on either side   415
Disparted *Chaos* over-built exclaim'd,
And with rebounding surge the bars assail'd,
That scorn'd his indignation: through the Gate,
Wide open and unguarded, *Satan* pass'd,
And all about found desolate; for those   420
Appointed to sit there, had left thir charge,
Flown to the upper World; the rest were all
Far to th'inland retir'd, about the walls
Of *Pandæmonium*, City and proud seat
Of *Lucifer*, so by allusion call'd,   425
Of that bright Star to *Satan* paragon'd.

390. Satan's triumph in Eden is matched by the triumphal work of Sin and Death, their bridge, the *Causey* of l. 415 below.
397. So Satan drops to earth "amongst innumerable Stars" in III, 565, and Raphael descends "between worlds and worlds" in V, 268.
407–409. Milton thought of a formula used in giving Roman consuls supreme power in crises to protect Rome against all *detriment* (*detrimentum*) or injury.
413. Popular astrology regarded people who suffered from unfavorable influences from the stars as "planet-struck." At Christmas time says Marcellus, "No planets strike" (*Hamlet* I, i, 162). Milton regards the stars themselves as being blasted by Sin and Death.
426. The *Star* is Lucifer or Venus as the light-bringing morning star. Cf. VII, 132, n.

There kept thir Watch the Legions, while the Grand
In Council sat, solicitous what chance
Might intercept thir Emperor sent, so hee
Departing gave command, and they observ'd.   430
As when the *Tartar* from his *Russian* Foe
By *Astracan* over the Snowy Plains
Retires, or *Bactrian* Sophi from the horns
Of *Turkish* Crescent, leaves all waste beyond
The Realm of *Aladule*, in his retreat   435
To *Tauris* or *Casbeen:* So these the late
Heav'n-banisht Host, left desert utmost Hell
Many a dark League, reduc't in careful Watch
Round thir Metropolis, and now expecting
Each hour their great adventurer from the search   440
Of Foreign Worlds: he through the midst unmark't,
In show Plebeian Angel militant
Of lowest order, pass't; and from the door
Of that *Plutonian* Hall, invisible
Ascended his high Throne, which under state   445
Of richest texture spread, at th' upper end
Was plac't in regal lustre. Down a while
He sat, and round about him saw unseen:
At last as from a Cloud his fulgent head
And shape Star-bright appear'd, or brighter, clad   450
With what permissive glory since his fall
Was left him, or false glitter: All amaz'd
At that so sudden blaze the *Stygian* throng
Bent thir aspect, and whom they wish'd beheld,
Thir mighty Chief return'd: loud was th' acclaim: 455
Forth rush'd in haste the great consulting Peers,
Rais'd from thir dark *Divan*, and with like joy
Congratulant approach'd him, who with hand
Silence, and with these words attention won.

    Thrones, Dominations, Princedoms, Virtues, Powers,   460
For in possession such, not only of right,

---

427. The *Grand* are the *great consulting
Peers* of l. 456 below.
432. In *Moscovia* Milton often mentions *Astracan*, a Russian frontier town on the Volga, not far from the Caspian Sea.
433–436. A. H. Gilbert spots Hakluyt's *Voyages* I, 351, as Milton's authority for the *Bactrian* ruler then reigning as "nothing valiant," and as having been driven back by the Turks "even nigh unto the Citie of *Teveris*, wherein he was wont to keepe his chiefe court. And now having forsaken the same, is chiefly resiant at *Casbin*." *Tauris* (or Tebriz) was an important

Persian city under king *Aladule* in the wars with the Turks.
438. *Reduc't* keeps its Latin military meaning of "lead back" (an army in retreat).
445. *state:* canopy over a chair of state or throne like Satan's in II, 1–4, where he is compared with a Turkish Sultan as he is in l. 458 below.
451. *permissive:* permissible or permitted (i.e. by God).
458. The Turkish council of state was known as the *Divan*.
461. *Possession* of the world that Satan has won for them as well as their claim to their lost heavenly ranks, entitles the devils to Satan's titles for them.

I call ye and declare ye now, return'd
Successful beyond hope, to lead ye forth
Triumphant out of this infernal Pit
Abominable, accurst, the house of woe,   465
And Dungeon of our Tyrant: Now possess,
As Lords, a spacious World, to our native Heaven
Little inferior, by my adventure hard
With peril great achiev'd. Long were to tell
What I have done, what suffer'd, with what pain   470
Voyag'd th' unreal, vast, unbounded deep
Of horrible confusion, over which
By Sin and Death a broad way now is pav'd
To expedite your glorious march; but I
Toil'd out my uncouth passage, forc't to ride   475
Th' untractable Abyss, plung'd in the womb
Of unoriginal *Night* and *Chaos* wild,
That jealous of thir secrets fiercely oppos'd
My journey strange, with clamorous uproar
Protesting Fate supreme; thence how I found   480
The new created World, which fame in Heav'n
Long had foretold, a Fabric wonderful
Of absolute perfection, therein Man
Plac't in a Paradise, by our exile
Made happy: Him by fraud I have seduc'd   485
From his Creator, and the more to increase
Your wonder, with an Apple; he thereat
Offended, worth your laughter, hath giv'n up
Both his beloved Man and all his World,
To Sin and Death a prey, and so to us,   490
Without our hazard, labor, or alarm,
To range in, and to dwell, and over Man
To rule, as over all he should have rul'd.
True is, mee also he hath judg'd, or rather
Mee not, but the brute Serpent in whose shape   495
Man I deceiv'd: that which to mee belongs,
Is enmity, which he will put between
Mee and Mankind; I am to bruise his heel;
His Seed, when is not set, shall bruise my head:
A World who would not purchase with a bruise,   500
Or much more grievous pain? Ye have th' account
Of my performance: What remains, ye Gods,
But up and enter now into full bliss.
    So having said, a while he stood, expecting
Thir universal shout and high applause   505

---

471. Cf. the *unapparent Deep* in VII,
103. Its formless elements make it *un-*
real.
    477. *Night*, which in II, 962, is *eldest*

of things, is *unoriginal* because nothing
existed before it to originate it. Night
does not oppose Satan and Chaos helps
him on his way in II, 999–1009.

To fill his ear, when contrary he hears
On all sides, from innumerable tongues
A dismal universal hiss, the sound
Of public scorn; he wonder'd, but not long
Had leisure, wond'ring at himself now more; 510
His Visage drawn he felt to sharp and spare,
His Arms clung to his Ribs, his Legs entwining
Each other, till supplanted down he fell
A monstrous Serpent on his Belly prone,
Reluctant, but in vain: a greater power 515
Now rul'd him, punisht in the shape he sinn'd,
According to his doom: he would have spoke,
But hiss for hiss return'd with forked tongue
To forked tongue, for now were all transform'd
Alike, to Serpents all as accessories 520
To his bold Riot: dreadful was the din
Of hissing through the Hall, thick swarming now
With complicated monsters, head and tail,
Scorpion and Asp, and *Amphisbæna* dire,
Cerastes horn'd, *Hydrus*, and *Ellops* drear, 525
And *Dipsas* (not so thick swarm'd once the Soil
Bedropt with blood of *Gorgon*, or the Isle
Ophiusa) but still greatest hee the midst,
Now Dragon grown, larger than whom the Sun
Ingender'd in the *Pythian* Vale on slime, 530
Huge *Python*, and his Power no less he seem'd

508. In the devils' hiss James Hutton makes the plausible suggestion (in *English Miscellany*, ed. by M. Praz, V, 1955, p. 59) that Milton intended an antithesis to the music of the angels at the creation of the world in VII, 558–74.

513. *supplanted* has its Latin force of "tripped by the heels."

514–533. Though there are traces of Ovid's story of the metamorphosis of Cadmus into a serpent (*Met.* IV, 575–89) and of Lucan's account in *The Civil War* IX, 700–733, of the varieties of serpents that sprang from the blood dripping from the Gorgon's head as Perseus carried it over Libya, Milton's lines rest on a belief which Jakob Boehme interpreted religiously when he wrote in *A Description of the Three Principles of the Divine Essence* (tr. John Sparrow, 1648), iv, 64, that, after "the divine light went out of the Devils, they lost their beauteous forme and Image, and became like Serpents, Dragons, Wormes, and evill Beasts: as may be seen by *Adam's* Serpent." In Vondel's *Lucifer*, as the devil falls under Michael's sword in the battle in heaven, he is suddenly changed into a monster mingling serpent features with those of six other fierce animals (*Cycle*, p. 414).

See the Introduction 15.

521. *Riot:* revolt.

523. *complicated* has its Latin meaning of "intertwined."

524. Like all Milton's serpents, the fabulous *Amphisbæna*, which had a head at each end, was understood to be real and symbolic. In the *Serpentum et draconum historiae Libri II* (Bologna, 1640) of Ulisse Aldovrandus the *Amphisbæna* is both scientifically described and then "hieroglyphically" made a symbol of inconstancy and adultery.

525. Aldovrandus says that the *Cerastes* symbolizes the devil and lust for power. The *Hydrus* was a watersnake; the *Ellops* perhaps originally the swordfish.

526. The *Dipsas* was familiar from Lucian's dialogue "The Thirst Snake" and from Lucan's account of it in *The Civil War* IX, 737–50. Aldovrandus and Topsell in his *Historie of serpents* both interpret the thirst provoked by its bite as an allegory like the thirst of Tantalus in hell. Cf. II, 614.

528. *Ophiusa*, the "snaky" or "snake-filled," was a name given by the Greeks to some Balearic islands.

531. Ovid tells the story of the primi-

Above the rest still to retain; they all
Him follow'd issuing forth to th' open Field,
Where all yet left of that revolted Rout
Heav'n-fall'n, in station stood or just array,   535
Sublime with expectation when to see
In Triumph issuing forth thir glorious Chief;
They saw, but other sight instead, a crowd
Of ugly Serpents; horror on them fell,
And horrid sympathy; for what they saw,   540
They felt themselves now changing; down thir arms,
Down fell both Spear and Shield, down they as fast,
And the dire hiss renew'd, and the dire form
Catcht by Contagion, like in punishment,
As in thir crime. Thus was th' applause they meant,   545
Turn'd to exploding hiss, triumph to shame
Cast on themselves from thir own mouths. There stood
A Grove hard by, sprung up with this thir change,
His will who reigns above, to aggravate
Thir penance, laden with fair Fruit, like that   550
Which grew in Paradise, the bait of *Eve*
Us'd by the Tempter: on that prospect strange
Thir earnest eyes they fix'd, imagining
For one forbidden Tree a multitude
Now ris'n, to work them furder woe or shame;   555
Yet parcht with scalding thirst and hunger fierce,
Though to delude them sent, could not abstain,
But on they roll'd in heaps, and up the Trees
Climbing, sat thicker than the snaky locks
That curl'd *Megæra:* greedily they pluck'd   560
The Fruitage fair to sight, like that which grew
Near that bituminous Lake where *Sodom* flam'd;

---

tive earth's unwilling engendering of the mountainous serpent *Python* (*Met.* I, 438–40). Cf. *El.* VII, 31.

535. *in station:* on posts.

536. *sublime* has its Latin meaning of "uplifted."

545–572. This "cartoon scene," which Waldock condemns as crude allegory in "*PL*" *and Its Critics,* p. 91, is shown by Stein in *PMLA* LXV (1950), 226, to be a "psychological" and "physical climax" in the drama of the poem. In *MLQ*, XVI (1961), 321–335, J. M. Steadman reviews the tradition of demonic theriomorphosis and treats the scene as an epic reversal of Satan's fortune. For Addison in *Spectator,* 357, for L. Abercrombie in *The Idea of Great Poetry* (London, 1925), p. 80, and for Edith Sitwell in *The Pleasures of Poetry* (New York, n.d.), p. 25, the lines are a poetic triumph.

551. The trees loaded with the *bait of Eve* suggest the graft of the Tree of Knowledge below which Dante found a host of famished spirits in *Purgatory* (xxix, 103–117).

560. *Megæra*, one of the Furies or goddesses who avenge crime, and who appear with *snaky locks* as the chorus in Aeschylus' *Eumenides.*

562. Throughout the popular encyclopaedias — Swan's *Speculum Mundi* and Caxton's *Mirrour of the World* especially — Svendsen (*M.&S.*, pp. 28–29) traces repetitions of Josephus' story of *that bituminous Lake* (the Dead Sea) and the city of *Sodom,* which, "for the impiety of its inhabitants, was burnt by lightning; . . . and the traces are still to be seen, as well as the ashes growing in their fruits, which fruits have a color as if they were fit to be eaten; but if you pluck them with your hands, they dissolve into smoke and ashes" (*Wars* IV,

This more delusive, not the touch, but taste
Deceiv'd; they fondly thinking to allay
Thir appetite with gust, instead of Fruit   565
Chew'd bitter Ashes, which th' offended taste
With spattering noise rejected: oft they assay'd,
Hunger and thirst constraining, drugg'd as oft,
With hatefullest disrelish writh'd thir jaws
With soot and cinders fill'd; so oft they fell   570
Into the same illusion, not as Man
Whom they triumph'd, once lapst. Thus were they plagu'd
And worn with Famine long, and ceaseless hiss,
Till thir lost shape, permitted, they resum'd,
Yearly enjoin'd, some say, to undergo   575
This annual humbling certain number'd days,
To dash thir pride, and joy for Man seduc't.
However some tradition they dispers'd
Among the Heathen of thir purchase got,
And Fabl'd how the Serpent, whom they call'd   580
Ophion with *Eurynome*, the wide-
Encroaching *Eve* perhaps, had first the rule
Of high *Olympus*, thence by *Saturn* driv'n
And *Ops*, ere yet *Dictæan Jove* was born.
Meanwhile in Paradise the hellish pair   585
Too soon arriv'd, *Sin* there in power before,
Once actual, now in body, and to dwell
Habitual habitant; behind her *Death*
Close following pace for pace, not mounted yet

viii, 4).   Sodom and Gomorrah, upon
which "the Lord rained . . . brimstone
and fire from the Lord out of heaven"
(Gen. xix, 24), are conspicuously shown
all aflame together with Zeboim and
Admah on Fuller's map of southern
Palestine. (See p. xxx.)
565. *gust:* keen relish, gusto.
566–570. In the background is a popu-
lar belief that snakes eat nothing but dust
which Topsell in his *Historie of Serpents*,
p. 16, challenged, though he thought it
possible that snakes of the kind that
figures in Eve's temptation might have
no food but dust.
568. *drugg'd:* nauseated.
572. *triumph'd:* triumphed over, van-
quished.
572–577. Again folklore may be in the
background in stories like Ariosto's ac-
count in the *Orlando Furioso* XLIII, 98,
of the confession of the fairy Manto that
she and all her kind are obliged every
seventh day to assume the form of ser-
pents.
581. In the *Argonautica* I, 503–506,
Apollonius recalls that Olympus was
ruled by the Titans *Ophion* ("the ser-
pent") and his wife *Eurynome* until their

expulsion by Saturn and his wife Rhea,
whom Milton calls *Ops*. *Ophion* seems to
be the Titan Ophioneus who — according
to the sixth century B.C. philosopher
Pherecydes — led an unsuccessful attack
on Olympus. Ophioneus was identified
by Origen (*contra Celsum* VI, 43) with
"the serpent which was the cause of man's
expulsion from the divine paradise, and
deceived the female race with a promise of
divine power of attaining to greater
things." Ophioneus' identification with
the serpent of Eden survived as a tradi-
tion in George Sandys' introduction to his
version of Ovid's *Metamorphoses* II, and
it was extended by Jean Bodin in *Le
Fleau des Demons et Sorciers* (Nyort,
1616), pp. 3–4, and by Cornelius Agrippa
in *De Occulta Philosophia* III, xviii, to
include "that old serpent called the
devil" in Rev. xii, 9. Since *Eurynome*
means "wide-encroaching," punctuation
with the comma immediately after the
word rather than immediately before it
(as in the early editions), seems justified.
Cf. IX, 507–510, n., and the Introduc-
tion 16.
586. *Sin* was in Eden *in power* when
Adam and Eve fell.

On his pale Horse: to whom *Sin* thus began.   590
   Second of *Satan* sprung, all conquering *Death*,
What think'st thou of our Empire now, though earn'd
With travail difficult, not better far
Than still at Hell's dark threshold to have sat watch,
Unnam'd, undreaded, and thyself half starv'd?   595
   Whom thus the Sin-born Monster answer'd soon.
To mee, who with eternal Famine pine,
Alike is Hell, or Paradise, or Heaven,
There best, where most with ravin I may meet;
Which here, though plenteous, all too little seems   600
To stuff this Maw, this vast unhide-bound Corpse.
   To whom th' incestuous Mother thus repli'd.
Thou therefore on these Herbs, and Fruits, and Flow'rs
Feed first, on each Beast next, and Fish, and Fowl,
No homely morsels, and whatever thing   605
The Scythe of Time mows down, devour unspar'd,
Till I in Man residing through the Race,
His thoughts, his looks, words, actions all infect,
And season him thy last and sweetest prey.
   This said, they both betook them several ways,   610
Both to destroy, or unimmortal make
All kinds, and for destruction to mature
Sooner or later; which th' Almighty seeing
From his transcendent Seat the Saints among,
To those bright Orders utter'd thus his voice.   615
   See with what heat these Dogs of Hell advance
To waste and havoc yonder World, which I
So fair and good created, and had still
Kept in that state, had not the folly of Man
Let in these wasteful Furies, who impute   620
Folly to mee, so doth the Prince of Hell
And his Adherents, that with so much ease
I suffer them to enter and possess
A place so heav'nly, and conniving seem
To gratify my scornful Enemies,   625
That laugh, as if transported with some fit
Of Passion, I to them had quitted all,
At random yielded up to their misrule;
And know not that I call'd and drew them thither

---

590. The *pale Horse* is from Revelation vi, 8: "And I looked, and behold a pale horse; and his name that sat on him was Death."

617. *havoc* was a battle-cry used when troops were ready to begin plundering. It was often used as a transitive verb.

624. *conniving* reflects its Latin meaning of "shutting the eyes."

629–633. Among many vague parallels to this scene in Du Bartas which are noted by G. McColley in *SP*, XXXV (1938), 87, the closest is to these lines. To make the parallel McColley collects the following scattered phrases from *The Divine Weeks*, p. 273:

"God . . . summon'd-up/With thundering call the damned *Crew*, that sup/Of . . . Bloody *Cocytus*, muddy *Acheron*./ Come snake-trest Sisters, com . . ./

My Hell-hounds, to lick up the draff and filth 630
Which man's polluting Sin with taint hath shed
On what was pure, till cramm'd and gorg'd, nigh burst
With suckt and glutted offal, at one sling
Of thy victorious Arm, well-pleasing Son,
Both *Sin*, and *Death*, and yawning *Grave* at last 635
Through *Chaos* hurl'd, obstruct the mouth of Hell
For ever, and seal up his ravenous Jaws.
Then Heav'n and Earth renew'd shall be made pure
To sanctity that shall receive no stain:
Till then the Curse pronounc't on both precedes. 640
  He ended, and the heav'nly Audience loud
Sung *Halleluiah*, as the sound of Seas,
Through multitude that sung: Just are thy ways,
Righteous are thy Decrees on all thy Works;
Who can extenuate thee? Next, to the Son, 645
Destin'd restorer of Mankind, by whom
New Heav'n and Earth shall to the Ages rise,
Or down from Heav'n descend. Such was thir song,
While the Creator calling forth by name
His mighty Angels gave them several charge, 650
As sorted best with present things. The Sun
Had first his precept so to move, so shine,
As might affect the Earth with cold and heat
Scarce tolerable, and from the North to call
Decrepit Winter, from the South to bring 655
Solstitial summer's heat. To the blanc Moon
Her office they prescrib'd, to th' other five
Thir planetary motions and aspects
In *Sextile*, *Square*, and *Trine*, and *Opposite*,
Of noxious efficacy, and when to join 660
In Synod unbenign, and taught the fixt

Com, parbreak heer your foul, black,
banefull gall."
  635. Cf. St. Paul: "Death is swallowed
up in victory" (I Cor. xv, 54).
  638. In *CD* I, xxxiii (C.Ed. XVI, 368),
Milton stated his faith in "a new heaven
and a new earth . . . coming down from
God out of heaven" and in the "destruc-
tion of the present unclean and polluted
world."
  642. "And I heard as it were the voice
of a great multitude, and as the voice of
many waters, . . . saying 'Alleluia' "
(Rev. xix, 6).
  651–706. Like all his contemporaries
Milton interpreted Genesis iii, 17, as
meaning that after the Fall nature "be-
came subject to mortality and a curse on
account of man" (*CD* I, xiii; C.Ed. XV,
216). The theme inspired such theo-
logical works as Godfrey Goodman's *The
Fall of Man, or the Corruption of Nature*

Proved by Natural Reason and such poetry
as Du Bartas' *Divine Weeks*. When
Adam sinned, said Henry Vaughan in
Corruption,
  He drew the curse upon the world
    and cracked
  The whole frame with his fall.
  651. *sorted:* corresponded.
  656. *blanc* was Milton's spelling when
he intended the word to mean "white"
or "pale-colored," as it does in French.
  657. *th' other five* are the other five
planets. Cf. V, 177.
  659. In a *Sextile* (60°), a *Square* (90°),
a *Trine* (120°), or *Opposite* (180°) aspect
to each other any two planets were re-
garded as exerting a harmful influence
upon the earth.
  661. In *Synod* (conjunction) in any
sign of the zodiac the planets were re-
garded as in an "indifferent" aspect,
neither benign nor malignant.

Thir influence malignant when to show'r,
Which of them rising with the Sun, or falling,
Should prove tempestuous: To the Winds they set
Thir corners, when with bluster to confound   665
Sea, Air, and Shore, the Thunder when to roll
With terror through the dark Aereal Hall.
Some say he bid his Angels turn askance
The Poles of Earth twice ten degrees and more
From the Sun's Axle; they with labor push'd   670
Oblique the Centric Globe: Some say the Sun
Was bid turn Reins from th' Equinoctial Road
Like distant breadth to *Taurus* with the Sev'n
Atlantic Sisters, and the *Spartan* Twins
Up to the *Tropic* Crab; thence down amain   675
By *Leo* and the *Virgin* and the *Scales*,
As deep as *Capricorn*, to bring in change
Of Seasons to each Clime; else had the Spring
Perpetual smil'd on Earth with vernant Flow'rs,
Equal in Days and Nights, except to those   680
Beyond the Polar Circles; to them Day
Had unbenighted shone, while the low Sun
To recompense his distance, in thir sight
Had rounded still th' *Horizon*, and not known
Or East or West, which had forbid the Snow   685
From cold *Estotiland*, and South as far
Beneath *Magellan*. At that tasted Fruit
The Sun, as from *Thyestean* Banquet, turn'd
His course intended; else how had the World
Inhabited, though sinless, more than now,   690
Avoided pinching cold and scorching heat?
These changes in the Heav'ns, though slow, produc'd
Like change on Sea and Land, sideral blast,
Vapor, and Mist, and Exhalation hot,

662. Contrast the "selectest influence" of the constellations in VIII, 513.

665. So in the seventh Holy Sonnet Donne commands the angels to blow "At the round earth's imagin'd corners."

668–678. Regarding the course of the sun as having originally coincided with the celestial equator, Milton imagines either that the angels tilted the earth's axis 23½ degrees or that the sun changed its course so as to approach the tropic of Cancer in the spring, when it reaches the constellation *Taurus* (the Bull), in whose neck are the *Atlantic Sisters* (the Pleiades, cf. VII, 374), and then to climb through the *Spartan Twins* (Castor and Pollux) to the *Crab*. In July, August, and September it descends through *Leo* (the Lion), the *Virgin*, and the *Scales* to cross the equator southward to the tropic of *Capri-*

corn. "No heat nor cold had touched them," said Boehme in *Mysterium Magnum* xviii, 13, "if Adam had not fallen, there had been no winter manifest upon the earth." Milton's passage seems — as M. Kelley suggests in *PMLA*, LXX (1955), 1098 — to reflect Aratus' survey of the Zodiac in *Phaenomena*, 741–50. Cf. "the penalty of Adam/The seasons' difference," in *As You Like It*, II, i, 5–6.

686–687. On the Mercator maps *Estotiland* lies on the northeastern coast of Labrador. *Magellan:* the straits of Magellan.

688. The myth of Atreus represented the sun as averting his face when Atreus served his brother Thyestes with the flesh of his own sons.

693. *sideral* (sidereal) *blast:* a blast from the stars.

Corrupt and Pestilent: Now from the North 695
Of *Norumbega,* and the *Samoed* shore
Bursting thir brazen Dungeon, arm'd with ice
And snow and hail and stormy gust and flaw,
Boreas and *Cæcias* and *Argestes* loud
And *Thrascias* rend the Woods and Seas upturn; 700
With adverse blast upturns them from the South
Notus and *Afer* black with thundrous Clouds
From *Serraliona;* thwart of these as fierce
Forth rush the *Levant* and the *Ponent* Winds
Eurus and *Zephir* with thir lateral noise, 705
Sirocco, and *Libecchio.* Thus began
Outrage from lifeless things; but Discord first
Daughter of Sin, among th' irrational,
Death introduc'd through fierce antipathy:
Beast now with Beast gan war, and Fowl with Fowl, 710
And Fish with Fish; to graze the Herb all leaving,
Devour'd each other; nor stood much in awe
Of Man, but fled him, or with count'nance grim
Glar'd on him passing: these were from without
The growing miseries, which *Adam* saw 715
Already in part, though hid in gloomiest shade,
To sorrow abandon'd, but worse felt within,
And in a troubl'd Sea of passion tost,
Thus to disburd'n sought with sad complaint.

O miserable of happy! is this the end 720
Of this new glorious World, and mee so late
The Glory of that Glory, who now become
Accurst of blessed, hide me from the face
Of God, whom to behold was then my highth
Of happiness: yet well, if here would end 725
The misery, I deserv'd it, and would
My own deservings; but this will not serve;
All that I eat or drink, or shall beget,

---

696. All northern New England was vaguely called *Norumbega,* where Burton thought that "in 45° lat. all the sea is frozen ice" (*Anatomy* II, ii, 3; Everyman Ed. II, p. 44). In *Moscovia* (C.Ed. X, 344) Milton describes the *Samoeds* as accustomed to live and travel over immense depths of snow.
699–706. Most of these winds will be found on Peter Apian's chart in his *Cosmographia,* which is reproduced on page 308 from the edition of 1580. It is oriented with the south at the top. K. Svendsen has collected much relevant meteorological lore in *M.&S.,* pp. 94–97, and in *Milieu,* pp. 79 and 121–22, Whiting connects this passage with Pliny's distribution of the winds to the four points of the compass and with their

representation in Jan Jansson's *Atlas.*
703. *Serraliona:* the modern Sierra Leone, on the west African coast.
704. *Levant,* like "Orient," refers to the east; *Ponent,* like "Occident," to the west. On the chart east winds like *Eurus* and west winds like *Zephyr* blow laterally.
706. The use of the Italian name, *Sirocco,* for the southeast wind, and of *Libecchio* for the southwest wind seemed natural to Milton because, as Peacham's *Compleat Gentleman* (1634, p. 64) explained, "the eight principall winds are commonly expressed in the *Italian.*"
718. The metaphor, which is elaborated at length in Vaughan's *The Storm,* goes back to Isaiah lvii, 20 — "The wicked are like the troubled sea, when it cannot rest."

Is propagated curse. O voice once heard
Delightfully, *Increase and multiply*,   730
Now death to hear! for what can I increase
Or multiply, but curses on my head?
Who of all Ages to succeed, but feeling
The evil on him brought by me, will curse
My Head; Ill fare our Ancestor impure,   735
For this we may thank *Adam;* but his thanks
Shall be the execration; so besides
Mine own that bide upon me, all from mee
Shall with a fierce reflux on mee redound,
On mee as on thir natural centre light   740
Heavy, though in thir place. O fleeting joys
Of Paradise, dear bought with lasting woes!
Did I request thee, Maker, from my Clay
To mould me Man, did I solicit thee
From darkness to promote me, or here place   745
In this delicious Garden? as my Will
Concurr'd not to my being, it were but right
And equal to reduce me to my dust,
Desirous to resign, and render back
All I receiv'd, unable to perform   750
Thy terms too hard, by which I was to hold
The good I sought not. To the loss of that,
Sufficient penalty, why hast thou added
The sense of endless woes? inexplicable
Thy Justice seems; yet to say truth, too late   755
I thus contest; then should have been refus'd
Those terms whatever, when they were propos'd:
Thou didst accept them; wilt thou enjoy the good,
Then cavil the conditions? and though God
Made thee without thy leave, what if thy Son   760
Prove disobedient, and reprov'd, retort,
Wherefore didst thou beget me? I sought it not:
Wouldst thou admit for his contempt of thee
That proud excuse? yet him not thy election,
But Natural necessity begot.   765
God made thee of choice his own, and of his own
To serve him, thy reward was of his grace,
Thy punishment then justly is at his Will.
Be it so, for I submit, his doom is fair,

---

730. *Increase and multiply* was part of
God's blessing in Genesis i, 28.
738. *Mine own* refers to *curses* in
l. 732.
739. *redound:* flow back (like a re-
turning wave).
743. Cf. Isaiah xlv, 9: "Woe unto
him that striveth with his maker! . . .

Shall the clay say to him that fashioneth
it, 'What makest thou?' "
748. *equal:* just, fair.
762. Cf. Isaiah xlv, 10: "Woe unto
him that saith unto his father, 'What
begettest thou?' "
764. *election:* choice.

That dust I am, and shall to dust return: 770
O welcome hour whenever! why delays
His hand to execute what his Decree
Fix'd on this day? why do I overlive,
Why am I mockt with death, and length'n'd out
To deathless pain? How gladly would I meet   775
Mortality my sentence, and be Earth
Insensible, how glad would lay me down
As in my Mother's lap! There I should rest
And sleep secure; his dreadful voice no more
Would Thunder in my ears, no fear of worse   780
To mee and to my offspring would torment me
With cruel expectation. Yet one doubt
Pursues me still, lest all I cannot die,
Lest that pure breath of Life, the Spirit of Man
Which God inspir'd, cannot together perish   785
With this corporeal Clod; then in the Grave,
Or in some other dismal place, who knows
But I shall die a living Death? O thought
Horrid, if true! yet why? it was but breath
Of Life that sinn'd; what dies but what had life   790
And sin? the Body properly hath neither.
All of me then shall die: let this appease
The doubt, since human reach no further knows.
For though the Lord of all be infinite,
Is his wrath also? be it, Man is not so,   795
But mortal doom'd. How can he exercise
Wrath without end on Man whom Death must end?
Can he make deathless Death? that were to make
Strange contradiction, which to God himself
Impossible is held, as Argument   800
Of weakness, not of Power. Will he draw out,
For anger's sake, finite to infinite
In punisht Man, to satisfy his rigor
Satisfi'd never; that were to extend
His Sentence beyond dust and Nature's Law,   805

770. The thought of the entire passage recalls the verse in Job (xxxiv, 15) which is echoed here.

782-794. Adam's rhetorical question parallels Milton's in *CD* I, xiii (C.Ed. XV, 22-28): "What could be more absurd than that the mind, which is the part principally offending, should escape the threatened death; and that the body alone, to which immortality was equally alotted, . . . should pay the penalty of sin by undergoing death, though not implicated in the transgression?" Milton's belief in the extinction of both soul and body at physical death and in their joint resurrection may be implicit, as G.

Williamson declares in *SP*, XXXII (1935), 553-79; but N. H. Henry is right in thinking — *SP*, XLVIII (1951) 248 — that for Milton the belief was "a thing indifferent, and no heresy." Cf. ll. 49-54 above, n.

799. Writing on the divine omnipotence, Milton said: "It must be remembered that the power of God is not exerted in things which imply a contradiction" (*CD* I, ii; C.Ed. XIV, 49).

805. *Nature's Law* is "that general law which is the origin of everything, and under which everything acts" (*CD* I, ii; C.Ed. XIV, 27).

By which all Causes else according still
To the reception of thir matter act,
Not to th' extent of thir own Sphere. But say
That Death be not one stroke, as I suppos'd,
Bereaving sense, but endless misery   810
From this day onward, which I feel begun
Both in me, and without me, and so last
To perpetuity; Ay me, that fear
Comes thund'ring back with dreadful revolution
On my defenseless head; both Death and I   815
Am found Eternal, and incorporate both,
Nor I on my part single, in mee all
Posterity stands curst: Fair Patrimony
That I must leave ye, Sons; O were I able
To waste it all myself, and leave ye none!   820
So disinherited how would ye bless
Me now your Curse! Ah, why should all mankind
For one man's fault thus guiltless be condemn'd,
If guiltless? But from me what can proceed,
But all corrupt, both Mind and Will deprav'd,   825
Not to do only, but to will the same
With me? how can they then acquitted stand
In sight of God? Him after all Disputes
Forc't I absolve: all my evasions vain
And reasonings, though through Mazes, lead me still   830
But to my own conviction: first and last
On mee, mee only, as the source and spring
Of all corruption, all the blame lights due;
So might the wrath. Fond wish! couldst thou support
That burden heavier than the Earth to bear,   835
Than all the World much heavier, though divided
With that bad Woman? Thus what thou desir'st,
And what thou fear'st, alike destroys all hope
Of refuge, and concludes thee miserable
Beyond all past example and future,   840
To *Satan* only like both crime and doom.
O Conscience, into what Abyss of fears

807. To explain *reception* Newton
quoted the axiom: "Every efficient [i.e.
everything which acts] acts according to
the powers of what receives its action,
not according to its own powers."
810. *Bereaving sense:* depriving of
power of sensation. The haunting dread
is like Hamlet's fear of consciousness
When we have shuffled off this mor-
tal coil.
815–844. The passage is related to the
lament over Adam's sin in II Esdras vii,
46–56, by K. Svendsen in *C.E.*, X (1949),
366–370, and briefly by J. B. Broadbent

in *Some Graver Subject*, p. 264.
816. *Am* agrees with the near subject
I. incorporate: united in one body.
828–834. Adam's conviction of sin
marks the first of the four steps in re-
generation in *CD* I, xix (C.Ed. XV, 384):
"Conviction of sin, contrition, confession,
departure from evil and conversion to
good."
840. Cf. the awakening of despair by
Conscience in Satan in IV, 23.
842–844. In the chapter "Of the
Punishment of Sin" — in *CD* I, xii
(C.Ed. XV, 204) — Adam's experience

And horrors hast thou driv'n me; out of which
I find no way, from deep to deeper plung'd!
Thus *Adam* to himself lamented loud　845
Through the still Night, not now, as ere man fell,
Wholesome and cool and mild, but with black Air
Accompanied, with damps and dreadful gloom,
Which to his evil Conscience represented
All things with double terror: On the ground　850
Outstretcht he lay, on the cold ground, and oft
Curs'd his Creation, Death as oft accus'd
Of tardy execution, since denounc't
The day of his offense. Why comes not Death,
Said he, with one thrice acceptable stroke　855
To end me? Shall Truth fail to keep her word,
Justice Divine not hast'n to be just?
But Death comes not at call, Justice Divine
Mends not her slowest pace for prayers or cries.
O Woods, O Fountains, Hillocks, Dales and Bow'rs,　860
With other echo late I taught your Shades
To answer, and resound far other Song.
Whom thus afflicted when sad *Eve* beheld,
Desolate where she sat, approaching nigh,
Soft words to his fierce passion she assay'd:　865
But her with stern regard he thus repell'd.
　Out of my sight, thou Serpent, that name best
Befits thee with him leagu'd, thyself as false
And hateful; nothing wants, but that thy shape,
Like his, and color Serpentine may show　870
Thy inward fraud, to warn all Creatures from thee
Henceforth; lest that too heav'nly form, pretended
To hellish falsehood, snare them. But for thee
I had persisted happy, had not thy pride
And wand'ring vanity, when least was safe,　875
Rejected my forewarning, and disdain'd
Not to be trusted, longing to be seen
Though by the Devil himself, him overweening
To over-reach, but with the Serpent meeting
Fool'd and beguil'd, by him thou, I by thee,　880
To trust thee from my side, imagin'd wise,
Constant, mature, proof against all assaults,
And understood not all was but a show
Rather than solid virtue, all but a Rib

---

is the first illustration of the "terrors of conscience" that follow "guiltiness." In *"Paradise Lost" as 'Myth,'* p. 117, Mrs. I. G. MacCaffrey quotes Augustine's saying in his *Commentaries on the Psalms* (xli, 13), that, "If by 'abyss' we understand a great depth, is not man's heart an abyss? For what is more profound than that abyss?"

867–868. In *MLN*, LXXII (1959), 679–681, D. C. Allen marked a pun in Hebrew on *Eve* and *Heve* (serpent).

872, *pretended* has its Latin force of "held out" (as a screen or disguise).

Crooked by nature, bent, as now appears,   885
More to the part sinister from me drawn,
Well if thrown out, as supernumerary
To my just number found. O why did God,
Creator wise, that peopl'd highest Heav'n
With Spirits Masculine, create at last   890
This novelty on Earth, this fair defect
Of Nature, and not fill the World at once
With Men as Angels without Feminine,
Or find some other way to generate
Mankind? this mischief had not then befall'n,   895
And more that shall befall, innumerable
Disturbances on Earth through Female snares,
And strait conjunction with this Sex: for either
He never shall find out fit Mate, but such
As some misfortune brings him, or mistake,   900
Or whom he wishes most shall seldom gain
Through her perverseness, but shall see her gain'd
By a far worse, or if she love, withheld
By Parents, or his happiest choice too late
Shall meet, already linkt and Wedlock-bound   905
To a fell Adversary, his hate or shame:
Which infinite calamity shall cause
To Human life, and household peace confound.

   He added not, and from her turn'd, but *Eve*
Not so repulst, with Tears that ceas'd not flowing,   910
And tresses all disorder'd, at his feet
Fell humble, and imbracing them, besought
His peace, and thus proceeded in her plaint.

   Forsake me not thus, *Adam*, witness Heav'n
What love sincere, and reverence in my heart   915
I bear thee, and unweeting have offended,
Unhappily deceiv'd; thy suppliant
I beg, and clasp thy knees; bereave me not,
Whereon I live, thy gentle looks, thy aid,
Thy counsel in this uttermost distress,   920
My only strength and stay: forlorn of thee,
Whither shall I betake me, where subsist?
While yet we live, scarce one short hour perhaps,
Between us two let there be peace, both joining,
As join'd in injuries, one enmity   925

886. The play on the literal meaning of *sinister* (left) and its figurative meaning rests on the tradition that Eve was made from a rib from Adam's left side (as in VIII, 465). The idea that woman was made from a bent rib and is "an imperfect animal — she always deceives," is traced by K. Svendsen — in *M.&S.*, 183–85 — to the *Malleus Maleficarum* of Henricus Institoris and Jacobus Sprenger (c. 1484).

887. *supernumerary* refers to a belief that Adam was created with an extra rib for the creation of Eve.

888. Cf. Euripides' invective against women in *Hippolytus* 616–18, and Milton's reflection on them in *SA*, 1053–60.

899. Cf. VIII, 450, n.

Against a Foe by doom express assign'd us,
That cruel Serpent: On me exercise not
Thy hatred for this misery befall'n,
On me already lost, mee than thyself
More miserable; both have sinn'd, but thou   930
Against God only, I against God and thee,
And to the place of judgment will return,
There with my cries importune Heaven, that all
The sentence from thy head remov'd may light
On me, sole cause to thee of all this woe,   935
Mee mee only just object of his ire.
   She ended weeping, and her lowly plight,
Immovable till peace obtain'd from fault
Acknowledg'd and deplor'd, in *Adam* wrought
Commiseration; soon his heart relented   940
Towards her, his life so late and sole delight,
Now at his feet submissive in distress,
Creature so fair his reconcilement seeking,
His counsel whom she had displeas'd, his aid;
As one disarm'd, his anger all he lost,   945
And thus with peaceful words uprais'd her soon.
   Unwary, and too desirous, as before,
So now of what thou know'st not, who desir'st
The punishment all on thyself; alas,
Bear thine own first, ill able to sustain   950
His full wrath whose thou feel'st as yet least part,
And my displeasure bear'st so ill. If Prayers
Could alter high Decrees, I to that place
Would speed before thee, and be louder heard,
That on my head all might be visited,   955
Thy frailty and infirmer Sex forgiv'n,
To me committed and by me expos'd.
But rise, let us no more contend, nor blame
Each other, blam'd enough elsewhere, but strive
In offices of Love, how we may light'n   960
Each other's burden in our share of woe;
Since this day's Death denounc't, if aught I see,
Will prove no sudden, but a slow-pac't evil,
A long day's dying to augment our pain,
And to our Seed (O hapless Seed!) deriv'd.   965
   To whom thus *Eve*, recovering heart, repli'd.
Adam, by sad experiment I know
How little weight my words with thee can find,
Found so erroneous, thence by just event

---

938. *Immovable* seems to qualify *Adam*, who is inflexible until Eve's confession of her fault brings *peace* between them.

The thought recurs in *Samson Agonistes*, 1003–1007.
   959. *elsewhere*, i.e. at "the place of judgment" (932 above).

Found so unfortunate; nevertheless,   970
Restor'd by thee, vile as I am, to place
Of new acceptance, hopeful to regain
Thy Love, the sole contentment of my heart
Living or dying, from thee I will not hide
What thoughts in my unquiet breast are ris'n,   975
Tending to some relief of our extremes,
Or end, though sharp and sad, yet tolerable,
As in our evils, and of easier choice.
If care of our descent perplex us most,
Which must be born to certain woe, devour'd   980
By Death at last, and miserable it is
To be to others cause of misery,
Our own begott'n, and of our Loins to bring
Into this cursed World a woeful Race,
That after wretched Life must be at last   985
Food for so foul a Monster, in thy power
It lies, yet ere Conception to prevent
The Race unblest, to being yet unbegot.
Childless thou art, Childless remain: So Death
Shall be deceiv'd his glut, and with us two   990
Be forc'd to satisfy his Rav'nous Maw.
But if thou judge it hard and difficult,
Conversing, looking, loving, to abstain
From Love's due Rites, Nuptial embraces sweet,
And with desire to languish without hope,   995
Before the present object languishing
With like desire, which would be misery
And torment less than none of what we dread,
Then both ourselves and Seed at once to free
From what we fear for both, let us make short,   1000
Let us seek Death, or he not found, supply
With our own hands his Office on ourselves;
Why stand we longer shivering under fears,
That show no end but Death, and have the power,
Of many ways to die the shortest choosing,   1005
Destruction with destruction to destroy.
    She ended here, or vehement despair
Broke off the rest; so much of Death her thoughts
Had entertain'd, as dy'd her Cheeks with pale.
But *Adam* with such counsel nothing sway'd,   1010
To better hopes his more attentive mind
Laboring had rais'd, and thus to *Eve* replied.
    Eve, thy contempt of life and pleasure seems

978. *As in our evils:* in such evils as
ours — a Latinism.
979. *descent:* descendants.
987. *prevent:* forestall, cut off in ad-
vance. Cf. IV, 996.
996. *the present object* is Eve herself,
standing in Adam's presence.
1013–1028. Adam's reasoning against

To argue in thee something more sublime
And excellent than what thy mind contemns;   1015
But self-destruction therefore sought, refutes
That excellence thought in thee, and implies,
Not thy contempt, but anguish and regret
For loss of life and pleasure overlov'd.
Or if thou covet death, as utmost end   1020
Of misery, so thinking to evade
The penalty pronounc't, doubt not but God
Hath wiselier arm'd his vengeful ire than so
To be forestall'd; much more I fear lest Death
So snatcht will not exempt us from the pain   1025
We are by doom to pay; rather such acts
Of contumacy will provoke the Highest
To make death in us live: Then let us seek
Some safer resolution, which methinks
I have in view, calling to mind with heed   1030
Part of our Sentence, that thy Seed shall bruise
The Serpent's head; piteous amends, unless
Be meant, whom I conjecture, our grand Foe
Satan, who in the Serpent hath contriv'd
Against us this deceit: to crush his head   1035
Would be revenge indeed; which will be lost
By death brought on ourselves, or childless days
Resolv'd, as thou proposest; so our Foe
Shall 'scape his punishment ordain'd, and wee
Instead shall double ours upon our heads.   1040
No more be mention'd then of violence
Against ourselves, and wilful barrenness,
That cuts us off from hope, and savors only
Rancor and pride, impatience and despite,
Reluctance against God and his just yoke   1045
Laid on our Necks. Remember with what mild
And gracious temper he both heard and judg'd
Without wrath or reviling; wee expected
Immediate dissolution, which we thought
Was meant by Death that day, when lo, to thee   1050
Pains only in Child-bearing were foretold,
And bringing forth, soon recompens't with joy,
Fruit of thy Womb: On mee the Curse aslope

Eve's proposal of suicide seems to G. Williamson — in *SP*, XXXII (1935), 570 — to be a reflection on the libertine arguments for suicide in Walter Charleton's *The Immortality of the Human Soul* (1657) and in Donne's *Biathanatos*, as well as on Hobbes's interpretation of the law of nature in *Leviathan*. But basically the thought is as general as Hamlet's wish that "th' Everlasting had not fix'd/His canon 'gainst self-slaughter."
1031–1036. Cf. ll. 168–84 above.
1045. *Reluctance* keeps its Latin meaning of "struggling."
1050. *that day* is the preceding day.
1053. The curse has struck only a glancing blow and fallen to the ground, like an arrow that has grazed its mark. Cf. l. 201 above.

Glanc'd on the ground, with labor I must earn
My bread; what harm? Idleness had been worse;   1055
My labor will sustain me; and lest Cold
Or Heat should injure us, his timely care
Hath unbesought provided, and his hands
Cloth'd us unworthy, pitying while he judg'd;
How much more, if we pray him, will his ear   1060
Be open, and his heart to pity incline,
And teach us further by what means to shun
Th' inclement Seasons, Rain, Ice, Hail and Snow,
Which now the Sky with various Face begins
To show us in this Mountain, while the Winds   1065
Blow moist and keen, shattering the graceful locks
Of these fair spreading Trees; which bids us seek
Some better shroud, some better warmth to cherish
Our Limbs benumb'd, ere this diurnal Star
Leave cold the Night, how we his gather'd beams   1070
Reflected, may with matter sere foment,
Or by collision of two bodies grind
The Air attrite to Fire, as late the Clouds
Justling or pusht with Winds rude in thir shock
Tine the slant Lightning, whose thwart flame driv'n down   1075
Kindles the gummy bark of Fir or Pine,
And sends a comfortable heat from far,
Which might supply the Sun: such Fire to use,
And what may else be remedy or cure
To evils which our own misdeeds have wrought,   1080
Hee will instruct us praying, and of Grace
Beseeching him, so as we need not fear
To pass commodiously this life, sustain'd
By him with many comforts, till we end
In dust, our final rest and native home.   1085
What better can we do, than to the place
Repairing where he judg'd us, prostrate fall
Before him reverent, and there confess
Humbly our faults, and pardon beg, with tears
Watering the ground, and with our sighs the Air   1090
Frequenting, sent from hearts contrite, in sign
Of sorrow unfeign'd, and humiliation meek.

1065. In IV, 132–72, Paradise has been
described as a *Mountain.*
1066. So Spenser speaks in *The Shep-
heardes Calendar (November,* l. 125) of
"faded lockes" that "fall from the loftie
oke."
1069. *this diurnal Star:* the sun. Cf.
the *Day-star* in *Lycidas,* 168.
1073. *Attrite* is felt as having its Latin
form as a perfect passive participle, and
as meaning "rubbed," or "worked by
friction."
1075. *Tine:* kindle.   *thwart:*   trans-
verse, slanting.
1075–1078. The theory that men first
secured fire from the kindling of the
forests by lightning is vividly stated in
Lucretius' *De rerum natura* V, 1091–95.
Cf. VII, 463–70, n.
1081. *praying:* if we pray.
1091. *Frequenting* has its Latin mean-
ing of "filling" or "crowding."

Undoubtedly he will relent and turn
From his displeasure; in whose look serene,
When angry most he seem'd and most severe,   1095
What else but favor, grace, and mercy shone?
So spake our Father penitent, nor *Eve*
Felt less remorse: they forthwith to the place
Repairing where he judg'd them prostrate fell
Before him reverent, and both confess'd   1100
Humbly thir faults, and pardon begg'd, with tears
Watering the ground, and with thir sighs the Air
Frequenting, sent from hearts contrite, in sign
Of sorrow unfeign'd, and humiliation meek.

The End of the Tenth Book.

BOOK XI

THE ARGUMENT

The Son of God presents to his Father the Prayers of our first Parents now repenting, and intercedes for them: God accepts them, but declares that they must no longer abide in Paradise; sends Michael *with a Band of Cherubim to dispossess them; but first to reveal to* Adam *future things:* Michael's *coming down.* Adam *shows to* Eve *certain ominous signs; he discerns* Michael's *approach, goes out to meet him: the Angel denounces thir departure.* Eve's *Lamentation.* Adam *pleads, but submits: The Angel leads him up to a high Hill, sets before him in vision what shall happ'n till the Flood.*

Thus they in lowliest plight repentant stood
Praying, for from the Mercy-seat above
Prevenient Grace descending had remov'd
The stony from thir hearts, and made new flesh
Regenerate grow instead, that sighs now breath'd   5
Unutterable, which the Spirit of prayer
Inspir'd, and wing'd for Heav'n with speedier flight
Than loudest Oratory: yet thir port
Not of mean suitors, nor important less
Seem'd thir Petition, than when th' ancient Pair   10

1. *stood* seems inconsistent with *prostrate* in X, 1099, but in IV, 720, Adam stands to pray. In *CD* II, iv (C.Ed. XVII, 90), Milton says that, "No particular posture of the body in prayer was enjoined, even under the law."
2. The image is the mercy-seat in Aaron's tabernacle with its "two cherubim of gold, of beaten work, . . . in the two ends" (Exod. xxv, 18), which was traditionally a type of the intercession of angels, or of Christ, in heaven.
3. *Prevenient Grace:* grace which anticipates repentance. Cf. Ezekiel xi, 19: "I will take the stony heart out of their flesh, and will give them an heart of flesh."
5. So St. Paul says that "the Spirit itself maketh intercession for us with groanings that cannot be uttered" (Rom. viii, 26).
10. *th' ancient Pair:* Deucalion and Pyrrha, whom Ovid describes (*Met.* I, 321–80) as praying effectually to "fate-revealing Themis," the goddess of justice, after their survival of a great flood.

In Fables old, less ancient yet than these,
Deucalion and chaste *Pyrrha* to restore
The Race of Mankind drown'd, before the Shrine
Of *Themis* stood devout. To Heav'n thir prayers
Flew up, nor miss'd the way, by envious winds   15
Blown vagabond or frustrate: in they pass'd
Dimensionless through Heav'nly doors: then clad
With incense, where the Golden Altar fum'd,
By thir great Intercessor, came in sight
Before the Father's Throne: Then the glad Son   20
Presenting, thus to intercede began.
   See Father, what first fruits on Earth are sprung
From thy implanted Grace in Man, these Sighs
And Prayers, which in this Golden Censer, mixt
With Incense, I thy Priest before thee bring,   25
Fruits of more pleasing savor from thy seed
Sown with contrition in his heart, than those
Which his own hand manuring all the Trees
Of Paradise could have produc't, ere fall'n
From innocence. Now therefore bend thine ear   30
To supplication, hear his sighs though mute;
Unskilful with what words to pray, let mee
Interpret for him, mee his Advocate
And propitiation, all his works on mee
Good or not good ingraft, my Merit those   35
Shall perfet, and for these my Death shall pay.
Accept me, and in mee from these receive
The smell of peace toward Mankind, let him live
Before thee reconcil'd, at least his days
Number'd, though sad, till Death, his doom (which I   40
To mitigate thus plead, not to reverse)
To better life shall yield him, where with mee
All my redeem'd may dwell in joy and bliss,
Made one with me as I with thee am one.
   To whom the Father, without Cloud, serene.   45
All thy request for Man, accepted Son,

---

15. These prayers are contrasted with the "fruits/Of painful superstition and blind zeal" in III, 451–52, which "a violent cross wind . . . blows . . . transverse" in the limbo of vanity.

17. *Dimensionless* implies the immateriality of the prayers; extensionlessness was basic in the Cartesian definition of non-corporeal or spiritual being. The prayer are *clad With incense*, like those which are presented by the angel in Revelation viii, 3, who "stood at the altar, having a golden censer; and there was given unto him much incense, that he should offer it with the prayers of all sants. . . ."

19. The *Intercessor* is the Son of God, who makes intercession by "appearing in the presence of God for us" and by "rendering our prayers agreeable to God" (*CD* I, xv; C.Ed. XV, 294).

28. *manuring:* dressing, cultivating. Cf. IV, 628.

33. Cf. "We have an advocate with the Father, Jesus Christ the righteous: And he is the propitiation for our sins" (I John ii, 1–2).

43. So Christ prays in John xvii, 11: "Holy Father, keep through thine own name those whom thou hast given me, that they may be one, as we are."

Obtain, all thy request was my Decree:
But longer in that Paradise to dwell,
The Law I gave to Nature him forbids:
Those pure immortal Elements that know   50
No gross, no unharmonious mixture foul,
Eject him tainted now, and purge him off
As a distemper, gross to air as gross,
And mortal food, as may dispose him best
For dissolution wrought by Sin, that first   55
Distemper'd all things, and of incorrupt
Corrupted. I at first with two fair gifts
Created him endow'd, with Happiness
And Immortality: that fondly lost,
This other serv'd but to eternize woe;   60
Till I provided Death; so Death becomes
His final remedy, and after Life
Tri'd in sharp tribulation, and refin'd
By Faith and faithful works, to second Life,
Wak't in the renovation of the just,   65
Resigns him up with Heav'n and Earth renew'd.
But let us call to Synod all the Blest
Through Heav'n's wide bounds; from them I will not hide
My judgments, how with Mankind I proceed,
As how with peccant Angels late they saw;   70
And in thir state, though firm, stood more confirm'd.
    He ended, and the Son gave signal high
To the bright Minister that watch'd: hee blew
His Trumpet, heard in *Oreb* since perhaps
When God descended, and perhaps once more   75
To sound at general Doom. Th' Angelic blast
Fill'd all the Regions: from thir blissful Bow'rs
Of *Amarantin* Shade, Fountain or Spring,
By the waters of Life, where'er they sat
In fellowships of joy, the Sons of Light   80
Hasted, resorting to the Summons high,
And took thir Seats; till from his Throne supreme
Th' Almighty thus pronounc'd his sovran Will.

49. Cf. *Nature's Law* in X, 805.

50–57. The *incorrupt* and *pure Elements* of Eden are regarded as expelling fallen man as Belial says that the *Ethereal mould* of heaven, *incapable of stain*, would automatically *purge off the baser fire* of the rebel angels if they were to invade heaven. Cf. II, 140.

64. Here and in XII, 427, Milton indicates his qualified assent to the Lutheran doctrine of justification by faith.

74. The *Trumpet*, which summoned Michael's forces in heaven (VI, 60), Milton says *may* have been heard on earth when God gave the Ten Commandments to Moses on Mount Sinai, or *Horeb*, and *may* be heard again when God "shall send his angels with a great sound of the trumpet" (Matt. xxiv, 31) for the last judgment. At the judgment — according to traditions recorded in the *Jewish Encyclopaedia* VIII, 537 — Michael will blow the trumpet. Cf. the comparison of "the wakeful trump of doom" to "such a horrid clang/As on Mount Sinai rang" in *Nativity*, 157-58.

79. The *waters of Life* are the *River of Bliss* of III, 358.

O Sons, like one of us Man is become
To know both Good and Evil, since his taste   85
Of that defended Fruit; but let him boast
His knowledge of Good lost, and Evil got,
Happier, had it suffic'd him to have known
Good by itself, and Evil not at all.
He sorrows now, repents, and prays contrite,   90
My motions in him; longer than they move,
His heart I know, how variable and vain
Self-left. Lest therefore his now bolder hand
Reach also of the Tree of Life, and eat,
And live for ever, dream at least to live   95
For ever, to remove him I decree,
And send him from the Garden forth to Till
The Ground whence he was taken, fitter soil.
   Michael, this my behest have thou in charge,
Take to thee from among the Cherubim   100
Thy choice of flaming Warriors, lest the Fiend
Or in behalf of Man, or to invade
Vacant possession some new trouble raise:
Haste thee, and from the Paradise of God
Without remorse drive out the sinful Pair,   105
From hallow'd ground th' unholy, and denounce
To them and to thir Progeny from thence
Perpetual banishment. Yet lest they faint
At the sad Sentence rigorously urg'd,
For I behold them soft'nd and with tears   110
Bewailing thir excess, all terror hide.
If patiently thy bidding they obey,
Dismiss them not disconsolate; reveal
To *Adam* what shall come in future days,
As I shall thee enlighten, intermix   115
My Cov'nant in the woman's seed renew'd;
So send them forth, though sorrowing, yet in peace:
And on the East side of the Garden place,
Where entrance up from *Eden* easiest climbs,
Cherubic watch, and of a Sword the flame   120
Wide waving, all approach far off to fright,

---

84. "And the Lord God said, Behold, the man is become as one of us, to know good and evil: and now, lest he put forth his hand, and take also of the tree of life, and eat, and live for ever: Therefore the Lord God sent him forth from the garden of Eden' (Gen. iii, 22–23).
86. *defended:* forbidden. Cf. XII, 207.
91. *My motions:* my influence, i.e. the *prevenient Grace* of l. 3 above.
93. *Self-left:* when left to itself.
99. Cf. the note on Michael in VI, 44.
102. In reply to those who would in-

terpret *in behalf of* as "implying Satan's good will towards man," R. Adams observes — in *Ikon*, p. 119 — that the *O.E.D.* makes the meaning "with regard to" clear as a usage of Milton's time.
105. *remorse:* sorrow or pity. Cf. V., 566.
118. "So he drove out the man; and he placed at the east of the garden of Eden cherubim, and a flaming sword which turned every way, to keep the way of the tree of life" (Gen. iii, 24).

And guard all passage to the Tree of Life:
Lest Paradise a receptacle prove
To Spirits foul, and all my Trees thir prey,
With whose stol'n Fruit Man once more to delude.   125
    He ceas'd; and th' Archangelic Power prepar'd
For swift descent, with him the Cohort bright
Of watchful Cherubim; four faces each
Had, like a double *Janus*, all thir shape
Spangl'd with eyes more numerous than those   130
Of *Argus*, and more wakeful than to drowse,
Charm'd with *Arcadian* Pipe, the Pastoral Reed
Of *Hermes*, or his opiate Rod. Meanwhile
To resalute the World with sacred Light
Leucóthea wak'd, and with fresh dews imbalm'd   135
The Earth, when *Adam* and first Matron *Eve*
Had ended now thir Orisons, and found
Strength added from above, new hope to spring
Out of despair, joy, but with fear yet linkt;
Which thus to *Eve* his welcome words renew'd.   140
    Eve, easily may Faith admit, that all
The good which we enjoy, from Heav'n descends;
But that from us aught should ascend to Heav'n
So prevalent as to concern the mind
Of God high-blest, or to incline his will,   145
Hard to belief may seem; yet this will Prayer,
Or one short sigh of human breath, up-borne
Ev'n to the Seat of God. For since I sought
By Prayer th' offended Deity to appease,
Kneel'd and before him humbl'd all my heart,   150
Methought I saw him placable and mild,
Bending his ear; persuasion in me grew
That I was heard with favor; peace return'd
Home to my Breast, and to my memory
His promise, that thy Seed shall bruise our Foe;   155
Which then not minded in dismay, yet now
Assures me that the bitterness of death
Is past, and we shall live. Whence Hail to thee,
Eve rightly call'd, Mother of all Mankind,

---

129. The cherubs are compared to the Roman god of gates *Janus*, who was usually sculptured with two, but sometimes with four faces, ·ike the angels of Ezekiel's vision. A. H. Gilbert notes in *PMLA*, LIV (1941), 1026–30, that Calvin interpreted the four faces of Ezekiel's cherubim as signifying their power in the four quarters of the earth — a symbolism which was also understood to attach to the Janus quadrifrons. Cf. VI, 750, n.

130–132. The allusions span the description of the cherubs as "full of eyes" in Ezekiel i, 18, and Ovid's description (*Met.* I, 625–26) of Juno's commission of *Argus*, whose "head was set about with a hundred eyes," to watch her rival Io, though later in the story *Hermes* lulls all the eyes to sleep with his medicated rod and his pipes.

135. *Leucóthea*, the "shining goddess," is identified by Ovid (*Fasti*, 479 and 545) with the Roman goddess of the dawn, Matuta.

159. "And Adam called his wife's name Eve; because she was the mother

Mother of all things living, since by thee   160
Man is to live, and all things live for Man.
   To whom thus *Eve* with sad demeanor meek.
Ill worthy I such title should belong
To me transgressor, who for thee ordain'd
A help, became thy snare; to mee reproach   165
Rather belongs, distrust and all dispraise:
But infinite in pardon was my Judge,
That I who first brought Death on all, am grac't
The source of life; next favorable thou,
Who highly thus to entitle me voutsaf'st   170
Far other name deserving. But the Field
To labor calls us now with sweat impos'd,
Though after sleepless Night; for see the Morn,
All unconcern'd with our unrest, begins
Her rosy progress smiling; let us forth,   175
I never from thy side henceforth to stray,
Where'er our day's work lies, though now enjoin'd
Laborious, till day droop; while here we dwell,
What can be toilsome in these pleasant Walks?
Here let us live, though in fall'n state, content.   180
   So spake, so wish'd much humbl'd *Eve*, but Fate
Subscrib'd not; Nature first gave Signs, imprest
On Bird, Beast, Air, Air suddenly eclips'd
After short blush of Morn; nigh in her sight
The Bird of *Jove*, stoopt from his aery tow'r,   185
Two Birds of gayest plume before him drove:
Down from a Hill the Beast that reigns in Woods,
First hunter then, pursu'd a gentle brace,
Goodliest of all the Forest, Hart and Hind;
Direct to th' Eastern Gate was bent thir flight.   190
Adam observ'd, and with his Eye the chase
Pursuing, not unmov'd to *Eve* thus spake.
   O *Eve*, some furder change awaits us nigh,
Which Heav'n by these mute signs in Nature shows
Forerunners of his purpose, or to warn   195
Us haply too secure of our discharge
From penalty, because from death release

---

of all living" (Gen. iii, 20).
162. *sad:* serious, grave. Cf. the angels' *sad resolution* in VI, 541.
165. Cf. the note on *Mate* in X, 899.
182–192. The *Air* is *eclips'd* or darkened probably by an eclipse of the sun such as sheds *disastrous twilight* in I, 597. The blight now beginning to fall on all nature is the consequence of the *influence malignant* of X, 662, that the heavenly bodies have begun to pour upon the earth. The "pathetic fallacy" involved

in the conception of nature as degenerating after man's fall is justified by A. Z. Butler in *Essays in Honor of Walter Clyde Curry* (Nashville, 1954), pp. 274–76, as logical in the light of the theory of the "great chain of being" which Raphael expounds in V, 469–90.
185. *The Bird of Jove*, the eagle, and the lion both feel their first hunting instinct. Stooping was a term in falconry for the swoop of a hawk from its *tower* (lofty flight) to strike its prey.

Some days; how long, and what till then our life,
Who knows, or more than this, that we are dust,
And thither must return and be no more.   200
Why else this double object in our sight
Of flight pursu'd in th' Air and o'er the ground
One way the self-same hour? why in the East
Darkness ere Day's mid-course, and Morning light
More orient in yon Western Cloud that draws   205
O'er the blue Firmament a radiant white,
And slow descends, with something heav'nly fraught.
   He err'd not, for by this the heav'nly Bands
Down from a Sky of Jasper lighted now
In Paradise, and on a Hill made halt,   210
A glorious Apparition, had not doubt
And carnal fear that day dimm'd *Adam's* eye.
Not that more glorious, when the Angels met
Jacob in *Mahanaim*, where he saw
The field Pavilion'd with his Guardians bright;   215
Nor that which on the flaming Mount appear'd
In *Dothan*, cover'd with a Camp of Fire,
Against the *Syrian* King, who to surprise
One man, Assassin-like had levied War,
War unproclaim'd. The Princely Hierarch   220
In thir bright stand, there left his Powers to seize
Possession of the Garden; hee alone,
To find where *Adam* shelter'd, took his way,
Not unperceiv'd of *Adam*, who to *Eve*,
While the great Visitant approach'd, thus spake.   225
   Eve, now expect great tidings, which perhaps
Of us will soon determine, or impose
New Laws to be observ'd; for I descry
From yonder blazing Cloud that veils the Hill
One of the heav'nly Host, and by his Gait   230
None of the meanest, some great Potentate
Or of the Thrones above, such Majesty
Invests him coming; yet not terrible,
That I should fear, nor sociably mild,
As *Raphaël*, that I should much confide,   235
But solemn and sublime, whom not to offend,
With reverence I must meet, and thou retire.
He ended; and th' Arch-Angel soon drew nigh,
Not in his shape Celestial, but as Man

---

204. The *light* is the glory of Michael's descending angels.
   214. *Mahanaim* (i.e. the two hosts) was Jacob's name for the place where "the angels of God met him" (Gen. xxxii, 1–2).
   217. After warning the king of Israel of a treacherous raid by the king of Syria,

the prophet Elisha was surrounded by the Syrians in *Dothan*. He would have been kidnapped if the mountain had not been "full of horses and chariots of fire round about Elisha" (II Kings vi, 17).
   234–235. Cf. the reference to Raphael as *the sociable Spirit* in V, 221.

Clad to meet Man; over his lucid **Arms**   240
A military Vest of purple flow'd
Livelier than *Melibæan,* or the grain
Of *Sarra,* worn by Kings and Heroes old
In time of Truce; *Iris* had dipt the woof;
His starry Helm unbuckl'd show'd him prime   245
In Manhood where Youth ended; by his side
As in a glistering *Zodiac* hung the Sword,
Satan's dire dread, and in his hand the Spear.
Adam bow'd low, hee Kingly from his State
Inclin'd not, but his coming thus declar'd.   250
   Adam, Heav'n's high behest no Preface needs:
Sufficient that thy Prayers are heard, and Death,
Then due by sentence when thou didst transgress,
Defeated of his seizure many days
Giv'n thee of Grace, wherein thou mayst repent,   255
And one bad act with many deeds well done
May'st cover: well may then thy Lord appeas'd
Redeem thee quite from Death's rapacious claim;
But longer in this Paradise to dwell
Permits not; to remove thee I am come,   260
And send thee from the Garden forth to till
The ground whence thou wast tak'n, fitter Soil.
   He added not, for *Adam* at the news
Heart-strook with chilling gripe of sorrow stood,
That all his senses bound; *Eve,* who unseen   265
Yet all had heard, with audible lament
Discover'd soon the place of her retire.
   O unexpected stroke, worse than of Death!
Must I thus leave thee Paradise? thus leave
Thee Native Soil, these happy Walks and Shades,   270
Fit haunt of Gods? where I had hope to spend,
Quiet though sad, the respite of that day
That must be mortal to us both. O flow'rs,
That never will in other Climate grow,
My early visitation, and my last   275
At Ev'n, which I bred up with tender hand

---

242. The Thessalian town of *Melibœa* was famous for its purple *grain* (dye), as Virgil suggests in the *Aeneid* V, 251.

243. *Sarra* was an ancient name for Tyre, which was famous for its dyes as early as its king's dispatch of "a man skilful to work . . . in purple, in blue, and in fine linen" to help build Solomon's temple (II Chron. ii, 14).

244. Cf. *Iris' Woof,* the colors of the goddess of dawn, in *Comus,* 83.

247. *Zodiac* keeps its Greek meaning of "a belt," but it also suggests the splendor of the celestial zodiac and its constellations.

254. *Defeated:* frustrated (in his attempt to arrest Adam). Cf. ll. 96–98 and 48–49 above.

272. *respite:* the remainder of the time granted by God's reprieve of the sentence of physical death.

273–285. The thought remotely parallels Henry More's interpretation of Adam's "casting out of Paradise" as "a descent from an 'aerial' to a 'terrestrial' world," the loss of an original state that was "wholly etherial" and was "an happy and joyful condition of the Spirit." Cf. ll. 50–57 above, n.

From the first op'ning bud, and gave ye Names,
Who now shall rear ye to the Sun, or rank
Your Tribes, and water from th' ambrosial Fount?
Thee lastly nuptial Bower, by mee adorn'd   280
With what to sight or smell was sweet; from thee
How shall I part, and whither wander down
Into a lower World, to this obscure
And wild, how shall we breathe in other Air
Less pure, accustom'd to immortal Fruits?   285
    Whom thus the Angel interrupted mild.
Lament not *Eve*, but patiently resign
What justly thou hast lost; nor set thy heart,
Thus over-fond, on that which is not thine;
Thy going is not lonely, with thee goes   290
Thy Husband, him to follow thou art bound;
Where he abides, think there thy native soil.
    Adam by this from the cold sudden damp
Recovering, and his scatter'd spirits return'd,
To *Michael* thus his humble words address'd.   295
    Celestial, whether among the Thrones, or nam'd
Of them the Highest, for such of shape may seem
Prince above Princes, gently hast thou told
Thy message, which might else in telling wound,
And in performing end us; what besides   300
Of sorrow and dejection and despair
Our frailty can sustain, thy tidings bring,
Departure from this happy place, our sweet
Recess, and only consolation left
Familiar to our eyes, all places else   305
Inhospitable appear and desolate,
Nor knowing us nor known: and if by prayer
Incessant I could hope to change the will
Of him who all things can, I would not cease
To weary him with my assiduous cries: 310
But prayer against his absolute Decree
No more avails than breath against the wind,
Blown stifling back on him that breathes it forth:
Therefore to his great bidding I submit.
This most afflicts me, that departing hence,   315
As from his face I shall be hid, depriv'd
His blessed count'nance; here I could frequent,

---

283. *to this:* in comparison with this.
294. Cf. Eve's *damp horror* in V, 65.
Fear *scattered* the vital and animal *spirits*
from their seats in the heart and head
throughout the whole body. Cf. V,
484–88, n.
309. Cf. Lovelace's transitive use of
can: "Yet can I music too" (*O.E.D.*).
310. *weary:* importune. Milton con-

trasts God with the unjust judge of
Luke xviii, 5–7, who could be made to
yield only by importunity.
316. Adam's words resemble Cain's
after his curse for the murder of Abel:
"Behold, thou hast driven me out this
day from the face of the earth; and from
thy face shall I be hid" (Gen. iv, 14).

With worship, place by place where he voutsaf'd
Presence Divine, and to my Sons relate;
On this Mount he appear'd, under this Tree   320
Stood visible, among these Pines his voice
I heard, here with him at this Fountain talk'd:
So many grateful Altars I would rear
Of grassy Turf, and pile up every Stone
Of lustre from the brook, in memory,   325
Or monument to Ages, and thereon
Offer sweet smelling Gums and Fruits and Flow'rs:
In yonder nether World where shall I seek
His bright appearances, or footstep trace?
For though I fled him angry, yet recall'd   330
To life prolong'd and promis'd Race, I now
Gladly behold though but his utmost skirts
Of glory, and far off his steps adore.
    To whom thus *Michael* with regard benign.
Adam, thou know'st Heav'n his, and all the Earth,   335
Not this Rock only; his Omnipresence fills
Land, Sea, and Air, and every kind that lives,
Fomented by his virtual power and warm'd:
All th' Earth he gave thee to possess and rule,
No despicable gift; surmise not then   340
His presence to these narrow bounds confin'd
Of Paradise or *Eden:* this had been
Perhaps thy Capital Seat, from whence had spread
All generations, and had hither come
From all the ends of th' Earth, to celebrate   345
And reverence thee thir great Progenitor.
But this preëminence thou hast lost, brought down
To dwell on even ground now with thy Sons:
Yet doubt not but in Valley and in Plain
God is as here, and will be found alike   350
Present, and of his presence many a sign
Still following thee, still compassing thee round
With goodness and paternal Love, his Face
Express, and of his steps the track Divine.
Which that thou may'st believe, and be confirm'd,   355
Ere thou from hence depart, know I am sent
To show thee what shall come in future days

335–338. The thought fuses Christ's
warning to the woman of Samaria against
worshipping God only "in this mountain"
(John iv, 21) with Jeremiah's question:
"Can any hide himself in secret places
that I shall not see him? saith the Lord:
do not I fill heaven and earth?" (xxiii, 24).
Cf. VII, 168–69.
338. *Fomented:* filled with life-giving
heat. Cf. IV, 669. *virtual:* possessed of

the power to instil virtue.
357. Adam's vision of the future of
mankind rests on epic precedent like the
vision of Rome's future that Aeneas sees
in the Elysian Fields (*Aen.* VI, 754–854)
and Britomart's vision of her progeny in
the *Faerie Queene* III, iii, 29–49; but it
rests also on Daniel's vision of "Michael,
one of the chief princes" coming to the
help of exiled Israel (Dan. x, 13). Cf.

To thee and to thy Offspring; good with bad
Expect to hear, supernal Grace contending
With sinfulness of Men; thereby to learn   360
True patience, and to temper joy with fear
And pious sorrow, equally inur'd
By moderation either state to bear,
Prosperous or adverse: so shalt thou lead
Safest thy life, and best prepar'd endure   365
Thy mortal passage when it comes. Ascend
This Hill; let *Eve* (for I have drencht her eyes)
Here sleep below while thou to foresight wak'st,
As once thou slep'st, while Shee to life was form'd.
　　To whom thus *Adam* gratefully repli'd.   370
Ascend, I follow thee, safe Guide, the path
Thou lead'st me, and to the hand of Heav'n submit,
However chast'ning, to the evil turn
My obvious breast, arming to overcome
By suffering, and earn rest from labor won,   375
If so I may attain. So both ascend
In the Visions of God: It was a Hill
Of Paradise the highest, from whose top
The Hemisphere of Earth in clearest Ken
Stretcht out to the amplest reach of prospect lay.   380
Not higher that Hill nor wider looking round,
Whereon for different cause the Tempter set
Our second *Adam* in the Wilderness,
To show him all Earth's Kingdoms and thir Glory.
His Eye might there command wherever stood   385
City of old or modern Fame, the Seat
Of mightiest Empire, from the destin'd Walls
Of *Cambalu*, seat of *Cathaian Can*,
And *Samarchand* by *Oxus*, *Temir's* Throne,
To *Paquin* of *Sinæan* Kings, and thence   390
To *Agra* and *Lahor* of great *Mogul*

VI, 44, n. Milton's closest precedent is in Du Bartas' *Divine Weeks*, in the parts from *The Handicrafts* through to *The Decay*.

363. The phrasing suggests the title of Petrarch's treatise *On the Remedies of both Kinds of Fortune* (i.e. of good and bad). The Stoic principle was assimilated very early by Christian humanism.

377–384. Milton recalls both "the visions of God . . . upon a very high mountain" of the prophet Ezekiel (x, 2) and the "exceeding high mountain" where the devil tempted Christ with "all the kingdoms of the world, and the glory of them" (Matt. iv, 8). Cf. *PR* III, 252.

388. In *Moscovia* (C.Ed. X, 344–47) Milton describes the glories of the wall of Cathay (China) and the *Can* (Khan), its ruler, whose seat is *Cambalu*. E. N. S. Thompson suggested — in *SP*, XVI (1919), 160–62 — that here he remembered *Cambalu* on Ortelius' map of Tartary, with the Khan pictured sitting in a great tent, sceptre in hand, under an inscription reading: "Magnus Cham, maximus Asie princeps." On the same map *Temir* or Timur (Tamberlane) is shown enthroned in his capital *Samarchand* on the river *Oxus*.

390. *Paquin*: Pekin. *Sinæan*: Chinese.

391. *Agra*, in northwestern India, is the site of the Taj Mahal. Like *Lahor* in the Punjab, it was a great *Mogul* capital.

Down to the golden *Chersonese,* or where
The *Persian* in *Ecbatan* sat, or since
In *Hispahan,* or where the *Russian Ksar*
In *Mosco,* or the Sultan in *Bizance,*   395
Turchestan-born; nor could his eye not ken
Th' Empire of *Negus* to his utmost Port
Ercoco and the less Maritime Kings
Mombaza, and *Quiloa,* and *Melind,*
And *Sofala* thought *Ophir,* to the Realm   400
Of *Congo,* and *Angola* fardest South;
Or thence from *Niger* Flood to *Atlas* Mount
The Kingdoms of *Almansor, Fez* and *Sus,*
Marocco and *Algiers,* and *Tremisen;*
On *Europe* thence, and where *Rome* was to sway   405
The World: in Spirit perhaps he also saw
Rich *Mexico* the seat of *Montezume,*
And *Cusco* in *Peru,* the richer seat
Of *Atabalipa,* and yet unspoil'd
Guiana, whose great City *Geryon's* Sons   410
Call *El Dorado:* but to nobler sights
Michael from *Adam's* eyes the Film remov'd
Which that false Fruit that promis'd clearer sight
Had bred; then purg'd with Euphrasy and Rue
The visual Nerve, for he had much to see;   415
And from the Well of Life three drops instill'd.
So deep the power of these Ingredients pierc'd,

392. Purchas suggests both Siam and Molucca or Samatra (*Pilgrimage,* pp. 557 and 697) as identifiable with the *golden Chersonese* of Ptolemy and also with the *Ophir* whence gold was brought for Solomon's temple (I Kings ix, 28). Cf. l. 400, n.
393–394. *Ecbatana* was the ancient capital of Persia; *Hispahan* (Ispahan) became its capital under Shah Abbás the Great about 1600.
395. *Bizance:* Byzantium, the modern Constantinople, conquered by the Turks in 1453.
397–398. The *Negus* or king of Abyssinia controlled the port of *Ercoco,* the modern Arkiko, on the Red Sea.
399. *Mombaza* in British East Africa, *Melind* on the East African coast, and *Quiloa* (Kilwa-Kisiwani), an island port off the Tanganyikan shore, are briefly mentioned by Purchas (*Pilgrimes,* II, 1024).
400. *Sofala* in Portuguese East Africa, was a port so famous for traffic in gold that it was sometimes identified with the *golden Chersonese.* Cf. l. 392, above, n.
401. Purchas mentions *Angola* as ruled by a king who was "but a Governour or

Deputie under the king of Congo" (*Pilgrimes,* II, 995).
403–404. *Almansor* (Mansur, 938–1002 A.D.) ruled *Fez* and *Sus* in Morocco, *Tremisen* (modern Tlemcen) in Algeria, and parts of Spain.
407. *Montezuma* was the Aztec emperor whom Cortez conquered in 1520.
408. *Cusco* was the capital of the Peruvian emperor *Atabalipa* or Atahuallpa whom Pizarro overthrew in 1533.
410. The *great City* is probably Manoa, the reputed residence of *El Dorado,* the Gilded King, in quest of whom Sir Walter Raleigh undertook to explore the Orinoco in 1595.
414. *Euphrasy* or Eiebright, says Gerard's *Herball,* p. 537, "is very much commended for the eies. . . . It preserveth the sight, increaseth it, and being feeble and lost it restoreth the same." On p. 1074 *Rue* is said, "when a little is boyled or scalded, and kept in pickle, . . . and eaten," to have virtue that "quickeneth the sight."
416. Cf. Psalm xxxvi, 9: "For with thee is the fountain of life: in thy light shall we see light."

Ev'n to the inmost seat of mental sight,
That *Adam* now enforc't to close his eyes,
Sunk down and all his Spirits became intranst: 420
But him the gentle Angel by the hand
Soon rais'd, and his attention thus recall'd.
    Adam, now ope thine eyes, and first behold
Th' effects which thy original crime hath wrought
In some to spring from thee, who never touch'd   425
Th'excepted Tree, nor with the Snake conspir'd,
Nor sinn'd thy sin, yet from that sin derive
Corruption to bring forth more violent deeds.
    His eyes he op'n'd, and beheld a field,
Part arable and tilth, whereon were Sheaves   430
New reapt, the other part sheep-walks and folds;
I' th' midst an Altar as the Land-mark stood
Rustic, of grassy sward; thither anon
A sweaty Reaper from his Tillage brought
First Fruits, the green Ear, and the yellow Sheaf,   435
Uncull'd, as came to hand; a Shepherd next
More meek came with the Firstlings of his Flock
Choicest and best; then sacrificing, laid
The Inwards and thir Fat, with Incense strew'd,
On the cleft Wood, and all due Rites perform'd.   440
His Off'ring soon propitious Fire from Heav'n
Consum'd with nimble glance, and grateful steam;
The other's not, for his was not sincere;
Whereat hee inly rag'd, and as they talk'd,
Smote him into the Midriff with a stone   445
That beat out life; he fell, and deadly pale
Groan'd out his Soul with gushing blood effus'd.
Much at that sight was *Adam* in his heart
Dismay'd, and thus in haste to th' Angel cri'd.
    O Teacher, some great mischief hath befall'n   450
To that meek man, who well had sacrific'd;
Is Piety thus and pure Devotion paid?
    T' whom *Michael* thus, hee also mov'd, repli'd.
These two are Brethren, *Adam*, and to come
Out of thy loins; th' unjust the just hath slain,   455
For envy that his Brother's Offering found
From Heav'n acceptance; but the bloody Fact
Will be aveng'd, and th' other's Faith approv'd
Lose no reward, though here thou see him die,

420. So Daniel sinks into trance in the vision to which l. 357 above refers.
430. *tilth:* land under cultivation.
432–460. Milton stresses the murder of Abel by Cain because of its symbolic importance, to which St. Augustine contributed in the *City of God* XIII, v, by making it an example of the danger of envy.
436. *Uncull'd:* unselected (in contrast with *Choicest and best* in 438).
441. *Fire from Heav'n* kindles sacrifices by sincere worshippers in Lev. ix, 24; I Chron. xxi, 26, etc.

Rolling in dust and gore. To which our Sire.   460
Alas, both for the deed and for the cause!
But have I now seen Death? Is this the way
I must return to native dust? O sight
Of terror, foul and ugly to behold,
Horrid to think, how horrible to feel!   465
To whom thus *Michaël*. Death thou hast seen
In his first shape on man; but many shapes
Of Death, and many are the ways that lead
To his grim Cave, all dismal; yet to sense
More terrible at th' entrance than within.   470
Some, as thou saw'st, by violent stroke shall die,
By Fire, Flood, Famine, by Intemperance more
In Meats and Drinks, which on the Earth shall bring
Diseases dire, of which a monstrous crew
Before thee shall appear; that thou may'st know   475
What misery th' inabstinence of *Eve*
Shall bring on men. Immediately a place
Before his eyes appear'd, sad, noisome, dark,
A Lazar-house it seem'd, wherein were laid
Numbers of all diseas'd, all maladies   480
Of ghastly Spasm, or racking torture, qualms
Of heart-sick Agony, all feverous kinds,
Convulsions, Epilepsies, fierce Catarrhs,
Intestine Stone and Ulcer, Colic pangs,
Dæmoniac Frenzy, moping Melancholy   485
And Moon-struck madness, pining Atrophy,
Marasmus, and wide-wasting Pestilence,
Dropsies, and Asthmas, and Joint-racking Rheums.
Dire was the tossing, deep the groans, despair
Tended the sick busiest from Couch to Couch;   490
And over them triumphant Death his Dart
Shook, but delay'd to strike, though oft invok't
With vows, as thir chief good, and final hope.
Sight so deform what heart of Rock could long

469. The *Cave* resembles an under-world such as the Sheol of the Hebrews or — as G. L. Loane suggests in *N&Q*, CLXXV (1938), 457 — "that invisible cave that no light enters," Hades, as Chapman describes it in the opening lines of the *Iliad*.

477–495. Godwin, in his *Life of Chaucer* (II, 412) suggested that Milton got the "first hint of a lazar-house from *Piers Plowman*, Passus XX," but the spirit of Milton's scene is rather like that of Du Bartas in the account of human misery that opens *The Furies* in *The Divine Weeks*. Cf. l. 357 above, n.

480–488. Milton's names for these diseases and his indications of their symp-

toms are studied by K. Svendsen in *M. & S.* pp. 174–200.

485–487. These lines were added by Milton in the second edition.

487. *Marasmus:* any wasting away or "consumption" of the body.

492. *oft invok't* is a vague allusion to many passages in the classics (e.g., Sophocles' *Oedipus Colonneus*, 1220, and *Philoctetes*, 797–98) which Milton may have remembered as echoed in Spenser's lines:

　　. . . death is an equall doome
　To good and bad, the commen in of
　rest.

　　　　　　　　(*F.Q.* II, i, 59)

Dry-ey'd behold? *Adam* could not, but wept,   495
Though not of Woman born; compassion quell'd
His best of Man, and gave him up to tears
A space, till firmer thoughts restrain'd excess,
And scarce recovering words his plaint renew'd.
  O miserable Mankind, to what fall   500
Degraded, to what wretched state reserv'd!
Better end here unborn. Why is life giv'n
To be thus wrested from us? rather why
Obtruded on us thus? who if we knew
What we receive, would either not accept   505
Life offer'd, or soon beg to lay it down,
Glad to be so dismist in peace. Can thus
Th' Image of God in man created once
So goodly and erect, though faulty since,
To such unsightly sufferings be debas't   510
Under inhuman pains? Why should not Man,
Retaining still Divine similitude
In part, from such deformities be free,
And for his Maker's Image sake exempt?
  Thir Maker's Image, answer'd *Michael*, then   515
Forsook them, when themselves they vilifi'd
To serve ungovern'd appetite, and took
His Image whom they served, a brutish vice,
Inductive mainly to the sin of *Eve*.
Therefore so abject is thir punishment,   520
Disfiguring not God's likeness, but thir own,
Or if his likeness, by themselves defac't
While they pervert pure Nature's healthful rules
To loathsome sickness, worthily, since they
God's Image did not reverence in themselves.   525
  I yield it just, said *Adam*, and submit.
But is there yet no other way, besides
These painful passages, how we may come
To Death, and mix with our connatural dust?
  There is, said *Michael*, if thou well observe   530

---

496. Here the reminiscence of *Macbeth* (V, viii, 37–39) must have been conscious:
  Though Birnam wood be come to Dunsinane,
  And thou oppos'd, being of no woman born,
  Yet I will try the last.
497. Again the reminiscence is of *Macbeth* (V, viii, 23–24):
  Accursed be that tongue that tels mee so;
  For it hath Cow'd my better part of man.
504. In making Adam guilty of what

Sir Thomas Browne called the "underweening of this life" Milton was probably thinking, like Browne, of the saying of "the Stoic [Seneca] that life would not be accepted if it were offered unto such as knew it" (*Christian Morals* III, xxv).
507–514. Adam has heard from Raphael (VII, 519) that God made man in his own image, and Milton represents the angel as adding the Platonic argument for human nobility from man's upright stature. Cf. VII, 509, n.
529. Cf. X, 246, and XI, 199–200 and 463.

The rule of not too much, by temperance taught,
In what thou eat'st and drink'st, seeking from thence
Due nourishment, not gluttonous delight,
Till many years over thy head return:
So may'st thou live, till like ripe Fruit thou drop   535
Into thy Mother's lap, or be with ease
Gather'd, not harshly pluckt, for death mature:
This is old age; but then thou must outlive
Thy youth, thy strength, thy beauty, which will change
To wither'd weak and gray; thy Senses then   540
Obtuse, all taste of pleasure must forgo,
To what thou hast, and for the Air of youth
Hopeful and cheerful, in thy blood will reign
A melancholy damp of cold and dry
To weigh thy Spirits down, and last consume   545
The Balm of Life. To whom our Ancestor.
    Henceforth I fly not Death, nor would prolong
Life much, bent rather how I may be quit
Fairest and easiest of this cumbrous charge,
Which I must keep till my appointed day   550
Of rend'ring up, and patiently attend
My dissolution. *Michaël* repli'd.
    Nor love thy Life, nor hate; but what thou liv'st
Live well, how long or short permit to Heav'n:
And now prepare thee for another sight.   555
    He look'd and saw a spacious Plain, whereon
Were Tents of various hûe; by some were herds
Of Cattle grazing: others, whence the sound
Of Instruments that made melodious chime

531. The idea that "health is destroyed by too much and too little food and drink" was already a commonplace when Aristotle stated it as one of many aspects of the *rule of not too much* in the *Nicomachean Ethics* II, ii, 6.

535. The simile of *ripe Fruit* came down from Cicero's *Of Old Age* (xix) through Dante's *Convito* (iv) and Spenser's image of being "made ripe for death by eld" (*F.Q.* II, x, 32, 2).

544. Cf. Burton on old age as the most frequent cause of melancholy, since it is "cold and dry, and of the same quality as melancholy is, . . . needs must cause it, by diminution of spirits and substance" (*Anatomy* I, ii, 5; Everyman Ed. I, 210).

551-552. *and patiently attend My dissolution:* Milton's insertion in the second edition. The reader of the first was expected to complete the thought from Job xiv, 14: "All the days of my appointed time will I wait, till my change come."

553. The maxim repeats Martial in his tenth *Epigram:* "Neither dread nor desire thy last hour," and similar advice in Horace's famous "Soracte" *Ode* (I, ix, 9) and in Seneca's *Epistles* xxiv, 24, and lxv, 18.

556-711. The basis for the scenes in the *spacious plain* is the account in Genesis iv, 20-22, of the sons of Lamech: Jabal, "the father of such as dwell in tents," Jubal, "the father of all such as handle the harp and organ," and Tubal-Cain, "an instructor of every artificer in brass and iron." Du Bartas embroidered the subject of the metalworkers, over whom

sweating *Tubal* stands,
Hastning the hot work in their sounding hands,
No time lost *Jubal:* th'unfull Harmony
Of uneven hammers, beating diversely,
Wakens the tunes that his sweet numbery soule
Yer birth (some think) learn'd of the warbling *Pole.*

(*Divine Weeks,* p. 304)

Was heard, of Harp and Organ; and who mov'd 560
Thir stops and chords was seen: his volant touch
Instinct through all proportions low and high
Fled and pursu'd transverse the resonant fugue.
In other part stood one who at the Forge
Laboring, two massy clods of Iron and Brass 565
Had melted (whether found where casual fire
Had wasted woods on Mountain or in Vale,
Down to the veins of Earth, thence gliding hot
To some Cave's mouth, or whether washt by stream
From underground); the liquid Ore he drain'd 570
Into fit moulds prepar'd; from which he form'd
First his own Tools; then, what might else be wrought
Fusile or grav'n in metal. After these,
But on the hither side a different sort
From the high neighboring Hills, which was thir Seat, 575
Down to the Plain descended: by thir guise
Just men they seem'd, and all thir study bent
To worship God aright, and know his works
Not hid, nor those things last which might preserve
Freedom and Peace to men: they on the Plain 580
Long had not walkt, when from the Tents behold
A Bevy of fair Women, richly gay
In Gems and wanton dress; to the Harp they sung
Soft amorous Ditties, and in dance came on:
The Men though grave, ey'd them, and let thir eyes 585
Rove without rein, till in the amorous Net
Fast caught, they lik'd, and each his liking chose;
And now of love they treat till th' Ev'ning Star
Love's Harbinger appear'd; then all in heat
They light the Nuptial Torch, and bid invoke 590
Hymen, then first to marriage Rites invok't;
With Feast and Music all the Tents resound.

561–563. The rhythm of the lines is analyzed in Whaler's *Counterpoint*, p. 74, as exactly corresponding to a fugal effect.

562. Jubal's art is inborn (*instinct*) because he has, as "some think," absorbed it before birth from "the warbling Pole" (the heavens).

564–573. The lines reflect Lucretius' account of the discovery of metals when they were first laid bare by lightning-kindled forest fires and accidentally fused in natural pits (*De rerum natura* V, 1241–68).

573–627. The scene shifts from east of Eden to *the hither side*, west. A tradition stemming from Genesis vi, 2–4, represents the sons of Seth as deservedly called the "sons of God" until they were lured from their mountain homes to marry and beget a giant race on the daughters of Cain. Many commentators, Jewish and Patristic, interpreted "sons of God" as meaning that the lovers of Cain's daughters were fallen angels, but Saint Augustine, Saint Thomas Aquinas, and most later commentators, Protestant as well as Catholic, condemned that view as heretical. Cf. D. C. Allen in *MLN*, LXI (1946), 78; R. H. West in *Angels*, pp. 129–31; and A. Williams in *Expositor*, p. 152. Cf. also V, 446–49, and *PR* II, 178–81.

588. The *Ev'ning Star* is Venus, as in VIII, 519.

591. Milton thought of many invocations of the god of marriage such as the cry of the groomsmen in Spenser's *Epithalamion*, l. 140:

Hymen, Iö Hymen, Hymen, they
do shout.

Such happy interview and fair event
Of love and youth not lost, Songs, Garlands, Flow'rs,
And charming Symphonies attach'd the heart   595
Of *Adam*, soon inclin'd to admit delight
The bent of Nature; which he thus express'd.
　　True opener of mine eyes, prime Angel blest,
Much better seems this Vision, and more hope
Of peaceful days portends, than those two past;   600
Those were of hate and death, or pain much worse,
Here Nature seems fulfill'd in all her ends.
　　To whom thus *Michael*. Judge not what is best
By pleasure, though to Nature seeming meet,
Created, as thou art, to nobler end   605
Holy and pure, conformity divine.
Those Tents thou saw'st so pleasant, were the Tents
Of wickedness, wherein shall dwell his Race
Who slew his Brother; studious they appear
Of Arts that polish Life, Inventors rare,   610
Unmindful of thir Maker, though his Spirit
Taught them, but they his gifts acknowledg'd none.
Yet they a beauteous offspring shall beget;
For that fair female Troop thou saw'st, that seem'd
Of Goddesses, so blithe, so smooth, so gay,   615
Yet empty of all good wherein consists
Woman's domestic honor and chief praise;
Bred only and completed to the taste
Of lustful appetence, to sing, to dance,
To dress, and troll the Tongue, and roll the Eye.   620
To these that sober Race of Men, whose lives
Religious titl'd them the Sons of God,
Shall yield up all thir virtue, all thir fame
Ignobly, to the trains and to the smiles
Of these fair Atheists, and now swim in joy,   625
(Erelong to swim at large) and laugh; for which
The world erelong a world of tears must weep.
　　To whom thus *Adam* of short joy bereft.
O pity and shame, that they who to live well
Enter'd so fair, should turn aside to tread   630
Paths indirect, or in the mid way faint!

---

607. Cf. Psalm lxxxix, 10: "I had
rather be a doorkeeper in the house of
my God, than to dwell in the tents of
wickedness."
　611. *Spirit* — as M. Kelley notes in
Argument, p. 109 — "does not refer to
the Third Person" of the Trinity, but
to "the virtue and power of God the
Father." Cf. XII, 485–95.
　618–625. The lines owe something to
the commentary on Genesis in the Geneva

Bible, which observes that the "men had
more respect to the beautie, and worldly
considerations, then to their manners
and godliness." G. W. Whiting collects
the Geneva marginal notes in *N&Q*,
CXCIV (1949), 75.
　620. *troll:* wag.
　624. *trains:* tricks, deceits.
　626. The play on *swim* anticipates the
flood in ll. 818–74 below.

But still I see the tenor of Man's woe
Holds on the same, from Woman to begin.
From Man's effeminate slackness it begins,
Said th' Angel, who should better hold his place   635
By wisdom, and superior gifts receiv'd.
But now prepare thee for another Scene.
He look'd and saw wide Territory spread
Before him, Towns, and rural works between,
Cities of Men with lofty Gates and Tow'rs,   640
Concourse in Arms, fierce Faces threat'ning War,
Giants of mighty Bone, and bold emprise;
Part wield thir Arms, part curb the foaming Steed,
Single or in Array of Battle rang'd
Both Horse and Foot, nor idly must'ring stood;   645
One way a Band select from forage drives
A herd of Beeves, fair Oxen and fair Kine
From a fat Meadow ground; or fleecy Flock,
Ewes and thir bleating Lambs over the Plain,
Thir Booty; scarce with Life the Shepherds fly,   650
But call in aid, which makes a bloody Fray;
With cruel Tournament the Squadrons join;
Where Cattle pastur'd late, now scatter'd lies
With Carcasses and Arms th' ensanguin'd Field
Deserted: Others to a City strong   655
Lay Siege, encampt; by Battery, Scale, and Mine,
Assaulting; others from the wall defend
With Dart and Jav'lin, Stones and sulphurous Fire;
On each hand slaughter and gigantic deeds.
In other part the scepter'd Heralds call   660
To Council in the City Gates: anon
Grey-headed men and grave, with Warriors mixt,
Assemble, and Harangues are heard, but soon
In factious opposition, till at last
Of middle Age one rising, eminent   665
In wise deport, spake much of Right and Wrong,
Of Justice, of Religion, Truth and Peace,
And Judgment from above: him old and young
Exploded, and had seiz'd with violent hands,
Had not a Cloud descending snatch'd him thence   670
Unseen amid the throng: so violence

633. To illustrate the popular etymology the *O.E.D.* quotes John Heywood's *Proverbs* II, vii: "A woman! As who saith, woe to the man!"
638–673. The panorama has many obvious Homeric echoes — particularly of the description of the shield of Achilles (*Il.* XVIII, 478–616).
646. *Band select:* a band of picked men.

660. The council of elders called together by heralds while a city is besieged is very close to *Iliad* XVIII, 503–10.
665. *Of middle Age one rising* is Enoch, who "walked with God" and was translated to heaven at the "middle age" (in comparison with that of most of the patriarchs) of 365 years (Gen. v, 21–24).
669. *Exploded:* hooted.

Proceeded, and Oppression, and Sword-Law
Through all the Plain, and refuge none was found.
Adam was all in tears, and to his guide
Lamenting turn'd full sad; O what are these,   675
Death's Ministers, not Men, who thus deal Death
Inhumanly to men, and multiply
Ten thousandfold the sin of him who slew
His Brother; for of whom such massacre
Make they but of thir Brethren, men of men?   680
But who was that Just Man, whom had not Heav'n
Rescu'd, had in his Righteousness been lost?
  To whom thus *Michael*. These are the product
Of those ill-mated Marriages thou saw'st;
Where good with bad were matcht, who of themselves   685
Abhor to join; and by imprudence mixt,
Produce prodigious Births of body or mind.
Such were these Giants, men of high renown;
For in those days Might only shall be admir'd,
And Valor and Heroic Virtue call'd;   690
To overcome in Battle, and subdue
Nations, and bring home spoils with infinite
Man-slaughter, shall be held the highest pitch
Of human Glory, and for Glory done
Of triumph, to be styl'd great Conquerors,   695
Patrons of Mankind, Gods, and Sons of Gods,
Destroyers rightlier call'd and Plagues of men.
Thus Fame shall be achiev'd, renown on Earth,
And what most merits fame in silence hid.
But hee the sev'nth from thee, whom thou beheld'st   700
The only righteous in a World perverse,
And therefore hated, therefore so beset
With Foes for daring single to be just,
And utter odious Truth, that God would come
To judge them with his Saints: Him the most High   705
Rapt in a balmy Cloud with winged Steeds
Did, as thou saw'st, receive, to walk with God
High in Salvation and the Climes of bliss,
Exempt from Death; to show thee what reward
Awaits the good, the rest what punishment;   710
Which now direct thine eyes and soon behold.
  He look'd, and saw the face of things quite chang'd;

683–697. For the Giants of l. 688 see the note on ll. 573–627 above. The tone of the passage — as Whiting notes in *N&Q*, CXCIV (1949), 75 — is that of the marginal comment on Genesis vi, 4–5 in the Geneva Bible: "All were given to the contempt of God, & oppression of their neighbours." Cf. IX, 27–31, *PR* III, 44–87, and *Lycidas*, 78:

Fame is no plant that grows on mortal soil.

700. *Hee the seventh from thee* is Enoch, who has been mentioned in l. 665. "God tooke him away," says the Geneva gloss, "To shew that there was a better life prepared, and to be a testimonie of the immortalitie of soules and bodies."

The brazen Throat of War had ceast to roar,
All now was turn'd to jollity and game,
To luxury and riot, feast and dance, 715
Marrying or prostituting, as befell,
Rape or Adultery, where passing fair
Allur'd them; thence from Cups to civil Broils.
At length a Reverend Sire among them came,
And of thir doings great dislike declar'd, 720
And testifi'd against thir ways; hee oft
Frequented thir Assemblies, whereso met,
Triumphs or Festivals, and to them preach'd
Conversion and Repentance, as to Souls
In Prison under Judgments imminent: 725
But all in vain: which when he saw, he ceas'd
Contending, and remov'd his Tents far off;
Then from the Mountain hewing Timber tall,
Began to build a Vessel of huge bulk,
Measur'd by Cubit, length, and breadth, and highth, 730
Smear'd round with Pitch, and in the side a door
Contriv'd, and of provisions laid in large
For Man and Beast: when lo a wonder strange!
Of every Beast, and Bird, and Insect small
Came sevens, and pairs, and enter'd in, as taught 735
Thir order; last the Sire, and his three Sons
With thir four Wives; and God made fast the door.
Meanwhile the Southwind rose, and with black wings
Wide hovering, all the Clouds together drove
From under Heav'n; the Hills to their supply 740

715. *luxury:* lust. Cf. "Fie on lust, and luxury" in *Merry Wives of Windsor* V, v, 98, and many other Shakespearian examples.
717. *fair:* beauty, i.e. beautiful women. Cf. IX, 606.
719–720. The *Reverend Sire* is Noah, who was "six hundred years old when the flood of waters was upon the earth" (Gen. vii, 6). Milton remembered Josephus' picture of Noah pleading with the giants to "change their dispositions," when he saw that they "were slaves to their wicked pleasures" (*Antiquities* I, iii, 1). In the main the account of the flood follows Genesis vi, 9–ix, 17; but it is influenced by the countless Renaissance pictures of it, many of which are reproduced in D. C. Allen's *The Legend of Noah* (Urbana, 1949), facing p. 176.
723. *Triumphs:* processions, entertainments. Cf. *L'Allegro*, 120.
724–725. "Spirits in prison" is a phrase applied by Saint Peter to the "slaves to their wicked pleasures" to whom Noah preached. (I Pet. iii, 19.)
735. Cf. Genesis vii, 2: "Of every clean beast thou shalt take to thee by sevens, the male and his female; and of beasts that are not clean by two."
737. With the detail that *God made fast the door* (Gen. vii, 16) Milton turned from the Bible story to Ovid's account of Deucalion's flood (cf. l. 10 above, n.), many details of which are also embodied in Du Bartas' description of Noah's flood in *The Divine Weeks*. Davis P. Harding in *Renaissance Ovid*, pp. 82–84, and Allen in *The Legend of Noah*, pp. 176–77, discuss Milton's belief that Ovid's story was a foil and (it may be added) a corroboration for the biblical account.
738. Milton could count on his readers to remember that in Ovid's account of Deucalion's flood (*Met.* I, 264), when Jove prepared vengeance on wicked mankind, he called the South Wind, Notus, to drown the earth with rain. Contemporary meteorologists — as Svendsen notes in *M.&S.*, p. 97 — confirmed Milton's theory of rain as caused by the action of the south wind on thick clouds.

Vapor, and Exhalation dusk and moist,
Sent up amain; and now the thick'n'd Sky
Like a dark Ceiling stood; down rush'd the Rain
Impetuous, and continu'd till the Earth
No more was seen; the floating Vessel swum   745
Uplifted; and secure with beaked prow
Rode tilting o'er the Waves, all dwellings else
Flood overwhelm'd, and them with all thir pomp
Deep under water roll'd; Sea cover'd Sea,
Sea without shore; and in thir Palaces   750
Where luxury late reign'd, Sea-monsters whelp'd
And stabl'd; of Mankind, so numerous late,
All left, in one small bottom swum embark't.
How didst thou grieve then, *Adam*, to behold
The end of all thy Offspring, end so sad,   755
Depopulation; thee another Flood,
Of tears and sorrow a Flood thee also drown'd,
And sunk thee as thy Sons; till gently rear'd
By th' Angel, on thy feet thou stood'st at last,
Though comfortless, as when a Father mourns   760
His Children, all in view destroy'd at once;
And scarce to th' Angel utter'd'st thus thy plaint.
    O Visions ill foreseen! better had I
Liv'd ignorant of future, so had borne
My part of evil only, each day's lot   765
Anough to bear; those now, that were dispens't
The burd'n of many Ages, on me light
At once, by my foreknowledge gaining Birth
Abortive, to torment me ere thir being,
With thought that they must be. Let no man seek   770
Henceforth to be foretold what shall befall
Him or his Children, evil he may be sure,
Which neither his foreknowing can prevent,
And hee the future evil shall no less
In apprehension than in substance feel   775
Grievous to bear: but that care now is past,
Man is not whom to warn: those few escap't
Famine and anguish will at last consume
Wand'ring that wat'ry Desert: I had hope
When violence was ceas't, and War on Earth,   780

---

750. The shoreless sea is a striking touch in Ovid's story (*Met.* I, 292). It reappears in Du Bartas' picture of "stormy waters" where

Rivers and Seas have all one common shoar,
(To wit) a Sable, water-loaden Skie,
Ready to rain new Oceans instantly.
                    (*Divine Weeks*, p. 310)
750-751. This is Ovid's picture (*Met.*

I, 299-303) with a touch of its quaintness in Du Bartas:

The Sturgeon, coasting over Castles, muses
(Under the Sea) to see so many houses.
                    (*Divine Weeks*, p. 59)
765. Cf. Matthew vi, 34: "Sufficient unto the day, is the evil thereof."
779. *Wand'ring* is transitive.

All would have then gone well, peace would have crown'd
With length of happy days the race of man;
But I was far deceiv'd; for now I see
Peace to corrupt no less than War to waste.
How comes it thus? unfold, Celestial Guide,   785
And whether here the Race of man will end.
　　To whom thus *Michael*. Those whom last thou saw'st
In triumph and luxurious wealth, are they
First seen in acts of prowess eminent
And great exploits, but of true virtue void;   790
Who having spilt much blood, and done much waste
Subduing Nations, and achiev'd thereby
Fame in the World, high titles, and rich prey,
Shall change thir course to pleasure, ease, and sloth,
Surfeit, and lust, till wantonness and pride   795
Raise out of friendship hostile deeds in Peace.
The conquer'd also, and enslav'd by War
Shall with thir freedom lost all virtue lose
And fear of God, from whom thir piety feign'd
In sharp contest of Battle found no aid   800
Against invaders; therefore cool'd in zeal
Thenceforth shall practice how to live secure,
Worldly or dissolute, on what thir Lords
Shall leave them to enjoy; for th' Earth shall bear
More than anough, that temperance may be tri'd: 805
So all shall turn degenerate, all deprav'd,
Justice and Temperance, Truth and Faith forgot;
One Man except, the only Son of light
In a dark Age, against example good,
Against allurement, custom, and a World   810
Offended; fearless of reproach and scorn,
Or violence, hee of thir wicked ways
Shall them admonish, and before them set
The paths of righteousness, how much more safe,
And full of peace, denouncing wrath to come   815
On thir impenitence; and shall return
Of them derided, but of God observ'd
The one just Man alive; by his command
Shall build a wondrous Ark, as thou beheld'st,
To save himself and household from amidst   820
A World devote to universal rack.
No sooner hee with them of Man and Beast

807. This climax to a passage which is filled with Milton's passionate political and ethical faith can be read as an attack upon the time-servers in his own party. Perhaps the best light in which to regard it is as the record of disillusion from the mood in which he painted England in *Areopagitica:* "a noble and puissant Nation," "entering the glorious ways of truth and prosperous virtue. destined to become great and honorable in these latter ages" (C.Ed. IV, 344).

821. *devote:* dedicated to destruction. Cf. III, 208.

Select for life shall in the Ark be lodg'd,
And shelter'd round, but all the Cataracts
Of Heav'n set open on the Earth shall pour   825
Rain day and night, all fountains of the Deep
Broke up, shall heave the Ocean to usurp
Beyond all bounds, till inundation rise
Above the highest Hills: then shall this Mount
Of Paradise by might of Waves be mov'd   830
Out of his place, push'd by the horned flood,
With all his verdure spoil'd, and Trees adrift
Down the great River to the op'ning Gulf,
And there take root an Island salt and bare,
The haunt of Seals and Orcs, and Sea-mews' clang.   835
To teach thee that God attributes to place
No sanctity, if none be thither brought
By Men who there frequent, or therein dwell.
And now what further shall ensue, behold.

He look'd, and saw the Ark hull on the flood,   840
Which now abated, for the Clouds were fled,
Driv'n by a keen North-wind, that blowing dry
Wrinkl'd the face of Deluge, as decay'd;
And the clear Sun on his wide wat'ry Glass
Gaz'd hot, and of the fresh Wave largely drew,   845
As after thirst, which made thir flowing shrink
From standing lake to tripping ebb, that stole
With soft foot towards the deep, who now had stopt
His Sluices, as the Heav'n his windows shut.
The Ark no more now floats, but seems on ground   850
Fast on the top of some high mountain fixt.
And now the tops of Hills as Rocks appear;
With clamor thence the rapid Currents drive
Towards the retreating Sea thir furious tide.
Forthwith from out the Ark a Raven flies,   855

831. So Virgil describes the Po as dividing its stream into horns:
> Po first issues from his dark abodes, . . .
> Two golden horns on his large front he wears,
> And his grim face a bull's resemblance bears.
> (*Georgics* IV, 370–73. Dryden's translation)

833. The *great River* is probably the Euphrates. The *Gulf* is the Persian Gulf.

834–835. *Orcs:* whales. J. B. Broadbent — in *MP*, LI (1954), 163 — notes that "islands of whales (orcs) were frequently described (as in *Hakluytus Posthumus* xix, 80)" by voyagers in eastern seas.

840–843. So "God made a wind to pass over the earth, and the waters assuaged" (Gen. viii, 1); and so also Ovid makes a north wind drive away the clouds after Deucalion's flood (*Met.* I, 328). But the picture — says E. M. W. Tillyard in *TLS*, 6 March, 1953, p. 153 — comes from Sidney's opening scene in the *Arcadia* of "a ship . . . hulling there, part broken, part burned, part drowned. . . . A number of dead bodies (as it were) filled the wrinkles of the sea visage."

845. Cf. the sun supping with the ocean in V, 426.

849. So in Genesis viii, 2· "The fountains of the deep and the windows of heaven were stopped," and the details of the raven, the dove, and the olive leaf follow.

And after him, the surer messenger,
A Dove sent forth once and again to spy
Green Tree or ground whereon his foot may light;
The second time returning, in his Bill
An Olive leaf he brings, pacific sign: 860
Anon dry ground appears, and from his Ark
The ancient Sire descends with all his Train;
Then with uplifted hands, and eyes devout,
Grateful to Heav'n, over his head beholds
A dewy Cloud, and in the Cloud a Bow   865
Conspicuous with three listed colors gay,
Betok'ning peace from God, and Cov'nant new.
Whereat the heart of *Adam* erst so sad
Greatly rejoic'd, and thus his joy broke forth.

  O thou who future things canst represent   870
As present, Heav'nly instructor, I revive
At this last sight, assur'd that Man shall live
With all the Creatures, and thir seed preserve.
Far less I now lament for one whole World
Of wicked Sons destroy'd, than I rejoice   875
For one Man found so perfet and so just,
That God voutsafes to raise another World
From him, and all his anger to forget.
But say, what mean those color'd streaks in Heav'n,
Distended as the Brow of God appeas'd,   880
Or serve they as a flow'ry verge to bind
The fluid skirts of that same wat'ry Cloud,
Lest it again dissolve and show'r the Earth?

  To whom th' Arch-Angel. Dext'rously thou aim'st;
So willingly doth God remit his Ire,   885
Though late repenting him of Man deprav'd,
Griev'd at his heart, when looking down he saw
The whole Earth fill'd with violence, and all flesh
Corrupting each thir way; yet those remov'd,
Such grace shall one just Man find in his sight,   890
That he relents, not to blot out mankind,
And makes a Cov'nant never to destroy
The Earth again by flood, nor let the Sea
Surpass his bounds, nor Rain to drown the World
With Man therein or Beast; but when he brings   895
Over the Earth a Cloud, will therein set
His triple-color'd Bow, whereon to look
And call to mind his Cov'nant: Day and Night,

---

867. The *Cov'nant* is the promise of
God, of which the rainbow with its *listed*
(striped) *colors* was the pledge, never
again to flood the world (Gen. ix, 11–17).
  898–901. Milton's account of the flood
ends like that in Genesis viii, 22, to which

he adds the promise of a "new heaven and
a new earth" after the melting of the
elements "with fervent heat" (II Peter,
iii, 12–13). Cf. *CD* I, xxxiii (C.Ed. XVI,
375 and 381). As a theme for poetry the
final conflagration of the world was strik-

Seed-time and Harvest, Heat and hoary Frost
Shall hold thir course, till fire purge all things new,   900
Both Heav'n and Earth, wherein the just shall dwell.

The End of the Eleventh Book.

BOOK XII

THE ARGUMENT

The Angel Michael *continues from the Flood to relate what shall succeed; then, in the mention of* Abraham, *comes by degrees to explain, who that Seed of the Woman shall be, which was promised* Adam *and* Eve *in the Fall; his Incarnation, Death, Resurrection, and Ascension; the state of the Church till his second Coming.* Adam *greatly satisfied and recomforted by these Relations and Promises descends the Hill with* Michael; *wakens* Eve, *who all this while had slept, but with gentle dreams compos'd to quietness of mind and submission.* Michael *in either hand leads them out of Paradise, the fiery Sword waving behind them, and the Cherubim taking thir Stations to guard the Place.*

As one who in his journey bates at Noon,
Though bent on speed, so here the Arch-Angel paus'd
Betwixt the world destroy'd and world restor'd,
If *Adam* aught perhaps might interpose;
Then with transition sweet new Speech resumes.   5
    Thus thou hast seen one World begin and end;
And Man as from a second stock proceed.
Much thou hast yet to see, but I perceive
Thy mortal sight to fail; objects divine
Must needs impair and weary human sense: 10
Henceforth what is to come I will relate,
Thou therefore give due audience, and attend.
This second source of Men, while yet but few,
And while the dread of judgment past remains
Fresh in thir minds, fearing the Deity,   15
With some regard to what is just and right
Shall lead thir lives, and multiply apace,
Laboring the soil, and reaping plenteous crop,
Corn, wine and oil; and from the herd or flock,
Oft sacrificing Bullock, Lamb, or Kid,   20
With large Wine-offerings pour'd, and sacred Feast,

---

ingly developed in Vida's *Hymn to the Son of God*, and as a scientific doctrine it found expression as late as 1696 in William Whiston's *A New Theory of the Earth, From its Original, to the Consummation of all Things, . . . the General Conflagration.* The history of the belief is traced in the *Harvard Theological Review,* LI (1958), 169–185, by C. A. Patrides.

1–5. These transitional lines were added in 1674 when the tenth book of the first edition was divided to form the eleventh and twelfth books of the second edition.

1. *bates:* abates, reduces speed or pauses.

Shall spend thir days in joy unblam'd, and dwell
Long time in peace by Families and Tribes
Under paternal rule; till one shall rise
Of proud ambitious heart, who not content   25
With fair equality, fraternal state,
Will arrogate Dominion undeserv'd
Over his brethren, and quite dispossess
Concord and law of Nature from the Earth;
Hunting (and Men not Beasts shall be his game)   30
With War and hostile snare such as refuse
Subjection to his Empire tyrannous:
A mighty Hunter thence he shall be styl'd
Before the Lord, as in despite of Heav'n,
Or from Heav'n claiming second Sovranty;   35
And from Rebellion shall derive his name,
Though of Rebellion others he accuse.
Hee with a crew, whom like Ambition joins
With him or under him to tyrannize,
Marching from *Eden* towards the West, shall find   40
The Plain, wherein a black bituminous gurge
Boils out from under ground, the mouth of Hell;
Of Brick, and of that stuff they cast to build
A City and Tow'r, whose top may reach to Heav'n;
And get themselves a name, lest far disperst   45
In foreign Lands thir memory be lost,
Regardless whether good or evil fame.
But God who oft descends to visit men
Unseen, and through thir habitations walks
To mark thir doings, them beholding soon,   50
Comes down to see thir City, ere the Tower
Obstruct Heav'n Tow'rs, and in derision sets

24–63. Nimrod, whose name means "rebel," is "a mighty hunter before the Lord" (Gen. x, 9), but he is not mentioned in the biblical account of the confusion of tongues at Babel (Gen. xi, 1–9). His character as the foiled empire-builder of St. Gregory's commentary on Genesis in *On the Trinity and its Works* and of Dante's *Purgatory* (xii, 34; cf. *Inf*. xxxi, 77) is first foreshadowed in Josephus' *Antiquities* I, iv, 2. For the fifteenth century lawyer, Sir John Fortescue, whom Milton quoted in the first *Defense* (C.Ed. VII, 476, 478), Nimrod's mighty hunting meant that he was "an oppressor and destroyer of men, as hunters are destroyers but not rulers of beasts" (*On the Nature of the Law of Nature* I, vii). Milton's public, like Sir Thomas Browne in *Vulgar Errors* VII, vi, thought of Nimrod as one whose "secret design to settle unto himself a place of dominion"

had been nipped by the confusion of tongues at Babel. For the popular conception of Nimrod see Starnes and Talbert, *Dictionaries*, pp. 264–68.

41–44. *The Plain* of Shinar has been mentioned in III, 467. The idea that the brick in the tower of Babel was "cemented with mortar made of bitumen" comes from Josephus, *Antiquities* I, iv, 3.

52–59. "Languages," said Milton in the *Logic* I, xxiv (C.Ed. XI, 220), "both that first one which Adam spoke in Eden, and those varied ones also possibly derived from the first, which the builders of the tower of Babel suddenly received, are without doubt divinely given." In *PQ*, XXVIII (1949), 11, D. C. Allen observes that, "Every philologist of the seventeenth century was quite ready to accept the Confusion as a miracle."

Upon thir Tongues a various Spirit to rase
Quite out thir Native Language, and instead
To sow a jangling noise of words unknown: 55
Forthwith a hideous gabble rises loud
Among the Builders; each to other calls
Not understood, till hoarse, and all in rage,
As mockt they storm; great laughter was in Heav'n
And looking down, to see the hubbub strange   60
And hear the din; thus was the building left
Ridiculous, and the work Confusion nam'd.
   Whereto thus *Adam* fatherly displeased.
O execrable Son so to aspire
Above his Brethren, to himself assuming   65
Authority usurpt, from God not giv'n:
He gave us only over Beast, Fish, Fowl
Dominion absolute; that right we hold
By his donation; but Man over men
He made not Lord; such title to himself   70
Reserving, human left from human free.
But this Usurper his encroachment proud
Stays not on Man; to God his Tower intends
Siege and defiance: Wretched man! what food
Will he convey up thither to sustain   75
Himself and his rash Army, where thin Air
Above the Clouds will pine his entrails gross,
And famish him of breath, if not of Bread?
   To whom thus *Michael*. Justly thou abhorr'st
That Son, who on the quiet state of men   80
Such trouble brought, affecting to subdue
Rational Liberty; yet know withal,
Since thy original lapse, true Liberty
Is lost, which always with right Reason dwells
Twinn'd, and from her hath no dividual being: 85

---

53. *A various Spirit:* a spirit of contradiction, a quarrelsome spirit.
62. The name *Babel* seems to have meant "gate of the Gods" or "of God." Josephus declared that "the tower is now called Babylon because of the confusion of that language which they readily understood before, for the Hebrews mean by the word *Babel*, Confusion" (*Antiquities* I, iv, 3).
82–101. Milton's political inference from his belief that through Adam's sin men at least partially lost "that right reason which enabled man to discern the chief good" (*CD* I, xii; C.Ed. XV, 206) was no less explicitly drawn by many commentators on Genesis — as A. Williams shows in *Expositor*, pp. 222–23. But his politics stemmed equally from Plato's *Republic* and its echoes in definitions of "true libertie" such as Castiglione's view of it in the *Book of the Courtier* (Hoby's translation, Everyman Ed. p. 275) as not living "as a man will," but rather as living "according to good lawes." The equally humanistic and biblical political creed of Sir John Eliot as he stated it in the closing sentence of *The Monarchie of Man* (written c. 1631) was the faith that man's "safety and tranquillity by God" (as Aristotle's *Ethics* "did expresse it) are made dependant on himselfe, & in that selfe dependance, . . . in the intire rule & dominion of himselfe, the affections being compos'd, the action soe divided, is the perfection of our government, that *summum bonum* in Philosophie, the *bonum publicum* in our pollicie, the true end and object of this Monarchy of man." Cf. IX, 352 and 654.

Reason in man obscur'd, or not obey'd,
Immediately inordinate desires
And upstart Passions catch the Government
From Reason, and to servitude reduce
Man till then free. Therefore since hee permits   90
Within himself unworthy Powers to reign
Over free Reason, God in Judgment just
Subjects him from without to violent Lords;
Who oft as undeservedly enthral
His outward freedom: Tyranny must be,   95
Though to the Tyrant thereby no excuse.
Yet sometimes Nations will decline so low
From virtue, which is reason, that no wrong,
But Justice, and some fatal curse annext
Deprives them of thir outward liberty,   100
Thir inward lost: Witness th' irreverent Son
Of him who built the Ark, who for the shame
Done to his Father, heard this heavy curse,
Servant of Servants, on his vicious Race.
Thus will this latter, as the former World,   105
Still tend from bad to worse, till God at last
Wearied with their iniquities, withdraw
His presence from among them, and avert
His holy Eyes; resolving from thenceforth
To leave them to thir own polluted ways;   110
And one peculiar Nation to select
From all the rest, of whom to be invok'd,
A Nation from one faithful man to spring:
Him on this side *Euphrates* yet residing,
Bred up in Idol-worship; O that men   115
(Canst thou believe?) should be so stupid grown,
While yet the Patriarch liv'd, who scap'd the Flood,
As to forsake the living God, and fall
To worship thir own work in Wood and Stone
For Gods! yet him God the most High voutsafes   120
To call by Vision from his Father's house,
His kindred and false Gods, into a Land
Which he will show him, and from him will raise
A mighty Nation, and upon him show'r
His benediction so, that in his Seed   125

101. The *irreverent Son* of Noah was Ham, the father of Canaan. "And [Noah] said, Cursed be Canaan; a servant of servants shall he be unto his brethren" (Gen. ix, 25).
111–113. Cf. *CD* I, iv (C.Ed. XIV, 99), where Milton condemns the Calvinistic doctrine of individual election to personal salvation by God, but recognizes "that general, or national election by which God chose the whole nation of Israel for his own people."
113–121. The *one faithful man* is Abraham, to whom God promised the land of Canaan (Gen. xii, 7). God called him "from his father's house," said Milton in *CD* I, xvii (C.Ed. XV, 348–50), although he "was even an idolator at the time."

All Nations shall be blest; he straight obeys,
Not knowing to what Land, yet firm believes:
I see him, but thou canst not, with what Faith
He leaves his Gods, his Friends, and native Soil
Ur of *Chaldæa*, passing now the Ford   130
To *Haran*, after him a cumbrous Train
Of Herds and Flocks, and numerous servitude;
Not wand'ring poor, but trusting all his wealth
With God, who call'd him, in a land unknown.
Canaan he now attains, I see his Tents   135
Pitcht about *Sechem*, and the neighboring Plain
Of *Moreh;* there by promise he receives
Gift to his Progeny of all that Land;
From *Hamath* Northward to the Desert South
(Things by thir names I call, though yet unnam'd)   140
From *Hermon* East to the great Western Sea,
Mount *Hermon*, yonder Sea, each place behold
In prospect, as I point them; on the shore
Mount *Carmel;* here the double-founted stream
Jordan, true limit Eastward; but his Sons   145
Shall dwell to *Senir*, that long ridge of Hills.
This ponder, that all Nations of the Earth
Shall in his Seed be blessed; by that Seed
Is meant thy great deliverer, who shall bruise
The Serpent's head; whereof to thee anon   150
Plainlier shall be reveal'd. This Patriarch blest,
Whom *faithful Abraham* due time shall call,
A Son, and of his Son a Grandchild leaves,
Like him in faith, in wisdom, and renown;
The Grandchild with twelve Sons increast, departs   155
From *Canaan*, to a Land hereafter call'd
Egypt, divided by the River *Nile;*

---

128. "By faith Abraham, when he was called to go out into a place which he should after receive for an inheritance, obeyed" (Heb. xi, 8).

130-131. Perhaps knowing that *Ur* was on the west bank of the Euphrates, Milton saw Abraham leaving it for Haran on the east of the river but far northwest of Ur. From Haran Palestine lay southwest over the Euphrates. Cf. IV, 211 n.

132. *servitude:* servants. The story of the migration as told in Genesis xii, 5–6 is traced below Ortelius' large map of Canaan in a diagram called *Abrahami Patriarchae Perigrinatio et Vita.* It shows *Sechem* (Schechem), lying between Mounts Ebal and Gerizim, where Abraham first camped in Canaan, and the plain of *Moreh.*

139. *Hamath*, on the Orontes in Syria, is mentioned as the northern frontier of Canaan in Numbers xxxiv, 8. The promise in Joshua xiii, 5–6, was that all the inhabitants of the region "under Mount Hermon unto the entering into Hamath" should be driven out "before the children of Israel."

143. "Carmel by the sea" (Jer. xlvi, 18) is a mountainous promontory jutting into the Mediterranean from the Palestinian shore.

144-145. The notion that the Jordan was formed by the confluence of two non-existent streams, the Jor and the Dan, seems ultimately to have stemmed from St. Jerome's commentary on Genesis xiv, 14. Cf. A. H. Gilbert, *Dictionary*, p. 163.

146. *Senir* was a peak of the ridge of Hermon (I Chron. v, 23).

153. *A Son:* Isaac. From this point the Bible story is briefly summarized.

See where it flows, disgorging at seven mouths
Into the Sea: to sojourn in that Land
He comes invited by a younger Son   160
In time of dearth, a Son whose worthy deeds
Raise him to be the second in that Realm
Of *Pharaoh:* there he dies, and leaves his Race
Growing into a Nation, and now grown
Suspected to a sequent King, who seeks   165
To stop thir overgrowth, as inmate guests
Too numerous; whence of guests he makes them slaves
Inhospitably, and kills thir infant Males:
Till by two brethren (those two brethren call
Moses and *Aaron*) sent from God to claim   170
His people from enthralment, they return
With glory and spoil back to thir promis'd Land.
But first the lawless Tyrant, who denies
To know thir God, or message to regard,
Must be compell'd by Signs and Judgments dire;   175
To blood unshed the Rivers must be turn'd,
Frogs, Lice and Flies must all his Palace fill
With loath'd intrusion, and fill all the land;
His Cattle must of Rot and Murrain die,
Botches and blains must all his flesh imboss,   180
And all his people; Thunder mixt with Hail,
Hail mixt with fire must rend th' *Egyptian* Sky
And wheel on th' Earth, devouring where it rolls;
What it devours not, Herb, or Fruit, or Grain,
A darksome Cloud of Locusts swarming down   185
Must eat, and on the ground leave nothing green:
Darkness must overshadow all his bounds,
Palpable darkness, and blot out three days;
Last with one midnight stroke all the first-born
Of *Egypt* must lie dead. Thus with ten wounds   190
The River-dragon tam'd at length submits
To let his sojourners depart, and oft
Humbles his stubborn heart, but still as Ice
More hard'n'd after thaw, till in his rage
Pursuing whom he late dismiss'd, the Sea   195
Swallows him with his Host, but them lets pass
As on dry land between two crystal walls,

171–172. By a dubious trick the Israelites "spoiled the Egyptians" (Exod. xii, 36) when they left the country. The summary of the ten plagues rests on Exodus vii, 19–xii, 51.
173. *denies:* refuses.
180. *imboss:* cover with bosses or swellings.
188. The *Palpable darkness* is the plague of "thick darkness" (Exod. x, 22).

191. "Behold, I am against thee, Pharaoh king of Egypt, the great dragon that lieth in the midst of his rivers" (Ezek. xxix, 3).
197. The *crystal walls* are a reminiscence of Du Bartas' description of the same scene:
And on each side is flanked all along
With walls of crystal, beautiful and strong.

Aw'd by the rod of *Moses* so to stand
Divided, till his rescu'd gain thir shore:
Such wondrous power God to his Saint will lend,   200
Though present in his Angel, who shall go
Before them in a Cloud, and Pillar of Fire,
By day a Cloud, by night a Pillar of Fire,
To guide them in thir journey, and remove
Behind them, while th' obdurate King pursues: 205
All night he will pursue, but his approach
Darkness defends between till morning Watch;
Then through the Fiery Pillar and the Cloud
God looking forth will trouble all his Host
And craze thir Chariot wheels: when by command   210
Moses once more his potent Rod extends
Over the Sea; the Sea his Rod obeys;
On thir imbattl'd ranks the Waves return,
And overwhelm thir War: the Race elect
Safe towards *Canaan* from the shore advance   215
Through the wild Desert, not the readiest way,
Lest ent'ring on the *Canaanite* alarm'd
War terrify them inexpert, and fear
Return them back to *Egypt*, choosing rather
Inglorious life with servitude; for life   220
To noble and ignoble is more sweet
Untrain'd in Arms, where rashness leads not on.
This also shall they gain by thir delay
In the wide Wilderness, there they shall found
Thir government, and thir great Senate choose   225
Through the twelve Tribes, to rule by Laws ordain'd:
God from the Mount of *Sinai*, whose gray top
Shall tremble, he descending, will himself

Two walls of Glass, built with a word
alone.
      (*Divine Weeks*, pp. 476-77)
The passage also left its mark on Milton's
boyish paraphrase of Psalm cxxxvi, 49.
200-204. "The Lord went before them
by day in a pillar of cloud; . . . and by
night in a pillar of fire, to give them
light" (Exod. xiii, 21). In *CD* I, v (C.Ed.
XIV, 296) Milton made a point of the
fact that God lent his name to an angel
who guided the Israelites.
207. *defends:* prevents (by coming be-
tween Pharaoh and the Israelites).
210. *craze:* shatter. The scene is de-
scribed in Exodus xiv.
217. The devious route of Israel during
its thirty-eight years in the wilderness on
the way to Canaan was clearly traced on
contemporary maps. Milton found the
explanation that he gives for it in Exodus

xiii, 17-18.
225-226. Milton thought of the Sev-
enty Elders in Exodus xxiv, 1-9, and
Numbers xi, 16-30, who witness some of
the acts of Moses. Though Roger
Williams was unwilling to see the charter
of the Colony of Massachusetts Bay
based upon "the sandy and dangerous
ground of Israel's pattern" (quoted by
Perry Miller in *Roger Williams: His
Contribution to the American Tradition*,
Cambridge, 1954, p. 153), Milton ac-
cepted the Seventy Elders as a divinely
constituted Senate which, with the sup-
port of the "Magistracy and People,"
were what James Harington regarded as
the perfect pattern of government by
law rather than by royal power, as it
was once for all revealed "in the fabrick
of the Commonwealth of Israel" (*Oceana*,
ed. by S. B. Liljegren, Heidelberg, 1921,
p. 26).

In Thunder, Lightning and loud Trumpet's sound
Ordain them Laws; part such as appertain   230
To civil Justice, part religious Rites
Of sacrifice, informing them, by types
And shadows, of that destin'd Seed to bruise
The Serpent, by what means he shall achieve
Mankind's deliverance. But the voice of God   235
To mortal ear is dreadful; they beseech
That *Moses* might report to them his will,
And terror cease; he grants what they besought,
Instructed that to God is no access
Without Mediator, whose high Office now   240
Moses in figure bears, to introduce
One greater, of whose day he shall foretell,
And all the Prophets in thir Age the times
Of great *Messiah* shall sing. Thus Laws and Rites
Establisht, such delight hath God in Men   245
Obedient to his will, that he voutsafes
Among them to set up his Tabernacle,
The holy One with mortal Men to dwell:
By his prescript a Sanctuary is fram'd
Of Cedar, overlaid with Gold, therein   250
An Ark, and in the Ark his Testimony,
The Records of his Cov'nant, over these
A Mercy-seat of Gold between the wings
Of two bright Cherubim, before him burn
Sev'n Lamps as in a Zodiac representing   255
The Heav'nly fires; over the Tent a Cloud
Shall rest by Day, a fiery gleam by Night,
Save when they journey, and at length they come,
Conducted by his Angel to the Land
Promis'd to *Abraham* and his Seed: the rest   260
Were long to tell, how many Battles fought,
How many Kings destroy'd, and Kingdoms won,
Or how the Sun shall in mid Heav'n stand still

236. In Exodus xx, 19, the Israelites say "unto Moses, Speak thou with us, and we will hear: but let not God speak with us, lest we die."

240. Christian commentators treated Moses as the first of the types of Christ as *Mediator* (cf. X, 60) mainly because Deuteronomy xviii, 15, is quoted in Acts iii, 22. "For Moses truly said unto the fathers, A Prophet shall the Lord your God raise up unto you of your brethren, like unto me."

247-256. The *Tabernacle* is described loosely as it is in Exodus xxv. Cf. the *Mercy-seat* in XI, 2, n.

255. Josephus describes the golden candle-stick as having "seven lamps

. . . in imitation of the number of planets" (*Antiquities* III, vi, 7).

260-277. The allusion is to the promise to Abraham in Genesis xxii, 18.

263-267. Du Bartas, in his dramatization of Israel's victory over the Amorites when the sun halted in heaven "until the people had avenged themselves upon their enemies" (Joshua x, 13), similarly paraphrased Joshua's command to the sun and moon:

Stay, stand thou still, stand still in *Gabaon;*
And thou, O Moone, i'th'vale of *Aialon.*

(*Divine Weeks*, p. 516)

A day entire, and Night's due course adjourn,
Man's voice commanding, Sun in *Gibeon* stand,   265
And thou Moon in the vale of *Aialon*,
Till *Israel* overcome; so call the third
From *Abraham*, Son of *Isaac*, and from him
His whole descent, who thus shall *Canaan* win.
   Here *Adam* interpos'd. O sent from Heav'n,   270
Enlight'ner of my darkness, gracious things
Thou hast reveal'd, those chiefly which concern
Just *Abraham* and his Seed: now first I find
Mine eyes true op'ning, and my heart much eas'd,
Erewhile perplext with thoughts what would become   275
Of mee and all Mankind; but now I see
His day, in whom all Nations shall be blest,
Favor unmerited by me, who sought
Forbidd'n knowledge by forbidd'n means.
This yet I apprehend not, why to those   280
Among whom God will deign to dwell on Earth
So many and so various Laws are giv'n;
So many Laws argue so many sins
Among them; how can God with such reside?
   To whom thus *Michael*. Doubt not but that sin   285
Will reign among them, as of thee begot;
And therefore was Law given them to evince
Thir natural pravity, by stirring up
Sin against Law to fight; that when they see
Law can discover sin, but not remove,   290
Save by those shadowy expiations weak,
The blood of Bulls and Goats, they may conclude
Some blood more precious must be paid for Man,
Just for unjust, that in such righteousness
To them by Faith imputed, they may find   295
Justification towards God, and peace
Of Conscience, which the Law by Ceremonies
Cannot appease, nor Man the moral part
Perform, and not performing cannot live.
So Law appears imperfet, and but giv'n   300
With purpose to resign them in full time
Up to a better Cov'nant, disciplin'd

267. The name *Israel* ("he that striv-
eth with God") was given to Jacob at
Peniel (Gen. xxxii, 28) and later to all
his descendants as "the children of
Israel."
290. The line fuses several Pauline
passages which teach that "what things
soever the law saith, it saith to them
who are under the law; that . . . all
the world may become guilty before
God" (Rom. iii, 19).

291. Milton describes the sacrifices as
shadows or types of Christ's expiation of
sin as the law is said to have been "a
shadow of good things to come" in He-
brews x, 1, though the "sacrifices which
they offered year by year continually"
could never "make the comers thereunto
perfect." Cf. Romans x, 5, where the
righteousness taught by the Mosaic law
is contrasted with Christian righteous-
ness.

From shadowy Types to Truth, from Flesh to Spirit,
From imposition of strict Laws, to free
Acceptance of large Grace, from servile fear   305
To filial, works of Law to works of Faith.
And therefore shall not *Moses*, though of God
Highly belov'd, being but the Minister
Of Law, his people into *Canaan* lead;
But *Joshua* whom the Gentiles *Jesus* call,   310
His Name and Office bearing, who shall quell
The adversary Serpent, and bring back
Through the world's wilderness long wander'd man
Safe to eternal Paradise of rest.
Meanwhile they in thir earthly *Canaan* plac't   315
Long time shall dwell and prosper, but when sins
National interrupt thir public peace,
Provoking God to raise them enemies:
From whom as oft he saves them penitent
By Judges first, then under Kings; of whom   320
The second, both for piety renown'd
And puissant deeds, a promise shall receive
Irrevocable, that his Regal Throne
For ever shall endure; the like shall sing
All Prophecy, That of the Royal Stock   325
Of *David* (so I name this King) shall rise
A Son, the Woman's Seed to thee foretold,
Foretold to *Abraham*, as in whom shall trust
All Nations, and to Kings foretold, of Kings
The last, for of his Reign shall be no end.   330
But first a long succession must ensue,
And his next Son for Wealth and Wisdom fam'd,
The clouded Ark of God till then in Tents
Wand'ring, shall in a glorious Temple enshrine.
Such follow him, as shall be register'd   335
Part good, part bad, of bad the longer scroll,
Whose foul Idolatries, and other faults
Heapt to the popular sum, will so incense
God, as to leave them, and expose thir Land,
Thir City, his Temple, and his holy Ark   340

307. Cf. *CD* I, xxvii (C.Ed. XVI, 134), where Christians are said to be "delivered" not from the ceremonial law alone, but from the whole law of Moses," because (*CD* I, xxvi; C.Ed. XVI, 110) "the imperfection of the law was manifested in . . . Moses himself; for Moses, who was a type of the law, could not bring the children of Israel into the land of Canaan, that is, into eternal rest; but an entrance was given to them under Joshua, or Jesus." In Charles Stephanus' *Dictionary* Joshua is identified with Jesus both as bearing the same name and as a "type" of Christ. Cf. Starnes and Talbert, *Dictionaries*, p. 261.
321. *The second:* David, to whom the prophet Nathan promised that his throne should "be established for ever" (II Sam. vii, 16).
332. The *next Son:* Solomon, whose building of the temple in Jerusalem is elaborately described in I Kings vi–vii and II Chronicles iii–iv.
337. Compare the allusion to Solomon's idolatries in I, 399–403.

With all his sacred things, a scorn and prey
To that proud City, whose high Walls thou saw'st
Left in confusion, *Babylon* thence call'd.
There in captivity he lets them dwell
The space of seventy years, then brings them back,   345
Rememb'ring mercy, and his Cov'nant sworn
To *David*, stablisht as the days of Heav'n.
Return'd from *Babylon* by leave of Kings
Thir Lords, whom God dispos'd, the house of God
They first re-edify, and for a while   350
In mean estate live moderate, till grown
In wealth and multitude, factious they grow;
But first among the Priests dissension springs,
Men who attend the Altar, and should most
Endeavor Peace: thir strife pollution brings   355
Upon the Temple itself: at last they seize
The Sceptre, and regard not *David's* Sons,
Then lose it to a stranger, that the true
Anointed King *Messiah* might be born
Barr'd of his right; yet at his Birth a Star   360
Unseen before in Heav'n proclaims him come,
And guides the Eastern Sages, who enquire
His place, to offer Incense, Myrrh, and Gold;
His place of birth, a Solemn Angel tells
To simple Shepherds, keeping watch by night;   365
They gladly thither haste, and by a Choir
Of squadron'd Angels hear his Carol sung.
A Virgin is his Mother, but his Sire
The Power of the most High; he shall ascend
The Throne hereditary, and bound his Reign   370
With earth's wide bounds, his glory with the Heav'ns.
He ceas'd, discerning *Adam* with such joy
Surcharg'd, as had like grief been dew'd in tears,
Without the vent of words, which these he breath'd.

347. Milton treats the return of the Hebrew exiles from Babylon to Jerusalem in 536 B.C. as a fulfilment of God's covenant with David to make "his throne as the days of heaven" (Psalm lxxxix, 29).

348. The *Kings* are Cyrus the Great, Darius, and Artaxerxes, under whom the Jews conducted the rebuilding of Jerusalem that is recorded in the Book of Ezra.

353–358. In summarizing the struggle for the high priesthood between Onias and Joshua in the second century B.C., Milton follows II Maccabees iii–iv, and Josephus' *Antiquities* XII, iv–v. In l. 356 *they* refers to the Asmonean family, which held the priesthood from 153 to 35 B.C. The *stranger* in l. 358 is Antipater the Idumaean, whom the Romans made governor of Jerusalem in 61 B.C. Under his son, Herod the Great, Christ was born.

366. *thither:* to Bethlehem, Christ's birthplace.

368–369. In *CD* I, xiv (C.Ed. XV, 280) Milton declares the "efficient cause" of the conception of Christ to be the "Holy Spirit," which he adds that he is inclined to regard as "the power and spirit of the Father."

371. The line blends the promise in Psalm ii, 8 (which was referred to Christ) — "Ask of me, and I shall give thee . . . the uttermost parts of the earth for thy possession" — with Virgil's prophecy that the fame of Augustus should be bounded by the stars (*Aen.* I, 287).

O Prophet of glad tidings, finisher   375.
Of utmost hope! now clear I understand
What oft my steadiest thoughts have searcht in vain,
Why our great expectation should be call'd
The seed of Woman: Virgin Mother, Hail,
High in the love of Heav'n, yet from my Loins   380.
Thou shalt proceed, and from thy Womb the Son
Of God most High; So God with man unites.
Needs must the Serpent now his capital bruise
Expect with mortal pain: say where and when
Thir fight, what stroke shall bruise the Victor's heel.   385
  To whom thus *Michael*. Dream not of thir fight,
As of a Duel, or the local wounds
Of head or heel: not therefore joins the Son
Manhood to Godhead, with more strength to foil
Thy enemy; nor so is overcome   390.
Satan, whose fall from Heav'n, a deadlier bruise,
Disabl'd not to give thee thy death's wound:
Which hee, who comes thy Saviour, shall recure,
Not by destroying *Satan*, but his works
In thee and in thy Seed: nor can this be,   395.
But by fulfilling that which thou didst want,
Obedience to the Law of God, impos'd
On penalty of death, and suffering death,
The penalty to thy transgression due,
And due to theirs which out of thine will grow: 400.
So only can high Justice rest appaid.
The Law of God exact he shall fulfil
Both by obedience and by love, though love
Alone fulfil the Law; thy punishment
He shall endure by coming in the Flesh   405
To a reproachful life and cursed death,
Proclaiming Life to all who shall believe
In his redemption, and that his obedience
Imputed becomes theirs by Faith, his merits
To save them, not thir own, though legal works.   410
For this he shall live hated, be blasphem'd,
Seiz'd on by force, judg'd, and to death condemn'd
A shameful and accurst, nail'd to the Cross
By his own Nation, slain for bringing Life;
But to the Cross he nails thy Enemies,   415.

---

383. *capital* plays on the literal Latin meaning, "pertaining to the head," where the serpent is to be bruised, and the derived meaning, "fatal."
393. *recure:* heal, restore.
401. *appaid:* satisfied. Cf. III, 210.
401–458. The doctrinal elements of this passage are expressly affirmed in

Milton's detailed assertion of Christ's "voluntary submission of himself to the divine justice both in life and in death . . . for man's redemption," and his resurrection and ascension "to a state of immortality and highest glory" in *CD* I, xvi (C.Ed. XV, 302).

The Law that is against thee, and the sins
Of all mankind, with him there crucifi'd,
Never to hurt them more who rightly trust
In this his satisfaction; so he dies,
But soon revives, Death over him no power   420
Shall long usurp; ere the third dawning light
Return, the Stars of Morn shall see him rise
Out of his grave, fresh as the dawning light,
Thy ransom paid, which Man from death redeems,
His death for Man, as many as offer'd Life   425
Neglect not, and the benefit embrace
By Faith not void of works: this God-like act
Annuls thy doom, the death thou shouldst have di'd,
In sin for ever lost from life; this act
Shall bruise the head of *Satan*, crush his strength   430
Defeating Sin and Death, his two main arms,
And fix far deeper in his head thir stings
Than temporal death shall bruise the Victor's heel,
Or theirs whom he redeems, a death like sleep,
A gentle wafting to immortal Life.   435
Nor after resurrection shall he stay
Longer on Earth than certain times to appear
To his Disciples, Men who in his Life
Still follow'd him; to them shall leave in charge
To teach all nations what of him they learn'd   440
And his Salvation, them who shall believe
Baptizing in the profluent stream, the sign
Of washing them from guilt of sin to Life
Pure, and in mind prepar'd, if so befall,
For death, like that which the redeemer di'd.   445
All Nations they shall teach; for from that day
Not only to the Sons of *Abraham's* Loins
Salvation shall be Preacht, but to the Sons
Of *Abraham's* Faith wherever through the world;
So in his seed all Nations shall be blest.   450
Then to the Heav'n of Heav'ns he shall ascend
With victory, triumphing through the air
Over his foes and thine; there shall surprise
The Serpent, Prince of air, and drag in Chains
Through all his Realm, and there confounded leave;   455
Then enter into glory, and resume

---

433. Cf. Milton's conception of *temporal death* in XI, 469.

442. *profluent* is derived from the Latin word used in Milton's discussion of baptism as ideally to be performed in running water (in *CD* I, xxviii; C.Ed. XVI, 168).

447. Cf. Galatians iii, 8: "And the scripture, foreseeing that God would justify the heathen through faith, preached before the gospel unto Abraham, saying, In thee shall all nations be blessed." In the next eighty lines countless reminiscences from the New Testament, the Psalms, and the Prophets are more or less clearly introduced.

His Seat at God's right hand, exalted high
Above all names in Heav'n; and thence shall come,
When this world's dissolution shall be ripe,
With glory and power to judge both quick and dead,   460
To judge th' unfaithful dead, but to reward
His faithful, and receive them into bliss,
Whether in Heav'n or Earth, for then the Earth
Shall all be Paradise, far happier place
Than this of *Eden*, and far happier days.   465
　So spake th' Arch-Angel *Michaël*, then paus'd,
As at the World's great period; and our Sire
Replete with joy and wonder thus repli'd.
　O goodness infinite, goodness immense!
That all this good of evil shall produce,   470
And evil turn to good; more wonderful
Than that which by creation first brought forth
Light out of darkness! full of doubt I stand,
Whether I should repent me now of sin
By mee done and occasion'd, or rejoice   475
Much more, that much more good thereof shall spring,
To God more glory, more good will to Men
From God, and over wrath grace shall abound.
But say, if our deliverer up to Heav'n
Must reascend, what will betide the few   480
His faithful, left among th' unfaithful herd,
The enemies of truth; who then shall guide
His people, who defend? will they not deal
Worse with his followers than with him they dealt?
　Be sure they will, said th' Angel; but from Heav'n   485
Hee to his own a Comforter will send,
The promise of the Father, who shall dwell
His Spirit within them, and the Law of Faith
Working through love, upon thir hearts shall write,
To guide them in all truth, and also arm   490
With spiritual Armor, able to resist

460. *quick and dead:* living and dead. The phrase is from the Apostles' Creed, with Christ's words, "all that are in the graves shall hear the voice" (John v, 28), in the background.
469–478. Adam's cry repeats the title of the medieval hymn *O Felix Culpa* (*O Happy Sin*). It is paraphrased by the chorus in Salandra's *Adamo caduto* II, xiv: "O happy Sin / O blessed crime / O precious theft / Dear Disobedience / Adam, blest thief not of the Apple / But of Mercy, Clemency, and Glory." The paradox is the climax of Giles Fletcher's *Christ's Triumph over Death* (1610) and Du Bartas' *Divine Weeks* (p. 261). The history of the belief is traced by Lovejoy in *ELH*, IV (1937), 161–79, by Williams

in *Expositor*, p. 138, by Madsen and Marshall in articles listed in the bibliography and by Ogden in *PQ*, XXXVI (1957), 11–19. Daiches and Kermode warn against its overstress in *The Living Milton*, pp. 59, 102 and 121.
478. Cf. Romans v, 20: "Where sin abounded, grace did much more abound."
486. So in *CD* I, vi (C.Ed. XIV, 389) Milton says that "the Holy Spirit, the Comforter, was sent by the Son from the Father." Cf. John xv, 26.
489. Hebrews viii, 10, echoes Jeremiah xxxi, 33, in describing God's laws as written on the heart.
491. The *spiritual Armor* comes from Ephesians vi, 11–17.

Satan's assaults, and quench his fiery darts,
What Man can do against them, not afraid,
Though to the death, against such cruelties
With inward consolations recompens't,   495
And oft supported so as shall amaze
Thir proudest persecutors: for the Spirit
Pour'd first on his Apostles, whom he sends
To evangelize the Nations, then on all
Baptiz'd, shall them with wondrous gifts endue   500
To speak all Tongues, and do all Miracles,
As did thir Lord before them. Thus they win
Great numbers of each Nation to receive
With joy the tidings brought from Heav'n: at length
Thir Ministry perform'd, and race well run,   505
Thir doctrine and thir story written left,
They die; but in thir room, as they forewarn,
Wolves shall succeed for teachers, grievous Wolves,
Who all the sacred mysteries of Heav'n
To thir own vile advantages shall turn   510
Of lucre and ambition, and the truth
With superstitions and traditions taint,
Left only in those written Records pure,
Though not but by the Spirit understood.
Then shall they seek to avail themselves of names,   515
Places and titles, and with these to join
Secular power, though feigning still to act
By spiritual, to themselves appropriating
The Spirit of God, promis'd alike and giv'n
To all Believers; and from that pretense,   520
Spiritual Laws by carnal power shall force
On every conscience; Laws which none shall find
Left them inroll'd, or what the Spirit within
Shall on the heart engrave. What will they then
But force the Spirit of Grace itself, and bind   525
His consort Liberty; what, but unbuild
His living Temples, built by Faith to stand,
Thir own Faith not another's: for on Earth
Who against Faith and Conscience can be heard
Infallible? yet many will presume: 530
Whence heavy persecution shall arise
On all who in the worship persevere

---

508. *grievous Wolves* is St. Paul's term (Acts xx, 29), which is echoed in *grim Wolf* in the attack on the corrupt clergy in *Lycidas*, 128, and again in the *hireling Wolves, whose gospel is their maw* of the *Sonnet to Cromwell.*

517–525. So in *CD* I, xxx (C.Ed. XVI, 280) Milton denounced all efforts to impose "human authority in matters of religion" as in effect efforts "to impose a yoke, not on man, but on the Holy Spirit itself." Cf. "Now the Lord is that Spirit: and where the Spirit of the Lord is, there is liberty" (II Cor. iii, 17).

527. St. Paul called the body "the temple of the Holy Ghost" (I Cor. vi, 19).

Of Spirit and Truth; the rest, far greater part,
Will deem in outward Rites and specious forms
Religion satisfi'd; Truth shall retire   535
Bestuck with sland'rous darts, and works of Faith
Rarely be found: so shall the World go on,
To good malignant, to bad men benign,
Under her own weight groaning, till the day
Appear of respiration to the just,   540
And vengeance to the wicked, at return
Of him so lately promis'd to thy aid,
The Woman's seed, obscurely then foretold,
Now amplier known thy Saviour and thy Lord,
Last in the Clouds from Heav'n to be reveal'd   545
In glory of the Father, to dissolve
Satan with his perverted World, then raise
From the conflagrant mass, purg'd and refin'd,
New Heav'ns, new Earth, Ages of endless date
Founded in righteousness and peace and love,   550
To bring forth fruits Joy and eternal Bliss.
    He ended; and thus *Adam* last repli'd.
How soon hath thy prediction, Seer blest,
Measur'd this transient World, the Race of time,
Till time stand fixt: beyond is all abyss,   555
Eternity, whose end no eye can reach.
Greatly instructed I shall hence depart,
Greatly in peace of thought, and have my fill
Of knowledge, what this Vessel can contain;
Beyond which was my folly to aspire.   560
Henceforth I learn, that to obey is best,
And love with fear the only God, to walk
As in his presence, ever to observe
His providence, and on him sole depend,
Merciful over all his works, with good   565
Still overcoming evil, and by small
Accomplishing great things, by things deem'd weak
Subverting worldly strong, and worldly wise
By simply meek; that suffering for Truth's sake
Is fortitude to highest victory,   570
And to the faithful Death the Gate of Life;

533. ". . . true worshippers shall worship the Father in spirit and in truth" (John iv, 23).

539–551. Milton interprets St. Peter's "times of refreshing . . . from the presence of the Lord" (Acts iii, 19) as the day of Christ's coming "with the clouds" (Rev. i, 7) at the last judgment, when, he says in *CD* I, xxxiii (C.Ed. XVI, 355), "Christ shall judge the evil angels and the whole race of mankind." Cf. XI, 900–901, and III, 334–38.

559. *this vessel*, as St. Paul called the human body (I Thess. iv, 4), Milton warns in *CD* I, ii (C.Ed. XIV, 61), is able to understand God only "in such manner as may be within the scope of our comprehension." Cf. VIII, 167–73.

565. The line repeats St. Paul's words in Romans xii, 21.

566–569. "God hath chosen the weak things of the world to confound the things that are mighty . . ." (I Cor. i, 27).

Taught this by his example whom I now
Acknowledge my Redeemer ever blest.
　To whom thus also th' Angel last repli'd:
This having learnt, thou hast attain'd the sum　　　575
Of wisdom; hope no higher, though all the Stars
Thou knew'st by name, and all th' ethereal Powers,
All secrets of the deep, all Nature's works,
Or works of God in Heav'n, Air, Earth, or Sea,
And all the riches of this World enjoy'dst,　　　580
And all the rule, one Empire; only add
Deeds to thy knowledge answerable, add Faith,
Add Virtue, Patience, Temperance, add Love,
By name to come call'd Charity, the soul
Of all the rest: then wilt thou not be loath　　　585
To leave this Paradise, but shalt possess
A paradise within thee, happier far.
Let us descend now therefore from this top
Of Speculation; for the hour precise
Exacts our parting hence; and see the Guards,　　　590
By mee encampt on yonder Hill, expect
Thir motion, at whose Front a flaming Sword,
In signal of remove, waves fiercely round;
We may no longer stay: go, waken *Eve;*
Her also I with gentle Dreams have calm'd　　　595
Portending good, and all her spirits compos'd
To meek submission: thou at season fit
Let her with thee partake what thou hast heard,
Chiefly what may concern her Faith to know,
The great deliverance by her Seed to come　　　600
(For by the Woman's Seed) on all Mankind,
That ye may live, which will be many days,
Both in one Faith unanimous though sad,
With cause for evils past, yet much more cheer'd
With meditation on the happy end.　　　605
　He ended, and they both descend the Hill;
Descended, *Adam* to the Bow'r where *Eve*
Lay sleeping ran before, but found her wak't;
And thus with words not sad she him receiv'd.
　　Whence thou return'st, and whither went'st, I know;　　　610
For God is also in sleep, and Dreams advise,

---

587. The *paradise within* (in contrast with the hell within Satan in IV, 20) recalls Robert Crofts's title for his *A Paradise within Us or the Happie Mind* (1640). Reasoning much as Milton does in ll. 469–78, Crofts pled that the possibility of an inward paradise proved that Adam's fall was fortunate. A case for Crofts's influence on Milton is made with some reservations by G. C. Taylor in *PQ,* XXVIII (1949), 208.

589. *Speculation* has its Latin meaning of "looking out." Cf. the *specular Mount* of *PR* IV, 236.

602. ". . . the days that Adam lived were nine hundred and thirty years: and he died" (Gen. v, 5).

611. Perhaps there is a trace of Achilles' words to Agamemnon: "A dream is from Zeus" (*Il.* I, 63). There

Which he hath sent propitious, some great good
Presaging, since with sorrow and heart's distress
Wearied I fell asleep: but now lead on;
In mee is no delay; with thee to go,   615
Is to stay here; without thee here to stay,
Is to go hence unwilling; thou to mee
Art all things under Heav'n, all places thou,
Who for my wilful crime art banisht hence.
This further consolation yet secure   620
I carry hence; though all by mee is lost,
Such favor I unworthy am voutsaf't,
By mee the Promis'd Seed shall all restore.
    So spake our Mother *Eve*, and *Adam* heard
Well pleas'd, but answer'd not; for now too nigh   625
Th' Arch-Angel stood, and from the other Hill
To thir fixt Station, all in bright array
The Cherubim descended; on the ground
Gliding meteorous, as Ev'ning Mist
Ris'n from a River o'er the marish glides,   630
And gathers ground fast at the Laborer's heel
Homeward returning. High in Front advanc't,
The brandisht Sword of God before them blaz'd
Fierce as a Comet; which with torrid heat,
And vapor as the *Libyan* Air adust,   635
Began to parch that temperate Clime; whereat
In either hand the hast'ning Angel caught
Our ling'ring Parents, and to th' Eastern Gate
Led them direct, and down the Cliff as fast
To the subjected Plain; then disappear'd.   640
They looking back, all th' Eastern side beheld
Of Paradise, so late thir happy seat,
Wav'd over by that flaming Brand, the Gate
With dreadful Faces throng'd and fiery Arms:
Some natural tears they dropp'd, but wip'd them soon;   645
The World was all before them, where to choose

---

is certainly a reminiscence of the distinction which Bacon said (*Essays* xlii) that a certain rabbi drew between a vision and a dream on the ground that the former is the clearer revelation of God.

635. *adust:* burnt. Milton had perhaps read John Salkeld's review of several theories about the swords of the cherubim guarding the entrance of Eden, and among them St. Thomas Aquinas' suggestion that the garden lay under the equator and that "the sword which the angel held before Paradise, is nothing else but the mighty heate of the torrida zona" (*A Treatise of Angels* — 1613 — p. 290); but like Salkeld he seems to have thought

that the cherubim were true angels. Cf II, 714, n.

640. *subjected* has its Latin meaning of "lying beneath."

646–649. John Crowe Ransom represents much modern interpretation when he writes in *Kenyon Review*, XXI (1959), 137, that God "deliberately and knowingly" endowed Adam and Eve "with a prodigious adventurousness" so as to be "pioneers of a happiness which only strength can win in a world of pain, sickness, and death." Actually their mood — as Broadbent observes in *Some Graver Subject*, p. 298 — corresponds with Michael's commission to "send them forth,

Thir place of rest, and Providence thir guide:
They hand in hand with wand'ring steps and slow,
Through *Eden* took thir solitary way.

The End

though sorrowing, yet in peace," and with a "new hope" born "of despair" (XI, 117 and 139). The ambivalence of their dismissal — as Kester Svendsen notes in *Studies in English Literature*, I (1961), 65–72 — was caught in Blake's drawing of the Expulsion from Eden. In John Martin's mezzotint (1827) the exiles descend from the shining gate of paradise to begin the human adventure of scientific exploration on a dark plain where a dinosaur feeds in the far distance. Milton's conception lay between the modern interpretations and that of Masaccio's Expulsion from the Earthly Paradise (1427), which presents the exiles close up, in attitudes of despair. As Miss Helen Gardner points out in *ESEA*, N.S. IX (1956), 35, Masaccio's painting — mediated by Raphael's Expulsion in the Vatican — was the model for the very poor illustration of Milton's closing lines by his first illustrator, J. – B. Medina, in 1688. All three illustrations are reproduced in *JEGP*, LVIII (1961) between pp. 672 and 673.

LIBRI COSMO.   Fol.XXVII

HARVM RERVM HANC SVME
FIGVRATIONEM.

THE LIFE OF MILTON

(1694)

By Edward Phillips *

Of all the several parts of history, that which sets forth the lives, and commemorates the most remarkable actions, sayings, or writings of famous and illustrious persons, whether in war or peace, whether many together, or any one in particular, as it is not the least useful in itself, so it is in highest vogue and esteem among the studious and reading part of mankind.

The most eminent in this way of history were, among the ancients, Plutarch and Diogenes Laertius, of the Greeks; the first wrote the lives, for the most part, of the most renowned heroes and warriors of the Greeks and Romans; the other, the lives of the ancient Greek philosophers. And Cornelius Nepos (or as some will have it Æmilius Probus) of the Latins, who wrote the lives of the most illustrious Greek and Roman generals.

Among the moderns, Machiavelli, a noble Florentine, who elegantly wrote the life of Castruccio Castracani, Lord of Lucca. And of our nation, Sir Fulke Greville, who wrote the life of his most intimate friend, Sir Philip Sidney; Mr. Thomas Stanley of Cumberlo-Green, who made a most elaborate improvement to the foresaid Laertius, by adding to what he found in him, what by diligent search and enquiry he collected from other authors of best authority; [and] Isaac Walton, who wrote the lives of Sir Henry Wotton, Dr. Donne, and for his divine poems, the admired Mr. George Herbert. Lastly, not to mention several other biographers of considerable note, the great Gassendus of France, the worthy celebrator of two no less worthy subjects of his impartial pen; *viz.* the noble philosopher Epicurus, and the most politely learned virtuoso of his age, his countryman, Monsieur Peiresk.

And pity it is the person whose memory we have here undertaken to perpetuate by recounting the most memorable transactions of his life (though his works sufficiently recommend him to the world), finds not a well-informed pen able to set him forth, equal with the best of those here mentioned; for doubtless, had his fame been as much spread through Europe in Thuanus's time, as now it is and hath been for several years, he had justly merited from that great historian, an eulogy not inferior to the highest by him given to all the learned and ingenious that lived within the compass of his history. For we may safely and justly affirm, that take him in all respects, for acumen of wit, quickness of apprehension, sagacity of judgment, depth of argument, and elegancy of style, as well in Latin as English, as well in verse as prose, he is

---

* Edward Phillips left the fullest and least unreliable of the early biographies of his uncle. He was the son of Anne Milton Phillips (the poet's sister) and Edward Phillips, senior, and was born in the autumn of 1630. He and his brother John were both pupils of Milton and must have lived with him for several years, but in the end both of them seem to have become sympathizers with the position of the Royalists. Edward, however, remained personally loyal to Milton and translated his *Letters of State* into English after his death.

scarce to be paralleled by any the best of writers our nation hath in any age brought forth.

He was born in London, in a house in Breadstreet, the lease whereof, as I take it, but for certain it was a house in Breadstreet, became in time part of his estate, in the year of our Lord 1606.[1] His father John Milton, an honest, worthy, and substantial citizen of London, by profession a scrivener; to which he voluntarily betook himself by the advice and assistance of an intimate friend of his eminent in that calling, upon his being cast out by his father, a bigoted Roman Catholic, for embracing, when young, the protestant faith, and abjuring the popish tenets. For he is said to have been descended of an ancient family of the Miltons, of Milton near Abingdon in Oxfordshire; where they had been a long time seated, as appears by the monuments still to be seen in Milton church; till one of the family having taken the wrong side, in the contest between the Houses of York and Lancaster, was sequestered of all his estate, but what he held by his wife. However, certain it is that this vocation he followed for many years, at his said house in Breadstreet, with success suitable to his industry and prudent conduct of his affairs. Yet he did not so far quit his own generous and ingenious inclinations as to make himself wholly a slave to the world; for he sometimes found vacant hours to the study (which he made his recreation) of the noble science of music, in which he advanced to that perfection that as I have been told, and as I take it by our author himself, he composed an *In Nomine* of forty parts; for which he was rewarded with a gold medal and chain by a Polish prin ce, to whom he presented it. However, this is a truth not to be denied, that for several songs of his composition after the way of these times (three or four of which are still to be seen in Old Wilby's set of Airs, besides some compositions of his in Ravenscroft's Psalms) he gained the reputation of a considerable master in this most charming of all the liberal sciences. Yet all this while he managed his grand affair of this world with such prudence and diligence that by the assistance of divine Providence favoring his honest endeavors, he gained a competent estate, whereby he was enabled to make a handsome provision both for the education and maintenance of his children; for three he had, and no more, all by one wife Sarah, of the family of the Castons, derived originally from Wales, a woman of incomparable virtue and goodness: John the eldest, the subject of our present work, Christopher, and an only daughter Ann.

Christopher, being principally designed for the study of the common law of England, was entered young a student of the Inner Temple, of which house he lived to be an ancient bencher, and keeping close to that study and profession all his life-time, except in the time of the civil wars of England; when being a great favorer and asserter of the King's cause, and obnoxious to the Parliament's side, by acting to his utmost power against them, so long as he kept his station at Reading; and after that town was taken by the Parliament forces, being forced to quit his house there, he steered his course according to the motion of the King's army. But when the war was ended with victory and success to the Parliament party by the valor of General Fairfax and the craft and conduct of Cromwell, and his composition made by the help o f is

---

[1] The correct date of Milton's birth was Dec. 9, 1608.

brother's interest with the then prevailing power, he betook himself again to his former study and profession, following chamber-practice every term; yet came to no advancement in the world in a long time, except some small employ in the town of Ipswich, where (and near it) he lived all the latter time of his life; for he was a person of a modest, quiet temper, preferring justice and virtue before all worldly pleasure or grandeur. But in the beginning of the reign of King James the II, for his known integrity and ability in the law, he was by some persons of quality recommended to the King, and at a call of sergeants received the coif, and the same day was sworn one of the barons of the Exchequer, and soon after made one of the judges of the Common Pleas. But his years and indisposition not well brooking the fatigue of public employment, he continued not long in either of these stations; but having his *quietus est*, retired to a country life, his study and devotion.

Ann, the only daughter of the said John Milton, the elder, had a considerable dowry given her by her father in marriage with Edward Philips, the son of Edward Philips of Shrewsbury, who, coming up young to town, was bred up in the crown-office in Chancery, and at length came to be secondary of the office under old Mr. Bembo. By him she had, besides other children that died infants, two sons yet surviving, of whom more hereafter; and by a second husband, Mr. Thomas Agar (who, upon the death of his intimate friend Mr. Philips, worthily succeeded in the place, which, except some time of exclusion before and during the Interregnum, he held for many years, and left it to Mr. Thomas Milton, the son of the aforementioned Sir Christopher, who at this day executes it with great reputation and ability), two daughters, Mary who died very young, and Ann yet surviving.

But to hasten back to our matter in hand. John, our author, who was destined to be the ornament and glory of his country, was sent, together with his brother, to Paul's school, whereof Dr. Gill the elder was then chief master; where he was entered into the first rudiments of learning, and advanced therein with that admirable success, not more by the discipline of the school and good instructions of his masters (for that he had another master, possibly at his father's house, appears by the *Fourth Elegy* of his Latin poems written in his 18th year, to Thomas Young, pastor of the English Company of Merchants at Hamburg, wherein he owns and styles him his master), than by his own happy genius, prompt wit and apprehension, and insuperable industry: for he generally sat up half the night, as well in voluntary improvements of his own choice, as the exact perfecting of his school exercises. So that at the age of 15 he was full ripe for academic learning, and accordingly was sent to the University of Cambridge; where in Christ's College under the tuition of a very eminent learned man, whose name I cannot call to mind, he studied seven years and took his degree of Master of Arts; and for the extraordinary wit and reading he had shown in his performances to attain his degree (some whereof, spoken at a *Vacation Exercise* in his 19th year of age, are to be yet seen in his *Miscellaneous Poems*), he was loved and admired by the whole university, particularly by the fellows and most ingenious persons of his house. Among the rest there was a young gentleman, one Mr. King, with whom, for his great learning and parts, he had contracted a particular friendship and intimacy; whose death (for he was drowned on the Irish seas in his passage from Chester to Ireland) he bewails in that most excellent monody in his forementioned poems, entitled *Lycidas*. Never was the loss of friend so elegantly lamented; and among the rest of his *Juvenile Poems*, some he wrote at the age of 15, which contain a poetical genius scarce to be paralleled by any English writer.

Soon after he had taken his Master's degree, he thought fit to leave the university: not upon any disgust or discontent for want of preferment, as some ill-willers have reported; nor upon any cause whatsoever forced to fly, as his detractors maliciously feign; but from which aspersion he sufficiently clears himself in his *Second Answer to Alexander Morus*, the author of a book called, *Clamor Regii Sanguinis ad Coelum*, the chief of his calumniators; in which he plainly makes it out that after his leaving the university, to the no small trouble of his fellow-collegiates, who in general regretted his absence, he for the space of five years lived for the most part with his father and mother at their house at Horton near Colebrook in Berkshire; whither his father, having got an estate to his content and left off all business, was retired from the cares and fatigues of the world.

After the said term of five years, his mother then dying, he was willing to add to his acquired learning the observation of foreign customs, manners, and institutions; and thereupon took a resolution to travel, more especially designing for Italy; and accordingly, with his father's consent and assistance, he put himself into an equipage suitable to such a design; and so, intending to go by the way of France, he set out for Paris, accompanied only with one man, who attended him through all his travels; for his prudence was his guide, and his learning his introduction and presentation to persons of most eminent quality. However, he had also a most civil and obliging letter of direction and advice from Sir Henry Wotton, then Provost of Eton, and formerly resident Ambassador from King James the First to the state of Venice; which letter is to be seen in the first edition of his *Miscellaneous Poems*.

At Paris, being recommended by the said Sir Henry and other persons of quality, he went first to wait upon my Lord Scudamore, then Ambassador in France from King Charles the First. My Lord received him with wonderful civility; and understanding he had a desire to make a visit to the great Hugo Grotius, he sent several of his attendants to wait upon him and to present him in his name to that renowned doctor and statesman, who was at that time Ambassador from Christina, Queen of Sweden, to the French king. Grotius took the visit kindly, and gave him entertainment suitable to his worth and the high commendations he had heard of him. After a few days, not intending to make the usual tour of France, he took his leave of my Lord, who at his departure from Paris, gave him letters to the English merchants residing in any part through which he was to travel, in which they were requested to show him all the kindness and do him all the good offices that lay in their power.

From Paris he hastened on his journey to Nice, where he took shipping, and in a short space arrived at Genoa; from whence he went to Leghorn, thence to Pisa, and so to Florence. In this city he met with many charming objects, which invited him to stay a longer time than he intended; the pleasant situation of the place, the nobleness of the structures, the exact humanity and civility of the inhabitants, the more polite and refined sort of language there than elsewhere. During the time of his stay here, which was about two months, he visited all the private academies of the city, which are places established for the improvement of wit and learning, and maintained a correspondence and perpetual friendship among gentlemen fitly qualified for such an institution; and such sort of academies there are in all or most of the most noted cities in Italy. Visiting these places he was soon taken notice of by the most learned and ingenious of the nobility and the grand wits of Florence, who caressed him with all the honors and civilities imaginable; particularly Jacobo Gaddi, Carlo Dati, Antonio Francini, Frescobaldo, Cultellino, Bonmatthei and Clementillo: whereof Gaddi hath a large, elegant Italian canzonet in his praise, [and] Dati, a Latin epistle, both printed before his Latin poems, together with a Latin distich of the Marquis of Villa, and another of Selvaggi, and a Latin tetrastich of Giovanni Salsilli, a Roman.

From Florence he took his journey to Siena, from thence to Rome, where he was detained much about the same time he had been at Florence; as well by his desire of seeing all the rarities and antiquities of that most glorious and renowned city, as by the conversation of Lucas Holstenius and other learned and ingenious men, who highly valued his acquaintance and treated him with all possible respect.

From Rome he travelled to Naples, where he was introduced by a certain hermit who accompanied him in his journey from Rome thither, into the knowledge of Giovanni Baptista Manso, Marquis of Villa, a Neapolitan by birth, a person of high nobility, virtue, and honor, to whom the famous Italian poet, Torquato Tasso, wrote his treatise *De Amicitia;* and moreover mentions him with great honor in that illustrious poem of his, entitled *Gierusalemme Liberata.* This noble marquis received him with extraordinary respect and civility, and went with him himself to give him a sight of all that was of note and remark in the city, particularly the viceroy's palace, and was often in person to visit him at his lodging. Moreover, this noble marquis honored him so far, as to make a Latin distich in his praise, as hath been already mentioned; which being no less pithy than short, though already in print, it will not be unworth the while here to repeat.

> *Ut mens, forma, decor, facies, [mos,] si pietas sic*
> *Non Anglus, verum hercle Angelus ipse foret.*

In return of this honor, and in gratitude for the many favors and civilities received of him, he presented him at his departure with a large Latin eclogue, entitled *Mansus,* afterwards published among his *Latin Poems.* The marquis at his taking leave of him, gave him this compliment: that he would have done him many more offices of kindness and civility, but was therefore rendered incapable, in regard he had been over-liberal in his speech against the religion of the country.

He had entertained some thoughts of passing over into Sicily and Greece, but was diverted by the news he received from England that affairs there were tending toward a civil war; thinking it a thing unworthy in him to be taking his pleasure in foreign parts while his countrymen at home were fighting for their liberty: but first resolved to see Rome once more; and though the merchants gave him a caution that the Jesuits were hatching designs against him in case he should return thither, by reason of the freedom he took in all his discourses of religion; nevertheless he ventured to prosecute his resolution, and to Rome the second time he went; determining with himself not industriously to begin to fall into any discourse about religion, but, being asked, not to deny or endeavor to conceal his own sentiments. Two months he stayed at Rome, and in all that time never flinched, but was ready to defend the orthodox faith against all opposers; and so well he succeeded therein, that, good Providence guarding him, he went safe from Rome back to Florence, where his return to his friends of that city was welcomed with as much joy and affection as had it been to his friends and relations in his own country, he could not have come a more joyful and welcome guest.

Here, having stayed as long as at his first coming, excepting an excursion of a few days to Lucca, crossing the Apennine and passing through Bononia and Ferrara, he arrived at Venice; where when he had spent a month's time in viewing of that stately city and shipped up a parcel of curious and rare books which he had picked up in his travels (particularly a chest or two of choice music-books of the best masters flourishing about that time in Italy, namely, Luca Marenzo, Monte Verde, Horatio Vecchi, Cifa, the Prince of Venosa, and several others), he took his course through Verona, Milan, and the Poenine Alps, and so by the lake Leman to Geneva, where he stayed for some time, and had daily converse with the most learned Giovanni Deodati, theology professor in that city; and so returning through France, by the same way he had passed it going to Italy, he, after a peregrination of one complete year and about three months, arrived safe in England about the time of the King's making his second expedition against the Scots.

Soon after his return and visits paid to his father and other friends, he took him a lodging in St. Bride's Churchyard, at the house of one Russel, a tailor, where he first undertook the education and instruction of his sister's two sons, the younger whereof had been wholly committed to his charge and care.

And here by the way, I judge it not impertinent to mention the many authors both of the Latin and Greek, which through his excellent judgment and way of teaching, far above the pedantry of common public schools (where such authors are scarce ever heard of), were run over within no greater compass of time, than from ten to fifteen or sixteen years of age. Of the Latin, the four grand authors *De Re Rustica,* Cato, Varro, Columella and Palladius; Cornelius Celsus, an ancient physician of the Romans; a great part of Pliny's *Natural History;* Vitruvius his *Architecture;* Frontinus his *Stratagems;* with the two egregious poets, Lucretius and Manilius. Of the Greek, Hesiod, a poet equal with Homer; Aratus his *Phaenomena,* and *Diosemeia;* Dionysius Afer *De Situ Orbis;* Oppian's *Cynegetics* and *Halieutics;* Quintus Calaber his *Poem of the Trojan War* continued from Homer; Apollonius Rhodius his *Argonautics:* and in prose, Plutarch's *Placita Philosophorum,* and Περι Παιδων 'Αγωγιας [*sic*]; Geminus's *Astronomy;* Xenophon's *Cyri Institutio,* and *Anabasis;* Ælian's *Tactics;* and Polyænus his *Warlike Stratagems.* Thus by teaching he in some measure increased his own knowledge, having the reading of all these authors as it were by proxy; and all this might possibly have conduced to the preserving of his eyesight, had he not moreover been perpetually busied in his own laborious undertakings of the book and pen.

Nor did the time thus studiously employed in conquering the Greek and Latin tongues, hinder the attaining to the chief oriental languages, *viz.*, the Hebrew, Chaldee, and Syriac, so far as to go through the *Pentateuch*, or Five Books of Moses in Hebrew, to make a good entrance into the *Targum*, or Chaldee Paraphrase, and to understand several chapters of St. Matthew in the Syriac Testament: besides an introduction into several arts and sciences, by reading Urstisius his *Arithmetic*, Riff's *Geometry*, Petiscus his *Trigonometry*, Johannes de Sacro Bosco *De Sphæra;* and into the Italian and French tongues, by reading in Italian Giovan Villani's *History of the Transactions between several petty States of Italy;* and in French a great part of Pierre Davity, the famous geographer of France in his time.

The Sunday's work was, for the most part, the reading each day a chapter of the Greek Testament, and hearing his learned exposition upon the same (and how this savored of atheism in him, I leave to the courteous backbiter to judge). The next work after this was the writing from his own dictation, some part, from time to time, of a tractate which he thought fit to collect from the ablest of divines who had written of that subject: Amesius, Wollebius, &c., *viz. A perfect System of Divinity*, of which more hereafter.

Now persons so far manuducted into the highest paths of literature both divine and human, had they received his documents with the same acuteness of wit and apprehension, the same industry, alacrity, and thirst after knowledge, as the instructor was indued with, what prodigies of wit and learning might they have proved! The scholars might in some degree have come near to the equalling of the master, or at least have in some sort made good what he seems to predict in the close of an elegy he made in the seventeenth year of his age, upon the death of one of his sister's children (a daughter), who died in her infancy:

> Then thou, the mother of so sweet a child,
> Her false, imagin'd loss cease to lament,
> And wisely learn to curb thy sorrows wild:
> This if thou do, he will an offspring give,
> That till the world's last end shall make thy name to live.

But to return to the thread of our discourse. He made no long stay in his lodgings in St. Bride's Church-yard; necessity of having a place to dispose his books in, and other goods fit for the furnishing of a good, handsome house, hastening him to take one; and, accordingly, a pretty garden-house he took in Aldersgate-street, at the end of an entry and therefore the fitter for his turn by the reason of the privacy; besides that there are few streets in London more free from noise than that. Here first it was that his academic erudition was put in practice, and vigorously proceeded, he himself giving an example to those under him (for it was not long after his taking this house, ere his elder nephew was put to board with him also) of hard study and spare diet; only this advantage he had, that once in three weeks or a month, he would drop into the society of some young sparks of his acquaintance, the chief whereof were Mr. Alphry and Mr. Miller, two gentlemen of Gray's Inn, the beaux of those times, but nothing near so bad as those now-a-days; with these gentlemen he would so far make bold with his body as now and then to keep a gawdyday.

In this house he continued several years, in the one or two first whereof he set out several treatises, *viz.*, that *Of Reformation;* that *Against Prelatical Episcopacy; The Reason of Church-Government; The Defence of Smectymnuus,* at least the greatest part of them, but as I take it, all; and some time after, one sheet *Of Education* which he dedicated to Mr. Samuel Hartlib, he that wrote so much of husbandry (this sheet is printed at the end of the second edition of his *Poems*), and lastly *Areopagitica.*

During the time also of his continuance in this house, there fell out several occasions of the increasing of his family. His father, who till the taking of Reading by the Earl of Essex his forces, had lived with his other son at his house there, was upon that son's dissettlement necessitated to betake himself to this his eldest son, with whom he lived for some years, even to his dying day. In the next place he had an addition of some scholars; to which may be added, his entering into matrimony; but he had his wife's company so small a time, that he may well be said to have become a single man again soon after.

About Whitsuntide it was, or a little.after, that he took a journey into the country; no body about him certainly knowing the reason, or that it was any more than a journey of recreation; after a month's stay, home he returns a married man, that went out a bachelor; his wife being Mary, the eldest daughter of Mr. Richard Powell, then a justice of peace, of Forresthill, near Shotover in Oxfordshire; some few of her nearest relations accompanying the bride to her new habitation; which by reason the father nor any body else were yet come, was able to receive them; where the feasting held for some days in celebration of the nuptials and for entertainment of the bride's friends. At length they took their leave and returning to Forresthill left the sister behind, probably not much to her satisfaction as appeared by the sequel. By that time she had for a month or thereabout led a philosophical life (after having been used to a great house, and much company and joviality), her friends, possibly incited by her own desire, made earnest suit by letter, to have her company the remaining part of the summer, which was granted, on condition of her return at the time appointed, Michaelmas, or thereabout. In the meantime came his father, and some of the forementioned disciples.

And now the studies went on with so much the more vigor, as there were more hands and heads employed; the old gentleman living wholly retired to his rest and devotion, without the least trouble imaginable. Our author, now as it were a single man again, made it his chief diversion now and then in an evening, to visit the Lady Margaret Lee, daughter to the —— Lee, Earl of Marlborough, Lord High Treasurer of England, and President of the Privy Council to King James the First. This lady being a woman of great wit and ingenuity, had a particular honor for him and took much delight in his company, as likewise her husband Captain Hobson, a very accomplished gentleman; and what esteem he at the same time had for her, appears by a sonnet he made in praise of her, to be seen among his other *Sonnets* in his extant *Poems.*

Michaelmas being come, and no news of his wife's return, he sent for her by letter; and receiving no answer, sent several other letters, which were also unanswered; so that at last he dispatched down a foot messenger with a letter, desiring her return. But the messenger came back not only without an answer, at least a satisfactory one, but to the best of my remembrance, reported that he was dismissed with some sort of contempt. This proceeding in all probability was grounded upon no other cause but this, namely, that the family being generally addicted to the cavalier party, as they called it, and some of them possibly engaged in the King's service, who by this time had his headquarters at Oxford, and was in some prospect of success, they began to repent them of having matched the eldest daughter of the family to a person so contrary to them in opinion; and thought it would be a blot in their escutcheon, whenever that court should come to flourish again.

However, it so incensed our author that he thought it would be dishonorable ever to receive her again, after such a repulse; so that he forthwith prepared to fortify himself with arguments for such a resolution, and accordingly wrote two treatises, by which he undertook to maintain, that it was against reason, and the enjoinment of it not provable by Scripture, for any married couple disagreeable in humor and temper, or having an aversion to each other, to be forced to live yoked together all their days. The first was his *Doctrine and Discipline of Divorce*, of which there was printed a second edition with some additions. The other in prosecution of the first, was styled *Tetrachordon*. Then the better to confirm his own opinion by the attestation of others, he set out a piece called *The Judgment of Martin Bucer*, a protestant minister, being a translation out of that reverend divine, of some part of his works exactly agreeing with him in sentiment. Lastly, he wrote in answer to a pragmatical clerk, who would needs give himself the honor of writing against so great a man, his *Colasterion*, or *Rod of Correction for a Saucy Impertinent*.

Not very long after the setting forth of these treatises, having application made to him by several gentlemen of his acquaintance for the education of their sons, as understanding haply the progress he had infixed by his first undertakings of that nature, he laid out for a larger house, and soon found it out.

But in the interim before he removed, there fell out a passage, which though it altered not the whole course he was going to steer, yet it put a stop or rather an end to a grand affair, which was more than probably thought to be then in agitation; it was indeed a design of marrying one of Dr. Davis's daughters, a very handsome and witty gentlewoman, but averse, as it is said, to this motion. However, the intelligence hereof, and the then declining state of the King's cause, and consequently of the circumstances of Justice Powell's family, caused them to set all engines on work to restore the late married woman to the station wherein they a little before had planted her. At last this device was pitched upon. There dwelt in the lane of St. Martin's le Grand, which was hard by, a relation of our author's, one Blackborough, whom it was known he often visited, and upon this occasion the visits were the more narrowly observed, and possibly there might be a combination between both parties; the friends on both sides concentring in the same action, though on different behalfs. One time above the rest, he making his usual visit, the wife was ready in another room, and on a sudden he was surprised to see one whom he thought to have never seen more, making submission and begging pardon on her knees before him. He might probably at first make some show of aversion and rejection; but partly his own generous nature more inclinable to reconciliation than to perseverance in anger and revenge and partly the strong intercession of friends on both sides, soon brought him to an act of oblivion and a firm league of peace for the future; and it was at length concluded that she should remain at a friend's house till such time as he was settled in his new house at Barbican, and all things for her reception in order; the place agreed on for her present abode was the widow Webber's house in St. Clement's Church-yard, whose second daughter had been married to the other brother many years before. The first fruits of her return to her husband was a brave girl, born within a year after; though, whether by ill constitution or want of care, she grew more and more decrepit.

But it was not only by children that she increased the number of the family; for in no very long time after her coming, she had a great resort of her kindred with her in the house, *viz.* her father and mother, and several of her brothers and sisters, which were in all pretty numerous; who upon his father's sickening and dying soon after, went away.

And now the house looked again like a house of the Muses only, though the accession of scholars was not great. Possibly his proceeding thus far in the education of youth may have been the occasion of some of his adversaries calling him pedagogue and schoolmaster; whereas it is well known he never set up for a public school to teach all the young fry of the parish, but only was willing to impart his learning and knowledge to relations, and the sons of some gentlemen that were his intimate friends; besides, that neither his converse, nor his writings, nor his manner of teaching ever savored in the least anything of pedantry; and probably he might have some prospect of putting in practice his academical institution, according to the model laid down in his sheet *Of Education*. The progress of which design was afterwards diverted by a series of alteration in the affairs of state; for I am much mistaken if there were not about this time a design in agitation of making him adjutant-general in Sir William Waller's army. But the new modeling of the army soon following proved an obstruction to that design; and Sir William, his commission being laid down, began, as the common saying is, to turn *cat in pan*.

It was not long after the march of Fairfax and Cromwell through the city of London with the whole army, to quell the insurrections Brown and Massey, now malcontents also, were endeavoring to raise in the city against the army's proceedings, ere he left his great house in Barbican, and betook himself to a smaller in High Holburn, among those that open backward into Lincoln's Inn Fields. Here he lived a private and quiet life, still prosecuting his studies and curious search into knowledge, the grand affair perpetually of his life; till such time as, the war being now at an end, with complete victory to the Parliament's side, as the Parliament then stood purged of all its dissenting members, and the King after some treaties with the army *re infecta*, brought to his trial; the form of government being now changed into a free state, he was hereupon obliged to write a treatise, called *The Tenure of Kings and Magistrates*.

After which his thoughts were bent upon retiring again to his own private studies, and falling upon such subjects as his proper genius prompted him to write of, among which was the history of our own nation from the beginning till the Norman Conquest, wherein he had made some progress. When (for this his last treatise, reviving the fame of other things he had formerly published) being more and more taken notice of for his excellency of style, and depth of judgment, he was courted into the service of this new commonwealth and at last prevailed with (for he never hunted after preferment, nor affected the tintamar and hurry of public business) to take upon him the office of Latin secretary to the Council of State, for all their letters to foreign princes and states; for they stuck to this noble and generous resolution, not to write to any, or to receive answers from them, but in a language most proper to maintain a correspondence among the learned of all nations in this part of the world; scorning to carry on their affairs in the wheedling, lisping jargon of the cringing French, especially having a minister of state able to cope with the ablest any prince or state could employ, for the Latin tongue. And so well he acquitted himself in this station that he gained from abroad both reputation to himself and credit to the state that employed him.

And it was well the business of his office came not very fast upon him, for he was scarce well warm in his secretaryship before other work flowed in upon him, which took him up for some considerable time. In the first place there came out a book said to have been written by the king, and finished a little before his death, entitled Εἰκὼν βασιλικὴ, that is, *The Royal Image;* a book highly cried up for its smooth style, and pathetical composure; wherefore to obviate the impression it was like to make among the many, he was obliged to write an answer, which he entitled Εἰκονοκλάστης or *Image-Breaker*.

And upon the heels of that, out comes in public the great kill-cow of Christendom, with his *Defensio Regis contra Populum Anglicanum;* a man so famous and cried up for his Plinian Exercitations and other pieces of reputed learning, that there could no where have been found a champion that durst lift up the pen against so formidable an adversary, had not our little English David had the courage to undertake this great French Goliath, to whom he gave such a hit in the forehead, that he presently staggered, and soon after fell. For immediately upon the coming out of the answer, entitled, *Defensio Populi Anglicani contra Claudium Anonymum,* &c. he that till then had been chief minister and superintendent in the court of the learned Christina, Queen of Sweden, dwindled in esteem to that degree that he at last vouchsafed to speak to the meanest servant. In short, he was dismissed with so cold and slighting an adieu, that after a faint dying reply, he was glad to have recourse to death, the remedy of evils and ender of controversies.

And now I presume our author had some breathing space, but it was not long. For though Salmasius was departed, he left some stings behind; new enemies started up barkers, though no great biters. Who the first asserter of Salmasius his cause was, is not certainly known but variously conjectured at, some supposing it to be one Janus, a lawyer of Gray's Inn, some Dr. Bramhal, made by King Charles the Second, after his restoration, Archbishop of Armagh in Ireland; but whoever the author was, the book was thought fit to be taken into correction; and our author not thinking it worth his own undertaking, to the disturbing the progress of whatever more chosen work he had then in hands, committed this task to the youngest of his nephews; but with such exact emendations before it went to the press that it might have very well passed for his, but that he was willing the person that took the pains to prepare it for his examination and polishment should have the name and credit of being the author; so that it came forth under this title, *Joannis Philippi Angli Defensio pro Populo Anglicano contra,* &c.

During the writing and publishing of this book, he lodged at one Thomson's next door to the Bull-head tavern at Charing-Cross, opening into the Spring-Garden; which seems to have been only a lodging taken till his designed apartment in Scotland-Yard was prepared for him. For hither he soon removed from the aforesaid place; and here his third child, a son, was born, which through the ill usage, or bad constitution, of an ill chosen nurse, died an infant.

From this apartment, whether he thought it not healthy, or otherwise convenient for his use, or whatever else was the reason, he soon after took a pretty garden-house in Petty-France in Westminster, next door to the Lord Scudamore's, and opening into St. James's Park. Here he remained no less than eight years, namely, from the year 1652, till within a few weeks of King Charles the Second's restoration.

In this house his first wife dying in childbed, he married a second, who after a year's time died in childbed also. This his second marriage was about two or three years after his being wholly deprived of sight, which was just going about the time of his answering Salmasius; whereupon his adversaries gladly take occasion of imputing his blindness as a judgment upon him for his answering the King's book, &c. whereas it is most certainly known that his sight, what with his continual study, his being subject to the headache, and his perpetual tampering with physic to preserve it, had been decaying for above a dozen years before, and the sight of one for a long time clearly lost. Here he wrote, by his amanuensis, his two *Answers to Alexander More,* who upon the last answer quitted the field.

So that being now quiet from state adversaries and public contests, he had leisure again for his own studies and private designs; which were his aforesaid *History of England,* and a new *Thesaurus Linguæ Latinæ,* according to the manner of Stephanus, a work he had been long since collecting from his own reading, and still went on with it at times, even very near to his dying day; but the papers after his death were so discomposed and deficient that it could not be made fit for the press; however, what there was of it was made use of for another dictionary.

But the height of his noble fancy and invention began now to be seriously and mainly employed in a subject worthy of such a Muse, *viz.* a heroic poem, entitled *Paradise Lost;* the noblest in the general esteem of learned and judicious persons of any yet written by any either ancient or modern. This subject was first designed a tragedy, and in the fourth book of the poem there are six verses, which several years before the poem was begun, were shown to me and some others, as designed for the very beginning of the said tragedy. The verses are these: —

O thou that with surpassing glory crown'd!
Look'st from thy sole dominion, like the god
Of this new world; at whose sight all the stars
Hide their diminish'd heads; to thee I call,
But with no friendly voice; and add thy name,
O Sun! to tell thee how I hate thy beams
That bring to my remembrance, from what state
I fell, how glorious once above thy sphere;
Till pride and worse ambition threw me down,
Warring in Heaven, against Heaven's glorious King.

There is another very remarkable passage in the composure of this poem, which I have a particular occasion to remember; for whereas I had the perusal of it from the very beginning, for some years, as I went from time to time to visit him, in a parcel of ten, twenty, or thirty verses at a time, which being written by whatever hand came next, might possibly want correction as to the orthography and pointing; having as the summer came on, not having been showed any for a considerable while, and, desiring the reason thereof, was answered: That his vein never happily flowed but from the autumnal equinoctial to the vernal,[2] and that whatever he attempted [otherwise] was never to his satisfaction, though he courted his fancy never so much, so that in all the years he was about this poem, he may be said to have spent but half his time therein.

It was but a little before the King's restoration that he wrote and published his book *In Defence of a Commonwealth*, so undaunted he was in declaring his true sentiments to the world; and not long before, his *Power of the Civil Magistrate in Ecclesiastical Affairs*, and his *Treatise against Hirelings*, just upon the King's coming over; having a little before been sequestered from his office of Latin secretary and the salary thereunto belonging.

He was forced to leave his house also in Petty-France, where all the time of his abode there, which was eight years as above-mentioned, he was frequently visited by persons of quality, particularly my Lady Ranalagh, whose son for some time he instructed; all learned foreigners of note, who could not part out of this city, without giving a visit to a person so eminent; and lastly, by particular friends that had a high esteem for him, *viz.* Mr. Andrew Marvel, young Lawrence (the son of him that was president of Oliver's council), to whom there is a sonnet among the rest, in his printed *Poems;* Mr. Marchamont Needham, the writer of *Politicus;* but above all, Mr. Cyriac Skinner whom he honored with two sonnets, one long since public among his *Poems,* the other but newly printed.

His next removal was, by the advice of those that wished him well and had a concern for his preservation, into a place of retirement and abscondance, till such time as the current of affairs for the future should instruct him what farther course to take. It was a friend's house in Bartholomew Close, where he lived till the act of oblivion came forth; which it pleased God, proved as

[2] The evidence about this much-controverted point has been reviewed by T. B. Stroup in "Climatic Influence on Milton," in *MLQ,* IV (1943), 185–89, incidentally showing that another of Milton's early biographers, John Toland, understood that he "composed best in warm weather."

favorable to him as could be hoped or expected, through the intercession of some that stood his friends both in Council and Parliament; particularly in the House of Commons, Mr. Andrew Marvel, a member for Hull, acted vigorously in his behalf and made a considerable party for him; so that, together with John Goodwin of Coleman Street, he was only so far excepted as not to bear any office in the Commonwealth.

Soon after appearing again in public, he took a house in Holborn near Red Lyon Fields; where he stayed not long, before his pardon having passed the seal, he removed to Jewin Street. There he lived when he married his 3d wife, recommended to him by his old friend Dr. Paget in Coleman Street. But he stayed not long after his new marriage, ere he removed to a house in the Artillery-walk leading to Bunhill Fields. And this was his last stage in this world, but it was of many years continuance, more perhaps than he had had in any other place besides.

Here he finished his noble poem, and published it in the year 1666. The first edition was printed in quarto by one Simons, a printer in Aldersgate Street; the other in a large octavo, by Starky near Temple-Bar, amended, enlarged, and differently disposed as to the number of books by his own hand, that is by his own appointment; the last set forth, many years since his death, in a large folio, with cuts added, by Jacob Tonson.

Here it was also that he finished and published his history of our nation till the Conquest, all complete so far as he went, some passages only excepted; which, being thought too sharp against the clergy, could not pass the hand of the licenser, were in the hands of the late Earl of Anglesey while he lived; where at present is uncertain.

It cannot certainly be concluded when he wrote his excellent tragedy entitled *Samson Agonistes*, but sure enough it is that it came forth after his publication of *Paradise Lost*, together with his other poem called *Paradise Regained*, which doubtless was begun and finished and printed after the other was published, and that in a wonderful short space considering the sublimeness of it; however, it is generally censured to be much inferior to the other, though he could not hear with patience any such thing when related to him. Possibly the subject may not afford such variety of invention, but it is thought by the most judicious to be little or nothing inferior to the other for style and decorum.

The said Earl of Anglesey, whom he presented with a copy of the unlicensed papers of his history, came often here to visit him, as very much coveting his society and converse; as likewise others of the nobility and many persons of eminent quality; nor were the visits of foreigners ever more frequent than in this place, almost to his dying day.

His treatise *Of True Religion, Heresy, Schism and Toleration*, &c. was doubtless the last thing of his writing that was published before his death. He had, as I remember, prepared for the press an answer to some little scribing quack in London, who had written a scurrilous libel against him; but whether by the dissuasion of friends, as thinking him a fellow not worth his notice, or for what other cause I know not, this answer was never published.

He died in the year 1673[3] towards the latter end of the summer and had a very decent interment according to his quality, in the church of St. Giles,

---

[3] Milton died November 8 [?], 1674.

Cripplegate, being attended from his house to the church by several gentlemen then in town, his principal well-wishers and admirers.

He had three daughters who survived him many years (and a son) all by his first wife (of whom sufficient mention hath been made): Anne his eldest as above said, and Mary his second, who were both born at his house in Barbican; and Deborah the youngest, who is yet living, born at his house in Petty-France, between whom and his second daughter, the son, named John, was born as above-mentioned, at his apartment in Scotland Yard. By his second wife, Catharine, the daughter of captain Woodcock of Hackney, he had only one daughter, of which the mother, the first year after her marriage, died in childbed, and the child also within a month after. By his third wife Elizabeth, the daughter of one Mr. Minshal of Cheshire, (and kinswoman to Dr. Paget), who survived him, and is said to be yet living, he never had any child.

And those he had by the first he made serviceable to him in that very particular in which he most wanted their service, and supplied his want of eyesight by their eyes and tongue. For though he had daily about him one or other to read to him; some persons of man's estate, who of their own accord greedily catched at the opportunity of being his readers, that they might as well reap the benefit of what they read to him as oblige him by the benefit of their reading; others of younger years sent by their parents to the same end; yet, excusing only the eldest daughter by reason of her bodily infirmity and difficult utterance of speech (which to say truth I doubt was the principal cause of excusing her), the other two were condemned to the performance of reading and exactly pronouncing of all the languages of whatever book he should at one time or other think fit to peruse; viz. the Hebrew (and I think the Syriac), the Greek, the Latin, the Italian, Spanish, and French. All which sorts of books to be confined to read, without understanding one word, must needs be a trial of patience almost beyond endurance; yet it was endured by both for a long time. Yet the irksomeness of this employment could not always be concealed, but broke out more and more into expressions of uneasiness; so that at length they were all (even the eldest also) sent out to learn some curious and ingenious sorts of manufacture that are proper for women to learn, particularly embroideries in gold or silver. It had been happy indeed if the daughters of such a person had been made in some measure inheritrixes of their father's learning; but since fate otherwise decreed, the greatest honor that can be ascribed to this now living (and so would have been to the others had they lived) is to be daughter to a man of his extraordinary character.

He is said to have died worth 1500£ in money (a considerable estate, all things considered) besides household goods; for he sustained such losses as might well have broke any person less frugal and temperate than himself; no less than 2000£ which he had put for security and improvement into the excise office, but neglecting to recall it in time could never after get it out, with all the power and interest he had in the great ones of those times; besides another great sum by mismanagement and for want of good advice.

Thus I have reduced into form and order whatever I have been able to rally up, either from the recollection of my own memory of things transacted while I was with him, or the information of others equally conversant after-wards, or from his own mouth by frequent visits to the last.

I shall conclude with two material passages which though they relate not immediately to our author, or his own particular concerns, yet in regard they happened during his public employ and consequently fell especially most under his cognizance, it will not be amiss here to subjoin them. The first was this:

Before the war broke forth between the States of England and the Dutch, the Hollanders sent over three ambassadors in order to an accommodation; but they returning *re infecta*, the Dutch sent away a plenipotentiary, to offer peace upon much milder terms, or at least to gain more time. But this pleni-potentiary could not make such haste but that the Parliament had procured a copy of their instructions in Holland, which were delivered by our author to his kinsman that was then with him, to translate for the Council to view before the said plenipotentiary had taken shipping for England; an answer to all he had in charge lay ready for him, before he made his public entry into London.

In the next place there came a person with a very sumptuous train, pre-tending himself an agent from the prince of Condé, then in arms against Cardinal Mazarin: the Parliament mistrusting him, set their instrument so busily at work, that in four or five days they had procured intelligence from Paris that he was a spy from King Charles; whereupon the very next morning our author's kinsman was sent to him with an order of Council commanding him to depart the kingdom within three days, or expect the punishment of a spy.

By these two remarkable passages, we may clearly discover the industry and good intelligence of those times.